V&R

Refo500 Academic Studies

Edited by
Herman J. Selderhuis

In co-operation with
Christopher B. Brown (Boston), Günter Frank (Bretten),
Barbara Mahlmann-Bauer (Bern), Tarald Rasmussen (Oslo),
Violet Soen (Leuven), Zsombor Tóth (Budapest),
Günther Wassilowsky (Frankfurt), Siegrid Westphal (Osnabrück).

Volume 94

Maria Crăciun / Volker Leppin / Katalin Luffy /
Ulrich A. Wien (eds.)

Prayer Books and Piety in Late Medieval and Early Modern Europe / Gebetbücher und Frömmigkeit in Spätmittelalter und Früher Neuzeit

Vandenhoeck & Ruprecht

Bibliographic information published by the Deutsche Nationalbibliothek:
The Deutsche Nationalbibliothek lists this publication in the Deutsche Nationalbibliografie;
detailed bibliographic data available online: https://dnb.de.

© 2023 by Vandenhoeck & Ruprecht, Robert-Bosch-Breite 10, 37079 Göttingen, Germany,
an imprint of the Brill-Group
(Koninklijke Brill NV, Leiden, The Netherlands; Brill USA Inc., Boston MA, USA;
Brill Asia Pte Ltd, Singapore; Brill Deutschland GmbH, Paderborn, Germany;
Brill Österreich GmbH, Vienna, Austria)
Koninklijke Brill NV incorporates the imprints Brill, Brill Nijhoff, Brill Hotei, Brill Schöningh,
Brill Fink, Brill mentis, Vandenhoeck & Ruprecht, Böhlau, V&R unipress and
Wageningen Academic.

All rights reserved. No part of this work may be reproduced or utilized in any form or by any means,
electronic or mechanical, including photocopying, recording, or any information storage and
retrieval system, without prior written permission from the publisher.

Cover design: SchwabScantechnik, Göttingen
Typesetting: satz&sonders GmbH, Dülmen
Printed and bound: Hubert & Co. BuchPartner, Göttingen
Printed in the EU

Vandenhoeck & Ruprecht Verlage | www.vandenhoeck-ruprecht-verlage.com

ISSN 2198-3089
ISBN 978-3-525-57345-7

Inhalt

Maria Crăciun
Worship of the Written Word:
Books and Piety in Late Medieval and Early Modern Religious Experience . .   7

Katalin Luffy
Von Süddeutschland nach Klausenburg:
Zur Geschichte der Handschrift Ms. 683   21

Regina Cermann
Individualstück oder Standardware?
Über das deutschsprachige Gebetbuch Ms. 683 in Klausenburg   31

Adrian Papahagi
A Medieval Flemish Book of Hours in Early Modern Transylvania
(MS 684, Lucian Blaga Central University Library, Cluj)   79

Constantin Ittu
A Sixteenth-Century Devotional Book: the *Brukenthal Breviary*   95

Kata Ágnes Szűcs
Saint Elizabeth of Hungary in Flemish Books of Hours 105

Volker Leppin
Eine Untersuchung anhand des *Hortulus animae* 131

Adinel C. Dincă
Absence of Evidence or Evidence of Absence?
On Prayer Books and Devotional Behaviour in Late Medieval
Transylvania 151

Paula Cotoi
Cum oratis, dicite:
Sermons on Prayer in Late Medieval Transylvania and Hungary 169

Carmen Florea
Between Norm and Practice:
Observant Franciscans and Religious Life at the End of the Middle Ages . . . 193

6 | Inhalt

András Bándi
Reste und Spuren vorreformatorischer Liturgie in siebenbürgischen
handschriftlichen Agenden 209

Ulrich A. Wien
Spirituelle Offenheit und ethische Akzentuierung der
Stadtreformation in Kronstadt/Siebenbürgen am Beispiel des
Gesangbuchs von Andreas Moldner (1543) 221

Edit Szegedi
Adiaphora und „recycling": protestantische Heiligengebete? 251

Maria Crăciun
Seeing the Word of God:
Daily Devotions and Modes of Communication in the Lutheran
Churches of Early Modern Transylvania 265

Niranjan Goswami
'Stinted Prayer':
Puritan Dilemmas of Common-Prayer Worship in England and New
England during the English Reformation 321

Kathrin Chlench-Priber
Gebetsliteratur im Spätmittelalter:
Ein Resümee aus literaturwissenschaftlicher Sicht 339

Christopher Ocker
Prayer Literature and the History of Prayer:
Material Conditions and Subjectivities 347

Gesamtbibliographie 359

Index 397

Maria Crăciun
Babeş-Bolyai University, Cluj

Worship of the Written Word:
Books and Piety in Late Medieval and Early Modern Religious Experience

The initial purpose of this project was to draw attention to a particular manuscript (MS 683) from the collection of the University Library of Cluj and to make this a centrepiece of a conference discussing late medieval Books of Hours and the fate of the genre in subsequent centuries. The ensuing conference inevitably widened the scope of the research as it progressed beyond the interest in the detailed analysis of individual examples of prayer books and towards the need to place them within the broader genre of devotional literature and to consider them in connection with prevailing cultural, religious and artistic developments in late medieval and early modern Europe, taking into account the advent of the Reformation, the revolution in communication brought about by the printing press and the growing interest in the religious life of the laity. Wishing to showcase an exceptional fifteenth-century manuscript, insufficiently explored in existing literature, which could be approached from the perspective of literary criticism, codicology, art history, cultural history of religion and the sociology of reading, the conference became a starting point for a lively debate concerning devotional literature analysed in inter and transdisciplinary manner. This fresh approach brought to the fore more general issues related to the role of books, prayerbooks, liturgical books, postils, catechisms, hymnals, psalters and songbooks, as well as bibles and biblical commentaries in late medieval and early modern piety and led participants to contextualise the broad category of devotional literature in all its guises, leading to more refined understandings of devotional practice and its relationship with the written word, while the fifteenth century manuscript, which had sparked the initial discussion remained the focus of some of the presentations (Katalin Luffy, Regina Cermann) and stimulated analysis of similar texts (Kata Szűcs and Adrian Papahagi).

In an attempt to underline the relevance of this volume it has to be noted that Regina Cermann's research has dated MS 683 to the end of the fifteenth or beginning of the sixteenth century and traced its origin to Augsburg on the basis of iconographical, stylistic and literary analysis. The comparative analysis has also clarified the nature of the manuscript, which Cermann deems to have been a workshop serial product rather than a unique and singular commission and thus

8 | Maria Crăciun

unable to shed light on individual spiritual expectations. She also suggests that the manuscript cannot be associated with the production of printed books developed at that time but is firmly inserted into the Augsburg manuscript tradition. A similar exercise undertaken by Adrian Papahagi has traced the origin and context of production for a second manuscript from the University Library's collection, MS 684, by using minute analyses of its features. Although these valuable items cannot be placed within a regional culture of prayer or lay devotional life in late medieval Transylvania, they have stimulated a discussion concerning the role of written texts in the religious life of the laity.

The idea of this volume was born from two observations made during the conference: the presence of late medieval prayer books in the collection of the University Library of Cluj, highlighted in this volume by the studies of Katalin Luffy and Adrian Papahagi, and the absence of any trace of the use of prayerbooks in the devotional patterns of the Transylvanian medieval laity, heralded by Paula Cotoi and Adinel Dincă. The fact that the prayer books from the collection of the University Library, as well as other libraries throughout present day Romania, were produced either in the Holy Roman Empire or the Netherlands and were acquired by early modern or modern collectors, as suggested by the studies of Katalin Luffy, Adrian Papahagi and Constantin Ittu, only serves to highlight their absence from Transylvanian medieval devotional patterns.

According to Katalin Luffy's article, which sets the scene for the discussion, the manuscript which acted as the initial focus of the volume, now part of the holdings of the University Library of Cluj, was previously included in the collection of the Transylvanian Museum Society. According to the Society's records, one of the librarians, Szabó Károly, bought it in 1870 from a certain Borosnyai, for 35 florins. The item was described in the inventory of the collection as a richly illuminated manuscript in German, an observation that has led to its subsequent identification with MS 683. The marginalia and annotations in the manuscript allow one to trace part of its journey until it found its way into the Transylvanian Museum Society's collection. The name Nemes, which appears several times is that of a rather famous antiquarian, Nemes Literáti Sámuel, active at the beginning of the nineteenth century. Apparently, he had bought the manuscript in Vienna and then given it to his sister in 1841. The manuscript must have remained in the family until it was acquired by the Transylvanian Museum Society, as Borosnyai was the son in law of Nemes Literáti's sister. Thus, despite its selection of texts and beautiful decorations, this particular manuscript will not enrich our knowledge concerning Transylvanian devotional culture at the end of the Middle Ages, but will throw some light on the elite's interest in collector's items during the nineteenth century.

The articles of Adrian Papahagi and Constantin Ittu suggest that prayerbooks produced in distant lands in late medieval context did not make their way to Transylvania until much later and were integrated into individual piety only in the early modern period. Thus, at the end of his codicological and artistic analysis, Adrian Papahagi concludes that the little book that caught his attention, MS 684, was produced in the third quarter of the fifteenth century or a little later in the Southern Netherlands, possibly in Bruges. In his opinion, the manuscript is the product of a minor workshop, and was probably intended for a client from Saint-Omer. More interestingly for its use in Transylvanian context, the book may have belonged to Francis I Rákóczy, Prince of Transylvania in the second half of the seventeenth century, while, in 1687, it belonged to a parish priest from the east of the province, who was using it for his private devotion. As the author points out, in the absence of Books of Hours demonstrably used by laymen in medieval Transylvania, MS 684 supplies one with precious evidence that aristocrats and parish priests still had recourse to medieval books of private devotion in the seventeenth century. In the same vein, analysing the so-called *Brukenthal Breviary*, which is in fact a Book of Hours, Constantin Ittu briefly mentions that this has been acquired by Brukenthal in the eighteenth century.

These observations have brought to the fore a number of questions concerning lay piety in late medieval and early modern times, revolving around the place and role of written texts in lay devotional practices, particularly in the culture of prayer fostered by traditional Catholicism and early modern Protestantism.

It has often been suggested that the development of a culture of prayer was the direct result of the involvement of the regular clergy, particularly the mendicants, in the shaping of lay piety and their commitment to pastoral duties, expressed primarily through their heightened interest in preaching. Particularly in the later Middle Ages, the clergy taught the laity that salvation could be obtained through the recitation of prayers at appointed times during the day (Bossy: 1991; Winston Allen: 1998; Duffy: 2006 a). This devotional exercise, aided by the use of prayer books, existed alongside and in harmony with ecclesiastical rhythms of prayer and reflected the structure of the mass (Wieck: 2008, 390–392, 395–396, 400, 412).Thus, it is generally acknowledged that the Book of Hours was designed for lay people seeking to imitate clerical prayer (Wieck: 1997; Wieck: 1998; Duffy: 1992; Fassler: 2004).

This stimulated the mendicants, particularly the observant branches of these orders to instruct the laity in the exercise of prayer (Duffy: 2006a, 143). The pious behaviour of the laity was to be modelled on that of the female members of the mendicant orders (Honée: 1994; Hamburger: 1989) and thus the devotional practices of a clerical society were transferred to the laity. Consequently, the laity began to use books in their private devotion and prayerbooks, particularly the Books of Hours became staples of affluent households (Wieck: 1997; Wieck: 1998, Duffy: 2006 a).

Considered to have been initially a luxurious product, and hence the preserve of royalty, aristocracy and the urban elite, during the fifteenth and sixteenth centuries, the Book of Hours became increasingly available to middling segments of society (Wieck: 2008, 389). According to Eamon Duffy, this democratization of the prayer-book can be explained by the invention of printing, which made it available to anyone capable of reading, and the marketing strategies of stationers, who produced these books in vellum and decorated them with illustrations bought in bulk from artists. In Duffy's opinion, these "assembly-line books" were favoured by individuals with social 'pretensions', keen to emulate their social superiors (Duffy: 2006a, 141–148; Duffy: 2006b, 4). Their popularity is suggested by the fact that many people owned more than one Book of Hours and these items were carefully transmitted from one generation to the next within families and kinships as well as outside them, as they were given or bequeathed to friends, chaplains and servants. They had thus become widely accessible to the point where bourgeois women "felt naked without these devotional fashion accessories" (Duffy: 2006a, 145–146; Wieck: 2008, 392). It was consequently concluded that, in the course of the fifteenth century, the Book of Hours and the religion it represented ceased to be the monopoly of the aristocracy and the upper gentry and became an integral part of the religious experience of the "urban and rural middling sort" (Duffy: 2006a, 148).

Consequently, Duffy suggests that, by the fifteenth century, Books of Hours were mass-produced and had become an increasingly common devotional accessory, superseding the Psalter, which until then had been the most popular prayer book for literate lay people (Duffy: 2006 a, 144; Wieck: 2008, 392–393). In Duffy's opinion, the prayer regimes inculcated by the use of the Book of Hours, which are often considered elitist, were in fact firmly rooted in the world of popular devotion and popular belief and not so far removed from magic (Duffy: 2006a, 142). They are thus presumed to have held together rather than polarized the conventions of lay and clerical piety, the belief systems and devotional practices of educated and ignorant, rich and poor, orthodox and marginal (Duffy: 2006a, 142). The divide between elite and 'popular' religion has sometimes been equated with the contrast between "the religion of the bead and the religion of the book", a contrast that, according to Eamon Duffy, implies "a gulf between a religion of uninformed mechanical repetition and a religion which is text-based, discursive, rational, verbalized". In challenging this assumption, Duffy suggests that "the exponents of the religion of the book and those of the religion of the bead have been, if not identical, then at least overlapping constituencies" (Duffy: 2006a, 141). The use of the book was thus located in a devotional regime which included, with no apparent sense of hierarchy, the recitation of the rosary, the use of devotional images, the recitation of the liturgical office and the cultivation of extended devotional meditation on the Passion (Wieck: 2008, 396–397, 400, 407). In Duffy's view, if Books of Hours were expressions of the religion of the word, or of a newly-awakened lay appetite for religious instruction and a more active and personalized devotional regime, they were also very much part of the religion of the image, where the pictures were at least as important to their users as the texts they accompanied (Duffy: 2006a, 143–144). Seeing Books of Hours as objects, other scholars have argued that they were imbued with the tension between public, ceremonial and ecclesiastical uses of texts and personal, private and individualized reading (Wieck: 2008, 393). In fact, scholars have suggested that the emergence of new and distinctive types of portable prayer books was closely tied to the development of reading habits in the late medieval period and that the proliferation of Books of Hours resulted from the advent of silent reading (Saenger: 1987, 139–142).

Duffy concludes by asking whether the popularity of the Book of Hours was a sign of the growth of individualism, associated with the privatization of religion, the proliferation of private pews and chapels, which could be construed as means by which the gentry were able to insulate themselves from the communal devotion of the rest of the parishioners. In his view, the use of the Book of Hours was part of the promotion of lay interiority, a personalization of religion, which provided the laity with an opportunity to share in monastic forms of piety (Duffy: 2006a, 150–152). After all, people used their Books of Hours alone, whether in a public space or in the privacy of their "closets". Duffy however counters that the essential feature of the Book of Hours is that it offered lay people a share in the church's official cycle of daily prayer. Moreover, he suggests that printed Books of Hours offered new opportunities for communal worship. Whereas manuscripts hindered communal recitation of prayers because they were not identical, printed versions encouraged it because they were uniform. Consequently, the lay person who recited prayers was best equipped to understand and appropriate words which they routinely heard recited by clergy and ministers in the public liturgy (Duffy: 2006a, 153). In the same vein, Paul Saenger suggests that Books of Hours proliferated in a milieu that accommodated different types of reading ability, involving the public act of reciting and silent prayer. In both cases however, reading a Latin prayer aloud or reciting a written text from memory were pious acts performed by individuals in public contexts (Saenger: 1987, 142; Wieck: 2008, 392).

One can only conclude that discussions in international scholarship have highlighted a complex culture of prayer which prevailed in the later Middle Ages, fostered as it was by a clergy committed to its pastoral duties, by macro-societal developments, such as urbanization and increased literacy, and by the revolution in communication brought about by printing. Engaging with the issues raised by international scholarship on the place of the written word in devotion in late medieval and early modern times, the contributors to this volume have raised several converging questions focused on the interplay between the apparent absence of prayerbooks and the development of a lay culture of prayer, taking into account both agency and regional traits, as well as the broader issue of the role of the word, handwritten or printed, in lay devotional practices. As Transylvanian society transitioned from the Middle Ages to the early modern period, a development strongly impacted by the emergence and appropriation of evangelical ideas, new questions were brought to the fore concerning the place of written texts in individual and communal piety when traditional Catholicism was replaced by confessions which privileged the Word of God. Consequently, attempts to identify the types of written texts deployed in these diverse contexts have naturally become part of this inquiry.

Some of these questions have benefited from tentative answers in existing literature. For instance, in her survey concerning book culture in medieval Hungary, Anna Boreczky has argued that devotional literature and particularly prayer books were not abundant in the manuscript production or in the book collections of the medieval Hungarian kingdom. The existing book culture was born in the context of royal and ecclesiastical patronage and responded to practical needs associated with the liturgy or the representation and legitimacy of royal authority. This was combined with a conspicuous absence of books in the private sphere, suggested by the very few examples of Books of Hours that have survived from medieval Hungary. This is explained by the fact that this type of literature did not benefit from clerical patronage as these books were preferred by women and wealthy, secular, and, mostly urban elites. In Boreczky's opinion, this segment of medieval society did not have the economic strength to sustain permanent workshops of illustrators, a fact that impacted on local production, but did possess books, even luxuriously illustrated ones, as sometimes attested by their testaments (Boreczky: 2018, 297–299).

Several scholars who have dealt with ownership of books in medieval Transylvania seem to concur with this conclusion. For example, in her previous work, Paula Cotoi has already suggested that the Transylvanian laity seems to have placed their salvation in the hands of the clergy and resorted to pious gifts, bequests and patronage in exchange for their prayers (Cotoi: 2021, 10–11). This falls within existing interpretative paradigms in international literature, which posited that religious books in the hands of the laity were proof of intense piety and an expression of devotion, even when they were not meant to be read. In these circumstances, they may have been part of a soteriological strategy, intended as pious gifts to ecclesiastical establishments (Pettegree: 2005, 156–159; Bischof: 2013, 46–49, 59–69).

Engaging with these previous efforts to unravel the mysteries concerning the role of the written word in medieval devotion, some of the articles in this volume have noted the absence of the prayer book from the religious experience of the Transylvanian laity as there are no surviving examples of this type of devotional literature nor any mentions in any other relevant documents. As Adinel Dincă has persuasively suggested, evidence that the typical prayerbook was not in use comes from notations of prayer on the margins of both handwritten and printed books, which seem to have acted as substitutes for prayerbooks.

These authors have concluded that devotional literature, designed for either public or private worship of the laity, seems to be the missing piece in the puzzle of the spiritual landscape that integrated simultaneously traditional piety with new European devotional practices.

Asking himself whether this could be considered a clue towards acknowledging that written texts were not a component of the standardized lay pious performance, or whether it implies an alternate devotional pattern, Adinel Dincă suggests that the only acceptable explanation for the absence of devotional literature in the religious behaviour of the Transylvanian laity – if one chooses to exclude the hypothesis of the complete, traceless destruction of such texts and books – is that lay religiosity in late medieval Transylvania was articulated without a significant implication of individual reading of inspiring texts or the contemplation of images, other than those from the ornately-decorated church buildings. Going against the grain of conclusions in international scholarship, Dincă suggests that there was no interest in luxury products as devotional accessories in late medieval Transylvania, that Books of Hours implied the presence of wealth and social status, that they were in fact a tool of representation, that the local book market was oriented towards the practical needs of the parish clergy or members of the religious orders, that owners of prayerbooks were members of the secular and ecclesiastical aristocracy and that use of Books of Hours implied literacy. Without explicitly discussing literacy, Dincă suggests that literate expressions of devotion and lay piety were shaped by local writing and reading processes.

Starting from the actual absence of the most common textual support of the devotional behaviour specific to the laity, Books of Hours and prayer books, and, in a sense, taking things one step further, Paula Cotoi focuses on the existence and circulation in Transylvania of homiletic literature addressing the topic of prayer and explores the content of the sermon collections written by two late medieval Hungarian authors, looking for the contexts in which the topic of praying was approached, highlighting specific issues they emphasized, and gleaning relevant information concerning lay engagement in devotion. This particular approach brings to the fore the issue of agency, more precisely clerical involvement in the shaping of lay piety, supplementing previous similar endeavours which have privileged visual material. It is the author's contention that the clergy's intentions in wishing to shape lay piety amounted to a need to control their behaviour rather than an encouragement of individual, private actions. The author also seems to suggest that the laity was subjected to clerical discourses disseminated through a diversity of channels, while sermons and images may have replaced prayer books as the necessary props in their pious behaviour.

Remaining in the realm of clerical agency, Carmen Florea explores the impact of norms on religious practice by focusing on Observant reform in relation to the Third Order. Building on the work of Marie Madeleine de Cevins (de Cevins: 2008), Carmen Florea starts from the premise that norm and practice are inextricably linked and proceeds to investigate the appropriation of the guidelines for devotion provided by the clerical hierarchy among the membership of the order. The daily devotional routine included communal and private prayer as well as the reading of the breviary. By analysing the texts, produced in the context of Observance, Florea appeals to the most suitable tool for the exploration of the aims and strategies of the regular clergy in shaping female piety within the Franciscan Order, among the Poor Clares and the Tertiaries. This is particularly relevant to the themes approached in this volume as the strategies developed by the regular clergy for female religious were subsequently deployed in fostering a culture of prayer among the laity. The article also explores the Christocentric piety encouraged by the Franciscan Order, which found particular expression in the spiritual life of Poor Clares and Tertiaries for whom identification with Christ's suffering was transformed into standardized religious practice, reduced to a literal imitation of Christ. The author ultimately suggests that the investigation of the functioning of the province's hierarchy and its structures of government could shed light on the norms which were imposed to the body of friars and sisters in their pious practices. As these were closely linked to devotions more generally promoted by the Observant Franciscans, they have the merit of highlighting the most relevant features that shaped the identity of this particular religious community.

Bringing to the fore the issue of piety and ultimately the culture of prayer, Volker Leppin analyses a *Hortulus animae* of German provenance, printed in Nüremberg in 1519. By the end of the fifteenth century, these had become the most popular and widely disseminated prayer books, possibly because they shifted the focus of prayer away from monastic routine and towards the personal and devotional (Haemig: 2016, 162). Leppin uses this to highlight the different strands of late medieval piety, fostered in this particular case in an environment that had much in common with the prevailing spirit that animated Luther in his endeavours. Starting from a subtle analysis of the prayer associated with the Mass of St Gregory, Leppin traces the spiritual development from forgiveness of sins to the internalising of Christ's suffering and the attainment of salvation. The author suggests that this particular medium of communication offered the faithful a rich variety of choices in the practice of piety.

One is thus led to conclude that use of the prayerbook was a specific form of devotion that was supplemented by the veneration of saints through images and relics. Viewed up-close rather than from afar and manipulable/portable, images in prayerbooks served several functions. First of all, they helped orient the reader within a manuscript and even suggested the correct comprehension or proper meaning of the text (Chartier: 1987, 2–5; Wieck: 2008, 393). Secondly, images contributed to the enhancement of personal piety as the owner often requested to be depicted with the patron saint. In fact, more often than not, prayer books were personalised either by the inclusion of donor portraits or by the depiction of a particular selection of saints (Wieck: 1991, 172; Wieck: 2008, 409). In this volume, preference for a specific saint is illustrated by Kata Szűcs' article focused on depictions of St Elizabeth of Hungary in prayerbooks, often shown accompanying the donor. For instance, Isabella of Portugal is portrayed with St Elizabeth, as the latter was her personal patron saint, the two were distant relatives and they were both connected to the Franciscans. By analysing these images, Szűcs suggests that Books of Hours offer insight into an individual's private devotion as the prayers to specific saints were customized to suit the spiritual needs and preferences of the owner.

As evangelical ideas spread from Wittenberg to all corners of Europe, a new practice of piety was developed alongside the new theology proffered by reformers. The emphasis on the Word of God made knowledge of the Bible a desirable component of lay piety, as the clergy encouraged congregations to become familiar with the Scriptures. Prayer consequently acquired a sound scriptural basis, as the laity was urged to address God by using the Lord's Prayer, which was instituted by Christ himself. One is thus compelled to ask whether prayer books continued to be used in the new confessional context, or whether they were gradually replaced with other types of text. As Mary Jane Haemig has suggested, sixteenth-century reformers, Martin Luther particularly, condemned prayer books because they contained beliefs and practices directly opposed to his views by presenting prayers as good works conducive to salvation (Haemig: 2004, 522–523). Moreover, as Virginia Reinburg has astutely remarked, Martin Luther's commentaries on the Lord's Prayer expressed hope that this would replace the "deceptions" of the Book of Hours and teach lay people how to pray in a "simpler, more direct and more heartfelt way" (Reinburg: 1993, 22,29, 32–34). Moreover, Haemig argues that Martin Luther wished to change both the theology and practice of prayer and encouraged simple and direct prayer to God, as prayer was no longer perceived as a good work but rather as communication with the divine. Consequently, the prayer book produced by Luther in 1522 was intended to shape people's piety, but reflected the structure of the catechism and provided direction and advice concerning prayer, instead of including a sample of written prayers (Haemig: 2016, 163). Moreover, book collections throughout Europe suggest that the laity's daily devotions were structured by a mixture of genres and that people's libraries were flooded by hymn books, catechisms, postils, prayer books and handbooks as well as bibles in smaller formats (Dahl: 2011, 47–58). What all of these genres had in common was a preference for a mixture of texts anchored in the Creed, the Ten Commandments, the Lord's Prayer and explanations of the sacraments, consisting mainly of biblical excerpts, as the ultimate goal was knowledge of the bible and the Lutheran articles of faith.

It has been suggested, notably by Mary Jane Haemig, that, during the Middle Ages, boundaries were not finely drawn between prayer book, catechism and breviary, nor between texts created for communal worship and those deemed suitable for individual and sometimes private devotion, while, after the Reformation, prayer books became decidedly catechetical (Haemig: 2016, 162–163). In fact, some scholars, for instance Roger Chartier, had already suggested that Books of Hours contained parts designed for ritual use, which were read aloud during communal worship, while others were designed for private devotions and based on silent reading (Chartier: 1987, 2; Saenger: 1982; Saenger: 1987, 139–141). Thus, while Haemig points to a significant shift in emphasis from the Middle Ages to the Reformation, by suggesting, albeit implicitly, that medieval Books of Hours were mostly used during the liturgy or at least reminiscent of it, while Protestant prayer books were more firmly anchored in individual piety, scholars working on central Europe have highlighted continuities as well as breaks with the past. For example, in the peripheral territory of Transylvania, prayers continued to be used in, sometimes surprising, continuity with the medieval period. Thus, András Bándi's study focuses on the medieval liturgical tradition, which survived in printed and handwritten Lutheran agendas from the early modern period, bestowing particular attention to prescriptions concerning the saints and prayers addressed to them, which were only gradually eliminated during the eighteenth century. Using the agenda of 1653, Edit Szegedi posits that the recycling of prayers addressed to saints inherited from the medieval period was not an *adiaphoron* but rather a political statement laden with confessional meaning, especially since the agenda was printed the same year as the compilation of Transylvanian laws, *Approbatae Constitutiones*.

Peripheries are also explored in Niranjan Goswami's article, which gives the collection a much broader perspective. Any attempt to understand devotional practices in Europe benefits from a discussion of the multifarious developments within Protestantism in England and their continuities in New England during the sixteenth and seventeenth centuries. By examining a few early texts written in both England and New England, Goswami explores the increasingly intolerant attitudes towards the Prayer Book that offered set prayers as opposed to spontaneous ones. This attitude heralds a break rather than continuities with medieval practice and focuses one's attention on the realignments that occurred in the transition from traditional Catholicism to reformed piety, in both individual and communal worship.

In this volume, changes in communal worship are highlighted by Ulrich Wien's study. Focused on the analysis of the first Protestant Songbook printed in Transylvania in 1543 by Honterus' press at Braşov (Kronstadt, Brassó), the study explores the context for its production, the early development of the Reformation in urban environment under Humanist influence. Compiled by Andreas Moldner, these songs reflect the influence of the Bohemian Brethren (*Unitas Fratrum*), which was gradually expunged from later copies of the book. The production of a songbook highlights alternative uses of the word, in this case sung in unison during the service. Communal worship focused on the word, in this case read, spoken and memorized, is the underlying issue in Maria Crăciun's study dedicated to the intricate web of communication established between clergy and laity in the Lutheran churches of Transylvania, where the Words of God, in the form of "kernels of knowledge", brief biblical quotations, were placed on church furnishings, particularly altarpieces. Familiar with these words because of having memorized them in catechism classes or from readings of the Gospel performed by the minister during the service, the congregation recognized and responded to them when they saw these fragments displayed in church, despite their limited literacy.

Besides tracing the development of a regional culture of prayer in the longue durée, highlighting continuities and changes from the late Middle Ages to early modern times, this volume emphasizes differences between regional devotional cultures and the norms set by the universal Church. The volume can also show the complexity of a specific culture of prayer, where use of the prayer book was often replaced by oral instruction and visual interaction with the sacred through contemplation and meditation, which both placed images at the centre of religious practice. Some of the articles in this volume seem to suggest that devotional behaviour in Transylvania was less connected with written texts, and more with memorized psalms and prayers, recited orally, as well as with devotional objects owned privately or placed in public settings like the ecclesiastical buildings.

By focusing on prayerbooks or lack thereof, the volume also highlights the tension between private and public devotion. Scholars mostly agree that prayer was an individual exercise conceived of as private. Moreover, use of the prayerbook is generally associated with domestic devotion and, if not, at least with individual devotion performed in a private chapel or chamber, or privatized space, a chapel or an altar cut off from the public realm. Contrary to this general belief, the contributions to this volume suggest that public, rather than private settings for worship seem to have been the norm in late medieval piety, as people seemed more attached to communal acts of devotion performed in church than to individual piety performed in private. While communal recitation of prayers and congregational singing emphasized the public nature of worship after the Reformation, uses of the book, be it the bible or other genres that fell under the umbrella term of devotional literature, highlight individual devotional exercises, often performed in domestic setting. Use of the prayerbook in these devotional exercises, which can be equated with the private use of the written word, can be understood within a specific literate culture.

Consequently, by looking at the role of texts in lay devotion across the divide caused by the Reformation, this volume is able to make a contribution to the theme of continuity between late medieval and early modern religious cultures, particularly the so-called cultures of prayer. Studies in this volume highlight the fact that the basic prayers the laity was supposed to become familiar with, such as the

Lord's Prayer and The Creed, have stayed the same. This ultimately suggests that expectations concerning the laity's involvement in religious matters were limited in both traditional Catholic and Protestant contexts. However, the evidence analysed in this volume suggests a substantial involvement of the clergy in shaping the devotional life of the laity, whether by regular orders, particularly the mendicants, as highlighted by Paula Cotoi's article, or by the new type of parish priests, who had begun to be trained at university, particularly that of Vienna, as concluded by Adinel Dincă. Consequently, one is led to surmise that, in late medieval context, a new type of university-educated ecclesiastical figure was to guide the common man towards pious conduct, while in the early modern one, he was customarily replaced by ministers and preachers trained in the new Protestant universities and seminars. This leads one to conclude that the clergy was consistently involved in shaping the religious life of the laity before and after the Reformation.

Another area of continuity is highlighted by strategies of communication. Again, at least two articles in the volume suggest that the discourse contained in books was transmitted to the laity through different channels, sermons and images, highlighting the fact that oral and visual means of communication were intended to shape lay experiences of piety. This is best illustrated by the contributions of Paula Cotoi, who suggests that the absence of prayerbooks should not be equated with the absence of prayer from the devotional lives of the laity, and Maria Crăciun, who suggests that emphasis on the Word of God did not eliminate the visual from the realm of worship. Paula Cotoi's article highlights the emphasis on prayer that can be gleaned from sermons, which can be construed as a means of instruction for various audiences. Starting from deceptively simple questions about the prayers to be recited, the times best suited for prayer, the most appropriate places for this particular devotional exercise and the favoured postures and gestures of prayer, Paula Cotoi explores the clergy's expectations concerning the devotional behaviour of the laity in an attempt to reconstruct prescribed expressions of piety. Maria Crăciun, on the other hand, argues that the Bible reached the laity through oral and visual means and that the Words of God, in the guise of brief quotations, the already-mentioned "kernels of knowledge", were not only heard but also seen in church and that memorizing them and sometimes reciting them was an act of devotion. Both articles emphasize the role of memory and mnemonic techniques in expressions of devotion. On the one hand, prayers transmitted orally were learned by heart and recited from memory, on the other, brief excerpts from the Bible, including the Lord's Prayer, were committed to memory and reproduced during the service or in catechism classes.

Thus, uses of the written word were numerous and not restricted to private, individual reading. Lay piety was articulated without a significant involvement of personal engagement with the book, without reading or contemplation of images other than those present in church buildings. This means that literate behaviour did not overlap with devotional behaviour, because the faithful often relied on orality, listening to prayers read to them or reciting prayers that had been committed to memory. Improvised substitutes for prayer books suggest that memory and prayer learnt by heart, in the church or at home, were essential and surely dominant in comparison to the read prayers. Moreover, prayers were focused on representations of the sacred, whether these were images of Christ, the Virgin and other saints, or depictions of the Words of God. Lay devotion was organized around objects and orality, a pattern enhanced by impulses both visual and spoken coming from the parish clergy, which ultimately encouraged oral and collective prayer. While during the Middle Ages, the faithful seem to have been expected to recite a limited number of prayers committed to memory and to respond affectively to visual narratives, after the Reformation, individual efforts were directed towards instruction, a better grasp of the Bible and the articles of Lutheran faith, while recitation of prayers learnt by heart and sometimes addressed to saints remained surprisingly resilient.

Bibliography

BISCHOF, JANIKA (2013), Testaments, Donations and the Values of Books as Gifts. A Study of Records from Medieval England before 1450, Frankfurt am Main: Peter Lang.

BORECKY, ANNA (2018), Book Culture in Medieval Hungary, in: Xavier Barral i Altet, Pál Lővei, Vinni Lucherini, Imre Takács (ed.), The Art of Medieval Hungary, Roma: Viella, 283–306.

BOSSY, JOHN (1991), Christian Life in the Later Middle Ages. Prayer, Transactions of the Royal Historical Society 1, 137–148.

DE CEVINS, MARIE-MADELEINE (2008), Les franciscains observants hongrois de l'expansion à la débâcle (vers 1450 – vers 1540), Roma: Istituto Storico dei Cappuccini.

CHARTIER, ROGER (1987), The Culture of Print. Power and the Uses of Print in Early Modern Europe, Oxford: Polity Press.

COTOI, PAULA (2021), The Book as Object of Lay Devotion in Late Medieval Transylvania (15th–16th centuries), Studia Universitatis Babeș-Bolyai Series Historia 66, Special issue, 27–42.

DAHL, GINA (2011), Books in Early Modern Norway, Leiden/Boston: Brill.

DUFFY, EAMON (2006b), Marking the Hours: English People and Their Prayers 1240–1570, New Haven/London: Yale University Press.

DUFFY, EAMON (2006a), Elite and Popular Religion: The Book of Hours and Lay Piety in the Later Middle Ages, Studies in Church History 42, 140–161.

DUFFY, EAMON (1992), The Stripping of the Altars. Traditional Religion in England 1400–1580, New Haven/London: Yale University Press.

FASSLER, MARGO (2004), Psalms and Prayers in Daily Devotion: A Fifteenth-Century Devotional Anthology from the Diocese of Rheims, Beinecke 757, in: Karin Maag/John D.

Witvliet (ed.), Worship in Medieval and Early Modern Europe, Change and Continuity in Religious Practice, Notre Dame, Indiana: University of Notre Dame Press, 15–40.

HAEMIG, MARY JANE (2004), Jehoshaphat and His Prayer among Sixteenth Century Lutherans, Church History 73/3, 522–535.

HAEMIG, MARY JANE (2016), Little Prayer Book. 1522, in: Mary Jane Haemig (ed.), The Annotated Luther volume 4 Pastoral Writings, Minneapolis, Minnesota: Fortress Press, 159–165.

HAMBURGER, JEFFREY (1989), The Visual and the Visionary: The Image in Late Medieval Monastic Devotion, Viator. Medieval and Renaissance Studies 20, 161–182.

HONÉE, EUGÈNE (1994), Image and Imagination in the Medieval Culture of Prayer: a Historical Perspective, in: Henk van Os (ed.), The Art of Devotion in the Late Middle Ages in Europe 1300–1500, London: Merrell Holberton, 157–174.

PETTEGREE, ANDREW (2005), Reformation and the Culture of Persuasion, Cambridge: Cambridge University Press.

REINBURG, VIRGINIA (1993), Hearing Lay People's Prayer, in: Barbara Diefendorf/Carla Hesse (ed.), Culture and Identity in Early Modern Europe 1500–1800. Essays in Honor of Natalie Zemon Davis, Ann Arbor: Michigan University Press, 19–39.

SAENGER, PAUL (1982), Silent Reading. Its Impact on Late Medieval Script and Society, Viator. Medieval and Renaissance Studies 13, 367–414.

SAENGER, PAUL (1987), Books of Hours and the Reading Habits of the Later Middle Ages, in: Roger Chartier (ed.), The Culture of Print. Power and the Uses of Print in Early Modern Europe, Oxford: Polity Press, 141–173.

WIECK, ROGER S. (1997), Painted Prayers. The Book of Hours in Medieval and Renaissance Art, New York: George Braziller.

WIECK, ROGER S. (1988), Time Sanctified. The Book of Hours in Medieval Art and Life, New York: George Braziller.

WIECK, ROGER S. (1991), The Savoy Hours and Its Impact on Jean, Duc du Berry, The Yale University Library Gazette 66, 159–180.

WIECK, ROGER S. (2008), Prayer for the People. The Book of Hours, in: Roy Hammerling (ed.), A History of Prayer. The First to the Fifteenth Century, Leiden/Boston: Brill, 388–416.

WINSTON ALLEN, ANNE (1998), Stories of the Rose. The Making of the Rosary in the Middle Ages, University Park, PA: Pennsylvania State University Press.

Katalin Luffy
„Lucian Blaga" Zentrale Universitätsbibliothek, Klausenburg

Von Süddeutschland nach Klausenburg:
Zur Geschichte der Handschrift Ms. 683

Die Grundidee unserer Konferenz ergab sich durch den in unserem Besitz gehüteten, reich illuminierten kleinen Kodex mit der Signatur Ms. 683,[*] und durch dessen teilweise legendäre Geschichte. Die Konferenz ist das Ergebnis einer anregenden internationalen Zusammenarbeit. In meiner Darlegung versuche ich den Weg zu skizzieren, wie die Universitätsbibliothek aus Klausenburg in den Besitz dieses Kodex kam. Darüber hinaus werde ich mich mit dessen Legende beschäftigen.

Die Forschung bezieht sich auf zwei voneinander zu unterscheidenden Phasen dieses Weges. Sicherlich gäbe es noch mehr Zwischenphasen, die aber von Klausenburg aus schwer zu verfolgen sind. In umgekehrter zeitlicher Abfolge stellen sich der Forschung zwei Fragen: Erstens: Wann und wie kam der Band in den Besitz unserer Bibliothek? Und zweitens: Welchen Weg ging der Kodex bis er in die Bibliothek gelangte, durch wie viele Hände ist er gegangen, wer waren seine ehemaligen Eigentümer?

Der Band enthält das Siegel und die Inventarnummer[1] in dem alten Etikettenformat der Manuskriptenabteilung des Siebenbürgischen Museum-Vereins [Erdélyi Múzeum-Egyesület]. Der Siebenbürgische Museumsverein (SMV) wurde auf Initiative des Grafen Imre Mikó im Jahre 1859 in Klausenburg gegründet, nach einer langen Reihe von Vorbereitungen und Genehmigungen. Wie der Name schon andeutet, war das Vereinsziel, Museumsobjekte aus Siebenbürgen zu sammeln, zu bewahren und als Kulturgut öffentlich zugänglich zu machen.[2]

Acknowledgement: This article has been written with the support of the *MTA BTK Lendület Long Reformation in Eastern Europe (1500–1800) Research Project.*

[*] Online erreichbar: https://www.bcucluj.ro/public-view/vpdf.php?htsbt=dsf4RFdsfRT|BCUC LUJ_FCS_MS683.pdf (07.06.2022).

[1] Manuskriptenabteilung des Siebenbürgischen Museum-Vereins IV.A.18b – wo die römischen Zahlen auf die Schranknummer, die Kennbuchstaben auf das Regal und die arabischen Zahlen auf den Platz des Buches im Regal verweisen.

[2] Das 19. Jahrhundert ist die Blütezeit der Gründung ethnisch bestimmter Kultur-Vereine in Siebenbürgen. 1840 wurde der Verein für siebenbürgische Landeskunde, 1849 der Verein für Naturwissenschaften begründet, deren zunächst überethnischer Charakter sich aufgrund des sächsischen Schwerpunkts und Mitgliederstruktur sich verzweigte, gefolgt vom Erdélyi Múzeum-Egyesület im Jahre 1859 und im 1861 von der Siebenbürgischen Gesellschaft für rumänische Literatur und Kultur des rumänischen Volkes (ASTRA – Asociația Transilvană pentru Literatura Română și Cultura Poporului Român).

Überlegungen zur Vereinsgründung beschäftigten die Elite der siebenbürgischen Gesellschaft schon länger. Deshalb konnte er bereits im Gründungsjahr auf eine bedeutende Bibliothek zurückgreifen, weil die Grafen József Kemény und Sámuel Kemény schon 1841 ihre eigenen Sammlungen für einen zukünftigen Verein in weiter Vorausschau angeboten hatten. Dessen Zielsatz, siebenbürgische wissenschaftliche und museale (historische) Wertobjekte zu sammeln und zu bewahren, stand schon damals im Raum.

Nach seiner Gründung rief der Verein die siebenbürgische Gesellschaft mehrmals dazu auf, private Sammlungen und Wertobjekte an den SMV zu spenden. Dieser Aufruf fand in der breiten Öffentlichkeit rege Resonanz und hatte sich in eine echte gesellschaftliche Bewegung verwandelt. Spenden kamen aus ganz Siebenbürgen: Wertsachen aus Familienbesitz – egal ob es sich um Bücher, Manuskripte oder andere Wertgegenstände (Gemälde, Münzen, alte Waffen) handelte. Zu dieser Zeit entstand auch die Pflanzen- und Tiersammlung mit zahlreichen Fossilien.

Wirft man einen Blick auf die Liste der Spender, so wird die gesellschaftliche Zusammensetzung der Spender deutlich: Alte Adelsfamilien spendeten dem Verein beispielhaft, der Gründer Imre Mikó selber spendete dem SMV nicht nur den Großteil der Kulturgüter aus dem Familienbesitz, sondern kaufte auf eigene Kosten weitere Wertobjekte von anderen siebenbürgischen Familien oder Sammlungen früherer Gesellschaften für den SMV. Eine ähnliche Großzügigkeit zeigten weitere Familien, wie Bánffy, Teleki, Torma und Lázár.

Die städtische Mittelschicht und der ländliche Kleinadel haben es als ihre eigene Angelegenheit betrachtet, und haben alle zur Vervollkommnung der Sammlung am neuen Institut beigetragen. Im Laufe der Jahre wurden die SMV-Sammlungen durch Spenden, Ankäufe, Austausch und Dauerleihgaben vergrößert. 1950 wurde auch die Sammlung des SMV verstaatlicht, der Großteil seiner Bibliothekssammlung ist heute Teil der Klausenburger Universitätsbibliothek.[3]

Folgende Forschungs-Hypothesen zum hier behandelten Kodex seien vorgestellt:

Unter Berücksichtigung von Siegel und Inventarnummer wird deutlich, dass der Kodex nicht mit der Vorgeschichte des SMV verknüpft werden kann.[4] Das alte Etikettenformat verrät uns, dass der Kodex ganz bestimmt vor 1907 in den Besitz des SMV kam; zu diesem Zeitpunkt zog die Bibliothek des SMV in das neue Gebäude der Universitätsbibliothek um, danach wurden die alten Inventarnummern durch die neue Ms. Bezeichnung ersetzt. 1904 wurden neuartige Aquisitionsbü-

---

3 Über die Sammlungen des SMV siehe die Jubiläumsausgabe zum 150. Jahrestag des Vereins: Sipos: 2009. – mit ausführlichen fremdsprachlichen Resümees.

4 Die Hand- und Druckschriften, die in den ersten 10–15 Jahren nach der Gründung zum SMV gelangten, trugen nur das Siegel der Siebenbürgischen Museumsbibliothek, das kleiner war als das später verwendete Siegel.

Von Süddeutschland nach Klausenburg: | 23

cher geführt, aber der Kodex befindet sich weder im fachgemäßen Zugangsbuch, das 1904 eingeführt wurde, noch im vorherigen, in dem zwischen 1891 und 1904 geführten Aquisitionsbuch.

Nach einer Recherche anhand der Spendenakten der Bibliothek kommt – gemäß der Such-Kriterien – ein einziger Kodex in Frage: Graf Miklós Lázár spendete im Dezember 1862 „Ein Kodex aus Pergament (Gebetbuch) aus dem 15. Jahrhundert".[5] Eine solche Hervorhebung lässt darauf schließen, dass die Schönheit und der Wert des Kodex' nicht unbemerkt geblieben sind, wäre er eine Spende gewesen, so hätte er Spuren in den Spendenlisten hinterlassen. Wie wir später feststellen werden, ist der von Miklós Lázár stammende Kodex nicht der Ms 683.

Der wissenschaftlicher Bibliothekar Károly Szabó[6] leitete 1860–1891 die Bibliothek des Vereins und nach 1872 – nach der Gründung der Universität – die Universitätsbibliothek samt Vereinsbibliothek.

Szabó hat auch ein Zugangsbuch über die angekauften Bänder geführt, einige davon sind in der Dokumentensammlung unserer Bibliothek zu finden. Im zwischen den Jahren 1860 und 1872 geführten Register[7] gibt es von ihm einen Eintrag zum 15. Mai 1870: „Ein deutschsprachiger Kodex mit Bildern aus dem XVI. Jahrhundert. Angekauft von Borosnyai" – anbei die Kaufsumme: 35 Forint.[8] Der Verkäufer hieß also Borosnyai, den Namen sollen wir uns merken.

Dieser Eintrag von Károly Szabó wurde mit weiteren Akten des Vereins untersucht und korreliert. Die Leitung des SMV hielt monatlich mehrere Sitzungen, jährlich wurde eine Mitgliederversammlung abgehalten. In den Sitzungen wurde regelmäßig über die neuen Akquisitionen berichtet. Die Berichte und Beschlüsse wurden in der Vereinszeitschrift veröffentlich, zwischen 1860 und 1874 gelegentlich in der Gazette des Siebenbürgischen Museums, dann ab dem Jahr 1874 diese Dokumente regelmäßig in der Zeitschrift des Siebenbürgischen Museums publiziert. Zwischen 1869 und 1870 wurde der Versammlungsbericht in gedruckter Form nicht veröffentlicht. Die Originalprotokolle der Versammlungen befinden sich im Staatsarchiv Klausenburg. Betreffs der Sitzung vom 7. Mai 1870 wurde Folgendes eingetragen:

Vorgestellt wird ein auf Pergament geschriebenes Gebetbuch aus dem frühen 16. Jahrhundert oder spätem 15. Jahrhundert. Das Gebetbuch ist mit 30 Miniaturen geschmückt, steht zum Verkauf und wurde vom Besitzer der Vereinsbibliothek angeboten. Der Bibliothekar

---

5 Karteizettel: (undatiert); Liste: 1860–1890, 44.
6 Geschichtswissenschaftler, Bibliograph, Autor vieler Fachstudien. Sein Hauptwerk, die *Alte ungarische Bibliothek,* eine retrospektive Bibliographie, erschien zwischen 1879 und 1898 und enthält die bibliographische Beschreibung aller vor 1711 herausgegebenen Bücher mit ungarischem Bezug.
7 Signatur: Col. Doc. 105.
8 Bei Weitem der teuerste Kauf in diesem Register. Für die SMV war das ein guter Kauf. Damals war das 28,22 Gr. Gold wert.

wird aufgefordert und gleichzeitig bevollmächtigt, sich mit dem Besitzer auf einen guten Kaufpreis zu einigen und die Handschrift für die Bibliothek anzukaufen.[9]

Der Kassenführer berichtet nach der Sitzung am 16. Mai über den Kauf des Kodex' für 35 Forint.[10]

Mit einem Ausschlussverfahren können wir eine erste Hypothese formulieren: In unserer Bibliothek befinden sich drei deutschsprachige Kodizes aus dem 16. Jahrhundert: Der erste ist ein Hutterer-Manuskript, kopiert zwischen 1570–1580, ab 1907 im Besitz unserer Bibliothek, der andere ist *Der Tabernakelje* von Adam Reisner aus dem Jahr 1559 (es ist jedoch fraglich, ob er ein Original ist, ein Exemplar davon befindet sich in der Bibliothek von Wolfenbüttel, offensichtlich könnte es auch noch anderswo Kopien geben, er stammt aber ohne Frage aus der 16. Jahrhundert), diesen erwarb die Bibliothek 1903. Man vermutet also, dass das 1870 gekaufte Manuskript der heutige, mit der Referenznummer Ms. 683 signierte Kodex ist.

Über die Identität des Verkäufers lassen die unterschiedlichen Inschriften auf der Rückseite des Vorsatzblattes deuten.

Die erste Inschrift heißt:

Nro. 83. Saec. XV. 121 Blättern, 31 Bildern.
Nb. Folio 22 Recto:
Ablaß: Pii II. (Aeneas Sylvius) de Anno 1459

Dies ist eindeutig ein Antiquareneintrag, die Schrift wurde mit der Reihennummer 83 signiert. Ihr Wert und Alter werden mit dem auf Textabschnitt auf dem 22. Blatt hervorgerufen, bezüglich einer Verordnung von Pius II.

Darunter steht eine andere, durchstrichene Handschrift, die sogar verkratzt und mit einem dickeren Füller durchstrichen wurde. Nur ein paar Wörter sind lesbar: *Anna… Regina Hungariae.* Dieser Vernichtungsakt stammt wahrscheinlich nicht vom Antiquaren und zielte nicht darauf, einen Eintrag über das Alter des Kodex oder über die Identität der vorherigen Besitzer zu vernichten, denn der Eintrag hätte den Wert des Kodex vergrößert.

Der nächste, konkrete Eintrag: „Diese Rarität [wurde] mit dem geheimen Siegelabdruck aus feinem Gold, mit farbenprächtiger Emaille von König Ludwig der II. von Nemes. MP entdeckt."

---

9 Sitzungsprotokoll: 1870. Übersetzung aus dem Ungarischen von Beatrice Nicoriuc.
10 „Der Bibliothekar berichtet ebenfalls, dass im laufenden Jahr, bei der Sitzung vom 7. Mai laut Protokolleintrag – unter dem Punkt 90 – die angebotene Handschrift für 35 Forint gekauft wurde, die Kaufsumme wird genehmigt und dem Bibliothekar überwiesen." Ebd. In der Korrespondenz des Vereins gibt es über den Handlungsverlauf mit dem Verkäufer keine Spuren. Dessen Namen kennen wir nur aus den Akquisitionsbüchern von Károly Szabó: Borosnyai.

Dieser Eintrag entstand im Sommer 1841, ohne genauere Zeitangabe, dazu fügte dieselbe Hand Folgendes hinzu: „Geschenkt an seine geliebte Schwester am 20. August 1841. In Pest."

Durch diese Angaben können wir feststellen, dass der Kodex erst nach 1841 nach Siebenbürgen kam, früher war er sicherlich nicht in unseren Gegenden unterwegs.

Aus der Bindung des Kodex lässt sich feststellen, dass diese Eintragungen nach der Neubindung des Kodex abgefasst wurden. Die Buchbindung ist eine vergoldete Neorenaissance-Bindung aus dem 19. Jahrhundert; diese war üblich in Wien, aber solche, günstige Bindungen wurden auch in Pest angefertigt.[11]

Den Namen des Antiquars ausfindig zu machen, ist keine einfache Aufgabe, denn zu dieser Zeit kommen mindestens 15 Antiquare in Frage, die zwischen 1840–41 in Wien aktiv waren.[12]

Der Eintrag „Nemes" macht aber deutlich, dass es sich um einen einzigen Antiquaren-Buchhändler handelt: Sámuel Literáti Nemes aus Neumarkt am Mieresch. Diese Feststellung ist gleichzeitig erfreulich und auch unerfreulich, denn jede von Literátis Äußerungen erfordert eine gründliche Nachprüfung; er war nämlich einer der größten Fälscher seiner Zeit.

Der berühmt-berüchtigte Sámuel Literáti Nemes wird als der „Dritte Gründer" der Széchényi-Nationalbibliothek in Budapest bezeichnet (nach dem ersten, Ferenc Széchényi, und dem zweiten, Miklós Jankovich). Dieser Autodidakt und Antiquar war einer der „Lieferanten" des berühmten Antiquitätensammlers und Aristokraten Miklós Jankovich;[13] auf seinen Touren erwarb er Antiquitäten von unermesslicher Menge und Wert. Zugleich war er ein sehr begabter Fälscher: Er hat sogar die bedeutendsten Wissenschaftler seiner Zeit mit einigen gut gelungenen, in seiner Werkstatt angefertigten „Antiquitäten"[14] irregeführt. Mehrere seiner Fälschungen wurden erst nach Jahrzehnten enthüllt. In der Széchényi Nationalbibliothek wurde eine einzigartige, aus seinen Fälschungen bestehende Samm-

---

11 In Bezug auf die Einträge und die Buchbindung hat Marianne Rozsondai dankenswerterweise wertvolle Hinweise gegeben.

12 Meine Recherche zu den in Wien aktiven Antiquaren basiert auf der wissenschaftlichen Arbeit von Georg Hupfer: 2003.

13 Siehe dazu: Balázs Nemes: 2002, 389.

14 Seine ungarische Bilderchronik von 1301 wurde von Ferenc Toldy, einem der berühmtesten Literaturkritiker seiner Zeit, Mitglied der Ungarischen Akademie der Wissenschaften, als originales Sprachdenkmal 1854 aufgeführt; der Sprachhistoriker János Jerney hat seine ungarische Gebetsfälschung aus der Zeit von Andreas I. in zwei Bänden veröffentlicht und gewürdigt.

26 | Katalin Luffy

lung zusammengestellt.[15] Literáti Nemes ist in der Fachliteratur der Fälscher gut bekannt.[16]

Das *Athenaeum*, eine sich als fortschrittlich bürgerlich bezeichnende Zeitung aus Pest, veröffentlichte mehrmals Berichte von Literátis Sammeltouren und einige seiner kurzen Berichte von alten Büchern.[17] Das Blatt schreibt über Nemes als guten Patrioten und lobt dessen unermüdliche Arbeit, die Antiquitäten mit ungarischem Bezug aufzuspüren und ins Heimatland zurückzuholen. 1841 berichtet Ferenc Schedel[18] in der Ausgabe vom 17. August über eine neue Sammeltour von Literáti. Unter anderem steht im Bericht:

> Der geliebte Sohn unserer Heimat hat in diesem Jahr bereits zwei neue Antiquitäten-Sammeltouren durchgeführt. [...] Wir können den Patriotismus unseres Nemes nicht genug loben, oft ohne sein eigenes Nutzen zu sehen, strengt er sich an, alles von Interesse für unsere Heimat zu erwerben oder zu behalten. [...] Zu den zuletzt entdeckten und gesammelten Schätzen gehört *der geheime Siegelring aus emailliertem Gold unseres unglücklichen Königs, Ludwig II., den er in Wien aufgetrieben* hat [Hervorhebung K. L.], wo ihm dafür zunächst zwanzig, dann fünfzig Louis d'or angeboten wurden, sogar der freie Tausch aus einer reichen Sammlung, doch unser Patriot brachte unseren Schatz in die Heimat, um ihn hier aufzubewahren und nie wieder aufzugeben. [...]. (Schedel: 1841, 334)

Es ist offensichtlich, dass der Bericht vom Siegelring aus Wien fast mit dem Eintrag aus dem Kodex identisch ist. Damit können wir die Hypothese aufstellen, dass Literáti Nemes den vermeintlichen Ring des König Ludwig II. und den Kodex zur selben Zeit erworben hatte.

Aus dem nächsten Eintrag im Kodex erfahren wir, dass Nemes das Manuskript seiner Schwester geschenkt hat, am 20. August 1841, in Pest. Die Schwester von Sámuel Literáti Nemes war Zsuzsanna Literáti Nemes, wohnhaft in Neumarkt am Mieresch (Marosvásárhely, Târgu Mureş), ihr Gatte war Mihály Szathmári Ilyés, der mehrmals amtierende Stadtrichter. Diesem Paar wurden fünf Kinder geboren.[19] Der Ehemann ihrer Tochter Jusztina war Pál Borosnyai, der zwischen 1872–1875 und später zwischen 1884–1887 Bürgermeister der Stadt war.

---

15 Gábor Mátray, der ehemalige Direktor der Széchényi Nationalbibliothek, der selbst durch eine Fälschung von Literáti Nemes irregeführt worden war, fing systematisch an, die Fälschungen des Antiquars zu sammeln. Heutzutage verfügt diese Sammlung über 24 Stücke.

16 Über Nemes Literáti Sámuel vgl. Láng: 2014, 129–155; Kelecsényi: 1971, 317–330; Kelecsényi: 1975, 307–327; Kelecsényi: 1988, 108–114.

17 Die Berichte von Literáti Nemes wurden auch in anderen Zeitschriften zwischen 1839 und 1841 veröffentlicht, wie *Századunk* [Unser Jahrhundert], *Hirnök* [Der Bote], *Honművész* [Der Heimatkünstler].

18 Der Geburtsname des Literaturwissenschaftlers Ferenc Toldy.

19 Wir wissen wenig über Sámuel Literáti Nemes Lebensweg. Lexikaeinträge über seine Person: Szinnyei: 1891–1914; Kenyeres: 1967. Seine eigenen Aussagen helfen der Forschung nicht weiter. Den ausführlichsten Bericht über sein Leben finden wir bei Fodor: 2015, 276–277. Die Daten über seine Schwester und seine Familie entnahmen wir aus dem Nekrolog von Zsuzsanna Literáti Nemes, das in Neumarkt am Mieresch aufbewahrt wird. Zsuzsanna Li-

Meine vierte und letzte Hypothese bezüglich der Reise unseres Kodex: Der SMV hat im Mai 1870 von Pál Borosnyai, dem Ehemann der Literáti-Nichte, für 35 Forint unseren vielleicht wertvollsten Kodex gekauft.

Die siebenbürgische Reise unseres Kodex beginnt also nach 1841. Über die früheren Besitzer wissen wir wenig, zu dem könnte der zweite Eintrag aus dem Kodex näherbringen: ... *Anna... Regina Hungariae.* Auf der Rückseite des letzten Blattes (122-v. Blatt) steht etwas Ähnliches: *Anna regina ... filia ... regina filia.* Die verwischte bzw. zerkratzte Schrift mit grüner Tinte scheint ein Schmiereintrag zu sein, der Handschrift nach könnte er neuer als der Kodex sein. Es ist nicht auszuschließen, dass die neue Handschrift eine alte imitiert. Dieser Eintrag hat einen Bezug zu der, auf dem Vorsatzblatt erwähnten Anna, Schwester von Ludwig II. und Ehefrau Ferdinands I. Angeblich fand Nemes gleichzeitig den Siegelring von König Ludwig II. und den Kodex, die er später an Miklós Jankovich verkauft hat. So dachte er vielleicht, dass er während seiner Wiener Tour gleich zwei königliche Schätze gefunden habe. Die Geschichte des königlichen Siegelrings des Ludwig II. ist – wie im Folgenden dargestellt – in der Wissenschaft nicht unbekannt.

Die Ungewissheiten um die Todesumstände des Königs lieferten einen reichen Erzählstoff.[20] Durch die posthumen Dokumente, durch die Dekrete der Ehefrau, Königin Maria, und durch die Verordnungen des Pfalzgrafen István Báthori ist es eindeutig, dass der auf dem Schlachtfeld von Mohács verlorene Siegelring tatsächlich gefunden wurde und nach dem zeitgenössischem Rechtsgebrauch zerstückelt wurde (Prokopp: 1967). Gyula Prokopp schließt in seinen Argumenten die Möglichkeit aus, dass König Ludwig II. zwei Siegelringe besessen habe. Der Siegelring, den Sámuel Literáti Nemes gefunden und dem König Ludwig II. zugeschrieben hat, war sicherlich nicht der Ring des in der Schlacht von Mohács gefallenen Königs.

Wenn Nemes wirklich geglaubt hat, er habe den echten Ring gefunden, wie Jankovich oder Manó Andrássy (Andrássy: 1861), der nächste Besitzer, dann war es eine großzügige Geste seinerseits, den so wertvollen Kodex seiner Schwester zu schenken.

Wie der Siegelring war auch der Kodex mit großer Wahrscheinlichkeit nicht im Besitz des Umfeldes von König Ludwig II. gewesen. Trotz dieser Erkenntnis ist die Echtheit des Kodex' nicht zu bezweifeln. Er wurde Ende des 15. Jahrhundert, Anfang des 16. Jahrhundert in einer Werkstatt in Augsburg angefertigt.[21]

---

teráti Nemes ist am. 24. November 1883 gestorben. Für die Kopie des Nekrologs danke ich hiermit Réka Kovács Bányai, der Bibliothekarin der Teleki Bibliothek, Neumarkt am Mieresch.

20 Letzte Zusammenfassung: Farkas: 2015.
21 Siehe dazu die Studie von Regina Cermann aus diesem Band.

28 | Katalin Luffy

Bibliographie

Quellen

Ein GEBETTE von der hailigen drinaltikait, 16. Jh., Handschrift, Signatur Ms. 683, Zentrale Universitätsbibliothek „Lucian Blaga", Klausenburg.

KARTEIZETTEL (undatiert), Staatsarchiv Klausenburg: Bestand des Siebenbürgischen Museum-Vereins, Nr. 298, Ordner 94: Alphabetische Karteizettel der Spender des Siebenbürgischen Museum-Vereins.

LISTE (1860–1890), Staatsarchiv Klausenburg: Bestand des Siebenbürgischen Museum-Vereins, Nr. 298, Ordner 241: Liste der Spenden (Bücher, Manuskripte, Museumsstücke).

SITZUNGSPROTOKOLL (1870), Staatsarchiv Klausenburg: Bestand des Siebenbürgischen Museum-Vereins, Nr. 298, Ordner 17: Sitzungsprotokoll, 1870.

SZABÓ, KÁROLY (1866–1870), [Biblioteca Centrală Universitară „Lucian Blaga", Cluj] – Registru inventar-achiziții cărți, începând cu 27 aprilie 1866-31 decembrie 1872, [Register und Inventarbuch aus der Periode 27 April 1866-31 Dezember 1872], Signatur: Col. Doc. 105, Zentrale Universitätsbibliothek „Lucian Blaga", Klausenburg.

Sekundärliteratur

ANDRÁSSY, MANÓ, Graf (1861), Kiadatlan magyar érmek és pecsétgyűrűk saját gyűjteményemből, Archeológiai Értesítő 2, 49–64.

FARKAS, GÁBOR (2015), Új kérdések II. Lajos rejtélyes halálával és temetésével kapcsolatosan, Magyar Könyvszemle, 381–396.

FODOR, ISTVÁN (2015), Marosvásárhelyi krónikás füzetek I–II, Sebestyén Mihály (ed.), Erdélyi Ritkaságok 9, Neumarkt am Mieresch: Mentor.

HUPFER, GEORG (2003), Zur Geschichte des antiquarischen Buchhandels in Wien, Diplomarbeit zur Erlangung des Magistergrades der Philosophie aus der Studienrichtung Deutsche Philologie eingereicht des Geistes- und Kulturwissenschaftlichen Fakultät der Universität Wien. – https://www.wienbibliothek.at/sites/default/files/files/buchforschung/hupfer-georg-antiquariat-wien.pdf (30.01.2020).

KELECSÉNYI, ÁKOS (1975), Egy magyar régiségkereskedő a 19. században. Literáti Nemes Sámuel (1794-1842), in: Az Országos Széchenyi Könyvtár évkönyve – 1972, 307–327. Budapest: OSZK.

KELECSÉNYI, ÁKOS (ed.) (1988), A hamisítások és Literáti Nemes Sámuel,in: Múltunk neves könyvgyűjtői, Budapest, Gondolat, 108–114.

KELECSÉNYI, ÁKOS (1988), Literáti Nemes Sámuel 1794-1842, in: Múltunk neves könyvgyűjtői, Budapest: Gondolat, 102–107.

KELECSÉNYI, ÁKOS (1971), Literáti Nemes Sámuel útinaplója, in: Az Országos Széchenyi Könyvtár évkönyve, 1968-1669, Budapest: OSZK, 317–330.

KENYERES, ÁGNES (ed.) (1967), Magyar életrajzi lexikon. Budapest: Akadémiai.

LÁNG, BENEDEK (2014), Invented Middle Age in Nineteenth-century Hungary. The Forgeries of Sámuel Literáti Nemes, in: M. János Bak / Patrick J. Geary / Gábor Klaniczay (ed.), Manufacturing a Past for the Present. Forgery and Authenticity, in Medievalist Texts and Objects in Nineteenth-Century Europe, Leiden/Boston: Brill, 129–155.

NEMES, BALÁZS (2002), Die mittelalterlichen Handschriften des Miklós Jankovics im Spiegel zeitgenössischer Kataloge I, Magyar Könyvszemle, 387–410.

NEMES, BALÁZS (2003), Die mittelalterlichen Handschriften des Miklós Jankovics im Spiegel zeitgenössischer Kataloge II, Magyar Könyvszemle, 67–88.

PROKOPP, GYULA (1967), II. Lajos király pecsétgyűrűje, Vigilia, 527–530.

SCHEDEL (TOLDI) FERENC (1841), Literáti Nemes Sámuel, ,s a' közel legrégibb Magyar naptár, Athenaeum 17. August, 333–335.

SIPOS, GÁBOR (ed.) (2009), Az Erdélyi Múzeum-Egyesület gyűjteményei, Klausenburg: SMV.

SZINNYEI JÓZSEF (1891–1914), Magyar írók élete és munkái, Budapest: Hornyánszky Viktor.

Übersetzung: Beatrice Nicoriuc

Regina Cermann
Österreichische Akademie der Wissenschaften, Institut für
Mittelalterforschung, Abteilung Schrift- und Buchwesen

Individualstück oder Standardware?
Über das deutschsprachige Gebetbuch Ms. 683 in Klausenburg

Das mit 31 ganzseitigen Miniaturen üppig ausgestattete deutschsprachige Gebetbuch Ms. 683 in Klausenburg (Cluj-Napoca, Kolozsvár), das Anlass und Ausgangspunkt für die 2018 veranstaltete Tagung bildete, ist der Forschung bis vor einigen Jahren vollkommen unbekannt gewesen. Zum ersten Mal auf das Stück aufmerksam gemacht wurde ich im Jahr 2010 durch den in Freiburg ansässigen Germanisten Balázs J. Nemes,[1] der damals mit Vorarbeiten für einen Census der in rumänischen Bibliotheken aufbewahrten deutschen mittelalterlichen Handschriften beschäftigt war, wobei er selbst erst durch den ersten Referenten dieser Tagung, Adinel Dincă, über dessen Existenz in Kenntnis gesetzt worden war.[2] Er wollte sich seinerzeit vergewissern, ob mir der kleine Codex im Zuge meiner Arbeiten für die Stoffgruppe „Gebetbücher" innerhalb des „Katalogs der deutschsprachigen illustrierten Handschriften des Mittelalters" begegnet war.[3] Das war er nicht! Er musste folglich mit einer Nachtragsnummer bedacht werden und wird dort künftig nur mehr innerhalb der Online-Version behandelt werden können.[4] Umso erfreulicher ist es daher, wenn dieses beinah übersehene Manuskript drei Tage lang auf einer Konferenz das Scheinwerferlicht auf sich zieht.

Für eine/n Wissenschaftler/in kann es zuweilen recht angenehm sein, wenn der Forschungsgegenstand nicht übermäßig mit Sekundärliteratur verstellt ist.[5]

---

1 Email vom 30.3.2010. Im April 2010 erster Eintrag im HSC, vgl. ⟨http://www.handschriftencensus.de/22675⟩ (derzeitiger Stand: August 2014). Dort noch fälschlicherweise 30 statt 31 Miniaturen angegeben gemäß dem unvollständigen Digitalisat, welches unter der URI ⟨http://dspace.bcucluj.ro/handle/123456789/13246⟩ mit der Beschreibung verlinkt ist (es fehlen Aufnahmen von 31v–33v).

2 Vgl. Nemes: 2012.

3 Von 2002 bis 2014 sind in fünf Lieferungen die Bibliotheksorte A–F im Druck erschienen, die nun Band 5/1 füllen. Vgl. KdiH 5/1.

4 Vgl. KdiH 5/1, XIV, Nr. 43.1.42a, sowie KdiH digital unter ⟨https://kdih.badw.de/datenbank/stoffgruppe/43⟩, wo mittlerweile eine von Isabel von Bredow-Klaus angelegte rudimentäre Beschreibung von Ms. 683 unter ⟨https://kdih.badw.de/datenbank/handschrift/43/1/42a⟩ eingestellt worden ist.

5 An Literatur noch zu nennen ist: Papahagi: 2013, 36–37, 39, Fig. 6. Dort werden korrekt 31 Miniaturen angegeben und der bisher aufgrund einer Ablassrubrik auf 22r für die Handschrift vergebene Titel „Piccolomini-Codex" zu Recht kritisch in Frage gestellt. Außerdem Papahagi/Dincă/Mârza: 2018, 134, Nr. 362, Pl. 10.

32 | Regina Cermann

Auf diese Weise kann sie/er sich unmittelbar auf das Objekt konzentrieren und wird versuchen, es aus sich selbst heraus zum Sprechen zu bringen. Vordringliches Anliegen muss zunächst sein, dasselbe in einem historischen Umfeld sicher zu verankern, d. h. es zuvördert möglichst genau zu datieren und zu lokalisieren.

Einen sicheren *terminus post quem* liefert in diesem Fall ein Seelengebet, dem auf Folio 22r eine Rubrik vorangeht, der wir entnehmen können, dass Papst Pius II. (als humanistischer Autor und kaiserlicher Sekretär bekannter unter seinem bürgerlichen Namen Enea Silvio Piccolomini [1405–1464]), für dasselbe im Jahr 1459 auf dem Fürstentag in Mantua Markgraf Karl I. von Baden (1427–1475) einen Ablass verliehen hat.[6] Die gepflegte Hand des professionellen Schreibers steht einer solchen zeitlichen Ansetzung keineswegs entgegen, doch lässt sie durchaus noch etwas Luft nach oben (Abb. 9). Einen weiteren handfesten, deutlich später liegenden Anhaltspunkt erhalten wir durch eine für die Miniatur mit der hl. Katharina benutzte graphische Vorlage: Für die Darstellung ihres Martyriums zog der Buchmaler einen 39 × 28,5 cm großen Holzschnitt von Albrecht Dürer (1471–1528) zu Rate (Abb. 1). Das Blatt wird zumeist um 1498 angesetzt,[7] da es stilistisch auf der Höhe mit den in diesem Jahr herausgekommenen *Apokalypse*-Drucken des Nürnberger Künstlers rangiert.[8] Herausgegriffen aus der für seine Zwecke stark zu verkleinernden Komposition – das Gebetbüchlein misst nur 9 × 7 cm – hat der Buchmaler nur die beiden Hauptprotagonisten, wobei ihn hauptsächlich der rückansichtige Scherge in seiner modischen Gewandung interessiert hat, wohingegen er die Heilige eher pauschal, wohl in eigene, alte Gewohnheiten verfallend, ins Bild gesetzt hat. Genau beobachtet hat er hingegen das Momentum des vom Henker unpraktisch steil nach oben aus der Scheide zu ziehenden langen Schwertes, den knapp anliegenden, mit geschlitzten Puffärmeln versehenen Wams, an den mit Schnüren die in modischem Mi-parti gehaltenen Beinlinge geknüpft sind. Über derartige Details sich verlierend, hat er das eigentlich Interessante der Figur, nämlich deren ausgeprägten Kontrapost, also die Ponderation von Stand- und Spielbein sowie der damit einhergehenden Drehung des Oberkörpers um die eigene Achse, weitgehend außer Acht gelassen. Deutlich vereinfacht wird bei ihm der Bewegungsablauf durch einen seitlich erfolgenden Ausfallschritt, der stärker an herkömmliche Darstellungen erinnert, etwa an einen Holzschnitt aus einer heute nurmehr neunteiligen Serie, die man um 1480/90 angesetzt und

---

6 S. Anhang 3, Nr. 2. Vgl. allgemein Paulus: 1923, 166 (Mantua), 189 (Markgraf Karl von Baden erhält 1450 einen Jubelablass).

7 Bartsch: 1808, 141, Nr. 120. Vgl. Schoch/Mende/Scherbaum: 2002, 109–112, Nr. 128.

8 Bartsch: 1808, 127–130, Nr. 60–75. Es existiert eine lateinische und eine deutsche Ausgabe (GW M12930 und GW M12922). Vgl. Schoch/Mende/Scherbaum: 2002, 59–105, Nr. 109–126.

versuchsweise nach Augsburg lokalisiert hat (Abb. 3).[9] Dürers Holzschnitt hat offenkundig nachhaltig Eindruck bei verschiedenen Buchmalern gemacht. So benutzte ein Augsburger Illuminator 1504 erneut das Blatt als Vorlage, wobei er wie in Klausenburg das Geschehen weitgehend von Beiwerk befreit und auf das Notwendige reduziert hat (Abb. 4).[10]

Modische Details, die mit einer Datierung gegen Ende des 15., Anfang des 16. Jahrhunderts einhergehen, finden wir noch in anderen Miniaturen des Klausenburger Gebetbuchs: So etwa beim hl. Sebastian, der als Zeichen seines Soldatenstandes ein Barett auf dem Haupt trägt,[11] derweil sein bis auf einen Schurz gänzlich entblößter Körper schutzlos den tödlichen Pfeilen ausgesetzt ist (Abb. 5), oder bei dem männlichen Kirchgänger, der zu Beginn der Mess- bzw. Kommuniongebete jeweils in einer bodenlangen, pelzbesetzten Schaube abgebildet ist (Abb. 6, 7).[12] Leider sind dem andächtig Knienden beide Male keine weiteren Attribute beigegeben, so dass es vermessen erscheint, in dem betuchten Laien den Auftraggeber bzw. Erstbesitzer erblicken zu wollen, zumal er zunächst mit mittellangem blondem, dann mit fahlbraunem Haar dargestellt worden ist. Auch ein anderes Faktum spricht gegen die Annahme, es habe bei der Verfertigung von Ms. 683 bereits einen konkreten Abnehmer gegeben: Auf Folio 52v wurde in dem Gebet zum Eigenapostel mit Bedacht ein kleiner Freiraum für den Namen des individuell Anzurufenden gelassen (in der Regel hat man sich an solch einer Stelle mit einem „N" – stellvertretend für „nomen" – als Platzhalter beholfen). Die Auswahl bei den 13 Heiligengebeten – angerufen werden nach dem Pestheiligen Sebastian noch Alle Heiligen sowie Johannes der Täufer, Johannes Evangelista, Antonius

---

9 Vgl. Field: 1965, Nr. 79–87, hier Nr. 84. Vor derartigen, in der älteren Forschung üblichen Lokalisierungsversuchen von Graphik warnt jedoch Schmidt: 1998 sowie Schmidt: 2003, 15–16.

10 Freiburg, UB, Hs. 213, 142v. Vgl. KdiH 5/1, 303–310, Nr. 43.1.62, Volldigitalisat online unter ⟨http://dl.ub.uni-freiburg.de/diglit/hss213⟩.

11 Ursprünglich eine Kopfbedeckung für gebildete bzw. vornehme Stände, kam das Barett Ende des 15., Anfang des 16. Jahrhunderts besonders bei Landsknechten in Mode, vgl. Kühnel: 1992, 23–24, 155; Zander-Seidel: 1990, 219–224. Auf einem Holzschnitt in einem Augsburger Frühdruck von 1510 (VD16 T 198) trägt der hl. Sebastian ebenfalls ein Barett: *Taschenbüchlin auß einem closter in dem Rieß*, Augsburg: Hans Otmar für Georg Diemer, 4.4.1510, d$_{viij}$r. Vgl. das Digitalisat unter ⟨http://daten.digitale-sammlungen.de/bsb00008180/image_53⟩.

12 Vergleichbar mit Schaube gewandet ist der Adorant vor dem Schmerzensmann in dem für Graf Ulrich VII. von Montfort-Tettnang (†1520) hergestellten Gebetbuch in Wien, ÖNB, Cod. 2748, 60r (nach 1511 zu datieren, da für die historisierte Initiale mit dem hl. Christophorus auf 157v ein entsprechend datierter Kupferstich Albrecht Altdorfers als Vorlage genutzt wurde [Mielke: 1997, 27, Nr. e.21/I]). Im Laufe des 16. Jahrhunderts wird die Schaube dann sukzessive bis auf Höhe der Schenkel verkürzt. Vgl. Kühnel: 1992, 220–221, Zander-Seidel: 1990, 164–167. In Ansätzen zu erblicken sind beim Martyrium der hl. Apollonia auf 115v auch sog. Kuhmäuler bzw. Kuhmaulschuhe, die ebenfalls Ende des 15., Anfang des 16. Jahrhunderts modern wurden. Vgl. Kühnel: 1992, 151; Zander-Seidel: 1990, 217–218.

Eremita, Leonhard, Christophorus, Georg,[13] Maria Magdalena, Barbara, Ottilie, Katharina und Apollonia – lässt ob deren großer Popularität ebenfalls keine besonderen Vorlieben erkennen.[14] Stutzig macht allerdings die dem Gebet zu Allen Heiligen voranstehende Miniatur (Abb. 8): Nur vier aus der Heerschar der Fürsprecher sind durch Attribute eindeutig zu bestimmen, nämlich Ulrich, Petrus, Maria Magdalena und Katharina. Bischof Ulrich von Augsburg († 983), dem ein Fisch als Symbol dient, wurde als Volksheiliger zwar im gesamten süddeutschen Raum ob seiner reichspolitisch bedeutsamen Rolle bei der Schlacht auf dem Lechfeld (955) verehrt, doch könnte seine Hervorhebung in einem frei zur Disposition stehenden Zusammenhang möglicherweise einen gewollten Fingerzeig auf das nähere Entstehungsumfeld der Handschrift geben.[15] Zumal auch stilistische Gründe für eine Zuordnung des Klausenburger Gebetbuchs an die schwäbische Bischofsstadt am Lech sprechen.

Anders als etwa die Handelsmetropole Nürnberg hat Augsburg in der zweiten Hälfte des 15. Jahrhunderts einen charakteristischen Lokalstil in der Buchmalerei ausgebildet, der sich auf den umtriebigen Illuminator und Inkunabeldrucker Johannes Bämler (um 1425–1504) zurückführen lässt und sich im Verbund mit dem Buchdruck und der von Augsburg aus tatkräftig mitunterstützten Melker Reform als wahrer Exportschlager entpuppen sollte.[16] Typische Kennzeichen sind etwa die farblichen Wechselrahmen und die stilisierten Akanthusbordüren (Abb. 9, 10), die Text- und Miniaturseiten gleichermaßen umgeben (Abb. 11, 12). Gegen Ende des Jahrhunderts entwickelten einige der dort ansässigen Buchmaler zudem eine eigentümliche Vorliebe für mit Rotlack und Gold gemusterte Stoffe (Abb. 13, 14).[17]

---

13 Dem relativ kurzen Heiligengebet auf 102 r–102 v geht auffälligerweise als einzigem keine Miniatur voraus. Der Lagenformel und dem Inhalt nach fehlt an dieser Stelle jedoch kein Blatt. Lagenformel (Ist-Zustand): 3 IV^{24}, 2 III^{36}, 2 IV^{52}, 8 III^{100}, II+1^{105} (+105), III^{111}, II+2^{117} (+112, 117), II+1^{122} (+118).

14 Sechs von ihnen zählt man im süddeutschen/bayerischen Raum zu den 14 Nothelfern, nämlich Sebastian, Leonhard, Christophorus, Georg, Barbara, Katharina. Vgl. LCI 8, Sp. 546–550. Besondere Hilfe bzw. Schutz bei konkreten Anliegen versprachen: Sebastian (Pest), Antonius (Mutterkornvergiftung), Leonhard (Gefangene), Christophorus (jäher Tod), Barbara (gute Sterbestunde), Ottilie (Augen), Apollonia (Zahnschmerzen) usw.

15 Vergleichbare Darstellungen von Bischof Ulrich von Augsburg finden sich z. B. in München, BSB, Clm 4302, 77 v (historisierte Initiale in einem von Johannes Franck 1459 illuminiertem Antiphonar für St. Ulrich und Afra in Augsburg) oder Augsburg, SStB, 2° Cod. 154, 148 v (Federzeichnung in der *Heiligen Leben*). Vgl. die entsprechenden Digitalisate unter ⟨http://daten.digitale-sammlungen.de/bsb00110793/image_156⟩ bzw. ⟨http://daten.digitale-sammlungen.de/bsb00087192/image_304⟩.

16 Vgl. König: 1997; Beier: 2004; Cermann: 2018, 265, Folien 51–62; Cermann: in Vorbereitung, Kapitel II.36 sowie Anhang 17 und 18.

17 Vgl. Klausenburg, UB, Ms. 683, 36 v, 54 v, 103 v mit Wolfenbüttel, HAB, Cod. Guelf. 84.4 Aug. 12°, 65 v, 91 v, 114 v, wo Maria und Maria Magdalena bzw. Maria und Bischof Nikolaus ein solches (Unter-)Gewand tragen. Außerdem Cambridge, Fitzwilliam Museum, Ms 157; Esztergom, Erzdiözesanbibliothek, Mss. III. 171; Karlsruhe, BLB, Cod. Durlach 2; London, BL, Add. 24153.

Schrift und Schreibsprache zeigen hingegen keine ortsspezifischen Charakteristika: Die schleifenlose Bastarda in Ms. 683 weist nur leichte Anflüge an die in Augsburg besonders geschätzte und von den Humanisten zu einer veritablen Programmschrift deklarierten Rotunda auf (Abb. 15, 16), der insbesondere durch zwei professionelle Schreiber, nämlich Heinrich Molitor (†1482/83) und Leonhard Wagner (1453–1522), sowie den Augsburger Erstdrucker Günther Zainer (†1478) dort zum Durchbruch verholfen wurde.[18] Statt der italianisierenden Formen der Rotunda, bei der man die romanische Minuskel wieder belebt hat, tradieren sich im Klausenburger Gebetbuch gotische Brechungen weiter fort (Abb. 9). Bei der Schriftsprache hinwiederum handelt es sich zwar um Schwäbisch, doch fehlt die für Augsburg bzw. Bayerisch-Schwaben typische Diphthongierung von „a" zu „au" (so heißt es in Ms. 683 z. B. „hat" statt „haut").[19]

Näheren Aufschluss über die Herkunft des Büchleins können wir uns daher am ehesten über die Ausstattung und den Text bzw. mögliche Parallelüberlieferung erhoffen. Schaut man sich die Situation um 1500 in Augsburg näher an, so werden repräsentative Aufträge zu dieser Zeit etwa an Georg Beck im Verbund mit Hans Holbein d. Ä. oder Ulrich Taler vergeben: Von dem Ausstattungsniveau einer Kaiser Maximilian I. dedizierten *Vita Sancti Simperti* (Abb. 16) oder einem für Abt Mörlin von St. Ulrich und Afra entstandenen *Extractus Missae* (Abb. 17) ist das Klausenburger Gebetbuch weit entfernt.[20] Ungleich besser lässt es sich in eine Umbruchsphase situieren (Abb. 18–20), in der die normative Kraft einer Buchmaler-Kooperative, der sog. Augsburg-Salzburger Missalien-Werkstatt, die den von Johannes Bämler ausgebildeten Formenkanon über Jahrzehnte beflissen weiter tradiert hat, erste Auflösungserscheinungen zeigt und aus dem anonymen Kreis der dort Wirkenden wieder Einzelpersönlichkeiten mit ihren eigenen Stilidiomen hervortreten. Dazu zähle ich Georg Beck (um 1450–1512), Ulrich Taler (nachweislich tätig von 1497–1520/25), Nikolaus Bertschi (um 1480/90–1541/2) und Narziß Renner (1501/2–1536).[21] Der Vater des exzentrischen Narziß Renner namens Hans Renner, der sich ebenfalls als Buchmaler betätigte, wurde 1496 wegen der schlechten Qualität seiner Arbeiten verklagt.[22] Leider verfügen wir über keine gesicherten Werke von demselben. Lediglich hypothetisch hat man ihm ei-

---

18 Vgl. Wehmer: 1955; Schneider: 1995; Schneider: 1999, 80–81.
19 Vgl. Paul/Moser/Schröbler/Grosse: [22]1982, 133.
20 Vgl. die Digitalisate von München, BSB, Clm 30044 unter ⟨http://mdz-nbn-resolving.de/urn:nbn:de:bvb:12-bsb00103265-3⟩ bzw. von München, BSB, Clm 23322 unter ⟨http://mdz-nbn-resolving.de/urn:nbn:de:bvb:12-bsb00092591-1⟩ sowie Pächt: 1964; Merkl: 1999, 353–354, Kat. 47, Abb. 275, 276.
21 Vgl. Cermann: in Vorbereitung, Kapitel II.36, sowie allgemein zu diesen Buchmalern Pächt: 1964; Messling: 2004; Merkl: 1999, 31–35, 41–48, 50–57, 343–369, Kat. 41–54 (Ulrich Taler), 273–314, Kat. 1–26 (Nikolaus Bertschi), 319–343, Kat. 30–40 (Narziß Renner).
22 Vgl. Wilhelm: 1983, 64, 541.

nige deutschsprachige Gebetbücher zugewiesen,[23] darunter ein 1499 für den vermögenden Augsburger Kaufmann Melchior Stuntz geschriebenes in Wolfenbüttel (Abb. 12, 14, 21).[24] Eine dort vorkommende Marienkrönung finden wir ganz ähnlich in Ms. 683 (Abb. 21, 11). Neben dem kompositionellen Aufbau übernahm man dort auch weitgehend die Farbgebung. Der Sohn des Hans Renner, Narziß Renner, griff bei seinen ersten Gehversuchen auf dem Feld der Buchmalerei ebenfalls auf diese Bildfindung zurück und integrierte sie in ein größeres Ensemble (Abb. 22). Hierfür könnte ihm ein älteres Tafelbild eines anonymen Augsburger Meisters vor Augen gestanden haben (Abb. 23).[25] Die zentrale Szene mit der Erhöhung Mariens hat sich in Augsburg als äußerst langlebig erwiesen: Noch Nikolaus Bertschi besann sich 1526 darauf (Abb. 24), wenngleich er die etwas starren Formen durch ein Wolkenband und zwei Engel zu beleben suchte. Schon um 1480/90 hatte man die von der Hl. Dreifaltigkeit im Himmel aufgenommene Maria in dieser Manier in einem Holzschnitt verewigt (Abb. 25), der zu der neunteiligen Serie gehört, aus der das bereits erwähnte Martyrium der hl. Katharina stammt.

Weitere Parallelen zwischen der Holzschnittserie und den Klausenburger Miniaturen lassen sich beim Martyrium der hl. Barbara konstatieren (Abb. 26, 27): Beide Male sehen wir den seine eigene Tochter hinrichtenden Vater, indem er das Schwert in einer weit ausholenden Bewegung über seinen Kopf schwingt, um in einem barbarischen Akt seinem Kind das Haupt abzuschlagen. Die Wildheit seiner Person wird hier wie dort durch seine Kleidung angedeutet. Ein Motiv erfährt allerdings eine kleine Veränderung: Im Holzschnitt fasst der Henker die ihren Tod Erwartende bei den Haaren, in der Miniatur fixiert er ihr Haupt hingegen mit einem Griff an ihre Krone. Den ersten, sehr viel dramatischeren Einfall kennen wir insbesondere aus der Nürnberger Tradition, wo er um 1470 wohl aus Paris eingeführt wurde.[26]

Lässt sich der Buchschmuck des hiesigen Gebetbuchs stilistisch mehr oder minder problemlos in Augsburg verankern, so führt die Textanalyse zunächst zu keinem so klarem Ergebnis: Ms. 683 versammelt einige Spolien klassischer Andachtsliteratur, so etwa die *Sieben Tagzeiten zur Passion* des Prager Hofkanzlers Johann von Neumarkt (um 1315–1380),[27] wie auch einzelne Gebete aus den von Johannes von Indersdorf (1382–1470) für seine beiden berühmten Beichtkinder,

---

23 Vgl. Merkl: 1999, 50, 52; Merkl/Obhof/Neidl: 2002, 172; KdiH 5/1, 256–264, Nr. 43.1.56; Heitzmann/Kruse/Lesser: 2015, 30–31, Kat. 12.
24 Wolfenbüttel, HAB, Cod. Guelf. 84.4 Aug. 12°.
25 Vgl. Kemperdick: 2007; Cermann: 2018, 265, Folie 49.
26 Vgl. Cermann: 2010, 20–21, Abb. 6–8.
27 25r–40r. Vgl. Klapper: 1935, 3–13, Nr. I,2, 4, 6–13. Außerdem: 51r–52r Gebet zum Schutzengel, 55r–62r Übersetzung des Sancta Maria. Vgl. Klapper: 1935, 176–179, Nr. 23 und 335–343, Nr. 98,1.

Herzog Wilhelm III. von Bayern (1375–1435)[28] und Frau Elisabeth Ebran,[29] in den 20er und 30er Jahren des 15. Jahrhunderts zusammengestellten Sammlungen. Beide Autoren wurden im süddeutschen Raum weithin rezipiert. Speziell erscheint lediglich die ausführliche Ablassrubrik, von der zu Beginn schon einmal die Rede gewesen ist (Anhang 3, Nr. 2). Markgraf Karl I. von Baden nahm an dem von Papst Pius II. 1459 nach Mantua einberufenen Fürstentag als kaiserlicher Gesandter teil. Der Papst erhoffte sich, die weltlichen Vertreter zu einem Kreuzzug gegen die Türken bewegen zu können.[30] Um die beträchtlichen Kreuzzugskosten aufzubringen, verteilte er freigebig Ablässe.[31] Das Seelengebet, mit dem der 100tägige Ablass zu erwerben war, ist von alters her bekannt; es handelt sich um eine Übersetzung des „Miserere mei domine animabus, qui singulares apud te non habent intercessores …" (auf Deutsch heißt es in Ms. 683 „Erbarme dich gott mein herre vber alle selen die gegen dir nit sonder bitter haben …").[32] Ich kenne bislang nur fünf weitere deutschsprachige Handschriften,[33] die diese Ablassrubrik in unterschiedlicher Ausführlichkeit überliefern: Am faktenreichsten werden die Ereignisse in dem ältesten Textzeugen übermittelt, dem Gebetbuch der Margaret Zschampi, das wohl bereits um 1460 in Basel entstanden sein dürfte (vgl. Anhang 3, Nr. 1).[34] 1481 taucht die Rubrik möglicherweise in St. Gallen auf (Anhang 3, Nr. 5).[35] Undatiert sind die Versionen in Dallas (Anhang 3, Nr. 6),[36] Rastatt (Anhang 3, Nr. 4)[37] und Heidelberg (Anhang 3, Nr. 3).[38] Stellt man die sechs Überlieferungsträger in einer Übersicht zusammen, so fällt auf, dass kein einziger Textzeuge mit einem anderen wörtlich übereinstimmt. Sowohl hinsichtlich der Länge, als auch in Bezug auf

---

28 2r–2v Gebet zur Dreifaltigkeit, 8r–10v Gebet von der Geburt und Kindheit Christi, 49v Gebet zu Pfingsten. Vgl. Haimerl: 1952, 155, Anm. 965, Nr. 1; 156, Anm. 973; 155, Anm. 964.

29 19r und 20r zwei Seelengebete innerhalb der Messgebete; 24v weiteres Seelengebet. Außerdem: 92r–93v zwei Gebete zu Johannes d. Ev. sowie 104r–105v eines zu Maria Magdalena. Vgl. Haimerl: 1952, 156, Anm. 972, Nr. 4 und Nr. 5; 155, Anm. 962; 154, Anm. 957, Nr. 1 und Nr. 2; 155, Anm. 958.

30 Seit dem Fall von Konstantinopel 1453 hatte das Problem neue Dringlichkeit erhalten.

31 Vgl. Paulus: 1923, 166.

32 Vgl. Haimerl: 1952, 127, Anm. 786.

33 Daneben existiert auch eine verkürzte lateinische Version (ohne Nennung des Markgrafen und des Fürstentags in Mantua), z.B. in Karlsruhe, BLB, Cod. Schwarzach 5, 240v–243v „Anno domini 1459 in die Katherine beatissimus … Pius papa secundus anno secundo omnibus has oraciones pro animarum salute devote dicentibus tociens quociens contulit dies centum indulgenciarum de iniunctis penitenciis." Vgl. Schlechter/Stamm: 2000, 292. Ähnlich Innsbruck, UB, Cod. 402, 277v–278r; Rom, BAV, Cod. Pal. lat. 1794, 177r.

34 Basel, UB, Cod. A VIII 51, 146r–147v. Vgl. Binz: 1907, 106–108; VL² 2, Sp. 1125–1126 sowie das Digitalisat unter ⟨https://www.e-codices.unifr.ch/de/list/one/ubb/A-VIII-0051⟩.

35 St. Gallen, Stiftsbibliothek, Cod. 511, 18v–21v. Vgl. Scarpatetti/Lenz: 2008, 240–245.

36 Dallas (Texas), Bridwell Library, MS 91, 38r ff.

37 Rastatt, Ludwig-Wilhelm-Gymnasium, K 173, 298r. Vgl. Heinzer: 1989, 46–49, Abb. 24, 25; Stegmüller: 1958, 79–82.

38 Heidelberg, UB, Cod. Pal. germ. 443, 140r. Vgl. Miller/Zimmermann: 2007, 447–452. Digitalisat online unter ⟨https://digi.ub.uni-heidelberg.de/diglit/cpg443⟩.

38 | Regina Cermann

den Faktenreichtum variieren die Beispiele beträchtlich![39] Nirgends lässt sich eine direkte Abhängigkeit erweisen. Die Distributionswege müssen folglich weiter verzweigt gewesen sein.

Möglicherweise haben Einblattdrucke dabei eine Rolle gespielt: In Basel druckte Berthold Ruppel (um 1468–1494/95) vermutlich im Jahr 1477 das Gebet samt Rubrik in lateinischer und in deutscher Sprache nebeneinander ab.[40] Doch machte er zu den Entstehungsumständen dort nur ganz rudimentäre Angaben.[41] Auch im *Hortulus animae*, einer für den Buchdruck konzipierten Gebetsanthologie, die in gewisser Weise das Pendant zum *Livre d'heures* in Frankreich darstellt, findet man zu Anfang des 16. Jahrhunderts nur die unabdingbaren Informationen.[42] Interessanterweise unterscheiden sich die lateinische und die deutsche Version allerdings in einem Punkt: In der älteren lateinischen Fassung wurde ein Absatz hinzugefügt, in dem es heißt, Papst Johannes IV. (640–642) habe bereits zu dem nachfolgenden Gebet so viele Tage Ablass verliehen, wie Seelen auf dem Friedhof liegen.[43] Diese Erweiterung könnte von dem Humanisten Sebastian Brant (1457–1521) vorgenommen worden sein, der laut Impressum die Ausgabe redigiert hat.[44] (In der deutschen Fassung dürfte man aus Platzgründen auf diesen Zusatz wieder verzichtet haben).

Vielleicht handelt es sich bei der vordem nicht bezeugten Reminiszenz jedoch um eine fingierte Nachricht: Ähnlich wie beim Marienoffizium im *Hortulus animae*, wo proklamiert wird, der liturgische Gebrauch stimme mit demjenigen vom Konzil von Clermont von 1095 überein und wäre von Papst Urban II. (1088–1099)

---

39 In Basel wird verwirrenderweise z. B. der Agnetentag (21.1.) anstelle des Katharinentags (25.11.) als Datum genannt.

40 Basel, UB, UBH Einblattdruck XV 29. Vgl. GW 0009450N; VE15 P-231, Abb. 69.

41 Die Rubrik vor dem deutschen Text lautet: „[A]llen gloubigen die dis nachgeschriben gebet antechtlich sprechen zu trost allen gloubigen selen so offt so dick hat Babst pius der ander ablas geben hundert tag vffgesetzter buß."

42 Straßburg: Johann Wähinger, [6.3.] 1504, F_{viij}v (VD16 H 5080; Oldenbourg: 1973, L14). Es heißt dort: „Für all glöubig selen die do keynen besunderen trost habent hat Pius der ander babst geben hundert tag ablaß dötlicher sunden einem yeden menschen als offt er diß gebett sprichet mit andacht." Vgl. das Digitalisat unter ⟨http://daten.digitale-sammlungen.de/bsb00005610/image_472⟩, sowie künftig KdiH Nr. 43.3C.1.c.

43 Straßburg: Johann Wähinger, 20.10.1503, D_{iij}v+D_{iv}r (VD16 H 5042; Oldenbourg: 1973, L13). Es heißt dort: „Pius papa secundus largitus est omnibus et singulis infra scriptas orationes pro animarum salute deuote dicentibus totiens quotiens centum dies indulgentiarum de iniunctis penitentijs. Item Johannes papa quartus tot dies indulgentiarum concessit quot animarum corpora ibi sepulta sunt." Vgl. das Digitalisat unter ⟨http://daten.digitale-sammlungen.de/bsb00005695/image_466⟩ sowie Haimerl: 1952, 127, Anm. 786.

44 Vgl. VL² 1, Sp. 992–1005; VL² 4, Sp. 148; VL Deutscher Humanismus 1, Sp. 247–283, bes. 271 sowie das Digitalisat unter ⟨http://daten.digitale-sammlungen.de/bsb00005695/image_5⟩. Es heißt auf dem Titelblatt: „Hortulus anime denuo diligentissime per prestantissimos viros et dominos doctorem Brant et magistrum Jacobum Wympffelingum castigatus. Sebastianus Brant ad lectorem" [es folgen vier Distichen].

bestätigt worden.[45] Urban II. hatte seinerzeit Klerikern für den Erfolg des ersten Kreuzzugs das Beten des Marienoffiziums vorgeschrieben. Sebastian Brant wäre diese Form der historisierenden Annotation durchaus zuzutrauen. Erst seit der Drucklegung fand jedenfalls diese Version des Marienoffiziums Eingang in die handschriftliche Überlieferung, z. B. in das 1526 von Nikolaus Bertschi illuminierte Gebetbuch (Abb. 24).[46] In dieser Handschrift hat man sich außerdem noch andere Druckvorlagen einverleibt: *Das Testament Jhesu Christi, das man bißher genent hatt die Meß* war von dem zeitweilig in Augsburg wirkenden Theologen und Reformator Johannes Oekolampad (1482–1531) übersetzt und drei Jahre zuvor bei Heinrich Steiner in der Bischofsstadt verlegt worden.[47] Obzwar Augsburg offiziell erst 1537 zum Protestantismus übertreten sollte, beherbergte die Stadt seit 1522 keinen katholischen Drucker mehr in ihren Mauern.[48] Augsburg avancierte zu einem der wichtigsten Druckorte für reformatorisches Schrifttum. Gleichwohl haben hochstehende Protestanten nachfolgend ihre Handschriften offenbar lieber in Nürnberg ausgestalten lassen.[49]

Von dieser geistesgeschichtlichen Zeitenwende findet sich im Klausenburger Gebetbuch jedoch noch keine Spur. Dennoch erscheint die Überlegung berechtigt, ob die dort versammelten, reichlich unspezifischen Texte nicht einem Druck entnommen worden sein könnten, der auf eine überregionale Verbreitung abgezielt hat. In Augsburg sind über die Jahrzehnte verstreut vier verschiedene Gebetbuchtypen herausgebracht worden: Gleich der Erstdrucker Günther Zainer verlegte 1471 *Die siben psalmen, vesper, vigilij vnd die selmeß in teutsch, mit andern andaechtigen gebetten*.[50] Um 1485 verfolgte Anton Sorg mit seinen *Siben Curs auff*

---

45 Straßburg: Johann Wähinger, [6.3.] 1504, C$_{ij}$r (VD16 H5080; Oldenbourg: 1973, L14). Es heißt dort: „Diß seynt die syben zeyt oder der Curß von vnser lieben frawen als sie zu samen bracht vnd gemacht seynt in dem concilio zu Claromont. Und auff gesetzt zu sprechend vom babst vrbano dem andern." Vgl. das Digitalisat unter ⟨http://daten.digitale-sammlungen.de/bsb00005610/image_43⟩ sowie Cermann: in Vorbereitung, Anm. 57.

46 Ehem. München, Hartung & Karl, 19./20.11.1975, Nr. 9 (erneut Wien, Dorotheum, 12.6.2017, Nr. 1; 1526 dat.), 1v–86r. Außerdem ehem. Königstein, Reiss & Sohn, 25.–27.10.2000, Nr. 1491 (erneut Hamburg, Hauswedell & Nolte, 22./23.5.2012, Nr. 1081) und Salzburg, St. Peter, b I 30 (1555 dat.). Vgl. KdiH 5/1, XVII, Nr. 43.1.135, XVIII, Nr. 43.1.159.

47 Augsburg: Heinrich Steiner, 1523 (VD16 M4861). Vgl. das Digitalisat unter ⟨http://daten.digitale-sammlungen.de/bsb00038943/image_3⟩. Abschrift auf 105v–125v in ehem. München, Hartung & Karl, 19./20.11.1975, Nr. 9 (erneut Wien, Dorotheum, 12.6.2017, Nr. 1).

48 Vgl. Cermann: 1998, 8–9.

49 Z. B. Dorothea von Preußen (Toruń, UB, Ob.6.II.4489 [*Feurzeug Christenlicher andacht*, Nürnberg: Jobst Gutknecht 1536, bislang nicht im VD16], Wolfenbüttel, HAB, Cod. Guelf. 68.12 Aug. 8°), Johann II. von Pfalz Simmern (Wien, ÖNB, Cod. 1880) oder Dorothea von Mansfeld (ehem. London, Christie's, 28.6.1995, Nr. 26). Vgl. KdiH 5/1, XX, Nr. 43.1.205.

50 Augsburg: Günther Zainer, 12.3.1471 (GW 12981). Vgl. das Digitalisat unter ⟨http://mdz-nbn-resolving.de/urn:nbn:de:bvb:12-bsb00064141-6⟩.

40 | Regina Cermann

ain yeglichen tag der wochen ein anderes Konzept.[51] 1510 erschien das sogenannte *Taschenbuechlin. Auß ainem closter in dem Riess*,[52] 1520 der ausgesprochen schön gestaltete *Gilgengart*.[53] Nur in den beiden letztgenannten Frühdrucken lässt sich jeweils ein Gebet entdecken, das über eine Entsprechung im Klausenburger Konvolut verfügt: Das Pestgebet zum hl. Sebastian einerseits[54] sowie eine Übersetzung des Sancta Maria andererseits.[55]

Bei der Suche nach Parallelüberlieferung wird man sich folglich verstärkt unter den Handschriften umzuschauen haben. In einer Übersicht habe ich zehn Codices neben Ms. 683 gestellt und ihre Textbausteine jeweils einzeln aufgeführt (s. Anhang 2). *Kursiv* markiert sind dabei festgestellte Abweichungen, d. h. Textvarianten, Textumstellungen oder Textzusätze. Je weiter man nach rechts blickt, desto größer bzw. unsicherer werden die Diskrepanzen (nicht von allen angeführten Handschriften existieren derzeit Vollbeschreibungen). Die größte Übereinstimmung ergibt sich mit einem Manuskript in Dallas (Anhang 2, Spalte 2), das wir von der Ablassrubrik Papst Pius' II. her schon kennen. Interessanterweise zieht sich eine Abweichung zu Ms. 683 konsequent durch die Überlieferungsreihe: Die Gebete zur Geburt Christi (Anhang 2, Zeile d) und zum Jüngsten Gericht (Anhang 2, Zeile r) erscheinen in allen anderen Überlieferungszeugen an anderer Stelle; sie rahmen die *Tagzeiten zur Passion* (Anhang 2, Zeile h) und die drei daran anschließenden Gebete zur Auferstehung, Himmelfahrt Christi und zu Pfingsten ein (Anhang 2, Zeile i, j, k). Wenn auch im Klausenburger Gebetbuch keine Fehlbindung vorzuliegen scheint, steht doch zu vermuten, dass die ursprüngliche Anordnung hier lediglich aus Versehen zerstört worden ist:

---

51 Augsburg: Anton Sorg, [um 1485] (GW 12983). Vgl. das Digitalisat unter ⟨http://resolver. staatsbibliothek-berlin.de/SBB0001EFB300000000⟩. Vgl. künftig KdiH Nr. 43.3B.3.b.

52 Augsburg: Hans Otmar für Georg Diemer, 4. 4. 1510 (VD16 T 198). Vgl. das Digitalisat unter ⟨http://mdz-nbn-resolving.de/urn:nbn:de:bvb:12-bsb00008180-2⟩. Weitere Ausgaben 1512, 1514, 1516, 1520. Vgl. künftig KdiH Nr. 43.3C.6.a bis Nr. 43.3C.6.e.

53 Augsburg: Hans Schönsperger, 1520 (VD16 G 2035). Vgl. das Digitalisat unter ⟨http://mdz-nbn-resolving.de/urn:nbn:de:bvb:12-bsb00092329-6⟩. Weitere Ausgaben 1521, zwei sine anno. Vgl. KdiH 5/1, 139, 256–257, 260 sowie künftig KdiH Nr. 43.3C.5.a bis Nr. 43.3C.5.d.

54 Augsburg: Hans Otmar für Georg Diemer, 4. 4. 1510 (VD16 T 198), $d_{viij}r - e_jr$. Vgl. das Digitalisat unter ⟨http://daten.digitale-sammlungen.de/bsb00008180/image_54⟩ mit Klausenburg, UB, Ms. 683, 85 r–86 r.

55 Augsburg: Hans Schönsperger, 1520 (VD16 G 2035), $k_{vj}r - l_{iv}r$. Vgl das Digitalisat unter ⟨http://daten.digitale-sammlungen.de/bsb00092329/image_158⟩ mit Klausenburg, UB, Ms. 683, 55 r–62 r.

Geburt Christi

Gefangennahme (Matutin)
Christus vor Pilatus (Prim)
Ecce homo (Terz)
Kreuzannagelung (Sext)   } *Sieben Tagzeiten vom Leiden Christi*
Kreuzigung (Non)
Beweinung (Vesper)
Grablegung (Komplet)

Auferstehung
Christi Himmelfahrt
Pfingsten
Jüngstes Gericht.

D. h. die siebenteiligen *Tagzeiten zur Passion* des Johann von Neumarkt waren zu einem zwölfteiligen Leben- und Leiden Christi-Zyklus erweitert worden.

Noch ein anderer interessanter Aspekt ergibt sich aus dieser Übersicht. Bis auf zwei Handschriften, nämlich diejenigen in St. Gallen (Anhang 2, Spalte 3) und in Heidelberg (Anhang 2, Spalte 11), weisen sie alle verschiedenermaßen die für Augsburg typischen Stilmerkmale auf. Ein früher Repräsentant (Anhang 2, Spalte 10; Abb. 28, 32, 33) wurde von einem Mitarbeiter des Johannes Bämler ausgemalt (Abb. 28, 29), den der Meister im Zuge der von ihm serienmäßig betriebenen Ausstattung von Inkunabeln mit farbigem Dekor wohl eigens angelernt hat.[56] Dabei wurden die von Bämler in den 1450er, 60er Jahren entwickelten opulenten, abwechslungsreichen Zierformen von seinem Hilfsarbeiter zunehmend auf ein ökonomisches Mindestmaß reduziert. Der Unterschied wird offenbar, wenn man eine 1466 gedruckte Inkunabel daneben hält, die Bämler 1468 eigenhändig ausgemalt und signiert hat (Abb. 30).[57] Die übrigen Vertreter der Überlieferungsgruppe (Abb. 34–43) nähern sich dagegen bereits stärker den Produkten der Augsburg-Salzburger Missalien-Werkstatt an (Abb. 31).

Ms. 683 (Abb. 1, 5–9, 11, 13, 19, 27, 43) kann somit in eine handschriftliche Augsburger Tradition eingebettet werden, die sich nicht in den Buchdruck hinüber gerettet hat. Doch handelt es sich bei dem Klausenburger Codex weniger um ein singuläres Artefakt, als vielmehr um ein unpersönliches, wohl auf Vorrat gefertigtes professionelles Produkt, bei dem individuelle Wünsche eines Bestellers keine Rolle gespielt haben.

---

56 Vgl. Zöhl: 2018; Cermann: in Vorbereitung, Anhang 17.
57 Nach dem gedruckten Explicit steht in Blau geschrieben „Johannes Bämler de Augusta Illuminator libri huius anno etc. 68."

Anhang 1.

Inhalt von Klausenburg, Universitätsbibliothek, Ms. 683

1v	Miniatur: Marienkrönung
2r–3v	Johannes von Indersdorf, Gebet zur Dreifaltigkeit aus der Sammlung für Herzog Wilhelm III. von Bayern „O Du hailige driualtigkaite O ware ainigkeit O du heilige vnd göttliche mayestat ..." (Haimerl: 1952, 155, Anm. 965, Nr. 1)
3v–5r	Morgengebet „O Ewiger vnd barmhertziger got herr ihesu criste ich armer sunder dein creatur sag heut lob vnd danck deiner göttlichen genade dz du mich behüttet hast ..."
5v	Miniatur: Veronika mit dem Schweißtuch Christi
6r–8r	Gebet zum Antlitz Christi bzw. zur hl. Veronika „O Aller sälikait ain anschowung du göttliches angesicht vnnsers herren ihesu cristi ..."
8r–10v	Johannes von Indersdorf, Gebet von der Geburt und Kindheit Christi aus der Sammlung für Herzog Wilhelm III. von Bayern „O Herr ihesu criste du ewige vnd göttliche weyßheit deins himlischen vaters ..." (Haimerl: 1952, 156, Anm. 973)
11r	leer
11v	Miniatur: Elevation des Kelches, männlicher Stifter
12r–21r	Gebete zur Messe: „O Schöpfer himels vnd der erden kung aller kung ...", 15v Vor der Wandlung „O Du tieffer abgrunde der ewigen weyßhait ...", 17v Zur Elevation der Hostie „Gegrüsset seyestu warer fronlichnam ihesu cristi warlichen geboren von der iunkfrowen maria ...", 18r Zur Elevation des Kelches „O herr ihesu criste der du disen aller heiligsten leichnam von dem loblichen leybe der iunckfrowen marie hast empfangen ...", 19r Zum Totengedenken: Johannes von Indersdorf, Seelengebet aus dem Ebran-Gebetbuch „O du reicher schatz vnd brunn der barmhertzigkait tail mit dein vätterliche liebe ..." (Haimerl: 1952, 156, Anm. 972, Nr. 4), 20r Johannes von Indersdorf, Seelengebet aus dem Ebran-Gebetbuch „Ewiger vnd allmechtiger gott erbarm dich vber alle ellend vnd gelöbige selen ..." (Haimerl: 1952, 156, Anm. 972, Nr. 5), 20v Zum Segen „O Du kaiserliche kron aller seligen herre ewiger gott Gib mir täglichen deinen segen ..."
21v	Miniatur: Seelen im Fegefeuer
22r–22v	Ablass von 100 Tagen, von Papst Pius II. am 25.11.1459 auf dem Fürstentag in Mantua Markgraf Karl von Baden erteilt „Vff sant katrinen tag des iares da man zalt von cristi gepurt Im lix Jar zu montaw In der statt hat der aller hailigist in xpo vatter vnd herr Pius bapst der ander in seim andern iar In gegenwertigkait des durchleuchtigen fursten vnd herren her karolus margrauen zu baden vnd ettlicher seiner rätte geben hundert tag aplas töttlicher schuld ainem yeden menschen als offt er das gebet spricht (22v) gelöbigen selen also"
22v–25r	Ablassgebet „Erbarme dich gott mein herre vber alle selen die gegen dir nit sonder bitter haben vnd den kain trost ist in ir peinigung ..."; weitere Seelengebete: 23r „Gegrüsset seyent Ir alle gelöbige selen ...", 24r „O allmechtiger gott wir bitten dich vber sich die selen deiner diener vnd dienerin ...", 24v Johannes von Indersdorf, Seelengebet aus dem Ebran-Ge-

Individualstück oder Standardware? | 43

	betbuch „O Du reicher brun der barmhertzigkait tail mit dein vätterliche liebe …" (Haimerl: 1952, 155, Anm. 962)
25 r–40 r	Johann von Neumarkt, *Tagzeiten vom Leiden Christi* (Klapper: 1935, 3–13, Nr. I,2, 4, 6–13; am ähnlichsten Sigle K [Karlsruhe, BLB, Cod. Perg. Germ. XL])
26 v	Miniatur: Gefangennahme (Mette)
28 v	Miniatur: Christus vor Pilatus (Prim)
30 v	Miniatur: Ecce homo (Terz)
32 v	Miniatur: Kreuzannagelung (Sext)
34 v	Miniatur: Kreuzigung (Non)
36 v	Miniatur: Beweinung (Vesper)
38 v	Miniatur: Grablegung (Komplet)
40 v	Miniatur: Auferstehung
41 r–45 v	Gebet zur Auferstehung Christi „O Gewaltiger O starcker O sighafftiger gott …"
46 r	leer
46 v	Miniatur: Himmelfahrt Christi
47 r–48 r	Gebet zur Himmelfahrt Christi „O Gewaltiger schöpfer des himels vnd der erden nach deiner hailigen vrstende …"
48 v	Miniatur: Pfingsten
49 r–50 v	Zwei Gebete zu Pfingsten „O Du mein aller liebster schatze vnd trost meiner armen sel …", 49 v Johannes von Indersdorf, Gebet aus der Sammlung für Herzog Wilhelm III. von Bayern „Kom hailiger gaiste du barmhertziger got …" (Haimerl: 1952, 155, Anm. 964)
51 r–52 r	Johann von Neumarkt, Gebet zum Schutzengel „O Du säliger wirdiger vnd englischer geist der mir von dem allmechtigen …" (Klapper: 1935, 176–179, Nr. 23)
52 r–54 r	Gebet zum Eigenapostel „O Du besonder außerwelter mein heiliger zwölfbotte Sant […] mein firsprech vor dem allmechtigen gott …"
54 v	Miniatur: Mater dolorosa, Herz von zwei Schwertern durchbohrt
55 r–62 r	Johann von Neumarkt, Sancta Maria, dt. (Klapper: 1935, 335–343, Nr. 98,1)
62 v	Miniatur: Maria in sole
63 r–63 v	Salve regina, dt.
63 v–64 v	Goldenes Ave Maria
65 r	leer
65 v	Miniatur: Kommunionempfang
66 r–78 v	Kommuniongebete: „O Ewiger vnd barmhertziger gott herr ihesu criste entzunde mich mit dem feur …", 74 r nach dem Empfang „Die enpfencknus des zarten waren fronlichnames …" (Haimerl: 1952, 84, Anm. 490, Nr. 1 und 3)
78 v–83 v	Gebet zum Gründonnerstag (antlastag) 80 r „O Du aller güttigoster erlöser herre ihesu criste der du als auffheitt in diser nache willigclichen …"
79 r	leer
79 v	Miniatur: Gebet am Ölberg
84 r	leer
84 v	Miniatur: Martyrium des hl. Sebastian
85 r–86 r	Pestgebet zum hl. Sebastian „O hailiger herr Sant Sebastion dein geloub ist groß …" (Haimerl: 1952, 84, Anm. 489)

44 | Regina Cermann

86v	Miniatur: Alle Heiligen, anhand von Attributen erkennbar: Bischof Ulrich von Augsburg, Petrus, Maria Magdalena, Katharina
87r–88r	Gebet zu allen Heiligen „Herr ihesu criste allmechtiger vnd ewiger got ich bitte dich verleiche mir alle deine hailigen also zu erenen …“
88v	Miniatur: Johannes d. T.
89r–90v	Zwei Gebete zu Johannes d. T. „O hailiger Sant iohannes der von mutterleib vol des hailigen geistes …“, 89v „O hailiger herre sant Johannes gottes töffer Ich großer sünder manen dich …“
91r	leer
91v	Miniatur: Johannes d. Ev.
92r–93v	Johannes von Indersdorf, Zwei Gebete zu Johannes d. Ev. aus dem Ebran-Gebetbuch „Iohannes du himlischer adeler …“, „O hailiger herre sant iohannes du cantzler cristi …“ (Haimerl: 1952, 154, Anm. 957, Nr. 1 und 2)
94r	leer
94v	Miniatur: Antonius Eremita
95r–96v	Gebet zum hl. Antonius Eremita „Ein yeglicher geiste vnd alle creaturen loben got …“
97r	leer
97v	Miniatur: Leonhard
98r–98v	Gebet zum hl. Leonhard „O Du hailiger beichtiger ihesu criste Sant lienhart wann du got hie auff erden gedienet hast …“
99r	leer
99v	Miniatur: Christophorus
100r–101v	Gebet zum hl. Christophorus „O Du hailiger herre Sant cristoffel Du wirdiger martrer gotes …“
102r–102v	Gebet zum hl. Georg „O hailiger ritter Sannt Jörg du wirdiger martrer gottes …“ (ohne Miniatur)
103r	leer
103v	Miniatur: Maria Magdalena
104r–105v	Johannes von Indersdorf, Gebet zur hl. Maria Magdalena aus dem Ebran-Gebetbuch „Maria magdalena du liebhaberin cristi Du spiegel der barmhertzigkait gottes …“ (Haimerl: 1952, 155, Anm. 958)
106r	leer
106v	Miniatur: Martyrium der hl. Barbara
107r–109r	Gebet zur hl. Barbara „Gegrüsset seyest du edels kostbarliches gestein …“
109v	Miniatur: Ottilie erlöst ihren Vater aus dem Fegefeuer durch ihre Fürbitte
110r–111v	Gebet zur hl. Ottilie „O hailige Otilia vnd iunckfrow ihesu criste wir bitten dich …“
112r	leer
112v	Miniatur: Martyrium der hl. Katharina
113r–114v	Gebet zur hl. Katharina „Gegrüsset seyest du katrina ein edel gestein der clarheit …“
115r	leer
115v	Miniatur: Martyrium der hl. Apollonia
116r–117v	Gebet zur hl. Apollonia „O Ewiger vnnd allersterckister gott, der du deinen ausserwelten in der peinigung des fleisches …“
118r	leer
118v	Miniatur: Jüngstes Gericht

Individualstück oder Standardware? | 45

119r–121r	Gebet zum Jüngsten Gericht „O Ewige göttliche barmhertzikeit o menschliche gerechtigkeit …"
121v–[122v]	leer

46 | Regina Cermann

Anhang 2.

	1.	2.	3.	4.	5.
	Klausenburg, UB, Ms. 683[58]	Dallas, Bridwell Library, MS 91[59]	St. Gallen, StiftsB, Cod. 511[60]	Augsburg, UB, Cod. III.1.8° 55[61]	München, BSB, Cgm 140[62]
	Abb. 1, 5–9, 11, 13, 19, 27, 43	Abb. 40		Abb. 39	Abb. 38
a	Dreifaltigkeit	7r–10r	1r–?	36v–39v	3r–5r
b	Morgengebet	15r–18r *Variante*	3v–? *Variante*	39v–42r *Variante*	5r–7v *Variante*
c	Antlitz Christi	18r–22r *Variante*	5r–? *Variante*	43r–46v *Variante*	8r–11v *Variante*
d	Geburt Christi	*43r–48r*	*22v–?*	*82r–86r*	*38v–42v*
e	Messgebete	*22r–38r*	*6v–?*	*47r–71r*	*12r–29r*
f	Ablass Pius' II.	*38r Variante*	*18v?*	*(152v–154v Ersatz)*	*(94v–96v Ersatz)*
g	Seelengebete		21r		
h	Tagzeiten zur Passion	53v–75v	26v–37r	*87r–103v*	*43r–54v*
i	Auferstehung	*75v–84r*	*37v–?*	*(103v–105v Ersatz)*	*(54v–56v Ersatz)*
j	Himmelfahrt	*84r–86v*	*41r–?*	*105v–107r*	*56v–58v*
k	Pfingsten	*86v–88r*	*42v–?*	*107v–110r*	*58v–60r*
l	Schutzengel	*94r–97r*	*45v–?*	*(72r–73v Ersatz)*	*(29r–31r Ersatz)*

---

58 KdiH 5/1, XIV, Nr. 43.1.42a. Vgl. Eintrag im HSC unter ⟨http://www.handschriftencensus. de/22675⟩ sowie künftig KdiH digital unter ⟨https://kdih.badw.de/datenbank/handschrift/ 43/1/42a⟩.

59 Ehem. Paris/New York/Chicago, Les Enluminures [Sandra Hindman], Reference Number TM 14. 2005 von der Bridwell Library erworben. Vgl. Beschreibung sowie vier Abbildungen (Vorderdeckel, 31v+32r, 153v, 176v) unter ⟨https://www.lesenluminures.com⟩ bzw. ⟨https:// sites.smu.edu/bridwell/specialcollections/bridwellwesternms/ms91.htm⟩ sowie Eintrag im HSC unter ⟨http://www.handschriftencensus.de/21784⟩.

60 1481 geschrieben von Gabriel Nagel von Waltdorff. Vgl. Scarpatetti/Lenz: 2008, 240–245.

61 KdiH 5/1, 25–27, Nr. 43.1.7, Abb. 46 (46v+47r). Vgl. Schneider: 1988, 666–673.

62 KdiH 5/1, XVII, Nr. 43.1.124. Vgl. Petzet: 1920, 262–264, sowie Volldigitalisat unter ⟨https:// mdz-nbn-resolving.de/details:bsb00082394⟩.

	6.	7.	8.	9.	10.	11.
	Mainz, StB, Hs. I 428[63]	New York, PML, MS Stillman 14[64]	Iowa City, UL, xMMs.Pr3	ehem. Zürich, Koller, 24.9.2016, Nr. 573	ehem. Pforzheim, Kiefer, Auktion 89, 27./28.6.2014, Nr. 412	Heidelberg, UB, Cod. Pal. germ. 443
	Abb. 36, 37	Abb. 42	Abb. 41	Abb. 34, 35	Abb. 28, 32, 33	
a	8r–10v	132v–?		13r–?	4r–?	
b	10v–12v *Variante*	137v–? *Variante*		?–24v *Variante*	?	
c	13r–15v *Variante*	140r–? *Variante*		25r–? *Variante*		
d	*41r–44r*	*165r–?*	*26r–30v*	*?–?*	*?–?*	
e	*16r–31r*	*143r–?*	*1r–25v*	*33r–?*	*?*	*56r–63v*
f		*(203r–? Ersatz)*	*(87v–89v Ersatz)*	*(?)*		*140r Variante*
g				?		
h	*82r–93r*		*31r–52r*	*81r–??*		
i	*(94r–? Ersatz)*	*172r–?*		*?–?*	*?*	
j	*96r–?*	*179r–?*		*?–?*	*?*	
k	*97v–?*	*181r–?*		*?–?*	*?*	
l	*(32r–33v Ersatz)*	*186v–?*	*52r–54r*	*?–?*	*?*	

---

63 KdiH 5/1, XVII, Nr. 43.1.109a. Vgl. Projektinformationen zur Erschließung der Handschriften der Wissenschaftlichen Stadtbibliothek Mainz, Teil 4 (Hs I 351 – Hs I 490, Hs I 513 – Hs I 529). Mit Handschriftenbeschreibungen von Gerhard List und Annelen Ottermann, Stand 2007, eingestellt in Manuscripta Mediaevalia ⟨http://www.manuscripta-mediaevalia. de⟩ (unter Projekte). Fünf Abbildungen von Hill Museum & Manuscript Library Color Microfilms eingestellt in *Vivarium* ⟨https://cdm.csbsju.edu/digital/collection/HMMLClrMicr⟩ (7v+8r, 12v+13r, 15v+16r, 116v+117r, 130v+131r). Ich danke Christoph Winterer, Mainz, der die von List/Ottermann erstellte Listenbeschreibung durch Abgleich mit Augsburg, UB, Cod. III.1. 8° 55 im Juni 2018 ergänzt und präzisiert hat. Vgl. nun auch List: 2021, 102–105, Abb. 5.

64 KdiH 5/1, XVIII, Nr. 43.1.143a. Vgl. Hamburger: 2013, 111–113, Fig. 18, 19 (6v+7r), 145–146, Anm. 58, 152 sowie knappe Beschreibung und 14 Abbildungen unter ⟨https://www.themorgan.org/manuscript/161058⟩.

		1.	2.	3.	4.	5.
		Klausenburg, UB, Ms. 683	Dallas, Bridwell Library, MS 91	St. Gallen, StiftsB, Cod. 511	Augsburg, UB, Cod. III.1.8° 55	München, BSB, Cgm 140
		Abb. 1, 5–9, 11, 13, 19, 27, 43	Abb. 40		Abb. 39	Abb. 38
m	Eigenapostel		97r–101r	46v–?	74r–76v	31r–34r
n	Mariengebete:					
	Sancta Maria					
	Salve regina		106r–107v	50r–?	114r–115v	64r–65r
	Gold. Ave Maria		121r–123r	56v–?	131v–132r	75r–76v
o	Kommuniongebete		130r–140v?	62v–?	133r–148r	77r–87v
p	Gründonnerstag		145r–150r	75r–?	148r–152r	87v–94r
q	Heiligengebete:					
	Sebastian/Pest		154r–156r	83r–?	155r–156v	77r–99r
	Alle Heiligen		160r–161v	88r–? *Plural*	(157r–183v Ersatz)	(105r–119r Ersatz)
	Johannes d.T.		161v–163v	88v–?	184r–185v	119v–122r
	Johannes Ev.		163v–165v	90r–?	186r–188r	122r–124v
	Antonius Erem.		165v–167r	91r–?	188v–189r	125r–127r
	Leonhard		167v–168r	92v–?	197r–198r	132r–133v
	Christophorus		168v–169r	93v–?	*193r–194v*	*127v–128v*
	Georg		169v–171r	95r–?		
	Maria Magdalena		171r–173r	95v–?	198r–199v	
	Barbara		173r–175r	97r–?	200r–202r	136v–139r
	Ottilie		175r–177r	99r–?	202v–203v	*136r–136v*
	Katharina		177r–179r	100r–?	203v–205r	*134r–135v*
	Apollonia		179r–181r	101r–?	205r–206v	139v–141v
					(+ 189r–191v Peter & Paul)	
					(+ 194v–197r Erasmus)	*(+ 129r–132r Erasmus)*
					(+ 206v–207r Wolfgang)	
r	Jüngstes Gericht		*90v–94r*	*43v–?*	*110r–112v*	*60r–63v*

Individualstück oder Standardware? | 49

	6.	7.	8.	9.	10.	11.
	Mainz, StB, Hs. I 428	New York, PML, MS Stillman 14	Iowa City, UL, xMMs.Pr3[65]	ehem. Zürich, Koller, 24.9.2016, Nr. 573[66]	ehem. Pforzheim, Kiefer, Auktion 89, 27./28.6.2014, Nr. 412	Heidelberg, UB, Cod. Pal. germ. 443[67]
	Abb. 36, 37	Abb. 42	Abb. 41	Abb. 34, 35	Abb. 28, 32, 33	
m	34r–36r *Variante*	188r–?	55r–57r		*?*	
n						
			60r–61r	?–?		
o	117r–123v		76r–87r	?–?	*?*	142r–150v
p	124r–127r					150v Abbruch
q	131r–? (*138r–? Ersatz*) 142r–? 144r–? 145v–? 147r–? 149r–? *153r–?* *151r–?*	193v–?, 204v–? 211r–? *Plural,* (*215v–? Ersatz*) 212r–? 214r–? 241v–? 243v–?	90r–92r 92r–93v *Plural* 93v–94v 94v–96r *100v–102r* 98r–100r (*+ 96r–97v Peter & Paul*)	(*?–? Ersatz*) *?* *?* *?* *?* *?* *?* (*+ Erasmus*)		
r	*99r–?*	*184r–?*		*?*		

---

65 Vgl. Eintrag im HSC unter ⟨http://www.handschriftencensus.de/18259⟩ sowie knappe Beschreibung und Volldigitalisat unter ⟨https://digital.lib.uiowa.edu/cdm/compoundobject/collection/mmc/id/2713⟩. Auf 4r Besitzstempel FG = Franz Goldhann (1782–1856), zahlreiche Handschriften von diesem Altertumsforscher heute in der ÖNB in Wien.

66 Nachfolgend: Cayce, King Alfred's Notebook LLC [Scott Gwara], 2017, Nr. 239. Vgl. Eintrag im HSC unter Charleston, s. ⟨http://www.handschriftencensus.de/25838⟩.

67 Vgl. Miller/Zimmermann: 2007, 447–452, sowie Volldigitalisat unter ⟨http://digi.ub.uni-heidelberg.de/diglit/cpg443⟩.

Anhang 3.

Rubriken zum Ablass Papst Pius' II. von 1459

1). Basel, Universitätsbibliothek, Cod. A VIII 51, 146 r–147 r
„In dem ior als man zalt von gottes geburt 1459 jor an sant angnesen tag der heiligen jungfrowen *[21.1.]* hat der aller heiligst in got vatter vnd herre her Pius der ander bobst des nammen in dem andern ior sins böstums von anrüffen eines frommen edeln mannes den er lieb hatt Als sin heilikeit vff die zit zuo mantow vnd der hochgebornen fürst margroff karle von baden vnd groff zuo spomhem von keiser fryderichs wegen zuo siner heilikeit gesandt was des selben herren Des margroffen diener vnd hoffmeister der edelman ist gewesen Geben allen vnd ieglichen kristenen menschen diß noch geschriben gebet In güter andacht bettend vnd sprechend hundert tag applos töttlicher sünd so dick si die also sprechend.“

2). Klausenburg, Universitätsbibliothek, Ms. 683, 22 r–22 v
„Vff sant katrinen tag *[25.11.]* des iares da man zalt von cristi gepurt Im lix *[1459]* Jar zu montow In der statt hat der aller hailigist in xpo vatter vnd herr Pius bapst der ander in seim andern iar In gegenwertigkait des durchleuchtigen fursten vnd herren her karolus margrauen zu baden vnd ettlicher seiner rätte geben hundert tag aplas töttlicher schuld ainem yeden menschen als offt er das gebet spricht gelöbigen selen also.“

3). Heidelberg, Universitätsbibliothek, Cod. Pal. germ. 443, 140 r
„Vff Sanct Kathereinen tag des Tausentst vierhunderst Neunvndfunffzigst Jar *[25.11.1459]* zuo Montaw in der stat hat der allerheiligst in got vatter vnd here here pius Babst der ander in seinem andern Jar Inn gegenwurtigkeit des durchleuchtigen fursten vnd hern hern Karels marggrauen zuo Baden zuo dissem gebete geben jᶜ tag ablaß todlicher schuldt.“

4). Rastatt, Ludwig-Wilhelm-Gymnasium, K 173, 298 r
„Item zuo dißem nachvolgenden gebette haut Bapst Pius des ander zuo Mantowe uff bitte Margkraff Karlis zuo Baden raetten geben hundertt tag Ablauß toettlicher schulde so offt ain yeglicher mensche das mit rüwe und andachte sprichet und bettett in genaden.“

Außerdem überliefert in:

5). St. Gallen, Stiftsbibliothek, Cod. 511, 18 v–21 v: Von Papst Pius II. zu Mantua Markgraf Karl von Baden verliehen (Hs. datiert 1481). Kein Incipit für die Rubrik im Katalog angegeben. 19 r Gebetsbeginn „Erbarm dich gott min herr über alle selen die da gegen dir nit sonnder bitter habent …“ (= Klausenburg, Universitätsbibliothek, Ms. 683, 22 v).

6). Dallas, Bridwell Library, MS 91, 38 r ff
„Von disem hernach geschriben gebet hatt pabst pius der ander geben eynem iden menschen hundert tag ablas todlicher schulde als offt er das spricht zuo trost allen gelaubigen selen."

Bibliographie

BARTSCH, ADAM (1808), Le peintre graveur, 21 Bde., Wien: Degen, 1802–1821, Bd. 7.

BEIER, CHRISTINE (2004), Missalien massenhaft. Die Bämler-Werkstatt und die Augsburger Buchmalerei im 15. Jahrhundert, Codices Manuscripti 48/49, Textbd., 55–78, Tafelbd., 67–78, Abb. 1–42.

BINZ, GUSTAV (1907), Die deutschen Handschriften der Öffentlichen Bibliothek der Universität Basel, Bd. 1: Die Handschriften der Abteilung A, Basel: Universitätsbibliothek.

CERMANN, REGINA (in Vorbereitung), Das Stundenbuch deutsch.

CERMANN, REGINA (1998), Der Verfasser der Gebete: Thomas von Kempen, in: Das Glockendon-Gebetbuch, Biblioteca Estense Universitaria, α.U.6.7, Kommentar zum Faksimile, Luzern: Faksimile-Verlag, 7–30.

CERMANN, REGINA (2010), Über den Export deutschsprachiger Stundenbücher von Paris nach Nürnberg, Codices Manuscripti 75, 9–24.

CERMANN, REGINA (2018), Unter Druck? Buchmalerei im Wettstreit mit Reproduktionsmedien, in: Jeffrey F. Hamburger/Maria Theisen (Hg.), Unter Druck. Mitteleuropäische Buchmalerei im 15. Jahrhundert, Tagungsband zum internationalen Kolloquium in Wien, Österreichische Akademie der Wissenschaften, 13.1.–17.1.2016, Buchmalerei des 15. Jahrhunderts in Mitteleuropa 15, Petersberg: Michael Imhof Verlag, Abbildungsteil zu dem gleichnamigen Beitrag online unter der URL ⟨http://archiv.ub.uni-heidelberg.de/artdok/volltexte/2017/4926⟩, Heidelberg: ART-Dok 2017.

FIELD, RICHARD S. (1965), Fifteenth Century Woodcuts and Metalcuts from the National Gallery of Art, Washington, D.C., Washington D. C.: National Gallery of Art.

HAIMERL, FRANZ X. (1952), Mittelalterliche Frömmigkeit im Spiegel der Gebetbuchliteratur Süddeutschlands, Münchener theologische Studien I,4, München: Karl Zink Verlag.

HAMBURGER, JEFFREY (2013), Another Perspective. The Book of Hours in Germany, in: Sandra Hindman/James Marrow (ed.), Books of Hours Reconsidered, Studies in Medieval and Early Renaissance Art History, Turnhout: Harvey Miller, 97–152.

HEINZER, FELIX (1989), Aus Handschriften und Inkunabeln der Historischen Lehrerbibliothek des Ludwig-Wilhelm-Gymnasiums, Vortragsreihe der Historischen Lehrerbibliothek des Ludwig-Wilhelm-Gymnasiums in Rastatt 1, Rastatt: Stadtverwaltung Rastatt, 46–49.

HEITZMANN, CHRISTIAN/KRUSE, BRITTA-JULIANE/LESSER, BERTRAM (Hg.) (2015), Bilder lesen. Deutsche Buchmalerei des 15. Jahrhunderts in der Herzog August Bibliothek Wolfenbüttel, Katalog zur Ausstellung in der Herzog August Bibliothek vom 22. November 2015 bis 28. Februar 2016, Buchmalerei des 15. Jahrhunderts in Mitteleuropa 13, Luzern: Quaternio.

52 | Regina Cermann

KEMPERDICK, STEPHAN (2007), Kreis und Kosmos. Ein restauriertes Tafelbild des 15. Jahrhunderts, mit einem Beitrag von Amelie Jensen zu Maltechnik und Restaurierung, Kunstmuseum Basel, 18.8.–11.11.2007, Petersberg: Michael Imhof Verlag.

KLAPPER, JOSEPH (1935), Schriften Johanns von Neumarkt. Vierter Teil: Gebete des Hofkanzlers und des Prager Kulturkreises, Vom Mittelalter zur Reformation, Forschungen zur Geschichte der deutschen Bildung 6, Berlin: Weidmannsche Buchhandlung.

KÖNIG, EBERHARD (1997), Augsburger Buchkunst an der Schwelle zur Frühdruckzeit, in: Helmut Gier/Johannes Janota (Hg.), Augsburger Buchdruck und Verlagswesen. Von den Anfängen bis zur Gegenwart, Wiesbaden: Harrassowitz, 173–200.

KÜHNEL, HARRY (Hg.) (1992), Bildwörterbuch der Kleidung und Rüstung. Vom Alten Orient bis zum ausgehenden Mittelalter, Stuttgart: Alfred Kröner Verlag.

LIST, GERHARD (2021), Die Handschriften der Stadtbibliothek Mainz, Bd. IV (Bestandsliste): Hs I 351–Hs I 490. Mit Ergänzungen von Annelen Ottermann und Christoph Winterer, Redaktion: Annelen Ottermann, Christian Richter, Christoph Winterer, Wiesbaden: Harrassowitz.

MERKL, ULRICH (1999), Buchmalerei in Bayern in der ersten Hälfte des 16. Jahrhunderts. Spätblüte und Endzeit einer Gattung, Regensburg: Schnell und Steiner.

MERKL, ULRICH/OBHOF, UTE/NEIDL, MICHAELA (2002), Das deutsche Gebetbuch der Markgräfin von Brandenburg. Hs. Durlach 2, Badische Landesbibliothek Karlsruhe. Kommentar [zum Faksimile], Luzern: Faksimile-Verlag.

MESSLING, GUIDO (2004), Leonhard Beck als Buchmaler. Eine Untersuchung zu zwei Hauptwerken der religiösen Buchmalerei Augsburgs vom Ende des 15. Jahrhunderts, Münchner Jahrbuch der bildenden Kunst 55, 73–114. [tatsächlich 2006 erschienen].

MIELKE, URSULA (1997): Albrecht and Erhard Altdorfer, The New Hollstein German Engravings, Etchings and Woodcuts 1400–1700 vol. 2, Rotterdam: Sound & Vision Publishers.

MILLER, MATTHIAS/ZIMMERMANN, KARIN (2007), Die Codices Palatini germanici in der Universitätsbibliothek Heidelberg (Cod. Pal. germ. 304–495), Kataloge der Universitätsbibliothek Heidelberg VIII, Wiesbaden: Reichert-Verlag.

NEMES, BALÁZS J. (2012), Mittelalterliche deutsche Handschriften in rumänischen Bibliotheken. Eine vorläufige Bestandsübersicht, in: Astrid Breith (Hg.), Manuscripta germanica. Deutschsprachige Handschriften des Mittelalters in Bibliotheken und Archiven Osteuropas, Zeitschrift für deutsches Altertum und deutsche Literatur. Beiheft 15, Stuttgart: S. Hirzel Verlag, 61–72.

OLDENBOURG, M[ARIA] CONSUELO (1973), Hortulus animae [1494]–1523. Bibliographie und Illustration, Hamburg: Dr. Ernst Hauswedell & Co.

PÄCHT, OTTO (1964), Vita Sancti Simperti. Eine Handschrift für Maximilian I., Berlin: Deutscher Verlag für Kunstwissenschaft.

PAPAHAGI, ADRIAN (2013), Manuscrisele medievale occidentale aflate in colecțiile Bibliotecii Centrale Universitare din Cluj-Napoca, Revista română de istorie a cărții IX/9, 32–46.

PAPAHAGI, ADRIAN/DINCĂ, ADINEL CIPRIAN/MÂRZA, ANDREEA (2018), Manuscrisele medievale occidentale din România. Census, Iași: Polirom.

PAUL, HERMANN/MOSER, HUGO/SCHRÖBLER, INGEBORG/GROSSE, SIEGFRIED ([22]1982), Mittelhochdeutsche Grammatik, Sammlung kurzer Grammatiken germanischer Dialekte, A. Hauptreihe Nr. 2, Tübingen: Max Niemeyer Verlag.

PAULUS, NIKOLAUS (1923), Geschichte des Ablasses im Mittelalter, Bd. 3: Geschichte des Ablasses am Ausgange des Mittelalters, Paderborn: F. Schöningh.

PETZET, ERICH (1920), Die deutschen Pergament-Handschriften Nr. 1–200 der Staatsbibliothek in München, Catalogus codicum manuscriptorum Bibliothecae Monacensis V,1, München: Palm'sche Buchhandlung.

SCARPATETTI, BEAT MATTHIAS VON / LENZ, PHILIPP (2008), Die Handschriften der Stiftsbibliothek St. Gallen, Bd. 2: Abt. III / 2, Codices 450–546. Liturgica, Libri precum, deutsche Gebetbücher, Spiritualia, Musikhandschriften, 9.–16. Jahrhundert, Wiesbaden: Harrassowitz.

SCHLECHTER, ARMIN / STAMM, GERHARD (2000), Die kleinen Provenienzen, Die Handschriften der Badischen Landesbibliothek in Karlsruhe XIII, Wiesbaden: Harrassowitz.

SCHMIDT, PETER (1998), Rhin supérieur ou Bavière? Localisation et mobilité des gravures au milieu du XVe siècle, Revue de l'art 120, 66–88.

SCHMIDT, PETER (2003), Gedruckte Bilder in handgeschriebenen Büchern. Studien zum Gebrauch von Druckgraphik im 15. Jahrhundert, Pictura et poësis 16, Köln / Weimar / Wien: Böhlau.

SCHNEIDER, KARIN (1988), Deutsche mittelalterliche Handschriften der Universitätsbibliothek Augsburg. Die Signaturengruppen Cod. I. 3. und Cod. III. 1, Die Handschriften der Universitätsbibliothek Augsburg 2,1, Wiesbaden: Harrassowitz.

SCHNEIDER, KARIN (1995), Berufs- und Amateurschreiber. Zum Laien-Schreibbetrieb im spätmittelalterlichen Augsburg, in: Johannes Janota / Werner Williams-Krapp (Hg.), Literarisches Leben in Augsburg während des 15. Jahrhunderts, Studia Augustana 7, Tübingen: Max Niemeyer Verlag, 8–26.

SCHNEIDER, KARIN (1999), Paläographie und Handschriftenkunde für Germanisten. Eine Einführung, Sammlung kurzer Grammatiken germanischer Dialekte, B. Ergänzungsreihe Nr. 8, Tübingen: Max Niemeyer Verlag.

SCHOCH, RAINER / MENDE, MATTHIAS / SCHERBAUM, ANNA (2002), Albrecht Dürer. Das druckgraphische Werk, Bd. 2: Holzschnitte und Holzschnittfolgen, München / Berlin / London / New York: Prestel.

STEGMÜLLER, OTTO (1958), Aus Handschriften der Rastatter Gymnasialbibliothek, in: Humanitas. 1808–1958. 150 Jahre Ludwig-Wilhelm-Gymnasium Rastatt, Rastatt: Pabel, 74–82.

WEHMER, CARL (1955), Ne Italo cedere videamur. Augsburger Buchdrucker und Schreiber um 1500, in: Clemens Bauer / Bernhard Josef / Hermann Rinn (Hg.), Augusta 955–1955. Forschungen und Studien zur Kultur- und Wirtschaftsgeschichte Augsburgs, Augsburg: Rinn, 145–173.

WILHELM, JOHANNES (1983), Augsburger Wandmalerei 1368–1530. Künstler, Handwerker und Zunft, Abhandlungen zur Geschichte der Stadt Augsburg 29, Augsburg: Mühlberger.

ZANDER-SEIDEL, JUTTA (1990), Textiler Hausrat. Kleidung und Haustextilien in Nürnberg von 1500–1560, München: Deutscher Kunstverlag.

ZÖHL, CAROLINE (2018), Das Catholicon-Projekt – eine Augsburger Kooperation im frühen Medienwandel, in: Jeffrey F. Hamburger / Maria Theisen (Hg.), Unter Druck. Mitteleuropäische Buchmalerei im 15. Jahrhundert, Tagungsband zum internationalen Kolloquium in Wien, Österreichische Akademie der Wissenschaften, 13.1.–17.1.2016,

Buchmalerei des 15. Jahrhunderts in Mitteleuropa 15, Petersberg: Michael Imhof Verlag, 224–238.

Etablierte Literaturkürzel

GW = Gesamtkatalog der Wiegendrucke, hg. v. der Kommission für den Gesamtkatalog der Wiegendrucke, Bd. 1 ff. Leipzig/Stuttgart/Berlin: Anton Hiersemann Verlag, 1925 ff. Online-Datenbank ⟨www.gesamtkatalogderwiegendrucke.de⟩.

HSC = Handschriftencensus. Eine Bestandsaufnahme der handschriftlichen Überlieferung deutschsprachiger Texte des Mittelalters. Ein Projekt der Mainzer Akademie der Wissenschaften und der Literatur. [Online-Datenbank] ⟨http://www.handschriftencensus.de⟩.

KdiH 5/1 = Katalog der deutschsprachigen illustrierten Handschriften des Mittelalters, Bd. 5/1, hg. v. Ulrike Bodemann/Norbert H. Ott, [Stoffgruppe] 43. Gebetbücher A–F, bearb. v. Regina Cermann, München: C. H. Beck, 2014.

KdiH digital = Deutschsprachige illustrierte Handschriften des Mittelalters. Datenbank online unter ⟨https://kdih.badw.de/datenbank/start⟩.

LCI = Lexikon der christlichen Ikonographie, hg. v. Engelbert Kirschbaum/Günter Bandmann/Wolfgang Braunfels/Johannes Kollwitz/u. a.; ab Bd. 5 hg. v. Wolfgang Braunfels, 8 Bde., Rom/Freiburg/Basel/Wien: Herder, 1968–1976.

SCHREIBER = SCHREIBER, WILHELM LUDWIG, Handbuch der Holz- und Metallschnitte des XV. Jahrhunderts. Stark vermehrte und bis zu den neuesten Funden ergänzte Umarbeitung des Manuel de l'amateur de la gravure sur bois et sur métal au XVe siècle, 8 Bde., Leipzig: Karl W. Hiersemann, 1926–1930.

VD16 = Verzeichnis der im deutschen Sprachgebiet erschienenen Drucke des XVI. Jahrhunderts, hg. v. der Bayerischen Staatsbibliothek in München in Verbindung mit der Herzog August Bibliothek in Wolfenbüttel, [Red.: Irmgard Bezzel], 24 Bde., Stuttgart 1983–1997. Online-Recherche über den Opac der Bayerischen Staatsbibliothek (BSB) ⟨http://gateway-bayern.de⟩ bzw. den Karlsruher Virtuellen Katalog (KVK) ⟨https://kvk. bibliothek.kit.edu⟩.

VE15 = Falk Eisermann, Verzeichnis der typographischen Einblattdrucke des 15. Jahrhunderts im Heiligen Römischen Reich Deutscher Nation, 3 Bde., Wiesbaden: de Gruyter, 2004.

VL^2 = Die deutsche Literatur des Mittelalters. Verfasserlexikon, begr. v. Wolfgang Stammler, fortg. v. Karl Langosch, 2., völlig neu bearb. Aufl. unter Mitarbeit zahlreicher Fachgelehrter hg. v. Burghart Wachinger zusammen mit Gundolf Keil/Kurt Ruh/Werner Schröder/Franz Josef Worstbrock, 14 Bde., Berlin/New York: de Gruyter, 1978–2008.

VL Deutscher Humanismus = Deutscher Humanismus 1480–1520. Verfasserlexikon, hg. v. Franz Josef Worstbrock, 3 Bde., Berlin/New York: de Gruyter, 2008–2015.

Fotostrecke

Abb. 1: Miniatur: Martyrium der hl. Katharina. Klausenburg, UB, Ms. 683, 112v

Abb. 2: Holzschnitt: Albrecht Dürer, Martyrium der hl. Katharina (Bartsch 120). Nürnberg, um 1498. Wien, Albertina, Inv.-Nr. 1934/463

Individualstück oder Standardware? | 57

Abb. 3: Holzschnitt: Martyrium der hl. Katharina (Schreiber 1343). Augsburg?, um 1480/90. Washington, NGA, Inv.-Nr. 1943.3.598

Abb. 4: Miniatur: Martyrium der hl. Katharina. Augsburg, 1504. Freiburg, UB, Hs. 213, 142v

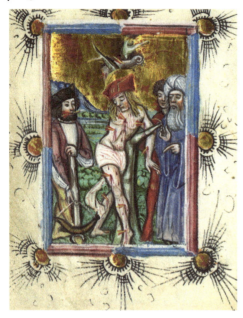

Abb. 5: Miniatur: Martyrium des hl. Sebastian (Pestheiliger). Klausenburg, UB, Ms. 683, 84v

Abb. 6: Miniatur: Männlicher Kirchgänger zu Beginn der Messgebete. Klausenburg, UB, Ms. 683, 11v

Abb. 7: Miniatur: Männlicher Kirchgänger zu Beginn der Kommuniongebete. Klausenburg, UB, Ms. 683, 65 v

Abb. 8: Miniatur: Alle Heiligen, identifizierbar Ulrich von Augsburg, Petrus, Maria Magdalena, Katharina. Klausenburg, UB, Ms. 683, 86 v

Abb. 9: Textseite mit Deckfarbeninitiale im farblichen Wechselrahmen und stilisierter Akanthusbordüre. Klausenburg, UB, Ms. 683, 2 r

Abb. 10: Textseite mit Deckfarbeninitiale im farblichen Wechselrahmen und Akanthusausläufern aus einem 1497 datierten *Obsequiale*. Freiburg, UB, Hs. 296, 4 r

Abb. 11: Miniatur: Marienkrönung, umgeben von vierseitiger Akanthusbordüre. Klausenburg, UB, Ms. 683, 1 v

Abb. 12: Miniatur: Dreifaltigkeit, umgeben von vierseitiger Akanthusbordüre, dt. Gebetbuch des Melchior Stuntz, Augsburg, 1499, illuminiert von Hans Renner? Wolfenbüttel, HAB, Cod. Guelf. 84.4 Aug. 12°, 1 v

Abb. 13: Miniatur: Beweinung Christi. Maria in gemustertem Gewand. Klausenburg, UB, Ms. 683, 36 v

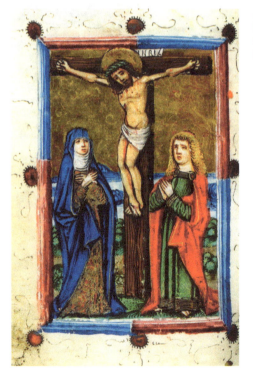

Abb. 14: Miniatur: Kreuzigung Christi. Maria in gemustertem Gewand. Wolfenbüttel, HAB, Cod. Guelf. 84.4 Aug. 12°, 65 v

Abb. 15: Dt. Psalter, geschrieben in einer für Augsburg typischen Rotunda. Augsburg, 1484, Dekor von der sog. Augsburg-Salzburger Missalien-Werkstatt. München, BSB, Cgm 82, 8 r

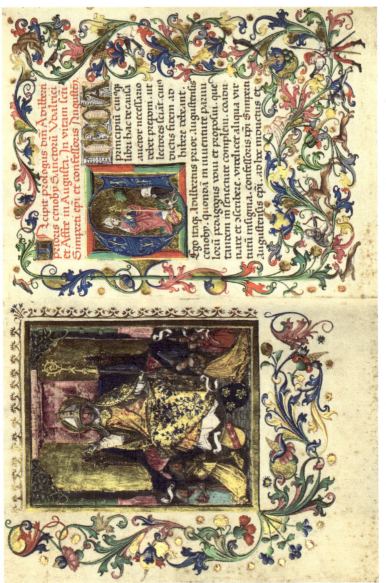

Abb. 16: *Vita Sancti Simperti* für Maximilian I. Augsburg, um 1492, illuminiert von Hans Holbein d. Ä. und Georg Beck, geschrieben von Leonhard Wagner. München, BSB, Clm 30044, 1v+2r

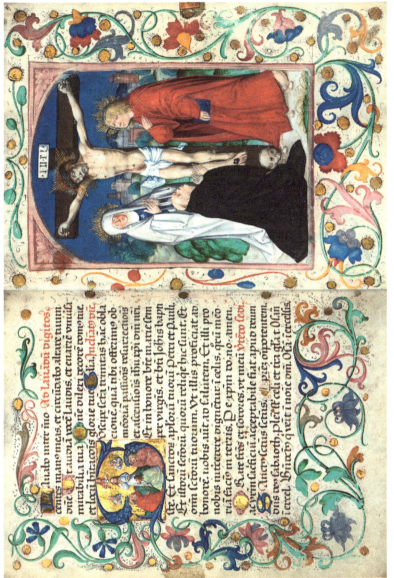

Abb. 17: *Extractus Missae* für St. Ulrich und Afra in Augsburg (Abt Konrad Mörlin als Adorant). Augsburg, um 1505, illuminiert von Ulrich Taler, geschrieben von Leonhard Wagner. München, BSB, Clm 23322, 4v+5r

Abb. 18: Miniatur: Maria Magdalena. Augsburg, um 1490, dt. Gebetbuch, illuminiert von der sog. Augsburg-Salzburger Missalien-Werkstatt. Wien, ÖNB, Cod. 2738, 322 r

Abb. 19: Miniatur: Maria Magdalena. Klausenburg, UB, Ms. 683, 1 v

Individualstück oder Standardware? | 67

Abb. 20: Miniatur: Maria Magdalena. Augsburg, 1504, dt. Gebetbuch, illuminiert von Ulrich Taler. Freiburg, UB, Hs. 213, 141 r

Abb. 21: Miniatur: Marienkrönung. Augsburg, 1499, dt. Gebetbuch des Melchior Stuntz, illuminiert von Hans Renner? Wolfenbüttel, HAB, Cod. Guelf. 84.4 Aug. 12°, 55v

Abb. 22: Miniatur: Marienkrönung. Augsburg, nach 1511/vor 1520, dt. Gebetbuch, Frühwerk von Narziß Renner (1501/2–1536)? Wien, ÖNB, Cod. 2748, 111r

Individualstück oder Standardware? | 69

Abb. 23: Tafelbild: Marienkrönung im Kreise von Engeln und Heiligen. Augsburger Meister, um 1470. Basel, Kunstmuseum, Inv.-Nr. 473

Abb. 24: Miniatur: Marienkrönung. Augsburg, 1526, dt. Gebetbuch, illuminiert von Nikolaus Bertschi. Ehem. Wien, Dorotheum, 12.6.2017, Nr. 1 (zuvor München, Hartung & Karl, 19./20.11.1975, Nr. 9), 63v

Abb. 25: Holzschnitt: Marienkrönung (Schreiber IX, 732c). Augsburg?, um 1480/90. Washington, NGA, Inv.-Nr. 1943.3.797

Abb. 26: Holzschnitt: Martyrium der hl. Barbara (Schreiber IX, 1260e). Augsburg?, um 1480/90. Washington, NGA, Inv.-Nr. 1943.3.586

Abb. 27: Miniatur: Martyrium der hl. Barbara. Klausenburg, UB, Ms. 683, 106 v

Abb. 28: Dt. Gebetbuch, Augsburg, Anfang der 1470er Jahre. Ehem. Pforzheim, Kiefer, Auktion 89, 27./28.6.2014, Nr. 412, 4r (s. Anhang 2, Spalte 10)

Abb. 29: Inkunabel, illuminiert vom sog. ersten Mitarbeiter des Johannes Bämler. Augsburg: Günther Zainer, 22.1.1470 (GW 9103). Dillingen, Studienbibliothek, XXIV 82

Individualstück oder Standardware? | 73

Abb. 30: Inkunabel, illuminiert und signiert von Johannes Bämler. [Straßburg: Johann Mentelin, nicht nach 1468] (GW 2883). Chantilly, Musée Condé, XXI¹ D.11

Abb. 31: Miniatur: Martyrium der hl. Apollonia. Augsburg, um 1490, dt. Gebetbuch, illuminiert von der sog. Augsburg-Salzburger Missalien-Werkstatt. Wien, ÖNB, Cod. 2738, 330v

 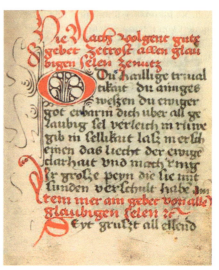

Abb. 32: Ehem. Pforzheim, Kiefer, 27./28.6.2014, Nr. 412, 88v

Abb. 33: Ehem. Pforzheim, Kiefer, 27./28.6.2014, Nr. 412

Individualstück oder Standardware? | 75

Abb. 34: Ehem. Zürich, Koller, 24.9.2016, Nr. 573, S. 32+33

Abb. 35: Ehem. Zürich, Koller, 24. 9. 2016, Nr. 573, S. 15

Abb. 36: Mainz, StB, Hs. I 428, 8r

Abb. 37: Mainz, StB, Hs. I 428, 130v

Abb. 38: München, BSB, Cgm 140, 129r

Individualstück oder Standardware? | 77

Abb. 39: Augsburg, UB, Cod. III.1 8° 55, 46v+47r

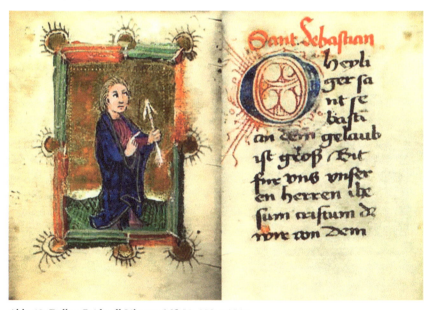

Abb. 40: Dallas, Bridwell Library, MS 91, 153v+154r

Abb. 41: Iowa City, UL, XMMs.Pr 3, 4r

Abb. 42: New York, PML, MS Stillman 14, 47v

Abb. 43: Klausenburg, UB, Ms. 683, 21v+22r

Adrian Papahagi
Babeş-Bolyai University of Cluj, Romania

A Medieval Flemish Book of Hours in Early Modern Transylvania (MS 684, Lucian Blaga Central University Library, Cluj)

Books of Hours are the undisputed "late medieval best-seller", to quote the formula consecrated by Léon Delaissé (1974, 203). As Christopher de Hamel writes, they "are now more widely scattered around the world than any other object made in the Middle Ages" (1997, 168). Victor Leroquais (1927), the pioneer of the systematic study of these books of private devotion identified over 330 volumes at the Bibliothèque Nationale in Paris, Eamon Duffy (2006, viii, 3) writes that "over 800 manuscript Books of Hours survive from the English Middle Ages", whilst Roger S. Wieck (1997, 9) informs us that the Pierpont Morgan Library in New York, and the Walters Art Gallery in Baltimore own around 370 manuscript and printed Books of Hours each. Similar considerations and estimates can be read in the introductions to most studies devoted to Books of Hours (e.g.Harthan: 1977, 9; Reinburg: 2012, 1, 20–21).

Since the early fourteenth century, Books of Hours were produced in large quantities in the major French cities – Paris, Amiens, Rouen, Tours, Lyon, Troyes etc. However, the Hundred Years' War weakened France, and by the time the English ceased occupying Paris, in 1436, this city was no longer the main producer of Books of Hours (Clark: 2013, 228; Dogaer: 1987, 13). Under Philip the Good and his successors, the Burgundian Netherlands, and especially Bruges and Gand now "seem to flood the local and international market" (Vanwijnsberghe: 2018, 110; see also Smeyers: 1999, 234–54) with standardised "shop-copy manuscripts" (Reinburg: 2012, 23). Until 1571, when Pope Pius V prohibited the use of existing Books of Hours, "nearly every European family of certain means" owned one (Hindman: 2013, 5).

Despite their incredible success in Western Europe, few Books of Hours can be found in Romanian libraries. We have been able to identify about a dozen volumes, none of which circulated on the territory of the Catholic dioceses of Alba Iulia (Weißenburg, Gyulafehérvár), Cenad (Csanád) and Oradea (Großwardein, Nagyvárad) in the Middle Ages, but were acquired by collectors from the eighteenth to the twentieth century (Papahagi/Dincă/Mârza: 2018, nrs 262, 284, 288, 325, 336, 342, 345, 361, 363, 500, 501). One little book, now kept at the Central University Library in Cluj (Klausenburg, Kolozsvár) (Biblioteca Centrală Universitară,

MS. 684) had entered Transylvania earlier, and shows traces of early modern use, which singles it out for discussion in the following pages (Papahagi/Dincă/Mârza: 2018, nr 363; Papahagi: 2013, 37, 40, 45).

The Central University Library was inaugurated in 1872, together with the "Franz-Joseph" University of Cluj, and incorporated the collections of the Society of the Transylvanian Museum (Erdélyi Múzeum-Egyesület), established in 1859. The library's medieval codices came from private donations to the Transylvanian Museum, which had already acquired 15,000 manuscripts, mostly modern, by 1867 (Radosav/Hentea: 1995). MS 684 appears to belong to the earliest collection of the Transylvanian Museum, and was donated by Ferenc Simó (1801–1869), as attested by a note on p. 1, reading "Simó Ferencz adom.⟨ánya⟩" – "donated by Simó Ferencz". Simó was a successful painter born in Odorheiu Secuiesc (Oderhellen, Székelyudvarhely), who studied and worked in Vienna and Budapest. He moved to Cluj in 1831, and taught at the Roman Catholic High School until his death. A label bearing the Transylvanian Museum shelfmark ("VI. A. 19a") appears on the front pastedown, and this institution's stamps are visible in various places.

More interestingly, on the opening page of the manuscript one can read the handwritten note "Serenissimus Princeps Franciscus Primus". In 1687 a subsequent owner, "Georgius Káldi" from Odorheiu Secuiesc, wrote his name on the codex ("Georgius Káldi. Sz. Udvar|hely 1687 m⟨anu⟩ p⟨ropria⟩", p. 3). This date suggests that the previous owner may have been Francis I Rákóczi (1645–1676), prince of Transylvania. (Fig. 1.)

Fig. 1. Cluj, BCU, MS 684, p. 1. Foto BCU, Cluj.

Francis I Rákóczi was born in Alba Iulia in 1645, and was elected prince of Transylvania by the Diet of 1652, during the lifetime of his father, George Rákóczi II (1621–1660). However, he never ruled, since the Turks removed his father from the throne in 1660, and forced the Rákóczis to retire to their fief in Royal Hungary. Francis I Rákóczi organised an unsuccessful uprising in Hungary, but never returned to Transylvania. After his father's death, Francis I abandoned the

Calvinist faith, and converted to Catholicism, the religion of his mother, Sophia Báthory (Kenyeres 1967: s.v. 'Rákóczi Ferenc, I.'). This may explain why he was using a Catholic book of private devotion, if he was indeed the owner identified as "Serenissimus Princeps Franciscus Primus" on p. 1 – or perhaps the book belonged to Sophia Báthory. Although Rákóczy left Transylvania in 1660, the book seems to have been left behind, and ended up on the market by 1687. (Fig. 2.)

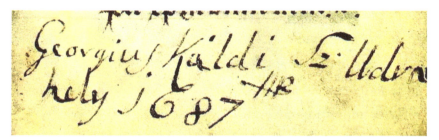

Fig. 2. Cluj, BCU, MS 684, p. 3. Foto BCU, Cluj.

The subsequent owner, Georgius Káldi was the Catholic priest of the parish of Leliceni (Csíkszentlélek) in 1687, and from about 1695 until the early 1700s functioned as a priest in Odorheiu Secuiesc, and was also head of the local school (Biró: 1937, 3; Mihály: 2012, 52, 54). Káldi added, in the same black ink and large script, notes and prayers in Latin and Hungarian on pp. 5–11, 14–15, 29, 30–32, and some clumsy drawings on pp. 57, 124. The prayers and such notes as 'Ad Vesperas' (p. 5), 'Cursus Conplectorij' (p. 20), 'Ad Letanias' (p. 57) suggest that Káldi was still using the book for private devotion. Thus, a medieval handwritten Book of Hours was still serving around 1700 in the Szekler counties, a predominantly Catholic region of the otherwise largely Protestant Transylvania. (Fig. 3.)

MS 684 is a small vellum book, trimmed down to 105 × 75 mm from an original size of about 120 × 85 mm. Only 63 leaves have survived; the pages were numbered in pencil on the recto of each leaf (from 1 to 125) when the book was rebound in the nineteenth century. It now displays a full modern binding, made of cardboard covered with brown leather. On the gold-tooled spine, one may read 'Breviar.' and 'Sæc. XV.' Decorated paper was used for the pastedown and flyleaves. The quires were originally *quaterniones*, but the leaves containing full-page paintings have been removed, so that the structure now looks as follows: I^{8-1} (1–14; wants first, p. 11 pasted to p. 10) II^{8-1} (15–28; wants first, p. 23 pasted to p. 22) III^2 (29–32) IV^{8-1} (33–46; stub at p. 35/36) $V–IX^8$ (47–126). No signatures or catchwords are visible. As Léon Delaissé pointed out, "the presence of a larger or smaller quire after a series of regular quires nearly always indicates the end of a part of the book" (Delaissé: 1974, 212). In this case, the third quire is a *binio*, and it does indeed correspond to the end of the Hours of the Virgin (on p. 32).

Fig. 3. Cluj, BCU, MS 684, p. 14. Foto BCU, Cluj.

The text was copied by one hand in a standard, but not extremely elegant Northern Gothic *textualis*, on sixteen long lines (68 × 43 mm). One may single out the two shapes of the *a* – called by Oeser (1971) 'Köpfchen-*a*', and by Albert Derolez (2003b, 84–86) 'double-bow *a*' (in initial position and erratically in central position, especially when a larger space is observed before it), and 'Kasten-*a*'/ 'box *a*' (generally, but not always, in final position, and in central position, especially in letter bitings such as *ba, ca, pa* etc. – Figure 4.7)

Fig. 4. Cluj, BCU, MS 684, morphology of letter 'a'. Foto BCU, Cluj.

The shape of *a* inside words seems to have been decided by the space the scribe observed before the letter: when the letters are squeezed against each other or even bite each other, he used the 'box-*a*' ('Kasten-*a*').

The ruling, made in red ink, consists of fifteen lines within single vertical and horizontal through lines extending over the full width and height of the page. All these codicological and palaeographical features are in keeping with the standards of Books of Hours made in the Southern Netherlands, as summarised by Albert Derolez (2003a). (Fig. 5.)

Fig. 5. Ruling pattern of Cluj, BCU MS 684. Drawn by author.

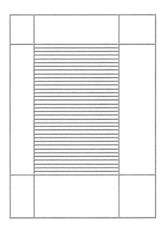

As already said, the major illustrations are missing. However, it is relevant to note that the extant section openings do not contain half-page pictures; consequently, the painted scenes must have been full-page. The rationalisation of production in Flemish centres, and especially in Bruges, led to the practice of pasting into the book full-page illustrations made by artists working as subcontractors; in France, miniatures and text generally coexist on the page (Smeyers: 1998, 195–96; Vanvijnsberghe: 2015, 135).

The extant artistic elements are decorated borders and five types of decorated initials of different grades. Only the beginnings of sections have decorated borders (the Seven Penitential Psalms, on p. 33, and the Vigils of the Dead, on p. 73); otherwise, the margins are undecorated. The border decoration surrounds the text box, and is surrounded by a red frame.[1] It includes green and red acanthus leaves, floating black seeds, berries and flowers common in Flemish manuscripts in the second half of the fifteenth century. However, one must note the absence of the yellow/orange/ochre colour that is so characteristic of Flemish manuscript painting. The quality of the paintings is relatively low: they lack the sharpness and the attention to detail that can be found in deluxe manuscripts from the 1440s – 1480s.[2] In order

---

1 On the classification of borders, see Farquhar: 1977, 67–75; on the borders of Flemish manuscripts, see also Smeyers: 1981, 27.
2 Compare to Malibu, J. Paul Getty Museum, Ludwig MS IX 7, the Llangattock Book of Hours from the school of Van Eyck, ca. 1440 (Dogaer: 1987, pl. 2); Vienna, ÖNB Cod. 2583, Privileges of Ghent and Flanders, ca. 1453 (Thoss: 1987, cat. 2, pl. 1); New York, Pierpont Morgan Library, MS M. 93, Bruges, ca. 1470 (Delaissé: 1974, 211, fig. 5); Malibu, J. Paul Getty Museum, Ludwig MS IX 8, Book of Hours from the school of Willem Vrelant, Bruges, ante 1481 (Dogaer: 1987, pl. 7).

to assess the quality of the paintings, one may compare the execution of characteristic flowers in the Cluj Hours, and in other Flemish manuscripts, such as Bruges, Groot Seminarie MS 158/189 (Valerius Maximus, *Dicta et facta memorabilia*, vol. II), decorated most likely in Bruges around 1470–1475 (Le Loup: 1981, 203–204, nr 97, kl. pl. 17).[3] (Fig. 6, 7.)

Fig. 6. Cluj, BCU, MS 684, flower detail. Foto BCU, Cluj.

Fig. 7. Bruges, Groot Seminarie, MS 158/189. Foto in Vlaamse kunst: 1981, 203–204, nr 97, kl. pl. 17.

The hierarchy of initials is dominated by major five-line blue or red/pink initials with foliage infill and white highlighting, on gold ground. The infill represents leaves and twisted stems bearing three-petalled blue and red/pink flowers with white dots. The intermediate level is represented by two-line "champie initials" using the same colour scheme as the larger ones. Finally, the lowest level is represented by one-line initials, alternately blue/red with red/blue pen flourishing, and burnished gold with black ink flourishing (Fig. 8.).

Fig. 8. Cluj, BCU, MS 684, hierarchy of decorated initials. Foto BCU, Cluj.

The same hierarchy and types of initials can be found in many manuscripts made in the Southern Low Countries, and especially in Bruges, from around 1430 to the end of the fifteenth century.[4] Below, just two examples of higher quality (Fig. 9–11.)

---

3 Compare also to Brussels, Bibliothèque Royale, MS 10977–9, Treaties on Nobility, 'Maître de la Cyropédie de Bruxelles', Bruges, s. XV² (Delaissé: 1959, cat. 117, pl. 42).
4 Compare to Watson: 2011, cat. nr 38, MS Reid 44 (MSL/1902/1691), Book of Hours, Use of Sarum, ca. 1430–40, Southern Netherlands (Bruges) and cat. nr 77, MSL/1978/4764, Book of Hours, Use of Rome, 1470–80, Southern Netherlands; As-Vijvers/Korteweg: 2018, cat. nr 59, The Hague, Koninklijke Bibliotheek, MS 76 G 21, Book of Hours for the use of Rome, Hainaut, ca. 1450–1475.

Fig. 9. Cluj, BCU, MS 684, p. 33. Foto BCU, Cluj.

Fig. 10. London, Victoria & Albert Museum, MSL 1978 4764. Foto Victoria & Albert Museum.

Fig. 11. The Hague, Royal Library, MS 76 G 21. Foto in Splendour: 2018, cat. nr 59.

For all purposes, however, the closest analogue to our manuscript is a Book of Hours from the Fitzwilliam Museum in Cambridge (MS 54, and two leaves from it, MSS 1261–1985 and 1262–1985). According to Nigel Morgan and Stella Panayotova (2009, cat. nr 225), the book was made for the use of Sarum, and probably in Bruges around 1480–90. As can be seen below and in the full-page pictures reproduced in the appendix, the border decoration and the main initials present striking similarities. Although the initial *D* is better executed in the Cambridge manuscript, it displays exactly the same elements of decoration (Fig. 12, 13).

Fig. 12. Cluj, BCU, MS 684, decorated initial D. Foto BCU, Cluj.

Fig. 13. Cambridge, Fitzwilliam Museum, MS 1261–1985, decorated initial D. Foto Fitzwilliam Museum.

As Gregory T. Clark (2013, 213) insists, it is important to record all the texts in a Book of Hours. A summary is provided here, but the reader can consult the detailed contents in the appendix. A standard fifteenth-century Book of Hours would begin with a Calendar, and would contain in variable order the Pericopes, the Hours of the Virgin (divided into the Infancy cycle and the Passion cycle, each with its pieces for the canonical hours of matins, lauds, prime, terce, sext, none, vespers and compline), the Hours of the Cross, the Hours of the Holy Spirit, the 'Obsecro te' and 'O intemerata' prayers, the Seven Penitential Psalms with the Litany, and the Office of the Dead (Harthan: 1977, 14–19; Wieck: 1997, 23).

Céline van Hoorebeeck (1997, quoted by Vanvijnsberghe: 2015, 132) studied a significant corpus of Flemish Books of Hours from the Royal Library in Brussels, most of which were made in Bruges, and showed that in 85 % of the cases they displayed a peculiar sequence, as opposed to books made for Paris use:

Cluj, BCU MS 684	Flemish Books of Hours (Bruges)	Paris use (first variant)	Paris use (second variant)
–	Calendar	Calendar	Calendar
–	Pericopes	Pericopes	Pericopes
–	Hours of the Cross	[Obsecro te/ O intemerata]	[Obsecro te/ O intemerata]
–	Hours of the Spirit	Hours of the Virgin	Hours of the Virgin
Hours of the Virgin (incomplete)	Hours of the Virgin	Hours of the Cross	Penitential Psalms + Litany
Penitential Psalms+ Litany	Penitential Psalms + Litany	Hours of the Spirit	Hours of the Cross
Office of the Dead (incomplete)	Office of the Dead	Penitential Psalms + Litany	Hours of the Spirit
–	[Obsecro te]	Office of the Dead	Office of the Dead

As can be seen, the order of the extant elements in our manuscript adheres to the sequence observed in Books of Hours produced in Bruges, but diverges from the Paris use, in which either the Hours of the Virgin or the Penitential Psalms and Litany were followed by the Hours of the Cross, which is not the case here (cf. Delaissé: 1974, 206–207).

Although in our manuscript the Hours of the Virgin are incomplete, the None, Vespers and Compline clearly indicate that the book follows the use of Rome, characterised by the following items according to Victor Leroquais (1927, vol. I, xxxviii; cf. Madan: 1927, 21–29):

None	*Hym.*	Memento ... [absent here]
	Ant.	Pulchra es ...
	Cap.	In plateis ...
Vespers	*Hym.*	Dum esset rex ...
	Cap.	Ab inicio ...
	Hym.	Ave, Maris stella ...
	Ant.	Beata mater ...

Compline	*Hym.*	Memento salutis ...
	Cap.	Ego mater ...
	Ant.	Cum iocunditate ...[5]

According to Dominique Vanvijnsberghe (2015, 128), "the Roman use, combined with other clues, may indicate a Bruges or Flemish origin". Due to mass production for export, this city and, to a lesser degree, other Flemish centres adopted the most universal use, that of Rome.

All the elements mentioned so far point to Bruges as the likeliest origin of MS 684. The calendar, litany and other personalised pictures, prayers and suffrages can sometimes indicate the private client, the institution or at least the diocese for which the book was customised. Since our manuscript is mutilated, one can only turn to the litany for clues concerning the destination of the book. The list of confessors is in this case the most eloquent (I transcribe it in the Vocative, and in the original spelling): "Sancte leonarde ..., bernarde, francisce, ludouice, bauo, remigi, eligi, egidi, dominice, andomare, bertine, liuine, amande". (Fig. 14, 15)

Figs. 14–15. Cluj, BCU, MS 684, pp. 62–63. Foto BCU, Cluj.

As can be seen, the list contains thirteen saints. The presence in the litany of Saint Omer (spelled 'Andomarus' rather than 'Audomarus'[6]) and Saint Bertin (founder of the Benedictine abbey of Saint-Omer) suggests that the manuscript

---

5 These elements are highlighted in the Appendix.
6 According to Vanvijnsberghe: 2015, 130, "in Flemish calendars, names are frequently misspelt".

88 | Adrian Papahagi

was made for use in the region of Saint-Omer. Saint Amand, also present in the litany, was worshipped especially in Flanders and in Picardy. However, the litany also includes Saint Louis of France, whose name seldom appears in Flemish Books of Hours after the middle of the fifteenth century, when the Southern Netherlands were annexed to Burgundy (Delaissé: 1974, 206). Although the client who ordered the book may have lived in the region Saint-Omer, it is perhaps more prudent to simply refer to the litany as "composite of North French and Flemish saints", as Lilian Randall does in several cases (Randall: 1997, 252, cat. nr 250, MS W. 197; 459, cat. nr 286, MS W. 440). For instance, she quotes a longer litany including many of these saints, in Baltimore, Walters MS 197, a Book of Hours made in Bruges around 1460: "Litany, headed 'Letania', composite of North French and Flemish saints: [...] 23 confessors, namely Silvester, Leo, Martin, Augustine, Nicholas, Amandus, Vedast, Gregory, Anthony, Ambrose, Jerome, Benedict, Bernard, Remigius, Eligius, Aegydius, Audomar, Bertin, Louis, Bavo, Francis, Dominic, Leonard...".

To conclude, the textual, codicological and artistic aspects of MS 684 suggest that the little book was produced in the third quarter of the fifteenth century or a little later in the Southern Netherlands, and possibly in Bruges, or imitated a product of Bruges. In any case, it is the product of a minor workshop, and was probably intended for a client from Saint-Omer. The book may have belonged to Francis I Rákóczi, Prince of Transylvania in the second half of the seventeenth century; in 1687, it belonged to a parish priest from the east of the province, who was using it for his private devotion. In the absence of Books of Hours demonstrably used by laymen in medieval Transylvania, MS 684 supplies us with the precious evidence that aristocrats and parish priests still had recourse to medieval books of private devotion in the seventeenth century.

Appendix
Contents of Cluj, BCU, MS 684

1–32. HOURS OF THE VIRGIN.

1–5. *[Ad nonam]. The text begins abruptly:* ... confundetur cum loquetur inimicis suis in porta (Ps. 126:5); *Psalmus dauid.* Beati omnes (Ps. 127); 2 *an.* Pulchra es; *capitulum.* In plateis sicut cynamomum; 3 *versus.* Post partum uirgo; *oracio.* Famulorum tuorum; 4 *De omnibus sanctis an.* Sancti dei omnes intercedere; *versus.* Letamini in domino; *r.* Et gloriamini; *Oracio.* Prestaque sumus omnipotens deus; *oracio.* Omnes sancti tui.

5–20. *[Ad vesperas]. an.* Dum esset rex; *psalmus.* Dixit dominus (Ps. 109); 6 *an.* Dum esset rex; *an.* Leua; 7 *ps.* Laudate pueri (Ps. 112); 8 *an.* Leuaeius sub capite; *an.* Nigra sum; *ps.* Letatus sum (Ps. 121); 10 *an.* Nigra sum; *an.* Iam enim; *ps.* Nisi

A Medieval Flemish Book of Hours in Early Modern Transylvania | 89

Dominus (Ps. 126); 11 *an.* Iam enim hyemps; 12 *an.* Speciosa; *ps.* Lauda iherusalem (Ps. 147); 13 *an.* Speciosa; 14 *cap.* Ab inicio; *hym.* Ave maris stella; 15 *v.* Diffusa est gracia; 16 *an.* Beata mater; *ps. (!)* Magnificat; 17 *an.* Beata mater; 18 *or.* Concede nos famulos tuos; 19 *De omnibus sanctis an.* Sancta (!) dei omnes; *v.* Letamini; *r.* Et gloriamini; *or.* Protege domine populum tuum; 20 *or.* Omnes sancti tui; *or.* Et pacem tuam.

21–32. *[Ad complectorium]. ps.* De profundis (Ps. 129); 23 *ps.* Domine non est exaltatum (Ps. 130); 24 *hym.* Memento salutis; 25 *cap.* Ego mater pulcre; *v.* Ora pro nobis; *an.* Sub tuum; Nunc dimittis; 26 *an.* Sub tuum presidium; 26 *or.* Beate et gloriose; 27 *De omnibus sanctis an.* Sancti dei omnes; *or.* Ex audinos deus; 28 *or.* Omnes sancti tui; *or.* Et pacem tuam; 30 Salue regina; *v.* Post partum; 31 *or.* Omnipotens sempiter ne deus.

33–56. Seven Penitential Psalms.

Septem psalmi penitentiales. Domine ne in furore (Ps. 6); 35 Beati quorum (Ps. 31); 38 Domine ne in furore (Ps. 37); 43 Miserere mei (Ps. 50); 47 Domine exaudi (Ps. 101); 52 De profundis (Ps. 129); 54 Domine exaudi (Ps. 142).

57–72. Litanies.

Incipiunt latenie (!)... The list of confessors consists of the following saints, in this order: Leonardus, Bernardus, Franciscus, Ludovicus, Bavo, Remigius, Eligius, Egidius, Dominicus, Andomarus (!), Bertinus, Livinus, Amandus (pp. 62–63).

73–126. Office of the Dead.

Incipiunt vigilie mortuorum. an. Placebo; *ps.* Dilexi quoniam exaudiet (Ps. 114); 75 *an.* Placebo; *an.* Ihesu me; *ps.* Ad dominum cum tribularer (Ps. 119); 76 *an.* Heu michi; *an.* Dominus custodit; *ps.* Leuaui oculos (Ps. 120); 78 *an.* Dominus custodit; *an.* Si iniquitates; *ps.* De profundis (Ps. 129); 79 *an.* Si iniquitates; 80 *an.* Opera; *ps.* Confitebor tibi domine (Ps. 137); 82 *an.* Opera; *v.* Audiui uocem; *r.* Scribe beati mortui; *an.* Omne; *ps. (!)* Magnificat; 84 *an.* Omne; *ps.* Lauda anima mea (Ps. 191); 86 *v.* A porta inferi; 87 *or.* Deus qui inter apostolos; 88 *or.* Quesumus; *or.* Fidelium deus omnium *[ad matutinum]* 89 Inuitatorium. Regem cui omnia viuunt; *an.* Dirige; *ps.* Uerba mea auribus (Ps. 5); 92 *an.* Conuertere; *ps.* Domine ne in furore (Ps. 6); 95 *an.* Conuertere; *an.* Ne quando; *ps.* Domine deus meus (Ps. 7); 99 *an.* Ne quando rapiat; *v.* A porta inferi; 100 *Lectio prima.* Parce michi domine (Job 9); 101 *r.* Credo quod redemptor; *v.* Quem uisurus; *Lectio secunda.* Sedet (!) animam meam (Job 10); 103 *v.* Qui venturus; 104 *Lectio tertia.* Manus tuas domine (Job 10); 105 *r.* Libera me; *v.* Tremens fac; *v.* Dies illa; 106 *an.* Exultabunt; *ps.* Miserere mei (Ps. 50); 110 *an.* Exultabunt domino; *an.* Exaudi; *ps.* Te decet hymnus (Ps. 64); 114 *an.* Exaudi; *an.* Me suscepit; *ps.* Deus deus meus (Ps. 62); 116 *ps.* Deus misereatur nostri (Ps. 66); 118 *an.* A porta inferi; Ego dixi in dimidio (Isa. 38:10); 122 *an.* Omnis; *ps.* Laudate dominum de celis (Ps. 148); 124 *ps.* Cantate domino canticum nouum (Ps. 149); 126 *ps.* Laudate dominum in sanctis eius laudate eum in firmament o uirtutis eius… (Ps. 150:1). *The rest of the manuscript is missing.*

Plate I. Cluj, Biblioteca Centrală Universitară, MS 684, p. 73. Foto BCU, Cluj.

Plate II. Cambridge, Fitzwilliam Museum, MS 1261–1985. Foto Fitzwilliam Museum.

Bibliography

As-Vijvers, Anne Margaret W./Korteweg Anne S. (2018), Splendour of the Burgundian Netherlands: Southern Netherlandish Illuminated Manuscripts in Dutch Collections, Zwolle: Wbooks/Utrecht: Museum Catharijneconvent.

Biró, Lajos (1937), Neves jezsuita-plebánosok és írók a székely anyavárosban, Székely Közélet 20.41 (9 Oct.), 3.

Clark, Gregory T. (2013), Variant Litany Readings and the Localization of Late Medieval Manuscript Books of Hours – The d'Orge Hours, in: Sandra Hindman / James H. Marrow (ed.), Books of Hours Reconsidered, London/Turnhout: Harvey Miller, 213–233.

DeHamel, Christopher (1997), A History of Illuminated Books, 2nd edn., London: Phaidon.

Delaissé, L. M. J. (1959), Le siècle d'or de la miniature flamande: Le mécénat de Philippe le Bon, Bruxelles: Palais des Beaux-Arts.

Delaissé, L. M. .J. (1974), The Importance of Books of Hours for the History of the Medieval Book, in: Ursula E. McCracken/Lilian M. C. Randall/Richard H. Randall, Jr. (ed.), Gatherings in Honor of Dorothy E. Miner, Baltimore: The Walters Art Gallery, 203–225.

Derolez, Albert (2003a), Masters and Measures. A Codicological Approach to Books of Hours, Quaerendo 33, 83–95.

Derolez, Albert (2003b), The Palaeography of Gothic Manuscript Books from the Twelfth to the Sixteenth Century, Cambridge: Cambridge University Press.

Dogaer, Georges (1987), Flemish Miniature Painting in the 15th and 16th Centuries, Amsterdam: B.M. Israël.

Duffy, Eamon (2006), Marking the Hours: English People and Their Prayers 1240–1570, New Haven/London: Yale University Press.

Farquhar, James Douglas (1977), The Manuscript as a Book, in: Sandra Hindman/ James Douglas Farquhar, Pen to Press. Illustrated Manuscripts and Printed Books in the First Century of Printing, College Park: University of Maryland Press, 67–75.

Harthan, John (1977), Books of Hours and Their Owners, London: Book Club Associates.

Hindman, Sandra (2013), Books of Hours: State of the Research. In Memory of L. M. J. Delaissé, in: Sandra Hindman/James H. Marrow (ed.), Books of Hours Reconsidered, London: Harvey Miller, 5–16.

Kenyeres, Ágnes, ed. (1967), Magyar Életrajzi Lexikon, Budapest: Akadémiai Kiadó.

Le Loup, Willi (1981), Vlaamse kunst op perkament. Handschriften en miniaturen te Brugge van de 12de tot de 16de eeuw, Brugge: Gruuthusemuseum.

Leroquais, Victor (1927), Les Livres d'heures manuscrits de la Bibliothèque Nationale, 3 vols., Paris: s.n.

Madan, Falconer (1927), The Localization of Manuscripts, in: H. W. C. Davis (ed.), Essays in History Presented to Reginald Lane Pool, Oxford: Clarendon Press (reprinted 1969), 7–29.

Mihály, Tibor (2012), A lelki és szellemi élet szolgálatában. Adatok az Oroszhegyi család történetéhez, Areopolisz 12, 45–59.

Morgan, Nigel/Panayotova, Stella et al. (2009), Illuminated Manuscripts in Cambridge: A Catalogue of Western Book Illumination in the Fitzwilliam Museum and the Cambridge Colleges, Part One, Volume Two: The Meuse Region, Southern Netherlands, London: Harvey Miller/The Modern Humanities Research Association.

Oeser, Wolfgang (1971), Das 'a' als Grundlage für Schriftvarianten in der gotischen Buchschrift, Scriptorium 25, 25–45, 250–52.

Papahagi, Adrian (2013), Manuscrisele medievale occidentale ale Bibliotecii Centrale Universitare din Cluj, Revista română de istorie a cărţii 9, 32–46.

Papahagi, Adrian/Dincă, Adinel/Mârza, Andreea (2018), Manuscrisele medievale occidentale din România: Census, Iaşi: Polirom.

Radosav, Doru/Hentea, Ioan (1995), La Bibliothèque Centrale Universitaire 'Lucian Blaga' de Cluj-Napoca. Bref historique, Transylvanian Review 4.2, 14–28.

Randall, Lilian M.C. (1992). Medieval and Renaissance Manuscripts in the Walters Art Gallery. Vol. II, France, 1420–1540, Baltimore: Johns Hopkins University Press/Walters Art Gallery.

Randall, Lilian M.C. (1997), Medieval and Renaissance Manuscripts in the Walters Art Gallery. Vol. III, Belgium, 1250–1530, Baltimore: Johns Hopkins University Press/Walters Art Gallery.

Reinburg, Virginia (2012), French Books of Hours: Making an Archive of Prayer, c. 1400–1600, Cambridge: Cambridge University Press.

Smeyers, Maurits (1981), De arte illuminandi, in: Vlamse kunst op pergament. Handschriften en miniaturen te Brugge van de 12de tot de 16de eeuw, Brugge: Gruuthusenmuseum, 19–43.

Smeyers, Maurits (1998), L'art de la miniature flamande du VIIIᵉ au XVIᵉ siècle, Tournai: La Renaissance du Livre, 1998.

Smeyers, Maurits (1999), Flemish Miniatures from the 8th to the Mid-16th Century: The Medieval World on Parchment, Turnhout: Brepols.

Thoss, Dagmar (1987), Flämische Buchmalerei: Handschriftenschätze aus dem Burgunderreich. Ausstellung der Handschriften- und Inkunabelsammlung der österreichischen Nationalbibliothek, Prunksaal, 21. Mai – 26. Oktober 1987, Graz: ADEVA.

Van Hoorebeeck, Céline (1997), Un corpus de vingt livres d'heures manuscrits du XVᵉ siècle du diocèse de Tournai: catalogue descriptif, hypothèses de localisation et modalités d'utilisation, unpublished BA dissertation, Louvain-la-Neuve: Université catholique de Louvain.

Vanvijnsberghe, Dominique (2015), Reconstructing Local Styles in the Southern Low Countries. The Importance of Books of Hours, in: Delmira Espada Custódio/Maria Adelaide Miranda (ed.), Livros de Horas. O imaginário da devoçao privada, Lisbon: Biblioteca Nacional de Portugal, 123–43.

Vanwijnsberghe, Dominique (2018), The Tastes of the Upper Classes, in: Splendour of the Burgundian Netherlands: Southern Netherlandish Illuminated Manuscripts in Dutch Collections, Zwolle: Wbooks / Utrecht: Museum Catharijneconvent, 110–119.

Watson, Rowan (2011), Victoria and Albert Museum: Western Illuminated Manuscripts, London: V&A Publishing, vol. 1.

Wieck, Roger S. (1997), Painted Prayers: the Book of Hours in Medieval and Renaissance Art, New York: George Braziller& The Pierpoint Morgan Library.

Constantin Ittu
Lucian Blaga University of Sibiu, Romania

A Sixteenth-Century Devotional Book: the *Brukenthal Breviary*

Umberto Eco, who was born in Alessandria, Italy, gave a lecture in English at the newly opened *Bibliotheca Alexandrina* from Egypt – this happened on November 1st, 2003 – in which he affirmed that there are three types of memory. The first one is *organic*, which is the memory made of flesh and blood and the one administered by our brain. The second is *mineral*, and in this sense, mankind has known two kinds of mineral memory: millennia ago, this was the memory represented by clay tablets and obelisks, pretty well known in Egypt, on which the ancient Egyptians carved their texts. This second type is also the electronic memory of today's computers, based upon silicon. There is another kind of memory, the *vegetal* one, represented by the first papyruses, and then on books, made of paper. He added: "Let me disregard the fact that at a certain moment the vellum of the first codices were of an organic origin, and the fact that the first paper was made with rugs and not with wood. Let me speak for the sake of simplicity of vegetal memory in order to designate books" (Ittu: 2017, 77–78).

Changing the topic, from books to libraries, the Italian scholar regarded libraries as being temples of vegetal memory. "Libraries, over the centuries, have been the most important way of keeping our collective wisdom. They were and still are a sort of universal brain where we can retrieve what we have forgotten and what we still do not know. If you will allow me to use such a metaphor, a library is the best possible imitation, by human beings, of a divine mind, where the whole universe is viewed and understood at the same time [..]. In other words, we have invented libraries because we know that we do not have divine powers, but we try to do our best to imitate them" (Eco: 2003, 665). Eco considered himself optimistic regarding the future of the classical books. In this respect, he believed that printed books have a future and that all fears *à propos* of their disappearance are only the last example of other fears, or of millenarist terrors about the end of something, the world included (Eco: 2003, 665). On that occasion, Umberto Eco apologized that he deliberately ignored *animal memory,* in other words, the fourth kind of memory, that of the parchment (Ittu: 2017, 78).

I mention this last aspect of Umberto Eco's lecture, because the topic of my essay is connected to a book, to a manuscript written on parchment – *The Brukenthal Breviary*. When I started my work, I took into consideration that Pythagoras stated, in his Sacred Hymns: "think before you start to act" (Pitagora: 2013, 43). Taking his words as advice, I would like to point out that specialists regard *The Brukenthal Breviary* as a *Book of Hours,* as a *Liber Horarum,* and not as a genuine breviary (Ordeanu: 2007, 7–9).

Generally speaking, a book of hours is a small, portable prayer book for laymen, a counterpart to the much more extensive breviary/breviaries for clergy. The core of a book of hours consists of a Calendar of Saints, the Hours of the Virgin, the Penitential Psalms with the Litany of the Saints and the Office of the Dead. In their turn, the Hours of the Virgin are a collection of psalms, hymns, lectures and prayers. They are arranged according to the hours of the day. A canonical day starts at midnight with Matins (*Matutinum* or *Matutinae* in Latin). In the Eastern (Orthodox) Churches, Matins is called *Orthros* in Greek (meaning early dawn or daybreak), and *Outrenia* or *Utrenia* (in Slavonic, respectively Romanian). In the Roman-Catholic framework, at daybreak the Dawn or Morning Prayers, known as *Lauds,* and during the day the *Terce* (*Tertia*) or the Midmorning Prayer, the *Sext* (*Sexta*) or Midday Prayer, the *None* (*Nona*) or Mid-Afternoon Prayer. The day closes with the *Vespers* and with the *Compline* or the Night Prayer (Poos: 2001, 33–38).

Basically, the *Book of Hours* known as the *Brukenthal Breviary* is an illuminated manuscript which had been made at the beginning of the sixteenth century in the Low Countries, as I already mentioned, and had been purchased, by Samuel Baron von Brukenthal, Governor of Transylvania. Written in Latin on parchment, with 630 pages – or in other words, 315 *bifolia*; dimension 212 × 150 mm – the book, which belongs to the Brukenthal National Museum Library, Sibiu, presents tiny Gothic letters as well as miniatures in painting (De Maere: 2007, 7).

The illuminators solved the extraordinary task of decorating every page of the 315 *bifolia* of the *Brukenthal Breviary* by exploring several model sources. Because I mentioned earlier the Master of the David Scenes, I would like to add that the Austrian art historian Otto Pächt (1902–1988) first identified this painter as a distinct artistic personality in the *Grimani Breviary* in 1966, basing his somewhat unwieldy name on a cohesive series of dynamic illuminations illustrating the life of David in the famous breviary, which now is located in Venice. Nothing definitive is known about the training of the Master of the David Scenes, but his precise draftsmanship and the occasional appearance of fine half-length portraits in his work have led some scholars to speculate that he was trained in the workshop of a panel painter. In the first decade of the sixteenth century the Master of the David Scenes attained a more mature style, distinguished by greater attention to naturalistic detail and increasingly distinct contours, which impart a cleaner, more linear quality to all his work. In manuscripts of this period, such as the *Brukenthal Breviary*, the stocky figures have more weight; no longer lost within their settings, they dominate the space (Kren/McKendrick: 2003, 383).

Without a title page, the *Brukenthal Breviary* contains, in its first part, a calendar which is divided according to the ancient Roman system, into three: *calendae, nones* and *ides*, each month being displayed on two pages augmented with miniatures and zodiacal signs. To be more precise, each month has three fixed points: Kalends or *calendae*, in Latin, being always the first day of the month and from which derives our term *calendar*, followed by *nones*, the ninth day before the *ides* counting inclusively (it fell on the fifth or seventh of the month) and *ides*, or the middle of the month, either of thirteenth or fifteenth. All the days in between were counted backward from these three fixed points (Gould: 1989, 229–233). The zodiacal signs were closely related to astrology, which used to be regarded as a part of learned scientific culture, practiced on a large scale in medieval courts, as "the supreme natural science of the medieval world" (Carey: 2010, 888).

The miniatures which border the calendar depict scenes from medieval everyday life having either rural or urban topics. They are different images of the economic practices during the four seasons of the year. On the one hand, according to ethnology of religions – which has, as its main focus, the study of religion/religiosity as it is practiced in everyday life, in the past, as well as in the present – it is emphasized that during the Middle Ages an economic aspect is, in the same time, a social, spiritual, religious, as well as a juridical and political one (Gavriluță: 2015, 23). On the other hand, the social time of that epoch can be regarded as divided in two categories: the first category including religious, working and resting time(s), while the second one consists of charitable social practices and of voluntary actions. According to a contemporary point of view, there does not exist today only one social time, but more such times, suitable to be analyzed from a fractalic perspective (Gavriluță: 2003, 15).The assumption that the medieval social time was orchestrated by the presence of the *sacred* is argued by the importance put on the *past*, because everything in everyday life was regarded as rooted in the *Genesis* (Gavriluță: 2015, 97).

Neither the *Genesis* nor any other biblical text can be read as a common text, – or can be regarded as a literary fragment of a book. As Thor Strandenaaes pointed out, "pure knowledge of a language or the ability to read it has never been sufficient for understanding biblical texts, even in New Testament times" (Strandenaaes: 2002, 181). In the Old Testament, the problem of understanding has begun with the story of Babel Tower (*Migdal Bavel* in Hebrew – Gen 11:1–9) as its touchstone; it was the first example of *confusio linguarum*. In that incident, the people decided to make it impossible for them to be spotted, a decision God regarded as a sin. Despite the fact that the Lord commanded Noah and his family to "fill the earth" after the flood, that generation decided they did not wish this, but rather to concentrate themselves in one place. If, at the beginning, "all the earth had one language and one tongue", later on, during the elevation of the Babel tower by the new generation, "the Lord came down to see the tower which the children of men

98 | Constantin Ittu

were building", and decided to "take away the sense of their language, so that they will not be able to make themselves clear to one another" (Gen 1:1–7). The divine punishment was *mida k'neged mida*, "measure for measure" for disobedience, and Jacques Derrida believes that the biblical story "can provide an epigraph for all discussions of translation" (Derrida: 1988, 100).

When, in the New Testament, Philip asked the Ethiopian dignitary, "Do you understand what you are reading", he got the following answer: "How can I, unless someone guides me?" (Acts 8:30–31). It is generally accepted that the translation of the sacred text needs interpretation. For example, talking about how could it be possible to translate the divine names (of God), some authors have pointed out that "to translate is to interpret, and one never translates without remainder. They must be multiple names of God, for there are many languages among which there can never be exact replication, but always interpretation" (Cunningham: 1995, 426). Regardless of a name, a sentence or a fragment, the difference between one's native language and the *Ur*-text of a sacred book would not stand as a barrier for the message to be understood. There are scholars who distinguish between three methods of reading the Bible critically: a) reading behind the text – focusing on the historical and sociological framework; b) reading the text itself – focusing on literary and narrative context; c) reading in front of the text – focusing on the major metaphors, themes and symbols that are projected by the text (Strandenaaes: 2002, 184).

In its next part, the *Brukenthal Breviary* comprises scenes from the Old and from the New Testament, painted on gold or coloured background with predominance of pink, blue and purple nuances (De Maere: 2007, 19). In her study, "Iconographic Originality in the Oeuvre of the Master of the David Scenes", Elisabeth Morrison notes that "beginning in the last quarter of the fifteenth century, the explosion of demand for Flemish paintings and manuscripts throughout Europe produced endless opportunities for narrative and compositional creativity among Flemish artists. A number of these artists turned for inspiration to the dramatic possibilities inherent in Old Testament stories" (Morrison: 2006, 149).

On the pages of the *Brukenthal Breviary* with sacred images, the first illumination is The Creation (p. 27), and the second one, Temptation or, in other words, Adam and Eve Fall into Sin (p. 26). The two scenes are complementary, taking into consideration that God made the world during a seven-day holy time ("In the beginning, when God created the universe, the earth was formless and desolate" – Gen 1:1), and, within this seven-day circle, he created the human being ("Then God said, 'And now we will make human beings; they will be like us and resemble us'" – Gen 1:26). The artist placed the scene of Creation in an Ancient Greek temple with a landscape in the background, as this kind of building was a frequent architectural element in the fifteenth and sixteenth century Flemish painting. In the temple, angels, as musicians, celebrated the Creation.

The scene of Temptation is a pendant image of the first one, Adam and Eve being already sinners, but the presence of an iris flower with its purple inflorescence in a bush behind them suggested hope, salvation. The iris flower – which earned its name from the Ancient Greek Goddess Iris, a messenger of gods who was thought to use the rainbow as a bridge between heaven and earth – symbolizes, in the Christian framework, the second Adam, Jesus Christ. The miniature of the Temptation is surrounded by a border into which the artist has incorporated a version of the Expulsion, two naked characters being expelled by an angel with a sword (Kren/McKendrick: 2003, 383).

As *Salvator Mundi* (p. 37), Christ wears a blue tunic and a purple mantle. Taking into consideration that Christ is regarded as a prophet, a high priest, and a king, the blue colour suggests his divinity, while red represents his royal dimension (not his royal status, because he does not regard himself as earthly king, as he said in John18:36: "My kingdom is not of this world"). At the same time, Christ blesses with his right hand, and keeps in his left hand a *globus crucicer* (globe bearing a cross), used not only as a symbol of royal power, but here, in this prayer book, also as a representation of Heavenly Jerusalem, as it is written in the Rev (21:2 "And I John saw the holy city, new Jerusalem, coming down from God out of heaven, prepared as a bride adorned for her husband." 21:23 "And the city had no need of the sun, neither of the moon, to shine in it: for the glory of God did lighten it, and the Lamb is the light thereof").

The *Brukenthal Breviary* provides important evidence of the miniaturist's predilection for rare Old Testament stories which were regarded as prophecies for the New Testament. For example, while the Annunciation to Abraham and Sarah – or The Hospitality of Abraham and Sarah – is paired with the Annunciation to the Virgin, the story of Esau and Jacob is paired with the Flight into Egypt (Matt 2:13–23), (Morrison: 2006, 151). I would like to add that The Hospitality of Abraham and Sarah is the main source for Andrei Rubliov's icon *The Holy Trinity*. The fifteenth century Russian icon-painter portrayed what has become the quintessential icon of the Holy Trinity in the Orthodox East, by depicting the three mysterious strangers who visited Abraham (Gen 18:1–15). The Lord visited Abraham in the form of three men who are apparently angels representing God. In his icon, Rubliov depicted the three heavenly guests sitting at the table with a cup placed before them on the table. Most scholars understand the visitors to be seated left to right in their doxological order: God-Father, Christ-Son and the Holy Spirit (Ittu: 2012, 103–104).

The Flight into Egypt is a story recounted in the Gospel of Matthew (2:13–23), being a quotation after Hosea (11:1), and, in this framework, the significance of the chapter resides in the following message: "This was to fulfill what the Lord had spoken by the prophet: 'Out of Egypt I called my son'" (Matt 2:15). The text refers to the son of God – in other words, Jesus Christ – about whom the Gospel tells us:

"Whoever believes in the Son has eternal life; whoever does not obey the Son shall not see life, but the wrath of God remains on him" (John 3: 36). The Flight into Egypt is also a topic of an apocryphal text, The Gospel of Pseudo-Matthew (17:2), in which Joseph is warned by an angel about Herod's intention and said: "Take Mary and the child and go by the desert road to Egypt". Over the centuries, the earliest Christian ascetics who lived in Egypt often invoked the idea of the desert as an escape from society into wilderness (Markus: 1990, 157–159).

The paired scene of The Flight into Egypt, the scene of Esau and Jacob, deals with the well-known story of two brothers, of twin brothers born to Isaac and Rebecca. Esau was born first and thereby became legal heir to the family birthright. In contrast to Esau, who was a skilful hunter, and his father's favorite, Jacob was a plain man, and his mother's favourite. The word plain refers to Jacob's character as a man of God, unlike his brother Esau who was a godless human being – [Esau], "who sold his birthright for a single meal" (Heb12:16). This peculiar birthright was a link in the line of descendants through which the Promised Messiah was to come, as it is written in Num (24:17–19): "The oracle of Balaam the son of Beor,/the oracle of the man whose eye is opened,/ the oracle of him who hears the words of God,/ and knows the knowledge of the Most High,/ who sees the vision of the Almighty// 'I see him, but not now;/ I behold him, but not near:/ a star shall come out of Jacob'".

The story of Esau and Jacob can be also found in the apocryphal writing The Second Book of Ezra: "For Esau is the end of this age, and Jacob is the beginning of the age that follows" (2Ezra 6:9).

The consistency of the *Brukenthal Breviary* sequences and the fact that the New Testament pictures are often made by different artists suggest that the Master of David Scenes had a personal interest in Old Testament iconography. He apparently recognized the obscurity of some of the scenes because titles were included beneath the Old Testament types along with citations of the biblical chapters and verses from which they are derived (Morrison: 2006, 151).

There is also a little-known story from I Samuel, the slaying of the priests of Nob. The Priests were cruelly murdered by order of Saul, who was punishing the servants of the Lord for having helped David. He also put to the sword Nob, the town of the priests, with its men and women, its children and infants, and its cattle, donkeys and sheep (I Sam 22:19). Saul appears at the right, personally overseeing the slaying, while the distant background shows the beginning of the story with David running for protection to the shrine of Nob. This Old Testament event appears as pairing with the Massacre of the Innocents, a scene depicted on the following page (Morrison: 2006, 150–151).

Anne Margreet W. As-Vijvers, who is a specialist in manuscript decorations, pointed out that the rich marginal decoration of the *Brukenthal Breviary* includes "the typical Ghent-Bruges border, consisting of flowers depicted in *trompe-l'oeil* (as if they are spotted upon a gold background), as well as several other types. The spacious architectural borders of the manuscript at the text incipits are a well-known hallmark of the David Master's workshop" (As-Vijvers: 2017). She also mentioned that all the illuminators were able to solve the extraordinary task of decorating every page of the manuscript by exploring several model sources. They derived motifs from historiated borders (such as calendar illustrations), from subsidiary elements in miniatures (e.g. the Lion of St. Mark), from models for earlier types of marginal decoration consisting of acanthus leaves interspersed with flowers and drolleries, from playing cards and other engravings. The illuminators concentrated on those motifs which were easy to isolate from the context of larger border designs or illustrations. There is evidence for the use of tracing and other methods of reproduction, and for the existence of model drawings as well as models in full colour. The illuminators made a deliberate choice in using specific motifs deemed appropriate for each margin, using simple flowers for the narrow upper margin, more complicated flowers and several other motifs in the side margins, and mammals in the spacious lower margins. The marginal motifs display a preference for diversity. The working method of the illuminators was to make variations on existing marginal motifs, in the process of which the models were adapted and changed, and sometimes became obscured. At the same time, there was the (opposite) tendency to a standardization of the motifs and the processes by which the variations were made (As-Vijvers: 2017).

From a certain perspective, the message sent by this *Liber Horarum* to those who had owned it in the sixteenth century should be understood as a spiritual support, in other words, as a spiritual daily meal, in the light of Jesus Christ's invitation "They need not go away: you give them something to eat" (Matt 14:16). The above-mentioned invitation refers to the spiritual nourishment – "Nourished up in the Words of Faith" (1 Tim 4:6) – suitable for all believers, and not only for a part of them, not for "about five thousand men, besides women and children" (Matt14:21). One of the earliest references to the parallel between physical and spiritual food, and which has become a landmark in the church during the centuries, can be found in Deut 8:2–3, "And you shall remember the whole way that the Lord your God [...] man does not live by bread alone, but man lives by every word that comes from the mouth of the Lord." This Old Testament fragment is mirrored in the Gospel of John, where Lord Jesus affirms that he is the Eucharistic bread: "I am the bread of life; whoever comes to me shall not hunger, and whoever believes in me shall never thirst" (John 6:35). Gregory the Great even used a rhetorical question concerning the Eucharistic bread: "Can any of the faithful doubt that at the hour of [Eucharistic] sacrifice the heavens open at the priest's calling, that in this mystery of Jesus Christ the choirs of angels are present, the heights joined to the depths, earth linked with heaven, the visible united with the invisible." (Markus: 1990, 21).

In the Orthodox East, St John Chrysostomos affirmed that there are three kinds of liturgy: the Eucharistic liturgy (in church), another one for the neighbour, as Jesus says: "You shall love your neighbor as yourself" (Matt 22:39), and, finally, the personal liturgy, as it is written in the Gospel: "but when you pray, go into your room and shut the door and pray to your Father who is in secret. And your father who sees in secret will reward you" (Matt 6:6), (Ittu: 2017, 89). In this context, *The Brukenthal Book of Hours* or *the Brukenthal Breviary*, as it is generally known, was the perfect devotional book for the personal liturgy, in which the book illuminations opened the door to a spiritual realm (Belting: 2011, 63).

Bibliography

As-Vijvers, Anne Margreet W. (2017), Creation by Variation: The Uses of Models in Ghent-Bruges Marginal decoration, https://hnanews.org/wp-content/uploads/2017/08/Abstracts-of-Antwerp-Conference-Papers.pdf

Belting, Hans (2011), An Anthropology of Images: Picture, Medium, Body, Princeton / Oxford: Princeton University Press.

Carey, Hilary M. (2010), Astrology in the Middle Ages, History Compass, 8/8, 888–902.

Cunningham, David S. (1995), On Translating the Divine Name, Theological Studies, 56/3, 415–440.

DeMaere, Jan (2007), Flämische Kunst in Siebenbürgen. Das Brukenthal-Museum in Hermanstadt/Sibiu, Antwerpen.

Derrida, Jacques (1988), The Ear of the Other, trans. by Peggy Kamuf, Lincoln: University of Nebraska.

Eco, Umberto (2003), Vegetal and Mineral Memory: the Future of Books, Al-Ahram, November 20–26, 665 (http://www.umbertoeco.com/en/bibliotheca-alexandrina-2003.html

Gavriluță, Nicu (2003), Fractalii și timpul social, Cluj-Napoca: Dacia.

Gavriluță, Nicu (2015), Mit, magie și manipulare politică, Iași: Institutul European.

Gould, Karen (1989), Roger Wieck, Time Sanctified: the Book of Hours in Medieval Art and Life (Book Review), The Papers of the Bibliographical Society of America 83/1, 233–237.

Ittu, Constantin (2012), Omilii nerostite ['Unspoken Homilies'], Sibiu: Editura Andreiana.

Ittu, Constantin (2017), Instantia Crucis, Sibiu: Editura Andreiana, Editura Universității Lucian Blaga.

Kren, Thomas/Mckendrick, Scot (2003), Illuminating the Renaissance: The Triumph of Flemish Manuscript Painting in Europe, Los Angeles: Paul Getty.

Markus, Robert Austin (1990), The End of Ancient Christianity, Cambridge: Cambridge University Press.

MORRISON, ELISABETH (2006), Iconographic Originality in the Oeuvre of the Master of the David Scenes, in: Elisabeth Morrison/Thomas Kren (ed.), Flemish Manuscript Painting in Context / Recent Research, Los Angeles: Paul Getty.

ORDEANU, MARIA (2007), Gloria in Excelsis Deo. Liber horarum Brukenthal, Sibiu/Alba Iulia: Altip.

PITAGORA (2013), Imnurile Sacre, București.

POOS, RAYMOND LAWRENCE (2001), Social History and the Book of Hours, in: Roger S. Wieck, Time Sanctified: The Book of Hours in Medieval Art and Life, New York: Braziller, 33–38.

STRANDENAAES, THOR (2002), Translation as Interpretation, in: Mogens Müller/Henrik Tronier (ed.), The New Testament as Reception, New York: Sheffield Academic Press, 181–200.

Kata Ágnes Szűcs
University of Szeged, Hungary

Saint Elizabeth of Hungary in Flemish Books of Hours

One of the most popular female saints of the Middle Ages was Saint Elizabeth of Hungary also known as Elizabeth of Thuringia (1207–1231). She was the daughter of Andrew II of the Árpád dynasty. The royal child was raised in the court of the Thuringian margrave and became the wife of Louis IV. Elizabeth lived a religious and charitable life, and by her canonization in the early thirteenth century she was the first to represent the new model of female sanctity focusing on the apostolic life. Accordingly, the princesses and noble women (mostly in Central Europe), who renounced their worldly possessions transmitted the glory of the royal family (Klaniczay: 2000, 169–239).

Saint Elizabeth's figure is bound to devotion. She quickly became one of the most popular female saints in the Middle Ages. Several prayers, hymns, and legends immortalized her life and deeds in devotional books, such as Breviaries, Missals and Books of Hours. In this study, however, I will examine the miniatures presented in these devotional books and through them the iconography of Saint Elizabeth in the fifteenth-sixteenth century. Looking at the different types of representations I will try to create a typology as well. The classification, in some cases, will bring us in a closer proximity to identify the original author or at least the guild where certain images were created.

Analysing the illuminations rather than the text gives an insight into the veneration of the Hungarian saint. Even more so, since these prayer books seem to invest her figure with a new iconographical feature. In the fifteenth and sixteenth-century Netherlands, Elizabeth is depicted with three crowns instead of the usual attributes known and used since the Middle Ages. The loaf of bread, the pitcher, the church building, and even the subsequently interpolated roses are often neglected in the Flemish books of hours.[1] The novelty of the paper is to analyse the iconography of

---

1 Naturally, the iconography of Saint Elizabeth has been subject to change and modification over the centuries, adapting to the religious needs of a particular place or era. One of the most well-known attributes of the Hungarian saint is a result of a later interpolation as well. The miracle of the roses was only linked to her legend in the late thirteenth and early fourteenth centuries, which cannot be fully dissociated from the mystical religious trends of Italy. For more on this subject see Pieper: 2000. Other scholars, however, state that the rose-motif is a phenomenon particularly associated with a region of Central and Eastern Europe and has become popular and well-known throughout Europe. On Saint Elizabeth of Hungary and the history of the miracle of the roses see Falvay: 2007; Gecser: 2005, 2007; Klaniczay: 2004.

Saint Elizabeth of Hungary in a group of images that were collected from various online databases, therefore, they have never been analysed together as a group.[2] I would also like to broaden the analysis by establishing the origin of the three-crown motif and highlighting the interpretations of its possible meanings. I will also try and answer some of the emerging questions. Does the motif originate from the Books of Hours, or do the first extant examples emerge from panel painting? Why would Elizabeth, depicted with three crowns, have such appeal among the Flemish elite?

The books of hours discussed in this paper may also give evidence of a religious-cultural change in the western part of Europe from the fifteenth century onwards, where the three-crown representation for Elizabeth first appeared.

Before discussing the images, I would like to look at the socio-historical context in which they were born. The Netherlands were ruled by the dukes of Burgundy from the middle of the fourteenth to the end of the fifteenth century. The last period of their regency coincided with the flourishing of illuminated manuscripts, as demonstrated by the numerous devotional and secular books produced for members of the court (Wisse: 2002). The Valois dynasty's French background, education and princely lifestyle gave Dutch culture a new impulse. Corresponding with their commissions, the era was also marked by artistic productivity and cultural growth. This era saw the emergence of the school of the so-called Flemish primitives, a realist tendency in portrait and landscape painting that reproduced the visible world in as detailed a manner as possible (Ainsworth/Christiansen: 1998).

Philip the Good's (1396–1467, r. 1419–67) foreign policy was characterized by territorial expansion and political control, while in internal affairs strong centralization and an extravagant court life was prevalent. Philip had no fixed residence and moved the court between his various palaces, the main ones being in Brussels, Bruges, and Lille. Due to his patronage, cultural and artistic centres were forming in these cities; Jan van Eyck, Petrus Christus, and later Hans Memling and Gerard David also worked at Philip's Bruges Court (Wisse: 2002).

The duke was also a remarkable book collector. During his regency, his library grew by approximately 600 volumes. In his court, the masterpieces of the flourishing book manufacture, especially the richly illuminated manuscripts were in heavy demand. Due to Philip's patronage, the codex painting workshops of the Netherlands became a true rival for big European centres like Paris (Kren/McKendrick: 2003).

The book of hours was a characteristic type of manuscript of this era. It emerged from the laicization of the breviary that was used for private devotional practices by the clerical society.

---

2 The images can be accessed through the British Library; The Morgan Library and Museum; The Cleveland Museum of Arts; Biblioteca Lazaro Galdiano and their online databases.

Among the 16 miniatures I will discuss in this paper that represent Saint Elizabeth of Hungary 12 are from books of hours.

The prayer books were small, therefore easy to transport, and their content was easily customizable. Finally, the rich illustrations opened a new level of personal devotion. With these qualities, the books of hours seem to have satisfied an emerging need for experiencing a personalized, private devotion, and they became popular in the centuries to come. These manufactured, lavishly illustrated books were so popular that, parallel with the rise of printing, they managed to survive on the market for at least another century (Wehli: 1986).

The first owners of these richly decorated codices were the members of the secular and ecclesiastical aristocracy, accordingly, they often served as diplomatic gifts, for instance during the celebration of courtly events, such as dynastic marriages.

The Divine Office and Hours of the Virgin formed an essential part of the book of hours with its own set of prayers, hymns, and antiphons but its content may include five to twenty-five further elements, of which the most common are the following: a calendar (to help the owner keep track of saints' days and other feasts), a set of gospel lessons, hours focusing on the Cross, a group of psalms that express penitence or regret, and finally, prayers to saints, called the Suffrages (Stein: 2017). The Suffrages of the Saints is the section that perhaps varies the most from one book of hours to another, as it can be customized with the patron's favourite saints.

The thus far collected books, which contain a prayer for Elizabeth and a personal miniature depicting the saint had aristocratic and even royal owners. Elizabeth, as a royal descendant, spent her life helping the poor. This particular attention towards her from the upper class at the end of the fifteenth century underlines the concept of a good monarch as socially considerate and pious.

This may be especially true in the case of female-owned books of hours. The two prayer books made for Isabella the Catholic, for instance, both contain an image of Elizabeth of Hungary, and her significance becomes even more layered. Apart from being a ceremonial gift, one should also consider the possibility of personal devotion, especially since Isabella the Catholic was able to honour not only her namesake and patron saint but also a distant family member in Saint Elizabeth of Hungary.

Not only the content but also the decoration of the books varied greatly depending on the imagination and the financial means of the patron. One could decide on the number and size of painted initials and miniatures, it could contain quarter-, half- or even full-sized illustrations.

Besides being decorative, the images fulfilled a rather practical purpose as well, serving as text markers. In the absence of page numbers, tables of contents, and indices, images provided an easy way for the users to orient themselves. On the other hand, the miniatures also contributed to the enhancement of personal piety. The owner could decide which of the saints should be represented by a miniature

108 | Kata Ágnes Szűcs

in the book. To further intensify the experience of a closer relationship the owner could request to be depicted with the patron saint (Wehli: 1986).

Considering the genre, it is not self-explanatory that a miniature of Elizabeth is presented in the books of hours. Therefore, my research aimed to find such prayerbooks that included her. The following table contains all the devotional books I have so far collected that meet this requirement. From now on, the paper will focus on these images, more specifically on those which depict Saint Elizabeth with three crowns.

The representations of Saint Elizabeth of Hungary in the sixteen collected prayer books vary according to the time and place of their provenience. For example, in the two, remarkably early paintings from the second half of the thirteenth century, she holds a book (MS M.440) and an angel brings her a mantle (MS M.729).[3] The first one was painted in Liège, Netherlands, and the second in Amiens, France.

There are three other paintings from the fifteenth century. In the two French specimens (Yates MS 3 and MS M.919), Elizabeth is depicted holding a book while in the Italian miniature, she holds a rosary in her hand (MS G.14). As an iconographical feature, the book often means piety or knowledge (Pál/Újvári: 2001). The rosary can refer to her devotion as well, however it has a particular meaning in the Italian context, where the miracle of the roses became widespread in the fourteenth and fifteenth centuries. The mantle, on the other hand, is a special attribute for Elizabeth of Hungary. This miracle is presented in one of her earliest legends which makes the manuscript quite exceptional.

The rest of the eleven miniatures represent Elizabeth with the three-crown attribute. Interestingly, all of these were manufactured in the Netherlands between 1420 and 1515. There is one exception, the MS M.917/945 painting was made in the Netherlands, although for a French noblewoman, which could explain the one-crown attribute.[4]

---

3   1. *Psalter-Hours*, 1261, The Morgan Library and Museum, MS M.440, 183 r. http://ica.themorgan.org/manuscript/page/38/77322 (16.11.22).
2. *Psalter-Hours*, 1280–1299, The Morgan Library and Museum, MS M.729, 260 v. http://ica.themorgan.org/manuscript/page/65/128492 (16.11.22).
3. *Book of Hours*, 1418, The Morgan Library and Museum, MS M.919, 199 v. http://ica.themorgan.org/manuscript/page/298/159955 (16.11.22).
4. *The Dunois Hours*, 1439–1450, The British Library, Yates MS 3, 286 r. http://www.bl.uk/manuscripts/FullDisplay.aspx?ref=Yates_Thompson_MS_3&index=11 (16.11.2022)
5. *Book of Hours*, 1470–1480, The Morgan Library and Museum, MS G.14, 46 r. http://ica.themorgan.org/manuscript/page/18/76806 (16.11.22).

4   The one exception is the *Hours of Catherine of Cleves*, where Elizabeth holds one crown in her hand. Nevertheless, as a consequence of the owner's identity we can presume the French provenience of the Master, where the motif was not widespread at the time. The French influence can also be observed by the style of the board decorations cf. *Hours of Catherine of Cleves*, The Morgan Library and Museum, MS M.917/945, fol. 321. https://www.themorgan.org/collection/hours-of-catherine-of-cleves/353 (16.11.22).

Saint Elizabeth of Hungary in Flemish Books of Hours | 109

The miniatures created in the Netherlands have a common way of representing the Hungarian Saint. But, according to the different placement of the three crowns and the general setting of the image, they can be further classified into four categories. Based on this differentiation, we can obtain information about their painter. The first group of illustrations that I would like to highlight is organized around the Master of the First Prayer Book of Maximilian I (generally known as the Maximilian Master).[5] There are three seemingly completely different books of hours, but the composition of the full-page miniature of Saint Elizabeth is the same (Fig. 1, 2).[6]

The first one is the so-called *The Hastings Hours* or *London Hours of William Lord Hastings* and was created by the Maximilian Master *ca.* 1480 in Ghent or Bruges. The uniformity of the so-called Hastings Hours suggests that the whole book was the work of one hand (Kren/ McKendrick: 2003, 192–194). Elizabeth dressed as a nun distributes alms to the poor, mainly food, and a piece of clothing. The three crowns appear above her head, held by an angel. (Fig. 2.)[7]

The second one is called *The London Rothschild Hours*, or *The Hours of Johanna I of Castile* illuminated *ca.* 1500 and later owned by Johanna I of Castile. According to relevant literature, the illumination of the prayer book was performed by two artists, and the Maximilian Master painted *The Suffrages of the Saints*, including of course the miniature of Saint Elizabeth.[8] It is obvious at first sight that there are differences between the two miniatures. The main figure and gestures of the female saint remain the same, however, the other parts of the miniature – the angel with the crowns, the donations, the poor and even the surrounding city – seem as if they have been cropped. Perhaps it was the Maximilian Master's personal invention that he later omitted these parts of his miniatures. (Fig. 3.)[9]

And finally, the last Elizabeth-miniature of this first group is in the *Da Costa Hours,*[10] painted *ca.* 1515. It was commissioned by the Sá-family in Porto, but later it came into the possession of Alvaro da Costa, the chamberlain of king Manuel I of Portugal. The illustration faithfully follows the complete composition of the first miniature presented in the Hastings Hours in 1480. Scholars identify the author of this later work as Simon Bening (Kren/McKendrick: 2003, 451–452).

---

5 The name of the illuminator is based upon a manuscript from 1486 whose owner was Maximilian I, the prayer book is now located in Vienna, ÖNB, under the shelf mark Cod. 1907.

6 http://www.bl.uk/manuscripts/Viewer.aspx?ref=add_ms_54782_fs001ar.

7 *St Elizabeth of Hungary*, Parchment miniature, *ca.* 1500, 235 v., British Library and Museum, http://www.bl.uk/manuscripts/Viewer.aspx?ref=add_ms_35313_fs001r#.

8 The British Library, Digitised Manuscripts, Book of Hours, Add MS 35313, http://www.bl.uk/manuscripts/FullDisplay.aspx?ref=Add_MS_35313 (05.12.17).

9 The right to publish the images indicated by Fig. 3. and Fig. 5. was funded by the University of Szeged under the UNKP grant, ID: UNKP-18-3-III-SZTE-27.
   Specific acknowledgement to the Morgan Library & Museum. Photographic credit: The Morgan Library & Museum, New York.

10 The Morgan Library and Museum, MS M.399, 328 v. http://ica.themorgan.org/manuscript/page/102/112362 (16.04.18).

Type	Name (if any)	Owner (if known)	Country	City
Psalter-Hours			Netherlands	Liège
Psalter-Hours	Psalter-Hours of Yolande de Soissons.		France	Amiens
Book of Hours			France	Paris
Missal			Belgium	Bruges
Book of Hours	The Dunois Hours	Jean, Count of Dunois	France	Paris
Book of Hours			Netherlands	Tournai
Book of Hours	Hours of Catherine of Cleves	Catherine of Cleves	Netherlands	Utrecht
Book of Hours			Netherlands	Tournai
Book of Hours			Italy(?)	Milan(?
Book of Hours			Belgium	Bruges Valenci
Book of Hours	Hastings Hours, or London Hours of William Lord Hastings	Edward IV; Edward V.	Netherlands	Ghent Bruges
Breviary	Breviary of Isabella the Catholic	Isabella I of Castille	Belgium	Bruges
Book of Hours	First Hastings Hours, or Madrid Hastings Hours		Belgium	Ghent Bruges
Book of Hours	Hours of Isabella the Catholic	Isabella I of Castille	Belgium	Ghent Bruges
Book of Hours	London Rothschild Hours	Johanna I of Castile	Netherlands	Ghent(
Book of Hours	Da Costa Hours	Sá family of Porto	Netherlands	Bruges

ter of the abeth-miniature	Date	Press mark	Page number	Motif 1	Location
	1261	MS M.440	183 r	Book	The Morgan Library and Museum
	1280–1299	MS M.729	260 v	Mantle/ Habit	The Morgan Library and Museum
	1418	MS M.919	199 v	Book	The Morgan Library and Museum
ter of the Gold lls	1420	Ms. M.374	147 v	Three crowns	The Morgan Library and Museum
	1439–1450	Yates MS 3	286 r	Book	The British Library
llower of Master of lebert de Mets	1440	MS M.357	fol. 014 v	Three crowns	The Morgan Library and Museum
ter of Catherine of es	1440	MS M.917/945	fol. 321	One crown	The Morgan Library and Museum
ter of Morgan 78	1450–1460	MS M.78	162 v	Three crowns	The Morgan Library and Museum
	1470–1480	MS G.14	46 r	Rosary	The Morgan Library and Museum
	1470	MS M.285	fol. 257 v	Three crowns	The Morgan Library and Museum
ter of the First erbook of Maximil-	1480	Add MS 54782	64 v	Three crowns	The British Library
ter of James IV of land	1480–1490	Add MS 18851	488 v	Three crowns	The British Library
ander Bening(?); or ter of Edward IV(?)	1480	Mss. I15503	46 v	Three crowns	Biblioteca Lazaro Galdiano
rd David	1495–1500	1963.256.197.b	197 v	Three crowns	The Cleveland Museum of Arts
ter of the First erbook of Maximil-	1500	Add MS 35313	235 v	Donations	The British Library
on Bening	1515	MS M.399	328 v	Three crowns	The Morgan Library and Museum

112 | Kata Ágnes Szűcs

	Collection	Type	Use	Name	Owner (if known)	Miniaturist	Date	Elizabeth	Figure
1.	The British Library	Book of Hours	Use of Sarum	Hastings Hours[11]	Edward IV; (or Edward V)	Maximilian Master	c. 1480	64v	1. Fig.
2.	The British Library	Book of Hours	Use of Rome	London Rothschild Hours	Johanna I of Castile	Maximilian Master	1500	235v	2. Fig.
3.	The Morgan Library and Museum	Book of Hours	Indeterminate	Da Costa Hours	The Sá-family of Porto; D. Alvaro da Costa	Simon Bening	1515	328v	3. Fig.

11 The coat of arms of the English nobleman is represented on several pages. (ff. 13r, 74r, 151r, and 184v). The latter owner was either king Edward IV (1442–1483), or Edward V (1470–1483).

Codex painting was no longer an ecclesiastical privilege in the fifteenth century when painters' guilds (generally named after Saint Luke) were founded. The masters and apprentices often divided the work among themselves. The masters' responsibility was to execute the complex parts and most importantly to elaborate the composition of the miniature, while the apprentices dealt with the more mechanical parts of the working process (Alexander: 1992; Kren/ McKendrick: 2003). The other consequence of working in guilds was that the masters soon elaborated patterns first for the floral decorative motifs, and only then the miniatures themselves. The pattern books could significantly accelerate the work of the workshop.

There are several theories for the identification of the Maximilian Master, one of which connects him with Alexander Bening (Kren/McKendrick: 2003, 190–198), the father of Simon Bening. However, due to limited biographical data, the identification rests on circumstantial and stylistic information.[12] The above-listed Saint Elizabeth miniatures may serve as another argument for this identification, as it was not unusual in the great Dutch painter dynasties, such as the Bening family, that a large body of patterns was passed on from father to son. And in this case the portrayal of Saint Elizabeth in the manuscript clearly shows that Simon Bening copies carefully: the gestures and the facial expressions are the same as those of the 1480s miniature, and this precision probably could not have been achieved without a book of patterns in hand, considering the restricted accessibility of the genre, produced for private use.

Along with the scene of the angel holding three crowns over Elizabeth's head, there are other patterns to be distinguished depicting the same motif. I created a second group that seems to continue the Maximilian Master's concept of Elizabeth depicted outdoors, helping the poor with alms. A piece of clothing in the paintings is not just a part of the alms for the poor, it can also be interpreted as a reference to the miracle of the mantle.[13] This hypothesis would also impact the meaning of the crown, and its heavenly nature and in case of the first group, even the presence of the angels would be more meaningful. Thus, the set of images is similar to those in the first group, without the presence of the angel. The miniatures in this group, however, differ in their placement of the three crowns: Elizabeth holds two of them in one hand and the third one, surrounded by a nimbus, is put on her head and in some cases, she holds a book in one of her hands as well.

---

12 Attempts have been made to identify him with the Master of Mary of Burgundy as well. See Marx/Krén: 2015.

13 According to her legend on one occasion, distinguished guests came to the court of Thuringia, wishing to see the princess famous for her piety. However, she could not arrive at the repeated messages of Count Louis of the province, because she gave all her suitable clothes to the poor. Praying in her cell, an angel of God suddenly appears, bringing her an ornate cloak and a crown of gold inlaid with precious stones, which evoked everyone's admiration and amazement.

114 | Kata Ágnes Szűcs

There are two miniatures in this group, and the first is in *The First Hastings Hours*' or the so-called *Madrid Hastings Hours*, which is made in Ghent or Bruges and dates around 1480.[14] The saint is wearing a grey tunic and hands over a piece of red clothing to a beggar, standing in front of the outlines of a city or an inner court. According to relevant literature, two artists may come into consideration as the painter of the Saint Elizabeth-miniature, Alexander Bening (who is probably the same as the Maximilian Master) or the Master of Edward IV (Ogáyar: 1983, 127–131). Comparing the two miniatures attributed to the Maximilian Master in the previous group of paintings with this one, the Master of Edward IV plausibly seems like the better candidate.

The miniature in the *Hours of Isabella I of Castile* has a similar composition, and represents Elizabeth handing out what appears to be the same red piece of clothing to a beggar. In this picture she wears a blue dress enfolded with a grey cloak and instead of a city there are city walls depicted in the background. This Saint Elizabeth-miniature is attributed convincingly by Scillia to the panel painter Gerard David. Although David was a panel painter, he also worked as a miniaturist and, as Scillia points out, the resemblance between his female figures and Elizabeth of Hungary[15] in this miniature makes him the illuminator in this case (Scillia: 2002, 50–67). The illustration was executed between 1495–1500 in Ghent or in Bruges. (Fig. 4.)

In the third group the same composition can be observed for the three crowns (two in one hand, one on the head) on three more representations of St Elisabeth. The difference is that she is portrayed under arches suggesting a monastic environment. The miniatures are preserved in a variety of books (breviary, missal, and a book of hours), but all of them were illustrated in Bruges. A Missal, from ca. 1420 is one of the earliest, so far discovered representations of Saint Elizabeth of Hungary with three crowns. Within the initial T,[16] Elizabeth holds two crowns in her hands and the third one on her head with a nimbus. Its illuminator was a Follower of Master of Guillebert de Mets. (Fig. 5.)

The second Elizabeth-miniature is from the *Breviary of Isabella the Catholic,* an unfinished Book of Hours made ca. 1480–1497. The miniature has nearly the same composition, it is only supplemented by a book that she holds in her hand (Karl: 1912, 30–33). The third image is unfinished (ca. 1470), but the general idea

---

14 Cf. Biblioteca de la Fundación Lázaro Galdian, Colección de manuscritos medievales, Hora B. M. V. secundum usum Sarum [Manuscrito], Mss. I15503, 46v. http://www.bibliotecalazarogaldiano.es/mss/i15503l.html(18.05.18).

15 David even registers an oil painting, the right wing of a triptych, painting Saint Elizabeth with three crowns. The oil painting was executed at least five years after the miniature, but the position of the crowns corresponds. Triptych of Jan Des Trompes, 1505, Groeninge Museum, Bruges. https://www.wga.hu/html/d/david/2/trompe.html (20.10.17).

16 Missal, M.374 fol. 147v – Images from Medieval and Renaissance Manuscripts – The Morgan Library & Museum, http://ica.themorgan.org/manuscript/page/55/112374 (04.05.18).

is alike: Elizabeth dressed as a nun, holds one crown in her hand, one on an opened book, and the third one is on her head surrounded by a nimbus.[17] (Fig. 6.)

In the fourth category of the miniatures Elizabeth is portrayed in a monastic environment as well, but the position of the crowns is somewhat different. In these pictures, Elizabeth holds the two crowns in each hand and the third one is, like before on her head surrounded by a nimbus. Both books containing this composition were illustrated in the Netherlands, Tournai – one in 1440[18] and the second one between 1450–1460.[19]

A possible origin of the motif

The composition, the different placement of the crowns, or the background of an image, may help us to identify a possible painter. Based on the already mentioned manuscripts and Saint Elizabeth-illuminations the three-crown motif is popular in the prayerbooks; however, the exact meaning and the origin of these crowns are still vague.

The only medieval or contemporary written record that contains a reference to something similar is the *vita* of Caesarius von Heisterbach (ca. 1180–ca. 1240), a Cistercian monk (Schmoll: 1914). However, it is not three crowns, rather a triple coronation by a heavenly crown (aureola). According to Caesarius, there are three groups of people to whom this celestial crown is due, the martyrs, the virgins, and the priests; and Elizabeth is part of all three groups. She is a martyr because of self-restraint and ascetic life, a virgin because of her widowhood purity, and she can be classified among priests because of her sacred way of life, and her encouraging revelations to others.

It is important, however, that this is an interpretation of a non-figural representation. Schmoll, however, argues that the three-crown depictions spread mainly in the Lower Rhine and the Netherlands precisely because the Cistercian monk was active in this region.

Although its origin can be traced back to the Lower Rhine region, the hagiography of the Cistercian monk was known also beyond this immediate geographical

---

17 Book of Hours, MS M.285 fol. 257v – Images from Medieval and Renaissance Manuscripts – The Morgan Library & Museum, http://ica.themorgan.org/manuscript/page/74/77087 (25.04.18).
18 Virgin Mary: Coronation, MS M.357. Fol. 014v – Images from Medieval and Renaissance Manuscripts – The Morgan Library & Museum, http://ica.themorgan.org/manuscript/page/1/112382 (12.02.18).
19 Book of Hours, MS M.78 fol. 162v – Images from Medieval and Renaissance Manuscripts – The Morgan Library & Museum, http://ica.themorgan.org/manuscript/page/19/76828 (18.05.18).

116 | Kata Ágnes Szűcs

environment. And respectively, this still does not explain how and why the pictorial representation spread with a "delay" of about 200–300 years. So, the question requires further research.

As far as pictorial representations are concerned, the ones that were discussed so far raise a great many questions, maybe even more than what can be answered within the current state of research. What is the meaning of this new attribute, what do the crowns symbolize, is there a difference between their placements? Several interpretations can be read in Rechberg (Rechberg: 1983) and Rexroth (Rexroth: 1981).

Brigitta Rechberg emphasizes in her paper the Dutch origins of the three-crown motif, regarding Saint Elizabeth of Hungary. More specifically she connects its invention to Jan van Eyck and the panel painters of fifteenth century Netherlands. Rechberg claims that the first known painting of Saint Elizabeth of Hungary with three crowns is from a 1441 oil painting that was ordered for the consecration of a Carthusian monk, Jan Vos (Ainsworth/Martens: 1995). The work was started by van Eyck but after his death, it was supposedly finished by his apprentice Petrus Christus in 1443.

In one of Christus's later paintings Saint Elizabeth of Hungary is also portrayed with three crowns. Since it shows great similarity to van Eyck's concept in the placement of the crowns, it simultaneously underlines his possible contribution to the Jan van Eyck-painting. Isabella of Portugal (1397–1471), the third wife of Philip the Good ordered the triptych after her retirement to a Franciscan convent in Nieppe, France in 1457 (see Web Gallery of Art, searchable fine arts image database 2015). I must stress the importance of the fact that Saint Elizabeth was not only Isabella's namesake and patron saint, but they were distant relatives as well. Their connection to the Franciscans further fortified this relationship. In the painting Isabella kneels before an opened book and prays while Elizabeth stands behind her holding three crowns in her hand. (Fig. 7.)

We can see that van Eyck's panel painting is dated to 1441–1443 which makes at least one of the miniatures earlier and a couple of them contemporary to it. However, Jan van Eyck's and Petrus Christus's oil paintings have something in common which none of the aforementioned prayerbooks share. The three crowns are depicted on top of each other in Elizabeth's hands. This exact motif also appears in a textual context. First, Jodocus Clichtoveus (1472–1543)[20] mentions the crowns in his sermon written for Elizabeth's feast day.[21]

---

20 Clichtove, Josse van (d. 1543), Belgian theologian, received his education at Louvain and at Paris under Jacques Lefèbvre d'Etaples. He became librarian of the Sorbonne and tutor to the nephews of Jacques d'Amboise, bishop of Clermont and abbot of Cluny. In 1519 he was elected bishop of Tournai, and in 1521 was appointed to the see of Chartres. He is best known as a distinguished antagonist of Martin Luther, against whom he wrote a good deal. When Cardinal Duprat convened his Synod of Paris in 1528 to discuss the new religion,

And when Johannes Molanus (1533–1585)[22] writes about the iconography of the Hungarian saint – referring to Clichtoveus from the second edition of his book – he also connects the attribute to Elizabeth. Molanus's post-Tridentine book about the representation of saints is particularly important because it led to the subsequent spreading of the motif.[23] Finally, I would like to mention a third, celebrated personality who, however shortly, also refers to and continues the Flemish tradition of the iconography of the Hungarian Saint. Justus Lipsius (1547–1606) in the *Diva Virgo Hallensis* claims the following: "Quantis iamtum sanctimoniae indiciis, longum sit dicere: hoc moneo, puellam, vxorem, viduam, mira pietatis laude celebrem fuisse: ideoque a pictoribus aut sculptoribus passim caput eius triplici corona insigniri, qua min quoque ordine illo iure sibi poscit." (Lipsius: 1605, 6).

All three of the authors concluded that three crowns symbolize the holiness of Saint Elizabeth during her youth (virginity), her married life, and her widowhood as well. When there is a reference to the position in the descriptions, the crowns are held on top of each other in Elizabeth's hands. The written texts also give the impression in each case that the authors have already seen such a representation. (Fig. 8.)

Interestingly, however, there is another painting by Christus which depicts the wife of the donor praying while in the background there is a xylography nailed on the wall (Parshall/Schoch: 2005, 41–43). This leaflet represents Saint Elizabeth of

---

Clichtove was summoned and was entrusted with the task of collecting and summarizing the objections to the Lutheran doctrine. This he did in his *Compendium veritatum [...] contra erroneas Lutheranorum assertions*, 1529). He died at Chartres on the 22nd of September 1543.

21 "Attamen eadem nunc recte possunt applicari et accomodari in laudem S. Elisabeth viduae, cuius hodie solennitatis in ecclesia celebratur: quem non unica, sicut in capite Aaron, sed triplex super caput huius beatae mulieris corona refulsit, et in aeternum fulgebit, quantum ad aeternae retributionis praemieum, quemadmodum ex praesentis sermonis deductione latius constabit. Et id quidem expresse repraesentatur per sacram eius imaginem, pro more Christianae pietatis in ecclesijs reponi solitam quem triplicem coronam manu gestare continereque effigiatur, primam reliquis duabus subsidentem, secundam mediam, et tertiam caeteris duabus superpositam." (Clichtoveus: 1575, 460).

22 Molanus was born in Lille, in Walloon Flanders, in 1533. His father, Hendrik Vermeulen was from Holland and his mother Anna Peters from Brabant. He matriculated at Louvain University in 1554, graduating in the Liberal Arts in 1558 and as Doctor of Theology in 1570. He became a canon of St. Peter's Church, Leuven, and a professor of Theology, serving both as dean of the Faculty of Theology and as rector of the university. In 1579 he was appointed president of King's College (Wauters: 1899, 48–55). Molanus was one of the first authorities to turn the Council of Trent's short and inexplicit decrees on sacred images (1563) into minutely detailed instructions for artists, which were then widely enforced in Catholic countries mostly (Freedberg: 1971, 34).

23 "Die decima nona Natalem habet Elisabeth, regis Hungarorum filia, xenodochiorum et pauperum amantissima. Haec pingitur cum tribus coronis, ut significetur vitam sanctissime transegisse in statu virginali, maritali, et viduali. Quomodo hanc picturam explicat Iodocus Clichthouenus integro sermone, quem unicum edidit de Natali hujus sanctissimae Viduae. In quo pro themate assumit illud Ecclesiastici, Corona aurea super caput ejus." (Molanus: 1594).

Hungary, who once again, and now on a *print*, holds two crowns in each hand and the third is placed on her head. A composition which could be familiar from the previously mentioned prayerbooks as well.

Conclusion and further questions

In the fifteenth century the art of painting had not yet crystallized as a profession: there was no clear distinction between panel painting and miniature painting, it is enough to mention Jan van Eyck or Petrus Christus as examples – whom we consider primarily as panel painters, but they also painted several miniatures as well (Kren/McKendrick: 2003).

During the period of the Burgundian Duchy in the Netherlands manuscript manufacture has begun its mass production – at least compared to the contemporary context. Therefore, the book of patterns played an important role in a miniaturist workshop to fulfil the incoming orders. These patterns were initially taken from panel or oil paintings, but this practice could not hinder individual inventions.

We can assert that the occurrence of the three crown-motifs in Saint Elizabeth's iconography is in fact strongly connected to the Netherlands. But the so far discovered earliest representation of Saint Elizabeth of Hungary with the three crown-attribute is not a panel painting but a miniature placed in a Missal circa 1420.

In addition to the above-mentioned issues, the following questions arise. Could this be an individual invention of its master, the so-called Master of the Golden Scroll? Can we assume that Jan van Eyck borrowed the motif applied on his panel painting from a book of hours or another devotional book or even a xylographic leaflet? Or rather, that there is a lost or destroyed panel painting dated earlier than 1441 which could have been used as a model for the miniatures?

At this point of the research, it is hard to tell. But according to the so far collected data it seems like the three crown-motif regarding Saint Elizabeth of Hungary was commonly used among the codex illuminators in the early fifteenth century Netherlands. Nevertheless, the invention that we can attribute to Jan van Eyck resides in the placement of the three crowns. One must consider that none of the already mentioned miniatures from before and even contemporary with the 1441 oil painting depicts the saint holding all three crowns put together in her hands.

In conclusion we can assert that the appearance of the three-crown motif in Saint Elizabeth's iconography is in fact strongly connected to the Netherlands. But the so far discovered earliest representation of Saint Elizabeth of Hungary with the three crown-attribute is not a panel painting but a miniature placed in a Missal circa 1420. It is not always possible to determine the exact date of origin, however several miniatures come from the 1440s, that is to say before or at the same time as the panel painting of Jan van Eyck and Petrus Christus.

Could this mean that the motif is the individual invention of its master, the so-called Master of the Golden Scroll? Can we assume that Jan van Eyck borrowed the motif applied on his panel painting from a devotional book or even a xylographic leaflet? Or rather, that there is a lost or destroyed panel painting dated earlier than 1441 which could have been used as a model for the miniatures?

At this point of the research, it is hard to tell. But according to the so far collected data it seems like the three crown-motif regarding Saint Elizabeth of Hungary was commonly used among the codex illuminators in the early fifteenth century Netherlands. It is also interesting to see that the cult of Saint Elizabeth is very popular amongst the female monarchs of the era. Especially those related to her. Their role is significant in the context of this new attribute; however, the nature of their role has not yet become perfectly clear.. Nevertheless, an invention that we can attribute to Jan van Eyck resides in the placement of the three crowns, considering that the herein mentioned miniatures from before and even contemporary with the 1441 oil painting portray the saint holding the crown in different positions. None of them depicts Saint Elizabeth with the three crowns placed together in her hands.

Bibliography

AINSWORTH, MARYAN W./MARTENS, MAXIMILIAAN P.J. (1995a), Jan van Eyck et atelier. Vierge à l'Enfant avec sainte Barbe, sainte Elisabeth et Jan Vos, in: Maryan W. Ainsworth/Maximiliaan P. J. Martens, Petrus Christus, Ghent/New York/Ludion: Metropolitan Museum of Art, 72–78.

AINSWORTH, MARYAN W./MARTENS, MAXIMILIAAN P.J. (1995b), Portrait d'un donateur, Portrait d'une donatrice, in: Maryan W. Ainsworth/Maximiliaan P. J. Martens, Petrus Christus, Ghent/New York/Ludion: Metropolitan Museum of Art, 131–135.

AINSWORTH, MARYAN WYNN/CHRISTIANSEN, KEITH (ed.) (1998), From Van Eyck to Bruegel: Early Netherlandish Painting in the Metropolitan Museum of Art, New York: Metropolitan Museum of Art.

ALEXANDER, JONATHAN J.G. (1992), Medieval Illuminators and Their Methods of Work, New Haven / London: Yale University Press.

CLICHTOVE, JOSSE VAN (1911), Article "Châtelet – Constantine", Encyclopædia Britannica, vol. 6, 507.

CLICHTOVEUS, JODOCUS (1575), Homiliae seu sermones Iudoci Clichtovei. Colonae: apud Heredes Iohannis Quentely et Geruuinum Calenium.

FALVAY, DÁVID (ed.) (2009), Árpád-házi Szent Erzsébet kultusza a 13–16. században: az Eötvös Loránd Tudományegyetem Bölcsészettudományi Karán 2007. május 24-én

120 | Kata Ágnes Szűcs

tartott konferencia előadásai, Budapest: Magyarok Nagyasszonya Ferences Rendtartomány.

FREEDBERG, DAVID (1971), Johannes Molanus on provocative paintings. De historia sanctarum imaginum et picturarum, book II, chapter 42, Journal of the Warburg and Courtauld Institutes, 34, 229–245.

GECSER, OTTÓ (2005), Il miracolo delle rose, in Annuario 2002–2004: Conferenze e convegni, Roma, 240–247.

GECSER, OTTÓ (2007), Aspects of the Cult of St. Elizabeth of Hungary with a Special Emphasis on Preaching, 1231–ca.1500, PhD thesis, Budapest: Central European University.

KLANICZAY, GÁBOR (2000), Az uralkodók szentsége a középkorban. Magyar dinasztikus szentkultuszok és európai modellek, Budapest: Balassi.

KLANICZAY, GÁBOR (2004), Proving sanctity in the canonization processes. (Saint Elizabeth and Saint Margaret of Hungary), in: Klaniczay, Gábor, Procès de canonisation au Moyen Âge. Aspects juridiques et religieux – Medieval Canonization Processes. Legal and Religious Aspects, Roma: École Française de Rome, 117–148.

KREN, THOMAS/MCKENDRICK, SCOT (2003), Illuminating the Renaissance: The Triumph of Flemish Manuscript Painting in Europe, Los Angeles: Getty Publications.

LIPSIUS, JUSTUS (1605), Diva virgo Hallensis: Beneficia eius & miracvla fide atque ordine descripta. Antverpiae: ex Officina Plantiniana, apud Ioannem Moretum.

MARX, DÁNIEL/KRÉN, EMIL (2015), Master of Mary of Burgundy, Biography, Web Gallery of Art, searchable fine arts image database, last accessed on 2015.07.10.

MOLANUS, JOHANNES (1594), De Historia sanctorum: Imaginum et picturarum. Lovanii: apud Ioannem Bogardum, Typographum iuratum.

OGÁYAR, JUANA HIDALGO (1983), Libro de Horas de William Hastings, Goya: Revista de arte, 177, 127–131.

PÁL, JÓZSEF/ÚJVÁRI, EDIT (ed.) (2001), Szimbólumtár: Jelképek, motívumok, témák az egyetemes és a magyar kultúrából, Budapest: Balassi.

PARSHALL, PETER W./SCHOCH, RAINER(2005), Die Anfänge der europäischen Druckgraphik. Holzschnitte des 15. Jahrhunderts und ihr Gebrauch. (Ausstellungskatalog) National Gallery of Art, Washington, 4. September – 27. November 2005; Germanisches Nationalmuseum, Nürnberg, 15. Dezember 2005.–19. Mä. Nürnberg.

PIEPER, LORI (2000), A New Life of St. Elizabeth of Hungary, Archivum Franciscanum Historicum, 93, 29–78.

RECHBERG, BRIGITTA (1983), Königstochter, Fürstin, Heilige Bemerkungen zum Drei-Kronen-Attribut der hl. Elisabeth, in: Elisabeth in der Kunst – Abbild, Vorbild, Wunschbild. Ausstellung im Marburger Universitätsmuseum für bildende Kunst, Marburg: Elwert, 109–134.

REXROTH, KARL HEINRICH (1981), Das Kronenattribut der heiligen Elisabeth in der Kunst des Spätmittelalters und der Renaissance, Hessische Heimat, 31/4–5, 116–121.

SALLAY, DÓRA (2012), V. Manuscript Illumination, in: Vladimir Baranov/Kateřina Horníčková/Elena Lemeneva/Gerhard Jaritz (ed.), Medieval Manuscript Manual [online], Budapest: Central European University, Department of Medieval Studies.

SCILLIA, DIANE G. (2002), Gerard David's "St. Elizabeth of Hungary" in the "Hours of Isabella the Catholic", Cleveland Studies in the History of Art, 7, 50–67.

Saint Elizabeth of Hungary in Flemish Books of Hours | 121

SCHMOLL, FRIEDRICH (1914), Zur Ikonographie der heiligen Elisabeth im 13. bis 16. Jahrhundert. Dissertation, Giessen: Hof- und Universitätsdruckerei Otto Kindt.

STEIN, WENDY (2017), The Book of Hours: A Medieval Bestseller, Heilbrunn Timeline of Art History, 2017, New York: Metropolitan Museum of Art.

WAUTER, ALPHONSE (1899), Article "Molanus, Joannes", Biographie Nationale de Belgique, vol. 15, Brussels.

WEHLI, TÜNDE (1986), A flamand hóráskönyv: kísérőtanulmány az Országos Széchényi Könyvtárban őrzött Cod. lat. 205-ös jelzetű Gent-brüggei kódex hasonmás, Budapest: Helikon.

WISSE, JACOB (2002), Burgundian Netherlands: Court Life and Patronage, Heilbrunn Timeline of Art History, New York: The Metropolitan Museum of Art. Gebet im späten Mittelalter zwischen Ablassverheißung und identifikatorischer Internalisierung.

Illustrations

Fig. 1. 'The Hastings Hours', or 'London Hours of William Lord Hastings', The British Library, Add MS 54782, 64 v.

Saint Elizabeth of Hungary in Flemish Books of Hours | 123

Fig. 2. 'The London Rothschild Hours', or 'The Hours of Johanna I of Castile', The British Library, Add MS 35313, 235v.

Fig. 3. Da Costa Hours, The Morgan Library and Museum, MS M.399, 328 v.

Fig. 4. 'Hours of Isabella I of Castile' The Cleveland Museum of Arts, 1963.256.197.b. 197 v. (Scillia 7(2002), 51.)

Fig. 5. Missal, The Morgan Library & Museum M.374 fol. 147 v.

Fig. 6. The 'Breviary of Isabella the Catholic', The British Library, Add MS 18851, 488 v.

Fig. 7. Petrus Christus, Isabel of Portugal with St Elizabeth 1457–1460, Web Gallery of Art.

Fig. 8. Petrus Christus, Wife of a donator, ca. 1450. Web Gallery of Art.

Volker Leppin
Yale Divinity School

Eine Untersuchung anhand des *Hortulus animae*

> „Unter andern vil schedlichen leren unnd buchlin, da mit die Christen
> verfuret und betrogen unnd untzehlich mißglawben auffkommen sind,
> acht ich nicht fur die wenigsten Die betbuchlin, darynnen ßo mancher-
> ley iamer von beychten und sunde tzelen, Szo unchristliche narheyt ynn
> den gepettlin tzu gott unnd seynen heyligen, den eynfeltigen eyngetrie-
> ben ist Und dennoch mit ablaß unnd rotten tittel hoch auffgeblassen,
> datzu kostlich namen drauff geschrieben. Eynß heyst Hortulus anime,
> das andere Paradyßus anime und ßo fort an, das sie woll wirdig we-
> ren eyner starcken, gutter reformacion oder gar vertilget werden" (WA
> 10/2, 375,3-11.)

Mit diesen scharfen Worten wandte Luther sich gegen Gebetbücher seiner Zeit.
Seine Kritik unterfüttert er im Einzelnen nicht. Es bleibt vielmehr bei der pau-
schalen Abwertung, die im konkreten Kontext der Einführung des eigenen „Bet-
büchleins" dienen soll. Dem mag die Kontrastierung geholfen haben – und zum
Teil dürfte sie durch diese Motivation auch verursacht sein. Doch die überscharfe
Entgegensetzung dürfte ihren Anhalt auch in bestimmten inhaltlichen Akzentuie-
rungen gehabt haben. Angesichts Luthers wiederholter Wendung gegen das bloß
äußerliche, plappernde Gebet (gem. Mt 6,7)[1] ist anzunehmen, dass er die inkrimi-
nierten Gebetbücher als Repräsentanten eben solcher Veräußerlichung verstand.[2]

Nun lässt sich deutlich machen, dass Luther mit seiner eigenen Betonung
des Innerlichen selbst Erbe einer bestimmten, schon innermittelalterlich der Veräußerlichung entgegenstehenden Frömmigkeitsströmung ist (Leppin: 2017). Vor
diesem Hintergrund verdient die Frage Aufmerksamkeit, ob beziehungsweise in
welchem Ausmaß die Einordnung unter veräußerlichte Frömmigkeit die genannten Gebetbücher trifft.

---

1 S. z.B. WA 38, 364,20–25: „Fur war, es findet sich, das es der rechte Meister gestellet und
geleret hat, Und ist jamer uber jamer, das solch gebet solchs Meisters sol also on alle andacht
zu plappert und zu klappert werden jnn aller welt. Viel beten des jars vileicht etlich tausendt
Pater noster, Und wenn sie tausent jar also sollten beten, so hetten sie doch nicht einen buch-
staben oder tuettel davon geschmeckt noch gebettet." Luther suggerierte, sich hierdurch von
der päpstlichen Kirche abzuwenden. Tatsächlich findet sich genau dieselbe Kritik bereits in
der mystischen Tradition des späten Mittelalters; s. Meister Eckhart: 1994, 322, 3–6.
2 Zu den Polaritäten des späten Mittelalters, zu denen neben der Polarität von Klerikern und
Laien wie der von Zentralität und Dezentralität auch die von äußerlicher und innerlicher
Frömmigkeit gehörte, s. Leppin: 2015, 31–68.

132 | Volker Leppin

Während der *Paradisus animae* nur in einem Baseler Druck von 1498 erhalten ist,[3] ist der *Hortulus animae* auf Deutsch wie Lateinisch in mehreren Ausgaben erhalten und kann als eines der erfolgreichsten Gebetbücher der Zeit unmittelbar vor der Reformation gelten. Er bietet sich daher in besonderer Weise für eine Untersuchung des Gebets um 1500 an.

Der *Hortulus animae*, Nürnberg, 1519

Der *Hortulus animae*, auf Deutsch „Das Seelenwürzgärtlein", auf den Luther rekurriert, stellt ein außerordentlich erfolgreiches Werk aus dem Umfeld der Straßburger „Gottesfreunde" (Achten: 1980, 137) in lateinischer wie deutscher Sprache dar. Erstmals erschien eine lateinische Ausgabe 1498 in Straßburg, wo das Werk auch entstanden ist (Achten: 1980, 137), 1501 dann ebendort eine deutsche Ausgabe (Achten: 1980, 137). Insgesamt kam das Büchlein auf 103 erhaltene Druckausgaben bis 1523, wobei der Charakter als Gebrauchsliteratur auch annehmen lässt, dass viele Editionen verloren gegangen sind.[4] Diese Vielzahl von Drucken erlaubt es, den *Hortulus animae* tatsächlich als ein repräsentatives Werk spätmittelalterlicher Frömmigkeitskultur Anfang des 16. Jahrhunderts anzusehen.

Eben als solches soll es im Folgenden betrachtet werden. Angesichts des Standes der Forschung ist dabei ein umfassender Überblick über die Überlieferung nicht nötig, sondern es muss ein einzelner Druck herausgegriffen werden, für welchen zwar anzunehmen ist, dass es das Werk in seiner Breite repräsentiert,[5] der aber eben angesichts von mindestens fünf identifizierten unterschiedlichen Fassungen[6] doch zunächst einmal als Repräsentant seines regionalen Entstehungs- und Verbreitungskontextes zu verstehen ist.

Da der Ausgang dieser Überlegungen bei Luther und seiner Kritik an der mittelalterlichen Frömmigkeit genommen wurde, konzentrieren sich die folgenden Überlegungen auf ein Exemplar, das recht nah an ein Luther vertrautes Milieu heranreicht: einen Nürnberger Druck des Jahres 1519.[7] Er enthält unter dem Ti-

---

3 Paradisus: 1498; nicht gemeint haben dürfte Luther den sehr verbreiteten pseudo-albertinischen *Paradisus animae*, bei dem es sich nicht um ein Gebetbuch, sondern um einen Tugendtraktat handelt, Söller: 1989.

4 Achten: 1980, 137; vgl. Matter: 2017, 293. Noch eine geringere, bibliographisch aber gründlich erfasste Anzahl von Ausgaben verzeichnet Oldenbourg: 1973, 18–67, mit 109 laufenden Nummern.

5 Vgl. Ochsenbein: 1983, 147, zur großen Nähe der frühen Drucke zueinander.

6 Ochsenbein: 1983, 147; vgl. Ochsenbein: 2004, 185f, zu Unterschieden im Einzelnen Matter: 2017, 294. Besonders interessant ist die Bearbeitung durch Sebastian Brant; s. hierzu Knape/Wilhelmi: 2015, 130f.

7 *Hortulus anime*: 1519. Es handelt sich hier um die Ausgabe L 86, bei Oldenbourg: 1973, 55.

tel „Hortulus anime zu tewtsch Selen wuertzgertlein genant" die deutschsprachige Fassung. Der Drucker Friedrich Peypus (*Hortulus animae*, g7^v.) gilt als einer der ersten Sortimentsbuchhändler Nürnbergs mit einem eigenen Laden am Markt (Pallmann: 1887, 25; Reske: 2007, 664f), sicherte also eine rege und rasche Verbreitung. Er arbeitete im Auftrag von Johann Koberger.[8] Konkret ist der *Hortulus animae* aber auf Veranlassung der Nürnberger Bruderschaft zum himmlischen Rosenkranz entstanden.[9] Offenkundig gehört der Druck einem Nürnberger Milieu an, das durch die von Wittenberg ausgehenden Veränderungen noch nicht grundlegend in seiner Frömmigkeitspraxis erschüttert war. Tatsächlich erfolgte der Druck von Luthers „Sermon von dem Hochwürdigen Sakrament" mit dem Anhang „von den Bruderschaften" (WA 2, 742–758) erst in eben dem Jahr 1519, in welchem auch das Würzgärtlein erschien.

Diese Beobachtung einer weitgehenden Unberührtheit von der reformatorischen Bewegung ist für Nürnberg insofern bedeutsam, als die Reichsstadt insgesamt einer der ersten Orte ist, an welchen sich eine intensive Luther-Rezeption greifen lässt: Im Zusammenhang mit Staupitz' Predigten im Advent 1516 in Nürnberg hatte sich eine *sodalitas Staupitziana* gebildet, deren Name sich gerade im Jahr 1518 in *sodalitas Martiniana* verändert hatte (Hamm: 2004, 67). Insbesondere über den ehemals in Wittenberg tätigen Juristen Christoph Scheurl gab es einen regen Briefverkehr zwischen Nürnberg und der kleinen Universitätsstadt an der Elbe.[10] Mit dem Druck des *Hortulus animae* aber steht man auf der Seite fortdauernder Orientierung an Frömmigkeitspraktiken, die durch die Reformation in die Defensive geraten sollten.

Das Würzgärtlein ist recht umfangreich: Auf 16 Blätter mit Kalenderüberblicken und Berechnungstabellen besonderer Festtage folgen 230 foliierte Seiten und darauf wiederum 6 nur durch Lagenzählung gekennzeichnete Blätter mit dem Register. Diesem kann man die aus Sicht der damaligen Herausgeber entscheidenden Inhalte entnehmen. Allerdings stellen die Rubrizierungen eher eine Hervorhebung des besonders Wichtigen dar als eine klare Einteilung des Inhalts. Dessen Kern sind „die 6 wichtigsten Elemente eines Stundenbuches (...): Kalender, Kleines Marienoffizium, sieben Bußpsalmen, Allerheiligenlitanei, Suffragien (...) und Totenoffizium" (Ochsenbein: 1983, 147), die aber um vielfältiges Andachtsmaterial erweitert sind:

---

8 Oldenbourg: 1973, 117. Johann Koberger ist offenbar Sohn und Erbe von Anton Koberger (s. Reske: 2007, 655).

9 S. Bild und Text in *Hortulus animae,* g2^v; der „himmlische Rosenkranz" war ein dreizehnzeiliges, weit verbreitetes Lied (Wachinger: 2004), auf das sich offenbar die Nürnberger Bruderschaft bezog.

10 S. in Christoph Scheurl: 1867, die auf beide Bände der Edition (also ab 1505) verweisenden Registereinträge zu Nicolaus von Amsdorff, Christian Bayer, Otto Beckmann, Andreas Carlstadt, Johann Doltz, Martin Luther, Georg Spalatin und Johann von Staupitz.

134 | Volker Leppin

- Am Anfang steht der erwähnte Kalender, der Heiligentage benennt und besonders hohe Feste in Rot hervorhebt, aber die kalendarischen Angaben auch mit den Tierkreiszeichen korreliert. Freilich bietet er auch Regelhinweise, die nicht unmittelbar mit devotionaler Haltung und Praxis zu tun haben, sondern eher mit Bauernweisheiten und astrologischen Kenntnissen wie etwa:

Der Wider hat das haubt in hut
Warm / drucken / sunst ist lassen gut
Des Mertzen zeychen ist wol kundt
Huot dich / nit wuer im haubt wundt" (*Hortulus animae*, IV[r])

- Die Gebete beginnen mit einem marianischen Reigen, der das Benedictus (den Lobgesang des Zacharias), das Magnificat, das Nunc dimittis (den Lobgesang des Simeon) und das Regina coeli enthält, also eine Erinnerung an die Geschichte und Vorgeschichte von Weihnachten – weswegen es auch Sonderbestimmungen für den Umgang mit diesen Gebeten in der Weihnachtszeit gibt – und den Preis Mariens. [11]
- Dem folgt ein auf die Stundengebete („sieben tagzeyt" – *Hortulus animae*, g3[r]) bezogener Passionszyklus, unter anderem mit den sieben letzten Worten Jesu, einem Bedenken der fünf Wunden Christi und einer Erinnerung an die Gregorsmesse, der abgeschlossen wird durch eine lange Widergabe der Passionsgeschichte nach Joh. [12]
- Darauf folgen die sieben Bußpsalmen. [13]
- Danach sind die Einschnitte nicht mehr einfach durch Rubrizierungen zu finden und für die nächste Gruppierung auch nicht ganz klar. Offenbar geht es nun um Gebete in Schwellensituationen: am Abend und Morgen, aber auch für ein seliges Ende, ebenso wie zum Verlassen des Hauses und dem Gang in die Kirche. [14]
- Es folgt ein Gebet zur Trinität und dann wieder eine längere marianische Sektion. [15]
- Danach handeln zwei Gebete von Michael und dem je eigenen Engel. [16]
- Ein Gebet von Johannes dem Täufer[17] leitet über zu einer Sektion in welcher von den Evangelisten und den Aposteln die Rede ist. [18]

---

11 Die Angaben hierzu beziehen sich im Register auf *Hortulus animae*, f. 2–30.
12 Bezogen auf *Hortulus animae*, f. 2–48.
13 Bezogen auf *Hortulus animae*, f. 48.
14 Bezogen auf *Hortulus animae*, f. 59–73.
15 Bezogen auf *Hortulus animae*, f. 74–89.
16 Bezogen auf *Hortulus animae*, f. 89.
17 Bezogen auf *Hortulus animae*, f. 91.
18 Bezogen auf *Hortulus animae*, f. 92–105.

Eine Untersuchung anhand des *Hortulus animae* | 135

- Ihnen folgen die Märtyrer[19] und dann die Bekenner und Lehrer der Kirche[20] sowie die Jungfrauen und Witwen.[21]
- Daraufhin werden die Hochfeste von Neujahr bis zum Tag der unschuldigen Kindlein behandelt.[22]
- Ein Passus zum „angesicht vnsers herrn", dem Schweißtuch der Veronika,[23] leitet über zu Anleitungen zu kirchlichen Riten wie Kirchenweihe, Altarweihe und Beichte.[24]
- Damit ist der Übergang zur sakramentalen Frömmigkeit geschaffen: Großen Raum nimmt die Begleitung der Eucharistie im Gebet ein.[25]
- Das Abendmahl leitet noch zu Vaterunser, Ave Maria und Glaubensbekenntnis über,[26] danach aber reiht sich eine Anzahl von Gebeten an, deren Aufnahme zum Teil liturgisch begründet wird,[27] zum Teil durch Autoritäten,[28] zum Teil durch verschiedene Anlässe[29] – unter diesen Gebeten finden sich dann auch Gebete zum Angelusläuten: „Ein gebet so man das Ave Maria leutet" (*Hortulus animae*, f. 175[r])
- Diese wenig geordnete Reihe schließt mit Gebeten zur Totenvesper und -vigil.[30]

Diese Inhaltsreihe gibt über die Ausrichtung des Gebetsbüchleins noch keine klaren Auskünfte – dieser soll nun im Folgenden anhand der oben erwähnten spätmittelalterlichen Polarität von äußerlicher und innerlicher Frömmigkeit weiter nachgegangen werden. Dabei ist grundsätzlich zwischen den Gebetstexten selbst und ihren – meist rot gedruckten[31] – Paratexten zu unterscheiden. Der Untersuchung liegt beides zugrunde: sowohl Gebetsinhalte als auch Anweisungen zu den Zeiten und Erläuterungen zum Nutzen der Gebetstexte werden daher Thema – Letztere entstammen in der Regel den Paratexten. Aus diesen wird man die Intention des Herausgebers des *Hortulus animae* deutlicher erschließen können als durch die Gebetstexte selbst, welche er der Tradition entnommen hat und in de-

---

19 Bezogen auf *Hortulus animae*, f. 105–111.
20 Bezogen auf *Hortulus animae*, f. 112–122.
21 Bezogen auf *Hortulus animae*, f. 122–131.
22 Bezogen auf *Hortulus animae*, f. 132–141.
23 Bezogen auf *Hortulus animae*, f. 142.
24 Bezogen auf *Hortulus animae*, f. 143–147.
25 Bezogen auf *Hortulus animae*, f. 156–166.
26 Bezogen auf *Hortulus animae*, f. 190f.
27 Bezogen auf *Hortulus animae*, f. 171: Das Quicumque als Gebet zur Prim.
28 Bezogen auf *Hortulus animae*, f. 174: Verse Bernhards.
29 Z.B. bezogen auf *Hortulus animae*, f. 180: um schönes Wetter; andere Gebete zielen auf bestimmte Tugenden bzw. die Vermeidung bestimmter Laster.
30 Bezogen auf *Hortulus animae*, f. 190–234.
31 Auch hier gilt aber, dass diese Einfärbung zwar eine Hervorhebung bedeutet, nicht aber den zwingenden Hinweis auf Paratexte: Auf derselben Seite kann eine Gebetserläuterung wie auch der Hinweis auf das Vaterunser rot eingefärbt sein (als ein Beispiel für viele: *Hortulus animae*, f. 38[r]).

136 | Volker Leppin

ren Auswahl er möglicherweise auch an vorhandene Sammlungen gebunden bzw. durch diese geprägt war.

Regulierung des äußeren Alltags

Als ein wichtiger Strang innerhalb des *Hortulus animae* lässt sich das Bemühen identifizieren, das Leben der Gläubigen christlich durchzuformen. Schon der Beginn mit dem Kalender ist trotz der darin enthaltenen astrologischen Elemente ein deutlicher Hinweis hierauf. Zwar sind die meisten, aber nicht alle Tage mit einem klaren eigenen Patron versehen. So wird etwa der 2. Januar als „Stepffans achter" geführt, also als Ende der Oktav seit dem Stephanustag am 26. Dezember (*Hortulus animae*, i^v), und manche Tage werden nur unter astronomischen Gesichtspunkten benannt – so wird dem 13. März die Tag- und Nachtgleiche zugeordnet (*Hortulus animae*, iii^v). Damit der Kalender zeitlos wirken kann, wird ein kompliziertes Buchstabensystem eingeführt, das es ermöglicht, für jedes Jahr nach einer ausführlich angegebenen Rechnungsanweisung mit Hilfe von Tabellen die Sonntage zu identifizieren (*Hortulus animae*, ¶vi^v). So gibt der Beginn des Gebetbuches eine monats- und wochenorientierte Struktur vor.

Stärker auf die devotionale Praxis ausgerichtet sind im fortlaufenden Text die Strukturierungen von Woche und Tag. Beides erscheint immer wieder und kann daher hier nur exemplarisch benannt werden: Für die Woche sieht der *Hortulus animae* einen sich über sieben Tage erstreckenden Reigen von Meditationen der letzten Dinge vor (*Hortulus animae*, f. 209^v–217^v): Er beginnt am Sonntag mit der Betrachtung der himmlischen Freude (*Hortulus animae*, f. 209^v). Hierauf folgt am Montag eine allgemeine Betrachtung des Todes beziehungsweise des unvermeidlichen Weges jedes Menschen zum Tod (*Hortulus animae*, f. 211^r), am Dienstag eine Betrachtung der Wohltaten Gottes (*Hortulus animae*, f. 212^r) dann am Mittwoch der Blick auf das erschreckende Urteil Gottes (*Hortulus animae*, f. 212 [recte: 213]^r), am Donnerstag eine Betrachtung der höllischen Qual (*Hortulus animae*, f. 214^r), am Freitag das Leiden Christi (*Hortulus animae*, f. 215^r) und schließlich am Samstag eine Betrachtung der Sünde (*Hortulus animae*, f. 216^r).

So wie die Woche liturgisch gestaltet wird, gilt dies auch für den Tag: Der *Hortulus animae* beginnt mit marianischen Stundengebeten, welche der Redaktor auf eine Anweisung Papst Urbans II. auf der Synode von Clermont zurückführt.[32] Dass dem marianischen Stundengebet das oben schon erwähnte passionsmeditative Stundengebet folgt, macht deutlich, wie das Gebetbuch verstanden werden

---

32 *Hortulus animae*, f. 1^v; zur Anordnung des sonnabendlichen marianischen Stundengebetes durch Urban II. auf der Synode von Clermont s. Benrath: 1886, 216, Anm. 2.

Eine Untersuchung anhand des *Hortulus animae* | 137

will: Zwar sind die liturgischen Anweisungen im Einzelnen umfassend – so finden sich etwa auch liturgisch korrekte Anweisungen zum Fortlassen des Halleluja im Stundengebet während der Fastenzeit (*Hortulus animae*, f. 2^r), was deutlich macht, dass ein Gebrauch des Stundengebets durch das ganze Jahr hindurch im Blick ist (*Hortulus animae*, f. 25^v–26^r). Doch erwartet der Redaktor darum keineswegs, dass alle von ihm vorgeschlagenen Texte jederzeit und von allen gleichermaßen genutzt werden. Das Nebeneinander der Stundengebete ist vielmehr so zu verstehen, dass hier alternative Angebote gemacht werden, die unterschiedliche Personen oder gar dieselben Personen zu unterschiedlichen Zeiten unterschiedlich nutzen können. Das Würzgärtlein bildet also keineswegs den durchgängigen Alltag eines frommen Menschen im ausgehenden Spätmittelalter ab, sondern präsentiert Möglichkeiten, solche Möglichkeiten allerdings, die dem Frömmigkeitsleben eine klare Struktur geben.

So gehören zu der möglichen liturgischen Gestaltung des Tages auch ein Abend- und ein Morgensegen. Dass sie in dieser Abfolge präsentiert werden, bildet den Beginn des Tages mit dem Abend, aber wohl auch die Vorgängigkeit des den Abendsegen bestimmenden Sündenbekenntnisses ab. Dieser (*Hortulus animae*, f. 49$^{r–v}$) nämlich besteht zunächst im Dank für die Führung durch Gott am vergangenen Tag, für Errettung vor jähem Tod und allem Übel an Leid und Seele und die Reue beziehungsweise unmittelbar vor Gott gebrachte Beichte darüber, „dz ich diesen tag so vnfruchtbarlich vnnd mer in eytelkeit dieser welt / dann in deiner dienstbarkeit verzeret hab" (*Hortulus animae*, f. 49^r). Der Segen impliziert so eine christliche Normierung des Alltags und zugleich als wiederholter Vorgang die permanente Verfehlung eben dieser Normierung. Gerade die Diskrepanz zur intendierten christlichen Lebensführung wird wiederholt hervorgehoben, auch etwa, wenn es heißt, „dz ich leider gethon hab / in die nachhellunge vnnd verwilligunge der verdamlichen lustparkeit vnnd handel dieser zergencklichen welt" (*Hortulus animae*, f. 49^v). Diese Aussagen passen recht genau in das Milieu des städtischen Bürgertums hinein, das sich in einem kaufmännisch orientierten Wertehorizont bewegen muss, welcher nicht durchgängig christlich geprägt, sondern vielmehr einer Eigenlogik verpflichtet ist, welcher sich die Agierenden wohl nicht entziehen, die sie gleichwohl bereuen können.

Der Betonung der Sündhaftigkeit des Lebens entspricht es, dass noch im Anschluss an das Abendgebet die Sünden, die dem oder der Betenden bewusst sind, in Reue unmittelbar vor Gott gebracht werden sollen (*Hortulus animae*, f. 49^v). Das ist insofern eine bemerkenswerte Empfehlung, als der *Hortulus animae* sonst durchaus die Bedeutung des Bußsakramentes in keiner Weise minimiert, im Gegenteil sogar vielfach einschärft. Hier aber erscheint als angedeutete Möglichkeit etwas, das sonst eher aus dem Bereich mystischer Frömmigkeit bekannt ist (Leppin: 2015, 179f): das unmittelbare Bringen der Sünden vor Gott, das wohl mindestens in dieser Situation vor dem Schlafengehen, die aus äußeren Gründen den

138 | Volker Leppin

Gang zum Beichtvater nicht mehr erlaubt, für das Bekenntnis vor dem vermittelnden Priester einen Ersatz schaffen kann. Anders als im Falle der mystischen Konzepte wird man hier kein schleichendes Unterlaufen der klerikalen Leitung des Lebens sehen dürfen[33] – dazu ist das Einverständnis mit den hierarchischen Strukturen im gesamten Text viel zu groß. Es zeigt sich unter anderem in der an Maria gerichteten Bitte: „Bitt Fraw fuer das gemein volck/fuer die geweyheten/ vnnd fuer das andechtig freulich geschlechte" (*Hortulus animae*, f. 7^r). Die Kirche hat ihre Gliederung in Laien, Kleriker und, so ist die dritte Gruppe wohl zu verstehen, Ordensleute, und genau in dieser Ordnung soll sie auch bewahrt bleiben. Vielmehr steht hinter der Anweisung, ungebeichtete Sünden vor Gott zu bringen, der Drang, nichts zu versäumen, was der Buße bedarf. Er zeigt sich auch in einer weiteren hinzugefügten Möglichkeit: für die unbewussten Sünden nämlich solle man vor dem Schlafengehen noch eine allgemeine Beichte vor Gott für allerlei Sünden „in gedenkcen/wortten/oder in wercken" ablegen (*Hortulus animae*, f. 60^v).

Anders als der Abendsegen ist der Morgensegen (*Hortulus animae*, f. 62^v–63^r) akzentuiert: Hier kann es der Sache nach ja nicht um Beichte für Vergangenes gehen, sondern – neben dem Dank für Behütung in der vergangenen Nacht – darum, den Tag unter dem Segen Gottes und unter dem Kreuz zu beginnen: Insbesondere Letzteres findet seinen Ausdruck nicht allein in den Worten der Gebetstexte, sondern auch in der umfassenden Gestik: Der oder die Betende soll das Kreuzeszeichen über Stirn, Mund, Brust und Rücken machen – und so vielfach bezeichnet in den Tag gehen.

Formen äußerlich quantifizierter Frömmigkeit

Auf der Suche nach unterschiedlichen Frömmigkeitsmustern stößt man im *Hortulus animae* unweigerlich auf eine Fülle von Ablassverheißungen – und es ist durchaus denkbar, dass es genau diese waren, die Luthers zitierte harsche Kritik an dem Gebetbuch provoziert haben. Freilich muss man nicht immer reflexhaft auf das Wort Ablass reagieren, wenn es erscheint, und in ihm erwartete Muster spätmittelalterlicher Frömmigkeit wiederfinden: Mit dem Ablass konnte durchaus variabel umgegangen werden, das heißt: Auch das ablassbewehrte Gebet war multivalent: Der *Hortulus animae* verweist auch auf eine Ablassverheißung von Papst Alexander VI. von 1494, also gemessen an der Entstehung des Gebetbuches eine relativ rezente Entwicklung: Ein Gebet, dreimal vor einem Annenbildnis ge-

---

33 Insofern besteht auch kein Anlass, an dieser Stelle die erkennbare Polarität von innerlicher und äußerlicher Frömmigkeit mit der von Laien und Klerus zu verbinden (s. hierzu Leppin: 2015, 40–43).

Eine Untersuchung anhand des *Hortulus animae* | **139**

sprochen, bringe tausend Jahre Ablass für Todsünden und 20000 Jahre für lässliche Sünden, „vnnd ist auch zuosprechen fuer die pestilentz" (*Hortulus animae,* f. 127^v–128^r). Der jenseitigen Hoffnung auf Minderung der Fegfeuerstrafen wird also kommentarlos und ohne erkennbare Abstufung der innerweltliche Nutzen an die Seite gestellt.

Wie gewichtig das Thema des Ablasses dennoch ist, zeigt die Schlussverheißung des gesamten Buches: Auf der letzten Seite vor dem Register findet sich eine Abbildung des himmlischen Rosenkranzes, nach welchem die oben erwähnte Bruderschaft benannt war: Im Zentrum des Bildes befindet sich ein Kruzifix, über ihm am obersten Rand des Holzschnitts ein Antlitz Gottes des Vaters, welches durch den Nimbus und einen an ein Veronikatuch erinnernden seitlich gerefften Vorhang die Vaterebenbildlichkeit Christi durchscheinen lässt. Zwischen beiden sind der Heilige Geist als Taube und Maria mit segnender Hand abgebildet – der Eindruck einer um Maria erweiterten Trinität lässt sich jedenfalls optisch schwer negieren. Weit um das Kruzifix herum erscheint ein Rosenkranz, dessen Perlenreihe durch fünf Kreuzeszeichen unterbrochen ist. Das so geschaffene Rund ist in vier Register unterteilt. Das oberste zeigt fürbittend auf der einen Seite Maria mit dem Kind, auf der anderen einen Engel. Aus Betrachtersicht links sind darunter die Propheten des Alten Bundes von Mose bis Johannes dem Täufer dargestellt, rechts die Apostel, unter denen insbesondere Petrus mit dem Schlüssel und Johannes mit dem Kelch erkennbar sind. Das dritte Register zeigt die geistlichen Amtsträger links des Alten, rechts des Neuen Bundes, das unterste Register die Laienpersonen. Unten in der Mitte, Gott Vater gegenüber und unter dem Fuß des Kreuzes, ist die Auferstehung abgebildet: Engel ziehen die Verstorbenen nach oben – links von ihnen kommen Papst, Kardinäle und Bischöfe, also die geistliche Gewalt herbei, rechts die weltliche Gewalt mit König und Kurfürsten. In den Zwickeln oben schließlich erscheint links eine Eucharistie und rechts ein Mönch, der eine Standarte mit dem Kruzifix trägt. Ob darin ein Ablassprediger zu sehen ist, muss offen bleiben. In jedem Falle weist der Text unter dieser Abbildung klar auf den Ablass: Wer nämlich, so heißt es hier, den himmlischen Rosenkranz bete, erhalte allen Ablass „vnser lieben Frawen Rosenkrantz" (*Hortulus animae,* f. 230^v) – ein Maß, das anscheinend als bekannt vorausgesetzt wird. Dessen Umfang ist nicht klar angegeben, jedenfalls kommen hinzu hundert und sieben Jahre und 100 „quadragen", also offenbar 100 mal 40 Tage plus 1780 Tage. Die mit der Bruderschaft, welche das Gebetbuch gestiftet hatte, verbundene Ablassverheißung, ist also außerordentlich umfangreich, ohne dass jedem Leser sofort das exakte Maß bewusst gewesen sein muss. Dennoch ist es offenkundig, dass die Verheißung mit exakten Zahlen arbeitet, und diese finden sich wiederholt im *Hortulus,* auch in der Weise, dass Ablasstarife ineinander umrechenbar sind. Für ein sehr demütig ausgerichtetes und ausführlich zitiertes Gebet etwa wird verheißen, man erhalte durch dieses so viel Ablass wie für tausend Vaterunser und tausend Ave Maria (*Hortulus animae,* f. 42^v).

140 | Volker Leppin

Das gewaltige Maß an hier wie dort verheißenem Ablass für relativ geringe eigene Leistungen setzt sich fort, wobei unter Leistungen durchweg nur Gebete zu verstehen sind: Von der Welt des käuflichen Ablasses ist dieses Frömmigkeitswerk weit entfernt. Um so mehr wird den recht Betenden verheißen. Unter Berufung auf einen angeblich von Papst Gregor III. (731–741) einer englischen Königin gestifteten und von allen anderen Päpsten bestätigten Ablass[34] etwa preist der *Hortulus animae* Gebete vor einem Kruzifix an. Wer diese halte, der empfange dafür so viele Tage Ablass, wie Christus – wohl durch die Geißelung – Wunden empfangen hatte, nämlich 5475 (*Hortulus animae*, f. 38[r]). Im Rahmen dieser massiven Quantifizierung macht es dann überhaupt nichts aus, dass in demselben Werk im Rahmen der Visionen Birgittas von Schweden die Anzahl von Christi Wunden mit 5460 angegeben wird:[35] Die Angabe von Zahlen ist nicht sensu stricto mathematisch zu nehmen, sondern zu verstehen als Ausdruck einer gewaltigen, schier unermesslichen Menge, die im Detail durchaus variieren darf.

Dieses Streben nach immer höhen Zahlen drückt sich auch in dem Hinweis auf eine Ablassverheißung in San Giovanni in Laterano aus: Wer „einmal im tag" das hier in Stein gemeißelte, auf Augustin zurückgeführte Gebet spreche, der erhalte 80000 Jahre Ablass für Todsünden (*Hortulus animae*, f. 39[r]). Bemerkenswert ist hier weniger die auch sonst zu beobachtende Abstufung des Ablasses für Todsünden gegenüber lässlichen Sünden (Vgl. *Hortulus animae,* f. 39[v]) als die Totalisierung: Wer das Gebet vierzig Tage lang bete, erhalte unter Berufung auf Bonifaz VIII. und Benedikt XI. nach vollzogener Beichte „vergebung aller suende" (*Hortulus animae*, f. 39[r]). Die Zuordnung beider Anweisungen ist nicht ganz klar: Versteht man das „einmal im tag" als täglich wiederholte Handlung, so ist die Verheißung viel geringer als für den genannten Vierzigtageabschnitt. Es ist also wohl so zu verstehen, dass für ein bloß einmaliges Beten an einem Tag die Verheißung der 80000 Jahre gilt und dies beliebig wiederholbar (und entsprechend multiplizierbar) ist. Hält man es aber quadragesimal, vierzig Tage, durch, so ist der Ablass vollkommen.

Im Grunde steigert sich damit das quantifizierende Denken schon zu einer Ebene, auf welcher es die Quantitäten hinter sich lässt, weil aus der vielfachen Wiederholung ein unendlicher Gewinn wird.[36] So kommt es gelegentlich auch zu einem völligen Verzicht auf quantifizierende Angaben: Für ein Gebet vor einem Bild der „marter christi" – gemeint ist wohl ein Schmerzensmann oder auch eine Abbildung der *arma Christi* – oder einem Kruzifix wird schlicht „groß gnad vnd ablaß" verheißen (*Hortulus animae*, f. 42[r]), ohne dass es nötig schiene, die Jahre,

---

34 Der Ablass ist Inhalt und Gestalt nach gewiss nicht mit einem Papst des 8. Jahrhunderts zu verbinden; s. Ochsenbein: 2004, 187 f.

35 *Hortulus animae*, f. 218[v]; vgl. zu diesen Zahlenangaben Hamm: 2016, 197 – Anm. 359.

36 Vgl. Zu diesem Phänomen Hamm: 2016, 110 f.

Monate oder Tage zu zählen, in welchen der Ablass sich ausdrückt, Ganz ähnlich steht es mit Verheißungen über ein Mariengebet: „Ein schoen gebet von der jungkfrawen Maria/wer das andechtiglichen spricht .xxx. tag nacheinander/der wurd gewert an seel vnd leyb was er zymlich bitten ist." (*Hortulus animae*, f. 81[r])

Die Angabe erfolgt nicht ohne Quantifizierung – diese liegt aber allein in der Praxis des Betenden. Ein Berechnungsverhältnis zur göttlichen Gnade, wie man es sonst vielfach beobachten kann, findet sich nicht, vielmehr wird man den Verweis auf Gewährung des angemessenerweise („zymlich") zu Erbetenden als eine fast umfassende Gnadenverheißung zu verstehen haben. Die Rede vom Ablass ist also selbst dort, wo sie massiv quantifizierend erscheint, nicht einfach nur als Ausdruck einer quantifizierten Frömmigkeitsform zu bezeichnen. Um das Phänomen auszudrücken, drängt sich die hegelianisierende Rede vom Umschlag quantitativer Veränderungen in qualitative geradezu auf: Die Steigerung der quantitativen Ablassverheißung ins Unermessliche lässt letztlich genau den Aspekt der Quantifizierung hinter sich.

Übergänge: Ablassverheißung als Anreiz für innerliche Frömmigkeit

Die beschriebenen Phänomene machen deutlich, dass die eingeführte Unterscheidung von äußerlicher und innerlicher Frömmigkeit nur begrenzt trägt: Es lässt sich im *Hortulus animae* nicht allein der Umschlag quantitativer Veränderungen in qualitative beobachten, sondern auch der Umstand, dass die massive Verheißung von Ablass auf eine paradoxale Weise Frömmigkeitsformen provoziert, die das Innere des glaubenden Menschen zur Hinwendung zu Gott und zum Leiden Christi bringen sollen. Das lässt sich deutlich machen anhand des berühmten Motivs der Gregorsmesse, die auch im *Hortulus animae* abgebildet ist.[37] Gewöhnlich gilt dieses Bildmotiv von der Erscheinung des Schmerzensmannes in einer Messe, die Papst Gregor der Große zelebrierte, als Kulmination spätmittelalterlicher veräußerlichter eucharistischer Frömmigkeit mit ihrer Verbindung aus päpstlichem Amtshabitus und Einschärfung der Realpräsenz Christi in den Elementen. Thomas Lentes und Berndt Hamm haben bereits darauf hingewiesen, dass eine solche Deutung zu kurz greift, weil sie den im Schmerzensmann mitgegebenen Appell an Leidensfrömmigkeit unterschätzt (Hamm: 2011, 484–497): Die Gregorsmesse ist nicht als dogmatisch orientiertes Lehrbild zu verstehen, sondern wie es auch die Verwendung im *Hortulus animae* deutlich macht, als Andachtsbild im strengen

---

37 *Hortulus animae*, f. 36[v]–37[v]; zur Verbreitung der Gregorsmesse s. den umfangreichen Katalog in Kelberg: 1983, 147–267.

142 | Volker Leppin

Sinne, das die Repräsentation des leidenden Christus in den Vordergrund hebt (Lentes: 2007, 13–35). Eben diese Destruktion klassischer Deutungsmuster lässt sich nun auch im *Hortulus animae* nachvollziehen. Auf den ersten Blick scheint die der Abbildung beigegebene Aufforderung eine veräußerlichende Deutung zu unterstützen:

> Wer diese nachgeschribene gebet/vnnd zu yedem gebet ein Vatter vnser. vnnd ein Gegruesset seyestu Maria. mit waren rewen vnnd lautere beycht vor einer figur sant Gregorien erscheynung andechtigklichnn spricht/der verdienet do mit: xxiiii. tawsent/sechßhundert jar/vnnd .xxiiii. tag ablaß/die von demselben bapst Gregorio vnnd andern nachvolgenden baebsten do von geben seint. (*Hortulus animae*, f. 37ʳ)

Offenkundig wird hier ein einfach und rasch erreichbarer Ablass verheißen: Der Ablass wird durch das Gebet übertragbar und wird so dem Beter oder der Beterin zuteil, wo immer sie oder er sich eben befindet. Doch geschieht mehr als dies. Der erste wichtige Aspekt liegt in der Einschärfung, dass eine solche Übertragung allein an diejenigen erfolgt, die ihr Gebet mit Reue und Andacht sprechen: Der scheinbar äußere Ablass ist also dergestalt konditioniert, dass er nur funktioniert, wenn die innerlichen Bedingungen geschaffen sind.

Vor allem aber folgt im Verlauf des Gebetbuches auf die Verheißungen zur Gregorsmesse eine bemerkenswerte Sammlung von Gebeten, die zu einer inneren Identifikation mit dem Leiden Christi führen sollen: Sie handeln von dessen Wunden und seiner Grablege, sie bitten durch diese hindurch um Erlösung und ewiges Leben (*Hortulus animae*, f. 37ᵛ). Der Ablass also soll hier motivieren zu einer innerlichen Aneignung des Leidens Christi, er ist letztlich ein äußerer Anreiz für innerliche Identifikation mit dem leidenden Erlöser.

Ganz ähnlich funktioniert ein Gebet zum Leiden Christi, das zu 3000 Jahren Ablass für Todsünden und 3000 Jahren Ablass für lässliche Sünden führen soll. Dieser Ablass ist nicht etwa mechanistisch gedacht. Hier wie auch an anderen Stellen des Gebetbuches, an welchen vom Ablass die Rede ist, spielt die theologisch so wichtige und in „*Salvator noster*" durch Sixtus IV. abgesicherte Lehre von einer kirchlichen Ablassvermittlung aufgrund des *thesaurus ecclesiae* nicht die geringste Rolle.[38] Christi Leiden und damit nach der *thesaurus*-Lehre seine Verdienste werden nicht in dieser Weise mittelbar zugeteilt, sondern der oder die Glaubende eignet sich diese unmittelbar devotional an aufgrund der „bewelhung in das leyden Christi":

> Die marter und das leyden Jesu christi meines herren vnnd gottes sey mir ein suesser eingang in alle tugent/(…) sein tieffe wunden sey meiner seel ein ware ertzney fuer die manigfeltigen versurung vnd wunden der suenden an meiner seel/sein heylig blutuergiessen vnd das wasser mit dem blut auß seynem heiligen hertzen durch die wunden der

---

38 S. hierzu Denziger/Hünermann: 2017, 1398.

rechten seyten geflossen ist / sey mir ein reynigung vnd abwaschung aller meiner suenden. (*Hortulus animae*, f. 40[r])

Nicht die mechanistische Abrechnung über den *thesaurus ecclesiae* also ist hier entscheidend, sondern im Fokus steht die echte innere Reinigung, die das Leiden Christi sündenbefreiend in das Leben der Glaubenden hineinzieht und auf dieses appliziert.

Solche Verbindungen mit Anreizen zu einer verinnerlichten Frömmigkeit scheinen selbst dort durch, wo auf den ersten Blick mechanistisch-ritualisierte Verfahren zur Heilsvermittlung empfohlen werden. So heißt es in Bezug auf ein Beda zugeschriebenes Gebet von den sieben letzten Worten Christi am Kreuz:[39]

Von demselben gebet spricht man / wer es alle tag andechtigklich mit gebognen knyen spricht / das der weder des tewfels / noch des boesen menschen schaden wuert leyden. Er wuert nit von hynnen scheyden ungebeichtet / vnnd wuert dreyssig tag vor seinem todt die gar erwirdige jungkfraw Mariam zu seiner hilff bereyt sehen. (*Hortulus animae*, f. 34[r+v])

Zunächst erscheint dieses Gebet wie eine Absicherung gegenüber der allezeit drohenden Furcht vor dem jähen Tod.[40] Aber was rein ritualisiert erscheint, ist auf bemerkenswerte Weise konditioniert, und zwar nicht allein durch den Rückzug auf ein Hörensagen – „spricht man" –, sondern vor allem durch die Rückkoppelung zur inneren Frömmigkeit: Das beschriebene Geschehen vollzieht sich nur dann, wenn das Gebet „andechtigklich" erfolgt: Gerade wer in der verheißenen Weise auf den Tod hin versichert sein will, muss sich selbst um rechte Andacht bemühen.

Dieser Rückbindung an die Innerlichkeit entspricht es auch, dass im Blick auf das Heil gegenüber der quantitativen Vorstellung vom Ablass, welche immer mit einem Mehr oder Weniger der Strafen im Fegefeuer hantiert, ein umfassenderer Aspekt des Heilsgewinns in den Blick gerät: Es geht bei einer rechten inneren Haltung nicht nur darum, auf der Seite derer, die, wenn auch im Fegefeuer, schon auf dem Weg zum Heil sind, die Zeit der Leiden zu verkürzen, sondern es geht auch darum, Menschen überhaupt von der Unheilsdrohung – dem Verderben in der Hölle – hinüber auf die Seite des möglichen und dann auch zu erwartenden Heils zu ziehen. So führt der *Hortulus animae* fünf Gebete ein, denen der Name Maria als Akrostichon zugrunde liegt und verspricht hierzu: „Wer dz alle tag spricht mit andacht vnnd mit rewen seiner suend / der kuembt nit in die hell. als das ein

---

39 S. dazu: Honemann: 1978, 662.
40 S. etwa die (neben vielen anderen) an die Heiligenlitanei angeschlossene Bitte: „Erloeß vns herr (…) Von dem gehen vnnd vnversehenem tod" (*Hortulus animae*, f. 56[v]) und das angeblich von Bernhard verfasste Gebet gegen einen jähen und schnellen Tod (ebd. 183[v]–184[r]); vgl. auch die Bitte, bereitet auf den Tod zugehen zu dürfen, d. h. zuvor rechte Buße getan und das Sakrament empfangen zu haben, ebd. 36[v].

144 | Volker Leppin

Johanser herr zu Straßburg offentlich geprediget vnnd sein seel zu pfand gesetzt hat." (*Hortulus animae,* f. 87ᵛ)

Die Zusage, durch wahre Reue und tägliches Gebet der Hölle zu entkommen, stellt ein radikalisiertes Heilsversprechen dar, und zudem eines, das im Rahmen eines sich sonst völlig selbstverständlich innerhalb der klerikalen und sakramentalen Welt bewegenden Gebetbuches auf ganz erstaunliche Weise genau ohne den üblichen Weg der sakramentalen Heilsvermittlung auskommt. Wer, so klingt die Verheißung, allein durch Reue und Gebet der Hölle entgehen kann, der bedarf vor allem nicht der Kraft des Bußsakraments, das in der Lage ist ewige Strafen – Höllenstrafen – in zeitliche – im Fegefeuer abzubüßende – zu verwandeln. Diese elementare und prinzipielle Aufgabe des Bußsakramentes wird so unterlaufen und angesichts der individuellen devotionalen Praxis obsolet.

Und dieser radikale Gedanke findet sich im *Hortulus animae* auch keineswegs singulär an der hier vorgestellten Stelle: In einem langen – auffälligerweise durchweg rot eingefärbten – Bericht über Birgitta von Schweden findet sich, als Wort des Kruzifix, der zu ihr redete, unter anderem auch die Verheißung, dass die Person, welche die dann im Folgenden niedergeschriebenen Gebete andächtig spreche, alle ihre Sündern vergeben bekomme, selbst wenn sie dreißig Jahre in Todsünde gelebt habe (*Hortulus animae,* f. 219ᵛ). Auch hier wird also das unmittelbare Gebet an Stelle eines Vorgangs gesetzt, den man üblicherweise mit dem Bußsakrament verbände. So scharf die daraus für das Sakrament entstehenden Anfragen sind – eine grundsätzliche Infragestellung verbindet sich hiermit nicht. Denn gleich darauf folgt für das Beten derselben Gebete die Verheißung von vierzig Tagen Ablass (*Hortulus animae,* f. 219ᵛ). Dies mag deutlich machen, dass die Heilszusagen, die der *Hortulus* gibt, in sich nicht unbedingt konsistent sind. Es ist nicht möglich und auch gar nicht nötig, sie in ein geschlossenes System der Heilsvermittlung einzuordnen. Wichtig ist für die Lesenden offenbar die Verheißung, dass das Heil, das ihnen geschenkt wird und das sie bis zu einem gewissen Grade auch erwerben können, groß und umfassend ist.

Formierung des Inneren

Schon diese Vermengungen, Inkonsistenzen und Überlagerungen zeigen, dass es zu kurz griffe, Luthers Kritik in wissenschaftlichem Gewande fortzuführen und den *Hortulus animae* in der hier vorliegenden Form als bloßen Ausdruck veräußerlichter, womöglich rein ablassorientierter Frömmigkeit zu sehen. Diese spielt eine enorm wichtige Rolle, und doch entwickelt das Würzgärtlein auch deutlich erkennbare Gegenakzente: Die Beter, die das Buch im Auge hat, müssen gar nicht immer eigens motiviert werden, sich auch innerlich auf das Gebet einzulassen

Eine Untersuchung anhand des *Hortulus animae* | 145

und Gott zuzuwenden. Die Erinnerung an diese innerliche Dimension begleitet vielmehr auch ohne solche Anreize die Anweisungen und Ratschläge. So heißt es beispielsweise bei einer Aufzählung von fünf Gebetsworten, die darum kreisen, dass im Sterben Jesus Christus der Begleiter sein soll:[41] „Wer diese fuenff wort hie nachgeschrieben mit wolbedachten synnen vnd mit guter andacht spricht / der soll wissen das er von got nymmer gescheiden wirt." (*Hortulus animae,* f. 35ᵛ)

Die Verheißung ist hier ähnlich umfassend wie in den oben angeführten Beispielen – nie von Gott geschieden zu sein, ist mindestens als Verheißung zu verstehen, der Hölle zu entgehen, reicht aber möglicherweise noch darüber hinaus, insofern das Fegefeuer gewiss ein Ort der Gottesferne ist. Es könnte also so verstanden werden, dass der Beter unmittelbar in den Himmel aufgenommen wird.

Selbst wenn diese Interpretation zu weitreichend sein sollte, bleibt die Zusage in ihrem sehr klaren Verzicht auf Quantifizierungen auffällig, wird doch in keiner Weise erklärt oder auch nur angedeutet, welches Maß an Beten erforderlich ist. Gegenüber den sonst immer wieder begegnenden Fristen mehrerer Tage und der verlangten Häufigkeit bestimmter Gebete fällt auf, dass hier nichts dergleichen aufscheint. Nicht die zeitlichen Angaben konditionieren den Erfolg des Gebetes, sondern die rechte Haltung: Die Verheißung gilt dem, der bewusst und „mit guter andacht" betet – die wahre Andacht, so scheint es, erübrigt eine Angabe zur Häufigkeit, da sie Wiederholungen entweder ersetzt oder ohnehin aus sich heraussetzt. Aus einer quantifizierenden Perspektive könnte man sagen: Diese Anweisung verheißt für äußerlich minimalen Einsatz maximalen Gewinn. Das ist nur deswegen möglich, weil ein Maximum inneren Engagements verlangt wird.

Schon in den Anfangspassagen des *Würzgärtleins* liegt ein besonderer Akzent auf der Innerlichkeit im Zusammenhang der auf das Leiden Christi ausgerichteten Stundengebete, nicht nur in den Paratexten, sondern auch in den Gebeten selbst: Während die davor aufgeführten mariologischen Horen weitgehend aus traditionellem Material, den Psalmen und den üblichen marianischen Gebeten – *Magnificat, Salve regina* und anderen – zusammengesetzt sind, finden sich hier tief innerliche Gebete. Markant ist schon der Beginn der passionsmeditativen Stundengebete: Hier zeigt das Buch eine Darstellung Jesu am Kreuz, an dessen Fuß stehen andächtig Maria und Johannes. Darunter steht ein Vers für den Beter: „Lieber herr kumm in mein gedencken / das mein hertz mit bitterer andacht vnnd betrachtung deiner heyligen marter zu aller stunde in meine gedencken / wortten vnnd wercken sey" (*Hortulus animae,* f. 31ʳ⁺ᵛ)

Der Passus „zu aller Stunde" konterkariert geradezu Sinn und Verfahren des Stundengebets. Er hebt gerade nicht auf die oben beschriebene Rhythmisierung des Tages durch das Gebet ab, sondern verlangt im Gebet selbst nach einer perma-

---

41 Z.B.: „Jesu christe ich begere dz dein heyliger nam sey mein juengstes wort das mein mundt ymmer gesprechen soll. Amen." (*Hortulus animae,* f. 35ᵛ).

146 | Volker Leppin

nenten Devotion: Das Stundengebet setzt aus sich eine Permanenz heraus, die es selbst nicht zu leisten vermag oder braucht. Dies aber geschieht, so legt es der Text nahe, durch die radikale Verinnerlichung in Gestalt einer Identifikation mit dem Leiden Christi. Gedanken, Worte und Werke, die klassische Trias der Bußterminologie wird hierauf ausgerichtet, das heißt: Das Leiden ändert die Haltung und das Verhalten des Menschen in der Welt.

Eine solche Perspektive kann dann auch den Ablass einbeziehen, ohne noch irgendeine Vorstellung von Quantität vorzubringen:

> Herr Jesu christe des lebendigen gottes sun / setze dein marter / leyden vnnd sterben / vnnd dein barmhertzigkeit zwischnn mein seel vnnd dein gericht nun vnnd in der stund meines tods / vnnd verleyhe gnad vnnd barmhertzigkeit den lebenden / den todten rwe vnnd ablaß / deiner kirche frieden vnnd vereynigung / vnnd vns suendern das ewig leben. A. (*Hortulus animae*, f. 31^v)

Der Ablass, der hier begegnet, ist nicht quantifiziert, auch wenn er durchaus mit dem klassischen Ablass zu tun hat: Er gilt ja den Toten, also den schon Verstorbenen, doch wohl den Seelen im Fegefeuer. Die eigene innere Devotion also ermöglicht – wohl im Sinne eines praktizierten devotionalen *modus suffragii*[42] – die Hoffnung auf Reduktion der Fegefeuerstrafen. Wie oben schon mehrfach beobachtet, ist es nicht die Vermittlung über den *thesaurus ecclesiae*, die eine solche Strafenreduktion ermöglicht, sondern die Gebetspraxis der einzelnen Glaubenden – und an dieser wiederum ist es nicht deren Menge, sondern deren tiefe Innerlichkeit.

Diese Gedankengänge verweisen darauf, dass der *Hortulus animae* nicht allein die sakramentale Buße einschärft, sondern auch an jenen Formen verinnerlichter Bußfrömmigkeit Anteil hat, die sich in vielen Bereichen spätmittelalterlicher Spiritualität finden: Buße ist mehr als ein äußerlich ritualisiertes Geschehen. So enthält der *Hortulus animae* auch einen ausführlichen Beichtspiegel, der, streckenweise katechismushaft, der Selbstprüfung vor der Beichte dient (*Hortulus animae*, f. 147^r–155^r). Das Bemühen ist dabei, einerseits den individuellen Ort des oder der Beichtenden in der Kirche zu bestimmen: Der erste Schritt ist, den eigenen Stand – Geistlicher oder Weltlicher, unverheiratet oder verheiratet – zu bestimmen, das eigene Alter, das eigene Vermögen, den Bekanntenkreis, Beschäftigung, Wohnort, Zeitumstände, eigene Gedanken, Worte und Werke (*Hortulus animae*, f. 147^r). Dann werden die verschiedenen Tugenden, aber auch die zehn Gebote im Einzelnen durchgenommen und zum Teil in geradezu scholastischer Manier noch einmal unterteilt. Dies kann hier nur am ersten Beispiel, der Hoffart, deutlich gemacht werden (*Hortulus animae*, f. 147^{r-v}): Diese kann, so der *Hortulus animae*, innerlich oder äußerlich sein. Die innerliche kann den Intellekt betreffen oder die

---

42 S. hierzu Denzinger / Hünermann: 2017, 1405–1407.

Begierde. Die intellektive Hoffart wiederum besteht erstens darin, was an einem gut ist, auf sich statt auf Gott zurückzuführen, zweitens zu meinen, das eigene Gute im Angesicht Gottes verdient zu haben, drittens sich Qualitäten einzubilden, die man gar nicht hat, viertens andere Leute zu verachten. Damit beginnen erst die Differenzierungen, die hier nicht weiter im Detail ausgeführt werden können. Deutlich ist: Im Blick auf die Beichte wird das eigene Innere auf den Prüfstand gestellt. Letztlich spiegelt sogar auch die äußere Hoffart, etwa in zu luxuriösen Kleidern, die innere falsche Haltung wider.

Dieser innerlichen Vertiefung sakramentaler Frömmigkeit entspricht eine lange Liste von Gebeten, die man im Zusammenhang des Empfangs des Sakraments sprechen soll (*Hortulus animae*, f. 156^r–162^r). Demgemäß zeigt die zugehörige Abbildung eine Person, die die Eucharistie empfängt und dabei eine Gebetskette in der Hand hält (*Hortulus animae*, f. 156^r). Hier geht es um die rechte Andacht, z. B. in der Anrufung der heiligen Bekenner: „bitten fuer mich dz ich heuot in diesem elend zu der wirtschafft des fronleichnams vnnd bluts vnsers herrn Jesu mit warer rew meines hertzen/vnnd lauterer beycht meines munds wirdigklichen geen moeg". (*Hortulus animae*, f. 157^v–158^r)

Offenkundig geht es hier um die Einweisung in den rechten Vollzug des Bußsakraments, betont wird aber der innere Vorgang, der die Lauterkeit der Beichte ermöglicht. Noch deutlicher zeigt dies ein Gebet zur Bereitung auf den Empfang der Eucharistie: „So du yetzund hyenzugeen wilt: ist nit not das du vil bettest sonder dein gemout gantz zuosamen ziehest/vnnd got warlich erkennest/rechten glauben habest/vnnd in gnaden seyest: vnnd jnnnerlich betrachtest das schmertzlich leyden Christi". (*Hortulus animae*, f. 158^v–159^r)

Der *Hortulus animae* lebt ganz offenkundig innerhalb der sakramentalen Welt des späten Mittelalters. Nur selten unterläuft er sie, aber er vertieft sie im Sinne einer innerlichen Dimension des Geschehens.

Schlussüberlegungen

Aus Druckwerken auf die Auffassung ihrer Leserinnen und Leser zu schließen, ist ein komplexer Prozess. Im Falle eines mehrfach aufgelegten Gebetsbuches, dessen pragmatischer Sinn im Gebrauch liegt, kann man aber etwas optimistischer sein als bei meinungsbildenden Traktaten, die einem mehrfachen Filterungsprozess unterliegen. Der Umstand der vielen Ausgaben des *Hortulus animae* lässt annehmen, dass die darin enthaltenen Anweisungen wenigstens zu guten Teilen auch in die Praxis umgesetzt werden. Daher stellt es ein besonders gutes Medium dar, um sich der praktizierten Frömmigkeit um 1500 zu nähern: Deutlich zeigen sich die Unterschiede zwischen innerlichen und äußerlichen Aspekten spätmittelalterlicher Frömmigkeit. Die Untersuchung hat allerdings auch noch einmal herausgestrichen, dass eben diese Unterscheidung von innerlicher und äußerlicher Frömmigkeit lediglich idealtypische Gestalt haben kann. Beide Formen von Frömmigkeit liegen ineinander. Sie finden sich nicht nur in ein und demselben Gebetbuch, sie finden sich sogar in ein und demselben Vorgang: Ein Gebet angesichts einer Gregorsmesse, um nur das gerne herbeigezogene scheinbar typischste Beispiel veräußerlichter Frömmigkeit aufzugreifen, verheißt erwartungsgemäß Ablass. Eine etwas subtilere Analyse der damit verbundenen Anweisungen und Verheißungen lässt erkennen, dass das Ablassversprechen zugleich zur verinnerlichten Aneignung des Leidens Jesu Christi und des Heilsgeschehens führt. Die Frömmigkeitswelt des späten Mittelalters, wie sie sich hier widerspiegelt, erweist sich als außerordentlich vielfältig. Für das Gebetbuch als Medium gesprochen bedeutet dies: die frömmigkeitstheologischen und praktischen Angebote, die den Nutzern gemacht werden, sind ambige beziehungsweise deutungs- und nutzungsoffen: Je nach eigener Frömmigkeitsdisposition führen sie in unterschiedliche, in sich möglicherweise auch gar nicht ganz konsistente Nutzungsformen hinein. Allein schon die Vielfalt der Anweisungen macht deutlich, dass das Buch nicht so gedacht ist, dass ein einzelner Nutzer alle befolgt. Pragmatisch sind sie eher Angebote, die den Raum für eine multiple Frömmigkeitspraxis im späten Mittelalter öffnen.

Bibliographie

Quellen

DENZINGER, HEINRICH / HÜNERMANN, PETER (ed.) (2017), Kompendium der Glaubensbekenntnisse und kirchlichen Lehrentscheidungen = Enchiridion symbolorum definitionum et declarationum de rebus fidei et morum, Freiburg / Basel / Wien: Herder.

HORTULUS ANIME | zu tewtsch Selen wuertz-| gertlein genant / mit viel schoe- | nen gebeten vnd figuren, Nürnberg: Peypus, 1519.

LUTHER, MARTIN (1907), Betbüchlein, 1522, WA 10/2, 331–501.

LUTHER, MARTIN (1912), Eine einfältige Weise zu beten für einen guten Freund, 1535, WA 38, 351–375.

LUTHER, MARTIN (1884), Ein Sermon von dem hochwürdigen Sakrament des heiligen wahren Leichnams Christi und von den Bruderschaften, 1519, WA 2, 738–741, 742–758.

MEISTER ECKHART (1994), Die deutschen und lateinischen Werke. Die lateinischen Werke, Bd. 3: Expositio Sancti Evangelii secundum Iohannem, Karl Christ u. a. (ed.), Stuttgart: Kohlhammer.

PARADISUS ANIME: pro orationum | delitijs affluit : velut alter delitia-| rum ortus: operandus et custodiensus, Basel: Jakob Wolff 1498.

SCHEURL, CHRISTOPH (1867) Christoph Scheurl's Briefbuch, ein Beitrag zur Geschichte der Reformation und ihrer Zeit (1867), Franz von Soden/J.F.K. Knaake (ed.). Zweiter Band: 1517–1540, Potsdam: Gropius. Neue Edition: Aalen: O Zeller, 1962.

Sekundärliteratur

ACHTEN, GERARD (1980), Das christliche Gebetbuch im Mittelalter. Andachts- und Stundenbücher in Handschrift und Frühdruck, Wiesbaden: Reichert.

BENRATH, KARL (1886), Zur Geschichte der Marienverehrung, Theologische Studien und Kritiken 59, 7–94, 197–267.

HAMM, BERNDT (2016), Ablass und Reformation – Erstaunliche Kohärenzen, Tübingen: Mohr Siebeck.

HAMM, BERNDT (2004), Lazarus Spengler (1479–1534). Der Nürnberger Ratsschreiber im Spannungsfeld von Humanismus und Reformation, Politik und Glaube, Spätmittelalter und Reformation. NR 25, Tübingen: Mohr Siebeck.

HAMM, BERNDT (2011), Religiosität im späten Mittelalter. Spannungspole, Neuaufbrüche, Normierungen, Reinhold Friedrich/Wolfgang Simon (ed.), Tübingen: Mohr Siebeck.

HONEMANN, VOLKER (1978), Art. „Beda", VerLex 1, Berlin/New York: De Gruyter, 660–663.

KELBERG, KARSTEN (1983), Die Darstellung der Gregorsmesse in Deutschland, Münster: Univ. Diss.

KNAPE, JOACHIM/WILHELMI, THOMAS (2015), Sebastian Brant Bibliographie. Werke und Überlieferungen, Gratia 53, Wiesbaden: Harrassowitz.

LENTES, THOMAS (2007), Verum Corpus und Vera imago. Kalkulierte Bildbeziehungen in der Gregorsmesse, in A. Garmans/Th. Lentes (ed.), Das Bild der Erscheinung. Die Gregorsmesse im Mittelalter, Berlin: Reimer, 13–35.

LEPPIN, VOLKER (2015), Die Wittenberger Reformation und der Prozess der Transformation kultureller zu institutionellen Polaritäten, in: ders., Transformationen. Studien zu den Wandlungsprozessen in Theologie und Frömmigkeit zwischen Spätmittelalter und Reformation, Spätmittelalter, Humanismus, Reformation 86, Tübingen: Mohr Siebeck.

LEPPIN, VOLKER (2017), Die fremde Reformation. Die mystischen Wurzeln Martin Luthers, München: C.H. Beck, 2. Aufl.

MATTER, STEFAN (2017), Transkulturelle Gärten. Zu den frühen Ausgaben des Hortulus animae, des Seelengärtleins und des Wurtzgartens, in: Ingrid Kasten/Laura Auteri (ed.), Transkulturalität und Translation. Deutsche Literatur des Mittelalters im europäischen Kontext, Berlin/Boston: De Gruyter, 293–299.

OCHSENBEIN, PETER (1983), Art. ‚Hortulus animae', VerLex 4, Berlin / New York: De Gruyter, 147–154.

OCHSENBEIN, PETER (2004), Das Gebet „Christus am Kreuz" – ein frühes Prosagebet aus Böhmen?, in: V. Bok/H. J. Behr (ed.), Deutsche Literatur des Mittelalters in und über Böhmen II. Tagung in České Budějovice/Budweis 2002, Schriften zur Mediävistik 2, Hamburg: Kovač 2004, 185–198.

OLDENBOURG, M. CONSUELO (1973), Hortulus animae. [1494]–1523. Bibliographie und Illustration, Hamburg: Hauswedell.

PALLMANN, HEINRICH (1887), Art. Peypus, Friedrich, ADB 25, 569.

RESKE, CHRISTOPH (2007), Die Buchdrucker des 16. und 17. Jahrhunderts im deutschen Sprachgebiet. Auf der Grundlage des gleichnamigen Werkes von Josef Benzing, Beiträge zum Buch- und Bibliothekswesen 51, Wiesbaden: Harrassowitz.

SÖLLER, BERTRAM (1989), Art. „Paradisus animae", VerLex 7, Berlin/New York: De Gruyter, 293–298.

WACHINGER, BURKHARD (2004), Art. „Der himmlische Rosenkranz", VerLex 11, Berlin/New York: De Gruyter, 676–680.

Adinel C. Dincă
Babeş-Bolyai University of Cluj, Romania / Researcher at 'George Bariţiu'
Institute of History, Romanian Academy, Cluj-Napoca, Romania

Absence of Evidence or Evidence of Absence?
On Prayer Books and Devotional Behaviour in Late Medieval Transylvania[*]

This short essay merits little introduction: the usual textual basis for the devotion of the laity during the later Middle Ages within the area of the Catholic Church – the prayer book and the book of hours[1] – is completely missing from the extant records pertaining to late-medieval Transylvania. Because this fact may be perceived instantly as very surprising, especially for the researcher of devotional behaviour in the "medieval West" (Kieckhefer: 1989; Bartlett/Bestul: 1999; Erler: 1999; Jakobi-Mirwald: 2004; Vulić/Uselmann/Grisé: 2016), my sketchy account of the matter attempts to offer not only an interpretative discussion regarding the meaning of such an absence in the East-Central part of Europe, which also formed a cultural borderland with the Greek-Slavic-Orthodox world (Kührer-Wielach: 2015), but also considers what the consequences of this striking lack of evidence might be for the religious landscape of late medieval Transylvania.

Reading devotional texts (and likewise producing them) during medieval times, in conjunction with contemplating their complementary illustrations is part of a communication strategy[2] that accurately reflects the development stage of literate mentality in a certain region and during a defined time span, a phenomenon which often includes social and political manifestations.[3] This is the key element

---

[*] This work was supported by a grant from the Romanian National Authority for Scientific Research, CNDI – UEFISCDI, project PN-III-P4-ID-PCCF-2016-0064: 'Naşterea elitei intelectuale în Europa Centrală. Formarea profesorilor la Universitatea din Viena (1389–1450)/ The Rise of an Intellectual Elite in Central Europe: Making Professors at the University of Vienna, 1389–1450'. I give special thanks to Prof. Maria Crăciun (Cluj-Napoca, Romania) for her comments on an earlier draft of this essay.

[1] A subject that has received academic attention during the last three decades mainly in Western Europe, see Schreiner: 1992; Lobrichon: 1994; Hamm/Lentes: 2001; Schreiner: 2002; Duffy: 2006a; Hindman/Marrow: 2013; Dondi: 2016.

[2] Communication strategy and piety was the theme of a conference held in Hungary more than a decade ago: "15th Symposium of the International Medieval Sermon Studies Society Piliscsaba – Budapest (Hungary), 14–18 July 2006. Texts to Read and Texts to Preach: Medieval Sermons for Private Reading and Public Dissemination". An enquiry into the changing history of manuscripts as objects of devotional, antiquarian and scholarly interest in Lähnemann: 2016.

[3] See Trio/Smet: 2006.

152 | Adinel C. Dincă

to be taken into consideration when discussing this individualized form of textual evidence, or better said in the case of the afore-mentioned territory, the lack of it.

It has already been argued on several occasions that due to specific historical conditions of development, writing and general concern for literate communication reached the easternmost territorial body of the Hungarian crown[4] in a delayed, abbreviated and transformed manner (Adamska: 2004; Adamska: 2016; Dincă: 2011). Such an adapted reception and adoption of written expressions of political, social, legal and religious transactions, which occurred progressively from the centre(s) towards the Transylvanian periphery, is best described by the academic expression of "pragmatische Schriftlichkeit".[5] The use of written records of various natures is almost exclusively circumscribed to areas of what would today be called the "public sphere", usually the administration of secular affairs or churchly matters. Certainly, this image dominated by administrative pragmatism of the sources preserved in Transylvania – or abroad, with respect to the same province – is engendered by the filter and fate of transmission and chance survival. Successive depositories, overseen in the late medieval and early modern period by Saxon institutions, later by the Hungarian administration and over the last century by the Romanian archival framework, have handled medieval textual material over troublesome times. Within these institutions of memory, the traces of private use of the written word, such as correspondence or texts for personal use, are scarce and rather accidental.[6]

Beside the functions of the public word, the intersection of private individuals with written forms of religiosity points out, first of all, the level of literacy within a given community. Domestic devotion (Deane: 2013) was considered a moral self-improving exercise, according to the model of Christ, the Virgin Mary and the Saints, thus pious women and men were encouraged towards a private spirituality[7] outside the church through prayers learnt by heart[8] or, if able to read and

---

4 On medieval piety in the pre – Reformation Hungarian Kingdom see Pásztor: 1940; Erdélyi: 2012.

5 This specific term, present in German scholarship since the late 1950s, was later circumscribed as "pragmatic literacy" by English and other European academics in the last two decades of the 20th century. A short bibliographical list comprising aspects of historical evolution together with theoretical and terminological approaches: Clanchy: 1979; Bäuml: 1980; Keller/Grubmüller: 1992; Ehlich: 1993; Assmann/Assmann: 1994; Assmann: 1999.

6 A recent discussion revolves around some letters and fragments of letters discovered in rather unusual circumstances, namely in manuscripts and printed books from Sibiu (within the Library of the Brukenthal National Museum), that were already circulating within the same region in the Late Middle Ages, see Dincă: 2020a.

7 Brantley: 2007; Ehrstine: 2012; Martin/Ryrie: 2012; Williamson: 2013; a special issue dedicated to Domestic Devotions in Medieval and Early Modern Europe was published by Religions in 2020, vol. 11, nr. 1.

8 According to 15th-century reforms of the clergy and monastic communities, prayer was divided in: vocal prayer, either read or learnt by heart, the latter suited for the illiterate, then

Absence of Evidence or Evidence of Absence? | 153

write, by means of Breviaries, psalter-books and books of hours,[9] accompanied by the reverence and contemplation of material items,[10] such as devotional images (*Andachtsbilder*), relics, rosaries, and the use of portable altars. However, actual objects came for much of the time in luxurious forms,[11] not affordable to common townspeople or villagers.

There is also an additional limitation regarding the spread of writing and reading in medieval Transylvania. Expressions of literacy are not extant uniformly throughout the province: they may be considered a distinctive feature of the network of urban settlements – together with their surrounding and closely connected villages – that were almost exclusively founded and populated by Western (notably German) colonists, arriving in several waves from the middle of the twelfth century onwards and under the protection of the Hungarian kings.[12]

Literate expressions of devotion and lay piety[13] are therefore, in Transylvania's case, drastically shaped by the overall identity of local writing and reading practices. Although some nuances in pace and coverage cannot be overlooked, one may surely define the written communication in Transylvania from the fourteenth to the early sixteenth century according to three parameters, as (1) mostly serving official purposes rather than private ones, (2) mostly clerical rather than secular and (3) preponderantly associated with the clusters of German settlements concentrated around urbanized commercial and artisanal centres, briefly mentioned before, than with any other ethnic and occupational groups. What also must not be forgotten is the overwhelming prevalence of Latin over vernacular, an additional factor that limited the larger, passive or active, involvement of laypeople to the dynamics of local literacy.

Browsing through the very first attempt to count and identify the medieval manuscripts written in Latin now preserved in Romanian collections (Papa-

---

    meditation, oriented towards deliberate inner focus and reflection, and contemplation, utterly silent, which is considered the highest form of prayer, see Baier: 2003, 345.

9 This type of devotional text, a compendium of prayers, hymns, eucharistic devotions, etc. that imitated the monastic model of Canonical Hours, is considered to have been the bestseller of the late Middle Ages and the Renaissance, comparable in popularity only to the Bible, see Wieck: 2008, 389.

10 See Laugerud/Ryan/Skinnebach: 2016.

11 One such example is the *Festetics Codex* (1492–1494), a prayer book written in Hungarian, with rich Renaissance decoration, made about 1493 on the commission of Pál Kinizsi for his wife. The same workshop of illumination that produced the *Corvinas* has painted the decoration of this luxury item. See Abaffy: 1996.

12 Gündisch: 1987; Roth: 1996. The relation between the medieval town and written communication has been mentioned by Dincă: 2011. The network of towns in the Hungarian Kingdom is described and analysed in Szende: 2018.

13 In spiritual terminology, piety (*pietas, Frömmigkeit*) is defined as a virtue which includes religious devotion (through various actions), spirituality (life conduct according to religious teachings) and humility.

hagi/Dincă: 2018), one sees immediately that certain texts usually related to the laity's taste for reading are completely absent: besides literature for spiritual perfection as a preparation for eternal life – such as (vernacular) history or poetry –, military treatises, travel literature, illustrated religious compendia etc. are also missing. This emphasizes once more that the local book market was orientated towards the practical needs of the parish clergy (Dincă: 2015a) or members of the religious orders, especially the Dominicans (Lupescu Makó: 2017). Historical catalogues and book lists, moreover, cannot fill this informational gap, as these records were exclusively produced, preserved and transmitted within ecclesiastical contexts. A natural assumption that such devotional texts for the Transylvanian laity must or could have been destroyed and scattered as a result of the Protestant Reformation would clearly be a reductionist assertion that is not supported by the initial observations in a very complex research field, which is the study of medieval book fragments, remnants of obsolete volumes that were taken apart and reused as binding elements.[14] Regardless of how limited our current knowledge regarding this subject is (Papahagi: 2017; Dincă: 2017), at least isolated traces of religious literature for lay usage would have come to the surface. Furthermore, Sibiu (Hermannstadt, Nagyszeben) and Brașov (Kronstadt, Brassó), the main urban centres of the Saxon population in Transylvania, did not experience a violent transition from the Catholic to the Lutheran denomination and many books of the medieval past were treasured and included in the libraries of the sixteenth century *gymnasia* (Müller; 1877; Gross: 1883; Gross: 1887; Dincă: 2018). Precious objects as they usually were, because of their accompanying illustrations and decorative embellishments, handwritten or printed devotional books would have been kept even if only for their aesthetic and material relevance, as happened with liturgical textiles, for instance.[15]

This observation does not unavoidably imply that the laity in Transylvania was irrecoverably illiterate. Leaving aside for now the fact that laypersons prove quite often and usually in official circumstances the ability to read and write (sometimes only as a mimetic gesture) (Dincă: 2015c), several documentary sources suggest private ownership of religious books (usually sermons) by the laity. However, evidence of this sort is somewhat misleading, as has been recently argued by a thorough investigation showing that laypeople (men and women alike) did indeed possess books (Cotoi: 2021). Their intention was not to read them, but to donate them to churches,[16] being aware of the continuous need of the Church for good written apparatus. So, the religious book in the hands of the Transylvanian laity

---

14 For the potential of this line of study, see Duba: 2019.
15 A parallel phenomenon documented by Wetter: 2015.
16 As alluring as this conclusion may appear, there are some nuances that should be considered, because the reading of Latin sermons was not an entirely isolated occurrence in lay circles throughout medieval Europe, see Thayer: 2012, 43–44.

may be really understood as proof of engaged devotion, though as an element of a different soteriological strategy, through pious gifts, not through personal conduct and attitude inspired by the reading of sacred and religious writings.

Testimonies such as the ones selectively evoked above seem to indicate that in what concerns the devotional and spiritual literature read by laypeople, the lack of evidence in late medieval Transylvania convincingly supports the assumption that this category of readings, rites, and prayers textually compiled in books – in their generally accepted form in Central and Western Europe – was missing. Confronted with different realities of an economic or political nature, even the most elevated circles of local society at the eastern frontier of the Latin Church showed no interest in such luxury products of private devotion, a personal religious behaviour that sometimes was displayed publicly as a means of social representation.[17] Furthermore, throughout the entire Hungarian kingdom such a book tailored for private devotion is rarely mentioned and only in highly restricted circles. Analysing the "Books in the Service of Liturgy and Devotion: Fourteenth-Fifteenth Centuries", Anna Boreczky concludes that "only a few examples of the Book of Hours, a prayer book that enjoyed great popularity in Western Christianity in the fourteenth and fifteenth centuries, have survived from medieval Hungary" (Boreczky: 2018, 297), all of them associated with the highest-ranking officials of the Church or of the royal court. This Hungarian scholar's conclusion regarding the scarcity or the complete absence of typical categories of texts read by European educated men and women (Boreczky: 2018, 298; Scott-Stokes: 2006) endorses the empirical observations regarding the Transylvanian source material I have suggested above, in the introduction to this essay. But can this be considered a clue towards acknowledging that written texts were not a component of the standardized lay pious performance, or does it imply an alternate devotional pattern?

Another illuminating detail in this respect is the fact that around 1500 several astonishingly sophisticated book and charter decorators (not necessarily itinerant artists) have left substantial traces of their mastery in southern Transylvania (Dincă: 2019a); their activity must have been quite ample, as it needed special regulation within the local statutes of artists and artisans (Firea/Dincă: 2015–2016). The elaborated "Crucifixion" scene added to the "Codex Altemberger" at Sibiu in 1481, or the rich embellishment of the initials featured in the works of the "Vigiliale-Group" around 1507, both in Sibiu and Brașov, maybe also in Albești (Weisskirch, Fehéregyháza), as well as the lavish use of gold in the town-book of Sighișoara (Schässburg, Segesvár), commissioned in 1487, not to mention highly

---

17 Tomaszewski: 2016, 51 quotes the verses of the well-known poet Wacław Potocki (1621–1696) *"Tak ta niwa Rodzi"* [*Thus this land bears*] on the matter: "Today in gilt sacks/lads carry prayer books for their masters/Books to remember what should be/Asked for and what should be thanked for . . . /And what are these costly sacks for? For vanity, for pride,/The prayer is pleasanter when read from a velvet cloak" [translated in English by Tomaszewski].

156 | Adinel C. Dincă

skilled calligraphers,[18] prove that resources for producing locally intricate prayer books were at hand. Although the printing press was only introduced in Transylvania during the third decade of the sixteenth century (Simon: 2007; Rother: 2002), printed material was imported earlier and a local specialized commerce had taken shape relatively early, around 1500 (Dincă: 2019d). The only acceptable explanation for the absence of devotional literature in the religious behaviour of the Transylvanian laity – if we choose to exclude the theory of the complete, traceless destruction of such texts and books – is that lay religiosity in late medieval Transylvania was articulated without a significant implication of personal reading of inspiring texts or the contemplation of images, other than those from the ornately-decorated church buildings.

For the analysis of medieval religiosity, Arnold Angenendt in his textbook "Grundformen der Frömmigkeit im Mittelalter" (Angenendt: 2004) understands the Latin terms *devotio* and *pietas* ("devotion", "piety"/*Andacht, Frömmigkeit* in the German text) in a more general sense and noticeably defines them not only a limited and clearly outlined range of religious actions but the phenomenon of religiosity as a whole, an idea which encompasses along practical, performative accomplishments also notions and norms. In the same work, he uses two auxiliary concepts dialectically organised: *Hochreligion* and *Einfachreligion* (Angenendt: 2004, 74). Accepting that objections can be raised against each of these terms, the German historian describes the so-called "high religion" as related to a developed (or higher) form of culture. Mysticism as initiated by Bernard de Clairvaux or scholastic theology may serve as examples in this respect. For this form of religious experience, however, *hochkulturelle* (Angenendt: 2004, 75) prerequisites are needed, where the transcending human intellectual faculties play the main role – this spiritual path leads to "contemplative prayer" and imaginative forms of meditation (Baier: 2009). Nonetheless, in opposition to this profoundly intellectualized "high religion", one also speaks of primitive, natural, primary or "simplified religion". This second form of religious behaviour is described as featuring a society that often lacks a vocational priesthood or has no professional theologians to bring the religious ideas into a harmonious system. Outside the framework of liturgical worship, popular piety is manifested, in public as well as in private, through gestures, recited texts and formulae, song and music, sacred places, times or processions (Webb: 2005; Duffy: 2006b; Corbellini: 2013). Certainly, late medieval Transylvania lies from this perspective on a long path of transition from popular, simplified understanding of the Christian religion towards a more profound comprehension of theological ideas illuminated by a clerical group, which becomes itself better in-

---

18 An indulgence issued by the Sibiu Chapter, SJAN Sibiu, Episcopia Bisericii Evanghelice C.A. din Transilvania, Colecția de documente episcopale, no. 30.

structed, especially starting with the mid-fourteenth century, after the foundation of universities in Central Europe.[19]

Institutions of higher education took upon themselves to reform the secular clergy – including in Transylvania – in the spirit of the reform councils from Basel, Pavia etc (Dincă: 2015b). In the first decades of the fifteenth century, the so-called "Wiener Schule der Pastoraltheologie" (Haberkern: 2003, 60), a divergent group within the Faculty of Theology of the Vienna University, adhered to an innovative theological practice, concerned mainly with bringing religion closer to the needs of a wider segment of the population by the "practice of piety" (*praxis pietatis*). The new type of priest assumed as his mission to support and educate the common man towards a pious conduct of life. According to the theologians of the "Vienna School", the communication channel between the scholar and layman was ensured by the sermon. In this new context, preaching suffered some changes in content, style and vocabulary, in order to better adapt to its newly-designated catechetical responsibility.

In addition to this, several other facts indicate that the devotional behaviour of laypeople in Transylvania was built on different foundations over a period of two centuries prior to the Protestant Reformation. The most important were perhaps the visual *stimuli* present in churches (van Os:1994; Marrow: 1979; Possas: 2018). The relevance of the devotional image in Transylvania has been so far clearly the best investigated aspect of local religiosity and it benefits from the expertise of established scholars (Firea: 2012a; Crăciun: 2013; Jenei: 2014a; Jenei: 2014b; Crăciun: 2002). Private devotion outside clerical groups has always involved objects. The variety of such material incentives of religious feelings is impressive, from prayer-nuts (Wetter/Scholten: 2017), for example, through relics[20] and rosaries, to home and portable altars.[21] While the first left no evidence in medieval Transylvania, the last type of objects is generously documented mostly in the Vatican

---

19 An antagonistic perspective on Transylvanian popular devotional exercises in Crăciun: 2011, 37; Crăciun: 2012, 108, who disconsiders the role of the "weak parish clergy (both in terms of number and in education)" and commends the active role of mendicant orders in secular religious life. The idea of poorly educated, inadequate and uninvolved Transylvanian parish clergy, especially in the Saxon cultural environment, has been recently revised with the help of solid documentary support, see especially Dincă: 2015a; Dincă: 2015b; Dincă: 2019c; Dincă: 2021; Dincă: 2022.

20 For relics in medieval Transylvania, see Florea: 2005; Covaciu: 2018.

21 Local archives preserve some evidence of this sort: first, there is the positive reply addressed to an anonymous citizen from Cluj, who received the permission of the holy father, Pope Leo X, to visit Compostela together with his wife and to have a portable altar [SJAN Cluj, Fond Primăria municipiului Cluj-Napoca, Seria C – Socotelile orașului și registre cu caracter economic, Subseria C1 – Socotelile orașului, 6/XXIX]. This happened in the second decade of the 16th century. Additionally, two earlier examples from the mid-15th century, the golden age of these portable altars in this part of the world: *Johannes Zaz, iudex regius* from Sibiu/Hermannstadt, was allowed to have such an altar [SJAN Cluj, Colecția generală, Seria 2 – BCU, no. 82], and the parish priest from Slimnic/Stolzenburg, received permission

158 | Adinel C. Dincă

sources.[22] Consequently, devotional behaviour in late medieval Transylvania must have been less connected with written texts and centred around memorized psalms and prayers, recited orally, as well as various devotional objects, owned privately.

Turning back to the textual basis of devotion, I consider that there are two main aspects of this discussion that in the light of the source material available at this moment deserve much closer attention. Possibly additional evidence that the typical prayer book was not in (general) use at all locally is the multitude of random notations of prayers (*preces, orationes*) of all kinds, extant in various parts of handwritten or printed books. While Thomas Wal in 1517, at that time not yet ordained priest, noted a prayer in his private agenda/calendar (*almanach*),[23] other manuscripts dating from the fifteenth and early sixteenth century include various notations of *Pater Noster*[24] or *Credo.*[25] These annotations made, evidently, by members of the clergy (or men, like Wal, who aspired to become priests) are examples of what may have been improvised substitutes for the actual prayer books. The only example of a small, typical *liber precum* that I was able to find among the preserved documentary sources is a text written on parchment from the fifteenth century. Its context of transmission speaks for a probable (?) Transylvanian use.[26] Such details, especially the mnemotechnic formulas[27] or the explanations of various prayer texts,[28] both provided by the parish clergy, suggest that memory

---

to have a *viaticum*, or portable altar [SJAN Sibiu, Colecția "Brukenthal", Seria 40: RS 1–10, no. 527].

22 In the Vatican documentary sources, Transylvanian supplications regarding permission to have a portable altar represents the second most important category of *petentes* after the so-called *Pfründenjäger* ("hunter" of ecclesiastical benefices).

23 Sibiu, Biblioteca Muzeului Național Brukenthal, no. V II 618, front page: *Tu pater immensi residens qui culmine coeli/foelix initinm tribuas, quo pectore laeto/Traducat spatium vivat foeliciter anni/Cuius in arbitrio praesens liber iste probatur.*

24 In various forms: Sibiu, Biblioteca Muzeului Național Brukenthal, Ms. 637; Sibiu, Biblioteca Muzeului Național Brukenthal, Ms. 651: f. Frater Siboto, *Commentarius in Pater Noster* (187 r). The latter example illustrates the use of mnemonic formulas to remember the start of each verse of the prayer: f. 1r: *Pater noster/Adveniat/Ffiat voluntas/Panem nostrum/Et dimitte/Et ne nos/Sed libera.*

25 Sibiu, Biblioteca Muzeului Național Brukenthal, Ms. 715.

26 SJAN Sibiu, Colecția de manuscrise, no. II-97: *Orationes ad sanctos, pro horis canonicis, de passione Domini, de compassione Beatae Mariae Virginis.* This collection was compiled in the 19th century from donations of local Saxon intellectuals, yet it is difficult to precisely determine whether the manuscript was of local origin or a modern bibliophile acquisition from abroad.

27 Mnemonic devices – repetition, rosary-based sequencing, rhyming, acronyms, etc. – were commonly used as learning techniques of verbal rituals: prayer, psalms and Scripture, see various examples in the special issue of Gesta: 2009.

28 Sibiu, Biblioteca Muzeului Național Brukenthal, Ms. 651, f. 1v renders (with a minor oversight) the short contemporary poem, based on Jacobus de Voragine's *Legenda Aurea*, regarding the Holy Kinship: *Anna solet dici tres conceuisse Marias/Quas genuere viri Joachim, Cleophas, Salomeque./Has duxere viri ⟨Joseph,⟩ Alpheus, Zebedeus./Prima parit Christum, Ja-*

and prayer learnt by heart, in the church or at home, were essential and surely dominant in comparison to the read prayers.

The second relevant aspect for the current discussion involves also a dynamic dialogue between writing and orality. After failing to find devotional literature designed for lay usage, the logical next step was to identify devotional themes in the available texts, especially in pastoral writings. Sermons form in Transylvania, as in any other region of the Latin Middle Ages, one of the most important categories of texts. An important media channel, preaching was an extremely important intermediary of devotional messages for the Christian communities, with *Passio Christi*[29] as one of the focal points of the textual basis for preaching activity in this peripheral province of the Hungarian crown. Acknowledging the low survival rate of manuscripts here, the result of the search is amazingly good,[30] especially for the southern part of the land, alongside the Carpathian Mountains.[31] All these examples of the Christocentric turn of late medieval piety may reflect a concentrated attitude of the secular clergy to broadcast a message regarding the model of Christ, and thus a strong suggestion for individual meditation (Erdei: 1990; Enenkel/Melion: 2010) for the audience.

Literate behaviour from medieval Transylvania did not intersect with the devotional behaviour of the land – or could have existed only marginally – because of the pragmatic, or professional orientation of writing and reading. The term "aspirational literacy" has been suggested elsewhere (Dincă: 2015a; Dincă: 2019c) to describe this reduced use of the written word. There are so far potential elements indicating a private or lay devotion in Transylvania during the fifteenth century

---

    cobum secunda minorem,/Et Joseph iustum peperit cum Symone Iudam,/Tertia majorem Iacobum volucremque Johannem.

29 Haug/Wachinger: 1993; Bestul: 1996, or the more recent Rittgers: 2012.

30 Sibiu, Biblioteca Muzeului Național Brukenthal Ms. 605: … b. *Passio Domini exposita compendiose* (f. 252v–270r); Sibiu, Biblioteca Muzeului Național Brukenthal Ms. 657: a. *Sermo Johannis Zekel* (f. 1r–11v, 212r–216v) … c. *Passio Christi, exemplum* (f. 210v–211r); Sibiu, Biblioteca Muzeului Național Brukenthal Ms. 683: … d. Iordanes de Quedlinburgo (sive de Saxonia): *Tractatus de passione Christi* (f. 9r–43v); e. *Tractatus anonimi de passione Christi* (f. 43v–55v); … ac. Alcherus Clarevallensis (Ps. Bernardus Clarevallensis), *Meditationes* (f. 135v–147r).

31 An inventory of the parish church of St Mary in Sibiu/Hermannstadt describes in a rather detailed manner the evolution of book accumulation from the second half of the 14th century until 1442, quoting: *Item duo passionalia, vnum in pergameneo et vnum in papirio*, Biblioteca Națională a României, filiala Alba-Iulia (Batthyaneum), Ms. R. II. 135, *Matricula plebaniae Cibiniensis*, 1442, f. 28r. Another medieval collection, preserved *in situ* in the Cisnădie Parish Archive, counts among its books: Ms. D 5 a. Nikolaus de Dinkelsbühl, *Passionale* (f. 1r–93r) …; Ms. D 7 a. *Sermones variae* (*de assumptione Beatae Virginis, de Passione Domini, in festo Pascae* etc.) (f. 1r–298v) … d. *"Pater noster" cum commento*, (f. 395r–441v); Ms. D 11 a. [Nikolaus de Dinkelsbühl?], *Tractatus de passione Christi. Sermones variae* (*in vigilia Nativitatis Domini, in circumcisione Domini* etc.) (f. 1r–88r) …; Ms. D 27 … b. *Tractatus sermonibus de corpore Christi* (f. 195r–280r).

160 | Adinel C. Dincă

organized around objects and orality, a pattern enhanced by impulses both visual and spoken coming from the parish clergy. That this clergy was indeed concerned with the spiritual needs and the right religious conduct of the flock is shown by another theme found in the sermons available in Transylvania, superstitions and bad habits.[32]

This microanalysis of lay forms of pious behaviour should mention, nonetheless, other well-documented local devout practices: owning a portable altar or relics, donations to the local parish churches or to mendicant convents (Florea: 2013a), bequests/testamentary clauses,[33] patronage of religiously-themed works of art (panel painting (Firea: 2013) or book decoration[34] with a public or semi-public display), cult of local saints[35] or dedication of votive masses (Firea: 2012b, 288–289), joining a lay confraternity (Gross: 2003; Fara: 2008; Florea: 2009), pilgrimage to Rome (Rehberg: 2012) or other holy places. Within this ample context, the lack of written evidence of private devotion in the late medieval Transylvanian Saxon settlements raises the question whether this specific habit existed in terms of coordinated regulation (demand/commission – offer/production) and its traces were swept away by time and/or hazard, or it never represented a constant factor, just a circumstantial occurrence, probably imported.[36]

Devotional books, designed for either public or private worship of the laypeople, seem to be the missing mosaic-piece from a spiritual landscape that integrated simultaneously traditional piety with new European devotional practices.[37] So far, the material evidence confirms the absence of such devotional accessories in the German parts of medieval Transylvania – the cultural space with the highest development of literate mentality in the province – despite the prerequisite documented presence of both the means of producing such items and a book-trade channel.

---

32 Cisnădie, Biserica Evanghelică, Oficiul Parohial, Ms. D 4: 5a. *De superstitionibus et malis consuetudinibus* (f. 2 r–113 r).

33 Lupescu Makó: 2001 noticed that by the late Middle Ages a large number of testators bequeathed monetary provisions to churches and convents and requested that mendicant friars would pray for the salvation of their souls. See a list of such donations made by lay people to various ecclesiastical institutions in Jenei: 2004, 23–24.

34 In 1481 Thomas Altemberger, the mayor of Sibiu, commissioned the decoration of a page in one of Sibiu's legal compendia (now known as *Codex Altemberger*) with the Crucifixion scene, together with the oath taken by the public officials of the town council, see Dincă: 2019a; Dincă: 2019b. See also Sand: 2014.

35 Regarding the cult of parish patron saints in Transylvania, see Florea: 2008 and Florea: 2013b. See also the sermons of Johannes Zeckel, Sibiu, Brukenthal Library, Ms. 657, f. 7r: *Hunc sermonem colegi* (sic) *et feci in ecclesia mea, in festo Sancti Georgii, ego Ioannes Zeckel anno 1502*.

36 Duffy: 2006a, 25 points out the fact that in the course of the fifteenth century textual religious experience ceased to be an aristocratic monopoly and became part of the urban and rural people's lives, decisively democratised with the arrival of print. The Low Countries and Northern France benefited from the activity of stationers' shops, who mass – produced manuscript books of hours in "assembly-lines".

37 Kühne/Bünz/Müller: 2013.

This conclusion is additionally supported by the observations regarding the entire Hungarian Kingdom, where this type of books was scarce, as Anna Boreczky eloquently asserts, extant exclusively in the hands of high aristocracy. Even the earliest Transylvanian bibliophiles, interested in recovering valuable medieval books circulating locally, have acquired their most aesthetically adorned items (Bibles, breviaries, psalters, and books of hours) from abroad. By the time Baron Samuel von Brukenthal (1721–1803) was assembling his private collection,[38] such evidence of pious behaviour was missing in Transylvania altogether.[39] And yet, the investigation of documentary source material is for the moment far from satisfactory: Transylvanian textual items have been displaced and scattered over the last centuries, some surfacing in collections abroad, or even dismembered, recycled and re-used fragmentarily within the bindings of hundreds of modern tomes. The indirect evidence given by the absence of devotional books (especially) in Saxon Transylvania points towards a complex and contingent research field, conditioned by the chance survival of documentary testimonies. Future inferences on these particular elements of local devotional conduct and their impact on the literate mentality of Latin Europe's peripheral regions depend mostly on thorough archival investigations. Hopefully, the discussion opened by this essay will clarify the aspects related to the relationship between the compendia of pious texts devised for reading in the lay household and their physical presence/absence in the settlements of the region.

Bibliography

Primary Sources / Manuscripts

Alba Iulia, Biblioteca Națională a României (*Batthyaneum*), Ms. R. II. 135.
Cisnădie, Biserica Evanghelică, Oficiul Parohial, Ms. D 11.
Cisnădie, Biserica Evanghelică, Oficiul Parohial, Ms. D 27.
Cisnădie, Biserica Evanghelică, Oficiul Parohial, Ms. D 5.
Cisnădie, Biserica Evanghelică, Oficiul Parohial, Ms. D 7.
Cisnădie, Biserica Evanghelică, Oficiul Parohial, Ms. D 45.
Cluj, National Archives, Colecția generală, Seria 2 – BCU, no. 82.
Cluj, National Archives, Fond Primăria municipiului Cluj-Napoca, Seria C – Socotelile orașului și registre cu caracter economic, Subseria C1 – Socotelile orașului, no. 6/XXIX.
Sibiu, Biblioteca Muzeului Național Brukenthal, Ms. 605.

---

38 Vlaicu/Gündisch: 2007.
39 The only such book in Baron von Brukenthal's collection, Ms. 763 (Book of Hours), see Papahagi/Dincă: 2018, no. 501.

162 | Adinel C. Dincă

Sibiu, Biblioteca Muzeului Național Brukenthal, Ms. 657.
Sibiu, Biblioteca Muzeului Național Brukenthal, Ms. 683.
Sibiu, Biblioteca Muzeului Național Brukenthal, Ms. 637.
Sibiu, Biblioteca Muzeului Național Brukenthal, Ms.651.
Sibiu, Biblioteca Muzeului Național Brukenthal, Ms. 657.
Sibiu, Biblioteca Muzeului Național Brukenthal, Ms. 715.
Sibiu, Biblioteca Muzeului Național Brukenthal, Ms. 763.
Sibiu, National Archives, Colecția "Brukenthal", Seria 40: RS 1-10, no. 527.
Sibiu, National Archives, Colecția de manuscrise, no. II - 97.
Sibiu, National Archives, Episcopia Bisericii Evanghelice C.A. din Transilvania, Colecția de documente episcopale, no. 30.

Printed Works

Sibiu, Biblioteca Muzeului Național Brukenthal, no. V II 618.

Secondary Literature

Abaffy, Csilla N. (ed.) (1996), Festetics-kódex, 1494 előtt. A nyelvemlék hasonmása és betűhű átirata bevezetéssel és jegyzetekkel, Budapest: Argumentum, Magyar Nyelvtudományi Társaság.

Adamska, Anna (2004), The Study of Medieval Literacy: Old Sources, New Ideas, in: Anna Adamska/Marco Mostert (ed.), The Development of Literate Mentalities in East Central Europe (Proceedings of the Fourth Utrecht Symposium on Medieval Literacy, 28-30 June 2001), Turnhout: Brepols, 13-47.

Adamska, Anna (2016), Intersections: Medieval East Central Europe from the Perspective of Literacy and Communication, in: Katalin Szende/Gerhard Jaritz (ed.), Medieval East Central Europe in a Comparative Perspective: From Frontier Zones to Lands in Focus, Abingdon, UK: Routledge, 225-238.

Angenendt, Arnold (2004), Grundformen der Frömmigkeit im Mittelalter, 2nd ed., München: R. Oldenbourg.

Assmann, Aleida/Assmann, Jan (1994), Das Gestern im Heute. Medien und soziales Gedächtnis, in: Klaus Merten/Siegfried J. Schmidt/Siegfried Weischenberg (ed.), Die Wirklichkeit der Medien. Eine Einführung in die Kommunikationswissenschaft, Opladen: Westdeutscher Verlag, 114-140.

Assmann, Jan (1999), Das kulturelle Gedächtnis. Schrift, Erinnerung und politische Identität in frühen Hochkulturen, München: C.H. Beck.

Baier, Karl (2009), Meditation and Contemplation in High to Late Medieval Europe, in: Eli Franco (ed.), Yogic Perception, Meditation and Altered States of Consciousness, Wien: Österreichischen Akademie der Wissenschaften, 325-349.

Bartlett, Anne Clark/Bestul, Thomas H. (ed.) (1999), Cultures of Piety: Medieval English Devotional Literature in Translation, Ithaca: Cornell University Press.

BÄUML, FRANZ H. (1980), Varieties and Consequences of Medieval Literacy and Illiteracy, Speculum, 55, 237–265.

BESTUL, THOMAS H. (1996), Texts of the Passion: Latin Devotional Literature and Medieval Society, Philadelphia: University of Pennsylvania Press.

BORECZKY, ANNA (2018), Book Culture in Medieval Hungary, in: Xavier Barral i Altet/Pál Lővei/Vinni Lucherini/Imre Takács (ed.), The Art of Medieval Hungary, Roma: Viella, 283–306.

BRANTLEY, JESSICA (2007), Reading in the Wilderness: Private Devotion and Public Performance in Late Medieval England, Chicago: University of Chicago Press.

CLANCHY, MICHAEL T. (1979), From Memory to Written Record. England 1066–1307, Cambridge: Harvard University Press.

CORBELLINI, SABRINA (2013), Cultures of Religious Reading in the Late Middle Ages: Instructing the Soul, Feeding the Spirit and Awakening the Passion, Turnhout: Brepols.

COTOI, PAULA (2021), The Book as Object of Lay Devotion in Late Medieval Transylvania, Studia Universitatis Babeș-Bolyai. Historia 66 (Sp. Issue), 27–42.

COVACIU, CĂTĂLINA (2018), Bunuri fără preț. Relicvele în context privat în Transilvania medievală, Buletinul Cercurilor Științifice Studențești, 24, 139–162.

CRĂCIUN, MARIA (2002), Eucharistic Devotion in the Iconography of Transylvanian Polyptych Altarpieces, in: José Pedro Paiva (ed.), Religious Ceremonials and Images: Power and Social Meaning (1400–1750), Lisbon: Palimage Press, 191–230.

CRĂCIUN, MARIA (2011), Mendicant Piety and the Saxon Community of Transylvania c. 1450–1550, in: Maria Crăciun/Elaine Fulton (ed.), Communities of Devotion. Religious Orders and Society in East Central Europe, 1450–1800, Farnham: Ashgate, 29–70.

CRĂCIUN, MARIA (2012), "Ora pro nobis sancta Dei genitrix": Prayers and Gestures in Late Medieval Transylvania, in: Gerhard Jaritz (ed.), Ritual, Images and Daily Life. The Medieval Perspective, Wien/Zurich: Lit Verlag, 107–138.

CRĂCIUN, MARIA (2013), Communities of Devotion: the Saxons in Early Modern Transylvania, Studia Universitatis Babeș-Bolyai. Historia 58, 156–195.

DEANE, JENNIFER (2013), Pious domesticities, in: Judith M. Bennett/Ruth Mazo Karras (ed.), The Oxford Handbook of Women and Gender in Medieval Europe, Oxford: Oxford University Press, 262–278.

DINCĂ, ADINEL C. (2011), Formen und Funktionen der Schriftlichkeit in spätmittelalterlichen Hermannstadt. Zum Schriftgebrauch in einer vormodernen Rechtsgemeinschaft, Berichte und Forschungen. Jahrbuch des Bundesinstituts für Kultur und Geschichte der Deutschen im östlichen Europa, 18, 290–296.

DINCĂ, ADINEL C. (2015a), Medieval Literacy in Transylvania. Selective Evidence from the Parish Church, Transylvanian Review, 24/1, 109–121.

DINCĂ, ADINEL C. (2015b), Reading Nicholas of Dinkelsbühl in Medieval Transylvania: Surviving Texts and Historical Contexts, in: Monica Brînzei (ed.), Nicholas of Dinkelsbühl and the Sentences at Vienna in the Early XVth century, Turnhout: Brepols, 453–471.

DINCĂ, ADINEL C. (2015c), Scrieri autografe în Transilvania medievală: de la cele mai timpurii mărturii, până în secolul al XVI-lea, in: Susana Andea/Avram Andea / Adinel Dincă (ed.), Autographa et signaturae Transilvaniae (sec. XIV–XVII), Cluj-Napoca/ Gatineau: Argonaut/Symphologic Publishing, 11–85.

DINCĂ, ADINEL C. (2017), The Medieval Book in Early Modern Transylvania. Preliminary Assessments, Studia Universitatis Babeș-Bolyai, Historia 1, 23–34.

DINCĂ, ADINEL C. (2018), "Biblioteca orașului Sibiu" în evul mediu. Câteva considerații pe marginea unei confuzii istoriografice, in: Lupescu Makó Mária (ed.), Cluj – Kolozsvár – Klausenburg 700: várostörténeti tanulmányok = Studii de istorie urbană, Cluj-Napoca: Erdélyi Múzeum-Egyesület, 431–436.

DINCĂ, ADINEL C. (2019a), Illuminating the Page in Transylvania around 1500. The First Contact, Étude bibliologiques / Library research studies, 1, 5–38.

DINCĂ, ADINEL C. (2019b), Codex Altemberger, in: Ginel Lazăr (ed.), Codex Altemberger. Primul cod de legi al sașilor din Sibiu, București: MNIR, 24–50.

DINCĂ, ADINEL C. (2019c), The University and the Parish. The Medieval Books from Heltau/Cisnădie, Philobiblon: Transylvanian Journal of Multidisciplinary Research in Humanities, 24/2, 337–352.

DINCĂ, ADINEL C. (2019d), La Transilvania nel commercio europeo di libri intorno al 1500. Stampe veneziane nella Sibiu (Cibinium – Nagyszeben – Hermannstadt) medievale, in: I Convegno della medievistica italiana. Bertinoro (Forlì-Cesena), 14–16 giugno 2018, Roma: Open Archive di Reti Medievali, 580–599.

DINCĂ, ADINEL C. (2020a), Scrisori private din Transilvania medievală în context local și european, Anuarul Institutului de Istorie "George Barițiu" din Cluj-Napoca, Series Historica, vol. LIX, 361–384.

DINCĂ, ADINEL C. (2022), Die Prädikatur in der siebenbürgisch-sächsischen Pfarrkirche vor der Reformation. Quellenauswertung und locale Zesammenhänge in: Ulrich A. Wien (ed.), Anfänge der Reformation in Siebenbürgen, Berlin: De Gruyter, forthcoming.

DINCĂ, ADINEL C. (2021), Dorfkirche und Schriftlichkeit in Siebenbürgen um 1500, in: Ulrich A. Wien (ed.), Common Man, Society and Religion in the 16th century. Piety, morality and discipline in the Carpathian Basin/Gemeiner Mann, Gesellschaft und Religion im 16. Jahrhundert. Frömmigkeit, Moral und Sozialdisziplinierung im Karpatenbogen, Göttingen: Vandenhoeck & Ruprecht, 39–54.

DONDI, CRISTINA (2016), Printed Books of Hours from Fifteenth-century Italy. The Texts, the Books, and the Survival of a Long-lasting Genre, Florence: Olschki.

DUBA, WILLIAM B. (2019), Fragmentarium, Das Mittelalter. Perspektiven mediävistischer Forschung, 24/1, 221–223.

DUFFY, EAMON (2006a), Marking the Hours: English People and Their Prayers 1240–1570, London: Yale University Press.

DUFFY, EAMON (2006b). Elite and popular religion: The Book of Hours and lay piety in the Later Middle Ages, Studies in Church History, 42, 140–161.

EHLICH, KONRAD (1993), Text und sprachliches Quellen. Die Entstehung von Texten aus dem Bedürfnis nach Überlieferung, in: Aleida Assmann/Jan Assmann/Christof Hardmeier (ed.), Schrift und Gedächtnis. Beiträge zur Archäologie der literarischen Kommunikation, München: Fink, 24–43.

EHRSTINE, GLENN (2012), Passion Spectatorship between Private and Public Devotion, in Elina Gertsman/Jill Stevenson (ed.), Thresholds of Medieval Visual Culture: Liminal Spaces, Woodbridge: Boydell and Brewer, 302–320.

ENENKEL, KARLA. E./MELION, WALTER (2010), Meditatio – Refashioning the Self: Theory and Practice in Late Medieval and Early Modern Intellectual Culture, Leiden: Brill.

ERDEI, KLÁRA (1990), Auf dem Wege zu sich selbst: Die Meditation im 16. Jahrhundert: Eine funktionsanalytische Gattungsbeschreibung, Wiesbaden: Otto Harrassowitz.

ERDÉLYI, GABRIELLA (2012) The Consumption of the Sacred: Popular Piety in a Late Medieval Hungarian Town, Journal of Ecclesiastical History 63/1, 31–60.

ERLER, MARY C. (1999), Devotional Literature, in: Lotte Hellinga/J. B. Trapp (ed.), The Cambridge History of the Book in Britain, Vol. III: 1400–1557, Cambridge: Cambridge University Press, 495–525.

FARA, ANDREA (2008), L'ordine e la Confraternita del Santo Spirito dalle origini allo sviluppo di una vocazione di frontiera ai confini orientali della Christianitas latina: la Transilvania tra Medioevo e prima Età moderna (XIV–XVI secolo), in: Cesare Alzati/Gabriella Rossetti (ed.), Profili istituzionali della santità medioevale. Culti importati, culti esportati e culti autoctoni nella Toscana Occidentale e nella circolazione mediterranea ed europea, Pisa: Edizioni ETS, 369–442.

FIREA, CIPRIAN/DINCĂ, ADINEL C. (2015–2016), Breslele artistice din Transilvania medievală și regulamentele lor. Un statut nou descoperit de la Bistrița, Ars Transsilvaniae, 28, 173–184.

FIREA, CIPRIAN (2012a), The Great Altarpiece of the Passion from Sibiu and its Painters, Brukenthal. Acta Musei, VII/2, 229–246.

FIREA, CIPRIAN (2012b), Liturgie médiévale et architecture gothique dans l'église paroissiale de Sibiu (1350-1550), in Arhitectura religioasă medievală din Transilvania/Középkori egyházi építészet Erdélyben/Medieval Ecclesiastical Architecture of Transylvania, V, Satu-Mare: Ed. Muzeului Sătmărean, 275–318.

FIREA, CIPRIAN (2013), Donatio pro memoria: Lay and Female Donors and their Remembrance in Medieval Churches of Transylvania. A Research on Visual and Documentary Evidence, Studia Universitatis Babeș-Bolyai. Historia, 58, 107–135.

FLOREA, CARMEN (2005), Relics at the Margins of Latin Christendom: the Cult of a Frontier Saint in the Late Middle Ages, Pecia, 8/11, Reliques et sainteté dans l'espace médiéval, 471–497.

FLOREA, CARMEN (2008), Identitate urbană și patronaj marian în evul mediu târziu, Studia Universitatis Cibiniensis. Series Historica V, 59–81.

FLOREA, CARMEN (2009), The Construction of Memory and the Display of Social Bonds in the Life of Corpus Christi Fraternity from Sibiu (Hermannstadt, Nagyszeben), in Lucie Doležalova (ed.), The Making of Memory in the Middle Ages, Leiden/Boston: Brill, 283–309.

FLOREA, CARMEN (2013a), Beyond the late medieval economy of salvation: the material running of the Transylvanian mendicant convents, Hereditas Monasteriorum 3, 97–110.

FLOREA, CARMEN (2013b), Civic Control of Sainthood in Late Medieval Transylvania, Studia Universitatis Babeș-Bolyai. Historia 58, 136–156.

GESTA (2009), Making Thoughts, Making Pictures, Making Memories: A Special Issue in Honor of Mary J. Carruthers, 48/2.

GROSS, JULIUS (1883), Katalog der von der Kronstädter Gymnasialbibliothek ausgestellten Druckwerke aus dem Reformationszeitalter, Kronstadt: Gött.

GROSS, JULIUS (1887), Zur ältesten Geschichte der Kronstädter Gymnasialbibliothek, Archiv des Vereins für siebenbürgische Landeskunde 21, 591–708.

166 | Adinel C. Dincă

GROSS, LIDIA (2003), Confreria Capitlului de Sibiu, Anuarul Institutului de Istorie "George Barițiu" – Series Historica, XLII, 161–170.

GÜNDISCH, GUSTAV (1987), Die Oberschicht Hermannstadts im Mittelalter, in: Gustav Gündisch, Aus Geschichte und Kultur der Siebenbürger Sachsen. Ausgewählte Aufsätze und Berichte, Köln/Wien: Böhlau, 182–200.

HABERKERN, ERNST (2003), Die "Wiener Schule" der Pastoraltheologie im 14. und 15. Jahrhundert: Entstehung, Konstituenten, literarische Wirkung, I–II, Göppingen: Kümmerle.

HAMM, BERNDT/LENTES, THOMAS (ed.) (2001), Spätmittelalterliche Frömmigkeit zwischen Ideal und Praxis, Tübingen: Mohr Siebeck.

HAUG, WALTER/WACHINGER, BURGHART (1993), Die Passion Christi in Literatur und Kunst des Spätmittelalters, Tübingen: M. Niemeyer.

HINDMAN, SANDRA/MARROW, JAMES (ed.) (2013), Books of Hours Reconsidered, Turnhout: Brepols.

JAKOBI-MIRWALD, CHRISTINE (2004), Das mittelalterliche Buch. Funktion und Ausstattung, Stuttgart: Reclam.

JENEI, DANA (2004), Art and Mentality in late Middle Age Transylvania, Getty-NEC Yearbook, 2000–2001, 2001–2002, București: NEC, 13–71.

JENEI, DANA (2014a), The Passion, Death and Resurrection of Jesus Christ painted inside St. Matthias Church in Râșnov (1500), Studii și Cercetări de Istoria Artei. Artă Plastică 4(48), 9–27.

JENEI, DANA (2014b), Thèmes iconographiques et images dévotionnelles dans la peinture murale médiévale tardive de Transylvanie (deuxième partie du XVe siècle – premier quart du XVIe siècle), Revue Roumaine d'Histoire de l'Art: Série Beaux-Arts, 51/1, 11–35.

KELLER, HAGEN/ GRUBMÜLLER KLAUS (ed.) (1992), Pragmatische Schriftlichkeit im Mittelalter. Erscheinungsform und Entwicklungsstufen, München: Fink.

KIECKHEFER, RICHARD (1989), Major Currents in Late Medieval Devotion, in: Jill Raitt et alii (ed.), Christian Spirituality: High Middle Ages and Reformation, vol. II: High Middle Ages and the Reformation, London: Routledge & Kegan Paul, 75–108.

KÜHNE, HARTMUT/ BÜNZ, ENNO / MÜLLER, THOMAS T. (ed.) (2013), Alltag und Frömmigkeit am Vorabend der Reformation in Mitteldeutschland. Katalog zur Ausstellung "Umsonst ist der Tod", Petersberg: Michael Imhof Verlag.

KÜHRER-WIELACH, FLORIAN (2015), Siebenbürgen als administrative Einheit und diskursives Konzept, in: Oliver Jens Schmitt/Michael Metzeltin (ed.), Das Südosteuropa der Regionen. Wien: Verlag der Österreichischen Akademie der Wissenschaften, 349–409.

LAUGERUD, HENNING / RYAN, SALVADOR / SKINNEBACH, LAURA KATRINE (ed.) (2016), The Materiality of Devotion in Late-Medieval Northern Europe: Images, Objects and Practices, Dublin: Four Courts.

LÄHNEMANN, HENRIKE (2016), The Materiality of Medieval Manuscripts, Oxford German Studies 45/2, 121–141.

LOBRICHON, GUY (1994), La religion des laïcs en Occident : XIe–XVe siècles, Paris: Hachette.

LUPESCU MAKÓ, MÁRIA (2001), "Item lego…". Gifts for the Soul in Late Medieval Transylvania, Annual of Medieval Studies at CEU 7, 161–185.

Lupescu Makó, Mária (2017), The Book Culture of the Dominican Order in Transylvania, Philobiblon: Transylvanian Journal of Multidisciplinary Research in Humanities 22/1, 187–204.

Marrow, James (1979), Passion Iconography in Northern European Art of the Late Middle Ages and Early Renaissance: A Study of the Transformation of Sacred Metaphor into Descriptive Narrative, Brussels: Van Ghemmert.

Martin, Jessica/Ryrie, Alec (ed.) (2012), Private and Domestic Devotion in Early Modern Britain, Farnham and Burlington, VT: Ashgate.

Müller, Friedrich (1877), Die Incunabeln der Hermannstädter "Capellenbibliothek", Archiv des Vereins für siebenbürgische Landeskunde N. F., 14, 293–358, 489–543.

Papahagi, Adrian/Dincă, Adinel C./Mârza, Andreea (2018), Manuscrisele medievale occidentale din România: Census [The Western Medieval Manuscripts in Romania: A Census], București: Polirom.

Papahagi, Adrian (2017), A Fragment of the Graduale Varadiense at the Romanian Academy Library in Cluj (Kolozsvár), Magyar Könyvszemle, 133, 455–459.

Pásztor, Lajos (1940), A magyarság vallásos élete a Jagellók korában [The religious life of Hungarians in the age of the Jagiellos], Budapest: Királyi Magyar Egyetemi Nyomda.

Possas, Stephanie (2018), Art of the Northern Renaissance: Courts, Commerce and Devotion, London: Laurence King Publishing.

Rehberg, Andreas (2012), Religiosi stranieri a Roma nel Medioevo: problemi e prospettive di ricerca, Rivista di storia della chiesa in Italia 66/1, 3–63.

Rittgers, Ronald K. (2012), The Reformation of Suffering: Pastoral Theology and Lay Piety in Late Medieval and Early Modern Germany, New York/Oxford: Oxford University Press.

Roth, Harald (1996), Kleine Geschichte Siebenbürgens, Köln/Weimar/Wien: Böhlau.

Rother, Christian (2002), Siebenbürgen und der Buchdruck im 16. Jahrhundert: mit einer Bibliographie "Siebenbürgen und der Buchdruck", Wiesbaden: Harrassowitz.

Sand, Alexa (2014), Vision, Devotion, and Self-Representation in Late Medieval Art, New York: Cambridge University Press.

Schreiner, Klaus (ed.) (1992), Laienfrömmigkeit im späten Mittelalter. Formen, Funktionen, politisch-soziale Zusammenhänge, München: R. Oldenbourg.

Schreiner, Klaus (ed.) (2002), Frömmigkeit im Mittelalter: Politisch-soziale Kontexte, visuelle Praxis, körperliche Ausdrucksformen, München: Fink.

Scott-Stokes, Charity (2006), Women's Books of Hours in Medieval England, Cambridge: Boydell & Brewer.

Simon, Zsolt (2007), Primele tipărituri din Transilvania (Sibiu, 1525), Anuarul Institutului de Istorie "George Barițiu" din Cluj-Napoca. Series Historica 46, 89–106.

Szende, Katalin (2018), Towns and Urban Networks in the Carpathian Basin between the Eleventh and the Early Sixteenth Centuries, in: Xavier Barral i Altet/Pál Lővei/Vinni Lucherini/Imre Takács (ed.), The Art of Medieval Hungary, Roma: Viella, 65–82.

Thayer, Anne T. (2012), The Medieval Sermon: Text, Performance and Insight, in: Joel Thomas Rosenthal (ed.), Understanding medieval primary sources: using historical sources to discover medieval Europe, London: Routledge, 43–58.

Tomaszewski, Jacek (2016), Girdle Books and Leather Overcovers in Poland. Relics and Iconographic Sources, Polish Libraries 4, 84–180.

TRIO, PAUL/SMET, MARJAN (ed.) (2006), The Use and Abuse of Sacred Places in Late Medieval Towns, Leuven: Leuven University Press.

VAN OS, HENK et alii (1994), The Art of Devotion in the Late Middle Ages in Europe. 1300–1500, Princeton, NJ: Princeton University Press.

VLAICU, MONICA/GÜNDISCH, KONRAD (ed.)(2007), Der Nachlaß Samuel von Brukenthals: Einblicke in Haushalt und Lebenswelt eines siebenbürgischen Gouverneurs der Barockzeit, Sibiu: Hora.

VULIĆ, KATHRYN R./USELMANN, SUSAN/GRISÉ, C. ANNETTE (ed.) (2016), Devotional Literature and Practice in Medieval England: Readers, Reading, and Reception, Turnhout: Brepols.

WEBB, DIANA (2005), Domestic Space and Devotion, in: S. Hamilton/A. Spicer (ed.), Defining the Holy: Sacred Space in Medieval and Early Modern Europe, Aldershot: Ashgate Pub, 27–47.

WETTER, EVELIN/SCHOLTEN, FRITS (ed.), (2017), Prayer Nuts, Private Devotion and Early Modern Art Collecting, Riggisberg: Abegg-Stiftung.

WETTER, EVELIN (2015), Liturgische Gewänder der Schwarzen Kirche zu Kronstadt in Siebenbürgen, 2 Vol., Riggisberg: Abegg-Stiftung.

WIECK, ROGER S. (2008), Prayer for the People: The Book of Hours, in Roy Hammerling (ed.), A History of Prayer: The First to the Fifteenth Century, Leiden / Boston: Brill, 389–416.

WILLIAMSON, BETH (2013), Sensory Experience in Medieval Devotion: Sound and Vision, Invisibility and Silence, Speculum, 88/1 1–43.

Paula Cotoi
Lucian Blaga University Library of Cluj, Romania

Cum oratis, dicite:
Sermons on Prayer in Late Medieval Transylvania and Hungary[1]

The study of devotional practices and, in particular, of the lay expression of piety, in medieval context usually involves two main approaches, determined by two major categories of sources: images and texts. While the visual material was analysed and discussed with respect to Transylvania in various occasions (Crăciun: 2005, 2010a, 2010b, 2010c, 2011, 2012; Firea: 2010, 2016), one would have to dig deep into the historiography to find at least some hints regarding the presence, nature and use of devotional literature in the Eastern periphery of the Medieval Latin *Christianitas*. Such circumstances are related, on the one hand, to the limited interest and insufficient research of medieval manuscripts and early printed books from this region and, on the other, to the actual absence of the most common textual supports of the devotional behaviour specific to the laity: books of hours and prayer books. Recent examination of book ownership suggests that the Transylvanian laity was not unfamiliar with this phenomenon although the practice was not necessarily widespread. However, even in those limited cases the written word did not function as a means of spiritual edification for the laity, who only assumed the role of donator (Cotoi: 2021). Such pious donations, testamentary bequests, as well as patronage of churches, chapels or altars (Lupescu Makó: 2001, 2004, 2013; Firea: 2013) – made in exchange for the clergy's intervention in favour of the salvation of their *benefactores* – seem to be the most consistent expressions of lay active religiosity in medieval Transylvania. While all these were individual acts and would have conveyed deeply personal choices, they manifested in the public sphere and seem to have entrusted the communication with God to the clergy.

Starting from these premises, in order to get a sense of what prayer could have meant for the Transylvanian laity, I will direct my attention towards sermons, as means of instruction of a wide range of lay audiences, accessible with the single

---

1 This work was supported by a grant of the Romanian National Authority for Scientific Research, CNDI – UEFISCDI, project PN-III-P4-ID-PCCF-2016-0064: 'Nașterea elitei intelectuale în Europa Centrală. Formarea profesorilor la Universitatea din Viena (1389–1450)/The Rise of an Intellectual Elite in Central Europe: Making Professors at the University of Vienna, 1389–1450'. I would like to thank Prof. Dr. Maria Crăciun for her valuable and constructive suggestions and comments on the manuscript of this study, as well as Sandy Gale (University of Bristol) for reading it and providing me with the perspective of the English sermons on the topic, helping me to identify further aspects to be explored.

condition of accomplishing one of the basic Christian duties, namely attending the Mass on Sundays and feast days. Written preaching material definitely served the needs of the clergy,[2] but their content was often addressed to the laity and reflected the message it plausibly received. In the following pages, I intend to examine the existence and circulation of homiletic literature addressing the topic of prayer in Transylvania and to scrutinize the content of the sermon collections written by two late medieval Hungarian authors, looking for the contexts in which the topic of praying was approached, specific problems they emphasized, and possible suggestions regarding concrete engagement of the laity in devotional matters. This approach conveys the possibility of exploring the level of clerical involvement in modelling lay piety and the intentions expressed in this respect, supplementing previous similar endeavours which focused mostly on the visual material.

Among the Medieval Latin manuscripts preserved in Transylvania, sermons are frequently found within composite codices which mirror a certain thematic or functional selection. Related to prayers, quite common examples are the homiletic texts commenting on the Lord's Prayer, such as Nicolaus de Dinkelsbühl's *De oratione dominica* or *Commentarius in Pater Noster* of the Dominican preacher known as Frater Siboto (Papahagi/Dincă/Mârza: 2018, nr. 347, 353, 469). Equally numerous are the expositions of the Apostles' Creed, like those authored by Nicolaus de Graetz or Iohannes de Kwidzyn (Papahagi/Dincă/Mârza: 2018, nr. 468, 470). Although not a prayer in the proper sense, it was perceived so in the Middle Ages (cf. Schmitt: 1981) and sermons on this topic could provide, alongside instruction on the basic articles of faith, explanations about the usefulness of its reciting (Reeves: 2010, 64). In the same category could be included the sermons on Psalms, either commenting on all of them or interpreting a single one, as Frater Siboto's *Sermones super psalmum Misere* (Papahagi/Dincă/Mârza: 2018, nr. 347, 469). These examples argue towards a catechetical function of preaching for which the explanation of the seven petitions from *Pater Noster* and of the dogmatic content of the *Credo* was essential. Such a purpose was a main feature of the sermons delivered in front of a lay audience, especially in a parish church (cf. Reeves: 2010, 41–42, 49–50; Thayer: 2010, 124), and it perfectly fitted the medieval contexts in which these manuscripts seem to have been used, namely two Transylvanian parishes pertaining to the Saxon communities of Sibiu (Hermannstadt, Nagyszeben) and Cisnădie (Heltau, Nagydisznód).

However, a more concrete concern for the practice of praying itself should not be excluded and Ms. 683 from the Brukenthal Library in Sibiu (Papahagi/Dincă/Mârza: 2018, nr. 487) could stand as evidence in this respect. Not only

---

2 The use of sermon collections as devotional reading, even by the laity (Valente Bacci: 1993, 319), is encountered in the late Middle Ages, but does not apply for the Transylvanian milieu (Cotoi: 2021).

of Transylvanian provenance, but also copied in this region, it comprises a great variety of texts, among which sermons or small treatises on religious topics are well represented. They include some writings of Robert Holcot on *Devota oratio* and *De impedimento orationis*. In addition, the manuscript appears to put a strong emphasis on penitence and devotional exercises, as suggested by the presence of two texts on confession, many others on temptations, vices and virtues, as well as of two treatises *de passione Christi* and a series of meditations by Alcherus Claravallensis. This kind of association with texts elaborating on Christ's Sorrows is not singular. To offer just one additional example, another manuscript from the same library (Ms. 657; Papahagi/Dincă/Mârza: 2018, nr. 470), containing two rare instances of personal sermons composed and delivered in Transylvania (cf. Reinerth: 1979, 2–5; Cotoi: 2019a, 164), also include *Expositio Symboli Apostolorum* of Nicolaus de Graetz, *Expositio symboli apostolorum* of Iohannes de Kwidzyn and an exemplum upon *Passio Christi*. Highly relevant for late medieval spirituality,[3] it might not be hazardous to assume this was also a beloved subject for Transylvanian preachers, with great potential for encouraging meditation and devotional exercises among parishioners.

The theme is also present in early printed books distributed in Transylvania soon after their availability on the market, although separate works on the subject are rather infrequent. An eloquent example is the text of the observant Franciscan Daniel Meyer (Agricola) entitled *Passio Domini nostri Iesu Christi secundum seriem quatuor evangelistarum,*[4] edited as an appendix to *Postilla super Epistolas et Evangelia totius anni* of Guillelmus Parisiensis, which at the beginning of the sixteenth century belonged to a priest from a Szeckler rural community in Transylvania (Spielmann et al.: 2001, G99). More specific preaching material about prayers is somewhat difficult to identify with precision, as the homiletic literature transmitted through the new media – a well-represented genre – usually came in the form of voluminous preaching anthologies, elaborating on virtually all religious and theological matters. These model sermon collections – conceived in order to support the pastoral tasks of those who were less trained[5] – also addressed

---

3 The subject was intensely studied in relation with the kind of devotion promoted by the mendicant orders, especially the Friars Minor, with *Devotio Moderna*, the cult of *Corpus Christi* and of Eucharist, exploring visual sources and the development of the iconography associated with such expressions of piety, as well as the vast literature inspiring prayer, contemplation, meditation (cf. Kieckhefer: 1989; Haug/Wachinger: 1993).

4 The work of this Swiss friar and preacher, with a clear homiletic function (cf. Landmann: 1927), seems to have enjoyed great popularity, being reprinted several times (VD 16: B 4701 – B 4721).

5 Prologues often mention such an intended audience, consisting especially of parish priests, and ownership marks from various copies testify that this goal was reached. In Transylvania as well, model sermon collections belonged in some instances to parish libraries, but were also part of what seems to have been small book collections of individual priests, as in the

172 | Paula Cotoi

the topic of prayer, as some of the Biblical readings assigned to specific Sundays and feast days brought the subject into discussion. In order to exploit this type of sources and to come into contact with the content itself, I chose as a case study, relevant for medieval Hungary and Transylvania, the homiletic works of Pelbartus de Themeswar (*ca.* 1435–1504) and Osvaldus de Lasko (*ca.* 1450–1511).

These two Observant Friars Minor, living in the second half of the fifteenth century in Hungary, became popular all over Europe thanks to the preaching aids they compiled and which successfully took advantage of the printing technology. Volumes preserved in Transylvania do not suggest that their sermons were preferred by the clergy from this province over those of other authors (Cotoi: 2019b). But although proximity does not seem to have greatly influenced the reception of their works, most likely since they were not printed locally, this proximity might be relevant in the sense of a shared cultural, intellectual and religious setting. The content of these sermon collections was previously tackled from similar positions, mainly by scholars interested in the origins of Hungarian literature and medieval religion in general.[6] Closer to my own intentions are some studies of Marie Madeleine de Cevins, who made use of the works of Pelbartus de Themeswar and Osvaldus de Lasko in her inquiries on the religiosity of lay people and on the role played by the Order of the Friars Minor in shaping popular piety in medieval Hungary (de Cevins: 2001; 2003; 2011). Her studies include even some references to prayer, which will be discussed in due course.

Both authors compiled full cycles of sermons *de tempore, de sanctis* and *quadragesimales*, gathered in distinct volumes with hundreds of ready-made discourses. The collection authored by Pelbartus, entitled *Pomerium* or *Sermones Pomerii*, started being published in 1489, while the one of Osvaldus – with the title *Biga salutis* – appeared from 1497 onwards. In addition, Pelbartus composed a separate work in honour of the Virgin who allegedly saved his life during a Plague outbreak, which could have functioned as a preaching aid as well.[7] Osvaldus on his part

---

case of the mentioned priest from a Szekler village owning the postils of Guillelmus Parisiensis.

6 Especially the collections comprising *sermones de sanctis* were investigated (Bárczi: 2009; Gecser: 2014; Dias: 2016), as a result of both a genuine interest in the local cults of saints, including those of Hungarian origin, and of the greater accessibility of these works after they were edited on-line on http://sermones.elte.hu.

7 Although the volume is organized as a treatise on the fundaments of Marian devotion, the structure of the comprised texts allowed for them to be used as sermons. Pelbartus himself in the prologue to *Pomerium* explains that he did not include Marian sermons in his new collection, as they can be found in *Stellarium*: *Scire quoque te volo quod de beata virgine Maria nullum sermonem in hoc opera conscripsi specialem pro hac ratione quia ex speciali devotione qua beatissime dei matri tenebar, precipuum librum nomine Stellarium corone beate virginis intitulatum iam antea conscripseram ubi pro singulis festivitatibus eiusdem gloriosissime virginis Marie abundantissimi extant sermones pro quibus illuc recurrendum iudicavi quem librum huic opera coniungendum dignum duxi* (Pelbartus: PH). Moreover, there is ev-

Cum oratis, dicite: | **173**

wrote one more sermon collection for Lent, *Gemma fidei,* discussing the demands of the good Christian. Different questions about prayer found their answers in all of these works.[8] However, only five sermons compiled by Pelbartus and five by Osvaldus are entirely dedicated to this matter.

During the liturgical year, the days preceding the feast of the Ascension and especially the foregoing Sunday represented habitually the context for preaching on prayer (Robinson: 2008). Accordingly, within the two collections of these Hungarian authors comprising *sermones dominicales,* those written for the Rogation Days offer the most extensive and in-depth discussions of the subject. Pelbartus de Temeswar included no less than four sermons for *Dominica Rogationum,* developing different arguments based on Biblical citations from the Gospel of John, while also proposing as alternative *themae* two verses from the Epistle of James. Osvaldus de Lasko, without precisely designating this Sunday as a special time consecrated to prayers, offered two sermons with quite elaborate structure, starting alike from John 16. This liturgical setting *per se* occasioned some reflections on the significance and effects of prayer, mirroring the motivations behind the institution of this feast. The theological and spiritual fundaments are related to the Ascension, which incited humans to raise their minds to God through prayers and also implied that Christ got closer to the Father, being able to intercede for people in front of Him. Therefore, litanies to angels and saints surrounding Him were intended to strengthen their intercession.[9] On a more pragmatic note, prayer in general and the rituals appointed for these days were alleged to intervene in removing harmful propensities and preventing unfortunate events frequent during that time of the year.[10] This kind of remarks were used only for introducing the topic of the ser-

---

    idence that texts from *Stellarium* were translated and incorporated in sermon collections (Mazurkiewicz: 2014).

8 As tables of contents of all their works, as well as some of the sermons were edited on-line, references to text will be given according to the style established in the edition, including the abbreviated form of the title, the number of the sermon and the section within the sermon, marked with a letter, allowing for the identification of the indicated passage in any of the medieval editions. For unedited sermons I will provide the transcription of relevant passages in footnotes.

9 *Sancta mater ecclesia hodie incipit diem vel festum Rogationum continuando usque ad festum Pentecostes. Unde hec dominica dicit rogationum. Hoc autem ordinavit primo propter propinquum diem Ascensionis Domini quod Christus in celum ascendit ad interpellandum pro nobis tanquam advocatus ut dicit Apostolus Hebrei VII. Et quod nos non possumus eum sequi in celum nunc corporaliter ascendendo, ideo ut sequemur saltem mente exorando ordinavit fieri rogationes pro hoc tempore quatenus ascendamus saltem mente, quod secundum Damascenum: Oratio est ascensus mentis in deum. Item, secundo, quod Christus in dextra Patris residens regnat cum omnibus beatis angelis et sanctis qui nos iuvant ad exaudiendum, suis intercessionibus, ideo etiam ecclesia hiis diebus rogationum letanias de singulis ordinibus angelorum et sanctorum diei processionaliter instituit* (Pelbartus: TP 27P).

10 *Primo quidem ut carnalis concupiscentia qua hoc tempore fervet magis in hominibus mortificetur per ieiunium et orationem. Secundo ut Dei iram quam pro peccatis nostris demeremur*

mons that further elaborated on subjects such as: the commandment of praying, trust in God's favorable answer, the relation of this response with merit, predestination, devotion and God's mercy, the virtues of prayer, good and bad petitions, the signs of God's love towards those who pray, reasons for one's eagerness for praying, hindrances to prayer and means of enhancing its effectiveness.

Besides, both authors dedicate a sermon for explaining the *Pater noster*, even though choosing different Sundays for this purpose, as the accounts regarding the institution of this prayer were not included among the readings appointed for the church year (Robinson: 2008, 448). Pelbartus considered the parable of the Pharisee and the Publican read in *Dominica X post Pentecostes* as a good pretext to approach in his second sermon for that day the worth and usefulness of reciting the Lord's Prayer. In his turn, Osvaldus discussed the subject in *Dominica XX post Pentecostes* in connection with one of Jesus' miracles recounted in the Gospel of John, the healing of a royal official's son, as a response to the father's plea. More than just clarifying in detail each of the seven petitions (Pelbartus: TA 29F-P; Osvaldus: OD 116Q), the authors demonstrate the importance of this prayer and the benefits of its reciting for the health of the body, the liberation of the soul and for worldly and heavenly achievements (Pelbartus: TA 29 R).

In addition, Osvaldus also used the period of Lent to answer questions on prayer throughout two entire sermons, one included in *Quadragesimale Bige salutis* – based on the third commandment *Memento ut diem sabbati sanctifices* – and the other in *Gemma fidei* – for the Tuesday of the Holy Week. If the one included in the collection, destined to clarify the precepts of good faith insists more on theological teachings and abstract aspects, the sermon from *Quadragesimale Bige salutis* is explicitly intended for *rusticanis et simplicibus populis*, teaching them what prayer is and which prayers to recite.

Other feasts and Biblical readings offered further occasions to include more specific matters on prayer among *divisiones*. St Stephen's feast provided the opportunity to speak about prayers for the enemies. Sermons on female saints enabled preachers to talk about women's special call to practice devotion. For instance, on the feast of St Dorothea, Osvaldus discussed how marriage can interfere with the fulfilment of pious duties (Osualdus: OS 26), while Pelbartus exhorts widows to pray like St Elizabeth (Pelbartus: PA 98G). St Francis is also presented as a model, for his spiritual achievements through frequent prayer and fervent meditation (Pelbartus: PA 72C). With a different approach, on St James's feast Pelbartus referred to his Epistle as well, including the passage about prayer. More generally, sermons *de sanctis* relate to their faculty of interceding in people's favour. If usually

---

avertamus, ne nobis Deus immittat guerras et bella qua hoc tempore solent magis exurgere vel etiam acres intemperiem et fructuum terre devastationem quam plus consuevit fieri his temporibus vel etiam pestilentias et mortem subitaneam (Pelbartus: TP 29K).

intercession is briefly mentioned, within the sermon for All Saints Day, Pelbartus discussed it thoroughly, as I shall point out later. Likewise, on the Day of the Dead, the two Hungarian authors commented on whether it is right or not to pray for the deceased and on the effects of prayer for souls in Purgatory (Pelbartus PA 86A, I; Osvaldus: OS 102, 103).

Instead of presenting each of these sermons, given that many questions are approached by both authors and reiterated in different contexts, I will further develop my argument by focusing on the treatment of specific matters, which concretely describe what clerics expected of the laity. Therefore, I choose to leave aside some rich demonstrations regarding more abstract notions that are rather informative about the theological training and positioning of the author. Translating such argumentations in more specific terms, the necessity of avoiding formalism in religious practices, which was most likely frequently encountered, was mainly emphasized. Hence, I will focus on four questions: what prayers were to be recited, when, where and how?

The clearest advice regarding the prayers a Christian should know and use are offered by Osvaldus de Lasko in *Quadragesimale Bige salutis*. Discussing *orationis quiditate*, the author states that for the simple people a single division is sufficient, including the three prayers established by the church for them: *oratio dominica, salutatio angelica, professio christiana*. Although only *Pater noster* was defined as a prayer in the proper sense, as the other two did not formulate any petitions,[11] their recitation was pleasing to the Holy Trinity[12] and necessary to salvation.[13] However, those who wanted to ask something of the Virgin Mary were provided with the right formula: *Regina celis, domina mundi, intercede pro me ad Deum qui te elegit* (Osvaldus: OQ 15T). Similar assistance was offered by Pelbartus, who, while making the difference between petitions that should be directed to God and the ones addressed to saints, also specifies the words that people should use: *Et propterea Ecclesia orando Deum vel Christum dicit: 'Miserere nobis' vel: 'Da nobis, quaesumus, Domine', et huiusmodi. Sed orans sanctos dicit: 'Orate vel intercedite pro nobis'* (Pelbartus: PA 82G). Returning to the three prayers, it is clear they were orally transmitted, learned by heart and recited from memory. Each sermon on the Lord's Prayer mentioned the obligation for each Christian to learn it, being excused only by means of *invincibili ignorantia*. Parents were responsible for teaching their children both the content and the interpretation, before the age of seven (Pelbartus: TA29D), together with the *Credo* and the Ten Commandments (Os-

---

11 *Et hec angelica salutatio proprie non est oratio, quod in ea non est aliqua petitio, sed quedam laudatio.*[…] *Tertia in super oratio est instituta comuni populo christiano fidei christiane confessio, que tamen improprie dicit oratio* (Osvaldus: OQ 15T).

12 *Angelica salutatio que quidem valde grata est Summe Trinitati* (Osvaldus: OQ 15T).

13 *Ipsa est ad salutem tam necessaria, quod sine ea nec elemosynarum largitio, nec prolixa oratio, nec carnis maceratio, imno nec mortis perpenssio valet ad salutem* (Osvaldus: OQ 15T).

176 | Paula Cotoi

valdus: OS 107 c04). In order to accomplish this obligation, Osvaldus de Lasko encourages his audience by emphasising the brevity of the prayer, which allowed for an easier recollection, a clearer understanding and a more zealous devotion, making it accessible to everyone.[14] Moreover, he teaches people to recite the *Pater noster* before any petition as *captatio benevolentie*.[15]

In addition to these three compulsory prayers, Osvaldus elaborates on possible modes of praying (*de orationis modalitate*), providing two models, in fact devotional exercises combining prayer and meditation. One of them, introduced as *Modus Corone Virginis Gloriose* was nothing else than the so-called Franciscan Crown or Rosary (Bracaloni: 1932), a series of sequential meditations on the seven joys of the Virgin intercalated by reciting one time the Lord's Prayer and ten times *Ave Maria* (Osvaldus: OQ 15U). Very popular during the later Middle Ages, the cult of the Rosary seems to have also gained the hearts of Transylvanian worshipers, especially lay women, being stimulated by the Order of the Friar Preachers, the traditional promoter of this devotion (Florea: 2011). The other pious exercise proposed by Osvaldus consisted of thirty-three phrases – corresponding to Christ's years spent on earth – which incited the devout to contemplate His life, each followed by one *Pater noster* and one *Ave Maria* (see Appendix II; Osvaldus: OQ 15U). The set of meditations begins with Christ's conception and the first nine phrases recount His life until the Baptism, with a clear emphasis on the Virgin. The ministry of Christ is brutally condensed in a single sentence simply stating that He was baptized, He preached and performed miracles, while the greatest part of the text (twenty-three sequences) focuses on the Passions, evoking the events starting with the Holy Supper until the Ascension. This resembles the *vita Christi* rosaries, dating back to as early as the beginning of the fourteenth century, but widespread especially towards the end of the fifteenth century, which knew various versions, with higher or lesser numbers of meditations, usually combining scenes from the life of the Saviour and of the Virgin. This type of contemplation technique marked a shift from a Marian devotion to an exercise of *imitatio Christi* aiming to inspire not only fervent affection towards God, but also a life shaped on Christ's model (Winston: 1993; 1998, 26–30), which naturally fitted the preaching of an Observant Franciscan. The included episodes put a strong emphasis on the pain Christ

---

14 *Primo, fecit eam Christus sic brevem pro faciliori recordatio et hoc quo ad memoriam ut scilicet homo faciliter addiscat doctrinam salutis sue atque inexcusabili sit de eius ignorantia [...] Secundo, Christus dominus hanc orationem dominicam voluit tam brevem institere pro clariori cognitione et hoc quo ad intelligentiam, facilius enim intelliguntur a simplicibus brevia quam prolixa et involuta. [...] Tertio, Christus, Deus noster, brevem instituit orationem pro ferventiori devotione et hoc quo ad voluntatem plerumque enim per orationis prolixitatem devotion impeditur* (Osvaldus: OD 116P).

15 *Ipsa dominica oratio commendatur a captanda benivolentie rationabilitate, sicut enim homines petituri aliquid ab aliquot prius premittunt ipsius commendationem ut capta benivolentia facilius impetrent.* (Osvaldus: OD 116P).

Cum oratis, dicite: | 177

had to endure. For instance, when praying in the Garden of Gethsemane Jesus is described as sweating blood. Moreover, the crucifixion is thoroughly presented in no less than four phrases. This insistent focus on Christ's suffering, mirroring the iconography of *Christus Patiens* (Derbes: 1996, 5–8, 64–68), together with several allusions to His nudity and repeated mentions of the ropes used in His torture not only tone with the Franciscan spirituality and imagery, but are also recurrent motifs in the Passion cycles depicted on Transylvanian altarpieces (Crăciun: 2008, 197–201; 2010b, 25–27). The narrative form of the text associated with these devotional exercises, invoking a familiar story, easy to be visualized, combined with prayers which were anyways mandatory could provide a successful recipe for an illiterate audience (Winston: 1998, 30). Included in a sermon meant to be preached during Lent, this exercise was probably intended to help worshipers prepare for Easter. However, when offering advice for women's pious behaviour Pelbartus (PA 124I) also mentioned *orationis frequentia, cum devota passionis Christi memoria,* suggesting this was a theme to be always remembered during prayers. More intriguing is the structuring of the religious exercise presented by Osvaldus de Lasko according to canonical hours, echoing the pursuit of the ideal of imitating monastic life in the ordinary routine of the laity. To a certain point it also resembles the Hours of the Cross included in the Book of Hours. The fact that Osvaldus de Lasko considered it appropriate to reproduce two entire prayers in his sermons suggests a consciousness of the potential or even necessity of preaching as substitute for such written texts.

In a society which cherished the memory of its predecessors and, moreover, expressed a constant concern for assuring the remembrance after death as part of its efforts towards salvation (cf. van Bueren: 2005; Gordon/Marshall: 2000; Geary: 1994), sermons had to provide guidance regarding the prayer for the dead. The two Hungarian authors approached this topic within the model discourses for the Day of the Dead, as well as in the ones about prayer in general. Even though praying for one's fellowman / woman was considered proof of *charitas,* not all petitions for the deceased were welcomed.[16] While the souls of the righteous, spending time in Purgatory, benefited from the prayers,[17] those who were damned could not be saved.[18] Quoting Augustinus, Pelbartus compared praying for the souls believed to be in hell with praying for the devil (Pelbartus: PA 82F; TP 30Z). Likewise, people were advised not to pray for those who lived a saintly life on earth, as this

---

16 *In duplici statu existentibus nullo modo est orandum, videlicet existentibus in beatitudine et existentibus in eterna damnatione* (Osvaldus: OD 64I).
17 *Orandum est pro animabus purgandis que acerbissime affliguntur ab igne Purgatorii.* (Osvaldus: OD 64I) *Sed pro fidelibus defunctis in purgatorio existentibus orandum est, quod indigent suffragiis vivorum et orationibus ut liberentur* (Pelbartus: TP 30Z).
18 *Non est orandum pro damnatis, quod pro illis solum orare debemus pro quibus impetrare presumimus.* (Osvaldus: OD 64I).

178 | Paula Cotoi

would be proof of disrespect and distrust in their salvation.[19] Regarding prayers that could provide help to the dead, Osvaldus offered further explanations, clearly emphasising the superiority and greater effectiveness of the *missa pro defunctis*, which also comprised specially formulated prayers (Osvaldus: OS 102).

Even if without indications concerning the specific words to be pronounced, prayers to saints are often mentioned. Both authors advised on the content of petitions addressed to saints, excluding grace and glory as gifts offered by God alone (Osvaldus: OD 63B; Pelbartus: 82G). Pelbartus de Themeswar goes into more details explaining even which saints should be implored in order for the prayer to be effective. In this regard, Marie Madeleine de Cevins (2011, 82) has drawn the conclusion that the two Hungarian preachers "opposed the view that prayers should be made to one saint in a specific context". Answering whether it is more useful to invoke the protection of a major saint, rather than of a minor one, Pelbartus' final response is that all saints are helpful and appealing to many of them cannot be other than beneficial. However, the entire demonstration is more complex, showing that experience proves that devotion of the worshiper weighs more than the rank of the one addressed. Consequently, if one feels closer to a minor saint and thus prays to him more fervently, the benefits are easier to reap. Furthermore, Pelbartus argues that God's will is for us to honour the smaller saints as well and so some of them were assigned to intervene on behalf of and patronise specific issues (Pelbartus: PA 82F). Therefore, people were instructed that in certain needs they could ask for the intercession of any Holy figure, as well as of particular saints.

This leads us to the second question: when should lay people pray? A first answer is indirectly offered by the contexts implied by these sermons. Beside the Rogation Days, all Sundays were to be honoured with prayers (de Cevins: 2001, 126–127), as proven by the *thema* chosen by Osvaldus for his Lent sermon *de oratione*, namely the third commandment. Not accidentally, issues related to praying are also included in the immediately previous discourse based on the same Biblical quotation (Osvaldus: OQ 14P) and in the seventy ninth sermon from the collection *de tempore*, for the second Sunday after Pentecost entitled *De missa* (Osvaldus: OD 79N). Explicitly, Pelbartus addressed this question in his third sermon for *Dominica Rogationum*,[20] under the second *distinctio* concerning the obligation of praying. He first refers to the law of the Holy Scriptures, which demanded

---

19 *Tertio quod in eis nulla est eventus dubietas, non enim est dubium quin eternaliter in ipsa beatitudine sint permansuri et ideo pro beatis orandum non est. Hinc Augustinus ait "Iniuria est pro martyre in ecclesia orare"* (Osvaldus: OD 64I). *Item nec pro beatis orandum est quod ut Augustinus dicit: "Iniuriam facit martyri qui orat pro martyre", ratio quod ipsi adepti sunt beatitudinem quam impossibile est eis perdere* (Pelbartus: TP 30Z).

20 On a more general note, in his second sermon for *Dominica infra octavas Epiphaniae*, Pelbartus asks: *quo tempore debet quaeri Christus, ut inveniatur?* His answer refers to a spiritual time of mercy, penitence and grace and insists on the need to search for God during life and not expect for death to come as then it might be too late (Pelbartus: TH 21O).

that the faithful honour Sundays, and in this respect the sermon taught people to pray on feast days, while attending church services.[21] Secondly, according to *lege instructionis apostolice*, humans were called to pray without ceasing. This demand was further clarified in relation with four rules which should be observed: 1. celebrating every day the Divine Office, a rule which applied to the clergy and to members of religious orders; 2. keeping one's special vow of prayer; 3. fulfilling the praying obligations related to penitence by obeying the confessor; 4. praying in accordance with free will, without any certain obligations.[22] Summarizing, Pelbartus concludes that each Christian is required to pray on feast days, as much as his/her conscience dictates him/her and as much as it takes to avoid sin (Pelbartus: TP 29P), therefore outlining moderate requirements for the laity. Similarly, the devotional exercises recommended by Osvaldus de Lasko were intended for *festivis diebus*. The same author provides further detail on the time people were expected to pray, instructing that prayers were not to be recited during the Mass (de Cevins: 2001, 131; 2011, 81). Worshipers were exhorted to focus on the words of the celebrant and pay attention even when they could not properly hear everything.[23] However, the author notes that, if performed with great devotion, a prayer said during the liturgy is unlikely to be a mortal sin, excepting the case when someone intended to fulfil multiple praying obligations at one time (such as the Divine Office or prayers imposed as penitence).[24] Therefore a distinction is made between the act of praying as a form of participation in the liturgy, considered so when Osvaldus allowed for people to pray while the priest recited in silence, and as a

---

21 Likewise, Osvaldus commenting on the third commandment explains: *Ecclesia ordinavit certum tempus orationi videlicet dies festivos* (Osvaldus: OQ 14P).

22 *Prima regula, de persolvendo divino officio et hec obligat illos qui tenentur, videlicet primo omnes beneficia tenentes ecclesiastica etiam si non sint ordinati* [...] *Et secundo omnes in sacris ordinibus constituti etiam si non sint beneficiati. Tertio religiosi. Secunda regula, de implendo voto orationis specialiter facto ab aliquo talis enim ad istud tenetur. Tertia de oratione iniuncta in penitentie sacramento.* [...] *Quarta regula, de oratione libero arbitrio facienda sine obligamento ut talibus attendatur orantis devotio* (Pelbartus: TP 29P). Osvaldus instructs in the same manner: *Sed quid aut quantum debet orare ecclesia non determinavit, nisi quod viri ecclesiastici tenentur dicere horas canonicas, alii vero ea que illis in penitentia sunt iniuncta vel ad que ex voto sunt obligati.* (Osvaldus: OQ 14P).

23 *Quomodo missa audiri debeat? Respondetur quod cum devotione et attentione, ut scilicet attendat ad verba que sacerdos alte dicit, non tunc debet orare. Et dicat quis non intelligo sacerdotis verba, quare ergo non debeam orare. Dico quod propter effectum divini verbi. Nam et serpens non intelligit verba incantantis, sed si audierit non potest incantanti nocere* (Osvaldus: OD 79N).

24 *Utrum audiens missam dicendo suas orationes satisfaciat huic precepto? Respondetur quod non, tamen si dicat ex devotione aliquas orationes infra missam non credo quod peccet mortaliter. Sed si dicat illas ad quas tenetur, sicut horas canonicas vel oratio in penitentia iniuncta, talis non excusatur tunc a mortali, pro eo quod tenetur ad audiendum missam et etiam tenetur ad illas orationes, ideo non satisfacit simul pro duobus debitis* (Osvaldus: OQ 14N).

form of distraction, when the focus moved from the liturgy to a different scope.[25] Discussing the topic in terms of being or not a mortal sin, these considerations suggest that collective prayer was somehow superior to that recited individually.

Such a hierarchy is also visible in instructions concerning the places where people should pray. Whereas the omnipresence of God implied that Christians could address him anywhere and no specific place was necessary for God Himself,[26] a special location was however necessary to worshipers. Both Pelbartus de Themeswar and Osvaldus de Lasko elaborated on this subject in their model sermons *de dedicatione ecclesie*. The two authors explained that prayers pronounced in a consecrated place were more prone to obtain a favourable answer since people could achieve there a higher state of devotion thanks to images and the Eucharist. These two elements not only inflamed worshipers' religious fervour, but also meant that Christ was present in flesh and blood, listening to people's petitions (Pelbartus: PA 103B). Since especially in the later Middle Ages the Eucharist became the object of adoration,[27] desired and experienced through all senses (Rubin: 1991), such an argument must have been particularly convincing. Secondly, in the church Christians could benefit from the help of all saints whose relics were present in the altar,[28] who were buried there, who were depicted in frescoes and, last but not least, of the saint to whom the church was dedicated. Thirdly, collective prayer was more effective, as people joined forces towards the same purpose (Pelbartus: PA 103B; Osvaldus: OS 112). If the context in which these sermons were to be delivered – the consecration of a church – naturally implied an exposition of arguments in favour of the usefulness of the church, such instructions are still informative regarding the appropriate ambiance for devotional exercises, especially concerning the importance and functionality of images. On a more general note, Pelbartus mentioned somewhere else that God could not be found in vitiated places, such as markets where vanities, fraud and slander prevailed or taverns where the devil resided, but rather where He lives, in places where there is harmony, in churches and wherever people gather in His name (Pelbartus: TH 21N). Instructions of the two authors regarding appropriate places for prayers fit

---

25 It has been alluded that because the Mass was recited in Latin and frequently in an inaudible voice (aspect evoked by Osvaldus as well), it was hard for laymen to hear, understand and get involved, so they began saying their own prayers (Crockett: 1989, 122).

26 *Ad Deum non est necessarius locus aliquis ad orandum deputandus, quia ubicumque, sive in agro, sive in domo, sive etiam in lecto, quo iaces, aut in carcere optime et aeque bene adorari potest Deus* (Pelbartus: PA 103B).

27 The articulation of such a Eucharistic devotion in Transylvania was explored mainly in relation with the iconography, Maria Crăciun (2005, 2010c) approaching the altarpieces, while recently Anna Kónya (2017) examined wall paintings in Transylvanian churches. Regarding the cult of the Eucharist in connection with Corpus Christi see Firea (2018) and Florea (2009).

28 Godefridus J. C. Snoek (1995, 353–380) argues that veneration of relics is to a certain point comparable with that of the Eucharist, in the same sense of *presentia realia*.

Cum oratis, dicite: | **181**

well within an evolution described by Patrick Henriet (2006: 204–205) as "spatialisation de la prière".

Finally, the two Hungarian authors offered advice regarding the manner in which Christians should or could pray. Two distinctions, partially overlapping, are involved in the description and definition of such manners: vocal/mental, public/private. While for Pelbartus the vocal prayer was equivalent with public devotion, and the silent, mental one with individual exercises of piety[29] – similar to the position expressed by Nicolaus de Lyra in his Postils (Saenger: 1989, 143) –, for Osvaldus the use of the spoken word did not essentially distinguish between public and private, but was a means of expression. In what the *oratio communis* was concerned, words had to be pronounced out loud by the celebrants in order for participants to hear, understand and not get distracted. On the other hand, the personal engagement in pious practices could be limited to a mental exercise and the voice was to be added in order to arouse devotion, display reverence and express affection (Osvaldus: OD 63E), in agreement with Hugo de Saint Victor (Saenger: 1989, 143). Coming from a Friar Minor, such a perspective seems somewhat surprising, given that within the Order instructions about prayer tended to establish an opposite hierarchy, in which meditation and mental prayer reflected a higher stage of spiritual progress (cf. Roest: 2007). This shift could indicate that they did not expect the laity to reach the same spiritual level. Moreover, for the two Hungarian authors the use of the spoken word was more of a formal aspect, less significant than the intention of prayer, the content of petitions and the inner state of the worshiper. Therefore, when discussing the demand for attention during prayer they did conform to this view, sketching a hierarchy in which the lower level meant paying attention to words, the intermediate one involved paying attention to their meaning and the optimal approach was to focus on the final goal of prayer, which was God or the (spiritual) things intended to be achieved through prayer (Pelbartus: TP 28G; Osvaldus: OD 63F). In fact, avoiding formalism was one of their main concerns, usually translated into advice on what is good to ask God. Spiritual benefits were constantly presented as pleasant supplications, while *temporalia* were to be requested with great care and only if useful for salvation (Pelbartus: TP 28E, TP 29N, PH 26F, PA 34F; Osvaldus: 63A). Furthermore, Christians were exhorted to demonstrate perseverance and patience in prayers, to address God with faith and humility (Pelbartus: TP 28D; Osvaldus: OD 64H), all opposite attitudes being presented as *impedimenta orationis* (Pelbartus: TP 30T; Osvaldus: OD 63G). Little is said about gestures and only in connection with Mass attendance, in which context Osvaldus insisted that people had to stand during the

---

29 *Preceptum ergo legis nature obligat hominem ad orandum saltem mentaliter et communiter, etiam orare vocaliter quod communes homines non possunt habere mentalem orationem* (Pelbartus: TP 29P).

182 | Paula Cotoi

reading of the Gospel (Osvaldus: OD 79N). Similarly, almost nothing is revealed about the use of books for praying. A single *exemplum* provided by Pelbartus mentions a friar who avoided sadness and bad disposition by praying and reading from the books received from his master. More relevant for the laity might be one of Osvaldus' remarks, instructing that during the liturgy when the celebrants pray out loud Christians should not read anything else.[30] On the other hand, the function of images is better emphasized. In strict relation with prayer, Pelbartus argued that the presence of visual representations of Christ and the saints within churches was able to incite worshipers' devotion and to ensure the intercession of those depicted. In at least two other sermons the same author referred to paintings as *libri laicorum* (Pelbartus: PH 44E, PA 68I), while also requesting preachers in various instances to use images when addressing their audiences (Ádám: 2009).

To sum up, both homiletic texts preserved in Transylvania and those composed in Hungary display a centrality of the Lord's Prayer, accompanied by the Apostle's Creed and Hail Mary. Not only were these three prayers introduced as the most important ones, comprising the compulsory doctrinal apparatus for a good Christian, but they were also almost the sole clear recommendations in terms of lay practice of piety. While these prayers were memorized and transmitted orally, sermons could have supported their learning and a more conscious reciting, constantly reminding worshipers the meaning of their words. A second observation is that the most elaborate sermons about prayer are those composed for Rogation Sunday, since this was a day specially dedicated to prayer and also the single moment in the liturgical calendar when the Epistle (Jas 1:22–27) and the Gospel (John 16:23–33) directly prompted the approach of the subject in the sermon. Articulated in a context of public devotion *par excellence*, all exhortations towards praying would have been primarily perceived as incitements to join the collective religious exercises, which would become more effective and pleasant to God as participants got an in-depth understanding of their acts and set their minds on the right direction and intention. The message itself focused usually on the most common form of public devotion, attendance of the Mass, during which individual prayer had to be reduced to moments when the priest recited in silence. Then, the moments when prayers were required are feast days, nothing being said about the rest of the time. Therefore, intentions towards shaping the engagement of the laity in devotional practices seem to reflect more a need of controlling lay behaviour, than an encouragement of individual, private actions, a situation that might be associated with the evolution of the prayer described by Patrick Henriet (2006, 204) as "une cléricalisation de la prière. S'il n'y a pas confisçation, il y a bien hiérarchisation et spécialisation à outrance". The single detailed account of a more complex

---

30 *Propterea utilius est illi qui audit missam quod cum sacerdos in missa aliquid alte dicit tunc ipse nihil legat* (Osvaldus: OQ 14N).

recommendation for private devotion consists of the models offered by Osvaldus in his sermon for Lent. If the practice of the Rosary is attested in Transylvania by the existence of a confraternity and of a chapel dedicated to it (Florea: 2011; Crăciun: 2012), contemplative exercises involving meditation on the life or passions of Christ might have also been a reality, since texts on such matters existed in medieval book collections, frequently associated with preaching aids. Although not explicitly presented as such by Osvaldus, the meditations he suggested might have been performed by the laity during *Quadragesima,* a period of intensified manifestations of piety, which could stimulate religious acts in preparation for the yearly communion. It was already demonstrated that the Passion cycle, depicted in versions characteristic for the Franciscan visual repertoire, penetrated the iconography present in Transylvanian altarpieces produced at the end of the fifteenth and the beginning of the sixteenth century, receiving special attention and being used during the Holy Week (Crăciun: 2008, 2010b, 2012). Therefore, it might be right to assume that in this particular time of the year the theme of Christ's Passions was exploited by all means and senses: displayed to be seen, preached to be heard, invoked in meditations and prayers to be mentally and emotionally perceived. On a different page, this means that laity was exposed to the same discourse transmitted via different channels and while prayer books for their use seem to have been missing, sermons and images together could have supplemented this lack.

Although written sermons do not always mirror spoken discourses and the response of the audience is almost impossible to grasp, their content discloses ideas that became common at a certain time and place. This is particularly true for model sermon collections which reflect the kind of predication regularly performed in front of lay people, able to produce impact over time (D'Avray: 1995). Hence, the sermons compiled by Pelbartus de Themeswar and Osvaldus de Lasko might not have been delivered in front of Transylvanian laymen. However, the fact that they encapsulate, more than the vision of these two authors, a shared understanding of prayer, spread throughout Hungary and mostly among the Friars Minor combined with a proven sympathy of Transylvanian people towards mendicants (Crăciun: 2011a; Florea: 2011), makes them a valuable source. Describing an ideal and setting a standard, the messages about prayers transmitted by the two Hungarian authors imply rather limited expectations concerning the laity's involvement in religious matters. However, they suggest a substantial involvement of the clergy in shaping the devotional life of the laity and especially a firm commitment of the mendicants, or at least the Franciscans, towards the pastoral mission. All the elements summarized in the previous paragraph build up the image of a prayer which can be broadly described by two words: oral and collective. In the light of these sermons, prayers would have been recited from memory and possibly assisted by images, occurring more often in churches, while private acts of this kind seem rather exceptional. Less inclined to contemplation, but still not simply liturgical, the kind of piety described

184 | Paula Cotoi

by these sermons fits within the devotional type defined by Kieckhefer (1996) and specific for the late Middle Ages. However, among the three main manifestations of devotion emphasized by the mentioned author – literary expression, artistic depiction and performance – the last two seem to have been of greater importance for Transylvania, while devotional texts might have been transmitted more often orally and preaching must have played an important role, as 'although there were many laypeople who might read the ever-proliferating devotional literature of the age, there were far more who would gladly have it preached to them' (Kieckhefer: 1996, 77). After all, attending sermons was itself a pious act.

Appendix I.

Sermons entirely dedicated to prayer within the collections of Pelbartus de Themeswar and Osvaldus de Lasko

Pelbartus de Temeswar

Sermones Pomerii de Tempore. Pars pascalis

- Sermo XXVII. Dominica Rogationum sermo I, iuxta evangeliam de orationis fiducia et dei complacentia ac potentia
  Amen amen dico vobis si quid petieritis patrem in nomine meo dabit vobis (John 16:23).
- Sermo XXVIII. De eadem dominica sermo II, de orationis exauditione certa conditione et dilectione Dei.
  Siquid petieritis Patrem in nomine meo dabit vobis (John 16:23).
- Sermo XIX. De eadem dominica sermo III, scilicet de orationis inductione, obligatione et fructificatione.
  Petite et accipietis ut gaudium vestrum sit plenum (John 16:24).
  Multum valet deprecatio iusti assidua (Jas 5:16).
- Sermo XXX. De eadem dominica sermo IIII, scilicet de orationis impedimentis et eius sanctitate ac commendatione.
  Usque modo non petistis quicque in nomine meo petite et accipietis (John 16:24).
  Petitis et non acciptitis, eo quod male petatis (Jas 4:3).

Sermones Pomerii de Tempore. Pars aestivalis

- Sermo XXIX. Dominica eadem [i.e. Dominica X post Pentecosten] sermo II, scilicet de orationis dominice dignitate et salubri utilitate.
  Duo homines ascenderunt in templum ut orarent. (Luke 18:10).
  Sic enim orabitis: Pater noster qui es in celi sanctificetur nomen tuum (Matt 6:9).
  Cum orates, dicite: Pater sanctificetur nomen tuum (Luke 11:2).

Osvaldus de Lasko

Sermones dominicales Biga salutis intitulatis

- Sermo LXIII. Dominica quinta post Pasca
  Amen amen dico vobis quid petieritis Patrem in nomine meo dabit vobis (John 16:23).
- Sermo LXIIII. De eadem dominica quinta
  Petite et accipietis ut gaudium vestrum sit plenum (John 16:24).
- Sermo CXVI. De eadem dominica XX post Pentecosten,
  Erat quidam regulus cuius fillis infirmabatur Capharnaum. Hic cum audisset quod Iesus venire ad Iudea in Galileam abiit ad eum et rogabat eum ut descenderet et sanaret filium eius (John 4:46–47).

Quadragesimale Bige salutis

- Sermo XV – in presenti sermone gratia dei de oratione tria daremus salutis documenta
  Memento ut diem sabbati sanctifices (Exod 20:8).

Quadragesimale Gemma fidei

- Sermo LIX. Feria tertia maioris hebdomadae de orationis congruentia, quod congruit orare Deum, probant auctoritates, rationes, distinctiones et exempla. Et quam multae sunt orationis efficaciae.
  Dico vobis: Omnia, quaecumque orantes petitis, credite (Mark 11:24).

Appendix II.

An example of private devotional exercise provided by Osvaldus de Lasko[31]

[…] Unde si vis de salute certus esse certitudine fidei et virtutibus ac devotione sublimari, tunc cum bona intentione festivis saltem diebus mente elevate intendas Deum et Dominum nostrum Iesum Christum cum dominica oratione glorificare hoc modo:

Primo, incipias a Summa Trinitate ut cuncta nostra oratio et actio ab ipso incipiat et per ipsum finiatur. Et ideo dic tria *Pater noster* et totidem *Ave Maria.* Deinde incipias meditare Christum Dominum in humanitate et ad singula inferius notanda dic unum *Pater noster* et unum *Ave Maria.* Primo igitur:

I. Cogita angelicam salutationem, virginis consensionem et dominicam conceptionem. *Pater noster. Ave Maria.*

---

31 The text is edited from Osvaldus de Lasko, Quadragesimale Bige salutis, Hagenau: Henricus Gran, 1501, ff. g2r–g3 r.

186 | Paula Cotoi

II. Meditare quomodo virgo beata concepto filio Elisabet visitavit et ibi Deum iubilando laudavit. *Pater noster. Ave Maria.*

III. Contemplare quomodo virgo in Bethleem Deum et hominem genuit adoravit et in presepio reclinavit. *Pater. Ave.*

IV. Cogita quomodo Christus octavo die circumciditur, sanguis illius effunditur ac eius nomen publicatur. *Pater. Ave.*

V.   Quomodo Christus tertio decimo die a magis adoratur, remunerator et pia collocutio cum virgine tractatur. *Pater noster. Ave Maria.*

VI. Quomodo virgo pia quadragesima die filium in templum presentavit. Symeon cognovit et de eo prophetavit. *Pater noster. Ave Maria.*

VII. Quomodo mater virgo Christum lactavit, balneavit ac in Egyptum angelo revelante portavit. *Pater noster. Ave Maria.*

VIII. Quomodo in Egypto Christum nutrivit et post septem annos inde iterum reportavit. *Pater noster. Ave.*

IX. Quomodo anno duodecimo in templo mater filium amisit et cum dolore quesitum invenit. *Pater noster. Ave Maria.*

X.   Quomodo tricesimo anno a Johanne est baptisatus, in predicatione fatigatus ac miracula operatus. *Pater noster. Ave Maria.*

Ad matutinum hec meditare

XI. Quomodo in cena legem veterem terminavit, pedes discipulorum lavit ac sacrum altaris consecravit. *Pater noster. Ave Maria.*

XII. Quomodo in monte oliveti devote oravit, angelus ipsum confortavit ac sanguinem sudavit. *Pater noster. Ave.*

XIII. Quomodo a Iuda osculatur, a iudeis capitur et a discipuli suis derelinquitur. *Pater. Ave.*

XIV. Quomodo ad Annam est ductus, ibi examinatus ac a servo alapis cesus. *Pater. Ave.*

XV. Quomodo inde ad Caypham ducitur, ibi examinatur, false accusatur, ceditur et a Petro negatur. *Pater noster. Ave Maria.*

XVI. Quomodo pie matri captivitas filii nunciatur, qua lacrymans cum suis filium visura regreditur Hierusalem. *Pater noster. Ave Maria.*

Hore prime meditatio

XVII. Quomodo mane Christum iterum examinaverunt ac dominum ad Pylatum turpiter duxerunt. *Pater noster Ave Maria.*

XVIII. Quomodo Iesum Pylatus examinatum, ad Herodem misit, quem ille examinatum veste alba illusit. *Pater Noster. Ave Maria.*

Hora tertie

XIX. Quo Herodes Christum ilusum Pylato remisit et ille interrogatum flagellari iussit. *Pater noster. Ave Maria.*

Cum oratis, dicite: | **187**

XX.   Quomodo Christus flagellatur purpura induitur, spinis coronatur, alapis et arundine ceditur et ad mortem sententiatur. *Pater noster. Ave Maria.*

XXI.   Quomodo crucem baiulat, mater illi obviat et usque mortis locum associat. *Pater. Ave.*

Hora sexte

XXII.   Quomodo ante crucem denudatur, oratione effuse in cruce extenditur ac dextra illius manus conclavatur. *Pater noster. Ave Maria.*

XXIII.   Quomodo sinistra Christi manus nudi et spinis coronati fune tracta transfigitur. *Pater. Ave.*

XXIV.   Quomodo pedes Christi funibus ad foramen tracti, primum pes dexter confoditur. *Pater. Ave.*

XXV.   Quomodo tandem pes Christi sinister dure confoditur et sic Christus crucifixus elevatur. *Pater noster. Ave Maria.*

Hora none

XXVI.   Quomodo Christus a iudei blasphematur et in cruce a latrone irridetur, a suis deplangitur et moritur. *Pater noster. Ave Maria.*

XXVII.   Quomodo Christum in cruce post mortem vulneraverunt unde sanguis et aqua fluxerunt. *Pater noster. Ave Maria.*

Hora vesperarum

XXVIII. Quomodo Christus de cruce deponitur coram matre nudus statuitur et in sinum ponitur a qua deplangitur. *Pater noster. Ave.*

Hora completorii

XXIX.   Quomodo a Christi corpore sanguinis extergitur, unguento ungitur, linteo involuitur et sepelitur. *Pater noster. Ave Maria.*

XXX.   Quomodo Christi sepulcrum lapide grandi custodibus et sacerdotum sigillis munitur. *Pater noster. Ave Maria.*

XXXI.   Quomodo Christi anima in limbum ad patres descendit et eos sua divinitate beatificavit. *Pater noster. Ave Maria.*

XXXII.   Quomodo Christus tertia die resurrexit, pie matri ac discipulis apparuit et se eisdem declaravit. *Pater noster. Ave Maria.*

XXXIII. Quomodo Christus in die ascensionis suos discipulos benedixit et coram illis in celum ascendit. *Pater noster. Ave Maria.*

Hec sunt trigintatria *Pater noster*, significantia triginta tres annos quibus dominus Iesus vixit hoc mundo. Unde tu, Christi Domini devote discipule, postquam sic mentaliter Dominum tuum in celum secutus fueris, tunc iterum ad honore Sanctissime Trinitatis dic tria *Pater noster* et totidem *Ave Maria* et devote te Sancte Trinitati ac domini Iesu recommenda!

188 | Paula Cotoi

Bibliography

Ádám, Edina (2009), Pelbart of Temesvar and the Use of Images in Preaching, Annual of Medieval Studies at CEU 15, 131–143.

Bárczi, Ildikó (2009), Morálteológiai tanítások Laskai Osvát és Temesvári Pelbárt Szent Erzsébet-napi beszédmintáiban, in: Dávid Falvay (ed.), Árpád-házi Szent Erzsébet kultusza a 13–16. században. Saint Elizabeth of Hungary's Cult in the 13th-15th Century. Az Eötvös Loránd Tudományegyetem Bölcsészettudományi Karán 2007. május 24-én tartott konferencia elöadásai, Budapest: Magyarok Nagyasszonya Ferences Rendtartomány, 83–104.

Bracaloni, Leone (1932), Origine, evoluzione ed affermazione della Corona francescana mariana, Studi francescani 21, 257–295.

Cotoi, Paula (2019a), Predica medievală între oralitate și scris. Abordări metodologice și perspective transilvănene, Anuarul Institutului de Istorie "George Barițiu". Series Historica 58/Supl., 159–174.

Cotoi, Paula (2019b), So Near and Yet so Far Away. The Reception of the Homiletic Works of Pelbartus de Themeswar and Osualdus de Lasko in Transylvania, Philobiblon: Transylvanian Journal of Multidisciplinary Research in Humanities 24/2, 311–335.

Cotoi, Paula (2021), The Book as Object of Lay Devotion in Late Medieval Transylvania (15th – 16th centuries), Studia Universitatis Babeș-Bolyai. Historia 66 (Sp. Issue), 27–42.

Crăciun, Maria (2005), Polipticul și devoțiunea euharistică în Transilvania evului mediu târziu, Caiete de Antropologie Istorică 4/1, 45–110.

Crăciun, Maria (2008), Frații minori și societatea seculară: impactul spiritualității mendicante în Transilvania medievală târzie, in: Ovidiu Cristea/Gheorghe Lazăr (ed.), Vocația Istoriei. Prinos Profesorului Șerban Papacostea, Brăila: Istros, 191–220.

Crăciun, Maria (2010a), The Cult of St Barbara and the Saxon Community of Late Medieval Transylvania, in: Ana Marincović/Trpimir Vedriš (ed.), Identity and Alterity in Hagiography and the Cult of Saints, Zagreb: Hagiotheca, 137–163.

Crăciun, Maria (2010b), Attitudes to Religious Art and the Confessional Identity of the Saxon Community. Passion Cycles in the Context of Lenten Observance and Easter Celebrations in Late Medieval and Early Modern Transylvania, Yearbook of the New Europe College, GE-NEC 2 Program, 13–70.

Crăciun, Maria (2010c), Eucharistic Iconography and the Confessional Identity of the Saxon Community in Early Modern Transylvania, in: Jaroslav Miller/László Kontler (ed.), Friars, Nobles and Burghers-Sermons, Images and Prints. Studies of Culture and Society in Early Modern Europe. In memoriam István György Tóth, Budapest: Central European University, 49–71.

Crăciun, Maria (2011), Mendicant Piety and the Saxon Community of Transylvania c.1450-1550, in: Maria Crăciun/Elaine Fulton (ed.), Communities of Devotion. Religious Orders and Society in East Central Europe, 1450–1800, Farnham: Ashgate, 29–70.

Crăciun, Maria (2012), "Ora pro nobis sancta Dei genitrix": Prayers and Gestures in Late Medieval Transylvania, in: Gerhard Jaritz (ed.), Ritual, Images and Daily Life. The Medieval Perspective, Wien, Zurich: Lit Verlag, 107–138.

Cum oratis, dicite: | **189**

CROCKETT, WILLIAM R. (1989), Eucharist: Symbol of Transformation, New York: Pueblo Publishing Company.

D'AVRAY, DAVID (1995), Method in the Study of Medieval Sermons, in: Nicole Bériou/ David D'Avray (ed.), Modern Questions about Medieval Sermons. Essays on Marriage, Death, History and Sanctity, Spoleto: Centro Italiano di Studi Sull'Alto Medioevo, 8–14.

DE CEVINS, MARIE MADELEINE (2001), La religion des laïcs, vue par les prédicateurs franciscains hongrois de la fin du Moyen Âge, Specimina Nova 1, 147–168.

DE CEVINS, MARIE MADELEINE (2003), Le stéréotype du bon laïc dans les sermons franciscains hongrois de la fin du Moyen Âge, in: M. Grandière/M. Molin (ed.), Le stéréotype, outil de régulations sociales, Rennes: Presses Universitaires de Rennes, 15–49.

DE CEVINS, MARIE MADELEINE (2011), The Influence of Franciscan Friars on Popular Piety in the Kingdom of Hungary at the End of the Fifteenth Century, in: Maria Crăciun/Elaine Fulton (ed.), Communities of Devotion. Religious Orders and Society in East Central Europe, 1450–1800, Farnham: Ashgate, 71–90.

DERBES, ANNE (1996), Picturing the Passion in Late Medieval Italy. Narrative Painting, Franciscan Ideologies, and the Levant, New York: Cambridge University Press.

DIAS, ISABEL (2016), Le sermon "De sanctis martyribus quinque fratribus" de Pelbart de Themeswar, in: Eleonora Lombardo (ed.), Models of virtues. The roles of virtues in sermons and hagiography, Padova: Centro Studi Antoniani, 189–210.

FIREA, CIPRIAN (2010), Art and its Context. Late Medieval Transylvanian Altarpieces in their Original Setting, New Europe College. GE-NEC Program, 2004–2007, 317–360.

FIREA, CIPRIAN (2013), "Donatio pro memoria": lay and female donors and their remembrance in late medieval Transylvania. Research on visual and documentary evidence, Studia Universitatis Babeş-Bolyai. Historia 58, Sp. Issue, 107–135.

FIREA, CIPRIAN (2018), The Pietà of Sibiu: Patronage of the Urban Elite in Transylvania around 1400, in: Susan Marti/Richard Němec/Marius Winzeler (ed.), Pražská Pieta v Bernu: předmět obchodu – modla – muzejní exponát / Die Prager Pietà in Bern: Handelsgut – Götzenbild – Museumsexponat, Praze: Národní Galerie, 191–202.

FLOREA, CARMEN (2009), The Construction of Memory and the Display of Social Bonds in the Life of Corpus Christi Fraternity from Sibiu (Hermannstadt, Nagyszeben), in: Lucie Doležalova (ed.), The Making of Memory in the Middle Ages, Leiden/Boston: Brill, 283–309.

FLOREA, CARMEN (2011), The Third Path: Charity and Devotion in Late Medieval Transylvanian Towns, in: Maria Crăciun, Elaine Fulton (ed.), Communities of Devotion. Religious Orders and Society in East Central Europe, 1450–1800, Farnham: Ashgate, 91–120.

GEARY, PATRICK (1994), Living with the Dead in the Middle Ages, Ithaca/London: Cornell University Press.

GECSER, OTTÓ (2014), Predicazione, formazione scolastica e modelli culturali nell'Osservanza francescana ungherese alla fine del medioevo, in: Francesca Bartolacci/ Roberto Lambertini (ed.), Osservanza francescana e cultura tra Quattrocento e primo Cinquecento: Italia e Ungheria a confronto. Atti del Convegno Macerata-Sarnano, 6–7 dicembre 2013, Roma: Viella, 33–52.

GORDON, BRUCE/MARSHALL, PETER (2000), The Place of the Dead: Death and Remembrance in Late Medieval and Early Modern Europe, Cambridge: Cambridge University Press.

HAUG, WALTER / WACHINGER, BURGHART (ed.) (1993), Die Passion Christi in Literatur und Kunst des Spätmittelalters, Tübingen: Niemeyer.

HENRIET, PATRICK (2006), Prière, expérience et fonction au Moyen Age: Remarques introductives, in: Jean-François Cottier (ed.), La prière en latin, de l'Antiquité au XVIe siècle. Formes, évolutions, significations, Turnhout: Brepols, 197–207.

KIECKHEFER, RICHARD (1987), Major Currents in Late Medieval Devotion, in: Jill Raitt/ Bernard McGinn/John Meyendorff (ed.), Christian Spirituality: High Middle Ages and Reformation, New York: Crossroad, 75–108.

KÓNYA, ANNA (2017), Eucharistic references in the representations of saints: A case study of Late Gothic wall paintings in Transylvania, Acta Historiae Artium Academiae Scientiarum Hungaricae AHistA 58/1, 85–113.

LANDMANN, FLORENZ (1927), Zum Predigtwesen der Straßburger Franziskanerprovinz in der letzten Zeit des Mittelalter, Franziskanische Studien 14, 297–332.

LUPESCU MAKÓ, MÁRIA (2001), Item lego… Gifts for the soul in late medieval Transylvania, Annual of Medieval Studies at CEU 7, 161–185.

LUPESCU MAKÓ, MÁRIA (2004), Death and Remembrance in Late Medieval Sighişoara (Segesvár, Schässburg), Caiete de Antropologie Istorică 1–2, 93–106.

LUPESCU MAKÓ, MÁRIA (2013), The Transylvanian Nobles: Between Heavenly and Earthly Interests in the Middle Ages, Studia Universitatis Babeş-Bolyai. Historia 58, Sp. Issue, 78–106.

MAZURKIEWICZ, ROMAN (2014), The Newly Identified Latin Prototype of the Marian Homilies of Jan of Szamotuły, Studia Slavica Academiae Scientiarum Hungaricae 59/1, 93–112.

PAPAHAGI, ADRIAN/DINCĂ, ADINEL C./MÂRZA, ANDREEA (2018), Manuscrisele medievale occidentale din România. Census, Iaşi: Polirom.

REEVES, ANDREW (2010), Teaching the Creed and the Articles of Faith in England (1215–1281), in: Ronald Stansbury (ed.), A Companion to Pastoral Care in the Late Middle Ages (1200–1500), Leiden/Boston: Brill, 41–72.

REINERTH, KARL (1979), Die Gründung der Evangelischen Kirchen in Siebenbürgen, Köln/Wien: Böhlau.

ROBINSON, PAUL W. (2008), Sermons on the Lord's Prayer and the Rogation Days in the Later Middle Ages, in: Roy Hammerling (ed.), A History of Prayer. The First to the Fifteenth Century, Leiden: Brill, 441–462.

ROEST, BERN (2007), The Discipline of The Heart: Pedagogies of Prayer in Medieval Franciscan Works of Religious Instruction, in: Timothy J. Johnson (ed.), Franciscans at Prayer, Leiden: Brill, 413–448.

RUBIN, MIRI (1991), Corpus Christi: The Eucharist in Late Medieval Culture, Cambridge: Cambridge University Press.

RUBIN, MIRI (2012), Popular Attitudes to the Eucharist, in: Ian Levy/Gary Macy/Kristen Van Ausdall (ed.), A Companion to the Eucharist in the Middles Ages, Leiden: Brill, 447–468.

Saenger, Paul (1989), Books of hours and the reading habits of the later Middle Ages, in: Roger Chartier (ed.), The Culture of Print. Power and the Uses of Print in Early Modern Europe, Princeton: Princeton University Press, 141–173.

Schmitt, Jean-Claude (1981), Du bon usage du *Credo*, in: Faire croire. Modalités de la diffusion et de la réception des messages religieux du XIIe au XVe siècle. Actes de table ronde de Rome (22–23 juin 1979), Rome: École Française de Rome, 337–361.

Snoek, Godefridus J. C. (1995), Medieval Piety from Relics to the Eucharist: A Process of Mutual Interaction, Leiden: Brill.

Spielmann, Mihály/Balázs, Lajos/Ambrus, Hedvig/Mesaroş, Ovidia(2001), Catalogus Librorum Sedecimo Saeculo Impressorum Bibliothecae Teleki-Bolyai Novum Forum Siculorum, Târgu-Mureş: Lyra.

Thayer, Anne T. (2010), Support for Preaching in Guido of Monte Rochen's *Manipulum Curatorum*, in: Ronald J. Stansbury (ed.), A Companion to Pastoral Care in the Late Middle Ages (1200–1500), Leiden/Boston: Brill, 123–144.

Valente Bacci, Anna Maria (1993), The Typology of Medieval German Preaching, in: Jacqueline Hamesse/Xavier Hermand (ed.), De l'homélie au sermon. Histoire de la prédication médiévale: Actes du Colloque international de Louvain-la-Neuve (9–11 juillet 1992), Louvain-la-Neuve: Université catholique de Louvain, 313–329.

Winston, Anne (1993), Tracing the Origins of the Rosary: German Vernacular Texts, Speculum 68/3, 619–636.

Winston, Anne (1998), Stories of the Rose. The Making of the Rosary in the Middle Ages, University Park: The Pennsylvania State University Press.

van Bueren, Truus (2005), Care for the Here and a Hereafter: A Multitude of Possibilities, in: Truus van Bueren (ed.), Care for the Here and a Hereafter: Memoria, Art and Ritual in the Middle Ages, Tournhout: Brepols, 13–28.

Carmen Florea
Babeş-Bolyai University of Cluj, Romania

Between Norm and Practice:
Observant Franciscans and Religious Life at the End of the Middle Ages

In 1446 Pope Eugene IV issued the bull *Ut sacra ordinis* which sanctioned the autonomy of the Observance within the Order of St Francis. After two centuries of dissensions, tensions, and persecutions, the movement (or rather various movements) seeking the restoration of the pristine ideal of poverty, humility and charity had finally found official confirmation. The Regular Observance benefited decidedly from the reform councils of Pisa, Constance and Basel, from the support provided by the papacy and surely not least from the activity of talented, charismatic preachers and highly trained theologians such as Bernardino of Siena, Alberto of Sarteano, John of Capistrano and James of the Marches, the so-called four pillars of the Observance (Roest: 2009, 446–457). Two years later, in 1448, *Vicaria Hungariae* has been established by the decision of Pope Nicholas V. It was an autonomous unit, enjoying increased independence as, from 1458 onwards, it was placed under the direct jurisdiction of the Minister General of the Order. This status remained unchanged until the turn of the fifteenth to sixteenth centuries when, with the active involvement of Osvaldus of Laska (Laskai Osvát), it was integrated (or rather re-integrated) within the Cismontane family (which also comprised the Observant Franciscans from Italy, Austria, Poland and the East) (Kertész: 2017, 179–182; Viallet: 2017, 92–95). With the bull *Ite vos in vineam meam* issued by Leo X in 1517, its status changed to that of a Province, headed not by a vicar, but by a minister provincial. In 1523, the chapter of Burgos authorized the functioning of two provinces in Hungary: the Province of the Virgin Mary (comprising the former Conventual branch of the Franciscans which has also adopted the Observant way of life) and the Province of the Holy Saviour (Kertész: 2017, 186).

The chronology of the emergence and functioning of the Observant vicariate in Hungary has been divided as follows: the decades between 1450 and 1490, characterized by a sustained rhythm of convents' foundation, supported by the royal house, the barons, the aristocrats and the noblemen; the years between 1490 and 1510 considered to be the golden age of the Observant presence in the kingdom when the number of the Observant houses grew to seventy and there were around 1700 friars (the largest monastic community in Hungary) and the influence and prestige of the Observants within the royal court, the ecclesiastical circles and among the laity was at its highest (De Cevins: 2008, 140–146). The decades between 1510 and 1540 were those of profound crisis as illustrated by the involvement of some Observant Franciscan friars in the peasant revolt of 1514 (in some cases personally, but also on an ideological level through the dissemination of eschatological beliefs), by the defeat at Mohács in 1526 that led to the disintegration of the kingdom and by the spread of the Evangelical ideas that made a severe impact on the functioning of the Observant province. Despite the fact that the number of convents decreased significantly, following either destruction or desertion, the number of friars, although diminished, still remained higher around 1520 than at the very beginning of the fifteenth century (Romhányi: 2017, 126).

Somewhat paradoxically, precisely the decades marked by several and profound crises coincided with the flourishing of the Observant reform in Transylvania, therefore an overview of its history would shed more light on this success. The dynamic of the Observant foundations in Transylvania reflects accurately the support provided by the kings, aristocrats, noblemen and, to a certain extent, the urban population, a situation which largely impacted on the spread of the Observance not only in the kingdom, but in other parts of Europe as well (Roest: 2009, 146–147). The convent of Hațeg (Hatzeg, Hátszeg) established by the King of Hungary, Louis the Great, in the second half of the fourteenth century was followed in 1422 and 1427–1431 by the foundations initiated by the members of the aristocratic families Jakcs of Kusaly and Losonci on their estates from Coșeiu (Kusaly) and Suseni (Pränzdorf, Felfalu) respectively. Emulation of the royal policy regarding the pastoral usefulness and missionary undertakings of the Observants was further motivated by the prestige and self-representation that these aristocrats derived from founding and endowing Observant friaries (De Cevins: 2008, 133–146; Romhányi: 2016, 242–243).

The mid-fifteenth century, particularly the decade between 1440 and 1450, can be regarded as the golden period of the Observant mission in Transylvania. Three friaries were founded during this time frame, two at the behest of John of Hunedoara, at that time the greatest supporter of the Observant reform in the kingdom, those from Șumuleu Ciuc (Csíksomlyó) (1441–1448) and Teiuș (Dreikirchen, Tövis) (1444–1449), whereas the third one was established in Albești (Weisskirch, Fehéregyháza) (1440–1448) by the Nádas family (De Cevins: 2008, 579, 581, 598). In 1444 the Conventual friary of Târgu Mureș (Neumarkt, Marosvásárhely) was transferred to the Observant family at the initiative of John of Hunedoara. It has been observed that the foundation and the transfer of convents in the 1440s were largely the result of the activity of the noteworthy Observant friar James of the Marches, who was actively engaged in missionary undertakings in the kingdom and indeed in Transylvania between 1436 and 1439 (Galamb: 1997, 213–216; De Cevins: 2008, 37–38). Thus, the ruler's and nobles' support remained firmly attached to the Observant reform as proven by the Transylvanian foundations from between 1440 and 1450. It must also be mentioned that the scope of the friars' apostolate during this decade seems to have widened and diversified as they started to be concerned with the population of the market-towns where their friaries functioned.

This increasing interest in the urban population is strongly highlighted by the foundations from the second half of the fifteenth century. To be sure, once again, royal support was essential as illustrated by the foundations from Hunedoara (Eisenmarkt, Vajdahunyad), Cluj (Klausenburg, Kolozsvár) and Brașov (Kronstadt, Brassó), friaries which were founded and generously supported by King Matthias Corvinus and his mother Elizabeth Szilágyi, as well as King Vladislas II (De Cevins: 2008, 587, 599; Salontai: 2017, 124–125). Moreover, with the active involvement of the urban population, the Observant friary from Mediaș (Mediasch, Medgyes) underwent significant reconstruction work at the end of the fifteenth century. This example further proves the reformed friars' success in Transylvania at the end of the Middle Ages (De Cevins: 2008, 589).

From both an institutional and hierarchical perspective it must be added that in 1517 the Transylvanian custody with its eleven convents was the largest one in the Observant Province of Hungary, the number of friars reaching 218 in 1523 (De Cevins: 2008, 571). However, the understanding of the functioning of the Observant Franciscans' network in Transylvania must necessarily be enriched by exploring the emergence of establishments belonging to the Third Order in the region. The greatest majority of the Observant friaries that existed in Transylvania in the first half of the sixteenth century were associated with a house of the Third Order and the dynamic of their foundation accurately reflects the impact of the Observant reform on religious life. Thus, the earliest such foundations, those from Coșeiu and Teiuș (both documented in 1501) were functioning with the direct involvement of the wives and widows of the patrons on whose estates the Observant friars pursued their apostolate (Karácsonyi: 1924, 553; 558; Lupescu: 2003, 838). The tertiaries from Târgu Mureș, firstly attested in 1503, as well as those from Șumuleu Ciuc (mentioned for the first time in 1535) most likely were organized as a result of the importance of these Observant friaries at local level, undoubtedly enhanced by the indulgences granted by the papacy (Soós: 2003, 253–263; Karácsonyi: 1924, 26–28). Significantly enough, houses of the Third Order were recorded in towns where the Observant friars had recently settled, for example at Cluj, where the construction of the convent started in 1486 and the tertiaries were attested before 1522, or their convent had been newly rebuilt, as happened at Mediaș where the tertiaries were attested in 1525 (De Cevins: 2008, 587, 589).

Even more significant to Observant success is the example of Brașov where the friary had come into existence with great difficulties at the beginning of the sixteenth century, functioning for three decades only, but where the community of the tertiaries, attested in 1534 managed to survive until 1556 under the super-

196 | Carmen Florea

vision of a confessor from the friary of Şumuleu Ciuc, thus enduring for almost two decades after the friars were expelled from the town and their friary demolished (Karácsonyi: 1924, 19). Very limited information has reached us about the communities of the tertiaries from Albeşti and Suseni. According to the surviving sources, it has been established that the former functioned between 1535 and 1556, whereas the latter between 1535 and most likely 1540 and, given the local apostolate pursued by the friars, it can be supposed that recruitment into the Third Order was similarly local (De Cevins: 2008, 261, 581).

Some noteworthy observations can be proposed at this stage already. Nine out of the twenty houses of the Third Order attested in the Observant Franciscan Province of Hungary functioned in Transylvania, a figure which reflects with great accuracy the success of the Observant movement in this region (De Cevins: 2008, 373–376, 396–397; De Cevins: 2011, 8, 18–21). Furthermore, this success is even more clearly revealed by the fact that, with the exception of the Târgu Mureş friary, which had been founded in the fourteenth century and transferred to the Observant family in mid fifteenth-century, all the other friaries and the houses of the Third Order were foundations *ex-nihilo*. In itself this effort of creating new, both male and female, houses illustrates the major accomplishments of the Observant Franciscans in Transylvania. Another main feature concerning the communities of the tertiaries derives from the profile of their members and supporters. Similarly, to the situation in the rest of the kingdom, the houses of the Third Order comprised exclusively female members and the involvement of the widows, particularly those of aristocrats and nobles, in the creation and support of such communities is well attested by Transylvanian sources (Karácsonyi: 1924, 101–102, 553, 558; De Cevins: 2008, 267). Yet, once more, a specific regional trait must be highlighted. As suggested by the example of the tertiaries from Cluj and Mediaş, it was the urban population and civic authorities that, next to the nobility's support, contributed to the maintenance of the Third Order (Entz-Kovács: 1995, 14–15; Lupescu Makó: 2001, 173–174, 178, 181; Karácsonyi: 1924, 554), a feature largely derived from the very nature of the Observant Franciscan network in Transylvania.

Observant reform is perhaps among the best suited phenomena to illustrate the impact of the norm on religious practice. Insistence on the return to the pristine ideal of the founders, on the reinforcement of the original model embodied by the Rule and surely not least, attempts at translating such exigencies into one's daily religious life, constitute strong justification for such an approach (Elm: 2001, 489–501). In her impressive monograph on the Observant friars in Hungary, Marie-Madeleine De Cevins made some highly interesting observations concerning norm and practice. When examining the surviving sources, which are worth investigating in connection to the Observant Franciscans, she concluded that they are predominantly of a normative kind, regulating, imposing, and monitoring the functioning of the friaries and the activities the friars were engaged in. The sources at our disposal are mainly issued by the papacy and by the leaders of the province. Therefore, they disclose the expectations of the Church officials. However, in order to find out what has been done and how it has been done, one has to start from the premise that norm and practice are inextricably linked. Therefore, as further argued by De Cevins, comprehending the difference between norm and practice could reveal more about the latter, something that can be achieved by a refined and subtle analysis of the interrelatedness of norm and practice (De Cevins: 2008, 19–25, 195).

The nature of the sources at our disposal thus decisively shapes our understanding of the Observant Franciscan reform as the movement has been designed and implemented from above. The normative centering seems indeed a more than appropriate tool to investigate and bring to light the modalities through which the rules and standards prescribed by the officials of the Observant Franciscans in Hungary were followed and the extent to which they formed, but also transformed devotional practices (Hamm: 2004, 3–22). Once more, the main traits of the Observant Franciscan reform, with its emphasis on obedience, Christ-centred devotion and penitence constitute a privileged area of research. Norm impacts practice in so far as the friars and the tertiaries, the main focus of this analysis, were instructed how to integrate obedience as the main virtue of their daily conduct, how to display devotion, particularly for the Passion of Christ and how to imitate Christ's sufferings through adopting a penitential way of life.

Observant identity is further enhanced by the very functioning of this branch of the Franciscan Order. As a highly centralized and hierarchical body, which closely supervised the functioning of the friaries, as revealed by the Constitutions of Atya (designed by the vicar Osvaldus of Laska and adopted in 1499), with several amendments brought by the decisions of provincial chapters held in the following years and the renewed Constitutions of Újlak (adopted in 1518), the Observant Province was thus characterized by great uniformity and internal cohesion (Viallet: 2017, 95; Kertész: 2017, 182–186; De Cevins: 2008, 146).

The norms imposed by the Constitutions referred first and foremost to the strict observance of the Rule, of obedience, poverty and humility (Kertész: 2017, 182; De Cevins: 2008, 93; Batthyány: 1827, 613). These were the main guidelines of the Observant governance both at central and local level. For example, in order to strengthen the internal organization of the province, the Constitutions of Atya were to be disseminated through the visits the custodians were to undertake in their custodies twice every year. They were explained to the friars in vernacular and read out loud to them on the occasion of each visit. To the custodians' effort was added that of the guardians who had to ensure that the Constitutions were available in their friaries and read to the friars (Batthyány: 1827, p. 613–614). The daily obligations of the friars mainly consisted of communal and private prayer, but they also had to read the breviary together, they had to work and embark on

198 | Carmen Florea

pastoral duties, preaching first of all, a task that was reserved only to those specifically appointed by the guardian, and hearing confessions (De Cevins: 2008, 83–93).

Submission to the authority of the Rule, to that of the guardian, custodian, vicar, then minister provincial is highly detectable in the norms governing the Observant province. A somewhat more nuanced submission can be observed in connection to the sisters of Poor Clare and the tertiaries. There is scarce reference in the surviving sources concerning either the Second or the Third Order. When it does occur, as happens in the regulation of the 1499 Constitutions, we find out that the friars were forbidden to enter the monasteries of Poor Clares (Batthyány: 1827, 617).

Whilst the Atya Constitutions concerned only the monasteries of the Poor Clares, the Constitutions of Újlak, adopted in 1518 devised strong supervision of the tertiary houses. The time spent between 1499 and 1518 can therefore be considered as the time when numerous houses of the tertiaries were organized to the extent that the officials of the Province needed to make decisions concerning their status. That indeed this was the case is additionally proven by the instructions sent by Pope Leo X in 1513 to the friars of the Hungarian Observant province. According to these, the tertiaries were allowed to live communally in a house (that was referred to as *cenobium*), to have a chapel for their liturgical needs, to be accommodated in separate cells and to wear the monastic habit (De Cevins: 2008, 271).

According to the 1518 Constitutions, the sisters of the Third Order were to live *sub clausura* under the supervision of the vicar (Batthyány: 1827, 648). These female religious were thus subjected to the authority of the leader of the province who also nominated their confessor, usually from among the friars of the convent next to which the houses of the Third Order were placed. The custodians who would have to visit the houses of the Third Order, as well as to allow the transfer of a tertiary from one house to another, were entitled to do so as a result of the vicar's decisions (De Cevins: 2008, 175). Thus, it can be observed that the houses of the Third Order were directly subordinated to the highest official of the province, having a hierarchically supervised contact with the local friars.

The rule of enclosure imposed on the tertiaries was a main feature of the Observant movement, an integral part of the reform it promoted, vigorously supported by its main artisans and considered to be an embodiment of the regular discipline these women adopted voluntarily (Zarri: 2015, 54; More: 2014, 298–313). The cloistered way of life the tertiaries had to follow according to the 1518 Constitutions was endorsed by several decisions taken by the Provincial Chapters held in the following decades. The collection of alms by the tertiaries was forbidden in 1533, being restricted only to their closest relatives (Bunyitay/Rapaics/Karácsonyi: 1904, 473), a decision that, although strongly derived from the difficult situation the Observant province underwent after 1526, and occurring within the context of the spread of the Reformation, could also be regarded as a desire for stricter control of these religious women.

Submission to the hierarchy of the Province regarding enclosure is further revealed by the chapter decisions from 1533, 1539 and 1542, which forbade the friars' visits to the tertiary communities and even devised penalties for those disobeying these prescriptions (De Cevins: 2008, 395–396). As a result, starting with the fourth decade of the sixteenth-century, the tertiaries were required not only to live cloistered, but also isolated from their families, within a context in which even institutional contacts with the friars were severely controlled. Such a development was not only due to the particular circumstances marking the history of this region during those decades, but was equally the result of Observant normative policy towards religious women, based as it was on submission and enforcement of male authority (Roest: 2018).

The exploration of the relationship between norm and practice, which cannot be understood as separate or even divergent factors impacting religious life is significantly enriched by two normative texts produced for the use of the tertiaries from the Province of the Holy Saviour. Both of these texts were compiled in the same year 1524, occurring thus at the time when the tertiaries' way of life was regulated through decisions taken by the officials of the Province and reflecting the increasing popularity of the Third Order in the kingdom.

The first set of rules I will discuss in what follows was edited in 2005 by András Korányi. The compiler or even the writer of these regulations was friar Michael of Besenyő, whose work is divided into two parts: *Constituciones Sororum Tertii ordinis de penitencia nuncupatarum* and *Modus Vivendi Circa Regulam Tercii Ordinis* (Korányi: 2005, 130–142). The Constitutions regulate in ten articles the governance of the order and the tertiaries' behavior during their daily and nightly routine, enforcing the basic tenets of cloistered and communal way of life (such as attendance at the divine services, the meal that was to be taken by all tertiaries in common, and the strict preservation of silence). Despite the fact that one cannot establish with certainty the extent to which these regulations were followed by all the tertiaries in the Province or whether they were addressed to a local house of the Third Order, still they are highly important for the understanding of the details which regulated the tertiaries' lives.

The second set of rules which deserves to be investigated is contained in the so-called Teleki codex and was authored by friar Francis of Sepsiszentgyörgy. This Hungarian language codex was produced between 1525 and 1531 for the use of the tertiaries from Târgu Mureş, and is considered to be the result of a local workshop. It contains the above-mentioned rules, but also an extended legend of St Anne, the legend of Macarius, several prayers and hymns dedicated to the Virgin Mary (Horváth: 1931, 139, 178). Ágnes Korondi has convincingly demonstrated that these rules were largely inspired by the works of Bonaventure, *De perfectione vitae ad sorores* and most importantly by his *Regula Novitiorum*. As such, the Teleki rules addressed those who had recently joined the Third Order and needed guidance and instruction in order to be able to live a true penitential life (Korondi: 2016, 166–169). It cannot be excluded therefore that Friar Francis was entrusted with the education of the novices entering the house of the Third Order in Târgu Mureş or even filled the office of confessor for the religious women residing there, a status which may have stimulated him in drafting these rules in vernacular.

At this point it would be worth discussing what affiliation to the Third Order meant in terms of ways of recruitment and preparation for a particular way of life. The support provided by women and their direct involvement in the functioning of the houses of the tertiaries, according to the available documentation, in most of the cases widows of noble status, has already been acknowledged. Significantly enough, this support coincided with a more open attitude the Observant Franciscans displayed towards integration of women within their ranks. Starting with the 1530s, there was an increase in the number of the letters of affiliations issued on behalf of women, who thus became associated with the merits and benefices of the Order (De Cevins: 2017, 113–116).

Despite the difficult situation marking the history of the Province of the Holy Saviour starting with the third decade of the sixteenth century, a growing interest and sustained support of the Observant Franciscans by women is well evidenced by existing documentation. Thus, the 1542 Provincial Chapter regulated the organization and functioning of the tertiary community from Cenad in the following manner: the widows or married women wishing to become tertiaries must live for one year in their own houses under the supervision of a *prelata* and of a confessor appointed to this task by the *custos* or the guardian of the friary, being allowed to become tertiaries only after completing the one year of novitiate and fulfilling the requirements connected to the tertiary way of life (Bunyitay/Rapaics/Karácsonyi: 1904, 497–498; Karácsonyi: 1924, 542).

Whilst this example further substantiates the support adult women provided to the Observant Franciscans more generally, there are also other cases which illustrate the Observant Franciscans' policy towards girls wishing to embrace the religious life they proposed. The Provincial Chapter of 1533 decided that no more girls should be received by the head of the custodies, a decision which reinforces the strong control of the hierarchy regarding female affiliation. It was by the same institutional means that this decision, which might have remained in use for a long time, was slightly modified in 1542. Then, at the request of the parish priest and of the city council from Mediaş, the Provincial Chapter allowed a girl to become a novice within the community of tertiaries (Bunyitay/Rapaics/Karácsonyi: 1904, 498).

The two discussed examples reveal that recruitment into the Third Order had to necessarily include one year of novitiate under both female and male supervision, a mandatory requirement to be fulfilled by anyone wishing to take the habit of the Third Order, no matter what the age of the candidate. Although distant in time from the moment friar Francis of Sepsiszentgyörgy compiled the Rules for the Novices, the decisions taken by the Provincial Chapters reveal on the one hand a certain enthusiasm on the part of women to become tertiaries. On the other, these decisions accurately demonstrate that the communities of female religious within the Observant Franciscans were regulated and closely supervised by the governing bodies of the Order.

It would be perhaps not too exaggerated to consider the two sets of rules concerning the tertiaries as further standardization of the norms devised by the Constitutions and the Provincial Chapters of the Observant Franciscans. In what concerns the Rule for the Tertiaries compiled by Michael Besenyő, even the way it is structured mirrors such standardization, as the first part concentrates in ten articles the main principles organizing the tertiaries' way of life, whereas the second part details the *modus vivendi* of the female religious according to the spirit of each of the articles contained in the Constitutions. The Rules for the Novices to be found in the Teleki codex offer an equally interesting example of the ways within which norms were imposed on those wishing to join the Third Order. Of key importance in this regard was the transformation of St Bonaventure into the father of the novices, whose advice and teachings were both a source of inspiration and justification for self-imposed discipline.

Bonaventure's immense prestige and authority in the last centuries of the Middle Ages were formally recognized through his canonization, a process started by Pope Sixtus IV in 1474 and concluded in 1482 (Finucane: 2011, 41–58). Although his cause was promoted by both the Conventual and the Observant branches of the Order, the reformed friars were using this modern cult in a way that would strengthen their own identity. Particularly relevant in this regard are the sermons authored by the two famous Observant preachers from Hungary, Pelbartus of Timişoara (Temesvári Pelbárt) and Osvaldus of Laska. As their works started to be published beginning with 1498, in Hagenau, in numerous editions, the two friars were considered to be amongst the earliest propagators Europe wide of the cult of St Bonaventure. Significantly enough, whilst for Pelbartus, Bonaventure was to be treasured because of his theological work, a true reflection of the divine grace he had been endowed with, Osvaldus of Laska emphasized the Seraphic Doctor's qualities in regard to the organization of the Franciscan friars, attempting to establish a direct link between Bonaventure's insistence on the context within which St Francis drafted the Rule and the Observant friars' efforts to fully obey it (Konrád: 2017, 400–415).

The close analysis of Osvaldus's sermons has brought to light that the vicar of the Observant Province in Hungary transformed Bonaventure into a true forerunner of the reform movement, as his role in the organization of the Franciscan Order (through the Constitutions he compiled, the official life of St Francis he authored and, not lastly his activity as the Master General of the Franciscans, an office he filled for almost two decades, between 1257 and 1274) was emphasized first and foremost (Berhidai: 2013, 31–41). To be sure, at the time Osvaldus of Laska wrote his sermons, he himself was actively engaged in the organization of the Observants in Hungary, as he also authored for his friars the Constitutions of 1499 (the Atya Constitutions), was elected vicar three times at the end of the fifteenth and beginning of the sixteenth century and compiled the chronicle of his order until 1501 (Kertész: 2017, 175–180). Not to mention that the Atya Constitutions were the first to include among the feasts to be celebrated in the province, that of St Bonaventure (Batthyány: 1827, 621), a decision that additionally proves Osvaldus's commitment to the institutional promotion of this recently established cult.

The pragmatic course of action undertaken by the Observant Franciscans in Hungary in what concerns the early and rapid diffusion of the cult of Bonaventure in their province can be integrated into the more general policy the reformed friars promoted, that of actively propagating those cults and devotions that defined their movement (Konrád: 2017, 426). Furthermore, Bonaventure's role in the organization of female monastic communities has been acknowledged and further developed by key figures of the Observant movement in the fifteenth century, such as Bernardino of Siena (Roest: 2011, 69–80). Taking into account that the normative role of St Bonaventure has been convincingly demonstrated by existing research concerning the vernacular texts compiled for and used by the female religious communities affiliated with the Observants (Korondi: 2016, 126–148), the strategy of the officials of the Hungarian Province is further revealed.

The Rules for the Novices to be found in the Teleki codex, compiled as they were with Bonaventure's ideas on monastic life at their centre, not only instructed those wishing to become tertiaries how to live in obedience, but also how to treasure the Seraphic Doctor himself. There are several instances in which Francis of Sepsiszentgyörgy praises the qualities of Bonaventure, who is called our Father or Doctor. His writing took on a more personal tone when he instructed the sisters about the useful and beautiful teachings that St Bonaventure had given to them (Volf: 1884, 401–402). The Teleki Rules reveal St Bonaventure as the true spiritual guide of the tertiaries, the authoritative voice they should hear at all times. Compared to the Rules for the Third Order compiled by Michael of Besenyő, regulations which detail the authority of the female superior (called either *magistra* or *prelata*) (Korányi: 2005, 134, 140), the Rules for the Novices did not make recourse to the authority coming from within the Order (either from a male or a female representative of the Observant Franciscan hierarchy), but to that of St Bonaventure, the Father whose instructions must be observed continuously.

The cult of St Bonaventure does not seem to have enjoyed great popularity in the kingdom of Hungary, yet it was ingeniously used by the Observant Franciscans for the edification of the communities of the tertiaries. The Rules for the Novices, written in vernacular, and the way they justified the need to obey Bonaventure's directives shaped the regular life of these religious women. Furthermore, this was indeed an ingenious strategy on the part of the Observant Franciscans, since the recently approved official cult of the Seraphic Doctor became an effective tool in strengthening the identity of the apostolate the friars undertook in regard with the recently emerged female communities of their Order.

Christ-centred devotion was perhaps the most important one in this process of identity construction on the part of the Observant Franciscans. Veneration for the Name of Jesus initiated and vigorously promoted by Bernardino of Siena became an integral part of the religious routine of the Observant Franciscans in Hungary. Late medieval evidence associates this cult to the daily religious practices of the friars. Thus, according to the Atya Constitutions, each time the Name of Jesus was pronounced, the friars had to bow their heads, whilst the provincial chapter of 1515 added that when Jesus's Name was heard the friars had to kneel (Batthyány: 1827, 621; Viallet: 2017, 103). Devotion for Christ had thus the tremendous potential of a universal cult that could be widely diffused and readily made available by the Observant apostolate. The emphasis placed on the Eucharistic cult is equally relevant from this point of view. Celebrating the Eucharist was defined by the Rule for the Tertiaries as both a process of preparing one's body and soul for the encounter with Christ and a way of meditating on the Holy Sacrifice (Korányi: 2005, 136). Indeed, evidence from the life of the tertiaries from Cluj reveals with great accuracy the importance attached to the Eucharist. In 1533 the provincial chapter allowed that, in the chapel these religious women used, the sacrament of the Eucharist would be celebrated with utmost devotion (Bunyitay/Rapaics/Karácsonyi: 1904, 473).

Devotion for Christ's sufferings was constantly enforced by the Rules for the Tertiaries and the Rules drawn for the Novices in a way that aimed at disciplining the daily conduct of these religious women and offering the most important example to imitate in their contemplative life (Korányi: 2005, 138). In fact, the Observant Franciscans encouraged the development of devotional practices that allowed partaking in the sufferings of Christ. Highly illustrative in this regard is the example of the confraternities of the flagellants, devotional organizations supervised by the friars that enjoyed tremendous success in the towns of Pápa and Baia Mare (Frauenbach, Nagybánya) in the second decade of the sixteenth century (De Cevins: 2008, 284).

However, it was perhaps in the world of the tertiaries where one's identification with Christ's sufferings was regulated in such a manner as to be transformed into a standardized religious practice. Both the 1524 Rules for the Tertiaries and the Rules for the Novices offer plenty of evidence to support this idea. Thus, the tertiaries had to flagellate themselves (*flagello disciplinare*) each Friday and to wear the *cillicium* two times each week. Self-inflicted pain was understood as a way to follow Christ. Before falling asleep and also the first thing a tertiary had to do in the morning in the solitude of her cell was to meditate on Christ's sufferings (Korányi: 2005, 138; Volf: 1884, 401). The Rules for the Novices also instructed them that, while silent in their cells, these young girls should remember the Passion of Christ and his last hours on the cross, such meditation being the way through which they could repent for their sins. Christ's holy death and the way his blood was shed from his wounds should always be carried in their hearts by those wishing to become tertiaries. In fact, the Rules for the Novices consider that those who desired to please God had to keep at all times the crucified Jesus Christ in their hearts and minds (Volf: 1884, 402).

Devotion to the Passion of Christ was assiduously promoted by the Observant Franciscans not only in their Province in the kingdom of Hungary, but also Europe-wide as exemplified by the support they provided to this end through the works they wrote and the sermons they preached (Roest: 2005, 429–433). The image of Christ crucified that was to be remembered by the tertiaries and the practice of flagellation that recreated and commemorated his sacrifice thus became constituent elements of the penitential life they lived. As it has been observed, the very act of focusing primarily on the sufferings of Christ reflected, at the end of the Middle Ages, a normative centering of piety, its reduction, albeit in a simplified and standardized form, to the literal imitation of Christ (Hamm: 2004, 12–13, 21–22).

Such a tendency is strongly suggested not only by the examples of the tertiaries or the members of the confraternities of flagellants. Visual evidence, mural and panel paintings alike, point to the same conclusion. The Observant Franciscan churches were decorated with impressive scenes of the Last Judgment and those of the Passion (De Cevins: 2008, 252). Furthermore, Christ's sufferings depicted intensely on a significant number of Transylvanian altarpieces reveal strong Franciscan influence. Great emphasis was laid on humility and obedience in the way the tormented body of Christ was represented by these works-of-art (Crăciun: 2011, 84–89). And indeed, the Passion of Christ was a constant presence in the friars' life, who devised means to further propagate this devotion. Thus, the seals of the so-called affiliation letters (*litterae confraternalis*) issued by the officials of the Observant Franciscans in Hungary for the lay persons who came to be associated to the spiritual merits of their Order represent in most of the cases the Crucifixion and scenes from the Passion of Christ. *Arma Christi* were depicted on the coat-of-arms of the province, significantly enough named, from 1523 onwards, as *Provincia Sancti Salvatoris in Hungaria Ordinis Minorum* (De Cevins: 2008, 251; De Cevins: 2017, 123–125).

What would be the observations that could be made concerning the interplay between norm and practice in relation to the devotions the Observant Franciscans promoted in the late Middle Ages? The investigation of the functioning of the province's hierarchy and its structures of government sheds light on the norms which were imposed to the body of friars and sisters in what concerns their religious practices. As these were closely linked to devotions more generally promoted by the Observant Franciscans, they have the merit of revealing the characteristic features according to which the identity of this particular religious community has been shaped. At the same time, mostly in what concerns the way of life conceived for the tertiaries, it can be observed that the very nature of the surviving sources at our disposal diminishes the supposedly inherent distance between norm and practice. The best illustration of this is the case of the cult of St Bonaventure who has been transformed into the Father of the novices in an attempt to associate him to the Third Order. Devotion for the Seraphic Doctor was to be embraced and constantly displayed through the practice of complete obedience to his teachings as revealed by the Teleki Rules.

The Observant reform's insistence on complete and total observance of the Rule (or rather prescriptions designed by the governing bodies of the Order in order to reach this end) would suggest that norm and practice were in harmony with the devotional routine promoted and developed by the Observant Franciscans. Standardization and reduction to the essential of religious life as illustrated for example by profound devotion and literal imitation of the sufferings of Christ crucified would argue in favour of this conclusion. At the same time, such a conclusion, whilst worthy of consideration, given its potential of illuminating our knowledge of the religious practices followed by Observant Franciscan communities in late medieval Transylvania, should nevertheless be espoused with caution. There are the sources at our disposal, in most of the cases issued, produced or emanated by those responsible for the governance of the Observant Franciscans (be they vicars, custodians, guardians or confessors) that justify such a point of view. This can be further nuanced by the close scrutiny of local and particular contexts within which certain norms were devised or imposed upon religious communities, particularly female ones. To be sure, the voices of the tertiaries remain silent to us and the way they must live in devotion reaches us only through the male authorities' decisions. Yet, the way they lived and expressed devotion can be deciphered through both a context-related and multifaceted approach.

206 | Carmen Florea

Bibliography

BAST, ROBERT J. (ed.) (2004), The Reformation of Faith in the Context of Late Medieval Theology and Piety. Essays by Berndt Hamm, London/Boston: Brill.

BATTHYÁNY, IGNÁC (ed.) (1827), Leges Ecclesiasticae Regni Hungariae et Provinciarum Adiacentium, Albae-Carolinae.

BERHIDAI, LAJOS PIUSZ (2013), Bonaventura-hagyomány Laskai Osvát prédikációiban, in: Judit Bogár (ed.), Misztika a 16–18. századi Magyarországon, Piliscsaba: Pázmány Péter Katolikus Egyetem. Bölcsészet- és Társadalomtudományi Kar, 31–41.

BUNYITAY, VINCE/RAPAICS, RAYMOND/KARÁCSONYI, JÁNOS (1904), Monumenta Ecclesiastica tempora innovatae in Hungaria religionis/Egyháztörténelmi emlékek a magyarországi hitújítás korából, vol. II, Budapest: Szent István Társulat.

CRĂCIUN MARIA (2011), Mendicant Piety and the Saxon Community of Transylvania, c. 1450–1550 in: Maria Crăciun/Elaine Fulton (ed.), Communities of Devotion. Religious Orders and Society in East Central Europe, 1450–1800, Farnham: Ashgate, 55–99.

DE CEVINS, MARIE-MADELEINE (2017), Le rayonnement des Franciscains de l'Observance en Hongrie à l'aune des entrées dans la confraternité de l'Ordre (v. 1450–v.1530), in: György Galamb (ed.), Chronica. Franciscan Observance between Italy and Central Europe. Proceedings of International Conference 4–6 December 2014, Franciscan Monastery of Szeged-Alsóváros (Hungary)/L'Osservanza francescana fra Italia ed Europa Centrale. Atti del Convegno internazionale 4–6 dicembre 2014, Convento Francescano di Szeged-Alsóváros (Ungheria), Szeged: University of Szeged, 105–125.

DE CEVINS, MARIE-MADELEINE (2011), Les travaux sur les orders mendiants en Transylvanie médiévale au regard des tendances actuelles de la recherche européenne, Studia Universitatis "Babeş-Bolyai". Historia vol. 56/1, 1–25.

DE CEVINS, MARIE-MADELEINE (2008), Les franciscains observants hongrois de l'expansion à la débâcle (vers 1450–vers 1540), Roma: Istituto Storico dei Cappuccini.

ELM, KASPAR (2001), Riforme e osservanze nel XIV e XV secolo. Una sinossi in: Giorgio Chittolini/Kaspar Elm (ed.), Ordini religiosi e società politica in Italia e Germania nei secoli XIV e XV, Bologna: Il Mulino, 489–504.

ENTZ, GÉZA/KOVÁCS, ANDRÁS (1995), A kolozsvári Farkas utcai templom címerei, Budapest: Balassi Könyvkiadó/Kolozsvár: Polis Könyvkiadó.

FINUCANE, RONALD C. (2011), Contested Canonizations: the Last Medieval Saints, 1482–1523, Washington D.C.: Catholic University Press.

GALAMB, GYÖRGY (1997), San Giacomo della Marca e gli eretici di Ungheria, in: Silvano Bracci (ed.), San Giacomo della Marca nell' Europa del'400. Atti del Convegno internazionale di studi. Monteprandone, 7–10 settembre 1994, Padova: Centro Studi Antoniani, 211–220.

HORVÁTH, JÁNOS (1931), A magyar irodalmi műveltség kezdetei, Budapest: Magyar Szemle Társaság.

KARÁCSONYI, JÁNOS (1924), Szent Ferenc rendjének története Magyarországon 1711-ig, Budapest: Magyar Tud. Akadémia kiadása.

KERTÉSZ, BALÁZS (2017), The 1499 Constitutions of the Hungarian Observant Franciscan vicariate, in: György Galamb (ed.), Chronica. Franciscan Observance between Italy and Central Europe. Proceedings of International Conference 4–6 December 2014, Fran-

Between Norm and Practice: | **207**

ciscan Monastery of Szeged-Alsóváros (Hungary)/L'Osservanza francescana fra Italia ed Europa Centrale. Atti del Convegno internazionale 4–6 dicembre 2014, Convento Francescano di Szeged-Alsóváros (Ungheria), Szeged: University of Szeged, 173–187.

KONRÁD, ESZTER (2017), The Representations of the Saints of the Mendicant Orders in Late Medieval Hungary, Doctoral Dissertation, Medieval Studies Department, Central European University, Budapest.

KORÁNYI, ANDRÁS (2005), Egy XVI. századi ferences beginaszabályzat in: Sándor Őze/ Norbert Medgyesy-Schmikli (ed.), A ferences lelkiség hatása az újkori Közép-Európa történetére és kultúrájára, Budapest – Piliscsaba: PPLE-METEM, 130–143.

KORONDI, ÁGNES (2016), Misztika a késő középkori magyar nyelvű kolostori kódexirodalomban, Kolozsvár: Egyetemi Műhely Kiadó, Bolyai Társaság.

LUPESCU, RADU (2003), A tövisi ferences kolostor középkori történetének és építéstörténetének néhány kérdése, Református Szemle 6:96, 830–844.

LUPESCU MAKÓ, MÁRIA (2001), Item lego... Gifts for the Soul in Late Medieval Transylvania, Annual of Medieval Studies at CEU 7, 161–185.

MORE, ALISON (2014), Institutionalizing Penitential Life in Late Medieval and Early Modern Europe: Third Orders, Rules, and Canonical Legitimacy, Church History 83:2, 297–323.

ROEST, BERT (2018), Observances "féminines" dans la famille franciscaine: phénomènes bouleversants, pluralistes et multipolaires, Mélanges de l'École française de Rome. Moyen Âge, 130:2.

ROEST, BERT (2011), Appropriating the Rule of Clare, Canterbury Studies in Franciscan History 3, 63–92.

ROEST, BERT (2009), Observant Reform in Religious Orders, in: Miri Rubin/Walter Simons (ed.), The Cambridge History of Christianity, Cambridge: Cambridge University Press, 446–457.

ROEST, BERT (2005), Franciscans between Observance and Reformation: the Low Countries (ca. 1400–1600), Franciscan Studies 63, 409–442.

ROMHÁNYI, BEATRIX F. (2017), Social Network and Resources of the Observant Franciscans in Hungary at the End of the Middle Ages, in: György Galamb (ed.), Chronica. Franciscan Observance between Italy and Central Europe. Proceedings of International Conference 4–6 December 2014, Franciscan Monastery of Szeged-Alsóváros (Hungary)/L'Osservanza francescana fra Italia ed Europa Centrale. Atti del Convegno internazionale 4–6 dicembre 2014, Convento Francescano di Szeged-Alsóváros (Ungheria), Szeged: University of Szeged, 125–137.

ROMHÁNYI, BEATRIX F. (2016), Das Konstanzer Konzil und die Ankunft der Franziskaner-observanz im mittelalterlichen Ungarn in: Attila Bárányi/Balázs Antal Bacsa (ed.), Das Konzil von Konstanz und Ungarn, Debrecen, 237–251.

SALONTAI, MIHAELA SANDA (2017), Repere dispărute din topografia ecleziastică a Brașovului medieval: capela Corpus Christi și claustrul Franciscanilor observanți, Historia Urbana XXV, 119–133.

SOÓS, ZOLTÁN (2003), The Franciscan Friary of Târgu Mureș (Marosvásárhely) and the Franciscan Presence in Medieval Transylvania, Annual of Medieval Studies at CEU vol. 9, 249–274.

VOLF, GYÖRGY (ed.) (1884), Teleki codex, Budapest: MTA.

208 | Carmen Florea

VIALLET, LUDOVIC (2017), L'Observance sans les vicaires: enjeux et conceptions de la vie franciscaine, Chronica (13) 15, 89–104.

ZARRI, GABRIELLA (2015), Ecclesiastical Institutions and Religious Life in the Observant Century, in: James D. Mixson/Bert Roest (ed.), A Companion to Observant Reform in the Late Middle Ages and Beyond, Leiden/Boston: Brill, 24–59.

András Bándi
Lucian-Blaga-Universität, Hermannstadt

Reste und Spuren vorreformatorischer Liturgie in siebenbürgischen handschriftlichen Agenden

Der Gottesdienst der Siebenbürger Sachsen ist von der Reformation nur marginal betroffen gewesen. Der siebenbürgische Reformator und Humanist Johannes Honterus hat in seiner „Kritik der mittelalterlichen Messe" hauptsächlich den Kanon als „gräuliche Gottlosigkeit, Beschmutzung des Testamentes Christi und Jahrmarkthandel" (EKO 24, 194) getadelt und abgetan. Seine Vorschläge zur Reform der Liturgie weisen einige Besonderheiten auf, wie z. B. das Vorlesen eines ganzen Kapitels aus dem Neuen Testament im Hauptgottesdienst oder die nachdrückliche Erinnerung an den seelsorgerlichen Charakter der Eucharistie. Der kontemplativ-meditative Grundzug der mittelalterlichen Messe bleibt im lutherischen Gottesdienst der Siebenbürger Sachsen erhalten (Schullerus: 1923, 424–426). In der Wittenberger Agende[1] des Birthälmer (Biertan, Berethalom) Predigers Laurentius Bombrecher, der 1560 in Wittenberg ordiniert worden war,[2] befindet sich eine Gottesdienstordnung mit Angabe der Sprache des jeweiligen liturgischen Stücks:

1. canatur Gloria in excelsis Deo Latine
2. canatur Dominus vobiscum germanicum
3. canatur oratio aliqua germanica
4. canatur oratio dominica germanica
5. fiat admonitio ad populum ante communionem germanica
6. Recitentur verba Coenae
7. canatur oratio germanica post communionem[3]
8. canatur dominus vobiscum germanicum
9. canatur oratio germanica post communionem
10. fiat publica benedictio ad populum

---

1 Ein Exemplar dieses Druckes (Sign. II-4899) befindet sich in der Bibliothek der Kreisdienststelle. Hermannstadt des Rumänischen Nationalarchivs (rum. Arhivele Naţionale ale României, Serviciul Judeţean Sibiu, biblioteca; künftig AN-SJ-SB). Die Gottesdienstordnung befindet sich auf dem hinteren Vorsatzblatt.

2 Laurentius Bombrecher hat im Jahr davor die Gymnasien in Kronstadt (Braşov, Brassó) und Klausenburg (Cluj, Kolozsvár) besucht: Wagner: 1998, 55.

3 In der handschriftlichen Eintragung ist die ganze Zeile, inkl. der Nr. 7, durchgestrichen.

210 | András Bándi

Es handelt sich um das Hochamt ohne Predigt. Als einzige Verkündigung hörte die Gemeinde eine Mahnrede vor dem Empfangen des Abendmahls. Im selben Band befindet sich auch ein Postkommuniongebet, datiert 1561, dessen Text nicht mit dem der Wittenberger Agende identisch ist:

Allemechtiger ewiger Gott, mir arm sunder dancken dir, deiner grosser guttigkeit, das du vns hast gespeist vnd gedrenckt, mit dem Leib vnd Bludt deines ewigen Sons vnsers Hern, Jesus Christus. Mir bitten dich, barmhercziger vatter, verleihe vns, das der Leib vnd das Bludt vnsers Hern Jesus Christus vns Armen sunderen sei czu einer sterckung vnsers schwagen Glaubens, vnd wircke in vns ein starcke hoffnung czu dir ewiger Vatter im Hÿmel, vnd ein wahrhafftige liebe gegen dir vnd vnseren nechsten. Durch Jesum Christum vnseren Herren. Amen.[4]

Die handschriftliche Agende (vor 1653) des Predigers Martin Czoltnerus/Zultner[5] aus Werd (Värd, Vérd) enthält dieses Gebet auch:

Allmechtiger Ewiger Gott, wir Arme Sunder dancken dir, der grosser gutte vnd Barmherzigkeit daß du vns hast gespeiset vnd getrunckt mitt dem Leib vnd blutt vnsers Herren Jesu Christi, wir bitten dich barmhercziger Vatter, verleÿ das der Leib vnd Blut vnsers Herren Jesu Christi vns arme Sünder bekomme czur sterckung vnsers schwachen Glaubens, vnd wirck in vns ein starcke hoffnung czu dir o Ewiger Gott, vnd eine wahrhafftige Lieb gegen dir vnd vnseren Nechsten durch Jesum Christum vnseren Herren. Amen.[6]

Die Ordnung des Gottesdienstes ist also auch nach der Reformation zum größten Teil dieselbe geblieben. Gebete konnten allerdings „importiert" werden. Wie von Erich Roth festgestellt, war der Bedarf an neuen und für alle Sonntage des Jahres bestimmten Gebeten groß, insbesondere bei den Kollekten. Die siebenbürgischen Geistlichen hatten im Grunde genommen nur zwei Möglichkeiten, um sich mit Kollekten zu „versorgen": entweder die schon vorhandenen vorreformatorischen Messbücher zu verwenden oder sich reformatorische Agenden anzuschaffen (Roth: 1954, 111–112).

Unter den Kollektengebeten befinden sich auch solche, die an Marien- und Apostelfeiertagen gesprochen worden sind. Dass man diese Feiertage bei den Sie-

---

4 Kirchenordnung: 1559, Rückseite des 2. hinteren Vorsatzblattes.
5 Martin Zultner, geboren in Agnethen (ung. Szentágota, rum. Agnita), bekleidete dieses Amt von 1634 bis 1654. Die handgeschriebene Agende wurde am 14. August 1653 von seinem Sohn angefertigt. Sie beinhaltet 35 Blätter mit Formeln zur Trauung, Beichte, Taufe, eine christliche „Haus-Taffel", eine „catechesis sacra", sowie Gebete zu den unterschiedlichsten Anlässen. Die Agende ist dem folgenden Druck beigebunden: Kirchenordnung, Wittenberg, 1554, im Exemplar mit Signatur 612-II-485, im Zentralarchiv der Evangelischen Kirche A. B. in Rumänien (ZAEKR) in Sibiu (Hermannstadt, Nagyszeben) aufbewahrt. Für die Lebensdaten des Besitzers, siehe: Series pastorum: 1865, I.
6 Kirchenordnung: 1554, handschriftlicher Anhang, p. 12.

Reste und Spuren vorreformatorischer Liturgie in siebenbürgischen Agenden | 211

benbürger Sachsen hielt, kann als ein Überbleibsel der vorreformatorischen Zeit angesehen werden. Bei der Kirchenvisitation im November 1650 in Broos (Orăştie, Szászváros) stellen die Kapitulare fest, dass hier nach reformiertem Vorbild auch der sächsische Pastor an „singulis diebus in sua ecclesia bis instituat preces publicas" (Kootz: 1890, 21). Pfarrer und Gemeinde werden gebeten:

> ut secundum ritus usitatus reliquarum ecclesiarum primaevae confessioni Augustanae addictarum omnes dies festos, Apostolorum, purificat[ionis] annunciat[ionis] visitat[ionis] Mariae e[t] c[um] t[empora] sanctificent diligenti et sedula verbi divini meditatione, auditu et praedicatione, sacramentorum administratione et usu. (Kootz: 1890, 21)

Die Marien- und Apostelfeiertage sind also mit dem Ende des 16. Jahrhunderts ein deutliches Merkmal lutherischer Identität der Superintendentur Birthälm, und ihre Vernachlässigung wird als Mangel an Frömmigkeit und Verbundenheit mit der Gesamtheit der sächsischen Kirche in Siebenbürgen empfunden.

Zur Zeit der Einführung der Reformation in Siebenbürgen, hatte Johannes Honterus bereits folgende Heiligenfeste aufgezählt: Bekehrung sanct Pauls. Purificationis Marie. Mathie des Apostels. Matthias, Annunciationis Marie.... Philippi und Jacobi.... Johannis des tauffers. Petri und Pauli. Visitationis Marie. Jacobi des apostels. Bartholomei apostoli. Mathei des apostels. Der tag Michaelis. Simonis und Jude. Andree des apostels. Thome des apostels. (EKO 24, 255)

Die theologische Grundlage zum Feiern dieser Feste sieht der Reformator in ihrem christologischen Bezug. Er nennt sie „feste des herrn Christi", von ihm gestiftet, um durch sie den Glauben zu bekennen, ihn zu erlernen und in ihm zu handeln (EKO 24, 255). Als solche sind sie bis zu Beginn des 19. Jahrhunderts gefeiert worden. Stefan Ludwig Roth[7] hat sie dementsprechend in seiner Agende bereits als solche bezeichnet, die „ehemals gehalten wurden" (Brandsch: 1941–1944, 181), und führt sie ohne Heiligenprädikat an.[8]

Zum Proprium dieser Feste gehören der Wochen- und Eingangsspruch, die Lesungen und das Kollektengebet, das letztere mit vorangestelltem Versikel. Der Fokus dieses Beitrags liegt auf den Kollektengebeten, da die Sprüche und Lesungen im Grunde genommen biblische Texte sind. Im Sprachgebrauch des 17. Jahrhunderts hießen sie „Collectae", „Orationes" oder „Praecationes". Die Kollekte besteht aus folgenden Teilen: Anrede – Prädikation – Bitte – Folgesatz – Konklusion – Amen (Arnold: 2011, 105).

Diese Gebete richten sich nicht an die Heiligen, erinnern bloß an sie, an ihr vorbildliches Leben oder ihre außergewöhnlichen Taten. Sehr oft schöpfen die unbe-

---

7 Stefan Ludwig Roth (1796–1849) war Pfarrer in Nimesch (Nemşa, Nemes), (1837–1847) und Meschen (Moşna, Muzsna), (1847–1849). Arz: 1955, 146/27, 169,26.

8 „30. Nov. Andreas", Brandsch: 1941–1944, 182.

212 | András Bándi

kannten Verfasser der Kollekten aus den Lesungen des Tages. Der Name des Heiligen muss gar nicht im Gebet vorkommen. Wie es uns die Gottesdienstordnung des konfessionell gemischten Doms zu Halberstadt zeigt, stammen viele protestantische Gebete der Heiligentage aus der Zeit vor der Glaubenserneuerung und sind ohne die Benennung der Heiligen und ihrer Verdienste weitergesungen worden (Odenthal: 2005, 111).

Dieser Beitrag zu den Kollektengebeten an Heiligentagen beschränkt sich auf handschriftliche Agenden, eine bisher nur oberflächlich behandelte Quelle einheimischer Liturgiegeschichte.[9] Folgende Agenden bieten gute Voraussetzungen zu einem Vergleich des Propriums dieser Feste: Radeln-Schäßburg (Roadeș-Sighișoara, Rádos, 1663–1739);[10] Seligstadt (Seliștat, Boldogváros, 1659–1689),[11] Denndorf

---

9 Die Agende des Predigers Andreas Teutsch aus Streitfort (Mercheașa, Mirkvásár) aus den Jahren 1703–1720, enthält laut Karl Reinerth deutsche Kollekten, wie auch „Collectae Latinae", 89 an der Zahl, die der Hermannstädter *Agenda Sacra* (1653) entnommen wurden. Reinerth bietet eine kurze Beschreibung der Handschrift, die Kollekten behandelt er allerdings nicht weiter eingehend. Die folgende Überschrift bringt eine Selbstbezeichnung der siebenbürgischen Lutheraner mit: „Formula confessionalis seu absolutionis in ecclesiis Transsilvaniae Lutherano-catholicis recepta et usitata". Reinerth: 1931, 130–134. Die Existenz dieser handschriftlichen Agenden bestätigt die Knappheit der *Agenda Sacra* von 1653 und rechtfertigt die nächste Ausgabe im Jahr 1748.
10 *Agenda*: undatiert. Bis zur S. 28 enthält die Agende Hauptgebete, die Kollekten beginnen mit S. 29, zuerst die deutschen, dann die lateinischen, beide für die gewöhnlichen Sonntage und Hochfeste. Zwischendurch sind Eingangssprüche und Absolutionsreden eingeschaltet. Auf S. 82–86 befinden sich, ohne Überschrift, die Heiligenkollekten. Ihnen folgen wieder solche „auff alle Sonn und Hohe Fest-Tage durchs gantze Jahr". Ab S. 112 sind die Amtshandlungen zu lesen. Die Handschrift ist in der Evangelischen Kirchengemeinde A. B. Radeln verwendet worden, ihrem Titel nach scheint es, dass sie für die Stadt Schäßburg (Sighișoara, Segesvár) bestimmt wurde.
11 *Agende: Seligstadt*. Diese Agende enthält bis S. 35 Hauptgebete für die unterschiedlichsten Gottesdienste. Es folgen einige thematische Kollekten: „Tempore Pestilentiae", „Umb Glauben Lieb und Hoffnung", „Für die Irrenden" usw. (S. 36–39). Die „Catechisation" (S. 40–52) und die „Orationes aliquot in Ecclesiis nostris consuetae & usitatae" (S. 53–56), hauptsächlich Morgen- Witterungs- und Friedensgebete (vor und nach den Lesungen), sind noch vor der Christlichen „Hauß-Taffel" (S. 57–64) zu lesen. Es folgt „Die Historia von der Zerstörung der Stadt Jerusalem" mit eingeschalteten Morgen- und Leichengebeten (S. 65–92). Nach den Amtshandlungen (S. 93–106) stehen die Kollektengebete (S. 107–168). Innerhalb dieser Rubrik liest man die Überschrift „Orationes de sanctis". Eingeschaltete Heiligenkollekten sind vereinzelt im ganzen Abschnitt vorzufinden. Der letzte Abschnitt (S. 169–219) behandelt seelsorgerliche Angelegenheiten wie Krankenkommunion, Beichte und Tröstung der Witwen und Waisen. Die Handschrift ohne Titelblatt wurde in Seligstadt angefertigt.

Reste und Spuren vorreformatorischer Liturgie in siebenbürgischen Agenden | 213

(Daia, Szászdálya, 1693),[12] Rode (Zagăr, Zágor, 1683–1812)[13] und Kronstadt (Brașov, Brassó, 1695).[14]

Bezüglich der gefeierten Feste gibt es gewisse Abweichungen in den unterschiedlichen Agenden. Zusätzlich zur Agende des Honterus wurde in Seligstadt und Kronstadt das Fest des Erzmärtyrers Stephanus gefeiert (*Agenda Ministrorum:* 1695, 94). In Seligstadt bediente man sich auch eines kollektiven Gebets für die Apostelfeiertage: „Oratio Generalis de Apostolis" (*Agende: Seligstadt,* 168). In Denndorf hatte man mit Ausnahme des Stephanstages dieselben Apostel- und Heiligenfeste wie in Kronstadt und Seligstadt gefeiert. In Rode fehlen die Kollekten für „Philippi et Jacobi", sowie am Tag Johannes des Täufers. In der Schäßburger Agende von Radeln fehlen sogar mehr Feste: „Thomae", „Andreae", „Purificationis Mariae", „Matthiae" und „Conversionis Pauli".

Es gab also Gemeinden, wo man nicht an allen Apostel- und Marienfeiertagen festhielt. Aber selbst in den drei Gemeinden mit den meisten Apostelfeiertagen, handelt es sich um eine Art Auswahl. Im Halberstädter Dom hatte man noch 1792 weiterer Heiligen gedacht, wie beispielsweise dem Evangelisten Markus, dem Apostel Barnabas, der Maria Magdalena, der Mariä Himmelfahrt, der Mariä Ge-

---

12 *Agende: Denndorf.* Nach den Morgen- und Pestgebeten (S. 1–14) folgen die „Orationes, sive Orationes Ecclesiasticae, quae vulgo collectae dicunt, et spirant adhuc Christianam et Catholicam Ecclesiam" (S. 15–62). In diesem Abschnitt befinden sich auch die Kollektengebete an den Feiertagen der Apostel und Mariä. Nach einem Morgen- und Abendgebet (S. 63–66) sind katechetische Fragen und deren Antworten zu lesen (S. 67–110). Nach der christlichen Haustafel (S. 111–117) stehen die Amtshandlungen mit Abendmahl und Beichte (S. 118–168). Die Handschrift ohne Titelblatt stammt aus Denndorf. In dieses Dorf scheint die Reformation spät Einzug erhalten zu haben. Antonius Schwartz, Pfarrer dieser Gemeinde von 1549 bis 1570 ist als Katholik verstorben. Mit der Begründung „pro Salute Animae meae" hinterlässt er den Klöstern in Schomlenberg, Schäßburg, Neumarkt und Sächsisch-Regen Teile seines Vermögens. Seinem Testament ist noch zu entnehmen, dass die Denndörfer Pfarrkirche das Patrozinium der „Virginis gloriosae S. Mariae" trug. Teutsch: 1853, 365.

13 *Agende: Rode.* Der Band hat folgenden Inhalt: Gebete für Matutinum und Vesper (S. 1–32), Eingangssprüche (Fragment; S. 33). Ab S. 34 beginnen die Kollektengebete. Auf S. 49–53 befinden sich die „Collecten an den Heiligen Feÿer-Tagen der Heiligen Aposteln, durchs gantze Jahr zu singen bräuchlich". Bis S. 58 sind thematische Kollekten zu finden („Contra Carnis et sathanae, De serenitate" etc.). Danach folgen bis zum Schluss Amtshandlungen, hie und da noch Gebete zu unterschiedlichen Anlässen. Die Handschrift ohne Titelblatt stammt aus Rode.

14 *Agenda Ministrorum:* 1695. Die Agende beginnt mit der Ordnung der Frühkirche, des Hochamtes, wie auch des Gottesdienstes an den Werktagen (S. 1–37). Es folgen die Amtshandlungen (S. 38–58). Der Teil mit den Kollektengebeten trägt die Überschrift: „Folgen etliche Gebet oder Collecten, so man brauchen mag in der Hohen-Meß oder zu VesperZeit" (S. 59–128). Nach ihnen sind die Gebete an den Feiertagen, darunter die Heiligengebete zu lesen. Die Agende endet mit der Passion (in 24 Gesängen), einem Verzeichnis der Schriftlesungen (mit Anfangszeilen), den unterschiedlichen Formen der Austeilung des Abendmahls (inkl. bei Kranken) und zwei Gebeten zur Einweihung der restaurierten Kanzel (28. Oktober 1696) und zur Einführung der Wöchnerinnen (S. 129–176). Die Handschrift befindet sich nach wie vor im Besitz der Evangelischen Kirchengemeinde A. B. Kronstadt.

214 | András Bándi

burt, dem Evangelisten Lukas, der Katharina usw. (Hennecke: [1792], 341–430) Das Breviarum des Doms enthält am Tag der Geburt Mariä eine christologische Kollekte: „Ut qui in Nativitate Dei genitricis congregamur, Filii ejus meritis … eruamur." (Hennecke: [1792], 406). Am Fest der Mariä Himmelfahrt wurden die Liturgischen Stücke vom Trinitatisfest verwendet. Das Gleiche gilt für den Katharinentag (Hennecke: [1792], 401, 430). Andreas Odenthal führt diese seltsame Lösung auf die konfessionell gemischte Zusammensetzung des Domkapitels zurück. Mit Rücksicht auf die Katholiken haben die Lutheraner diese Feste zwar halten müssen, dafür aber ihres Propriums beraubt (Odenthal: 2011, 329–330). Die Situation in Siebenbürgen war natürlich eine andere.

Die Kollekten können den Namen des jeweiligen Heiligen entweder in der Anrede oder im Folgesatz enthalten. Folgende Gebete erwähnen den Heiligen in der Anrede, z. T. auch im Folgesatz:

Ewiger Allmächtiger Gott, der du dein Wort in den Leib der Keuschen Jungfrauen Mariae hast laßen Fleisch werden, und solches durch den heiligen Engel Verkündiget. Verley uns gnädiglich, damit wir der Vorbitt deines lieben Sohnes mögen genießen, die weil wir glauben und bekennen, daß er von dem Heiligen Geist in der Maria empfangen und von ihr gebohren ist worden, durch den selben seinen lieben Sohn Jesum Christumm. unsern Herrn.[15]

Allemächtiger Ewiger Gott, wir dancken dir, daß du Sankt Johannem den ersten Prediger deß Neuen Testaments, daß freuden Feur deß Evangelij hast anzünden laßen und bitten Dich durch deine Gnad, du wollest dies heillige helle Liecht und Johannis Feur[16] in unsern Kirchen unnd Hertzen durch deinen Heiligen Geist erhalten, unnd uns mit der gantzen Christenheit Freud und Erkendnuß der Seeligkeit bekommen laßen, Durch Jesum Chrm unsern Herrn.[17]

Herre Gott, himmlischer Vater, der du den ersten Märtyrer Stephanum mit deinem Geist erfüllet, und ihn in seinen Nöthen, Hertz und Freudigkeit hast gegeben, hilf uns auch umb deines lieben Sohnes willen, daß wir dich und deinen Sohn mit Freudigkeit bekennen, und unser Leib und Bluth bey deinem Nahmen und Evangelio zusetzen, durch denselben etc.[18]

Kollekte mit Heiligennamen nur im Folgesatz:

Allmächtiger ewiger Gott, wir bitten dich hertzlich, gib uns, daß wir deinen Lieben Sohn erkennen unnd preißen, wie der Heilige Simeon ihn hertzlich in der Armen genommen unndt geistlich gesehen unndt bekandt hat, durch denselben deinen Lieben Sohn, Jesum Christum unsern Herren.[19]

---

15 „In Festo Annuntiationis Mariae", *Agende: Seligstadt*, 129–130. Maria kommt hier als Bestandteil der Biographie Jesu Christi auch im Folgesatz vor. Auf S. 146 und 156 befinden sich zwei weitere Kollekten zu diesem Fest, welches sie christologisch interpretieren.

16 Scheint eine geprägte Wendung zu sein, welche an den Brauch des Johannisfeuers erinnert. Also auch hier eine Wiederholung des Namens Johannes im Folgesatz.

17 „In Festo Johannis Baptistae", *Agende: Seligstadt*, 130.

18 „In die Stephani", *Agenda Ministrorum: 1695*, 94.

19 „In Festo Purificationis Mariae", *Agende: Seligstadt*, 165.

Kollekte ohne Heiligennamen:

Herr Gott himmlischer Vatter, wir dancken dir, daß du deinen gnädigen Willen und lieb-habendes Hertz uns in deinem Sohn Christus Jesus so klärlich angezeiget hast, und bitten dich hertzlich, du wollest uns in solchen Erkendtnuß[20] von Tag zu Tag laßen wachsen, auff daß wir in aller Anfechtungen uns damit trösten, unndt durch solche Hoffnung alles überwinden, unndt endlich selig werden. Durch deinen lieben Sohn Jesus Christus unse-ren Herren.[21]

Dem jeweiligen Apostelfeiertag wird ein bestimmter Bereich zugesprochen. So wird z. B. am Andreastag der Kirche, samt ihren Aposteln, Propheten und sons-tigen Dienern, gedacht. Am Thomastag geht es um die wahre Erkenntnis Jesu als fleischgewordener Gott, König, Priester und Mittler. Peter und Pauli ist der geist-lichen Gewalt der Kirche, der Sündenvergebung und der Heidenmission[22] gewid-met. Maria taucht immer in Verbindung mit Jesus auf und ist ein passiver Teil der Christologie und Heilsgeschichte. Die Zwölf als Kollegium stehen für das Prophe-ten-, Lehr-, und Priesteramt.

Über den tatsächlichen Ablauf der Apostelfesttage weiß man recht wenig. Der Großlogdeser (Ludoș, Nagyludas) Diakon (Prediger) Michael Honn hielt eine Pre-digt am Bartholomäustag des Jahres 1675 „de doctoribus ecclesiae" in der er seine Zuhörer ermahnte: „der fürnembste von euch sey wie ein diener" (Amtsschriften: 1593–1698, 126). Anschließend las er 1. Kor. 12 vor. In dieser Predigt nannte Honn den Ortspfarrer Martin Henning, seinen Vorgesetzten, „auß Rach öffentlig auff der Cantzel einen Esel" (Amtsschriften: 1593–1698, 128).

Der Pfarrer greift seinerseits am 11. Sonntag nach Trinitatis, in der Predigt über Lk. 18 den Diakon an. Nacherzählte Teile dieser Predigt sind schriftlich erhalten geblieben. Aus diesen erfahren wir, dass er Honn als Pharisäer abstempelt, weil er „mit dem munde, offt, schöne word giebt, ob schon das hertze falsch ist". Und im Bezug auf Gaben und Ämter, wirft er ihm vor:

Was darffstu mich dass lehren [...] dass die gaben mancherlaij sein, vnd fon Gott kom-men, eben darum soll man sie auch zu Gottes Lob vnd Ehre, dem nechsten zur erbawng

---

20 Anspielung auf die Bekehrung des äthiopischen Kämmerers durch Philippus (Apg. 8,26–39).

21 „In Festo Philippi & Jacobi", *Agende: Seligstadt*, 146.

22 Zwei Beispiele zum Tag der Bekehrung Pauli: „Ewiger Vater, gnädiger Gott, wir dancken dir von Hertzen, daß du uns zu gutt durch deinen Sohn, den außerwehlten WerckZeug S. Paulum vom Himmel beruffen, und czu einem Apostel der Heyden verordnet, und uns uns biß auf diese Stunde seine Episteln hast gelaßen, undt bitten alltag, du wollest seine Lehr in dieser unsrer Kirchen erhalten, und dieselbige durch deinen Geist recht verste-hen laßen", *Agenda Ministrorum*: 1695, 99–100. „Deus, qui universum mundum beati Pauli apostoli praedicatione docuisti, da nobis, quaesumus, ut cujus conversionem colimus, eius ad te exemplum gradiamur. Per Dominum nostrum Jesum Christum", *Agende: Seligstadt*, 156. Es fällt die Hervorhebung der Leistung Pauli als Briefschreiber im Kronstädter Gebet im Gegensatz zur moralischen Auslegung des Seligstädters auf.

216 | András Bándi

gebrauchen vnd nicht zu eijgnem lob, wie du thust [...] da du doch sonst ein grober Esel bist, [...] dass man dein nicht fill gebrauchen kan, weder in, noch außer der Kirchen. (Amtsschriften: 1593–1698, 129)

Wie am vorigen Beispiel ersichtlich, hat die Feier der Apostelfeste im Zuge der lutherischen Konfessionalisierung an Pietät verloren. Diakon Michael Honn missbraucht den Tag des aufrichtigen Bartholomäus, um seinen Vorgesetzten anzugreifen. Der Überlieferung nach war Bartholomäus Missionar und Märtyrer und steht für die Reinheit des Glaubens und der Lehre sowie die ehrliche Verkündigung.[23]

Spuren vorreformatorischer Liturgie findet man auch in der Praxis des kleinen und großen Exorzismus. Der kleine Exorzismus hat folgenden Wortlaut: „Far aus, du unreiner geist, und gib raum dem Heiligen Geist" (EKO 24, 248). Der große lautet: „Ich beschwere dich, du unreiner geist, bey dem namen des Vaters + und des Sones + und des Heiligen Geistes +, das du aus farest und weichest von diesem diener Jesu Christi. N. Amen" (EKO 24, 248). Den kleinen Exorzismus sprach man am Anfang der Taufe, nachdem man dem Pfarrer den Namen des Täuflings mitgeteilt hatte, nicht vor dem Altar, sondern „in porticu templi". Der große Exorzismus erfolgte nach dem sog. *Sintflutgebet*, also vor der Verlesung von Mk. 10,13ff: „Und sie brachten kindlin zu Jesu" (EKO 24, 248).

Im Burzenland (Ţara Bârsei, Barcaság) werden beide Formen des Exorzismus 1764 aufgegeben.[24] Der kleine Exorzismus wurde am 14. Januar 1793 per Synodalbeschluss in der ganzen Landeskirche abgeschafft. Der Burzenländer Prodechant und Kronstädter Stadtpfarrer Georg Preidt[25] argumentierte auf der Synodalsitzung folgendermaßen: „Exorcismum ad essentiam Baptismatis non facere, imo temporibus nostris minime accomodatum esse" (Synodi Generali: 1765–1801, 422). An ihm hielten allerdings die Laien fest, weil man Angst hatte, der Teufel könnte sich der Neugeborenen bemächtigen. Daher: „Quare cum Exorcismus multis gravi scandalo sit; abolendum eum omnino esse. Cui voto cum omnes unanimiter assentiuntur: Exorcismus Sÿnodaliter habetur abrogatus" (Synodi Gene-

---

23 Die Bitte der Bartholomäus-Kollekten aus Denndorf: „Wir bitten dich, du wollest uns den Geist der Wahrheit und des Friedes verleÿen", *Agende: Denndorf*, 58. In Rode wird um fleißige Kirchendiener gebeten, die, „durch Geitz und Hoffarth vom Sathan nicht bethört" würden, *Agende: Rode*, 53. In Seligstadt heißt es: „Da Ecclesiae tuae quaesumus, & amare, quod credidit, & praedicare, quod docuit", *Agende: Seligstadt*, 157. Diese letztere Kollekte wurde in Halberstadt auch am Andreas- und Thomastag gesungen. Es ist also ein allgemeines Gebet zu den Apostelfeiertagen. Hennecke: [1792], 341–342, 346.

24 Roth: 1954, 217. Die Hermannstädter *Agenda Sacra* von 1748 kennt nur noch den kleinen Exorzismus.

25 Georg Preidt (*18. April 1726 Zeiden † 21. September 1806 Kronstadt) hat die Gymnasien in Kronstadt, Straßburg am Mieresch (Aiud, Nagyenyed) und Preßburg (Bratislava, Pozsony), sowie die Universität Jena besucht und war zwischen 1752 und 1757 Lehrer am Kronstädter Gymnasium. 1762 wird er dessen Rektor. 1768 wird er Stadtprediger und 1771 Stadtpfarrer von Kronstadt. N. N.: 1808, 52–62.

Reste und Spuren vorreformatorischer Liturgie in siebenbürgischen Agenden | **217**

rali: 1765–1801, 423). Mitte des 19. Jahrhunderts wurde der kleine Exorzimus von Laien im Haus kurz vor der Taufe praktiziert (Roth: 1954, 218). Keiner der Exorzismen ist in den von mir angesehenen handgeschriebenen Agenden enthalten.

Ähnlich erging es der „Abrenuntiatio Diaboli", der Frage an die Taufzeugen, kurz vor dem Taufakt: „Entsagest du dem Teufel? […] Und allen seinen Wercken? […] Und allem seinem Wesen?" (*Agenda Sacra:* 1748, 233–234) Sie ist in der *Agenda Sacra* von 1748 enthalten, nicht aber in den handgeschriebenen Agenden.

Agendarische Stücke, deren Ursprung vorreformatorisch ist, wie auch Marien- und Apostelfeste, haben sich in der lutherischen Kirche der Siebenbürger Sachsen lange gehalten. Die Kollekten als Proprium dieser Feste sind, wie nachgewiesen, durchaus im lutherischen Sinne verfasst worden. Der Geist der Aufklärung hat in der Kirche der Siebenbürger Sachsen in der zweiten Hälfte des 18. Jahrhunderts diese Feste, wie auch den Exorzismus, Schritt für Schritt aufgelöst. Die Erinnerung an die Apostelfeiertage z. B. lebt in den Bauernregeln weiter. So hat z. B. Wolfgang H. Rehner (geb. 1936), Pfarrer i. R. aus Hermannstadt, in den Landgemeinden, wo er bis 2000 diente, folgende Regel zum Matthiastag (24. Februar) gehört: „Mattheis bricht das Eis, findet er keins, so macht er eins." [26]

Bibliographie

Quellen

AGENDA (undatiert), Das ist: Kirchen-Ordnung, wie sich die Seelen-Sorger in ihren Diensten halten sollen, für die Diener und Prediger der kirchen zu Schaesburg gestellet, Zentralarchiv der Evangelischen Kirche A. B. in Rumänien (ZAEKR), 400/109–200.

AGENDA MINISTRORUM ECCLESIAE CORONENSIS (1695), Archiv der Honterusgemeinde Kronstadt (AHK), Signatur: I-F-50.

AGENDA SACRA (1653), das ist Kirchen Ordnung in Hermanstadt, Auffs new vbersehen, gebessert und auffgelegt, Hermannstadt, Marcus Pistorius, 1653. ZAEKR, 612-II-286.

AGENDA SACRA (1748), das ist: Kirchen-Ordnung zum heiligen Gebrauch der Herrmann- städtischen, sowie auch der übrigen evangelischen Kirchen in Siebenbürgen von neuem übersehen, vermehrt und aufgelegt, Herrmannstadt, Stadt-Druckerey Samuel Sardi, ZAEKR, 612-III-2.

[AGENDE], DENNDORF, ZAEKR, 601-C-11.

[AGENDE], SELIGSTADT, ZAEKR, 400/118–293.

[AGENDE], RODE, ZAEKR, 400/278-29.

AMTSSCHRIFTEN (1593–1698) des Mühlbacher Bezirkskonsistoriums, ZAEKR, DA-209-14.

---

26 Vgl. Simrock: 1988, 352.

218 | András Bándi

BRANDSCH, GOTTLIEB (1941–1944), Die Agende Stephan Ludwig Roths, in Archiv des Vereins für Siebenbürgische Landeskunde, Fünfzigster Band, Erstes Heft. Hermannstadt und Bistritz: Michaelis, 149–238.

EKO 24: Armgart, Martin/Meese, Karin (ed.) (2012), Die Evangelischen Kirchenordnungen des XVI. Jahrhunderts. Bd. 24, Siebenbürgen, Tübingen: Mohr Siebeck.

HENNECKE, A. B. D., (ed.) ([1792]), Breviarium Ecclesiæ Cathedralis Halberstadiensis Juxta Ritum Antiquum Una Cum Missis Festorum Principalium Singularumque Dominicarum, Halberstadii: Delianus.

KIRCHENORDNUNG (1554), Wie es mit Christlicher Lere, reichung der Sacrament, Ordination der Diener des Euangelij, ordenlichen Ceremonien, in den Kirchen, Visitation, Consistorio vnd Schulen, Jm Hertzogthumb zu Meckelnburg etc. gehalten wird, Wittenberg, Hans Lufft.

KIRCHENORDNUNG (1559), Wie es mit Christlicher Lere, reichung der Sacrament, Ordination der Diener des Euangelij, ordenlichen Ceremonien, in den Kirchen, Visitation, Consistorio vnd Schulen, zu Witteberg, vnd in etlichen Chur vnd Fuerstenthum, Herrschafften vnd Stedte der Augsburgischen Confession verwand, gehalten wird, Wittenberg, Hans Lufft. Bibliothek der Kreisdienststelle Hermannstadt des Rumänischen Nationalarchivs (rum. Arhivele Naționale ale României, Serviciul Județean Sibiu, biblioteca, Signatur: II--4899.

SERIES PASTORUM VERDENSIS (1865), Pfarrarchiv Werd, ZAEKR, 400-246-99.

SYNODI GENERALI (1765–1801), Mühlbacher Bezirkskonsistorium, ZAEKR, DA-209-64.

Sekundärliteratur

ARNOLD, JOCHEN (2011), Was geschieht im Gottesdienst? Zur theologischen Bedeutung des Gottesdienstes und seiner Formen, Göttingen: Vandenhoeck & Ruprecht.

ARZ, GUSTAV (1955), Series Pastorum. Die Pfarrer der evangelischen Gemeinden A. B. in der R. V. R. von der Reformation bis zur Gegenwart, in: Siebenbürgische Familienforschung, mehrere Jahrgänge, Hermannstadt: [Typoskript] Druck.

KOOTZ, JULIUS (1890), Kirchenvisitationen im siebenbürgisch-deutschen Unterwald. Ein Beitrag zur Kirchen- und Kulturgeschichte des 17. Jahrhunderts, in: J. Wolff (ed.), Programm des vierklassigen Evangelischen Gymnasiums und der damit verbundenen Elementarschule in Mühlbach (Siebenbürgen) für das Schuljahr 1889/90, Hermannstadt: Krafft, 5–32.

N. N. (1808), Nekrolog auf Georg Preidt, in: Siebenbürgische Provinzialblätter, III. Band, Hermannstadt: Hochmeister, 52–62.

ODENTHAL, ANDREAS (2005), Die Ordinatio Cultus Divini et Caeremoniarium des Halberstädter Domes von 1591. Untersuchungen zur Liturgie eines gemischtkonfessionellen Domkapitels nach Einführung der Reformation, Münster: Aschendorff.

ODENTHAL, ANDREAS (2011), Liturgie vom Frühen Mittelalter zum Zeitalter der Konfessionalisierung. Studien zur Geschichte des Gottesdienstes, Tübingen: Mohr Siebeck.

REINERTH, KARL (1931), Eine Agende der Kirchengemeinde Streitfort, Vierteljahrschrift. Korrespondenzblatt des Vereins für siebenbürgische Landeskunde, 20/1, 130–134.

ROTH, ERICH (1954), Die Geschichte des Gottesdienstes der Siebenbürger Sachsen, Göttingen: Vandenhoeck & Ruprecht.

SCHULLERUS, ADOLF (1923), Geschichte des Gottesdienstes in der siebenbürgisch-sächsischen Kirche, Archiv des Vereins für siebenbürgische Landeskunde, Neue Folge, Band 41, Heft 2 und 3, Hermannstadt: Michaelis und Dück, 299–522.

SIMROCK, KARL (1988), Die deutschen Sprichwörter, Stuttgart: Reclam.

TEUTSCH, GEORG DANIEL (1853), Das Testament des Denndorfer Pfarrers Antonius Schwartz vom 8. Dezember 1570, Archivs des Vereins für siebenbürgische Landeskunde, Neue Folge, 1, Kronstadt: Michaelis, 363–374.

WAGNER, ERNST (1998), Die Pfarrer und Lehrer der Evangelischen Kirche A. B. in Siebenbürgen: I. Band: Von der Reformation bis zum Jahre 1700, Köln: Böhlau.

Ulrich A. Wien
Institut für Evangelische Theologie, Rheinland-Pfälzische Technische
Universität Kaiserslautern Landau

Spirituelle Offenheit und ethische Akzentuierung der Stadtreformation in Kronstadt / Siebenbürgen am Beispiel des Gesangbuchs von Andreas Moldner (1543)

Forschungsgeschichtliche Vorbemerkung

Der Mythos der Kronstädter Reformation suchte den Protagonisten Johannes Honterus aus den widersprüchlichen lokalen Erscheinungsformen herauszuhalten. Dies beginnt bereits mit dem reflektierenden Bericht des Organisten Ostermayer über die Ereignisse im Frühjahr 1544 und setzte sich fort bis hin zu den Deutungen der Gesangbuchgeschichte im 20. Jahrhundert.[1] Wenn in der siebenbürgisch-sächsischen Historiographie vom ersten Gesangbuch, nämlich dem bei Valentin Wagner wohl 1555/1556 erschienenen Gesangbuch in Kronstadt[2] (Brașov, Brassó) gesprochen wurde, war vielfach damit gleichzeitig intendiert, ein 1543 in der Druckerei von Honterus erschienenes Gesangbuch, das Acht-Liederbuch von Andreas Moldner, nicht nur wegen seines Umfangs, sondern besonders wegen seines Inhalts aus dem Gesamtbild der Einführung der Reformation in Kronstadt weitestgehend zurückzustellen (Gross: 1886, 1–5; Reinerth: 1972, 221–235; Reinerth: 1976, 172–176; Reinerth: 1973, 1–10; Plajer: 1980, 223–236). Mit seiner Herzensfrömmigkeit und Nähe zur anabaptistischen Theologie war ihm eine Resonanz in lutherisch-konfessioneller Perspektive versperrt. Es geht an dieser Stelle also darum, dieses Gesangbuch von 1543 angemessen in die Frühphase der Reformation in Kronstadt einzuordnen und nicht nur als das erste reformatorisch orientierte Gesangbuch in Siebenbürgen wahrzunehmen und zu rehabilitieren, sondern dessen spezifischen Charakter einer herzensfrommen, aber zugleich mit der stadtbürgerlichen humanistischen Ethik kompatiblen Ausrichtung herauszuarbeiten und darzulegen, also eine neue Facette zum Bild und Profil der Reformation in Kronstadt hinzuzufügen.

---

1 Zum allgemeinen Zusammenhang von Reformation und Musik vgl. u. a. Schilling: 2016, 187–201.

2 Franke: 2004, 65–134, 83, vermutet in dem nur durch eine briefliche Nachricht des Hermannstädter Bürgermeisters Petrus Haller belegten Druck von 1555 eine inhaltlich determinierte Bestellung, die „vorzüglich für Metten geeignet" gewesen war. Hingegen muss das aus druckspezifischen Gründen im Jahr 1556 anzusetzende Kronstädter Gesangbuch als weitgehende Übernahme des Babst'schen Gesangbuches bezeichnet werden.

222 | Ulrich A. Wien

Inkubationszeit: Hermannstadt als Resonanzraum der Reformation in den 1520er Jahren.

Um das Jahr 1519/20 soll im siebenbürgischen Hermannstadt (Sibiu, Nagyszeben) die von Wittenberg ausgehende reformatorische Bewegung bekannt geworden sein. Sie erfasste auch sofort die reformbereite sächsische, humanistisch gesinnte Bevölkerung (Teutsch: 1921, 197–198). Die Klageschrift des Pfarrers in Großscheuern (Şura Mare, Nagycsűr) und Dechanten im Hermannstädter Bezirk, Petrus Thonhäuser, berichtet 1526 relativ ausführlich über die Umstände: Kaufleute hatten die gedruckte religiöse Kontroversliteratur aus Zentraleuropa mitgebracht. Im städtischen Patriziat und in der Bürgerschaft waren die Drucke evangelischen Inhalts und die Lutherschriften gelesen und verbreitet worden sowie neugläubige Hausandachten – vor allem in der Muttersprache – gehalten worden. Auch hatten die Bürger erzwungen, dass vom neu entdeckten Evangelium inspirierte Gottesdienste in den Nebenkirchen der Stadt abgehalten werden konnten.[3] Auch Teile der Bevölkerung umliegender Ortschaften nahmen die Neuerungen wahr und an den Gottesdiensten teil (Herbert: 1883), d.h. die Reformation war mit dem Zentrum Hermannstadt ein städtisches Ereignis mit zugleich dörflichem Resonanzraum. Das verwundert nicht, wenn berücksichtigt wird, dass über sehr viele sächsische Dörfer schon im 14. und 15. Jahrhundert Notizen vorliegen, die Hinweise auf die Existenz von Schulen und also über Elementarbildung im dörflichen Milieu enthalten.

Schon 1523 besaß der Hermannstädter Georg Huet das 1522 in Basel gedruckte „new Plenarium oder ewangelybuch"[4] Luthers; im Privathaus des Ratsherrn Johannes Hecht wurden 1526 deutsche geistliche Lieder gesungen und muttersprachliche Predigten gehört, die reformatorischen Inhalt hatten (Schullerus:1923, 392). Antiklerikalismus artikulierte sich öffentlich.[5] Die gesellschaftlichen Wirkungen der reformatorischen Bewegung in der „Haupt- und Hermannstadt" waren unübersehbar: Die Nationsuniversität untersagte Stiftungen an die „tote Hand" (also an kirchliche Einrichtungen) und ermöglichte Bürgern, früheren familiären Immobilienbesitz, den die Kirche aufgrund von Vermächtnissengeerbt hatte, zurückzukaufen (Schullerus: 1923, 395–396). Legate und Stiftungen sind dementsprechend in den Folgejahren drastisch zurückgegangen, was auch der Dominikanerprior in Schäßburg (Sighişoara, Segesvár) beklagte (Teutsch: 1921, 1, 205–206; Reinerth: 1979, 30–31). Im Dorf Baumgarten (Bungard, Bongárd)

---

3 Schullerus: 1923, Teil 3 aus: Luthers Sprache in Siebenbürgen, 393; Oltard: 1650, 41 und 56–62; Teutsch: 1921, 1, 199–203; Reinerth:1979, 13–18, Quellen-Edition: Bunyitay/Rapaics/Karácsonyi: 258–262.

4 Schullerus:1923, 391, Fußnote 2; vgl. zur frühneuzeitlichen Lesekultur folgende Werke: Monok/Ötvös/Verók: 2004; Bándi/Monok/Verók: 2021.

5 Zu den Pasquillien vgl. Teutsch:1921, 1, 202–203.

Spirituelle Offenheit und ethische Akzentuierung der Stadtreformation in Kronstadt | **223**

trat – wohl durch den Hermannstädter Rat angeregt – die Bevölkerung in den Kirchenstreik, bis der von der Kirchenhierarchie aufgezwungene altgläubige Priester abgezogen worden war.[6] In Kleinscheuern hatte wohl Königsrichter Pempflinger („Dominus Magnificus") für den möglicherweise neugläubigen Gottesdienst die Kirchentüren gewaltsam öffnen lassen (Schullerus: 1923, 395, Fußnote 3).

Angesichts wachsender Zustimmung haben der Reichstag in Ungarn, König und Primas den Anhängern der reformatorischen Bewegung generell strenge Strafen angedroht. Der Reichstag von Rakosch (Racoş, Rákos) im Mai 1525 beschloss auf Druck des Nuntius als Sanktion gemäß dem Ketzerrecht die Todesstrafe (Fata: 2000, 65; Schullerus: 1923, 398, Fußnote 1; Bunyitay/Rapaics/Karácsonyi: 1902, 204). In der Bürgerschaft Hermannstadt machten diese Maßnahmen wenig Eindruck. Der Königsrichter Markus Pempflinger verstand es, mittels Symbolpolitik die Maßnahmen zu neutralisieren (Schullerus: 1923, 398; Fußnote 2). Doch eine offizielle Einführung der Reformation unterblieb, der Rat wartete ab. Der ‚Hermannstädter Frühling' blieb stecken und Fragment; die Bewegung „versandete" (Schullerus: 1923, 399).

Reformatorische Entwicklung im Zeitraffer

Mit der Niederlage des ungarischen Heeres und dem Tod König Ludwigs II. bei Mohács 1526 und der nachfolgenden Doppelwahl von Johann I. Szapolyai (1487–1540) sowie Ferdinand von Habsburg (1503–1564) ergab sich eine neue Situation in den Gebieten der *Universitas Saxonum:* Setzte man die Hoffnung darauf, dass die Habsburger das Territorium rückeroberten, musste deren antireformatorische Grundhaltung ins Kalkül gezogen werden. Aber auch König Johann, der mit der polnischen Jagiellonen-Prinzessin Isabella (1519–1559) verheiratet war, lehnte die Reformation ab. Die reformatorische Bewegung in Siebenbürgen erlahmte, wenngleich das humanistisch gesinnte Stadtbürgertum zu religiösen Reformen bereit schien. Man schickte einige Studenten nach Wittenberg; anscheinend wurde um 1540 in Hermannstadt das Abendmahl in der Spitalskirche *sub utraque* gefeiert. In Kronstadt wurde durch den aus dem Basler Exil zurückgerufenen Humanisten Johannes Honterus (1498/99–1549) (Wien: 2019, 19–41, 25–26) die Bildungsreform zum Wurzelboden der nachfolgenden Kirchenreform. Seine Druckerei veröffentlichte Lehrbücher für das *Trivium* und *Quadrivium* (Wien: 2015, [3]2020, 11–37; Şindilariu: 2017, 1–32, 3–9). Auch in Bistritz (Bistriţa, Beszterce) ist davon auszu-

---

6 Herbert: 1883, 4 (mit Fußnote 7 unter Verweis auf Capitelsprotokoll A, 43, 53, 57, 63–65, 75–76, 87, 92–93 und 188) und 10.

224 | Ulrich A. Wien

gehen, dass ab 1540 die Bürgerschaft nicht nur reformationsfreundlich, sondern auch aktiv den Transformationsprozess gestaltete.

Kronstädter humanistische Stadtreformation nach 1541

Erst mit der Besetzung Ofens (Buda) durch die Osmanen 1541 schwand bei den Sachsen in Siebenbürgen endgültig die Zuversicht auf habsburgische Hilfe. Der Weißenburger Bischof Johann III. Statilaeus (reg. 1528–1542) starb, und der Bischofsstuhl blieb vakant. Nach dem Tod des Kronstädter Stadtrichters Lukas Hirscher 1541 ergriff sein Nachfolger Johannes Fuchs (†1550) beherzt und nachdrücklich die Initiative zur offenen Kirchenreform. Im Oktober 1542 erfolgte die Gottesdienstreform, im Dezember 1542 die Kirchenvisitation im Kirchenbezirk des Kronstädter Umlandes, dem Burzenland (Țara Bârsei, Barcaság) und im Sommer 1543 der Druck des Reformationsbüchleins,[7] in welchem (höchstwahrscheinlich) der Ratsherr Johannes Honterus die ergriffenen Maßnahmen erläuterte. Schließlich verpflichtete sich dauerhaft der neu konstituierte Rat der Stadt Kronstadt nach Weihnachten 1543 auf die Reformation. Karl Reinerth hat bereits 1929 diesbezüglich festgestellt:

Geboren aber ist die siebenbürgisch-sächsische Reformation, insofern Honterus ihr Schöpfer ist, nicht aus dem Geist Wittenbergs, sondern des Humanismus, der Baseler Reformatoren und – des katholischen Augustin. Diese drei Größen geben uns auch den alleinigen Schlüssel zu ihrem Verständnis. (Reinerth: 1929, 97–114, 114).

Offenheit und Dynamik zeichneten die frühe reformatorische Bewegung in Siebenbürgen aus, welche „Möglichkeitskeime[n] verschiedenster Entwicklungen in sich" (Klein: 1935, 147) barg. Zoltán Csepregi ordnet den *reformatio*-Begriff der Kronstädter in den Verständnishorizont der von Erasmus geprägten, in umfassendem Sinn als katholisch verstandenen Reformversuche ein und erkennt in der Haltung der Kronstädter Reformatoren bei Einführung der Reformation eine „theologische und kirchenpolitische Umorientierung" (Csepregi; 2004, 1–18, 2). Edit Szegedi führt vor dem Hintergrund dieses gesamtchristlichen bzw. „katholischen" Selbstverständnisses („wir von der katholischen Kirche und dem orthodoxen Glauben und der wahren evangelischen Lehre in keiner Weise abgewichen sind" – Szegedi: 2012, 77–85, 78) aus: „Die Brücken zwischen einem reformfreudigen und -fähigen Katholizismus und der Reformation standen noch und schienen sogar konsolidierungsfähig." (Szegedi: 2012, 77–85, 78)

---

7 EKO 24, 177–190 und die deutsche Fassung 191–202; Gross: 1896, 33–64 (Faksimile) und deutsche Übersetzung ebenda, 65–96.

Nachträglich zur Einführung der Reformation suchten die Kronstädter Akteure Kontakt zu den Wittenberger Reformatoren, die das Kronstädter Vorgehen billigten und dem Hermannstädter Stadtpfarrer Matthias Ramser empfahlen (Luther am 1. September 1543, Melanchthon am 3. September 1543), sich an der Kronstädter Reform zu orientieren (Csepregi: 2004, 14, Verók: 2020, 123–138). Hatte der Kronstädter Magistrat schon vorreformatorisch seinen Einfluss auf die Verwaltung von Kirchengut ausgedehnt (Schullerus: 1923, 400), so übernahm beim Amtswechsel des Jahres (27. Dezember) 1543 der Rat definitiv das landesherrliche Kirchenregiment für Kronstadt und das Burzenland. Gemäß der Konzeption Melanchthons (1497–1560) übte der Rat die „Custodia utriusque tabulae" aus und schwor, den Inhalt des Reformationsbüchleins unerschütterlich für alle Zeiten in Geltung zu halten und zu verteidigen (Schullerus, 409). Wegen Differenzen bezüglich der Ausstattung der Kirchen (Altäre, *Vasa sacra ...*) nötigte der Rat Stadtpfarrer Jekel mit drei Stadtpredigern zum Rückzug. Mit dreimonatiger Verzögerung wurde der Ratsherr und Humanist Honterus als Jekels Nachfolger zum Stadtpfarrer inthronisiert (Csepregi: 2004, 6).

Neben der „Reformatio Coronensis ecclesiae" hatte Honterus 1543 auch die Schulordnung („Constitutio Scholae Coronensis") nach Nürnberger Vorbild gedruckt. Zugleich erschien ebenfalls 1543 in der Honterus-Druckerei ein Acht-Liederbuch von Andreas Moldner. Es gehört gleichfalls in die Frühphase der offiziellen Kronstädter Kirchenreform. Es hat ein eigenartiges Profil, weswegen an dieser Stelle vorweg die Kronstädter Reformation anhand einer kurz skizzierten Analyse des Reformationsbüchleins charakterisiert werden soll, um beide Drucke miteinander vergleichen zu können.

Reformationsbüchlein 1543

Die Kronstädter Reformation stellt eine Synthese zwischen Luthers Konzeption eines Priestertums aller Gläubigen und dem schweizerischen Konzept einer christlichen Reform des Gemeinwesens dar. Konkret wurden selektiv Ausstattungsgegenstände (vor allen Dingen Seitenaltäre und dazugehörige Geräte) entfernt; doch was noch für die evangelische Messe erforderlich war, wurde beibehalten, dagegen der Rest in den Besitz des Rates überführt. Die Einzelbeichte wurde zeitweilig fortgeführt, die neue Gottesdienstordnung sah (aus pädagogischen Gründen wurden lateinische Gesänge beibehalten) liturgische Zweisprachigkeit vor, und Heiligenfeste wurden beschränkt. Dennoch werden die Neuerungen eindeutig artikuliert: „dem Volk zugewandt" und „in der Volkssprache […] mit heller, lauter Stimme […] aus dem Schrifttext gelesen" und gepredigt steht das Evangelium im Mittelpunkt der Messe, d.h. die Verkündigung der Gnadenverheißung und die Reichung der

Eucharistie in beiderlei Gestalt. Die urchristliche Gestalt des Gottesdienstes war das Ziel der Reform, was die Apologie bereits als erreicht präsentierte: „niemals ist unter uns die Messe gemäß der Anordnung Christi reiner und mit größerer Ehrfurcht gefeiert worden, als es jetzt geschieht".[8]

Umso schärfer und radikaler wird die Sprache, wenn es um das vorreformatorische Mess-Verständnis geht. In der Kritik an der „missa privata" sowie an der „missa publica" wird von „eyn greuliche, scheuczlige gottlosenheit" (EKO 24, 194), „schändlichstem Schacher" (turpissimae nundinationes), einer „Pest absurdester Meinung", ja, von einem „gottlosen" Kanon (impium canonem) gesprochen, in dem „ohne Zeugnis der Schrift" (sine testimonio sacrae scripturae) eine Fälschung des ursprünglichen Sinns des Abendmahls praktiziert werde. Denn es sei „Teufelslehre" (*doctrinam Satanae*), „fluchwürdige Ruchlosigkeit und Profanierung des Testamentes Christi", wenn die Eucharistie als Opfer und gutes Werk verstanden würde, wo menschlicherseits „gar nichts zu leisten" sei, sondern „wir von ihm im Glauben das höchste Gut zur Vergebung der Sünden empfangen".[9] Auch wenn die äußere Gestalt der evangelischen Messe (inklusive der Weiternutzung der Paramente bis ins 19. Jahrhundert, einem bis heute bestehenden Paramentenschatz – Wetter/Kienzler/Ziegler: 2015) weiterhin einen katholischen Eindruck hervorrufen konnte, wie dies der französische Reisende Lescalopier berichtete, schlossen sich die Kronstädter Reformatoren uneingeschränkt einer evangelischen Gottesdienstauffassung an. Gebete richteten sich an den dreieinigen Gott, nicht mehr an die Heiligen. Entscheidend wurde der Gemeindegesang als Antwort der Gemeinde in der Volkssprache („lingua vernacula, lingua nostra, cantio vulgaris, psalmus Germanicus" – Schullerus: 1923, 425, Fußnote 1). An der Verbreitung und Durchsetzung der frühen Reformation, die auch als „Singbewegung" (Vgl. Mager: 1986, 25–38) bezeichnet worden ist, hatten die Lieder entscheidenden Anteil.

Das Profil des Kronstädter Gesangsbuchs von Andreas Moldner (1543). Forschungsgeschichte

In einem einzigen Exemplar ist das Acht-Liederbuch in Kronstadt überliefert worden. Der Prediger Andreas Moldner nimmt in der Überschrift (A2/r) die Autorschaft für sich in Anspruch; über ihn ist sonst nichts weiteres bekannt, er könnte eventuell ein Sohn eines Burzenländer Pfarrers gewesen sein. Nach einer Anzeige in Trauschs Schriftstellerlexikon (Trausch: 1983, 430–431) hat der damalige Gym-

---

8 Übersetzungen der Apologie der Reformatio des Johannes Honterus liegen vor von: Gross: 1927, 40. und von Binder: 1996, 197.
9 EKO 24, 181–183; deutsche Übersetzung der Zitate bei Schullerus: 1923, 420–421.

nasialdirektor Julius Gross (1855–1932) 1886 relativ ausführlich darauf aufmerksam gemacht. Aus dem Nachlass des für die Erforschung der Regionalgeschichte bedeutsamen Kronstädter Sammlers, Forschers und Editors Josef Franz Trausch (1795–1871) war das Werk in die Gymnasialbibliothek aufgenommen worden unter dem Titel: „Geistliche Lieder durch H. Andream Moldner gemacht. MDXLIII." (RMNy 53). Zusammen mit einem Kronstädter Nachdruck von Luthers Kleinem Katechismus (1548) und dem von Kaspar Helth (ca. 1510–1574) in Klausenburg herausgegebenen „Trostbüchlin" (1551, RMNy 94) hat Gross den Druck vorgestellt. Dabei wurde klar, dass es sich – nach damaligem Kenntnisstand – zumindest teilweise um Lieder handelte, deren Herkunft in der böhmisch-mährischen Brüder-Unität und im Täufer-Milieu zu verorten war. Das erste volkssprachliche Gesangbuch war 1501 in Böhmen gedruckt worden, und in vielen europäischen Ländern waren im Spätmittelalter geistlicher Gesang in der Volkssprache verbreitet gewesen und weithin geübte Praxis (Jürgens: 2015, 103–123, 105, mit Fußnote 4). Anhand von Wackernagels Kompendium (Wackernagel: 1870) konnte Gross vier Lieder eindeutig anderen Autoren als Moldner zuweisen, nämlich Michael Weiße (ca. 1488–1534) und dem Täufer Ludwig Hätzer (ca. 1500, hingerichtet 1529) (Gross: 1886; von Schlachta: 2020; Rempel: 2011, 389–424, 389–397; Stayer: 2011, 83–117, 99–109).

In der Forschung ist die Publikation des Acht-Liederbuchs Moldners zwar immer wieder genannt, aber erst durch Karl Reinerth (1891–1986) 1973 in einer kleinen Studie erneut behandelt und analysiert worden.[10] Dabei wertete er zunächst Moldners Liedsammlung ab, indem er es ablehnte, diese als Gesangbuch zu bezeichnen. Erst 2001 hat sich Martin Rothkegel unvoreingenommen mit der Publikation Moldners auseinandergesetzt (Rothkegel: 2001, 195–207). Er skizziert die Forschungsgeschichte und ihre Schwächen, die das schwärmerische Liederbuch nicht als direkten Vorfahren, sondern eher als „eine Art missratener Uronkel" (Rothkegel: 2001, 205) behandelt habe. Rothkegel erscheint es aber wahrscheinlich, dass die von Moldner herausgegebenen Täuferlieder „im Kontext der polyphonen Kronstädter Reformation gar nicht als Mißklänge empfunden wurden" (Rothkegel: 2001, 206), sondern bewusst für die Gemeinde dort, aber auch andernorts – wie dies ein literarischer Nachweis aus Bistritz bezeugt – im Gemeindegebrauch standen. Erhard Franke weist darauf hin, dass sich bereits im Titel indirekt die Kenntnis Wittenbergischer ‚Gesangbuchtradition' dokumentiert, weswegen – auch mit Verweis auf die in der „Reformatio" (1543) genannten deutschen liturgischen Stücke (*Te deum/Herrgott dich loben wir, Credo/Wir gleuben all, Jesus Christus/J.C. vnser heiland*) – eine Kenntnis auch lutherischer Lieder eigentlich vor-

---

10 Reinerth: 1973, 1–10. Darüber hinaus geht er in zwei aufeinander bezogenen Aufsätzen im JbLH 17 (1973), 221–235 und 20 (1976), 172–176 darauf ein und präsentiert eine Synthese in seiner Monographie: 1979, 157–160.

228 | Ulrich A. Wien

auszusetzen ist (Franke: 2004, 80–81). Moldner als Kompilator ergänzt mit seiner Auswahl wohl die bereits bekannten evangelischen Gesänge aus anderen Traditionsströmen und zwar mit Rückgriff auf die böhmische Tradition, die auch offiziell in Kronstadt als Referenz der Reform galt, indem auf dem Umschlag des Stadtrechnungsbuchs von 1544 neben Luther, Melanchthon, Erasmus, Kurfürst Johann Friedrich von Sachsen auch Jan Hus mit einem Porträt aufgepresst worden war (Gross: 1896, 252–253).

Theologie und Spiritualität

Wie bereits erwähnt enthält die Liedauswahl von Andreas Moldner acht Lieder. Ihre Verse sind im Druck nicht abgesetzt, sondern fortlaufend gedruckt. In Kürze sei ein Überblick vorangestellt.

Das erste Lied „Lob und ehr mit stettem danckopfer [...]" in fünf Strophen übernimmt mit wenigen orthografischen Abweichungen einen Lobgesang der deutschsprachigen Gemeinden der Böhmischen Brüder, der 1531 in dem deutschen Brüdergesangbuch des Michael Weiße erstmals gedruckt wurde und vermutlich Weiße auch zum Verfasser hat.

Das zweite Lied in elf Strophen „Mir dancken Gott von hertzen, seiner vetterlichen trew [...]" warnt vor dem falschen Glauben an die billige Gnade und ist sehr wahrscheinlich täuferischen Ursprungs. In einem Nürnberger Druck von 1550 (bei Valentin Neuber) ist die von Moldner gedruckte Fassung ebenfalls zu finden.

Das 18 Strophen umfassende, in täuferischen Kreisen weit verbreitete und in hutterischen Handschriften enthaltene Lied „Ein blümlein auf der heiden, ist Iesus Christus fein, umb das trag ich gros leiden, o möcht ich bei i[h]m sein" stellt die älteste bekannte Überlieferung dieses Liedes dar. Besonders wegen seiner noch näher zu bestimmenden Haltung zur Rechtfertigungslehre ist es für die Deutung der Kronstädter Reformation unverzichtbar.

Das vierte, achtstrophige Lied „Wiltu bei Gott dein wonung han, und seinen himmel erben" wird meist Ludwig Hätzer (alternativ auch Leonhard Schiemer) zugeschrieben. Ausdrücklich polemisiert dieses Lied gegen die lutherische Rechtfertigungslehre.

Als fünftes Lied übernahm Moldner mit geringen Abweichungen einen Christushymnus aus dem Gesangbuch Michael Weißes (1531): „O Iesu zu aller zeit, und in ewikeit gebenedeyt. Woll denen die dich hören, und sich nit lassen verfüren."

Zehn Strophen hat das Lied „Ein Klag zu Got", das sonst nicht nachzuweisen ist und eventuell von Moldner selbst stammt.

Nach einer leeren Seite folgen zwei Versdichtungen zu biblischen Stoffen; das Lied „Vom reichen Man und Lazaro" war in lutherischen Kreisen verbreitet, und ist

Spirituelle Offenheit und ethische Akzentuierung der Stadtreformation in Kronstadt | 229

auch in einem Marburger Gesangbuch von 1549 zu finden. Als letztes, das andernorts nicht nachzuweisen ist, beschließt „Von der Hochzeit in Cana Galilaeae" mit 24 Strophen das Kronstädter Achtliederbuch, das durch die allegorische Methode und die christliche Substitutionstheorie des Gottesvolkes heraussticht.

An dieser Stelle und angesichts des begrenzten Umfangs können nur einige Aspekte herausgegriffen und akzentuiert werden, die die geistlichen Dimensionen der Texte benennen. Die ersten beiden Lieder sind als Gesangbuchlieder gut geeignet und stimmen die Gemeinde auf das Lob Gottes ein. Das erste Lied ist der Hymnus von Michael Weiße: „Lob und ehr mit stettem danckopfer, sei Gott unserm vatter almechtigen schöpfer, sampt seinē sun, der hie für uns hat genug gethan. Dem heiligen geist gleicher weise, der mit seinē gaben die se[e]len kann[n] speisen, und sein gesetz, schreiben in der ausserwelten hertz."

Eröffnet mit der Trinitätstheologie, greift es die altkirchliche Terminologie der Dogmenentscheidungen der ökumenischen Konzilien auf und preist die Allmacht Gottes. Der Vater wird durchgehend angesprochen, ihm Dank gesagt für seine Wohltat, die er in Christus den Menschen erzeigt hat. Die Gemeinde, die in Anfechtung steht, wird im Glauben geprüft („wie golt zu probiren"), wird durch den Geist regiert und dankt dafür, dass sie auf Erden und in der Ewigkeit „im hellen Schein" und ewiger Freude lebt. Auch das zweite Lied (wohl von Jörg Steinmetz) nimmt eine Verfolgungs- und Prüfungssituation („Heimsuchung") in den Blick: auf Erden könne es wohl nicht anders sein, „der sünden los zu werdē, den[n] nur durch glauben und pein" Hier wird eine kleine, aber doch entscheidende Textvariante erkennbar: nicht durch „Leiden und Pein", sondern durch Glauben und Pein sei das Ziel zu erreichen, zu dem Gott viele berufen habe „zu seinem ewigen Licht". Auch in Strophe neun und zehn sind Textvarianten erkennbar: Um die Glaubensprüfung zu bestehen und der eschatologischen Strafe („straff ewiger pein") zu entgehen, erfolgt die Bitte „send uns den heiligen geist." Damit ist (im Unterschied zur Fassung bei Wackernagel) auch für die abschließende zehnte Strophe das Subjekt präzise benannt: der Heilige Geist.

Er thut gar klerlich sagen,
wol in der wahrheit gut.
Das mir nit solln verzagen,
sunder haben ein [ge]ringen mut,
das mir so fur sich lauffen
wol auf der engen ban.
leib und leben verkauffen
und also zum vatter gan.

Das dritte Lied ist nirgends sonst belegt. Es könnte also aus Siebenbürgen, vielleicht aus Kronstadt, eventuell sogar von Andreas Moldner stammen. Reinerth hält dies aus theologischen Gründen für äußerst unwahrscheinlich, denn die richtig verstandene Rechtfertigungslehre komme in diesem Lied zu kurz. Mit diesem Vorurteil (welches eine Wittenberg konforme Interpretation der Rechtfertigungslehre bei Moldner unterstellt) und der Meinung, die blumenreiche Sprache dieses Liedes deute auf den Entstehungskontext der Böhmischen Brüder hin, verstellt sich Reinerth den angemessenen Interpretationszugang. Martin Rothkegel hat auf die Schwächen der Argumentation Reinerths hingewiesen, denn die frühesten Belege der Rezeption dieses Liedes bei den Böhmischen Brüdern stammen vom Ende des 16. Jahrhunderts. Das Lied „Ein Blümlein auf der Heiden ist Jesus Christus fein" mit seinen 18 Strophen ist – im Kontext des gesamten Moldner-Gesangbuchs – meines Erachtens ein wichtiger Schlüssel zum Verständnis der dort ausgedrückten geistlichen Grundhaltung. Strophe vier appelliert an die Mitsingenden:

Wacht auf ir iungen hertzen, und bleibt in stetter hut,
Das[s] mir nit itz verschertzen, die edle blum so gut,
las[s]t euch niemant abschre[c]kē, lauft diser blumen noch,
eur sünd kan sie verde[c]ken, zum ewigen reich erwe[c]ken,
euch behüten vor der rach.

Wer ist gemeint mit den „jungen Herzen"? Entweder sind es die jugendlichen Gemeindeglieder, eventuell ist die Schuljugend gemeint, oder – wenn man Strophe acht berücksichtigt, in der als Adressat „du werter Christenmann" angesprochen wird –, die gewissermaßen neubekehrte, reformatorische Gemeinde. Ich halte letzteres für zwingend, weil ab Strophe neun die Kontroverse mit den einstmals reformfreudigen, nun aber an Tradition und Papsttum Orientierten geführt wird, also sich abgegrenzt wird von Christenmenschen, die sich von der Reformation zurückgezogen haben, also abgehängt worden sind. Mit einem Rückverweis auf den Durchzug des Volkes Israel unter der Führung Moses durchs Rote Meer wird die Situation der Einführung der Reformation verglichen. Vorbereitet wird diese Szene mit der Aufforderung, nicht zurück zu schauen, sondern vorwärts zu gehen, sich der Polemik und verfälschtem Gotteswort zu enthalten.

Diese Formulierung enthält den biblisch gesättigten Appell, nicht die Hand an den Pflug zu legen und dabei zurückzuschauen, weil sonst das Reich Gottes verfehlt werde. Analog dazu muss das Zurückbleiben bei (oder Zurückschrecken vor) der Einführung der Reformation einem Zaudern am Roten Meer verglichen werden. Die aktuellen Gegner waren zunächst die Vordenker, nun „bleiben sie hinten stan". Mehr noch, sie versuchten die jetzt Vorwärtsdrängenden zurückzurufen mit fragwürdigen Argumenten (Strophe zehn):

[…] nicht folgt götlicher lere,
sie ist unsicherlich,
das thun sie zu gefallen,
dem papst und seim gesind.

Spirituelle Offenheit und ethische Akzentuierung der Stadtreformation in Kronstadt | 231

Schließlich erfolgt in Strophe elf die Zurückweisung dieser Zumutung als Verrat an der Sache (Tragen des Judas-Beutels, Judas-Kuss) und die endgültige Feststellung der Trennung:

So lassen mir sie faren, und bleiben auf rechter fart.
Du wolst uns herr bewaren, erleuchten durch dein wort.

Wäre dieses Lied bei den Böhmischen Brüdern entstanden oder hätte einen täuferischen Entstehungskontext, dann richteten sich diese Strophen gegen eine nicht radikal genug durchgeführte Reformation. Wäre dies der Fall gewesen, hätte Moldner den Liedtext völlig missverstanden. Denn dann hätte sich eine radikale Reformation gegenüber einer gemäßigten Richtung abgegrenzt (als welche die Kronstädter bislang erscheint). Sinnvoller erscheint mir, dass es sich tatsächlich um einen Liedtext handelt, der in die Frühphase einer zur Einführung der Reformation entschlossenen Gemeinde einzuordnen ist, die sich in einem – polemischen – Abgrenzungsprozess gegenüber der katholischen Reform in der Prägung von Erasmus befindet oder diesen vollzogen hat. Wäre diese Deutung richtig, müsste erneut über die Frage der Einordnung der Kronstädter Reformation als „katholisch" diskutiert werden. Jedenfalls bleiben Fragen zu klären. Um aber die Deutung dieses Liedes und die Frage nach der Spiritualität fortzusetzen, sollen die abschließenden Strophen analysiert werden. „Solus Christus" ist der heimliche rote Faden dieses Liedes. In Strophe 15 wird metaphernreich geschildert, wie auf der Wurzel Jesse und dem Stamm Davids der „Geist in voller Blüt" gesessen war, also in der reinen Jungfrau der ewige Gott Mensch geworden war – „gestorben für uns alleine, hat geheiligt christlich gemeine." Die pneumatologische Dimension findet sich deutlich auch in diesem Lied; die Heiligung der christlichen Gemeinde ist der Weg zum eschatologischen Ziel: in Glaube, Liebe und Hoffnung werden Hindernisse und der versperrte Zugang zur Heide oder dem „Würtzgertelein" (die Verdeutschung des *hortulus animae* in Strophe 13), in dem das „Blümlein zart" steht, überwunden. Dies geschieht dadurch, dass die Sünde „mit Büßen" abgewaschen wird, die mit Dornen zugewachsene Tür schmerzvoll durchbrochen werden muss, indem man sich auf einem „schmalen steige", voll Gottvertrauen und Demut neigt, um dadurch „ins reich einge[h]en" zu können.[11] Das „solus Christus" ist aber nicht im Sinne Luthers verstanden, der den als Sühnetod verstandenen Kreuzestod Jesu als Grund der Rechtfertigung aus Glauben allein zur Basis seiner Theologie erklärt, sondern in diesem Lied wird der rechte Lebensstil und die praktische Nachfolge Christi zum Ausweis und zur Grundbedingung der Zulassung zum ewigen Leben

---

11 Diese Stelle bezieht sich auch auf Strophe drei, in der das Reich Gottes erwartet wird, in dem es unüberbietbar gut sein wird, und wo der ritterliche Streiter für die Gläubigen einen „bittern scharfen Tod" erlitten hat, womit er „uns bracht auß not".

232 | Ulrich A. Wien

deklariert. Die letzte Strophe bringt dies deutlich zum Ausdruck, wo die „Tat" gemäß Gottes Gebot herausgestrichen wird:

das gibt er denn alleine,/die do thun sein willen recht,
Vor ein christlich gemeine,/und leben christlich schlecht,
welch Got von hertzen lieben,/bekennen mit der that,
im glauben sie sich üben,/den nechsten nit betrüben,
als ers gepotten hat.

Damit liegt der Liedtext durchaus auf der Linie der Kronstädter Reformation. Valentin Wagner konnte in seinen *Praecepta vitae christianae* folgende humanistisch geprägte Frömmigkeit propagieren: „Sei gut und auch demütig, so wird dich sowohl deine Tugend als auch Gott in den Himmel hinaufheben und dir [dort] einen Platz bereiten."[12] In diesem reformbereiten humanistischen Kontext wird das Lied über das „Blümlein auf der Heiden" zum Ausweis der Stellung zur Rechtfertigungslehre Wittenberger Herkunft. Sie spielt in Kronstadt 1543 – ob nun das Lied dort entstanden ist oder nicht – keine Rolle.

Im Gegenteil: Das Lied von Ludwig Hätzer, das als nächstes in der Sammlung aufgenommen wurde, polemisiert ausdrücklich gegen die Rechtfertigungslehre. Hier heißt es in Strophe fünf:

Ja[,] spricht die welt[,] es ist nit not,/das ich mit Christo leide,
er lid doch selbst für mich den tod, /nu[n] zech ich auf sein kreyde,
er zalt für mich,/das selb glaub ich,/domit ists aufgerichtet.
O bruder mein,/es ist ein schein,/der teuffel hats erdichtet.

Eine radikale biblische Ethik, die einer Verfolgungssituation standhält und der Welt absagt, ist in diesem Lied zentral. Diese Situation spiegelt sich auch in Lied sechs „Ein Klag zu Got" wider. Es ist ein Klagelied der Gemeinde, endet aber als Vertrauenslied des Einzelnen. Der Satan tobt und schleicht sich hinterlistig, maskiert als Engel des Lichts, mit süßen, falschen Worten auf Erden ein, „zu schaden deinen frommen." Den glühenden Atem des Teufels kann nur das göttliche Wort zerschmettern und dreschen; es bleibt ewig stehen und erfreut in diesem Jammertal die Christen, deren Namen verborgen sind und auch ihre Zahl. Aus diesem Text treten eine Diasporasituation und die unklaren Gemeindeverhältnisse hervor. Wer zur wahren Kirche gehört, ist nicht offensichtlich. So erklingt die Bitte in der von allen Seiten sie umgebenden Gefahr: „Hilf iñ[,] herr frey in aller not, das[s] sie erkennen dich[,] mein Gott, und nit von dir abweichen [...]."[13] Das Lied endet in

---

12 Lateinisch: „Sis bonus atque humilis, sic te virtusque Deusque / Tollet in excelsum, constituetque locum", in: Wagner: 1554, 25–26.

13 Gott als „Herr" ist „frei" im Sinne von souverän, allmächtig in seinem Gnadenhandeln, den in Not Lebenden zu helfen; für die Verifizierung der Interpretation danke ich Cora Dietl (Gießen).

Spirituelle Offenheit und ethische Akzentuierung der Stadtreformation in Kronstadt | 233

der Vertrauensaussage, dass selbst die ‚outlaws', die Verworfenen und Ausgestoßenen, ihre Hoffnung unverbrüchlich auf Gott setzen:

Ich hoff auf dich [,] du wirst es thun,
durch deinen eingebornen son,
uns armen nit verlassen,
die wir sogar ellende sind,
verworfen und verstossen.

Anhand der hier vorgestellten Ausschnitte zeigt sich deutlich, dass die Liedauswahl eindeutig in den Kontext der Böhmischen Brüder und der Täufer gehört, dass die bislang nicht anderen Autoren zuzuweisenden Liedtexte ebenfalls in dieses Milieu einzuordnen sind, selbst wenn sie womöglich in Kronstadt entstanden sind. Die Reformation in Kronstadt zeigt sich in ihrem frühesten Gesangbuch von 1543, das durchaus Lieder für den gottesdienstlichen Gemeindegesang beinhaltet, in einer eigenartigen Profilierung. Sie zeigt eine Haltung von Menschen, die „mit Ernst Christen sein wollen",[14] die den trinitarischen Glauben, die Hoffnung auf die Erlösung durch das Kreuz Christi mit einer auf das Reich Gottes ausgerichteten Demutshaltung verbindet und eine radikale und schmerzhaft erlebte Kontrastethik als Nachfolge Christi proklamiert und zugrunde legt.

Da der Druck dieses Gesangbuchs unmittelbar mit der Publikation anderer entscheidender Texten bei der Einführung der Reformation in Kronstadt zusammenhängt, ist davon auszugehen, dass diese im Gesangbuch ausgedrückte Grundhaltung mit den Intentionen der humanistisch geprägten Stadtreformation in Einklang gesehen wurde. Für die Kronstädter Reformation ist also das Ziel einer vom Rat gesteuerten, besonders auf die ethischen Konsequenzen ausgerichteten Kirchenreform zu erschließen, die vermutlich vielfältige Traditionen (u. a. von Mystik und *Devotio moderna*, aber auch der Böhmischen Brüder und der Täufertheologie) zu integrieren wusste. Warum die Lieder Luthers (bis auf eines in den 1548 als Ergänzung der Triviumliteratur erschienenen „Odae cum harmoniis" von Honterus[15]) und verschiedener von der deutschen Reformation geprägter Gesangbücher, obwohl sie bekannt gewesen zu sein scheinen, in Kronstadt 1543 nicht in Moldners „Geistliche Lieder"-Buch aufgenommen wurden, muss offen bleiben. Deutlich ist aber festzuhalten, dass die für die frühe Wittenberger Reformation zentrale, mit der Kreuzestheologie verzahnte Rechtfertigungslehre in Kronstadt übergangen oder ausgeblendet wurde.

---

14 Formulierung Martin Luthers aus dessen Vorrede (1526): WA 19, 75.
15 Paraphrase auf Psalm 127 (Vulgata)/ 128 (Luther), Wittenberg 1543 in: Nussbächer/Philippi: 1983, 112–114.

Fortwirken der Liedersammlung Moldners

Während in der frühen Reformation das muttersprachliche Liedgut durch Luther (1483–1546) und Zwingli (1484–1531) sehr produktiv gefördert worden war und im Acht-Liederbuch von 1524 und den Erfurter Ausgaben (Enchiridien) sowie dem Klug'schen und dann Babst'schen Gesangbuch weite Verbreitung gefunden hatte, muss es verwunderlich erscheinen, dass es in der siebenbürgischen Reformation zunächst darauf keine Resonanz gab.

Das sogenannte erste Kronstädter Gesangbuch – in zwei verschiedenen Ausgaben – erschien wohl erst 1555/1556, obwohl im Reformationsbüchlein wie auch in der „Kirchenordnung aller Deutschen in Sybembürgen" (1547) deutsche Kirchengesänge und Kirchenlieder einen wesentlichen Anteil an den Werktags- und Sonntagsgottesdiensten einnehmen sollten.[16]

Vor diesem Hintergrund ist es bemerkenswert, dass Moldners Liedauswahl zunächst bei Honterus gedruckt wurde. Dann ist sie auch in dem aus der Barockzeit stammenden handschriftlichen Inhaltsverzeichnis der Ausgabe von 1555 immer noch mit vier Liedern repräsentiert. „Gott Vater in deinem Reich, erhöhe das Seufzen inniklich" (zehn Strophen), „O Jesu, zu aller Zeit und in Ewigkeit gebenedeit" (M. Weiße), „Ein Blümlein auf der heiden ist Jesus Christus fein" (mit 18 Strophen/hutterisch) sowie von Ludwig Hätzer „Willtu bey Gott dein Wonung han" (acht Strophen) sind aus Moldners Gesangbuch übernommen (Reinerth: 1976, 174). Im einzigen Exemplar des wohl 1556 erschienenen Gesangbuchs, das Valentin Wagner drucken ließ, sind alle Lieder der Moldner-Ausgabe bis auf die Cana-Versdichtung übernommen.[17]

Fazit

Moldners Achtliederbuch war das erste und früheste Gesangbuch in Kronstadt. Seine Lieder spiegelten die Frömmigkeit der städtischen Gemeinde – und ihrer Leitung – wider, sonst wären diese Lieder in dem Gesangbuch von 1556 nicht erneut aufgenommen worden. Die Liedsammlung von 1543 muss so populär und anerkannt gewesen sein, dass an ihr (bis auf das Cana-Lied) festgehalten wurde,

---

16 Zur liturgiegeschichtlichen Vorgeschichte vgl. Schullerus: 1923, 300–389; zu den liturgischen Bestimmungen der „Reformatio" (1543) vgl. für die lateinische Fassung EKO 24: 181–184 und 187, für die deutsche Version 194–196 und 199–200; die Angaben zur Liturgie in der Kirchenordnung (1547) die Artikel XVI–XIX, vgl. für die lat. Fassung EKO 24: 222–225 und für die deutsche Version 243–246.

17 Reinerth:1972, 225; Signatur der Ausgabe im Zentralarchiv der Evangelischen Landeskirche A. B. in Rumänien [ZAEKR]: 612-I, 23.

Spirituelle Offenheit und ethische Akzentuierung der Stadtreformation in Kronstadt | 235

als ergänzend dazu ein Großteil der Lieder des Babst'schen Gesangbuchs in Kronstadt offiziell eingeführt wurden. Berührungsängste oder inhaltliche Distanzierung scheint es, bis auf geringe Ausnahmen, die sich in Textvarianten zeigen, nicht gegeben zu haben. Die unterschiedlichen spirituellen Dimensionen, die die Kronstädter Reformation zu integrieren verstand, führten zwar zu theologischen Spannungen. Diese erwiesen sich wohl als nachrangig, wenn die vom Humanismus und seiner Fokussierung auf die christliche Ethik bestimmte Frömmigkeit sich mit der Orientierung an teilweise biblizistisch begründeten Normen aus dem Milieu der Täufer und Böhmischen Brüder verband. Dies konnte wohl unter anderem auch deshalb funktionieren, weil die Kronstädter Reformation aufgrund ihrer Vorordnung der Ethik zunächst auf die Rechtfertigungslehre Wittenberger Prägung schlechterdings verzichtete.

Anhang

Geistliche LIEDER DURCH H[errn] Andream Moldner gemacht. [Honterus-Druckerei Kronstadt] MDXLIII.

[1 r] DANCKSAGVNG H. Andreae Moldner [,] Prediger zu Cron.

Lob und ehr mit stettem danckopfer, sei Gott unserm vatter almechtigen schöpfer, sampt seinē sun, der hie für uns hat genug gethan. Dem heiligen geist gleicher weise, der mit seinē gaben die se[e]len kann[n] speisen, und sein gesetz, schreiben in der ausserwelten hertz. Disem Got[,] dem einigen Sabaoth sei zu allen zeytten, lob und ehr vom gantzen himlischen her, und auff allen seytten, auff dem gantzē erdreich dancksagung und klarheit, preis, heili[g]keit, benedeiung, krafft und herli[ch]keit.

Wer kan dich herr genugsam preisen, und dei[ne]m grossen namē wirdig ehr beweisen, du bist herrlich, und dein nam erschre[c]klich und ehrlich. Wer kan doch deine gewalt aussprechen, wer kā dein wunder und thatten aufrechnē, ey nu wol an, lobt Gott den herren[,] wer loben kan. Von auffgang biß zur sunnen undergang sey dir lob gesungē,[18] deine macht werd verkünde[t] tag und nacht frei von allen zungē, dein heiliger namē werdt itz[19] und alle zeit, in ewi[g]keit gelobt[,] gepreist vnd gebenedeit.

---

18 Ps 113,3.
19 jetzt.

236 | Ulrich A. Wien

Wer mag dich herre Gott durchgründen, wer kan deynes wesens orth und end erfinden, wer kan entgehn, oder deiner Gewalt sunst widersteen. Was mag an[20] dich auff erdē leben, was in luften schwebē

[1 v] und in wassern webē, welch mensch kan sich, oder welch fi[s]ch erneren an[21] dich. Herre Gott, almechtiger sabaoth[,] du bist der regiret, der die welt erhelt in irer gestalt, fruchtpar macht vnd zieret, den himmel umbwendet, lest dōnern und reg[n]en, o herr an[22] dich kan nichts leben[,] schweben noch weben.

Wer kann dir herre von uns krankē, deiner gnad und wolthat immermehr genug danckē, welch uns dein son, noch dei[ne]m willen thut und hat gethan. Disen hastu für vns gegeben, und in im versprochen das ewige lebē, gebenedeit und von sünd[,] tod und teufel erfreyt.[23] Herre Gott[,] wie gros ist deine genad über so vil sunder, die du nu durch deinen son führest zu[r] rhu[24], machest vberwinder, der welt und des fleisches, auch aller sünden kraft, durch den harnisch des glaubens in stetter ritterschafft.

Nu sey dir vatter danck gesaget, das[s] es deiner weisheit also hat behaget, durch deinen son, deinē völcklein so vil guts zu thun. Diß durch deinē geist zu regiren, vnd durch vil anfechtung wie golt zu probiren,[25] das allhie fein, und dort ewig wer im hellen schein. Freud euch heut, o ir christgläubige leut, den[n] euch ist gelungen, Christus hat als ein warer mensch und Gott,[26] hie für euch gerungen, erlanget ein[en] namen uber alle namē,[27] vnd disem sei lob und ehr in ewi[g]keit Amen.

[2 r] EIN ANDERS.

Mir dancken Gott von hertzen, seiner vetterlichen trew, Sein gnad sol niemant verschertzen, das[s] es yñ nit gerew,[28] an seinem letzten ende, wen[n] ehr verlassen ist, o herr hilff vns behende, ste vns bey Iesu Christ.

Ir vil hat Gott geruffen, zu seinem ewigē licht, Itzund thut er sie heimsuchen, wie alle welt wol sieht, wol hie auf dieser erden, kan es nit anders gesein, der sünden loszu werdē, den[n] nur durch glauben und pein.

---

20 ohne.
21 ernähren ohne.
22 ohne.
23 befreit.
24 Ruhe.
25 prüfen oder läutern.
26 Formulierung der altkirchlichen ökumenischen Konzilien und Bekenntnisse (Nizäa, Chalkedon).
27 Anspielung auf den urchristlichen Hymnus in Philipper 2.
28 gereue.

Spirituelle Offenheit und ethische Akzentuierung der Stadtreformation in Kronstadt | 237

Ia wölln wir selich werden, wir seien groß oder klein, Durch vil trübsal auf erden, mussen mir werden rein, von allen sünden schwerē, die uns beschuldigt han, wer folgt Christo dem herrē, derselb wirt gar wol bestan.

Christus[,] der spricht gar ebē, weg[29] und thür[30] will ich sein, Die warheit und das leben,[31] durch mich so gehet hinein,[32] vor im ist noch ein hagen,[33] das creutz im weg thut stan,[34] das mus ein ieder tragen,[35] wil er zum vatter gan.[36]

Die warheit wil ich iehē, wol hie zu dieser frist, Das creutz wirt angesehen, vil schwerer deñ es ist; darob thut manchem grausen, das ers nit tragen kann,[37] er spricht[,] ich will nach pausen, ich weiß ein ander ban.[38]

[2v] Zu Gott mag nimant kūmen, er trag deñ Christi ioch,[39] also hab ich vernūmen, vnd wer ein ander loch, im schaffstal ein will brechen,[40] ein mörder was er sein, Gott will sich an im rechnen,[41] durch straff ewiger pein.

Christus [,] der herr[,] will haben, ein menschen also rein, Der im das creutz nach thut tragen, und fölget im allein,[42] in allen seinen wegen, wie ich euch singen will, ioch Christi auf sich legen, vnd tragt bis an das zil.

Wer sein creutz nit wil tragen,[43] und wider hinder sicht,[44] Lest sich den teuffel iagen, nu hört wie Christus spricht, wer hie mein thut verlaugnē, wol hie auf diser erd, der darf sich nicht vertrawen, das[s] ich in bekennen werd.[45]

Wer Christū thut bekennen, find man geschribē stan, Behar[r]t bis an das ende,[46] der selb wird gar wol bestan,[47] o Gott[,] thu uns erhalten, zu deinem lob und preis, das[s] die lieb nit erkalte,[48] send uns den heiligen geist.

---

29 Joh-Evangelium: Ich bin der Weg, die Wahrheit und das Leben (Kapitel 14, Vers 6).
30 Joh-Evangelium: Ich bin die Tür, wenn jemand durch mich hinein geht, wird er selig werden (Kapitel 10, Vers 9).
31 Wie Anm 11.
32 Wie Anm. 12.
33 Einfriedung, Verhau, Hindernis.
34 stehen.
35 Anspielung auf Mk 8,34–36 par.
36 gehen.
37 Mt 11,29.
38 Bahn.
39 Joch, vgl. Anm. 17.
40 Joh 10,1.
41 rächen.
42 Vgl. Anm. 17.
43 Passionsmystische Tradition seit Bernhard von Clairvaux.
44 zurückschaut.
45 Mt 10,32f.
46 Mt 10,22.
47 Bestehen.
48 Mt 24,12.

238 | Ulrich A. Wien

Er thut gar klerlich sagen, wol in der warheit gut. Das[s] mir nit solln verzagen, sunder haben ein[en] [ge]ringen mut, das[s] mir so für sich lauffen, wol auf der engen ban,[49] leib und leben verkauffen und also zum vatter gan.

Mir dancken Gott dem [ge]rechtē, der uns geruffen

[3r] hat, Zu unwirdigen knechten, den willen[50] mir frü und spot, beyde[51] loben und preisen, immer und ewiklich, das[s] mir die ban durch reisen, im blut des lambs[52] so reich.

EIN ANDERS.

Ein blümlein auf der heiden, ist Iesus Christus fein, umb das trag ich gros leidē, o möcht ich bei im sein, darumb will ich mich massē, will all welt lassen stan, mein eigen willen hassen, wol durch die enge strassen, dort auf die heiden ausgan.

Die heide[,] die ich meine, man fint nit irē gleich. Vor Gott ist sie alleine, und nicht auf erden reich, die blum mag nit verterbē, sie gibt dē ewigen schein, ich ho[f]fs in Gott zu erwerbē, und solt ich darumb sterben, und geben das leben mein.

Vnd gib ich deñ das leben, wohl umb den herren mein, Sein reich wird her mir geben, wo mag mir besser sein, für uns hat er gelitten, ein bittern scharfen tod, hat ritterlich gestritten, sein leib hat er vor mitten,[53] und hat uns bracht auß not.

Wacht auf ir iungen hertzen, und bleibt in stetter hut, Das[s] mir nit itz verschertzen, die edle blum so gut, las[s]t euch niemant abschre[c]kē, lauft diser blumen noch, eur sünd kan sie verde[c]ken, zum ewigen reich erwe[c]ken, euch behüten vor der rach.

Willtu das blümlein brechē, auf die heiden mustu

[3v] auß gā. Zu diser welt solst sprechē, ade ich far darvon, gesegn dich Gott senft leben, hab urlaub fleisch und blut, ich will mich Gott ergeben, wider mein willen streben, und was mich dunket gut.

Ich hab also vernomē, und glaub das sicherlich, Zur blum kan niemant kūmen, er verlaugen den[n] selber sich[;] so schwing ich mich uber die heide, zu Christo[,] dem herren mein, mir geschicht lieb oder leiden, o welt mir mußen uns scheiden, es mag nit anders gsein.

Werd ich die welt verlassen, wol durch den herren mein, So wird sie mich verstossen, anlegen tod und pein, vor ir kan ich nicht pleibē, darūb ruf ich tzu Gott,

---

49 Mt 7,13 f. und Mt 19,24.
50 wollen.
51 sowohl früh als auch spät.
52 Blut des Lammes, vgl. Apk 12,11.
53 als Mittler stellvertretend gegeben.

Spirituelle Offenheit und ethische Akzentuierung der Stadtreformation in Kronstadt | 239

mit seuftzē und mit schreyen, das[s] er mich wolt erfrewen, von welt[,] sünd[,] hell[54] und tod.

Geestu[55] nu auf der strassen, du werder[56] Christenman, Du solt nit abelassen, du solst nur für sich gan[57], und nit zuruken gaffen,[58] saumen[59] an allem ort, als itz vil haben zuschaffen, mit zancken und mit klaffen, und felschen[60] Gottes wort.

Sie haben uns getriben, wol auß Egiptenland,[61] Das mir nit drin sein bliben, ir ler[62] ist uns bekannt, sie thetten uns recht füren, und gingen stetz für an, weil sie das mer[63] nu spüren, wie es sich fast[64] tut rürē, bleiben sie hinten stan.

Vnd schreien nach uns sere, ke[h]rt wider hinter

[4 r] sich, nicht folgt götlicher lere, sie ist unsicherlich, das thun sie zu gefallen, dem papst und seim gesind, und heuchlen fein mit allen, das[s] sie nur mügen erschallen, verratten uns geschwind.

So lassen mir sie farē, und bleibē auf rechter fart. Du wolst uns[,] herr[,] bewaren, erleuchten durch dein wort, das[s] uns nitpfetz[65] das eitel, sie seind der schlägenardt,[66] mir kennen dich[,] o kreutel du trechst[67] des Judas peytel,[68] sein kuß und süsse wort.

Dort ferr[69] auf iener heiden, wol in der tiefen aw,[70] Dar will ich dich bescheiden, merck eben auf und schaw, ein bechlein sichstu[71] fliessen, wol in dē tieffen grunt, gehe durch mit blossen füßē, dein sünd wasch ab mit bussen,[72] so wirt dein seel gesund.

---

54 Hölle.
55 gehst du.
56 werter.
57 vorwärtsgehen.
58 zurückschauen.
59 säumen, zögern.
60 fälschen.
61 Ägypten/dem „Sklavenhaus“ bzw. Gefangenschaft [der altgläubigen Lehre].
62 Lehre.
63 Meer.
64 sehr.
65 zwicke die Vergänglichkeit.
66 Schlangenart, Anspielung auf die Verführung und Sünde (Genesis 3).
67 trägst.
68 Beutel.
69 fern.
70 Au.
71 Siehst Du.
72 Büßen, Anklang an spätmittelalterliche Bußtheologie.

240 | Ulrich A. Wien

Darnoch so stet gar feine ein lust wurtzgertelein,[73] Das ist so hoch verzeumet,[74] niemand mag steigen hinein, die thür[,] die ist verleget, mit dörn[75] und stachel hart, hindurch mustu dich prechen, die dörn werdē dich stechen, do stet das blumlein zart.

Die thür die ist so enge, und niderig gebawt,[76] Hindurch mag niemand dringen, er hab deñ Gott vertrawt, in demut thu dich neigen, so kumstu wohl hinein, gee nach dem schmalen steige, dort auf dem grünen zweige, brich ab das blümlein fein.

Die wurtzel heisset Iesse, der stam[m] heisset David. Darauf so ist gesessen, der geist in voller blüt, von

[4v] einer Iunckfrawe reine, ward mēsch der ewig Got, gestorben für uns alleine, hat geheiligt christlich gemeine, Iesus[,] das Röslein rott.

Drei farben merck gar eben, die edle blummen hat, I[h]r deuttung dient zū leben, sie ist grün[,] gel[b] und rot, darbei solstu den glauben, die lieb[,] hofnūg vorsteen, gleich wie ein Gotes taubē, die blum ins hertz einklauben,[77] durch sie ins reich eingeen.

Das ist durch Iesum Christū, den waren Gottes son, Der hat das ewig bistum,[78] dem soltu leben nu, dein hertz solstu ihm geben, und allzeit bei im stan, damit du in dem leben, mit im in freuden schwebē, magst haben die ewige kron.[79]

Das gibt er deñ[80] alleine, die do thun sein[en] willen recht,[81] Vor ein christlich gemeine, und leben christlich schlecht, welch Got von hertzen lieben, bekennen mit der that, im glauben sie sich üben, den nechsten nit betrüben, als ers gepotten hat.

EIN ANDERS.

Wiltu bei Gott dein wonūg han, und seinē himmel erben, so far nur stetz auf seiner ban, mit Christo mustu sterben, Du must dein hertz, es gillt kein schertz, in Gottes kunst versencken, dein hab und gut, auch fleisch und blut, gentzlich dem vatter schencken.

On alle forcht und weibisch art, solst dich seins

---

73 Würzgärtchen, d. h. hortulus animae.
74 eingezäunt.
75 Dornen.
76 Zitatanklang: Enge Pforte, vgl. Mt 7,13 f.
77 aufnehmen?
78 Christus steht an der Spitze der ewigen Kirche, evtl. in Aufnahme von 1 Petr 5,4.
79 1 Petr 5,4 oder Joh 1,12.
80 denen.
81 Mt 7,21.

Spirituelle Offenheit und ethische Akzentuierung der Stadtreformation in Kronstadt | **241**

[5 r] willens halten, in frei bekennen ungespart, uñd in darnach la[sse]n walten, Greifs tapfer an, du must doch dran, ke[h]r dich an niemãds wüttē, wer nit mit streit wol aus ihm bleibt, all christen muße bluten.

Pracht, adel, gewalt, gestalt, sterck und kunst,[82] mag dich zu im nit bringen, es stinckt vor ihm, und ist umbsunst, nach demut mustu ringen. Auß all deiner kraft, do kumpt der saft, der macht dich freidich[83] lauffen, aufs hern stras, ia zil und maß, das heist all ding verkauffen.[84]

Hastu Gott lieb und kenst seinē son, als du dich berümpst mit worten, so mustu auch sein[e]n willen thun, auf erden an allen orten, Hie hilft kein glos,[85] die gschrifft ist bloß, ich kans nit anders lesen, wilstu sein from, so kanstu kurtz umb, fürs[86] teuffels gewalt nit genesen.

Ia[,] spricht die welt[,] es ist nit not, das[s] ich mit Christo leide, er lid doch selbst für mich den tod, nu zech ich auf sein kreyde,[87] Er zalt vor mich, das selb glaub ich, domit ists aufgerichtet. o bruder mein, es ist ein schein, der teuffel hats ertichtet.

Ia wers genug mit solchē wort, so het die welt gewunnen, glaub ist doch vil ein edler hort, wo er hat eingenōmen, Der weiß itz wol, von wem her sol, das kleinot zuwegen bringen, sagt ab der welt, dem gut und gelt, und hof[f]t im sol gelingen.

[5 v] Er ergibt sich Gott, acht keinen spot[t], lest alle menschē schelten, leid willig armut[,] ängst und not, obs schon das leben muß gelten, Er ist bereit, spart kein arbeit, den willen Gotts zu erhalten, er dul[de]t und lei[de]t, ist im ein freud, sein lieb mag niemant zu spalten.

Merck auf[,] o welt[,] mit sampt deiner pracht, ker ab[88] von deinem leben, gedenck den tod, und Gottes macht, schaw[,] was er dir will geben, Thustu hie buß[,] folgs[t] Christi fuß, er wirdt dich nicht verdammen, das ewig reich wirst haben gleich, mit Iesu Christo Amen.

IM THON DES SEQVUENTZ Congaudent ang. cho.

O Iesu[,] zu aller zeit, und in ewikeit gebenedeyt. Woll deñ[,] die dich hören, und sich nit lassen verfüren. Wo[h]l deñ[,] so dir leben, sich dir hertzlich undergeben.

---

82 Kunst, d. h. Können, Anstrengung bzw. Professionalität.
83 freudig.
84 Mt 19,21.
85 Glosse, erläuternde Randbemerkung.
86 von des.
87 trinke auf von ihm gewährten Kredit: Polemik gegen ethischen Libertinismus.
88 Kehre um!

Wol deñ[,] so auf erdē, deiner gnad und warheit teilhaftig werden, Wol deñ[,] die unschuldig, umb deinet wegen was leiden geduldig.

Den[n] du wirst in dort geben, mit den Englen das ewige Leben. Wo sie dich unverdriessen, recht loben und dein werden geniessen.

O Christe[,] guter hirt, du bist deiner kirchē haupt,[89]

[6r] die von hertzen deinen worten glaubt, sich an dich helt, und stetz befleist zu thun [,] was dir gefelt.

Du allein bist die ban, wie all geschrift zeiget an, durch dich kompt man zu ru gleichē zu, wol disen nu[n], so das wissen und sich schicken darzu.

Hy nu Iesu ste[h] uns bei, thu hilf und verlei[h], das[s] unser hertz mit dir verfüget sei. Du bist unser zuversicht, o verlas uns nicht, sunder zeig uns dein lieblich angesicht.

Den dyrsten und nach dir schreien, die altvetter erkantend sich als übertretter, desgleichen mir, darumb schreien mir auch wie sie zu dir.

Denn on dich kan kein lebendiger auf erden, vor Gott gerecht und selich werden, du bist die thyr, an dich kompt niemand in der Engel kyr.

Ey nu Iesu herrlich vorklert, und lobes werd, sich an[,] was unser hertz von dir begert, o ste uns bey[,] hilff und bewar, das[s] mir immerdar in dich allein vertrawen, und fest auf dich bawen.

Halt uns in deinen henden, das[s] mir uns nit abwenden, sunder deinen bund volenden.

EIN KLAG ZV GOT.

O Gott[,] vater[,] in deinem reich, erhör das seuftzen innikleich, welchs zu dir thut geschehen, von mancher frawen und auch von man, du wolst es[,] herr[,] ansehen.

[6v] Der satan ist gantz ledig zwar, er tobt und wüt In deiner schar, so gar gewalticklichen, was dein mund[,] herr[,] gebawet hat, fleist her selbs zu vernichten.

Er fert do her in grosser pracht, zum Engl des lichtes[90] sich gemacht, heimlich herein thut schleichen, mit seinen süssen falschen wort, wer kan ihm nur entweichen.

Zerstör[,] zerstör[,] o höchster Gott, des widersachers seinen rath, den er hat für genommen, mit seiner grosser hinderlist, zu schaden deinen frommen.

---

89 Kol 1,18: Haupt der Gemeinde.
90 2 Kor 11,14.

Spirituelle Offenheit und ethische Akzentuierung der Stadtreformation in Kronstadt | **243**

Wo du nit syhest[,] herr[,] darein, kein Mensch auf erd hie mag gesein, so gar bestendicklichen, den er nicht füret in sein netz, bestricket iemerlichen.

Verkürtz die tag[,] o herre Gott, umb der ausserwelten ir not, und laß sie nit beschmeissen, mits teuffels seiner argen list, von deinem wort abreyssen.

Der athem in dem munde sein, brennet wie ein glüender stein, wer sol in doch ausleschen, das wirt thun[,] herr[,] dein göttlichs wort, zuschmettern und zudreschen.

Auf das[s] dein wort bleib ewig stan, welchs sich erfreut manch christen man, in disem iamerthale, welcher namē verborgen ist, darzu auch ire zale.

Hilf iñ[,] herr frey[91] in aller not, das[s] sie erkennen dich[,] mein Gott, und nit von dir abweichen, in solcher grosser ferlikeit, umgeben auf allen seiten.

Ich hoff auf dich[,] du wirst es thun, durch deinen eingebornen son, uns armen nit verlassen, die mir sogar ellende sind, verworffen und verstossen. Amen.

[7r] VOM REICHEN MAN VND Lazaro.[92] And. Moldner.

Es war ein mal ein reicher man, mit samat und seiden angetan, der furt ein zartlichs leben, Sein hertz das rang noch grosser ehr, sein leib[,] den ziert und mestet ser, hieß im das beste geben, gar köstlich war erbaut sein hauß, er meint er wolt gar nimmer draus, darumb lebt er allzeit im sauß.

Sein weib und kind verstet man wol, sie waren freud und wolust vol, sie wüsten umb kein leiden, Sein gsind desgleichen het genug, einen vollen kropff ein ieder trug, sie lebten nur in freuden, ia[,] was nit mocht in iren mund, das gabē sie dem hauffen hund, also triben sie es alle stund.

Dar gegen dort ein betler lag, vors reichen tür mit grosser klag, hies Lazarus der arme, Sein leib[,] der war voll eiß und gschwer,[93] angst ūd schmertzen duldet er, seins wolt sich niemand erbarmen, er klaget hart sein grosse not, und wen[n] nur wollt der ewig Gott, so wer sein gwin der zeitlich tod.

Der arme gottes diener werd, begert allein die rintlein hert,[94] die bröcklein bei den füssen. Noch wolts im niemand bringen her, die hund leckten im sein geschwer, ließen sichs nit verdriessen, der hüger[,] durst und schuere pein, lernt uns hinauff ken himel schreien, mein Gott[,] sprach er[,] sich[95] schir darein.

---

91 Im Sinne von „souverän und allmächtig" im Gnadenhandeln.
92 Neutestamentliche Perikope: Lk 16,19-31.
93 Eiter und Geschwüre.
94 harte Brotrinde.
95 siehe.

244 | Ulrich A. Wien

[7 v] Nicht lang entschliff der betler lind, und ward gleich wie ein Gottes kind, von heiligen englen genommen. Sie furten in ins Abrahams schoß, do het er rue und freuden groß, bei allen gottes frommen[;] ein end het all sein wee und klag, dort schwebet er im ewigen tag, dass itz niemand aussprechen mag.

Es starb doch auch der reiche man, mit ach und wee musst er daran, nur eilends bald von hinnen, Er ward begraben in die erd, im was[96] das hellisch feur beschert, do must er brotten und brinnen,[97] o we[,] wie balt hat sich verkert, sein stoltzer pracht[,] den er auf erd, mit grosser hoffart hat verzert.

Vnd als er war in schwerer pein, do hub er auf die augē sein, sach Abraham vom ferren, Vnd Lazarum in seinē schos, er aber lid itz marter groß, die straff des gewaltigen herren, er sprach[,] mein vatter Abraham, wee mir[,] das[s] ich ie daher kam, erbarm dich mein[,] du Gottes son.

Schick umb ein wasser Lasarum, das[s] er zu mir her eilends kum, und frisch mir do mein zungen. Ia[,] nur ein tropf vom Finger sein, erkült mein hertz in diser pein, den[n] ich werd hart gedrungen, darzu gepeinigt in der flām, das feur schlecht oben mir zusam, erbarm dich mein durch Gottes nam.

Gedenck mein sun der gutten zeit, die dhast gehabt und zeitlich freud, sprach Abrahā zum reich

[8 r] en, Vnd Lazarus lid schwere pein, darum solt er in freuden sein, gepeinigt du deß gleichen, darzu ein graben dief und weit, ist zwischen uns und euch bereit,[98] das[s] jeder gwart von Gott sein bscheid.[99]

So bit[t] ich dich[,] o Abrahā, schick Lazarū in meinem nam, in meines vatters hause, Funf Brüder hab ich dorten noch, die sind gantz frech[,] ia [,] stoltz und roch,[100] sie leben nur im sause, damit in ia bezeuget werd, das[s] sie nit auch komen doher, sampt mir gepeinigt werden ser.

Sie haben Mosen alle gleich, darzu auch alle propheten reich,[101] die selben laß sie hören, O nein[,] du frōmer Abraham, so einer aus den toden kem, sie würden sich bekeren, sie würden haben rew und leid, ia trachten noch der ewigen weid, das[s] sie nicht kemen in das leid.

So sie dan Mose schetzen gering, propheten ler für lausig ding, sich selbest der freuden beraubē, Sie würdē noch vil spotten mer, eines toden menschen schreck-

---

96 war.
97 braten und brennen.
98 bereitet.
99 warte auf Gottes Urteil (im Jüngsten Gericht).
100 roh?
101 Sinn: Allgemein bekannt ist die Mose-Thora und die Gerichtspredigt der israelitischen Propheten.

Spirituelle Offenheit und ethische Akzentuierung der Stadtreformation in Kronstadt | 245

lich ler, darzu gar nichts nit glaubē, also beschloß Abraham schnel, der reich[,] der bleibt dort in der hell, do leidt er ewig pein und quel.[102]

Nun merckt gar wol ir Christen lewt, nempt fleissig war der gfehrlichen zeit, die Christus uns hie deutet, Fleucht diese welt[,] folgt Gottes rat, den er durch gschrift gegeben hat, sunst werd ir ausgereutet.

[8 v] erfors[ch]t die gschrift gar recht und woll, den[n] was man thū und laßē sol, des ist die heilig schrift gantz vol.

Der reich der schaw Gotts fürchtig sei, thu guts den armen auch dorbei, wiß das[s] er ist ein schaffer, Wer nöttig[103] ist [,] der hab gedult, gedenck[,] das[s] ers wol hab verschuldt, umb Gott den ewigen schöpfer, eins anderen bürd ein ieder trag, damit er mug am grossen tag,[104] entrinnen Gottes straf und plag.

Er wist[,][105] das[s] Gott noch diser zeit, kei[ne]m menschē weiter fristung geit, das ewig reich zu erwerbē, Derhalb versaum sich nit itzund, die weil noch ist der gnaden stund, wer anders sreich[106] will erben, das gespöt wird nichts nit gelten mer, verdampt[,] verflucht wirt ewig der, der itz veracht die gottes ler.

Der reich[,] von dem hie Christus meld, was het er geben für gold und gelt, het er möcht ledig werden, Es hilft in aber nichts nit mer, das sei uns allē ein starcke ler, das[s] mir buß thun auf erden, lob[,] ehr und preis zu diser frist, sei dir du starker Iesu Christ [,] der du ein rechter helffer bist.

Amen schreit all ir glaubigen hertz, den[n] gottes wort ist nit ein schertz, die wolthat Christi kēnet. Der hat schō sein gselschaft beweist, mit vatter[,] son[,] heiligē geist, ein Gott drei Namen genēnet, dem diēt ihr fleißig tag und nacht, o Gott[,] der du uns hast gemacht, halt uns in hut, sei drauf bedacht.

[9 r] VON DER HOCHZEIT in Cana Galilaeae.[107]

IN dem galileischen land, do lag ein stat Cana genant, dar ward der herr geladen, wol auf ein hochzeit[,] das ist war, mit sampt seinen zwelfpotē.[108]

Als in aber der Wein gebrach, Maria zu dē herren sprach, son[,] thu dich irer erbarmen, sie han kein wein, das merckstu wol, hilf in auß irē sorgen.

---

102 Qualen.
103 Not leidet.
104 beim Jüngsten Gericht.
105 Ihr wisst.
106 Das Reich.
107 Eines der sieben „Zeichen" (Wunder) Christi im Johannesevangelium: (Kapitel 2, Verse 1– 13).
108 Zwölfboten: Jünger Jesu bzw. Apostel.

246 | Ulrich A. Wien

Iesus antwort der mutter schon, weibs bild[,] was geet es mich dein [sic!] an, die stund ist noch nit kommen, die mir mein vatter hatt gesatzt, den glaubigen zu frommen.

Maria sprach zun dinern zwar, meines suns rede nempt ebē war, und losts euch nit verdrieße, was er euch heist[,] das solt ihr thū, ir werd sein wol genissen.

Sex krüg stunden all do bereit, nach der Iuden irer gewonheit, zur reinigung bestellet, wen[n] sie oftmals vom marcke quemen, das[s] in wasser nit felet.

Iesus hies wasser füllē ein, in die krüg gemachet von stein, gehorsam warn sie drotte, sie fulten sie gantz überaus, hielten seine gebotte.

Nu schencket ein und tragt es hin, dem bechermeister und gebts im, sie thetens schnellicklichen, als er den wein gekostet het, wundert sich innicklichen.

Er ruffet den breutgam zu im, sprach[,] wo hast du nur deine sin, soweit hin lassen sincken, anderleut

[9v] geben gutten wein, dem volck zu ersten zutrinken.

Du aber hast widersins thō, den gutten Wein zuletzt gelō, den leichten vorgegeben, das dünckt mich gantz unbillich sein, solchs merck selbest gar eben.

Das ist das erst zeichen gescheen, wie uns Iohānes thut vorichē,[109] in Cana Gallilaeae genant, sein herlikeit geoffembart, von allem volck aldo erkannt.

Nu hört und merket eben wol, was man alhie vorsteen sol, durch die hochzeit gescheen, man sehe den text nur fleißig an, wird in leichtli[c]h vorsteen.[110]

Galilaea unstet genant, von den Iuden gar wol erkant, da ward der herr geladen, durch die propheten immerdar, mit seuftzen und mit klagen.

Er solt das wasser wandlen thun, im gesetz angezeiget schon, das[s] sie es möchten trincken, verkerē in einen guten wein, vom glauben nicht lassen sincken.

Er kam mit sein zwelfpotten dar, verkündet das reich Gotts zuvor, den Iuden lengst versprochē, sie namens aber mitnichten an, es bleibt nit ungero[c]hē.[111]

Zun heiden wurden sie gesant, auf das[s] sein namen würd erkant, von inen angenōmen, die mutter[,] die muß darbei sein, der einikeit zufrommen.

Die krüg zur reinigung bestelt, das gsetz wirt dardurch gemelt, darein thut wasser ligen, vō außē uns nur waschē kan, im grunt bleibt es verschwigē.

Sex seind der tag von Gott gemacht, den sibentē

---

109 berichten.
110 Es folgt eine allegorische Auslegung.
111 ungerächt.

Spirituelle Offenheit und ethische Akzentuierung der Stadtreformation in Kronstadt | **247**

[10r] gar wohl betracht, was sexe han begangē, die werck im glaubē[,] vorste mich recht, die selikeit zu erlägen.

Steinen seind die herzen fürwar, der Juden gewest immerdar, das wirt alhie bedotten,[112] darūb mus man zum leiden gan, zu Christo sie auch laden.

Wasser wirt bekūmernus genant, dē wein Gotts wort lauter verstand, welchs trübsal uns kann lindern, die mir die hofnung zu im han, als rechte gottes kinder.

Die ausleger der Schrift bekant, werden bechermeister genant, wundern sich über die massen, das[s] er sein volck so lange zeit, im hunger hat gelassen.

Der breutgam wirt geruffen dar, warumb das[s] er der Iudenschar, den leichten Wein hat geben, das ist das creutz das niderschlecht, die gwissen merck gar eben.

Die hochzeit mit freuden geschicht, das macht sie hat ir tzuversicht, in Gott so gar gestellet, die lieb Gottes erforschen will, wie uns Paulus das meldet.

Das creutz gar bald vorhanden ist, welchs tragen muss ein frōmer Christ, in diesem stand verborgē. Gott hilfft im trewlich in der not, vor in will er auch sorgen.

Der gute Wein bleibt hinden stan,[113] das ist der frid darzu der lon,[114] den Christus uns wil geben, bei seinem vatter ewicklich, in dem ewigen leben.

Bibliographie

Quellen

Bándi, András/Monok, István/Verók, Attila (ed.) (2021), Lesestoffe der Siebenbürger Sachsen (1575–1800). Kronstadt und Burzenland/Adattár XVI–XVIII. századi szellemi mozgalmaink történetéhez = Materialien zur Geschichte der Geistesströmungen des 16–18. Jahrhunderts in Ungarn, 16/6. – Erdélyi könyvesházak = Bibliotheken in Siebenbürgen, VI, Budapest, MTA Könyvtár és Információs Központ = Bibliothek und Informationszentrum der Ungarischen Akademie der Wissenschaften.

Binder, Ludwig (1996), Johannes Honterus. Schriften, Briefe, Zeugnisse, durchgesehen und ergänzt von Gernot Nussbächer, Bukarest, Kriterion.

Bunyitay, Vincze/Rapaics, Rajmund/Karácsonyi, János (ed.) (1902), Monumenta Ecclesiastica tempora innovatae in Hungaria religionis illustrantia, vol. I (1520–1529), Budapest: Szent István-Társulat.

---

112 angedeutet / bedeutet.
113 wird zurückgehalten, kommt zum Schluss.
114 Der Lohn des Gottesreiches: Friede im ewigen Leben.

248 | Ulrich A. Wien

EKO 24 = ARMGART, MARTIN / MEESE, KARIN (ed.) (2012), Die evangelischen Kirchenordnungen des 16. Jahrhunderts, Bd. 24: Das Fürstentum Siebenbürgen. Das Rechtsgebiet und die Kirche der Siebenbürger Sachsen, Tübingen, Mohr Siebeck.

GROSS, JULIUS (1927), Honterus Schriften, Gross Julius (ed.), Schriften des Johannes Honterus, Valentin Wagner und Markus Fronius, Kronstadt, Gutenberg.

GROSS, JULIUS, (ed.) (1896), Quellen zur Geschichte der Stadt Kronstadt 3: Rechnungen aus (1475), 1511–1550 (1571), Kronstadt: Zeidner.

LUTHER, MARTIN (1897), Deutsche Messe und Ordnung Gottesdiensts, 1526, WA 19, 70–113.

MONOK, ISTVÁN / ÖTVÖS, PÉTER / VERÓK, ATTILA (ed.) (2004), Lesestoffe der Siebenbürger Sachsen (1575–1750, I–II), Adattár XVI–XVIII. századi szellemi mozgalmaink történetéhez = Materialien zur Geschichte der Geistesströmungen des 16.–18. Jahrhunderts in Ungarn; 16/4.1-4.2 – Erdélyi könyvesházak = Bibliotheken in Siebenbürgen, IV / 1–2, Budapest, Országos Széchényi Könyvtár.

NUSSBÄCHER, GERNOT / PHILIPPI, ASTRID (ed.) (1983), Odae Cvm Harmoniis 1548, Honterus, Faksimile Nachdruck, Transkription, Bukarest, Kriterion.

OLTARD, ANDREAS (1650), Concio solennis et extraordinaria complectens Initia et progressum reformationis prima eecclesiarum Saxonicarum in Sede Cibiniensi, in Transilvania, constitutarum. Elaborata et habita Cibinii Anno 1650. Ipsa Dominica Jubilate, quaeerat dies 8. MaiJ, dam ibidem Visitationem Ecclesiarum Saxonicarum, ordiretur et auspicaretur bono cum Deo, Reverendus et Clarissimus Vir Dominus Christianus Barthius Pastor Birthalbensis, Episcopus et Superintendens earundem. Ab Andrea Oltardo, Pastore Cibiniensi, nec non eiusdem Capituli Decano, Cibinii Transylvaniae, imprimebat Marcus Pistorius, Anno 1650, 41, 56–62 (RMNy 2343; VD 17 3:015394N).

TRAUSCH, JOSEPH (1983), Schriftsteller-Lexikon oder biografisch-literärische Denk-Blätter der Siebenbürger Deutschen, Kronstadt, 1870. = unveränderter Nachdruck: Schriftsteller-Lexikon der Siebenbürger Deutschen, Schriften zur Landeskunde Siebenbürgens 7/II, Köln / Wien: Boehlau.

WACKERNAGEL, PHILIPP (1870), Das deutsche Kirchenlied von der ältesten Zeit bis zum Anfang des XVII. Jahrhunderts, Bd. 3, Leipzig: Teubner.

WAGNER, VALENTIN (1554), Praecepta vitae Christianae Valent, Corona: [Wagner]. (RMNY 105)

Sekundärliteratur

CSEPREGI, ZOLTÁN (2004), Die Auffassung der Reformation bei Honterus und seinen Zeitgenossen, in: Ulrich A. Wien / Krista Zach (ed.), Humanismus in Ungarn und Siebenbürgen: Politik, Religion und Kunst im 16. Jahrhundert, Siebenbürgisches Archiv 37, Köln / Weimar / Wien: Boehlau, 1–18.

FATA, MÁRTA (2000), Ungarn, das Reich der Stephanskrone, im Zeitalter der Reformation und Konfessionalisierung. Multiethnizität, Land und Konfession 1500–1700, Katholisches Leben und Kirche im Zeitalter der Glaubensspaltung 60, Münster: Aschendorf.

FRANKE, ERHARD (2004), Kirchliches und schulisches Musizieren der Siebenbürger Sachsen im 16. Jahrhundert, in: Ulrich A. Wien / Krista Zach (ed.), Humanismus in Ungarn

Spirituelle Offenheit und ethische Akzentuierung der Stadtreformation in Kronstadt | **249**

und Siebenbürgen: Politik, Religion und Kunst im 16. Jahrhundert, Köln / Weimar / Wien: Boehlau, 65–134.

Gross, Julius (1886), Seltene Druckwerke in der Bibliothek des evang. Gymnasiums A. B., Kronstadt, Korrespondenzblatt des Vereins für siebenbürgische Landeskunde IX/1, 1–5.

Herbert, Heinrich (1883), Die Reformation in Hermannstadt und dem Hermannstädter Capitel: Festschrift zur 400-jährigen Gedächtnißfeier der Geburt Dr. Martin Luthers, Hermannstadt: von Closius.

Jürgens, Henning P. (2015), Das Evangelium singen. Gesangbücher und Psalter im europäischen Kontext, in: I. Dingel/U. Lotz-Heumann (ed.), Entfaltung und zeitgenössische Wirkung der Reformation im europäischen Kontext = Dissemination and Contemporary Impact of the Reformation in a European Context. Schriften des Vereins für Reformationsgeschichte 216, Gütersloh: Gütersloher Verlagshaus, 103–123.

Klein, Karl Kurt (1935), Der Humanist und Reformator Johannes Honter. Untersuchungen zur siebenbürgischen Geistes- und Reformationsgeschichte, Hermannstadt: Krafft und Drotleff.

Mager, Inge (1986), Lied und Reformation. Beobachtungen zur reformatorischen Singbewegung in norddeutschen Städten, in: Alfred Dürr/Walter Killy (ed.), Das protestantische Kirchenlied im 16. und 17. Jahrhundert: text-, musik- u. theologiegeschichtliche Probleme, Wiesbaden: Harrassowitz, 25–38.

Plajer, Dietmar (1980), Zur Geschichte des Kronstädter Gesangbuches, in: Christoph Klein (ed.), Bewahrung und Erneuerung. Festschrift für Bischof D. Albert Klein, Beihefte zu den Kirchlichen Blättern, 2, [Hermannstadt], 223–236.

Reinerth, Karl (1979), Die Gründung der evangelischen Kirchen in Siebenbürgen, Studia Transylvanica 5, Köln / Wien: Boehlau, 13–18.

Reinerth, Karl (1976), Nochmals: Das älteste siebenbürgisch deutsche Gesangbuch, Jahrbuch für Liturgik und Hymnologie 20, 172–176.

Reinerth, Karl (1973), H. Andreas Moldner aus Kronstadt und sein Gesangbüchlein aus dem Jahr 1543, Korrespondenzblatt des Arbeitskreises für Siebenbürgische Landeskunde 3, 1–10.

Reinerth, Karl (1972), Das älteste siebenbürgisch-deutsche evangelische Gesangbuch, Jahrbuch für Liturgik und Hymnologie 17, 221–235.

Reinerth, Karl (1929), Die reformationsgeschichtliche Stellung des Johannes Honterus in den Vorreden zu Augustins Sentenzen und Ketzerkatalog, Korrespondenzblatt des Vereins für siebenbürgische Landeskunde, 52/7–8, 97–114.

Rempel, John D. (2011), Anabaptist Religious Literature and Hymnology, in: John D. Roth/James A. Stayer (ed.), A Companion to Anabaptism and Spiritualism, 1521–1700, Leiden/Boston: Brill, 389–424.

RMNy, (1971) = Régi Magyarországi Nyomtatványok I.: 1473–1600, Borsa Gedeon et al. (ed.) Budapest: Akadémiai Kiadó.

Rothkegel, Martin (2001), Ein ‚schwärmerischer‘ Vorfahr des siebenbürgischen Gesangbuches: Täuferische und böhmisch-brüderische Lieder in einem Kronstädter Druck von 1543, Freikirchenforschung 11, 195–207.

Schilling, Johannes (2016), ‚Die Musik ist eine herrliche Gabe Gottes‘: Luther und die Reformation der Musik, in: von Dietrich Korsch/Jan Lohrengel (ed.), Das Evangelium

250 | Ulrich A. Wien

in der Geschichte der Frömmigkeit: Kirchengeschichtliche Aufsätze, Leipzig: Evangelische Verlagsanstalt, 187–201.

SCHLACHTA, ASTRID VON (2020), Täufer: Von der Reformation ins 21. Jahrhundert, Tübingen: A. Francke.

SCHULLERUS, ADOLF (1923), Geschichte des Gottesdienstes in der siebenbürgisch sächsischen Kirche, Teil 3 aus: Luthers Sprache in Siebenbürgen. Forschungen zur siebenbürgischen Geistes- und Sprachgeschichte im Zeitalter der Reformation, Archiv des Vereins für siebenbürgische Landeskunde 41/2, 299–522.

ŞINDILARIU, THOMAS (2017), Der Beginn der Reformation in Kronstadt: Ansätze zu einer Neubewertung, in: Bernhard Heigl/Thomas Şindilariu (ed.), Quellen zur Geschichte der Stadt Kronstadt, Band VIII, Beiheft 2: Johannes Honterus, Reformatio ecclesiae Coronensis ac totius Barcensis provinciae. Corona 1543, Kronstadt: Aldus, 1–32.

STAYER, JAMES M. (2011), Swiss-South-German Anabaptism, 1526–1540, in: John D. Roth/James A. Stayer (ed.), A Companion to Anabaptism and Spiritualism, 1521–1700, Leiden/Boston: Brill, 83–117, 99–109.

SZEGEDI, EDIT (2012), Wohin gehört die Kronstädter Reformation? Versuch einer theologischen Zuordnung von Johannes Honterus und der Reformation in Kronstadt, Banatica 22, 77–85, 78.

TEUTSCH, FRIEDRICH (1921), Geschichte der evangelischen Kirche in Siebenbürgen, Band 1: 1150–1699, Hermannstadt: Krafft und Drotleff.

VERÓK, ATTILA (2020), Melanchthon-Rezeption bei den Siebenbürger Sachsen im Reformationsjahrhundert, in: Andrea Seidler/István Monok (ed.), Reformation und Bücher: Zentren der Ideen – Zentren der Buchproduktion, Wolfenbütteler Schriften zur Geschichte des Buchwesens 51, Wiesbaden: Harrassowitz, 123–138.

WETTER, EVELIN/KIENZLER, CORINNA/ZIEGLER, ÁGNES (ed.) (2015), Liturgische Gewänder in der Schwarzen Kirche zu Kronstadt in Siebenbürgen, Riggisberg: Abegg-Stiftung.

WIEN, ULRICH ANDREAS (2015, 2020), Der Humanist Johannes Honterus, in: Robert Offner/Harald Roth/Thomas Şindilariu/Ulrich A. Wien (ed.), Johannes Honterus. Rudimenta Cosmographica: Grundzüge einer Weltbeschreibung, Corona/Kronstadt, 1542, Hermannstadt/Bonn: Schiller, 11–37.

WIEN, ULRICH ANDREAS (2019), Flucht hinter den Osmanischen Vorhang: Glaubensflüchtlinge in Siebenbürgen, Journal of Early Modern Christianity 6/1, 19–41.

Edit Szegedi
Babeş-Bolyai-Universität, Klausenburg

Adiaphora und „recycling": protestantische Heiligengebete?

Einleitung

1640 beschließt János Béldi, der Grundherr von Bodeln (Budila/Bodola), vom Katholizismus zum Calvinismus zu konvertieren, wobei die Untertanen ihrem Grundherrn folgen sollten (Ötvös:1859, 208) – laut dem Landtagsartikel von 1591 durften aber die Grundherren ihre Untertanen nicht zur Konversion zwingen.[1] Außerdem wäre eine radikale Konversion aus der Sicht von István Geleji Katona, Bischof der reformierten Kirche in Siebenbürgen, der über den Konversionsprozess der Gemeinde dem Fürsten Georg Rákóczi I. berichtete (Ötvös: 1859, 208– 211), kontraproduktiv gewesen, weshalb er einen graduellen Übergang von der einen zur anderen Konfession empfahl:

[…] wie ich sie ebenfalls instruiert habe: zum ersten, dass man ihnen das Fasten erhält; zum zweiten, dass sie die Heiligenfeste halten; zum dritten, dass ihre Altäre nicht entfernt werden […] Das [Heiligen]fest hat Herr Béldi ihnen genehmigt […] obzwar ich es nicht erlaube, dass das Fest von dem Predigerstuhl verkündigt werde […] an dem Tag soll der Prediger ihnen einmal [predigen], aber nicht über das Fest und auch nicht über den Heiligen, sondern über irgendeine heilige Materie; […] denn es ist schwer, sie dazu zu bringen, alles aufzugeben, vornehmlich weil sie vorher nicht unsrige waren, sondern Lutheraner und zu den Sachsen gehörten, die die Aposteltage und darüber hinaus einige Heiligen feierten. (Ötvös: 1859, 209)

Der Begriff Bischof ist hier bewusst anstelle von Superintendent gewählt, um auf die Episkopalstruktur der reformierten Kirche in Siebenbürgen[2] und somit auf die

---

1 A fejérvári egyetemes országgyűlés törvényei, 1591. nov. 1–20 [Landtag Weißenburg 1–20 November, 1591], in EOE: 1877, 385; bestätigt und erweitert in *Approbatae Constitutiones: 1815*, Prima Pars. Titulus Primus. Articulus VIII, 4.

2 Botond Gudor spricht von einem episkopalen Absolutismus in der reformierten Kirche des 17. Jahrhunderts, Gudor:2012, 39.

252 | Edit Szegedi

tatsächliche Macht und sowie Ambitionen[3] des genannten Superintendenten hinzuweisen.

Zu den Schwierigkeiten, die Geleji Katona bei der Konversion der besagten Gemeinde vom Katholizismus zum Calvinismus sah, gehörte neben der (nicht belegbaren) Zugehörigkeit der Dorfbewohner zum Luthertum (Ötvös: 1859, 209) die reale Gefahr der Nähe lutherischer Gemeinden Tartlau (Prejmer, Prázsmár) und Kronstadt (Brașov, Brassó). Der Kronstädter Stadtpfarrer Simon Albelius überprüfte nämlich die ungarischen untertänigen Gemeinden seit 1637 auf ihre Rechtgläubigkeit (Trausch: 1852, 54). Denn für die Lutheraner gehörten die Feste der Apostel wie auch einiger Heiligen zur konfessionellen Identität – d. h., die katholischen Bewohner von Bodeln hatten somit, egal ob sie einst Lutheraner gewesen waren oder „nur" in der Nachbarschaft des lutherischen Kerngebietes von Siebenbürgen lebten – eine evangelische d. h. „legitime" Form der Heiligenverehrung erlebt, was die Bestrebungen des streng calvinistischen Bischofs zusätzlich erschwert hätte.

Die Frage, ob es protestantische Heiligengebete in Siebenbürgen gegeben hat, beschränkt sich demnach nicht auf die religiöse Praxis. Es geht vielmehr um den Stellenwert des Heiligengedenkens in der Identität des siebenbürgischen Luthertums, sowie um die Rolle der Adiaphora und damit um den Umgang mit dem vorreformatorischen Erbe im politischen Kontext des Fürstentums im Zeitalter der reformierten Fürsten. Waren also die Adiaphora nur „schmückendes Beiwerk" einer Kirche auf der Suche nach ihrer Identität bzw. zur Verteidigung derselbigen oder gehörten sie zur Substanz des siebenbürgischen Luthertums, das durch eine „recycelte" Version der vorreformatorischen Frömmigkeit sich von der reformierten Kirche nicht nur dogmatisch greifbar, sondern auch sinnlich wahrnehmbar abgrenzte?

Adiaphora und Recycling – Adiaphora als Recycling?

Die zitierte Textstelle von Geleji enthält wichtige Hinweise auf die Bedeutung des Begriffs Adiaphora, auch wenn der Bischof den Begriff gar nicht gebraucht. Erstaunlich, denn unerwartet dabei ist, dass Geleji, der orthodoxe Calvinist, in seiner Auffassung über die Mitteldinge Luther sehr nahe kommt: es geht um Dinge, die nicht heilsnotwendig sind, demnach auch abgeschafft werden können, die aber um

---

3 Geleji Katona nannte sich „Episcopus seu Superattendens Ecclesiarum in Regno Transsylvaniae Orthodoxarum Ungaricarum, & quarundam etiam Walachicarum; ut & Lutherianarum Saxonicarum, nec non Samosatenianarum, vulgo Unitarianarum, reapse Dualistarum, Siculicarum Trisedensium, in Moralibus; Pastor Ecclesiae Albensis primarius, ac Senior Dioeceseos eidem annexae", in: Praeconium Evangelicum: 1638, Titelblatt des ersten Bandes.

Adiaphora und „recycling": protestantische Heiligengebete? | 253

der Schonung der Schwachen wegen trotzdem, wenn auch vorübergehend, beibehalten werden dürfen.[4] Für Geleji bedeutet Adiaphoron/Adiaphora eine Übergangslösung, wobei Teile des vorreformatorischen Erbes selektiv weitergeführt werden, obwohl sie mit dem neuen Glauben nicht vereinbar sind.

Für Geleji gehören aber die Mitteldinge nicht zur Sphäre dessen, „was nicht geboten und nicht verboten ist". Heiligenfeste jeder Art sind verboten, sie werden abgeschafft und unter keinerlei Bedingung mehr wiedereingeführt. Adiaphora sind somit keine Beliebigkeiten, auch wenn sie die theologische Substanz einer Kirche scheinbar nicht berühren. Die Feier der kaum noch als solche erkennbaren Heiligenfeste werden vom reformierten Bischof als Not- und Übergangslösung, als zeitweilig geduldeter Götzendienst betrachtet: in der Kirche selbst, im Raum des öffentlichen Gottesdienstes[5] also, darf das Fest nicht als solches begangen werden.

Die Verwendung des anachronistisch modernen Begriffs „recycling" ist kein Zufall, denn Adiaphora ist ohne „recycling" schwer möglich. Durch die Bearbeitung im weitesten Sinne (von minimalen Eingriffen bis hin zu Uminterpretation und Zweckentfremdung) des vorreformatorischen Erbes in jenen Bereichen, die die Grundlagen des Glaubens nicht berühren, wurde es zum Adiaphoron und nicht zum *casus confessionis*. Das vorreformatorische Erbe wurde selektiv weitergeführt, Teile davon konnten abgeschafft und wieder eingeführt werden, Erbstücke konnten von Übergangslösungen zu identitären Kennzeichen werden, die es zu verteidigen galt (Szegedi: 2008, 62–65). Adiaphora waren gleichzeitig eine politische Angelegenheit, vor allem wenn es um religionspolitische Duldung, Verfolgung oder Verbot ging. Sie konnten willkommene Gelegenheiten für Eingriffe seitens der politischen Macht bieten, so wie das die Unitarier schmerzlich erfahren mussten (Szegedi: 2008, 68–70, 72–74). Das Weiterleben der Heiligenfeste im siebenbürgischen Luthertum spielte somit im konfessionellen Grenzgebiet zwischen Königsboden, den Komitaten und den szeklerischen Dreistühlen neben der theologischen auch eine geradezu politische Rolle.

Die politische Dimension der Adiaphora geht aus den Approbaten hervor:

[…] In der kirchlichen Leitung und sowie in den Riten war es den Kirchen von vorne herein erlaubt zu ändern und zu verändern, was gemäß der christlichen Freiheit auch nicht eingeschränkt oder verboten sein wird, aber gleich den übrigen christlichen Ländern sowie das auch in unserem Land gebräuchlich war und ist, und zwar: dass in minoribus, die nur den geistlichen Stand betreffen, […] gleichermaßen darf es in externis ritibus directio-

---

4 WA 10/III,11–18, 22–27, 36–38, 60–62, WA 12, 205, 208, 214; ders., WA 19, 72–75, 85, 112–113; Confessio: [10]1986, Art. XXVI. Von Unterscheid der Speis/De discrimine ciborum, 106–107.
5 Dürr: 2006, 23, 24, 28.

254 | Edit Szegedi

neque Ecclesiastica reformatio und variatio geben (die [aber] keineswegs die Grundlagen und Artikel des Glaubens und des Bekenntnisses beeinträchtigen).[6]

Heiligengedenken als Adiaphora

Im Artikel XXI. des Augsburgischen Bekenntnisses *Vom Dienst der Heiligen. De cultu sanctorum* wird das Gedenken der Heiligen als Vorbilder im Glauben aber auch im Alltag ausdrücklich erlaubt, nicht aber ihre Anrufung. Somit sind Heilige keine Vermittler, Fürsprecher und Helfer mehr.[7]

Das Heiligengedenken bedeutete ursprünglich mehr als eine bloss pädagogische Erinnerung an große biblische oder außerbiblische Vorbilder (Knodt: 1998, 146; Steiger: 2002, 232; vgl. Szegedi: 2009, 95–115) – so war z.B. der Hl. Christophorus für Martin Luther das Ebenbild aller Gläubigen, da jeder Christ ein Christusträger sein sollte (Steiger: 2010, 14, 16, 18, 20, 29). Die Heiligenlegenden wurden zwar kritisiert, aber nicht ganz verworfen, sondern im Sinne der Rechtfertigungslehre umgearbeitet und reformuliert – ein Beispiel dafür ist das Lied *Es war ein gottfürchtiges und christliches Jungfräulein* von Nicolaus Hermann über Leben und Martyrium der Hl. Dorothea, welches in das Kronstädter handschriftliche Gesangbuch I. 78 aufgenommen wurde (Szőcs: 2009, 231).

In der *Agenda für die Seelsorger und Kirchendiener in Siebenbürgen* von 1547 wurden folgende Heiligenfeste in die Liste der Feiertage aufgenommen: Conversio Pauli; Purificatio Mariae; Matthias; Mariae Verkündigung; Philippus und Jacobus; Johannes der Täufer; Petrus und Paulus; Visitatio Mariae; Jakob; Bartholomäus; Matthäus; Erzengel Michael; Simon und Judas; Andreas; Thomas (Agenda:1547, unpaginiert). Außer dieser Liste enthält die Agende von 1547 keine Angaben mehr über die Art, wie diese Feste gefeiert werden.[8]

---

6 Approbatae Constitutiones: 1815, Prima Pars. Titulus Primus. Articulus III, 2. (Übersetzt von E. Sz.)

7 Vom Dienst der Heiligen. /Vom Heiligendienst wird von den Unseren also gelehret, daß man der Heiligen gedenken soll, auf daß wir unsern Glauben stärken, so wir sehen, wie ihnen Gnad widerfahren, auch wie ihnen durch den Glauben geholfen ist; darzu, daß man Exempel nehme von ihren guten Werken, ein jeder nach seinem Beruf [...] Durch Schrift mag man aber nicht beweisen, daß man die Heiligen anrufen oder Hilf bei ihnen suchen soll. „Dann es ist allein ein einiger Versuhner und Mittler gesetzt zwischen Gott und Menschen, Jesus Christus", 1.Timoth. 2., welcher ist der einige Heiland, der einig oberst Priester, Gnadenstuhl und Fursprech fur Gott, Rom. 8 /De cultu sanctorum./ De cultu sanctorum docent, quod memoria sanctorum proponi potest, ut imitemur fidem eorum et bona opera iuxta vocationem [...] Sed scriptura non docet invocare sanctos seu petere auxilium a sanctis, quia unum Christum nobis proponit mediatorem, propitiatorium, pontificem et intercessorem, in: Confessio: [10]1986, 83 b,c.

8 Die Liste der Feste, wie auch die Agende selbst, wird mit folgender Ermahnung abgeschlossen, die keinerlei liturgische Hinweise enthält: „Es sol aber das volck vermanet und darzu

Adiaphora und „recycling": protestantische Heiligengebete? | 255

Als die Synode von 1578 beschloss, zwei der Feste, nämlich Jakob und Michael, als Ganztagsfeste abzuschaffen, wurden diese 1580 auf Druck der Gemeinden wieder eingeführt.[9] Heiligenfeste konnten demnach abgeschafft, allerdings mit dem Risiko eines Konfliktes mit den Gemeinden, um danach unter dem Druck der Gemeinde wieder eingeführt zu werden. Das obige Beispiel ist aus zwei Gesichtspunkten relevant: einerseits belegt es den Stand des Heiligengedenkens als Adiaphoron, andererseits weist es auf die eigentliche Schwierigkeit im protestantischen Heiligengedenken hin, nämlich das Heiligenfest als Gedenken im liturgischen Rahmen im Gottesdienst.

Außerhalb der 1547 angeführten Heiligen konnte auch anderer gedacht werden, z. B. in Reden oder Predigten, aber nicht innerhalb der Liturgie.[10] Die Gemeinden waren wegen der Abschaffung des liturgisch gefeierten Heiligengedenkens unzufrieden, was auf immer noch vorhandene Kontinuität zur vorreformatorischen Frömmigkeit hinweist, die tiefer verwurzelt war, als es der amtskirchliche Rahmen erlaubte.

Die gottesdienstliche Form des Heiligengedenken übernahmen die Kollektengebete an den Heiligenfesten, für die es allerdings keine besondere und gesonderte Liturgie gab. Die Kollektengebete waren somit die einzige liturgisch eingebettete Form des Heiligengedenkens. Die Kollekte steht in der Tradition der alten Kirche und gehört zum Proprium der Messe; inhaltlich richtet sie sich nach dem Kirchenjahr. Sie ist immer an Gott gerichtet und schließt mit der Doxologie (Schulz: 2003, 749–750), wodurch somit die offensichtliche Anrufung der Heiligen ausgeschlossen wird.

Die Art und Weise, wie die Kollektengebete an Heiligenfesten von der lutherischen Gottesdienstordnung übernommen wurden, kann u. a. anhand der Agende von 1653 (Agenda Sacra: 1653, unpaginiert) untersucht werden. Als Vergleich dienen die Messbücher, die in Ungarn vor der Reformation im Gebrauch waren (Missale: 1486; Missale: 1507). Die Kollekten der Agende von 1653 sind zweisprachig, lateinisch und deutsch. Es gibt Kollekten, die nur eine lateinische Version haben und zwar jene für die Aposteltage, wobei die Apostel in zwei Gruppen eingeteilt werden, deren Gebetstexte aber identisch sind: Philippus und Jacobus, Petrus und Paulus, Simon und Judas; Andreas, Thomas, Matthias, Jacobus, Bartholomäus, Matthäus; Conversio Pauli. Conversio Pauli befindet sich im Anhang

---

angehalten werden / das sie der Feyrtag nicht missbrauchen zu füllerey und andern lastern / so aus müssig gang folgen / Sondern ein jeglicher daran Gottes worts und des gebots warte / und die seines solches auch lere / oder lernen lasse / So aber darneben ubrige zeit ist / mag ein jeglicher für müssig gehen wol seiner erbeit warten.", Agenda: 1547.

9 Teutsch: 1883, 225, 228–229, Anmerkung 1; vgl. Articul: 2002, 222; Haner: 1694, 302; Bod: 1890, 370; Teutsch: 1932, 331.

10 „ad diem Martis proxime futurae Septimanae, quae erit 13. Juli seu Margarethae (cum ea S. Margarethae virginis ac martyri sit sacra). 1. Nomen, 2. Vitae genus, 3. Fortuna, 4. Effigies", Articul: 2002, 293.

Edit Szegedi

der Agende, die nur lateinische Kollektengebete enthält, welche dem Vergessen entrissen werden sollen[11] – die Befürchtung war allerdings unbegründet, da in der Agende von 1748 (Agenda Sacra: 1748) die Anzahl der lateinischen Kollektengebete höher ist. Allerdings setzten sich deutschsprachige Kollekten durch, wie im Falle der Gebete an den Marienfesten, Johannes der Täufer und Erzengel Michael (Agenda Sacra: 1748, 29, 32, 37–38).

Bei den lateinischen Gebeten gibt es mehrere Arten der Übernahme: vollständig (Conversio Pauli, Michael – in diesem Fall ist die deutsche Version sogar eine Übersetzung der lateinischen, Johannes der Täufer – Vgl. Anhang 1); mit kleinen Änderungen (Purificatio Mariae, Philippus und Jacobus – Vgl. Anhang 1); verändert (Petrus und Paulus – Vgl. Anhang 1). Für den Andreastag gibt es einen völlig verschiedenen Text, weil die Vorlage die Anrufung des Heiligen enthält (Vgl. Anhang 1).

Die deutsche Version der Kollektengebete, die als genuin reformatorisch gelten können, kann anhand der Gebete für die Marienfeste untersucht werden. Die Marienfeste sind Christusfeste, sodass Jesus Christus im Mittelpunkt steht, wobei aber die Person der Jungfrau Maria nicht verschwindet (Steiger: 2002,232, 246–247). Die Ausnahme bildet das Fest Purificatio Mariae, welches aber auch in der katholischen Kirche als Darstellung Jesu im Tempel bekannt ist.

Die Kollekten beziehen sich auf Ereignisse des Marienlebens, die biblisch belegt sind. Die Kollekte für Purificatio besteht in einer Bitte, ein geistlicher Simeon zu werden, um Christus geistlich sehen und erkennen zu können (Vgl. Anhang 2). Der Kollektentext für das Fest Visitatio hingegen ist ein Beispiel des Heiligengedenkens: einerseits enthält er die Bitte um den Heiligen Geist, andererseits die ausdrückliche Bitte darum, die Erinnerung an das Ereignis (Marias Besuch bei Elisabeth und die Bewegung des noch ungeborenen Johannes) wachzuhalten (Vgl. Anhang 2). Somit enthält das Kollektengebet eine Heiligenmemoria im wahrsten Sinne des Wortes, während die Kollekte für das Fest Purificatio einem Modell entspricht, das mit dem Gedenken an den Hl. Christophorus verbunden ist, denn Simeon kann auch hier als ein idealtypisches Ebenbild eines Christen gedeutet werden, wobei er im Unterschied zu Christophorus eine biblische Gestalt ist.

Fazit

Gibt es protestantische Heiligengebete? Die deutschen Kollektengebete der Agenda Sacra von 1653 können als protestantische Heiligengebete betrachtet

---

11 „Sequuntur Collectae (totius Anni) Latinae, non sine gravi causa comportatae, & ad Calcem hujus AGENDAE, ne aeterna aliquando deleantur oblivione, conjectae."

Adiaphora und „recycling": protestantische Heiligengebete? | 257

werden, auch dann, wenn sie Übersetzungen der lateinischen Version sind. Die lateinischen Fassungen können ebenfalls als solche gelten – einerseits, weil das Bewusstsein der Kontinuität mit der mittelalterlichen Kirche existierte, andererseits weil die Gebete durch kleinere oder grössere Eingriffe in die tradierten Vorlagen an die reformatorische Theologie angepasst wurden. Daher ist es nicht abwegig zu sagen, dass das Heiligengedenken eine recyclete Form der vorreformatorischen Heiligenverehrung ist. Das Heiligengedenken konnte, ohne dass es eine Glaubensgrundlage bildete, durch die Kollektengebete, aber auch durch Predigt oder Kirchenlieder, gewisse Elemente der Lehre konsolidieren.

Die Gebete für die Heiligenfeste in der Agende von 1653 erhalten im politischen Kontext des Entstehungsjahres eine zusätzliche, politische Dimension. 1653 war das Jahr der Zusammenstellung der *Approbaten,* die die Gesetze des Fürstentums sammelten und synthetisierten. Die *Approbaten* wurden von der sächsischen Nation im Landtag heftig bekämpft.[12] Ebenfalls in diesem Jahr griff die Nationsuniversität durch, um die desaströsen Ergebnisse der Kirchenvisitation von 1652 im Kisder und Kosder Kapitel[13] zu beheben und die calvinisierenden Gemeinden auf den Weg des orthodoxen Luthertums zu bringen (Binder: 1990, 54).

Verglichen mit dem Jahr 1640 gab es eine neue politische Führung und einen neuen, weniger ehrgeizigen reformierten Bischof, doch die lutherische Kirche befand sich weiterhin im Legitimierungszwang – auch gegenüber den politischen Machthabern der sächsischen Nation. In diesem Kontext war das Heiligengedenken als Adiaphoron ein bedeutender Teil der konfessionellen Identität – protestantisch, aber mit katholisierendem Antlitz. Aus der Sicht der reformierten *de facto* Staatskirche war sie schwer einzuordnen und, anders als die Unitarier, schwer angreifbar. Für István Katona Geleji, den Vertreter des episkopalen Absolutismus, der sich als Bischof aller Konfessionen betrachtete, gefährdete genau diese von ihren religiösen Praxis her schwer einzuordnende aber religionspolitisch nicht angreifbare Spielart des Protestantismus seine Calvinisierungspläne in den konfessionellen Grenzorten wie Bodeln. Das Heiligengedenken, das in den lutherischen Nachbargemeinden praktiziert wurde, gehörte zu den Elementen, die einen konfessionellen Schwebezustand aufrechterhalten konnten, d. h. das Weiterleben des Katholizismus unter dem Deckmantel des Luthertums.

Genauso wie die Nationsuniversität und die lutherische Kirche Siebenbürgens keine Undeutigkeiten mehr dulden wollten und durften (egal, welcher Verkündigungssprache sich die jeweiligen Gemeinden bedienten), so war es auch für den reformierten Bischof grundlegend, dass in den von ihm visitierten Gemeinden in jeder Hinsicht Eindeutigkeit herrscht. Während aber für die Lutheraner die Heiligenfeste ein wesentliches Merkmal der konfessionellen Identität bildeten, waren

---

12 Simonius naplója, in EOE: 1888, 446–491.
13 Simonius naplója, in EOE: 1888, 442–444.

Edit Szegedi

sie für die Reformierten ein Greuel. Der zeitweilig geduldete Ersatz (im Falle Dorfes Bodeln) für die Heiligenfeste, in dem die Heiligen aber nicht erwähnt werden durften, war aus der Sicht von Geleji Katona ein Rest eines Götzendienstes, der nur außerhalb des Sakralraumes begangen werden durfte. Heiligenfeste gehörten für Bischof Geleji Katona nicht zu jenem Teil des kirchlichen Erbes, das in einer uminterpretierten Form bewahrt und in die eigene Identität eingebaut werden konnte – für ihn gab es kein Recycling der Heiligenfeste, denn sie waren kein Adiaphoron, sondern ein *casus confessionis*.

Anhang 1: Vergleich der vorreformatorischen und der lutherischen Kollektengebete

1. Unverändert übernommene oder nur unwesentlich geänderte Texte

Conversio Pauli
Missale 1486: DEUS, qui universum mundum beati Pauli Apostoli praedicationi docuisti; da nobis quaesumus, ut cuius conversionem colimus, eius ad te exemplo gradiamur, per Dominum nostrum IESUM CHRISTUM Filium tuum, qui tecum vivit et regnat
    Agenda Sacra 1653: DEUS qui universum Mundum Beati Pauli Apostoli praedicatione docuisti, da nobis quaesumus, ut cujus conversionem colimus ejus ad te exemplo gradiamur, per Dominum nostrum Jesum Christum Filium tuum, qui tecum vivit & regnat *in unitate Spiritus Sancti DEUS, per omnia secula seculorum. Amen*

Michaelis
Missale 1486: In Festo S. Michaelis Deus, qui miro ordine Angelorum Ministeria hominumque dispensas: Concede propitius, ut a quibus tibi Ministrantibus in coelo semper assistitur, ab his in terra nostra vita muniatur, per Dominum nostrum Jesum Christum Filium tuum, qui tecum vivit & regnat in unitate Spiritus Sancti Deus, per omnia secula seculorum. Amen
    Agenda Sacra 1653: In Festo S. Michaelis Deus, qui miro ordine Angelorum Ministeria hominumque dispensas: Concede propitius, ut a quibus tibi Ministrantibus in coelo semper assistitur, ab his in terra nostra vita muniatur, per Dominum nostrum Jesum Christum Filium tuum, qui tecum vivit & regnat in unitate Spiritus Sancti Deus, per omnia secula seculorum. Amen.
    Allmächtiger Ewiger Barmhertziger Gott/der du wunderbarlicher weise der Engel-und Menschen-Dienste verordnet hast/Wir bitten dich hertzlich/verleyhe uns gnädiglich/das unser Leben hie auff Erden/behüttet und beschirmet werde/

Adiaphora und „recycling": protestantische Heiligengebete? | 259

von denen die deiner Göttlichen Majestät allzeit beywohnen im Himmel / durch denselben deinen Sohn Jesum Christum unsern Herrn.

Johannes der Täufer

Missale 1486: Praesta quaesumus omnipotens Deus, ut familia tua per viam salutis in cedat, & Beati Johannis praecursoris hortamenta sectando, ad eum, quem praedixit, secuta perveniat, Jesum Christum Dominum nostrum Filium tuum, qui tecum vivit & regnat in unitate Spiritus Sancti Deus, per omnia secula seculorum. Amen.

Agenda Sacra 1653: Praestaquae sumus omnipotens Deus, ut familia tua per viam salutis in cedat, & Beati Johannis praecursoris hortamenta sectando, ad eum, quem praedixit, secuta perveniat, Jesum Christum Dominum nostrum Filium tuum, qui tecum vivit & regnat in unitate Spiritus Sancti Deus, per omnia secula seculorum. Amen.

2. In der Aussage leicht veränderte Varianten in der lutherischen Agende

Purificatio Mariae

Missale 1486: Omnipotens sempiterne Deus, Majestatem tuam supplices oramus, ut sicut Unigenitus Filius tuus hodierna die cum nostrae carnis substantia, in templo praesentatus est, ita nos facias tibi purificatis mentibus praesentari etc.

Agenda Sacra 1653: Omnipotens sempiterne Deus, Majestatem tuam supplices oramus, ut sicut Unigenitus Filius tuus ~~hodierna die~~ cum nostrae carnis substantia, in templo praesentatus est, ita nos facias tibi purificatis mentibus praesentari, *& vitam obtinere sempiternam* [...]

Philippus & Jacobus

Missale 1486: Deus qui nos annua beatorum Apostolorum tuorum Solennitate laetificas, praestaquae sumus, utquorum gaudemus meritis, virtutibus, eorumdem quoque instruamur Exemplis. Per Dominum nostrum Jesum Christum Filium tuum, qui tecum vivit & regnat in unitate Spiritus Sanctis Deus, per omnia secula seculorum.

Agenda Sacra 1653: Deus qui nos annua beatorum Apostolorum tuorum *Philippi & Jacobi* Solennitate laetificas, praestaquae sumus, utquorum gaudemus meritis ~~virtutibus, eorumdem quoque~~ instruamur Exemplis. Per Dominum nostrum Jesum Christum Filium tuum, qui tecum vivit & regnat in unitate Spiritus Sanctis Deus, per omnia secula seculorum.

260 | Edit Szegedi

3. Stark veränderter Text

Petrus & Paulus

Missale 1486: Deus qui Ecclesiam tuam Apostoli tui Petri martyrio consecrasti, da ecclesie tue eorum in omnibus sequi preceptum per quos religionis sumpsit exordium. Deus qui multitudine gentium beati pauli apostoli tui predicatione docuisti, da nobis quae sumus ut cuius natalicia colimus eius apud te patrocinia sentiamus quique illi Beatum Paulum ad praedicandum gentibus gloriam tuam sociare dignatus es; Concede, ut omnes qui Apostolorum tuorum memoriam agimus, Spirituali remuneratione ditemur, per D. N. J.C.F. tuum, qui tecum vivit & regnat in unitate Spiritus Sancti Deus, per omnia secula seculorum. Amen

Agenda Sacra 1653: Deus qui Ecclesiam tuam Apostoli tui Petri martyrio consecrasti, da ecclesie tue eorum in omnibus sequi preceptum per quos religionis sumpsit exordium. Deus qui multitudine gentium beati pauli apostoli tui predicatione docuisti, da nobis quaesumus ut cuius natalicia colimus eius apud te patrocinia sentiamus, per D. N. J.C.F. tuum, qui tecum vivit & regnat in unitate Spiritus Sancti Deus, per omnia secula seculorum. Amen

4. Völlig neuer Text

Andreas

Missale 1486: Quae sumus omnipotens Deus: ut beatus Andreas apostolus tuus pro nobis imploret auxilium: ut a nobis reatibus absoluti a cunctis etiam periculis eruamur.

Agenda Sacra 1653: Da nobis quaesumus aeterne Deus, beati Andreae (vel N.) Apostoli tui sollemnitati gloriari, ut filius fidei confessionem, congruad evotiones ectemur, per Dominum nostrum Iesum Christum Filium tuum, qui tecum vivit et regnat in unitate etc.

Anhang 2: nachreformatorische Kollekten der Marienfeste

1. Lateinische Fassung

Purificatio Mariae

Missale 1486: Omnipotens sempiterne Deus, Majestatem tuam supplices oramus, ut sicut Unigenitus Filius tuus hodierna die cum nostrae carnis substantia, in templo praesentatus est, ita nos facias tibi purificatis mentibus praesentari, & vitam obtinere sempiternam, per eundem Dominum nostrum Jesum Christum Filium

Adiaphora und „recycling": protestantische Heiligengebete? | **261**

tuum, qui tecum vivit & regnat in unitate Spiritus Sancti Deus, per omnia secula seculorum. Amen.

Agenda Sacra 1653: Omnipotens sempiterne Deus, Majestatem tuam supplices oramus, ut sicut Unigenitus Filius tuus Omnipotens sempiterne Deus, Majestatem tuam supplices oramus, ut sicut Unigenitus Filius tuus ~~hodierna die~~ cum nostrae carnis substantia, in templo praesentatus est, ita nos facias tibi purificatis mentibus praesentari, ~~& vitam obtinere sempiternam~~, per eundem Dominum nostrum Jesum Christum Filium tuum, qui tecum vivit & regnat in unitate Spiritus Sancti Deus, per omnia secula seculorum. Amen.

Annuntiatio Mariae

Missale 1486: Deus qui de Beatae Mariae Virginis utero verbum tuum Angelo nunciate, carnem suscipere voluisti: praesta supplicibus tuis, ut qui vere eam dei genitricem credimus eius apud te in intercessionibus adiuvemur, per eundem Dominum nostrum Jesum Christum Filium tuum, qui tecum vivit & regnat in unitate Spiritus Sancti Deus, per omnia secula seculorum. Amen.

Agenda Sacra 1653: Deus qui de Beatae Mariae Virginis utero verbum tuum Angelo nunciate, carnem suscipere voluisti: praesta supplicibus tuis, ut qui *vere Filium tuum a Spiritu Sancto in Maria conceptum, natumque credimus*, ejus Filii apud te intercessionibus adjuvemur, per eundem Dominum nostrum Jesum Christum Filium tuum, qui tecum vivit & regnat in unitate Spiritus Sancti DEUS, per omnia secula seculorum. Amen.

Visitatio Mariae

Missale 1486: Mariae: Deus, qui nos praesentem festivitatem Jesu Christi Filii tui, & Mariae Matris ejus, laudibus venerari fecisti, praesta quaesumus, ut qui ejusdem Virginis humilitatis & gaudiorum, quibus Elisabeth visitavit, solennia celebramus, in eorum memoria & gaudijs jugiter maneamus, per eundem Dominum nostrum Jesum Christum Filium tuum, qui tecum vivit & regnat in unitate Spiritus Sancti Deus, per omnia secula seculorum. Amen.

Agenda Sacra 1653: Deus, qui nos praesentem festivitatem Jesu Christi Filii tui, & Mariae Matris ejus, venerari fecisti, praesta quaesumus, ut qui ejusdem Virginis humilitatis & gaudiorum, quibus Elisabeth visitavit, solennia celebramus, in eorum gaudijs ~~memoria~~ jugiter *per*maneamus, per eundem Dominum nostrum Jesum Christum Filium tuum, qui tecum vivit & regnat in unitate Spiritus Sancti DEUS, per omnia secula seculorum. Amen.

2. Deutsche Fassung (Agenda Sacra 1653)

Auff Purificationis Mariae

Allmächtiger ewiger Gott / wir bitten dich hertzlich / gibe uns dasz wir deinen Sohn erkennen / und Preisen / wie der heilige Simeon. Ihn leiblich in die Arme genommen / und Geistlich gesehen und erkandt hat / durch denselben deinen lieben Sohn Jesum Christum unseren Herrn.

Auff Annunciationis Mariae

Allmächtiger Ewiger Gott und Vater / der du gewolt hast / dasz nach anzeigung des Englischen Grusses / dein Sohn von dem Leibe der Jungfrawen Marien solt Menschliche Natur an sich nehmen / Wir bitten dich / verleyhe uns / gnädiglich / das unsere sündliche Empfängnisz / durch seine heilige Empfängnis gereiniget werde / Durch denselben deinen Sohn Jesum Christum unsern Herrn.

Oratio Visitationis Mariae

Allmächtiger Barmherziger Vater / der du ausz uberschwenglicher Güte / die Jungfraw Mariam und Mutter deines Sohnes / Elisabeth zu grüssen / und Johannem dem Täufer noch im Mutter-Leibe verschlossen / beim zusuchen / beweget hast: Wir bitten dich hertzlich / verleyhe uns / dasz wir auch durch deine Barmhertzigkeit mit dem heiligen Geist erfüllet / und von allem ubel erlöset werden / und deiner Gnadenreichen Heimsuchung nimmermehr vergessen / Durch Jesum Christum deinen lieben Sohn unsern Herrn.

Bibliographie

Quellen

AGENDA (1547) für die Seelsorger und Kirchendiener in Sybembürgen, Kronstadt: [Honter].

AGENDA SACRA (1653). Das ist: Kirchen Ordnung in Hermannstadt Auffs new ubersehen, gebessert und augelegt, gedruckt bei Marcus Pistorius, [Hermannstadt].

AGENDA SACRA (1748). Das ist: Kirchen Ordnung zum heiligen Gebrauch der Hermannstädtischen, wie auch der übrigen Ewangelischen Kirchen in Siebenbürgen, von neuem übersehen, vermehret, und aufgelegt im Jahr 1748, Hermann-Stadt: Samuel Sardi.

APPROBATAE CONSTITUTIONES (1815): Regni Transylvaniae & Partium Hungariae Eidem Annexarum. Ex Articulis ab Anno Millesimo Quingentissimo Quadragesimo, ad praesentem huncusque Millesimum Sexcentesimum Quinquagesimum tertium conclusis, compilatae. Ac primum quidem per Dominos Consiliarios revisae, tandemque in Generali Dominorum Regnicolarum, ex Edicto Celsissimi Principis, D.D. Georgii Rákóczi

Adiaphora und „recycling": protestantische Heiligengebete? | 263

II. Dei Gratia Principis Transylvaniae, Partium Regni Hungariae Domini, & Siculorum Comitis, & Domini eorum Clementissimi, in Civitatem Albam Juliam ad diem decimum quintum mensis Januarii Anni praesentis 1653. Congregatorum, in: Fronius Mátyás/Érfalvi Halmágyi Mihály (ed.), Erdély Országának Három Könyvekre osztatott Törvényes Könyve Melly Approbata, Compilata Constitutiokbol és Novellaris Articulusokbol áll. Mostan újjabban, minden Haza-Fiaknak hasznokra ki-botsáttatott, Kolosváratt: Királlyi Lyceum Betüivel.

ARTICUL (2002), so in der Visitation beschlossen, Acta Capituli Barcensis in: Gross, Juilus/Nussbächer, Gernot/Marin, Elisabeta (ed.) Quellen zur Geschichte der Stadt Kronstadt, VIII/2, Annales ecclesiastici, Kronstadt: Aldus.

CONFESSIO (1986): oder Bekanntnuß des Glaubens etlicher Fürsten und Städte uber antwort Kaiserlicher Majestat zu Augsburg Anno 1530. Confessio fidei exhibita invictissimo Imperatori Carolo V. Caesari Augusto in comitiis Augustae Anno MDXXX in: Bekenntnisschriften der evangelisch-lutherischen Kirche, Göttingen: Vandenhoeck&Ruprecht.

EOE (1877, 1888), Erdélyi Országgyűlési Emlékek = Monumenta Comitialia Regni Transilvaniae, III, XIII, ed. Szilágyi Sándor, Budapest: MTA.

HANER, GEORG (1694), Historia ecclesiarum Transylvanicarum. Francofurti et Lipsiae, Fölginer.

GELEJI KATONA, ISTVÁN (1638), Praeconium Evangelicum in quo Evangelia omnia Anniversaria, vulgo Dominicalia vocitata, concionibus CCXII … explicantur ac enarrantur; … quod quidem in Aedificationem imprimis Aulae Transsylvanicae, ac Ecclesiae Albae-Juliensis … enuntiatum, nunc vero … recognitum, auctum, ac in gratiam neophitorum verbi Dei Praeconum publici juris et usus factum per Stepanum Katona Gelejinum … (Praeconii evangelici tomus primus, seu pars hymealis ac vernalis continens omnium evangelium Dominicalium a Dominica I. Adventus ad festum usque Pentecostes novae… concionibus C. et XIX. comprehensam analysin ac exegesin, cum indice triplici… studio et opera Stephani Katona Geleji …, Albae-Juliae: [typis principis].

LUTHER, MARTIN (1905), Acht Semone D. M. Luthers von ihm gepredigt zu Wittenberg in der Fasten, 1522, WA 10/III, 1–64.

LUTHER, MARTIN (1897), Deutsche Messe und Ordnung Gottesdiensts, 1526, WA 19, 70–113.

LUTHER, MARTIN (1891), Formula missae et communionis, 1523, WA 12, 205–220.

MISSALE ECCLESIAE STRIGONIENSIS (1507), Venetiis: Luc'Antonius de Giunta.

MISSALE secundum chorum almae ecclesiae Strigonienis, (1486), Venetiis: Erhardus Radtolt.

ÖTVÖS, ÁGOSTON (1859), Geleji István élete és levelei I. Rákóczi Györgyhöz [Leben und Briefe des Geleji István an Georg Rákóczi I.], Új Magyar Muzeum, IX, I, 199–329.

TEUTSCH, GEORG DANIEL (1883),Urkundenbuch der Evangelischen Landeskirche A.B. in Siebenbürgen, II, Hermannstadt: Michaelis.

Edit Szegedi

Sekundärliteratur

BINDER, LUDWIG (1990), Die Geistliche Universität, in: Wolfgang Kessler (ed.), Gruppenautonomie in Siebenbürgen. 500 Jahre siebenbürgisch-sächsische Nationsuniversität,Köln/Wien: Böhlau, 45–63.

BOD, PETRUS (1890), Historia Hungarorum ecclesiastica, inde ab exordio Novi testamenti ad nostra tempora ex monumentis partim editis, partim vero ineditis, fide dignis, collecta studio et labore Petri Bod de Felső-Csernáton, Lugduni-Batavorum, Brill.

DÜRR, RENATE (2006), Politische Strukturen in der Frühen Neuzeit: Kirchenräume in Hildesheimer Stadt- und Landgemeinden 1550–1750, Gütersloh: Gütersloher Verlagshaus.

GUDOR, BOTOND KUND (2012), Az eltűnt Gyulafehérvári Református Egyházmegye és egyházi közösségei. Inquisitoria Dioceseos Alba-Carolinensis Reformatae relatoria, Kolozsvár – Barót: Kriterion.

KNODT, GERHARD (1998), Leitbilder des Glaubens. Die Geschichte des Heiligengedenkens in der evangelischen Kirche, Stuttgart: Calwer.

SCHULZ, FRIEDER (2003), Das Gebet. A. Das Kollektengebet, in: Hans-Christoph Schmidt-Lauber/Michael Meyer-Blanck/Karl-Heinrich Bieritz (ed.), Handbuch der Liturgik. Liturgiewissenschaft in Theologie und Praxis der Kirche, Göttingen: Vandenhoeck & Ruprecht, 742–762.

STEIGER, JOHANN ANSELM (2010), Christophorus – ein ebenbild aller christen. Ein nichtbiblisches Bild und dessen Relevanz für die Schrift-und Bildhermeneutik. Aufgezeigt an Texten Martin Luthers und Sigmund von Birkens, in: Torbjörn Johansson/Robert Kolb/Johann Anselm Steiger (ed.), Hermeneutica Sacra. Studien zur Auslegung der Heiligen Schrift im 16. und 17. Jahrhundert. Studies of the Interpretation of Holy Scripture in the Sixteenth and Seventeenth Centuries, Berlin/New York: De Gruyter, 5–32.

STEIGER, JOHANN ANSELM (2002), Fünf Zentralthemen der Theologie Luthers und seiner Erben. Communicatio – imago – figura – Maria – exempla, Leiden/Boston/Köln: Brill.

SZEGEDI, EDIT (2009), Comemorarea sfinților în Transilvanian protestantă (sec. XVI–XVII), Banatica 19, 95–115.

SZEGEDI, EDIT (2008), Was bedeutete Adiaphoron/Adiaphora im siebenbürgischen Protestantismus des 16. und 17. Jahrhunderts, in: Evelin Wetter (ed.), Formierungen des konfessionellen Raumes in Ostmitteleuropa. Forschungen zur Geschichte und Kultur des östlichen Mitteleuropa (FGKOME) 33, Stuttgart:Franz Steiner Verlag, 57–74.

SZŐCS, TAMÁS (2009), Kirchenlied zwischen Pest und Stadtbrand. Das Kronstädter Kantional I.F.78 aus dem 17. Jahrhundert, Studia Transylvanica 38. Köln/Weimar/Wien: Böhlau.

TEUTSCH, FRIEDRICH (1921),Geschichte der evangelischen Kirche in Siebenbürgen, I, Hermannstadt: Michaelis, 1150–1699.

TRAUSCH, JOSEF (1852), Geschichte des Burzenländer Capituls, Kronstadt: Gött.

Maria Crăciun
Babeş-Bolyai University of Cluj, Romania

Seeing the Word of God:
Daily Devotions and Modes of Communication in the Lutheran Churches of Early Modern Transylvania

Image versus Word

It has generally been argued that late medieval religious experience was intensely sensual as people saw, heard, smelled, touched and tasted during their encounter with the sacred (Williamson: 2013; Brown: 2013). Among the senses, sight seems to have been privileged as indicated by the frequent use of images in liturgical, paraliturgical and mundane contexts, in both individual and communal devotions (Honée: 1994; Scribner: 1989a).[1] First of all, Gregory's qualification of images as bibles for the unlettered literally replaced words with images and carved a place for them in religious instruction, while at the same time placing them in a subordinate position to texts (Mâle: 1948; Baschet: 2008, 25–33; Chazelle: 1990; Camille: 1996). Moreover, the idea that God had created man in his own likeness (Gen 1:26) and the doctrine of the incarnation had made the representation of the divine possible, while it also allowed mankind to access the sacred through images (Baschet: 2008, 16–18). For instance, people had a visual experience of the mass, as the contemplation of the elevated host was equated with visual communion (Binski: 1999, 13; Duffy: 1992, 95–102; Scribner: 1989a, 458–459).[2] Moreover, people also integrated images in their daily devotions. Discussing altarpieces as images displayed on the altar, Beth Williamson rejects the dichotomy between liturgical and devotional reception of these artefacts. She suggests instead the existence of liturgically-structured or liturgically-related responses to images. Consequently, viewers of religious images used liturgical themes and concepts to structure their individual devotion. Viewers were thus encouraged to use images as a means of devotional meditation both within their private spiritual exercises and perhaps also in public, ostensibly liturgical settings (Williamson: 2004, 343–364, 381–383). Peo-

---

1 Scribner: 1989a, 456–457 understands medieval piety as specific ways of seeing "locating it in the context of worship in the Middle Ages and then within the framework of medieval epistemology and hermeneutics" and concluding that, for medieval people, worship was a visual experience.
2 Scribner: 1989a, 458–459 suggests that, during the medieval mass, Christ was made present by an act of "sacramental seeing". He discusses the "sacramental gaze" as a form of perception that was closer to popular epistemology.

266 | Maria Crăciun

ple prayed before images of Jesus, the Virgin and the saints and sometimes were rewarded with visions while engaged in these exercises of contemplation and meditation (Ringbom: 1969; Harbison: 1985; Scribner: 1989a, 457; Hamburger: 1989; Schmidt: 2001; Wilkins: 2002; Reiss: 2008).[3] Consequently, devotion was mostly focused on images of the sacred, whether material and perceived by corporeal sight or envisioned and seen only in the mind's eye (Sand: 2005; Williamson: 2013, 3, 13; Kennedy: 2015).[4] In conclusion, medieval religious experience was shaped by the prominent role of images in devotion and by the primacy of sight in contact with the sacred.

After the Reformation, the primacy of the image in devotion was replaced with the increasing importance of the word. As suggested by Ulinka Rublack, according to Luther's 1538 treatise, God's Word was the new sacred medium "which brought fruit whenever it was preached to the believers" (Rublack: 2010, 149). The principle of *sola scriptura* emphasized the Word of God and people were encouraged to become familiar with the Bible, which was to be firmly integrated into their religious experience (Stone: 1964, 42; Stone: 1969, 76–79; Kingdon: 1966, 26; Kingdon: 2004, 48; Razovsky: 1998, 6, 10, 12; Duffy: 1992, 450, 469, 499, 587; Hutton: 1987).[5] This leaves open the question of whether the growing value of words in comparison to images also diminished the importance of sight in accessing the sacred. Some scholars have claimed that the Reformation represented "a shift from the visual to the aural, from ritual to literary exposition, from the numinous and mysterious to the everyday" (Scarisbrick: 1984, 163).[6] Others, like Ulinka Rublack

---

3 Some authors however argue that the same type of exercise could be undertaken by reading, integrating meditation into their daily lives. Corbellini/Hoogvliet: 2015, 262, 269–270, 273–274. Corbellini: 2012, 15–39.

4 Scribner: 1989a, 457–458 distinguishes between a high cultural Augustinian tradition and a popular tradition that was essentially a sacramental tradition. The former allowed for three kinds of seeing, bodily, spiritual and intellectual and encouraged ascent from physical seeing, perhaps aided by a physical image to a form of devotional seeing, without a physical image, to an imageless devotion, a direct apprehension of the divine. In the latter tradition, seeing was set in the context where the sacred was apprehended through the senses, while visual perception was given a central role.

5 For some authors, the expectation that, after the Reformation, the laity would read and interpret the Bible has become a commonplace that needs no further argument. Others have concluded that although the provision of bibles for each parish was part of reformation programmes everywhere, both secular and ecclesiastical authorities experienced difficulties in implementing this programme. As Eamon Duffy has pointed out, it was often easier to enforce the removal of images than to make wardens equip their churches for the new worship, by purchasing bibles and service books. To prove the impact of the programme, Duffy: 1992 mentions that Morebath, where the parish had already bought a Bible in 1542, acquired the new common book, the Bible, the Homilies and the Paraphrases in 1560, but admits nonetheless, that in many parishes, ministers were content to collect the books of the old faith which were either destroyed or defaced.

6 This opinion was shared by other scholars to the point of becoming a historiographical commonplace. Stone: 1969, 77 emphasizes the role of print and quotes Elizabeth Eisenstein in

have persuasively suggested that "it would be misleading to think of Lutheranism as a disembodied, interiorized religion of the word located in a 'rationally reasoning' mind, in contrast to an equally generalized 'sensuous Catholicism'" (Rublack: 2010, 144). Still the question remains whether the new emphasis placed on words impacted on the hierarchy of the senses in reformed religious experience, particularly during worship, highlighting the issue of communication.

This leads one to consider whether, in the new confessional context, reading the Bible was encouraged among the laity or whether other means of communication, oral/aural and visual were deployed to achieve knowledge of the scriptures. This further compels one to reflect on the changes in devotional patterns, which occurred in the transition from traditional Catholic practice to Protestant religious experience, highlighting issues such as the place of the senses in individual and communal piety, visual engagement with images, ritual and texts and aural engagement with the Word of God.

In attempting to answer these questions, this study will explore the intricate web of communication between clergy and laity in the Lutheran churches of early modern Transylvania, reflecting on strategies, mechanisms, media, and messages. The study wishes to suggest that the biblical text was communicated to the laity in complex ways, which still involved the senses, particularly hearing, but also seeing. From this perspective, sensuality remained a significant feature of public worship. The main contention of the study is that, contrary to general belief, the visual held its place within the ecclesiastical space and coexisted with the oral/aural in the communication strategies deployed in early modern Transylvanian Lutheran churches.

The Word Read

If one starts from a simple question "how did the laity come into contact with the Bible?" one obvious answer would be that the laity became familiar with the scriptures by reading. Existing evidence suggests that reformers did help to make

---

claiming that an "image culture" was replaced by a "word culture". He further argues that Protestantism whitewashed images and replaced them with the Ten Commandments. Perhaps surprisingly, this view is shared by art historians. Belting: 1994, 14, 458, 490 advocates the change from "image culture" to "textual culture" and refers to a "desensualized religion that now puts its trust in the word". Parker: 1992, 52 suggests that "What had passed for piety in the fifteenth century- pilgrimages, processions, veneration of relics – was now normally execrated as superstition, instead familiarity with the Bible and Christian theology were seen as crucial, because faith alone could save." Pettegree: 2005, 10–101, although he takes into account other oral media besides preaching, such as singing and theatre, still upholds the primacy of the Word of God and oral/aural means of communication over visual ones.

268 | Maria Crăciun

the Bible more accessible to the laity by translating it into the vernacular and by fostering its printing in numerous editions (Gawthrop/Strauss: 1984, 39; Strauss: 1984, 116; Cole: 1984, 327–339; Edwards: 1994, 123).[7] However, individual private reading of the Bible was far from ubiquitous for three main reasons, the clergy's reluctance to make the Bible available to the widest possible public, the high cost of bibles and the modest levels of literacy, which often made direct contact with the Gospels impossible.

If one explores the position of the early reformers on this matter, one comes to the conclusion that Martin Luther was in favour of individual private reading of the Bible only until 1525. Afterwards, he strove to discourage unmediated contact between the scripture and the untrained mind. Consequently, most of the references to the reading of the Gospel by the laity were deleted from the 1546 edition of his German New Testament. Similarly, Philip Melanchton, in later editions of the *Loci communes theologici* omitted a prefatory passage exhorting all to read the Bible (Gawthrop/Strauss: 1984, 34, 43; Strauss: 1984, 112–113). Therefore, reformers seem to have reached a consensus that the laity needed guidance in order to understand the Bible. The Common Man and Woman were not given access to canonical biblical texts but rather to excerpts from it (Bottigheimer: 1993, 66–68).[8] From the very beginning, Martin Luther interpreted the New Testament by translating it into German, by writing prefaces and marginal glosses and even by choosing particular visual layouts of the text (Edwards: 1994, 109, 113, 117–118).[9] As Edwards has persuasively argued, Luther's translation reinforced his theological concerns and encouraged readers to understand the text as the reformer thought they should (Edwards: 1994, 118, 122). Moreover, in discussing Martin Luther's *Passional*, initially published in 1529 as the third part of the *Bettbüch-*

---

7 Gawthrop/Strauss: 1984, 39 point out that bibles poured out of the printing houses of Wittenberg, Augsburg, Basle, Zürich, Leipzig, Nürenberg, Strassburg and Erfurt. Luther's close connection with printers in Wittenberg (the Lotters – Melchior, Melchior the Younger and Michael-, the Grünerbergs – Johann, Hans and Georg- and Hans Lufft) is discussed by Cole: 1984, 327–339. Between 1534 and 1574 the Hans Lufft press printed thousands of Luther's bibles (p. 334). Edwards: 1994, 123 points out that statistics on reprints suggest that the German New Testament quickly became a sixteenth-century best-seller. Forty-three distinct editions appeared in approximately forty months between 1522 and 1525. Parker: 1992, 53 mentions that Luther's German New Testament had 253 editions between 1522 and 1546 while 500000 copies of the German Bible were issued between 1534 and 1574.

8 Gawthrop/Strauss: 1984, 34, 43 used school ordinances to support their claim that bible reading was absent from sixteenth and seventeenth century Protestant curricula. Lutheran children were provided with bible excerpts and edited bible stories. In attempting to revise Gawthrop's and Strauss' revisionist position, Bottigheimer: 1993, 66–68 notes the absence of the bible from modest households and comes to the conclusion that the Common Man read the Word of God not in canonical bible texts, but rather in a variety of excerpts from it.

9 Edwards: 1994, 109, 113, 117–118, 122 suggests that with these "visually unavoidable commentaries" Luther directed readers in their reading of the New Testament. Luther wanted readers to understand the New Testament as he himself did.

Seeing the Word of God: | **269**

lein, Ruth Bottigheimer noted that the Latin edition had more texts than the German one and concluded that Luther exposed the "broad German language, Bible reading public to the briefer of the two available textual versions" thus ensuring that they read less of the scriptures (Bottigheimer: 1993, 68–72).[10] Thus, as far as the first impediment is concerned, it is generally believed that the Reformation, while appearing to set the scriptures before everyone, in fact imposed a number of 'filters', designed to protect the 'common man' from inexpert handling of the holy writ and its far-fetched interpretation. Reading the Bible, gradually became the responsibility of the clergy, who were meant to interpret it for the broader public through sermons, biblical commentaries and catechisms (Cameron: 1991, 141–143; Gawthrop/Strauss: 1984, 33–35, 50–51; Strauss: 1984, 113; Bottigheimer: 1993, 74–75; Strauss: 1975, 33).[11] In this context, Luther began to publish "works of popular indoctrination" such as his two catechisms of 1529. Quoting Luther's words: "The catechism is the layman's Bible. It contains the whole of what every Christian must know of Christian doctrine" to give added strength to his argument, Gerald Strauss has argued that the catechism soon became the authorized method of religious instruction (Strauss: 1984, 113). Consequently, it should not surprise one that the clergy were compelled to provide religious instruction for the laity by teaching the catechism (Haigh: 2001, 41–43; Teutsch: 1883, 205).[12] Thus, from England to Transylvania, provisions that parishes should own a bible do not necessarily support conclusions regarding wide individual readership for the scriptures, but rather emphasize the role of the minister in disseminating the Word of God (Duffy: 1992, 485, 493). In fact, at least in Transylvania, parishes were

---

10 Bottigheimer: 1993, 68–72 suggests that "among Lutheran theologians there was limited interest in providing children and the simple folk with biblical texts even in minimal form."

11 Gawthrop/Strauss: 1984, 35 suggest that the catechism had become the authorized method of religious instruction to the point of becoming the layman's bible. Strauss: 1984, 114 argues that school ordinances ascribed only the catechism as an instrument of religious instruction for the school population at large: "They don't say very much about the Bible as a text for religious study in class or about individual Bible reading as a practice for the populace or a habit to be instilled in the young." Bottigheimer: 1993, 74–75 suggests that the notion of the Bible as a series of cautionary tales depicting the punishment of vice dominated the production of the bibles for children during the sixteenth and seventeenth centuries. Strauss: 1975, 33 quotes Martin Luther's Preface to Stephan Klingebeil's *Von Priester Ehe* (Wittenberg, 1528), published in WA 26, 528–533, to highlight the importance attached by the reformer to the use of the catechism. Strauss who uses knowledge of the Gospel to measure the success of the Reformation emphasizes the different expectations from clergy and laity. While ministers were required to read and retain passages from the Bible, parishioners were meant to learn the Catechism. Parker: 1992, 50 points out that hundreds of catechisms were produced and circulated by diligent pastors and schoolmasters.

12 "Catechesis magna diligentia indesinenter populo et juventuti proponatur, idque justa formam a Luthero propositam" Teutsch: 1883, 195. "Volumus in scholis urgeri parvam catechesin Lutheri, ac pueris memoriae mandari." Teutsch: 1883, 199. "Exercitatio catechismi diligentissime in scholis denuncietur cum interpretatione Lutheri et Philippi." Teutsch: 1883, 227.

270 | Maria Crăciun

to be equipped not just with bibles but also with postils and catechisms (Teutsch: 1862, 30–31).[13]

One other reason why bibles may not have been widely accessible was their price (Strauss: 1984, 116).[14] Andrew Pettegree and Matthew Hall have persuasively suggested that Luther's Bible became one of the publishing sensations of the century: "It was a book difficult to produce and, as such, understandably expensive to acquire" (Pettegree/Hall: 2004, 788). Despite this fact, people did buy Luther's Bible as Ulinka Rublack has inadvertently suggested when pointing out that many used Lufft's 1541 costly edition of the German Bible to paste in or bind in images and inscriptions and, very often, Luther's signature (Rublack: 2010, 157–161).[15] Moreover, as Mark Edwards has pointed out, the expensive *folio* reprints quickly made way for *quarto* and *octavo* editions. Although these smaller, less expensive books were very likely available to a larger audience from the *folio* editions, Edwards concludes that, in light of the expense involved in acquiring even the cheapest editions of the German New Testament, those able to afford them would not have been a big group. Even so, more people would have had access to a German New Testament than at any other time in the past (Edwards: 1994, 126–128). However, it has astutely been pointed out that it is dangerous to equate bible possession with bible reading and that "the bibles intended for the protestant Everyman that had poured off Canstein presses for nearly a century had not been read by him but placed reverently on a shelf in his rural home as a sacred talisman" (Bottigheimer: 1993, 89; Strauss: 1984, 116; Cressy: 1986, 92–94).

On the other hand, scholars were compelled to ask whether the laity were equipped to read the Bible; they consequently had to assess levels of secular literacy. Literacy is an elusive phenomenon, at once complicated to study and difficult to define. Initially, historians have confronted the dichotomy literacy-illiteracy and used terms such as illiterate, semi-literate and literate, in order to qualify this phenomenon (Biller: 1994, 1–19; Moore: 1994, 31–34; Scribner: 1994, 6).[16] Defi-

---

13 Duffy: 1992, 485, 493 argues that although the injunction of 1559 insisted on the provision of bibles and paraphrases for each parish, the emphasis was still placed on the suppression of the externals of Catholicism rather than on equipping the parish for reformed services. In Transylvania, the church order of 1547 recommended that each parish church should own a Latin and a German Bible, but also postils and catechisms: "Committendum insuper, ut in qualibet ecclesia parochiali Biblia latina et germanica, Postilla quoque, quam author domesticam inscripsit, cum Catechismo et similibus necessaijs libris in lingua vernacula habeantur, et quotidie ex illis aliqua lectio ad utilitatem populi, aut si auditores desint, ad laudem et honorem Dei pro populo legatur." Teutsch: 1862, 30–31.

14 Strauss: 1984, 116 suggests that most bibles went to parish churches and ministers' libraries purchased by governments or bought out of church revenues.

15 Rublack: 2010, 157–161 suggests that books with such inscriptions often remained in a family for generations and that many bibles carried beautiful sayings that Luther and other reformers had entered into them.

16 Moore: 1994, 31–34 uses the terms literacy, semi-literacy and passive literacy.

Seeing the Word of God: | 271

nitions, explicitly provided or implied tend to suggest a more nuanced view of the issue. Scholars have increasingly considered the existence of literacy in Latin and literacy in various vernaculars. For instance, Sabrina Corbellini has aptly pointed out that, while Latin was the preferred choice for members of the *republica clericorum* and thus the official and dominant language of culture, science and religion, the new reading communities were formed by non-Latinate but generally literate urban laity, strongly involved in political, financial and commercial activities (Corbellini/Hoogvliet: 2015, 259; Hoogvliet: 2013b, 240, 266–269).[17] Scholars have increasingly considered pragmatic literacy, which refers to the use of writing for practical purposes in various, mostly professional contexts, but also signals awareness of the importance of the written document and familiarity with the act of writing (Parks: 1973, 275; Aston: 1977, 347; Scribner: 1994, 2).[18] Others have opted for the concept of passive literacy, when referring to the habits of thought and social action of those affected by literate usages even when they were not literate themselves (Nelson: 1990, 269–270; Moore: 1994, 31–34). Semi-literate has also been used to describe people who were able to read, particularly texts that they were already familiar with, such as prayer books, but not to write (Scribner: 1994, 2; Tóth: 2007, 316, 331).[19]

Moving between these layers of complexity when trying to assess the literacy of a particular society, scholars are still compelled to rely on inference from collateral data. Consequently, circumstantial evidence from Transylvania, such as the availability and accessibility of schools (Seraphin: 1891, 791–792; Köpeczi: 1994, 344), attendance of foreign universities (Tonk: 1996, 119–121; Szögi: 2011), a rather lively book trade and active printing presses (Teutsch: 1881, 1–4; Bándi: 2016, 103; Rother: 2002; Jakó: 1977, 93–116; Nussbächer: 1977, 49–50), the increasing occurrence of private libraries, both clerical and lay (Gündisch: 1987a; Gündisch: 1987b; Gündisch: 1977; Gündisch/Nägler: 1992; Gündisch/Nägler: 1994), suggests the existence of fairly literate groups at least among the urban elites (Wagner: 1998; Flóra: 2014; Dincă: 2015). Even among the middling sector of urban society one could suspect the existence of at least a level of pragmatic literacy necessary in the

---

17 Hoogvliet: 2013b, 240, 266–269 includes servants and poor people among the new reading communities and even among those who owned and read bibles and suggests that it was not uncommon for middle class merchants and artisans to own a vernacular bible, particularly since, by the fifteenth century, books had become an easily accessible commodity. Hoogvliet also suggests that complete bibles were generally owned by the elite, whereas cheaper manuscripts reproducing parts of the bible were used by other social groups, signaling the existence of new reading communities.

18 Scribner: 1994, 2 uses pragmatic literacy when writing is used in professional context, as a "tool of trade" especially by artisans and merchants.

19 Scribner: 1994, 2 distinguishes between the ability to read and the ability to write. Tóth: 2007, 316, 331 argues that peasants were able to 'read' printed texts that they already knew by heart but unable to decipher a handwritten letter that they saw for the first time.

272 | Maria Crăciun

daily management of businesses and workshops (Szende: 2009, 110).[20] This leaves open questions relating to the lower strata of urban society, artisans who did not own their workshops, journeymen, apprentices and women.[21]

These tentative assessments concerning clerical guidelines, prices of books and levels of literacy do not allow firm conclusions concerning direct contact with the scriptures through individual private reading. So, if reading was not the answer, what other possible ways were there to access the biblical text?

The Word Spoken

While the definition of literacy is open to debate, its importance, as Robert Scribner has persuasively suggested, is relative and must be appreciated through the understanding of forms of communication specific to early modern Europe. In that particular social context, to be illiterate or partly literate did not mean that one was beyond the reach of the printed word: the laity may have gained access to the scriptures aurally, as the Bible was read and explained to them (Scribner: 1994, 257–259; Scribner: 1987, 50–54; Pettegree: 2005, 117–120; Hoogvliet: 2013b, 263).[22] Moreover, as Mark Edwards has pointed out, Luther did not need to reach everyone, only those in positions of "leadership and influence". The rest of the people would have been influenced by Luther's translation of the New Testament only through sermons and oral readings from scripture (Edwards: 1994, 128; Duffy: 1992, 450).[23]

---

20 Szende: 2009, 110 mentions that the urban population produced documents of practical and mostly administrative literacy. Scholars often presume the existence of a literate urban laity strongly involved in political, financial, and commercial activities. For the early emergence of new reading communities see Corbellini/Hoogvliet: 2015, 259 who argue in support of this idea using examples from Italy, northern France and the southern Netherlands.

21 Houston: 1983, 271–272 suggests that literacy was distributed in stratified fashion, which closely resembled the hierarchy of wealth, status, position, and gender. Moreover, an important feature of early modern literacy is the superiority of towns and cities over rural areas, although they were not homogeneous literacy environments. While data from Transylvania is insufficient for definite conclusions, Hoogvliet: 2013b, 265–266 includes servants and poor people among the new reading communities of western Europe.

22 Hoogvliet: 2013b, 263 quotes Jean de Rély's 'Prologue' in support of her contention that medieval texts were filled with numerous exhortations that the laity should become familiar with the Bible, but she does not mention that the author refers specifically to hearing, listening and learning by heart.

23 Duffy: 1992, 450 suggests that the reformation of the service involved shortening the Latin lections at matins and evensong to permit a chapter of the Bible in English to be read aloud to the people.

Seeing the Word of God: | 273

In Transylvania, as in many other parts of Europe, this happened primarily in church during the service.[24] In obedience to the third commandment, the clergy encouraged people to attend church (Teutsch: 1862, 28–29; Teutsch: 1883, 210–211; Szegedi: 2006, 258, 265, 267–269, 271). Although, at first glance the Transylvanian Lutheran service may seem disturbingly like its Catholic predecessor, in fact it was, distinctly and recognizably, Lutheran. The balance between the parts was different and more time was allocated to the sermon, to readings from the Old and New Testaments, to catechetical instruction, to music, particularly to the congregational singing of Hymns and Psalms, and to prayer (Crăciun: 2014; Crăciun: 2015).[25] All these actions, preaching, reading aloud, catechizing, singing and praying involved the biblical text.

If one returns to the provisions of the Church Order approved by the synod of the Lutheran Church in 1547, ministers were expected to read from the scriptures for the edification of the congregation (Netoliczka: 1896, 16–18; Teutsch: 1862, 31–33; Teutsch: 1883, 206; Szegedi: 2006, 258–262; for the quotation see footnote 13).[26] Moreover, in Transylvanian Lutheran churches, sermons were part of nearly every service (Netoliczka: 1896, 17; Teutsch: 1862, 32–35; Teutsch: 1883, 5, 107, 195, 227), while the morning service often included a reading from the Ten Commandments (Netoliczka: 1896, 16–17; Teutsch: 1862, 32–33, 35; Teutsch: 1883, 103–104). Finally, services generally opened and closed with prayer and the *Pater Noster* was frequently part of these proceedings (Netoliczka: 1896, 16–17; Teutsch: 1862, 33–34). Taking things one step further, the synod of 1565 asked the congregation to sing pious German songs explaining the doctrine concerning the Lord's Supper (Teutsch: 1883, 105).[27] In particular, Psalm number five was to be sung in German during Vespers for the building of the community (Netoliczka: 1896, 18, 176).[28] Systematic catechetical instruction was also provided, particularly for children, but also for adults, usually after the service. In an attempt to further involve the adults in this didactic endeavour, the girls from the school were supposed to quiz each other from the catechism and to explain the questions to the audience (Netoliczka: 1896, 18, 176, 181; Teutsch: 1862, 34, 48, 69–70; Teutsch:

---

24 For the German lands, Koerner: 2004, 303–304 mentions that ministers were expected to teach the catechism and that Luther's *Small Catechism* was to be read every Sunday from every village pulpit.

25 For the general importance of sermons and singing, see Pettegree: 2005, 19–39; Davis: 1999.

26 Some of the instructions mention that the text of the Bible should be read to and interpreted for the people. Netoliczka: 1896, 17–18, 22.

27 "Adhibeantur quoque inter distribuendum cantiones germanicae, piae, continentes doctrinae de institutione et usu coene dominae."

28 "In verspertinis precibus nihil penitus est immutatum, praeterquam quod quintus psalmus ad aedificationem ecclesiae canitur lingua vulgari". "Im Vesperamt ist gar nichts gerändert worden ausser dass der 5 Psalm zur Erbauung der Gemeinde in deutscher Sprache gesungen wird."

274 | Maria Crăciun

1883, 195, 199, 205–209, 227).[29] One is led to conclude that, in the context of public worship, the biblical text was disseminated orally to the congregations. This is further emphasized by the request that the words of institution would be recited in the vernacular, in a strong voice, while the minister faced the audience (Netoliczka: 1896, 16–17, 175–176).[30]

From the point of view of the clergy, oral dissemination of the Bible could also take place at home, as artisans, particularly masters, were encouraged to educate their dependents, children, apprentices and journeymen, and ensure their minimal religious instruction or at least the internalization of moral commandments. In fact, parental duties mostly included enforcing church attendance, particularly for hearing sermons, learning the catechism and instruction in the Word of God (Teutsch: 1883, 209; Szegedi: 2006, 265). It is not entirely clear whether this fostered direct contact with the Bible or mere participation in catechism lessons. It also seems that artisans did not undertake religious instruction themselves by reading the Bible to the household or by quizzing them from the catechism.[31] I have argued elsewhere that artisans were only eager to appropriate some of the suggestions of the clergy concerning religious instruction, particularly those that highlighted discipline (Crăciun: 2013, 185–186), as guild statutes merely tended to mention that all dependents had to be raised in the fear of God (Nussbächer: 1999, 237).

Local attitudes may have conformed to suggestions coming from the Lutheran heartlands, although the latter were hardly set in stone. For instance, while in 1523 Martin Luther had stated that each householder was obliged to teach the Bible to his children and domestic servants (WA 12, 11), by 1524 he had already abandoned this earlier notion that the fundamentals of Christian religion could be taught in the home (Strauss: 1975, 35). Moreover, domestic educational endeavours seem to have been restricted to the teaching of the catechism (Parker: 1992, 77).

This becomes obvious if one looks at the place of the Bible in the education of children over a longer time span. Scholars whose research has focused on the German lands have concluded that, in the eighteenth-century idealised urban home, a

---

29 "An der übrigen Tagen der Woche aber wird vor Sonnenaufgang nach vorangehendem Gesang eine freundliche Predigt zur Unterweisung der Jugend gehalten,...", "Wenn dies alles vollendet ist, singen die Schulmädchen entweder einige Gesänge in der Kirche oder stellen sich wechselseitig Fragen über Hauptteile des Katechismus und erklären sie zur Unterweisung der Zuhörer".

30 "...minister versus ad populum verba testamenti e scripto lingua vernacula super particulas panis iuxta numerum participantium praeparatas, mox etiam super calicem et vinum clarissima vox pronuntiat" ; "...wendet sich der Priester zum Volk und spricht mit klarer Stimme die Worte des Testaments aus der heiligen Schrift in heimischer Sprache."

31 Koerner: 2004, 303–304 suggests that, for the German lands, parents were not only expected to ensure their children's attendance at church but also to instruct them in the basis of the faith in the home. According to Koerner, in 1526 Luther still imagined the household as a busy classroom where fathers drilled their children in the catechism.

Seeing the Word of God: | **275**

tutor, governess or mother was expected to read bible stories aloud to children. This must have been a fairly recent phenomenon as, in 1615 Matthaeus Lunguvitius (Lungwitz) did not include reading the Bible among the official duties of the parents. In Bottigheimer's view, the total absence of canonical biblical texts in books for Lutheran children and a plethora of material in reworked form are consistent with Lunguvitius' precepts. Based on these two pieces of evidence she concludes that there was no expectation among sixteenth and seventeenth-century Lutheran parents that their children should or would have unimpeded access to the full canonical Bible (Bottigheimer: 1993, 78, 80–81). The emphasis was placed on catechetical instruction and children were expected to be familiar with the catechism by the time they were confirmed (Koerner: 2004, 303; Strauss: 1984, 119).

This was also true of Transylvania. The clergy paid particular attention to catechizing the young (Teutsch: 1883, 209; Szegedi: 2006, 255, 265–266; Netoliczka: 1896, 176, 181; Teutsch: 1862, 48, 69–70), and those who did not know the catechism were banned from communion (Teutsch: 1883, 209). While youngsters were examined at their confirmation, couples who wished to marry were granted approval only if they could demonstrate their familiarity with the catechism (Teutsch: 1883, 209). Meanwhile, artisans were responsible for the behaviour of their children and apprentices, as well as the journeymen and servants they employed (Nussbächer: 1999, 237). Journeymen, for instance, were required to attend catechism classes, come to church regularly and listen attentively to the sermon without talking or falling asleep (Vlaicu: 2003, 394).

One is led to conclude that housefathers took responsibility for the religious instruction of their children and dependents in an indirect manner by consistently sending them to catechism classes. In this sense they complied with the clergy's wish that the catechism would be committed to memory by the laity through its frequent recitation. Honterus' exhortation that children should quiz each other in church in front of an adult audience highlights the place of memory in this didactic exercise (Netoliczka: 1896, 18, 176, 181). This ultimately proves that Transylvanian educational practices fell within didactic strategies prevalent in the German lands and elsewhere in Europe. Scholars have concluded that, organized as a series of questions and answers meant to be memorized and recited aloud, the catechism was obviously considered to be ideally suited to these basic forms of religious instruction and able to strive in a moderately literate society (Haigh: 2001, 41–43; Strauss: 1984, 115, 119; Strauss: 1975, 47). Consequently, the laity came into contact with the Bible aurally, generally in the context of public worship, through readings from the scriptures, sermons, songs and prayer and above all by reciting regularly the answers from the catechism which they were meant to memorize.

One must further note that oral dissemination of the Bible, which took place in the context of public worship privileged specific parts of the scriptures, such as

276 | Maria Crăciun

the Creed (Netoliczka: 1896, 16, 175),[32] the Decalogue (Netoliczka: 1896, 17–18), the Words of Institution (Netoliczka: 1896, 16–17; Teutsch: 1862, 32–33; Teutsch: 1883, 103–104), the explanation of Baptism and the Lord's Prayer (Teutsch: 1862, 32–33; Teutsch: 1883, 207–208; Szegedi: 2006, 263). This was in keeping with practice elsewhere in the German lands, where Church Orders also emphasized the need for parishioners to become familiar with the Lord's Prayer, the Ten Commandments and the Creed and to understand the meaning of Baptism, the Lord's Supper and the Power of the Keys (Broadhead: 2005, 289). These carefully selected texts mirrored the structure of Martin Luther's catechisms, the *Great Catechism*, used for the instruction of the clergy and the *Small Catechism*, intended for the young and the laity (Crăciun/Ghitta/Murdock: 2002; Zach: 2002). Consequently, the texts that the clergy wished the laity to know and understand were the same as those discussed in catechetical instruction.

One is led to conclude that, within the context of its oral dissemination during the service, familiarity with the biblical text was ensured by its recitation throughout the liturgical year and by the memorization of excerpts equated with the core of the doctrine, the "kernels of knowledge", already appropriated through catechesis (Karant-Nunn: 1997, 116–126). Thus, as Joseph Leo Koerner has pointed out, the texts chosen to express piety belonged to a fixed and narrow canon of key biblical quotations, that served to interpret the rest of the scriptures. Luther termed these fragments 'text kernels' (*Kernstellen*), in a sense conveying their function as summaries of the summary (Koerner: 2004, 223).

Consequently, by devising a rather complex educational programme, the clergy made sure that lay audiences were familiar with the essential parts of the biblical text, i.e. a number of carefully selected quotations, by its oral dissemination. The emphasis placed on these oral means of transmitting biblical knowledge highlights the importance of aural rather than visual reception. So had the visual been completely ousted from Lutheran worship and from the prevalent modes of communication? To answer this question, one is compelled to consider the space where worship took place.

The Word Seen

During the early modern period, the Lutheran divine service took place in churches refashioned to fit its needs (Spicer: 2012). In Transylvania, as elsewhere in Europe, this involved the introduction of new furnishings, such as pulpits and

---

32 "…deinde symbolum fidei canitur lingua nostra, quandoque etiam Latina". "Dann singt man das Glaubensbekenntnis in unserer und manchmal in lateinischer Sprache."

pews, benches and galleries, lecterns and baptismal fonts, as well as altarpieces (Machat: 1985; Crăciun: 2014, 141–147; Crăciun: 2015a, 353–358; Crăciun: 2008, 102–114, Crăciun: 2015b). Although Lutheran theology had attempted to eliminate images from worship, these artefacts continued to be richly decorated, albeit with suitable visual programmes (Crăciun: 2016, 176–229; Christensen: 1979, 124–128). However, the most superficial glance at the various furnishings of a Lutheran church highlights the fact that, besides the images, most of the artefacts were decorated with a wealth of inscriptions, most of them biblical quotations. I have argued elsewhere that at the beginning of the reforming process, altarpieces were turned into text-retables precisely in order to replace images with the Words of God (Crăciun: 2018).[33] In these circumstances, one is compelled to ask whether the presence of inscriptions was yet another way to communicate the teachings of the Gospel to congregations. One way to answer this query is to think about the role of these inscriptions in relation to the artefact and particularly to the images that decorated it. The other is to think about their function in relation to the congregation/the public present in the church.

When one considers the relation between text and artefact and, ultimately between text and image, one is faced with five possible options in terms of presentation: the text is presented as an image, particularly in the case of text-retables, as a label, as a sign, as an emblem, and as an object.

Consequently, a first possible scenario is that the biblical text was presented as an image, beautifully written and displayed in the church, becoming, as Joseph Leo Koerner has suggested, an aesthetic emblem of the truths expressed (Koerner: 2004, 290–291, 297). This is obvious in the case of text-retables (text-altarpieces, catechism-retables or *Schriftikone*), such as the ones at Sibiu (Hermannstadt, Nagyszeben), Dobârca (Dobring, Doboka), Dârlos (Durles, Darlac) and Țapu (Abtsdorf, Csicsóholdvilág), where the text has replaced the images on the surface of the altarpiece (Diederichs-Gottschalk: 2005, 16–17; Belting: 2002, 22; Koerner: 2004, 282).[34]

---

33 Belting: 1994, 465 suggests more radically that the Reformation brought the domination of the word, which suppressed all other religious signs. Diederichs-Gottschalk: 2005, 16–17 chooses the term *Schriftikone*, which is equally suggestive.
34 Text-retables as a category have proved difficult to define and there is no consensus among scholars who either include altarpieces entirely covered in texts under this label, or also consider altarpieces that combine texts and images. Belting: 2002, 22 calls such artefacts "Antibild" and "Nichtbild" (an Anti-image or Non-image), ultimately contesting their value as images. Koerner: 2004, 289–303 tends to call them text-retables, text-altarpieces, text panels or catechism-retables suggesting that the two categories are interchangeable. Diederichs-Gottschalk: 2005, 16–17 calls them "Schriftikone", following Schuster: 1983, 116; Ruge: 1985, 14; Belting: 1994, 467; Göhler: 1997, 5, 45. Göhler: 1990, 224 had introduced the term catechism-retable. Although Diederichs-Gottschalk: 2005, 16–17 admits that this term is also used in reference to Scandinavian examples of text-retables, he is reticent to adopt it as ex-

The altarpiece of Sibiu, dated by inscription in 1519 was turned into a text-retable in 1545, when its central panel and the interior of its moveable wings were painted over and covered in inscriptions: Isa 53:11, Matt 11:28–29, the Ten Commandments (Exod 20), Gal, chapter 3:13–14 and chapter 4:4–5 (fig. 1; fig. 2).[35]

As the altarpiece from Sibiu had been produced as a Catholic artefact, one might say that, after the adoption of evangelical ideas, it underwent a process of adaptation, intended to render it more Protestant by affording a more important place to the word (Crăciun: 2018, 185–186).[36]

The altarpiece of Dobârca on the other hand was produced in 1629, very probably also as a text or catechism-retable (Crăciun: 2018, 179–182, 187–188). In its current presentation, which I have been able to photograph in 2016, the interior of the moveable wings is divided into a larger field painted in red and covered in inscriptions (the Words of Institution from 1 Cor 11:23–25 and Luke 22:19–20), and a smaller field with figurative decoration (fig. 3).

These two compositions also bear inscriptions, but they are different from the ones in the upper field, because they serve as captions or labels (Roth: 1916, 185) (fig. 4; fig. 5).

Restoration work, which has started in 2018 has suggested that the figurative compositions on the festive side of the altarpiece, visible in its open position, were painted over a red background covered in inscriptions (fig. 6).[37]

Thus, on the central panel, decorated with the Last Supper it is possible to discern underneath the painting an inscription from Matt 11 (VENITE AD ME OMNES QVI LABORATIS ET ONERATI ESTIS, ET EGO RE(FOC)I(L)A(BO) VOS./MAT. XI),[38] while on the semi-circular superstructure one can glimpse HIC EST FILIUS MEUS, which is part of Matt 3:17 (fig. 7, 8).[39]

This suggests that the figurative imagery was added at a later date and that, initially, this artefact had been conceived as a text-altarpiece. The inscriptions themselves, typical of seventeenth-century calligraphy,[40] lead one to deduce that the later intervention took place relatively soon after the installation of the artefact,

---

isting examples display other texts than just the catechism and often include images like the Last Supper and the Last Judgment. He tends to use the term *Schriftikone* generically to refer to all furnishings decorated with inscriptions.

35 Firea: 2010, 2, 306–307 identified the painter hired by the town council to paint the altarpiece. Roman: 2007, 254 published documents highlighting several similar engagements of the same painter and Mihály: 2014, 80 provided a reconstruction of the altarpiece's refurbishment.

36 Michalski: 1996, 34 discusses such adaptations elsewhere in the Lutheran world.

37 Thanks are due to Mirel Bucur who has shared his observations and photographs taken during the restoration process.

38 I am grateful to Heidrun König for generously providing this information.

39 Matthew 3:17: "et ecce vox de caelis dicens hic este filius meus dilectus in quo mihi complacui"

40 I would like to thank Katalin Luffy for her advice on this matter.

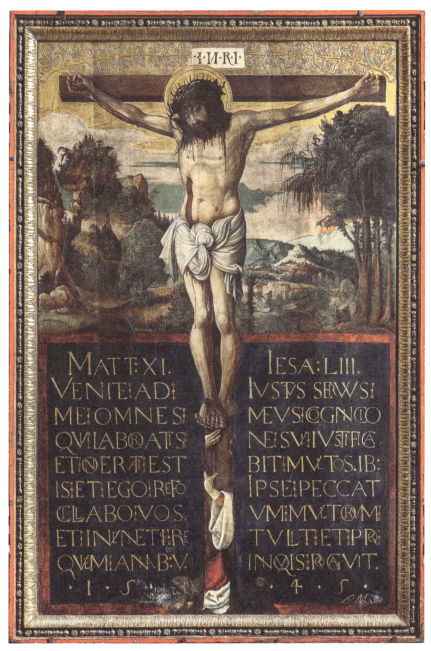

Figure 1: Central panel of the altarpiece from Sibiu (photo Ciprian Firea)

Figure 2: Reconstruction of the reformed altarpiece from Sibiu 1545 (drawing Mihály Ferenc)

perhaps in order to adapt to new trends in the production of altarpieces. One can only conclude that the altarpiece from Dobârca was initially a text-retable and that the image of the Last Supper together with the rest of the pictorial programme, visible when the artefact was open, was added at a later date.

Although the era of the text-retable may have been short-lived, as suggested by the commissioning of several figurative altarpieces with narrative imagery in the second half of the seventeenth century, the production of these particular artefacts seems to have continued in early modern Transylvania as indicated by at least two other examples, the altarpiece from Dârlos (fig. 9) and the one from Țapu (fig. 10), probably produced respectively in 1633 and 1699 (Crăciun: 2016, 199).

Although in its current presentation, the altarpiece from Dârlos only preserves a predella with an inscription dated to 1633 ("Christus Mortus Pro Pecatis Nostris et Resuscitatus est propter Iustificationem Nostram. Rom"), which may have come from a different artefact, its existence still suggests that this fragment may have been part of a text-retable. Similarly, in its current presentation, more precisely after the

Figure 3: The altarpiece from Dobârca, open (photo Ciprian Firea)

removal of overpainting probably introduced in 1712, the altarpiece from Țapu has an inscription on the central panel from John 3:14–15 and a paraphrase of John 3:16 together with a quotation from 1 Cor 11:28–29 on the predella (fig. 11).

In this case even more persuasively, the abundance of text suggests that this artefact may have been initially conceived as a text-retable (Crăciun: 2016, 199; Crăciun: 2018, 187).

As both the number and appearance of the inscriptions placed on the surface of these artefacts suggest, in the case of the text-retables the text has, in a certain sense, become an image and replaced the images in the decoration of the altarpieces (Belting: 1994, 467; Brückner: 2007, 106).[41] This is particularly obvious

---

41 Belting: 1994, 467 suggests that texts previously read in books were displayed in the place formerly occupied by the image and demanded the same kind of veneration. Later, Belting:

Figure 4: Wing from the altarpiece at Dobârca (photo Ciprian Firea)

Figure 5: Wing from the altarpiece of Dobârca (photo Ciprian Firea)

Figure 6: Wing from the altarpiece of Dobârca after restoration with letters visible on the red background (photo Mirel Bucur)

Figure 7: Detail from the central panel of the altarpiece from Dobârca (photo Ciprian Firea)

Figure 8: Detail from the superstructure of the altarpiece from Dobârca (photo Mirel Bucur)

when the text has been beautifully written on the surface of the altarpiece in bold, clear letters against a colourful background like at Sibiu and Dobârca (fig. 12).[42]

The text however can also play the role of a label that helped identify the image. In such cases, the text referenced the image and, if one were to believe Sergiusz Michalski, legitimized it by accounting for the articulation of the pictorial programme (Michalski: 1996, 39).[43] In practice, each chosen episode benefited from a biblical reference, thus justifying its inclusion in the visual narrative. For example, on the altarpiece from Agnita (Agnetheln, Szentágota), produced in 1650, each episode is associated with the relevant biblical quotation, taken mostly from the Gospels of John and Matthew (fig. 13).

This must have been the most common association of word and image, because as Koerner has suggested, Luther accepted images in church if they clearly recalled the Bible quotation they illustrated, which, for the sake of further clarity, ought to stand physically inscribed beside them (Koerner: 2004, 279).

2002, 22 has suggested that altarpieces like that in Dinkesbühl are equatable to an "Antibild" or "Nichtbild" ("dort, wo Du ein bild erwartest, findest Du Kein Bild, sondern einen Text zum Lesen"), Diederichs-Gottschalk: 2005, 21–23 considers the same altarpiece the result of late iconoclasm and claims that it cannot be interpreted as either "Nichtbild" or "Schriftikone". Koerner: 2004, 300 seems to believe that one is dealing with a text treated like an image, in a sense turned into an image. Brückner: 2007, 106 provides an interesting example of a sixteenth century altar painting where the words spoken during the Eucharist created a chalice and host.

42 Koerner: 2004, 223 suggests that texts, painted beautifully were framed and hung like beautiful pictures.

43 In Michalski's view the retable became a visual version of the biblical text.

Figure 9: Altarpiece from Dârlos (photo Ciprian Firea)

Figure 10: Altarpiece from Țapu (photo Ciprian Firea)

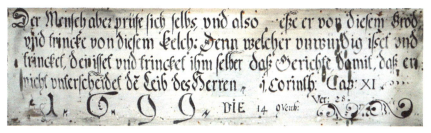

Figure 11: Predella of the altarpiece from Țapu (photo Ciprian Firea)

In a third scenario, the text acted as sign, indication or clue, as it complemented the image and decoded its meaning (Ginzburg: 1979, 280–282; Koerner: 2004, 279).[44] As Hans Belting has pointed out, Luther desired that mottoes – that is, biblical quotations – be added to pictures so that one "can have God's work and word always and everywhere before one's eyes" (Belting: 1994, 466). Thus, in Luther's view, images functioned best when accompanied by texts. It is thus tempting to see images as mere illustrations of the biblical text and agree with W. J. T. Mitchell's suggestion that "the image has always been policed by the word" (Mitchell: 1987, 43). In Peter Wagner's more optimistic view, representations in their visual and verbal varieties have two common denominators: rhetoric and signs. According to Wagner, signs are primarily units of basic meaning, of cognitive process and knowledge and only secondarily units of communication, although a process of signification is implied in the recognition of every object. Signs enable communication, the ability to share meaning, which is made more efficient by shared symbols and language (Wagner: 1996, 15–16, 32). Thus, in the Lutheran world, images are accompanied by texts in an effort to assign meaning and to communicate with the public through a complex system of signs. In fact, as Peter Burke has suggested, inscriptions could be used as a means of leading viewers to 'read' the image in the correct way (Burke: 2001, 177).

Interestingly enough, as some scholars have shown, this was not a new technique in conveying meaning. For example, Margriet Hoogvliet mentions an interesting medieval example, a set of tapestries representing scenes from the Old and New Testament, with poems of four lines in French and references to the corresponding bible books, ordered by cardinal Guillaume Fillastre around 1460, probably with the intention of donating them to the cathedral of Tournai (Hoogvliet: 2013b, 248). What seems to have changed between this particular medieval example and similar strategies deployed after the Reformation is the social scope of this manner of communication. If in the fifteenth century this technique seems to have been used among the elites, by the seventeenth century it had spread to a much

---

44 Koerner: 2004, 279 suggests that the relation of text to image mirrors that of signifier to signified.

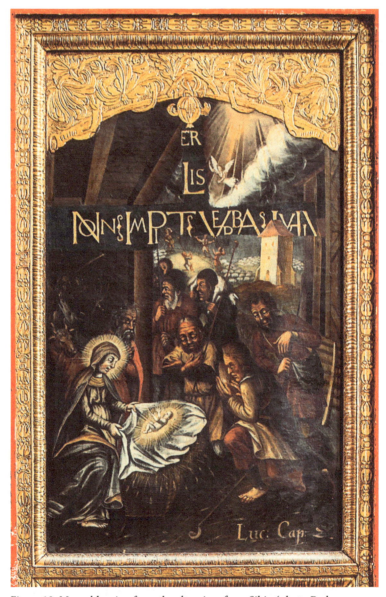

Figure 12: Moveable wing from the altarpiece from Sibiu (photo Radu Sălcudeanu)

Figure 13: The altarpiece from Agnita, closed (photo Ciprian Firea)

broader social segment and reached the outskirts of Europe. In the process it has also moved from the cathedral to the village church.

Thus, in the case of the Passion cycle at Dobârca, the compositions are commented on, not by their specific biblical references, but rather by Psalms, fragments from the prophecies (Isaiah and Hosea) and the Epistles (fig. 14).

It can be construed that the commissioners of the altarpiece and/or its makers were less interested in identifying the depicted episodes than in sharing their meaning with the congregation. In the context of pulpits, Krista Kodres has called such texts homiletic, because they focused on explaining the meaning of the images (Kodres: 2006, 369). The inscriptions attached to the Passion cycle at Dobârca definitely fit into this pattern because of the manner in which they emphasize the meaning of the images and not their direct textual reference, suggesting that edification rather than identification was the purpose behind their presence (fig. 15).

Moreover, if one looks at the visual programme that could be seen in its open position, the example of Dobârca further supports this view, as the texts present on the interior of the moveable wings, the Words of Institution, "Dominus Iesus in qua nocte tradebatur accepit panem et gratias agens fregit et dixit: accipite et manducate. Hoc est corpus meum, quod pro vobis tratur hoc facite in meam commemorationem" and "similiter et calicem postquam coenavit dicens: hic calix novum testamentum est in meo sanguine hoc facite ovotiescunque biberitis in meam commemorationem", initially related to the ritual, the administration of the sacrament, performed at the altar. Later, when the figurative images were added, the text also

Figure 14: The altarpiece from Dobârca, closed (photo Ciprian Firea)

Figure 15: Panel from the altarpiece of Dobârca (photo Mirel Bucur)

served to explain the meaning of the image of the Last Supper, which had been painted on the central panel of the altarpiece (see fig. 3).

Meanwhile, another set of texts, placed on the images in the lower field of the wings, in the manner of a caption, "Lex per Mosen data est" and "Gratia et veritas per Jesum Cristum facta est Joh 1:17" serve, not just to identify the two compositions, 'Moses Receiving the Tables of the Law' and the 'Descent of the Holy Spirit', but rather to emphasize the complex relationship between Law and Gospel (Christensen: 1979, 124–128; Scribner: 1989, 216–219; Noble: 2009, 27–37), antithetical and complementary at the same time (see fig. 4 and fig. 5).[45] This last point is further highlighted by a third inscription, from Paul's Epistle to the Corinthians, "Spiritus vivificat II Cor III" and "Litera occidit", which starts on the panel depicting the 'De-

---

45 Belting: 1994, 467 suggests that the very association of the Words of Institution with the Decalogue constituted a reference to the opposition between Law and Grace, between the Old Testament and the New.

292 | Maria Crăciun

scent of the Holy Spirit' and finishes on the panel depicting Moses receiving the Law on Mount Sinai.[46] The fact that the two panels are meant to be read together is highlighted by the way the inscriptions are juxtaposed on or arranged across the two panels. So, in the case of the altarpiece from Dobârca, the text signposted the meaning of the images and was deployed as a key that helped decode the messages transmitted to the congregation. One could almost suspect that image-makers attempted to control interpretation by adding relevant texts.

This may have proved extremely useful when, particularly in the case of allegorical images, the messages were not straightforward and the meanings somewhat obscure. For example, in the case of the pulpit from Şura Mare (Großscheuern, Nagycsűr), the decoding of the minimalist imagery – the Crucifixion associated with the Tables of the Law, encircled by a snake and decorated with a lily – is aided, to a certain extent, by the inclusion of references to biblical texts: 5 Book of Moses 6:4; 1 Book of Moses 9:11–14; 1 Book of Moses 3:15; Ps 50:14–15; Ps 141:2; Pred Salo. 12:13–14 and the Book of Tobit 12:8 (fig. 16).

The inscription at the top (the fifth book of Moses 6:4) is a fragment from Deuteronomy, which proclaims monotheist belief ("Hear Israel. The Lord our God is one Lord"). The inscription at the centre (the first book of Moses 9:11–14) is spread across two pillars and emphasizes the covenant between God and mankind, alluding to the realm of the Law and the world of the Old Testament.[47] The next inscription, placed between the Cross and the Tables of the Law comes from the first book of Moses 3:15, which is part of the story of original sin and is commonly interpreted as foretelling the victory of Christ over Satan (Cannon: 2010).[48] The two smaller pillars on the sides of the shrine are decorated with references to Psalms: Ps 50:14–15 and Ps 141:2.[49] The first emphasizes the reverence due to God, while the second stresses the importance of prayer. Underneath the Tables of the Law,

---

46 2 Cor 3: 6: "qui ct idoneos nos fecit ministros novi testament non litterae sed spiritus litterae enim occident spiritus autem vivificat".

47 "I establish my covenant with you, that never again shall all flesh be cut off by the waters of a flood and never again shall there be a flood to destroy the earth. And God said, this is the sign of the covenant which I make between me and you and every living creature that is with you, for all future generations; I set my bow in the cloud and it shall be a sign of the covenant between me and the earth."

48 "I will put enmity between you and the woman, and between your seed and her seed; he shall bruise your head and you shall bruise his heel." Cannon: 2010, 14.

49 Ps 50:14–15 "Offer to God a sacrifice of thanksgiving and pay your vows to the most high and call upon me in the day of trouble; I will deliver you, and you shall glorify me." Ps 141: 2 "Let my prayer be counted as incense before thee, and the lifting up of my hands as an evening sacrifice."

Figure 16: The pulpit of Șura Mare (photo Ciprian Firea)

there is another reference, Pred. Salo 12:13–14.[50] This again is a reminder of the imminence of judgement and the need to closely observe God's commandments.

In a fourth scenario, the text was used as an emblem, a concrete symbol of an abstract idea, where an image is associated with a set of verses for chiefly didactic

---

50 "The end of the matter; all has been heard. Fear God and keep his commandments; for this is the whole duty of man. For God will bring every deed into judgement, with every secret thing, whether good or evil."

294 | Maria Crăciun

purposes. Thus, in the case of some panels preserved in the church at Mediaş (Mediasch, Medgyes), each of the images is accompanied by two texts, one serving to identify the image while the other was used to explain its meaning. For example, the Image of the Brazen Serpent is accompanied by two inscriptions, Num 21 and John 3.[51] The Baptism of Jesus is decorated with Isa 61 and Matt 3 (fig. 17).[52]

Finally, the Lamb of the Resurrection is accompanied by Isa 33 and John 1 as well as Acts 5 (fig. 18).[53]

Jakub Pakora, when discussing pulpits, called this an emblematic use of texts (Pakora: 1987, 50). The fact that, in this case, the images, the Brazen Serpent, the Baptism of Jesus and the Lamb of the Resurrection are easily recognizable makes the arrangement even more interesting, as the texts were not needed to identify the images but to highlight links between the Old and New Testaments, emphasizing typological associations.

Dated to the eighteenth century, the panels in question are slightly intriguing as they have been labelled as epitaphs by the curators of the improvised gallery in the church at Mediaş, despite the fact that neither the formal features, nor their compositional structure evoke an eighteenth-century epitaph. This contention is also supported by the fact that neither the images nor the texts accompanying them overtly suggest a funerary context. It is far more likely that these panels were intended to function as "iconotexts". The term *iconotext*, borrowed by Peter Wagner from Michael Nerlich, refers to artefacts in which the verbal and the visual signs mingle to produce rhetoric that depends on the co-presence of words and images (Wagner: 1996, 15–16).[54] In this case communication strategies fully rely on the concomitant use of the verbal and visual.

Finally, a fifth scenario presents the text as object. The text, more precisely the Decalogue is placed on an object, the Tables of the Law, represented visually on

---

51 Numbers 21: "and the Lord said to Moses: Make a fiery serpent and set it on a pole; and everyone who is bitten, when he sees it, shall live. So Moses made a bronze serpent, and set it on a pole and if a serpent bit any man, he would look at the bronze serpent and live." John 3: "And as Moses lifted up the serpent in the wilderness, so must the son of man be lifted up that whoever believes in him may have eternal life."

52 Isaiah 61: "The spirit of the Lord God is upon me, because the Lord has anointed me to bring good tidings to the afflicted; he has sent me to bind up the broken hearted." Matthew 3: "And when Jesus was baptised, he went up immediately from the water, and behold, the heavens were opened and he saw the Spirit of God descending like a dove, and alighting on him; and lo a voice from heaven, saying: This is my beloved son with whom I am well pleased."

53 Although the panel is headed by Isa 33, in fact the quotation is from Isa 53: 7: "He was oppressed and he was afflicted, yet he opened not his mouth; like a lamb that is led to the slaughter, and like a sheep that before its shearers is dumb, so he opened not his mouth." John 1: "Ecce Agnus Dei qui tollit peccata mundi", that is "Behold the Lamb of God, who takes away the sin of the world.". Acts 5: "Agnus dignus est accipere virtutem divinitate fortitudinem honorem, gloriam et benedictionem."

54 Mitchell: 1994, 89 suggests that text and image form a whole that cannot be dissolved.

Seeing the Word of God: | 295

Figure 17: Panels from the church at Mediaș (photo Ciprian Firea)

Figure 18: Panel from the church at Mediaș (photo Ciprian Firea)

an actual, material object, the pulpit or the altarpiece, for example the altarpieces at Jidvei (Seiden, Zsidve), Dobârca and Buzd (Busd, Szászbuzd) and the pulpits at Brașov (Kronstadt, Brassó) and Șura Mare (fig. 19; fig. 20; fig. 21; fig. 22; see also fig. 16).

The fact that the Decalogue is most often reduced to the numerals that invoke the commandments transforms the text itself into an object with significant mnemonic potential (see fig. 20, 21, 22 and 16). On the other hand, the first three commandments are always inscribed on a different panel from the rest of the Decalogue. This is most obvious in the case of the altarpiece from Dobârca, where the first three commandments are actually written on the panel: "non habebis deos alienos coram me", "non assumens nomen deitu in vanum" and "memento ut dies sabbat" (see fig. 19). One is led to consider why the first three commandments are emphasized in this particular manner. One possible answer is that they are the ones

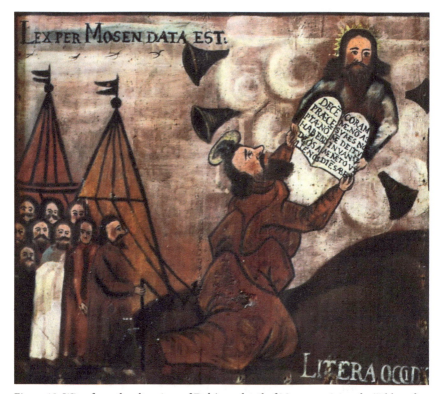

Figure 19: Wing from the altarpiece of Dobârca, detail of Moses receiving the Tables of the Law (photo Ciprian Firea)

that establish the proper relationship between God and mankind, taking a stand against blasphemy and idolatry, while requesting the observance of the Sabbath (Crăciun: 2017, 24–25).

One is led to conclude that, in relation to the artefacts they decorated, and to the images they accompanied, these texts, displayed for visual reception, had several functions, identifying and legitimizing these images while explaining their meanings. The idea of moving from identification to edification, from decoding the image to creating typological associations in reference to the same image suggests guided readings of the images and brings to the fore the public they were intended for.

The Word and Its Public

The dialogue between text and public is further suggested by the nature of these quotations, which were not always reproduced *verbatim* (see fig. 16, 20, 21, 22). In fact, viewers were presented either with references, which could stimulate mechanisms of recollection, or with fragments of text, brief and manageable portions of the scriptures, which could easily be committed to memory or brought to mind if they had already been assimilated through catechesis.

Consequently, the functions of these inscriptions have to be reconsidered while bearing the intended public in mind. The first question one feels compelled to ask concerns agency. Who decided to decorate ecclesiastical furnishings with inscriptions, choosing their content and their placement in relation to the images? The evidence from Transylvanian Lutheran churches examined so far suggests that the custom to decorate ecclesiastical furnishings with inscriptions had already reached this remote corner of Europe by mid-sixteenth century, when the altarpiece of

Figure 20: Moses from the pulpit at Brașov (photo Andreea Pocol)

Figure 21: Moses from the altarpiece at Busd (photo Ciprian Firea)

Figure 22: Superstructure of the altarpiece of Jidvei (photo Ciprian Firea)

Sibiu was painted with inscriptions on the initiative of the magistrate.[55] Although secular involvement may have been important in some cases, inscriptions on some of the images suggest that parish ministers played an important role in this process, even when they were not necessarily the commissioners of these furnishings.[56] One is thus compelled to question the reasons of ministers who made these decisions and decorated the ecclesiastical space in this particular manner.

It has been suggested that the practice of placing inscriptions, primarily scriptural passages, above, underneath, around and in paintings was sanctioned in Martin Luther's writings. Already in 1526, in the preface to the Wittenberg church ordinance, Luther instructed parents to write Bible quotations all over their houses (Koerner: 2004, 282). In 1530, the reformer suggested that a painting representing

---

[55] The painter Benedictus Moler was engaged by the magistrate on several occasions for work of this kind. Firea: 2010, 2, 306–307.

[56] I have argued elsewhere the involvement of Marcus Fronius, one of the preachers in Braşov and Martin Harnung, the parish priest, in the decoration of the pulpit placed in the parish church of the town after the fire of 1689. Crăciun: 2021a, 391–392.

the Last Supper should be surrounded by a scriptural sentence in golden letters (WA 1, 82; Koerner: 2004, 290).[57] Moreover, in the *Passional* included in the 1529 edition of the *Betbüchlein*, Martin Luther outlined the advantages of painting bible illustrations and quotations on the walls of the home "so that God's works and words might always be before one's eyes" (Bottigheimer: 1993, 69).[58] In response to these exhortations ministers displayed their learning and piety by filling their churches with writing, while in many Protestant homes, hostels and inns, pious sayings covered every available support, walls, ceilings and furniture (Koerner: 2004, 282). However, compliance with Luther's advice does not seem to have been reason enough to include texts on every image present in the church. One is thus compelled to consider other possible benefits perceived by the ministers who made these decisions.

According to Sergiusz Michalski, inscriptions proclaimed either the limitations of the work of art as a medium of religious instruction or emphasized elements in the composition which might be misinterpreted by the faithful. In his view the presence of inscriptions serves to demonstrate that the image as such may have been too restrictive a medium to express the full meaning of Christian doctrine (Michalski: 1996, 44–45). It is consequently possible that ministers sought to make the most of this new channel of communication and designed new functions for the inscriptions placed on ecclesiastical furnishings. In their view, besides decoding the meaning of the images, the biblical quotations deployed, particularly the oft-recurring John 6:51, present at Dupuş (Tobsdorf, Táblás) and John 3:16, reiterated at Biertan (Birthälm, Berethalom), Mediaş, Hălchiu (Heldsdorf, Höltövény) and Nemşa (Nimesch, Nemes), were able to make clear doctrinal statements, to shape the piety of the beholders and to act as markers of confessional identity, transforming these medieval altarpieces into Lutheran artefacts and practically adapting them to the new context of worship (fig. 23; fig. 24) (Crăciun: 2016, 122, 152–153, 160–161; Crăciun: 2012, 152).[59]

---

57 Michalski: 1996, 42–43 suggests that Luther also wanted to place "kräftige spräche" on church walls.

58 Rublack: 2010, 150 mentions that Luther wrote the verses of Ps 118: 17 in red letters on the walls of his room in Coburg castle to ward off Satan, with notes of a tune: "I shall not die, but live and I shall declare the words of God". This mechanism of communication was not new. Hoogvliet: 2013b, 259 mentions a letter by Jean Gerson where he insists that *Le Miroir de l'âme* should be disseminated as widely as possible and that it should be "published in a public place, entirely or partially, and attached to parish churches, schools, religious houses and hospitals in books or on tablets." Duffy: 1992, 454 mentions that walls were whitewashed and covered with texts against idolatry.

59 On the altarpiece from Dupuş one can read: "Ego sum panis vivus qui de caelo descendi si quis manducaverit ex…" (John 6: 51). The inscription is in fact incomplete as it should continue with "hoc pane vivet in aeternum". Roth: 1916, 72 provides the complete version of the quotation: "I am the living bread that came down from heaven. Whoever eats this bread will live forever. This bread is my flesh, which I will give for the life of the world."

Figure 23: Shrine of the altarpiece from Dupuș (photo Ciprian Firea)

Figure 24: Shrine of the altarpiece from Hălchiu (photo Ciprian Firea)

At Biertan, the inscription introduced in the shrine, John 3:16, allows a new reading of the narrative sequence, initially focused on the life of the Virgin, which was re-interpreted in the new Lutheran context as a life of Jesus (Crăciun: 2016, 160–161; Crăciun: 2012, 152–153). At Mediaș, Hălchiu and probably Nemșa, the same inscription was used throughout the early modern period, in order to shift the focus from the lives of saints to the role played by Jesus in the process of redemption. In these cases, the inscription managed to both transmit doctrinal messages and shape the piety of the beholders. Consequently, the text has become a more specific sign, namely a marker of confessional identity.

While in the case of these late medieval altarpieces, inscriptions were necessary in a process of adaptation which integrated medieval artefacts into Lutheran piety, in the case of the altarpieces from Agnita (1650), Meșendorf (Meschendorf, Mese) (1653) and Cincșor (Kleinschenk, Kissink) (1655) the inscriptions added at the base of the shrine, such as "Verbum Domini Manet in Aeternum Anno Domini 1653" (1 Pet 1:25) and "Sanguis Jesu Christi filii dei mundat nos ab omni peccato. Jon I" (John 1:7), simply made a clear and confessionally distinctive doctrinal statement, respectively proclaiming the primacy of the word and decoding the meaning of the narrative of the Passion while emphasizing Christ's role in the redemption of mankind (fig. 25; fig. 26) (Crăciun: 2016, 152–153, 215–218).

Moreover, besides emphasizing the primacy of the Word, *Verbum Domini Manet in Aeternum* may have had alternative uses. For instance, in the Lutheran heartlands, it had been adopted by Saxon princes to show their support for Lutheranism. On a personal level, a monogram of this inscription could act as a talisman but would also broadcast confessional identity (Koerner: 2004, 284). It is

Seeing the Word of God: | 301

Figure 25: Altarpiece from Agnita, open (photo Ciprian Firea)

Figure 26: Altarpiece from Meșendorf, open (photo Ciprian Firea)

thus within the realm of possibility that, in the confessionally tense climate of seventeenth and eighteenth-century Transylvania, Lutheran communities may have wished to proclaim their confessional identity publicly by displaying this motto on ecclesiastical furnishings.

This conclusion ultimately focuses attention on the content of these inscriptions. Particularly when compared to those in the German lands, inscriptions favoured in Transylvania for placement on ecclesiastical furnishings were not catechetical to the same extent as their counterparts from the heartlands of the Reformation. While in the German lands thoroughly catechetical altarpieces frequently grouped together the Decalogue, the Creed, the Words of Institution, the Lord's Prayer and statements concerning Baptism and Confession,[60] in Transylvania, the Creed and the Lord's Prayer are seldom present, allowing the Words of Institution to compete with the Decalogue for the first place. Explanations concerning baptism are provided by the use of Matt 3:17 (Dobârca), while the offer of grace is emphasized by the use of Matt 11:28 (Sibiu and Dobârca). These choices highlight concern for the core of the doctrine, the real presence of Christ in the sacrament, and for the behaviour of the congregation in the eyes of God and towards their fel-

---

60 See the examples from northwestern Germany (Niedersachsen, Ostfriesland and Harlingerland) studied by Diederichs-Gottschalk.

Seeing the Word of God: | 303

low Christians, in other words an emphatic promotion of right belief and proper conduct.

Even in this abbreviated form, emphasis on the catechism highlights the need to instil in the audience the fundamentals of faith and ultimately habits of correct thought, the right answer to questions concerning orthodoxy and orthopraxy. Moreover, texts emphasizing the primacy of the word, especially *Verbum Domini Manet in Aeternum*, together with quotes conveying specifically Lutheran doctrines, particularly concerning the Eucharist, not just the Words of Institution but also fragments from the Gospel of John (John 1, John 3 and John 6), were the most frequently used.

The frequent presence of the Decalogue on church furnishings, especially when compared with its rare occurrence in the writings of reformers, suggests that inscriptions on furnishings were intended especially for the benefit of the laity. The Decalogue, meant to instil correct behaviour, not just in church but also in the most mundane of contexts, held pride of place, located as it was on the interior of the movable wings, on the superstructure of altarpieces, on pulpits or on the Tables of the Law held aloft by Moses. Moreover, its referential rendering, with numbers used instead of texts, constituted additional proof of its appropriation through mnemonic exercises. Thus, the sight of the Roman numeral one, would recall the first commandment and so forth.

The Word Taught

One is led to conclude that some biblical quotations were more popular than others and it seems worth considering the frequency with which these texts appeared. The most often used inscriptions are the Ten Commandments (Exod 20), which make an appearance at Sibiu, Dobârca, Jidvei, Buzd, Brașov and Șura Mare, *Verbum Domini Manet in Aeternum* (1 Pet 1:25), which is present at Meșendorf, Jidvei, Sebeș (Mühlbach, Szászsebes), Mediaș and Ungra (Galt, Szászugra), John 3:16 ("Sic enim dilexit Deum mundum ....") which is inscribed in the shrine at Biertan and Mediaș and at the bottom of the shrine at Hălchiu and Nemșa, John 6:51, which appears on the predella at Sibiu and at the bottom of the shrine at Dupuș and parts of John 1, such as John 1:17 on the wings at Dobârca and John 1:7 ("Sanguis Jesu Christi Filii Dei mundat nos ab omni peccato"), which is present at Agnita and used to be present at Cincșor.[61] There is also frequent mention of Paul's epistles

---

61 In the case of the altarpiece from Cincșor, the inscription no longer exists on the artefact preserved in the collection of the museum of Făgăraș but it was mentioned by Roth: 1916, 189–191.

304 | Maria Crăciun

among which the first and the second epistles to the Corinthians seem to have found particular favour (especially 1 Cor 10 and 1 Cor 11). Finally, it is important to note that two of the text-retables produced in Transylvania, those of Sibiu and Dobârca included Matt 11:28–29 on the central panel.

The importance afforded by the clergy to these texts is reflected by their presence in some of the locally produced confessions of faith. In fact, Transylvanian reformers, such as Johannes Honterus, Matthias Hebler and Lukas Unglerus quoted some of these texts in their writings when making doctrinal points essential to Lutheran identity, such as the real presence of Christ in the sacrament, or supporting correct religious practice, for instance communion in both kinds. Thus, Paul's epistles, Eph 3 and 4, 1 Cor 10 and 11, and Gal 3 are all used in Honterus' *Reformatio ecclesiae coronensis ac totius barcensis provinciae* (1543), Hebler's *Brevis confessio de coena domini ecclesiarum Saxonicarum et conjunctarum in Transilvania* (1561), Unglerus' *Formula pii consensus inter pastores ecclesiarum Saxonicarum* (1572), *Propositiones de Coena Domini* (1561) and *Articuli Summam Doctrinae coelestis continentes* (1573) in support of the Lutheran interpretation of the Eucharist (Netoliczka: 1896, 15; Teutsch: 1883, 41, 44–46, 55, 160, 189). Among the issues discussed are the institution of the sacrament and its nature, the real presence of Christ in the sacrament and communion in both kinds. Moreover, Paul is quoted to illustrate the consequences of unworthy reception (Teutsch: 1883, 45). In the same vein, Paul 1 Cor 5, 6, and 11 and Matt 18, are used in *Reformatio Ecclesiae Coronensis* (1543), *Formula pii consensus* (1572) and *Articuli de pastorum vita et moribus* (1574) to justify the ban from communion and the exclusion of sinners from the community (Netoliczka: 1896, 20–21; Teutsch: 1883, 160, 193). Moreover, *Brevis confessio de coena domini* refers to John 6: 51 "Qui edit carnem meam et bibit meum sanguinem habet vitam aeternam" as an argument in support of consubstantiation (Teutsch: 1883, 45).

On the artefacts present in the church (Dobârca), Matt 3:17 is quoted in the context of Baptism proclaiming the status of Christ as the son of God. In the *Formula pii consensus* (1572) and *Articuli summam doctrinae* (1573), Matt 3 is mentioned in reference to penance rather than Baptism as the formulaic words of John the Baptist are mentioned: "Penitentiam agite et dignus fructus paenitentiae facite" (Teutsch: 1883, 169, 185). Gal 3 is used in reference to the meaning of Baptism in *Formula pii consensus* (1572) and *Articuli summam doctrinae* (1573) along with John 3, which is also invoked in *Articuli de praecipuis Christiane religionis capitibus* (1578) (Teutsch: 1883, 158, 188, 224). John 3 and John 6 are used in the writings of reformers, *Brevis Confessio de Coena Domini* (1561) and *Articuli de summam doctrinae* (1573) to support justification by faith and the promise of redemption (Teutsch: 1883, 46, 181).

One is led to conclude that several of the inscriptions chosen by ministers to be displayed on the furnishings of the church conveyed important tenets of

Lutheran doctrine to the congregations. Ministers clearly considered them 'kernels of knowledge' worthy of mention in their works and useful in educating the faithful.

By contrast, the Decalogue, which is frequently present on the furnishings placed in the church is rarely invoked in the writings of the local reformers. In fact, it's only mentioned once in the *Formula pii consensus* (1572) (Teutsch: 1883, 154). This is not entirely surprising as the Decalogue had no particular doctrinal relevance but was essential for instilling proper conduct among the laity. It was consequently a suitable choice for the decoration of altarpieces.

Moreover, many of these inscriptions echoed catechetic formulations. The altarpiece from Dobârca provides a relevant example as it contains fragments of the Decalogue and the Words of Institution prominently displayed on its moveable wings, while Matt 3:17 decorated the superstructure of the same altarpiece (see fig. 8). Benefiting from biblical references that explicitly refer to memory (Luke 22:19–20 and 1 Cor 11:23–25) the two quotations also resemble the explanations concerning the Eucharist from Luther's *Small Catechism* (Wandel: 2006, 115–116). As Koerner has persuasively suggested, in his *Small* and *Large Catechism*, Luther "sought to extract from Scripture and from its illuminating kernels a second order norm. Luther would further reduce these to thumbnail sketches where the Catechism was itself summarized." (Koerner: 2004, 303). This seems to suggest that whether disseminated visually or orally, the 'kernels' of biblical knowledge chosen by the clergy tended to be the same with catechetical pronouncements and were meant to instruct the congregations, but also to model their devotional patterns and to shape their behaviour, disciplining them as religious and social beings (Koerner: 2004, 306).

Further proof that these inscriptions were in fact considered 'kernels of knowledge' may come from yet another important source, as Koerner has persuasively suggested that in the 1541 edition of Luther's German Bible, text kernels were printed in a special type (Koerner: 2004, 299). This leads one to explore whether the biblical quotations recurrent on ecclesiastical furnishings are underlined in any way in the editions of the bible that circulated in Transylvania. A New Testament from 1534, now in the collection of the Brukenthal Museum of Sibiu, although it does not use a different font to mark 'kernels of knowledge', does spell the word "nemet" from the Words of Institution in capital letters, thus drawing particular attention to it ("NEMET, esset, das ist mein Leib der fur euch geboden wird. Sollen thut zu nemen gedechtnis"), while some passages, for example Matt 3, Matt 11, Gal 3, John 3 and John 6 have little comments or glosses written next to them. The most relevant part of John 6 ("Ich bin das brod des lebens…") has two glosses next to it. One of the comments states that the text does not refer to the sacrament, but rather to spiritual food. As these marginalia are printed together with the main body of the text they could be construed as guidelines for the readers in their interpretation of the Bible. They could also have been an incentive for the ministers to choose these particular paragraphs for display within the church.

This conclusion is further supported by an Old Testament from 1524 which belonged to Andreas Budacherus and, in 1606, to Martinus Seller of Cluj and then was acquired by the library of the gymnasium in Sibiu. This particular book includes an even more interesting marginal comment. The story of the Brazen Serpent (Num 21:6–9) has a typological link to John 3 indicated on the margins of the text. This is all the more interesting as one of the already-mentioned panels from Mediaş happens to be decorated with the Brazen Serpent accompanied by two inscriptions, Num 21 and John 3 (see fig. 17). This tends to confirm that inscriptions placed on church furnishings were not randomly picked but rather carefully chosen by the clergy for the instruction of the laity. These choices were not individual or spontaneous but rather recommended by prominent reformers. They resonate with the priorities highlighted by the writings of the local reformers such as Johannes Honterus, Matthias Hebler and Lukas Unglerus, which both espoused correct Eucharistic doctrine, consubstantiation and the real presence of Christ in the sacrament and encouraged correct practice, such as communion in both kinds. The importance of text kernels is further emphasized by the glosses printed next to them in Luther's German Bible that circulated in Transylvania. In this sense it may be noteworthy that Luther's *New Testament* printed in Wittenberg by Hans Lufft in 1558 and Luther's *Das Neue Testament Deutsch*, published in Wittenberg in 1589 by Zacharias Lehmann were present in local book collections (Gündisch: 1977; Gündisch/Nägler: 1992).

Moving from content to form, if one considers the way that these texts were arranged on the artefacts, leading viewers not just to read the images but rather to read them in specific ways, as was the case of the opposition between Law and Gospel signposted by the inscriptions placed on the 'Descent of the Holy Spirit' and 'Moses Receiving the Tables of the Law' from the altarpiece of Dobârca, one may get a clearer picture of the role inscriptions played in disseminating biblical messages and enhancing familiarity with the scriptures (see fig. 4 and 5).

Reproduced *verbatim* or as references, inscriptions on church furnishings acted as mnemonic devices reminding the congregation of the already familiar texts. One needs to remember in this context that the most familiar text was probably the catechism and perhaps other important quotes from the Bible often mentioned in sermons by the ministers. Seeing the numerals on the Tables of the Law may have stimulated the congregation to remember the Decalogue and inwardly recite the commandments. This created a rather complex web of communication since active participation was sometimes explicitly required of the laity, who were asked to recite in unison parts of the Bible, such as the Psalms and the Lord's Prayer. Thus, the efficacy of visual communication relied on cooperation with oral means of dissemination, reading aloud, preaching, catechizing, and singing.

One of the texts, rendered in full on the panel from the pulpit at Şura Mare is highly relevant in this respect as it reads: "Der Fürsten Heimlichkeit soll gantz verschwiegen bleiben: Von Gottes Werck soll man frey singen, reden, schreiben" (see fig. 16).[62] The message seems to be quite clear, as the Words of God needed to be preached, recited, written and sung in church.

Whether communication relied chiefly on the verbal or the visual, one needs to consider the language used in this exchange. The texts placed on the artefacts were almost always in Latin, rather than in the vernacular. This apparently peculiar choice may have had several explanations as, in Transylvania, Latin was a mediating language that facilitated communication between the various ethnic/linguistic groups (Szende: 2009, 209–210). Moreover, during the early modern period, Saxon communities did not have a shared and commonly accepted vernacular, speaking a variety of dialects. The choice of Latin may be explained by the absence of a literary form of the local language, while German used in print, for instance in Luther's German Bible was not necessarily understood by the laity. Consequently, according to some scholars, a model sermon in German would be delivered orally in the local dialect (Gündisch: 1987a, 345). In this situation Latin may have served as a common denominator that also rendered authority to the written text as it was the language used in governance, law, education and administration, the so-called language of prestige.

From this status, Latin bestowed upon its users the right to read and interpret the Bible (Szegedi: 2009, 274). Because they were familiar with Latin, as they had studied it either at local gymnasia or at foreign universities, the clergy fashioned themselves as its most suitable interpreters. Moreover, their familiarity with the local vernaculars, exercised in preaching and hearing confessions, turned them into the main protagonists in the parallel use of various languages (Szende: 2009, 221). Ministers could thus construct themselves as the only persons who had the ability and the right to interpret the Bible. Small wonder they wished to use the Bible as a symbol of their professional and social status and depicted themselves on their tombstones Bible in hand (fig. 27).

Having explored the complex web of communication created by the Lutheran clergy, one needs to examine the implications of the choice of contexts and settings for the dissemination of the Word of God. The evidence examined in this study has suggested that the Bible reached the laity primarily in liturgical context. This already gave the clergy the upper hand as ecclesiastical space was their 'realm' where they exercised their specific duties, the administration of sacraments, preaching and instruction of the laity.

As P.J. Broadhead has suggested, in the German lands, church orders made it clear that public worship was considered the most suitable context for dissemi-

---

62 Tob 12:8.

Figure 27: The tombstone of Michael Oltard (photo Ciprian Firea)

Seeing the Word of God: | **309**

nating the Bible among the laity. In the *Agendbüchlein*, ministers were instructed to read the Gospel passage for the day at the beginning of the sermon and then explain the text (Broadhead: 2005, 283–286). Thus, for both adults and children what they learned and assimilated through regular Sunday worship may have been of greater and more lasting significance than the results of catechetical instruction (Broadhead: 2005, 292). Adopting models from the German heartlands for their professional behaviour, Transylvanian ministers dutifully read passages from the Bible to their congregations and included sermons in every service, a decision with many-faceted consequences.

Uses of the Bible in the church meant that contact with the Word of God was mediated and controlled by the clergy, who presented the text to the laity in small instalments or in catechetical form, which suggests that the laity did not choose the fragments of the Bible they came into contact with, as they presumably would have done in individual private reading. Whether aural, when the text was recited in church, or visual, when the text was placed on church furnishings, in liturgical context, the laity's contact with the Bible was piecemeal and the emphasis was placed on the quotations necessary for teaching the fundamentals of the new faith. This paints a picture of a rather passive audience, which did not necessarily have any say in the choice of texts presented to them. They seem to have had no agency in their contact with the scriptures which was entirely controlled by the clergy.

Hearing, Sight and Memory

This conclusion brings us back to the issue raised at the beginning of this study, the break between a sensual medieval culture and the biblical culture fostered by the Reformation. The contention that the transition from sensual access to the sacred to a religious culture focused on the word, brought about by the Reformation, was recently refined in at least two ways: on the one hand by scholars (Strauss: 1975; Parker: 1992; Haigh: 2001) who, by focusing on the success or failure of the Reformation, suggested that the Bible did not enter the devotional world of the laity in the ways initially envisaged by reformers, on the other, by researchers (Corbellini: 2012; Hoogvliet: 2013a; Gow: 2005) who, by focusing on contesting what they called the "Protestant paradigm" wished to show that the Bible, in numerous vernacular editions was known within a broader segment of the laity, not just its upper echelons, long before the Reformation. These scholars contend that, in places like Italy, northern France and the Netherlands, there was a rich biblical culture in the various vernaculars, which was often adapted to specific religious practices and an active engagement of "religiously ambitious people" with biblical texts. They ultimately suggest that lay engagement with the Bible did not begin with the Reformation during the sixteenth century and that manuscripts were actually read rather than collected for their artistic and material value. Thus, while medievalists seem to support the existence of a lively biblical culture among the laity, Reformation scholars doubt that the latter were familiar with the biblical text even long after evangelical ideas were first espoused and zealously disseminated.

Emphasis on the content of published editions of the scriptures suggests that during the later Middle Ages complete bibles were relatively rare and manuscripts would contain a selection of Bible books, often with a strong focus on the New Testament, particularly on the Passion narrative. Produced with specific audiences in mind and adapted to their needs, these bibles were more affordable and reached a broader social spectrum, also encouraged by the fact that they were often translated into the various vernaculars. Thus, even if the Bible was better known than previously believed, it had been turned into narrative and practically reduced to stories from the life of Christ, particularly the Passion, in order to tug at the heartstrings of the laity triggering affective responses. Perhaps surprisingly, given the initial vision of the reformers, after the Reformation, the laity was not provided with the canonical text of the Bible either, but rather with interpreted and glossed versions of the scriptures. In fact, most of the time, the Bible was simply replaced by the Catechism as the principal tool of religious instruction.

The two camps also differ in the way they approach issues of agency and reception. On the one hand, the fact that these texts were mostly abridged bibles and collections of biblical quotations has been explained by medievalists as the reflection of selective and discontinuous reading practices, placing agency in the hands of the laity (Hoogvliet: 2013b, 245). On the other hand, Reformation scholars have come to the conclusion that the laity was fed 'kernels of knowledge' in catechetical format, bestowing responsibility for religious instruction upon the clergy who had authored these texts.

As far as reception is concerned, medievalists have suggested that the process of translation and the diffusion of the biblical text resulted in more intense cultural and religious participation of the laity, for instance through meditation and affective reactions to the narrative of the life of Christ (Corbellini/Hoogvliet: 2015, 262, 269–270, 273–274; Corbellini: 2012, 15–39). On the other hand, Reformation scholars have contended that catechisms did not leave room for speculation, as they provided the right answers to a set of preconceived questions. Thus, the laity was not encouraged to ask different questions or to give personal answers, engaging with the text in an individual way. As Gerald Strauss has suggested, relying on the Catechism instead of the Bible was a way of "playing it safe". Catechisms left no margin for error and instilled habits of correct thought (Strauss: 1984, 115).

Equating familiarity with the Bible among the laity with the success of the Reformation, scholars have been tempted to conclude that the process had failed as

Seeing the Word of God: | 311

the laity had no real engagement with the Gospel but rather with the catechism (Strauss: 1984, 109). The catechism taught the Creed, the Commandments and the Lord's Prayer, together with a short account of the sacraments. As Christopher Haigh has noted concerning the Reformation in England, it did not include any specifically Protestant doctrines (Haigh: 2001, 46–49). In fact, except for the absence of the Hail Mary, this minimal programme resembled to a great extent the prerequisites of the medieval Catholic Church. As pointed out by Margriet Hoogvliet, in his *Miroir de l'âme*, Jean Gerson included the basic biblical knowledge that every Christian was supposed to become familiar with, the Ten Commandments, the Lord's Prayer, the Apostolic Creed and the Hail Mary (Hoogvliet: 2013b, 259).

Consequently, by revising existing views and historiographical clichés, these two apparently opposing camps reached the same unexpected conclusion: the Bible was not known in its canonical form either before or after the Reformation. In both cases, the faithful were fed either narratives meant to tug at the heartstrings or pre-packaged answers to the simplest possible questions. According to existing scholarship, catechisms were best equipped to fulfil this end as they spelled out the approved tenets of faith and clearly conveyed the meaning of all the essentials of belief. Intended for memorization, incessantly repeated, catechisms rooted basic religious precepts in people's memory and thus incurred habits of correct thought. Moreover, catechism teaching and catechism recitation were primarily oral activities and could flourish in a culture of non-readers (Gawthrop/Strauss: 1984, 36–38; Strauss: 1984, 115; Parker: 1992, 54). Consequently, before and after the Reformation, contact with the scriptures was not direct, but rather mediated by a controlling clergy who presented the laity with already digested versions of the Word of God.

At the end of the analysis, one is compelled to wonder what the in-depth exploration of the Transylvanian example can bring to the issue under scrutiny here. In Transylvania, as elsewhere in Europe, by the time evangelical ideas were thoroughly adopted and implemented, reading the Bible had gradually become the responsibility of the clergy who interpreted it for the broader public through sermons, biblical commentaries and particularly catechisms, as they had become the preferred method of religious instruction. The Transylvanian evidence, by highlighting the need for parishes to equip themselves not just with bibles but also with postils and catechisms further supports this conclusion. One could mention that ministers' libraries were full of biblical commentaries and model sermons and many of them did not think it necessary to own a personal copy of the Bible (Crăciun: 2021b, 48.). Evidence concerning the price of bibles and levels of literacy in Transylvanian society suggests that direct contact with the scriptures through individual private reading must have been a limited phenomenon, particularly in the rural areas. One is led to conclude that the laity mostly came into contact with the

Bible aurally as it was read and explained to them in church, as suggested by church ordinances which prescribed more time allocated during worship to sermons and readings from the Old and New Testaments, and to catechetical instruction after the service. In this context, the use of the vernacular was encouraged while the minister was required to speak in a strong and clear voice.

More significantly, the oral dissemination of the Bible privileged specific parts of the scriptures, such as the Creed, the Decalogue, the Words of Institution, the explanation of Baptism and the Lord's Prayer, a selection of texts that closely mirrored the structure of Martin Luther's catechisms. Thus, within the context of its oral dissemination during the service, familiarity with the biblical text was ensured by its repeated recitation and the memorization of excerpts equated with the core of the doctrine, the same 'kernels of knowledge' that had already been appropriated through catechesis.

The evidence further suggests that the laity were not passive recipients of these educational endeavours. Although direct contact with the Bible was not explicitly encouraged, attendance at church and catechism classes became the responsibility of the housefathers who supervised in this manner the religious instruction of their children and dependents. As a consequence, youngsters were expected to be familiar with the catechism by the time they were confirmed and certainly before they married. This leads one to conclude that, in Transylvanian Lutheran churches, familiarity with the scriptures was not primarily achieved by individual reading in private contexts, but rather during the service, when individuals were engaged in communal worship within the public space of the church.

This attention bestowed on the interaction of the laity with the Bible has obscured somewhat the issue highlighted at the beginning of this study, the transition from a sensuous religious culture aided by the primacy of sight in accessing the sacred to a textual culture which privileged the word. The analysis has begun by asking whether the new emphasis placed on words impacted on the hierarchy of the senses in individual and communal worship and whether, ultimately, sight had lost its place in devotional behaviour.

The analysis undertaken in this study leads one to conclude that the prevailing oral mechanisms of dissemination highlight the mostly aural reception of the biblical text. However, the argument of this essay has been focused on the biblical texts that were seen by the congregation during the divine service because they had been placed on ecclesiastical furnishings. This highlights a manner of reception that hinted at visual not just oral dissemination of the scriptures. The cases analysed in this study have emphasized that texts were presented as images and transformed into the focus of the public's attention if not quite into the object of their devotion. They were also used as labels that identified images, legitimized their use by introducing a scriptural reference and placed them within pictorial programmes firmly anchored in textual tradition. Inscriptions were further posited as signs, encouraging communication between these texts and the public in a manner similar to the sermon, intended primarily to educate. Texts were also used as emblems meant to both identify and decode images, but also to establish typological associations between the Old and the New Testaments, by mingling verbal and visual signs in the manner of an "iconotext". Finally, these quotations were presented as objects, as material and didactic devices rendering the scriptures in fragments of brief and thus manageable size.

Thus, in a different medium, biblical texts were once more reduced to small quotations rendered in Latin on the surface of ecclesiastical furnishings. It is rather unlikely that congregations, particularly in Transylvanian villages were able to read them. One is consequently led to question the purpose of these visual mechanisms of communication along with their efficacy in conveying knowledge drawn from the Scriptures. The evidence analysed in this study provides a possible answer by suggesting that these brief kernels of knowledge functioned as mnemonic devices. People were already familiar with them from oral renditions of the same texts during the service or in catechism classes. It is fairly probable that they had already committed them to memory, by way of their frequent recitation. Associated as they were with images they became more easily understood. The sight of the Lamb of God, the Brazen Serpent or the Baptism of Christ was likely to trigger the recollection of the appropriate texts generally used by the minister to explain the image. One can only conclude that visual dissemination still proved effective in conveying biblical knowledge and that sight had not been dislodged from the features of early modern worship. The scriptures were disseminated to the laity in complex ways, which involved all the senses, especially hearing and sight. The visual still had a place within the ecclesiastical space where it coexisted with oral/aural communication.

Consequently, the Transylvanian example fits into the broader European context where, during the past few decades, scholarship has highlighted a story of continuity in the use of the Bible before and after the Reformation. The laity was fed small morsels of the Holy Writ by a well-meaning but ultimately controlling clergy. Moreover, views on the fundamentals of faith were very similar as the clergy wished the laity to become familiar with the Apostles' Creed, the Ten Commandments, the Lord's Prayer and the meaning of the Sacraments.

Differences between Protestants and Catholics were signposted by the removal of the Hail Mary, while the meaning bestowed on the sacraments traced a subtle border between the faiths, shaping the identity of each confessional group. Of all the doctrinal differences between the confessions, those related to the sacraments, especially to the Eucharist had practical and devotional consequences in ways that other distinctions, for example the offer of grace as opposed to good works or predestination, did not. It is small wonder then, that their significance was communicated to the congregation by all possible means, including the biblical texts

314 | Maria Crăciun

placed on church furnishings. The main tenets of faith were included in a visual catechism devised for the benefit of a moderately literate society.

Bibliography

ASTON, MARGARET (1977), Lollardy and Literacy, History LXII/206, 347–371.

BÁNDI, ANDRÁS (2016), Lectura sașilor în secolul al XVIII-lea, PhD thesis, Universitatea Babeș-Bolyai, Cluj-Napoca.

BASCHET, JÉRÔME (2008), L'Iconographie médiévale, Paris: Gallimard.

BELTING, HANS (2002), Macht und Ohnmacht der Bilder, Historische Zeitschrift 33, 11–32.

BELTING, HANS (1994), Likeness and Presence. A History of the Image before the Era of Art, Chicago/London: University of Chicago Press.

BILLER, PETER (1994), Heresy and Literacy. Earlier History of the Theme, in: Peter Biller/Anne Hudson (ed.), Heresy and Literacy, 1000–1530, Cambridge: Cambridge University Press, 1–19.

BINSKI, PAUL (1999), The English Parish Church and Its Art in the Later Middle Ages: A Review of the Problem, Studies in Iconography 20, 1–25.

BOTTIGHEIMER, RUTH B. (1993), Bible Reading, "Bibles", and the Bibles for Children in Early Modern Germany, Past & Present 139, 66–89.

BROADHEAD, P.J. (2005), Public Worship, Liturgy and the Introduction of the Lutheran Reformation in the Territorial Lands of Nuremberg, The English Historical Review 120/486, 277–302.

BROWN, JACOB M. (2013), From Incense to Idolatry: The Reformation of Olfaction in Late Medieval German Ritual, The Sixteenth Century Journal 44/2, 323–344.

BRÜCKNER, WOLFGANG (2007), Lutherische Bekenntnisgemälde des 16. bis 18. Jahrhunderts. Die Illustrierte Confessio Augustana, Regensburg: Schnell und Steiner.

BURKE, PETER (2001), Eyewitnessing. The Uses of Images as Historical Evidence, Ithaca, NY: Cornell University Press.

CAMERON, EVAN (1991), The European Reformation, Oxford: Clarendon Press.

CAMILLE, MICHAEL (1996), The Gregorian Definition Revisited: Writing and the Medieval Image, in: Jérôme Baschet/Jean Claude Schmitt (ed.), L'Image. Fonctions et usages des images dans l'Occident médiéval, Paris: Léopard d'Or, 89–107.

CANNON, JOANNA (2010), Kissing the Virgin's Foot: Adoration Before the Madonna and Child. Enacted, Depicted, Imagined, Studies in Iconography, 31, 1–50.

CHAZELLE, CELIA (1990), Pictures, Books and the Illiterate: Pope Gregory I's Letters to Serenus of Marseilles, Word and Image 6, 138–153.

CHRISTIANSEN, CARL C. (1979), Art and the Reformation in Germany, Athens, Ohio: Ohio University Press.

COLE, RICHARD G. (1984), Reformation Printers: Unsung Heroes, The Sixteenth Century Journal15/3, 3127–3139.

CORBELLINI, SABRINA/HOOGVLIET, MARGRIET (2015), Holy Writ and Lay Readers in Late Medieval Europe: Translation and Participation, in: André Lardinois/Sophie

Levie/Hans Hoeken / Christoph Lüthy (ed.), Texts, Transmissions, Receptions. Modern Approaches to Narratives, Leiden/Boston: Brill, 259–280.

CORBELLINI, SABRINA (2012), Instructing the Soul, Feeding the Spirit and Awakening the Passion: Holy Writ and Lay Readers in Late Medieval Europe, in: Bruce Gordon/ Matthew MacLean (ed.), Shaping the Bible in the Reformation: Books, Scholars and Readers in the Sixteenth Century, Leiden/Boston: Brill, 15–39.

CRĂCIUN, MARIA (2021a), The Voice of Pulpits. Word and Image in the Construction of Confessional Identity of Lutheran Communities in Early Modern Transylvania, in: Ulrich A. Wien (ed.), Common Man, Society and Religion in the Sixteenth Century/ Gemeindermann, Gesellschaft und Religion in 16. Jahrhundert. Piety, morality and discipline in the Carpathian Basin/Frömigkeit, Moral und Sozialdisziplinierung im Karpatenbogen, Götingen: Vandenhoeck &Ruprecht, 385–413.

CRĂCIUN, MARIA (2021b), The Minister's Reading List: Religious Books in the Libraries of Transylvanian Lutheran Clergy, in: Howard Louthan/Drew Thomas/Elizabeth Dillenburg (ed.), Print Culture at the Crossroads: The Book and Central Europe, Leiden/ Boston: Brill, 34–57.

CRĂCIUN, MARIA (2018), The Polyptych of Dobârca and the Issue of the Text-Retable in Early Modern Transylvania, Brukenthal Acta Musei XIII/2, 179–207.

CRĂCIUN, MARIA (2017), "Historiae Vero Sacrae et Similes Retineantur": Funcţia imaginilor produse pentru bisericile luterane ale Transilvaniei în epoca modernă timpurie, Studii şi Articole de Istorie LXXXIV, 18–38.

CRĂCIUN, MARIA (2016), Imaginea şi Reforma Luterană în Transilvania Modernităţii Timpurii, Cluj-Napoca: Editura Mega.

CRĂCIUN, MARIA (2015a), "Non in Mensis Ligneis sed in altaribus administratem esse Coena Domini": L'altare nelle chiese luterane della Transilvania nella prima età moderna, in: Ioan-Aurel Pop/Ovidiu Ghitta/Ioan Bolovan/Ana Victoria Sima (ed.), Dal cuore dell'Europa. Omaggio al Professor Cesare Alzati per il compimento dei 70 anni, Cluj-Napoca: Presa Universitară Clujeană, 209–228.

CRĂCIUN, MARIA (2015b), Transylvanian Lutheran Liturgical Practices in Comparative European Perspective, in: Irene Dingel/Ute Lotz-Heumann (ed.), Entfaltung und zeitgenössische Wirkung der Reformation im europäischen Kontext / Dissemination and Contemporary Impact of the Reformation in a European Context, Gütersloh: Gütersloher Verlagshaus, 345–375.

CRĂCIUN, MARIA (2014), Ritual şi Recuzită: practica liturgică luterană din Transilvania modernităţii timpurii (secolele XVI-XVII), Ars Transsilvaniae XXIV, 133–176.

CRĂCIUN, MARIA (2013), Communities of Devotion: The Saxons in Early Modern Transylvania, Studia Universitatis Babeş-Bolyai. Historia 58, Special Issue, 156–195.

CRĂCIUN, MARIA (2012), Marian Imagery and its Function in the Lutheran Churches of Early Modern Transylvania, in: Andrew Spicer (ed.), Lutheran Churches in Early Modern Europe, Farnham: Ashgate, 133–164.

CRĂCIUN, MARIA (2008), The Construction of Sacred Space and the Confessional Identity of the Transylvanian Lutheran Community, in: Evelin Wetter (ed.), Formierungen des Konfessionellen Raumes in Ostmitteleuropa, Stuttgart: Franz Steiner, 97–124.

CRĂCIUN, MARIA/GHITTA, OVIDIU/MURDOCK, GRAEME (2002), Religious Reform, printed books and confessional identity, in: Maria Crăciun/Ovidiu Ghitta/Graeme

316 | Maria Crăciun

Murdock (ed.), Confessional Identity in East-Central Europe, Aldershot: Ashgate, 1–30.

CRESSY, DAVID (1986), Books as Totems in Seventeenth-Century England and New England, The Journal of Library History, 92–106.

DAVIS, THOMAS J. (1999), "The Truth of the Divine Words": Luther's Sermons on the Eucharist, 1521–28 and the Structure of Eucharistic Meaning, Sixteenth Century Journal 30/2, 323–342.

DIEDERICHS-GOTTSCHALK, DIETRICH (2005), Die protestantischen Schriftaltäre des 16. und 17. Jahrhunderts in Nordwestdeutschland. Eine Kirchen und kunstgeschichtliche Untersuchung zu einer Sonderform liturgische Ausstattung in der Epoche der Konfessionalisierung, Regensburg: Schnell und Steiner.

DINCĂ, ADINEL CIPRIAN (2015), Notaries Public in Late Medieval Transylvania: Prerequisites for the Reception of a Legal Institution, Anuarul Institutului de Istorie "George Barițiu". Series Historica, Supplement 1, 33–47.

DUFFY, EAMON (1992), The Stripping of the Altars. Traditional Religion in England 1400–1580, New Haven/London: Yale University Press.

EDWARDS, MARK U. Jr. (1994), Printing, Propaganda, and Martin Luther, Berkeley/Los Angeles: University of California Press.

FIREA, CIPRIAN (2010), Arta Polipticelor medievale din Transilvania (1450–1550), PhD thesis, Universitatea Babeș-Bolyai, Cluj-Napoca.

FLÓRA, ÁGNES (2014), The Matter of Honour. The Leading Urban Elite in Sixteenth Century Cluj and Sibiu, PhD thesis, Central European University, Budapest.

GINZBURG, CARLO (1979), Clues: Roots of a Scientific Paradigm, Theory and Society 7/3, 273–288.

GOW, ANDREW (2005), Challenging the Protestant Paradigm: Bible Reading in Lay Urban Contexts of the Later Middle Ages, in: T.J. Heffernan/T.E. Burman (ed.), Scripture and Pluralism. Reading the Bible in the Religiously Plural Worlds of the Middle Ages and Renaissance, Leiden/Boston: Brill, 161–91.

GÖHLER, JOHANNES (1997), Aus der Geschichte des Kirchspiels, Debstedt.

GÖHLER, JOHANNES (1990), Ringstedt. Geschichte eines Kirchsspiel an der Oberen Geeste von der Christianisierung, bis zum Jahre 1900, Ringstedt.

GÜNDISCH, GUSTAV/NÄGLER, DOINA (1994), Die Bibliothek des Hermannstädter ev. Stadtpfarrens Andreas Oltard (1660) und seiner Familie, Zeitschrift für Siebenbürgische Landeskunde 17/2, 121–143.

GÜNDISCH, GUSTAV/NÄGLER, DOINA (1992), Die Bücherei des Hermannstädter ev. Stadtpfarrens Petrus Rihelius (1648) und seiner Söhne, Zeitschrift für Siebenbürgische Landeskunde 15/1, 41–62.

GÜNDISCH, GUSTAV (1987a), Die Bibliothek des Damasus Dürr (1585), in: Gustav Gündisch, Aus Geschichte und Kultur der Siebenbürger Sachsen. Ausgewählte Aufsätze und Berichte, Köln/Wien: Böhlau, 340–350.

GÜNDISCH, GUSTAV (1987b), Eine siebenbürgische Bischofsbibliothek des 16. Jahrhunderts. Die Bücherei des Lukas Unglerus, in: Gündisch, Aus Geschichte und Kultur der Siebenbürger Sachsen, Köln/Wien: Böhlau, 351–362.

GÜNDISCH, GUSTAV (1977), Die Bibliothek des Superintendenten der evangelischen Kirche Siebenbürgens, Matthias Schiffbäumer (1547–1611), Revue des Études Sud-Est Européennes, XV/3, 463–478.

HAIGH, CHRISTOPHER (2001), Success and Failure in the English Reformation, Past & Present 173, 28–49.

HAMBURGER, JEFFREY (1989), The Visual and the Visionary: The Image in Late Medieval Monastic Devotion, Viator 20, 161–182.

HAMBURGER, JEFFREY (1998), The Visual and the Visionary: Art and Female Spirituality in Late Medieval Germany, New York/London: Zone Books.

HARBISON, CRAIG (1985), Visions and Meditations in Early Flemish Paintings, Simiolus 15, 87–118.

HONÉE, EUGÈNE (1994), Image and imagination in the medieval culture of prayer: a historical perspective, in: Henk van Os (ed.), The Art of Devotion in the Late Middle Ages in Europe 1300–1500, London: Merrell Holberton, 157–174.

HONTERUS, JOHANNES (1896), Reformatio Ecclesiae Coronensis ac Totius Barcensis Provinciae, Coronae MDXLIII, in: Oskar Netoliczka (ed.), Johannes Honterus' ausgewählte Schriften. Im Auftrage des Ausschusses zur Errichtung des Honterusdenkmals in Kronstadt, Hermannstadt, 11–28.

HOOGVLIET, MARGRIET (2013a), The Medieval Vernacular Bible in French as a Flexible Text: Selective and Discontinuous Reading Practices, in: Eyal Poleg/Laura Light (ed.), Form and Function in the Late Medieval Bible, Leiden/Boston: Brill, 283–306.

HOOGVLIET, MARGRIET (2013b), Encouraging Lay People to Read the Bible in the French Vernaculars: New Groups of Readers and Textual Communities, Church History and Religious Culture 93/2, 239–274.

HOUSTON, RAB (1983), Literacy and Society in the West 1500–1850, Social History 8/3, 269–293.

HUTTON, RONALD (1987), The Local Impact of the Tudor Reformation, in: Cristopher Haigh (ed.), The English Reformation Revised, Cambridge: Cambridge University Press, 114–138.

JAKÓ, ZSIGMOND (1977), Tiparul cu litere latine din Sibiu în secolul al XVI-lea, in: Zsigmond Jakó, Philobiblon Transilvan, Bucureşti: Kriterion, 93–116.

KARANT-NUNN, SUSAN (1997), The Reformation of Ritual. An interpretation of early modern Germany, London: Routledge.

KENNEDY, KIRSTEN (2015), 'Seeing is Believing': The Miniatures of the Cantigas de Santa Maria and Medieval Devotional Practices, Portuguese Studies 31/2, 169–182.

KINGDON, R.M. (1966), Patronage, Piety and Printing in Sixteenth Century Europe, in: D. H. Pinkney/T. Rupp (ed.), A Festschrift for Frederick B. Artz, Durham, N.C.

KINGDON, ROBERT (2004), Worship in Geneva before and after the Reformation, in: Karin Maag/John D. Witvliet (ed.), Worship in Medieval and Early Modern Europe. Change and Continuity in Religious Practice, Notre Dame, Indiana: University of Notre Dame Press, 41–62.

KODRES, KRISTA (2006), Lutheran Internationalism of Estonian Art Production in the 16th-18th centuries: the Pulpit, in: Jan Harasimowicz/P. Oszczanowski/Marcin Wisłocki (ed.), On Opposite Sides of the Baltic Sea. Relations between Scandinavia and Central European Countries, Wroclaw: Via Nova, 381–393.

KOERNER, JOSEPH LEO (2004), The Reformation of the Image, London: Reaktion Books.

KÖPECZI, BÉLA et altri (ed.) (1994), History of Transylvania, Budapest: Akadémiai Kiadó.

LUTHER, MARTIN (1909), Von Priesterehe, 1528, WA 26, 528–533.

318 | Maria Crăciun

Luther, Martin (1891), Ordnung eines gemeinen Kastens, 1523, WA 12, 1-30.

Machat, Christoph (1985), Auswirkungen der Reformation auf die Ausstattung sieben-
bürgischen Kirchen, in: Renate Weber/Georg Weber (ed.), Luther und Siebenbürgen.
Ausstrahlungen von Reformation und Humanismus nach Südost Europa, Köln/Wien:
Böhlau, 309-326.

Mâle, Émile (1948), L'art religieux du XIIIe siècle en France. Étude sur l'iconographie
du Moyen Âge et sur ses sources d'inspiration, Paris: Armand Colin.

Michalski, Sergiusz (1996), Inscriptions in Protestant Paintings and in Protestant
Churches, in: Arja Leena Paavola (ed.), Ars Ecclesiastica. The Church as a Context for
Visual Arts, Helsinki: University Press, 34-47.

Mihály, Ferenc (2014), Contribuții la cercetarea polipticelor medievale transilvănene.
Observații privind tehnicile de execuție și intervențiile de restaurare, Ars Transsilvaniae, XXIV, 75-94.

Mitchell, W. J.T. (1994), Picture Theory. Essays on Verbal and Visual Representation,
Chicago: University of Chicago Press.

Moore, R. I. (1994), Literacy and the Making of Heresy, in: Peter Biller/Anne Hudson
(ed.), Heresy and Literacy, 1000-1530, Cambridge: Cambridge University Press, 19-
37.

Nelson, Janet L. (1990), Literacy in Carolingian Government, in: R. McKitteridge (ed.),
The Uses of Literacy in Early Medieval Europe, Cambridge: Cambridge University
Press, 269-270.

Noble, Bonnie (2009), Lucas Cranach the Elder. Art and Devotion in the German Reformation, Lanham: University Press of America.

Nussbächer, Gernot (1977), Johannes Honterus, București: Kriterion.

Nussbächer, Gernot/Marin, Elisabeta (ed.) (1999), Quellen zur Geschichte des
Stadt Kronstadt, vol. IX, (1420-1580), Kronstadt: Aldus.

Pakora, Jakub (1987), Word and picture as keys for solving the ideological programme
of Protestant Pulpits in Silesia, 1550-1650, Polish Art Studies 8, 45-56.

Palmer Wandel, Lee (2006), The Eucharist in the Reformation. Incarnation and Liturgy,
Cambridge: Cambridge University Press.

Parker, Geoffrey (1992), Success and Failure during the First Century of the Reformation, Past & Present 136, 43-82.

Parks, Malcolm B. (1973), The Literacy of the Laity, in: D. Daiches/A.K. Thorlby (ed.),
Literature and Western Civilization. The Medieval World, London: Aldus Books, 555-
576.

Pettegree, Andrew (2005), Reformation or the Culture of Persuasion, Cambridge:
Cambridge University Press.

Pettegree, Andrew/Hall, Matthew (2004), The Reformation and the Book: a Reconsideration, The Historical Journal 47/4, 785-808.

Razovsky, Helaine (1998), Remaking the Bible: English Reformation Spiritual Conduct
Books, Renaissance and Reformation / Renaissance et Réforme 22/4, 5-25.

Reiss, Athene (2008), Beyond "Books for the Illiterate": Understanding English Medieval Wallpaintings, The British Art Journal 9/1, 4-14.

Ringbom, Sixten (1969), Devotional Images and Imaginative Devotions: Notes on the
Place of Art in Late Medieval Piety, Gazette des Beaux Arts 673, 159-170.

Roman, Toma Cosmin (2007), Sibiul între siguranță și incertitudine în zorii epocii moderne 1528–1549, Alba Iulia: Editura Altip.

Roth, Victor (1916), Siebenbürgische Altäre, Strassburg.

Rother, Christian (2002), Siebenbürgen und der Buchdruck im 16. Jahrhundert. Mit einer Bibliographie Siebenbürgen und der Buchdruck, Wiesbaden: Harrassowitz.

Rublack, Ulinka (2010), Grapho-relics: Lutheranism and the Materialization of the Word, Past & Present Supplement 5, 144–165.

Ruge, Reinhard (1985), Der wiederentdeckte Schriftaltar, Festschrift Ludgerikirche, 14–24.

Scarisbrick, J.J. (1984), The Reformation and the English People, Oxford: Blackwell.

Schmidt, Victor M. (2001), Painting and Individual Devotion in Late Medieval Italy: the Case of St Catherine of Alexandria, in: Andre Landes/Shelley Zurow (ed.), Visions of Holiness: Art and Devotion in Italy, Athens: University of Georgia, 21–36.

Schuster, Peter Klaus (1983), Abstraktion, Agitation und Einfühlung. Formen protestantischer Kunst im 16. Jahrhundert in: Werner Hofmann (ed.), Kopie der Lutherzeit. Katalog der Ausstellung in der Hamburger Kunsthalle, München, 115–125.

Scribner, Bob (1994), Heterodoxy, literacy and print in the early German Reformation, in: Peter Biller/Anne Hudson (ed.), Heresy and Literacy 1000–1530, Cambridge: Cambridge University Press, 225–278.

Scribner, Bob (1989a), Popular Piety and Modes of Visual Perception in Late Medieval and Reformation Germany, The Journal of Religious History 15/4, 448–469.

Scribner, Robert (1989b), For the Sake of Simple Folk. Popular Propaganda for the German Reformation, Cambridge: Cambridge University Press.

Scribner, R. W. (1987), Oral Culture and the Diffusion of Reformation Ideas, in: R. W. Scribner, Popular Culture and Popular Movements in Reformation Germany, London: Hambledon Press, 49–70.

Seraphin, Friedrich Wilhelm (1891), Kronstädter Schulen vor der Reformation, Archiv des Vereins für siebenbürgische Landeskunde, Neue Folge, XXIII, 791–792.

Spicer, Andrew (ed.) (2012), Lutheran Churches in Early Modern Europe, Farnham: Ashgate.

Stone, Lawrence (1969), Literacy and Education in England 1640–1900, Past &Present 42, 69–139.

Stone, Lawrence (1964), The Educational Revolution in England, 1560–1640, Past & Present 28, 41–80.

Strauss, Gerald (1984), Lutheranism and Literacy: A Reassessment, in: Kaspar von Greyerz (ed.), Religion and Society in Early Modern Europe 1500–1800, London: George Allen and Unwin, 109–123.

Strauss, Gerald/Gawthrop, Richard (1984), Protestantism and Literacy in Early Modern Germany, Past & Present 104, 31–55.

Strauss, Gerald (1975), Success and Failure in the Reformation, Past & Present 67, 30–63.

Szegedi, Edit (2009), Hungarian and Saxon Culture in the Sixteenth Century, in: Ioan Aurel Pop/Thomas Nägler, Doina/András Magyari (ed.), The History of Transylvania, vol. II (from 1541 to 1711), Cluj-Napoca: Center for Transylvanian Studies, 273–280.

Szegedi, Edit (2006), Konfessionsbildung und Konfessionalisierung im städtischen Kontext. Eine Fallstudie am Beispiel von Kronstadt in Siebenbürgen (ca. 1550–1680),

320 | Maria Crăciun

in: Jörg Deventer(ed.), Berichte und Beiträge des Geisteswissenschaftlichen Zentrums Geschichte und Kultur Ostmitteleuropas an der Universität Leipzig. Heft 2, Konfessionelle Formierungsprozessen im Frühneuzeitlichen Ostmitteleuropa. Vorträge und Studien, Leipzig: GWZO, 126–253.

SZENDE, KATALIN (2009), Integration through Language: The Multilingual Character of Late Medieval Hungarian Towns, in: Derek Keene / Balázs Nagy / Katalin Szende (ed.), Segregation – Integration – Assimilation. Religious and Ethnic Groups in the Medieval Towns of Central and Eastern Europe, Farnham: Ashgate, 205–234.

SZÖGI, LÁSZLÓ (2011), Magyarországi diákok németországi egyetemeken és akadémiákon 1526–1700, Magyarországi diákok egyetemjárása az újkorban 17, 7–29.

TEUTSCH, FRIEDRICH (1881), Die Hermannstädter Buchdrucker und Buchhändler, Korrespondenzblatt des Vereins für Siebenbürgische Landeskunde IV / 1, 1–4.

TEUTSCH, GEORG DANIEL (ed.) (1862), Urkundenbuch der Evangelischer Landeskirche A. B. in Siebenbürgen, vol. I Hermannstadt.

TEUTSCH, GEORG DANIEL (ed.) (1883), Urkundenbuch der Evangelischer Landeskirche A. B. in Siebenbürgen,vol II, Hermannstadt.

TONK, SÁNDOR (1996), Siebenbürgische Studenten an ausländischen Universitäten, in: Walter König (ed.), Beiträge zur siebenbürgischen Schulgeschichte, Köln / Weimar / Wien: Böhlau, 119–121.

TÓTH, ISTVÁN GYÖRGY (2007), The Correspondence of Illiterate Peasants in Early Modern Hungary, in: Francisco Bethencourt / Florike Egmond (ed.), Correspondence and Cultural Exchange in Europe, Cambridge: Cambridge University Press, 313–332.

VLAICU, MONICA (ed.) (2003), Documente privind istoria orașului Sibiu II Comerț și meșteșuguri în Sibiu și în cele Șapte Scaune, 1229–1579, Sibiu: Editura Hora. Societatea de Studii transilvane din Heidelberg.

WAGNER, ERNST (1998), Die Pfarrer und Lehrer der Evangelischen Kirche A.B. in Siebenbürgen, Köln / Weimar / Wien: Böhlau.

WAGNER, PETER (1996), Introduction: Ekphrasis, Iconotexts and Intermediality – the State(s) of the Art(s), in: Peter Wagner (ed.), Icons-Texts – Iconotexts. Essays on Ekphrasis and Intermediality, Berlin / New York: Walter de Gruyten, 1–42.

WILKINS, DAVID G. (2002), Opening the Doors to Devotion: Trecento Triptychs and Suggestions Concerning Images and Domestic Practice in Florence, Studies in the History of Art 61, 370–393.

WILLIAMSON, BETH (2013), Sensory Experience in Medieval Devotions: Sound and Vision, Invisibility and Silence, Speculum 88/1, 1–43.

WILLIAMSON, BETH (2004), Altarpieces, Liturgy and Devotion, Speculum 79/2, 341–406.

ZACH, KRISTA (2002), Protestant vernacular catechisms and religious reform in sixteenth-century east-central Europe, in: Maria Crăciun / Ovidiu Ghitta / Graeme Murdock (ed.), Confessional Identity in East Central Europe, Aldershot: Ashgate, 49–63.

Niranjan Goswami
Chandernagore College, the University of Burdwan, India

'Stinted Prayer':
Puritan Dilemmas of Common-Prayer Worship in England and New England during the English Reformation

Before the Reformation the Roman Catholic liturgy comprised the Liturgy of the Word (Gathering, Proclaiming and Hearing the Word, Prayers of the People) and the Liturgy of the Eucharist (together with the Dismissal), but the entire liturgy itself is also properly referred to as the Holy Eucharist. The Mass contained public prayers like the Prayers at the Foot of the Altar or the Penitential Rite, *Kyrie eleison* ("Lord, have mercy"), *Gloria* ("Glory to God in the highest"), the prayers said in connection with the scripture readings, *Credo* ("I believe in one God"), the Nicene Creed, etc. Whereas private prayer also has a place in this faith but in the Mass the public prayers and sacraments are predominant. Reformation leaders wanted to do away with the Roman Catholic Eucharist as a sacrifice or practices like the intercession of the saints, etc. Even though some of the forms of prayer survived, an attempt was made to alter their sense. Unlike Reformation in Europe, in England a middle way was imposed by the English Church after first Henry VIII and later Elizabeth I imposed the Act of Supremacy making themselves the supreme leaders in religion in England.[1] Any attempt to understand devotional practices in Europe cannot do without a discussion of the multifarious developments within Protestantism in England and their continuities in New England in the sixteenth and seventeenth century.

Archbishop Cranmer and the Origins of the BCP

The Book of Common Prayers, the authorized Anglican Service Book has a chequered history. Designed probably by Archbishop Cranmer during the rule of

---

1 1534: Act of Supremacy, recognising that Henry VIII is rightfully head of the Church in England, enforced by an oath taken by all clergy. 1559: Act of Supremacy and Act of Uniformity (Mary's religious legislation undone, Elizabeth granted the title of Supreme Governor of the Church of England, conformity to Book of Common Prayer ordered) cf. https://journals.openedition.org/rfcb/1239#:~:text=The%20Elizabethan%20Reformation,-1558%3A%20Death%20of&text=1559%3A%20Act%20of%20Supremacy%20and,Book%20of%20Common%20Prayer%20ordered). Last accessed 19.08.20.

322 | Niranjan Goswami

Henry VIII and Edward VI it aimed to replace many Roman Catholic rites and make the liturgy and the services as much acceptable to a broad section of Protestants as possible:

Cranmer's intention was to suppress notions of sacrifice and transubstantiation in the Mass. To stress this, there was no elevation of the consecrated bread and wine, and eucharistic adoration was prohibited. The elevation had been the central moment of the medieval Mass, attached as it was to the idea of real presence.

Cranmer's theology of Christ's presence in the Eucharist was close to the Calvinist spiritual presence view and can be described as Receptionism and Virtualism: i.e. Christ is really present but by the power of the Holy Spirit. The words of administration in the 1549 rite were deliberately ambiguous; they could be understood as identifying the bread with the body of Christ or (following Cranmer's theology) as a prayer that the communicant might spiritually receive the body of Christ by faith.[2]

In order to satisfy most Protestants, it often underwent revisions. It was made compulsory by Elizabeth I in the English churches but after her death the so called 'Puritans'[3] or precisians began to raise many objections, being dissatisfied with the half-way Reformation. Eventually, the Parliament proscribed it after the victory of the Puritans in the English Civil War. After the Restoration in 1660 a nominally revised Prayer Book of 1662 was brought back in the English Church.[4] In spite of such extreme opposite reception of the Prayer Book in England, it appears that it was popular and tied to the daily lives of the masses. In this essay I argue by examining a few early texts of sixteenth and seventeenth century of both England and New England how the Puritans became increasingly intolerant towards the Prayer Book that had set prayers[5] as opposed to spontaneous prayers.

The first *Book of Common Prayer* was issued in England during the reign of Edward VI in 1549; it was supposed to replace the Latin liturgies which were traditionally used in English churches even after a break with the Papacy after Henry VIII. The book was probably issued by Archbishop Cranmer and its sources were the Latin *Sarum Rite* developed in the thirteenth century, the Reformed Roman breviary of the Spanish Cardinal Quiñones and a book on liturgies by Hermann von Wied, the Archbishop of Cologne. The first *Book of Common Prayers* was used only for three years and after thorough revision a second *Book of Liturgies* was

---

2 https://en.wikipedia.org/wiki/Book_of_Common_Prayer (Last accessed 19.08.20.)

3 'Puritan' and 'Puritanism' are terms used to refer to godly men who thought the law failed to conform to the pure model of religion placed by them to the queen. They represented all that distinguished real Protestants from merely formal ones. According to Collinson the difference between a Puritan and an Anglican is one of degree or 'theological temperature' rather than of fundamental principles. See Collinson: 1967, 26–27.

4 https://www.britannica.com/topic/Book-of-Common-Prayer (Last accessed 19.08.20.)

5 Translations of Latin prayers to be recited by the public in the church as opposed to spontaneous private prayers.

'Stinted Prayer': | 323

published in 1552.[6] The first book demanded in the King's name compliance to an interpretation of the Eucharist that had little difference with the Roman Catholic interpretation:

Edward by the grace of God King of England, France and Ireland, defender of the faith and of the Church of England and Ireland in earth the supreme head: To all and singular our loving subjects greeting: for so much as in our high court of Parliament lately holden in Westminster, it was by us with the consent of the lords spiritual and temporal, and Commons there assembled, most godly and agreeably to Christ's holy Institution enacted that the most blessed Sacrament of the body and blood of our Saviour Christ, should from thenceforth be commonly delivered and ministered unto all persons, within our Realm of England and Ireland and other our dominions under both kinds, that is to say of bread and wine (except necessity otherwise require) lest every man phantasying and devising a sundry way by himself, in the use of this most blessed Sacrament of unity, there might thereby arise any unseemly or ungodly diversity.[7] (Ketley: 1844, 1).

Though in the Proclamation, from which the above quotation has been taken, it is mentioned that the body and blood of Jesus Christ were consumed spiritually, the 1549 Prayer Book had always been very close to the Roman Catholic position on the issue and when much later King Charles attempted to thrust this Prayer Book on Scottish churches, it was considered as a great regression in the matter of Reformation leading to huge popular unrest. Diarmaid MacCulloch writes:

In 1637 he [King Charles] imposed on Scotland a version of the English Prayer Book modified in a fashion which Arminians would secretly have liked to achieve in England: a move back to the first English Prayer Book of 1549, which had many more Catholic features than the post-1552 English liturgies, in particular making it easier to proclaim a theory of the real presence in the Eucharist. (MacCulloch: 2003, 521.)

In this chapter I argue that in the peculiar case of the English Reformation where the condensation of an institutional Anglican Protestantism made the official religion look more like Roman Catholicism than the Reformed religion, we notice a gradual intolerance developing among the Puritans, or to be precise, among the Independents[8] and Congregationalists[9] towards forms of prayer authorised

---

6 http://justus.anglican.org/resources/bcp/1549/BCP_1549.htm. (Last accessed 07.04.18.)
7 https://archive.org/details/twoliturgiesad1500chur (Last accessed 29.03.18.)
8 "In English church history, Independents advocated local congregational control of religious and church matters, without any wider geographical hierarchy, either ecclesiastical or political. Independents reached particular prominence between 1642 and 1660, in the period of the English Civil War and of the Commonwealth and Protectorate, wherein the Parliamentary Army became the champion of Independent religious views against the Anglicanism or the Laudianism of Royalists and the Presbyterianism favoured by Parliament itself. The Independents advocated freedom of religion for non-Catholics." https://en.wikipedia.org/wiki/Independent_(religion) (Last accessed 19.08.20.)
9 "Congregational churches (also Congregationalist churches; Congregationalism) are Protestant churches in the Reformed tradition practicing congregationalist church governance, in

by the English Church. I survey the attitudes and opinions of some of the early English writers like John Brinsley and George Downame and compare them with New England preachers like Thomas Shepard and Increase Mather to suggest that the bitterness towards 'stinted prayer' or set forms of prayer gradually increased with time and that prayers, daily conduct and communion were looked upon as grave issues, a neglect of which would mean an adverse impact on the souls of the Christians. For New England Puritans prayer essentially stood for a habit of the old Church; in their eyes preaching was given a greater emphasis over prayer.[10]

The neglect of prayer and the primacy of preaching over prayer are first observed in the work of such a reputed minister and author as William Perkins (1558–1602). Through William Ames (1576–1633) of the University of Franeker the influence of Perkins was paramount on the Congregationalists of Massachusetts Bay colony. Perkins in his *Art of Prophesying* (1607) described prayer and preaching as the two parts of prophesying. However, in his hand prayer takes up only four pages out of the 148-page book, the rest of which is on preaching. Even in these four pages, prayer refers to conceived prayer[11] rather than set prayer.

John Brinsley (1566?–1647?), more famous for his school-book of grammar *Ludus Literarius*, a teacher of William Lyly, noted by him as a Puritan of the strict type, also wrote at least three treatises on prayer, published as three parts of the book with the same title. In his *Second Part of the True Watch containing the perfect rule and summe of Prayer* (1607) Brinsley writes a long but organised discussion of prayer. In his "Epistle to the Reader" he addresses the following kinds of readers: (a) those who do not pray at all; (b) those who pray in an unknown tongue; (c) those who desire to pray; (d) those who faint in their troubles; (e) those afraid to pray the Lord's Prayer; and (f) those fallen asleep. The principal discussion starts with (a) the necessity of prayer; (b) the special properties of them that can pray; and (c) the power of prayer rightly performed. Brinsley persuades the reader that only prayer can save him and that otherwise the wrath of God threatens him in many ways – salient examples of which are the death of Queen Elizabeth and the Gunpowder plot. Under the second division Brinsley speaks of the qualities of a good Christian. These are the following: faith in Christ; Christian love for others;

---

which each congregation independently and autonomously runs its own affairs." https://en.wikipedia.org/wiki/Congregational_church (Last accessed 19.08.20.)

10 See my comments below on William Perkins. The superior place of preaching over prayer in New England is commonplace knowledge. The preachers in New England flooded the country with sermons. There were sermons for every occasion, public and private. More than prayer, which is a direct communication with God the outcome of which was uncertain, preaching was considered a more efficacious way in which God's word entered via the priest through the ear and brought grace to the hearer. See below the issue of the "boring of the ear" in my discussion of Thomas Shepard. Also see Miller: 1939, 1953, 1954.

11 Conceived prayer means spontaneously imagined private prayer rather than recitation of pre-written prayers from the Prayer Book.

'Stinted Prayer': | 325

quest for heavenly kingdom and righteousness; humility for being dust and ashes; striving to know the will of God; looking for his providence and protection; consciousness of the burden of sin; God-fearing and acknowledging his sovereignty. In the main body of the text Brinsley gives a very long and detailed explanation and commentary on the Lord's Prayer. The unique quality of Brinsley's work is that in spite of his reputation of being a strict Puritan it is devoid of any controversy. The emphasis upon scholarly commentary of the Lord's Prayer makes prayer a matter of undisputed Christian duty.[12]

John Preston (1587–1628), a disciple of the famous John Cotton (1585–1682) who had a long and influential career as a Puritan in New England, himself remained within the English Church in spite of his Puritan tendencies. An astute politician, he replaced John Donne as preacher at Lincoln's Inn and Laurence Chaderton as Master of Emmanuel College at Cambridge. A critic of Arminianism,[13] Preston was yet able to get the favour of James I. In his *The Saints Daily Exercise* Preston discusses prayer more or less in the traditional manner without much controversy. However, in the 'Third Sermon' he deals with the topic of 'stinted prayers' showing rational ways to avoid controversy on the issue. He raises the issue as a question – whether we may use set forms of prayer and whether it is sufficient. He answers by emphatically saying that there is no doubt that set forms may be used because Christ used such forms and even in Luther's and Calvin's time such forms are used. Then he states the objection clearly:

That in stinted prayer the spirit is straitened, when a man is tyed to a forme, then hee shall have his spirit, as it were, bounded, and limited, that hee cannot go beyond that which is prescribed; and therefore, say they, it is reason a man should be left in more libertie, (as hee is in conceived prayers,) and not tyed to a strict forme. (Preston: 1630, 80–81.)

His answers to this are three-fold: (a) when one hears another pray it is a set form and constraining for his emotions; (b) one may pray freely at other times; (c) it is not a constraint because though it may be a constraint in words, but there is no restriction on one's affections. As to the question whether it is sufficient, Preston's

---

12 EEBO – TCP version of the 1607 Bodleian Library copy. No page numbers.
13 "The term 'Arminianism' in Protestant theology refers to Jacobus Arminius, a Dutch theologian, and his Remonstrant followers, and covers his proposed revisions to Reformed theology (known as Calvinism). 'Arminianism' in the English sense, however, had a broader application: to questions of church hierarchy, discipline and uniformity; to details of liturgy and ritual; and in the hands of the Puritan opponents of Laudianism, to a wider range of perceived or actual ecclesiastical policies, especially those implying any extension of central government powers over clerics. While the term 'Arminian' was widely used in debates of that time, and was subsequently co-opted as convenient to match later High Church views of Anglicanism, scholarly debate has not settled the exact content or historical role of English Arminianism." https://en.wikipedia.org/wiki/Arminianism_in_the_Church_of_England (Last accessed 19.08.20.)

answer is an unambiguous no. One may frequently attend public prayers but there one cannot unburden one's soul. Public prayers are only help or props for practising prayer as a child needs a prop to go. But Preston says that we cannot always behave like children. Preston's attitude to the question appears to be pragmatic. Public prayers had always been there and there is no point denying it. However, one cannot depend solely on such prayers. On the one hand he dilutes the idea that stinted prayers are constraining, on the other hand he admits that they are not sufficient.

Civil War and the BCP

In the intervening period between the texts of Preston and Downame, i.e. 1630–1656, a steady opposition to the Prayer Book was growing in the shadow of the Civil War. Isaac Stephens argues that:

Outcries against the Prayer Book only intensified as the Civil War drew near. In 1641, a publication appeared in which Richard Bernard urged Parliament to abolish the book: "wee againe and againe entreat you to pluck up that plant of the service-booke, which God neuer set." Based on such sources, it is easy to argue for a continuous strain of Puritan opposition to the Book of Common Prayer that stretched from the 1560s to the 1640s. Indeed, with Parliament's adoption of the *Directory of Public Worship*, we could conclude that this opposition reached a crescendo in 1645. (Stephens: 2011, 25.)

George Downham or Downame (d.1634), a Fellow of Christ's College, Cambridge was more well-known as a consummate teacher of logic. However, as the Bishop of Derry, he was involved in religious controversies of the day. He had written against Arminianism, early in his career and was well-known as a Calvinist preacher. His pursuit of Ramist [14] logic makes his treatise on prayer well-organised structuring his discussion into uses, reasons, objections and answers, a practice that will be found among many later Protestant and Calvinist/Ramist preachers. Such organisation made Downame's treatise very lucid and easy to follow despite his scholarly use of Greek, Latin and Hebrew words and phrases quite frequently. His *A Godly and Learned Treatise of Prayer,* posthumously edited by his brother John Downame, was not much different in subject matter from Brinsley but in the method of exposition it was much better laid out.

---

14 The French Huguenot philosopher Petrus Ramus or Peter Ramus, martyred in the Saint Bartholomew's Day Massacre was very influential in Protestant Calvinist circles in Europe and England, particularly in the matter of rhetorical and methodical organisation of writing. See Ong: 1958.

'Stinted Prayer': | 327

Downame's text also has a literary flavour as he begins by quoting Chrysostome that teaching prayer is the most excellent knowledge for a Christian man and then proceeds to define prayer logically, speaking of its general and special natures. "Invocation or prayer is a religious speech of the faithfull, directed unto God in the name of Christ, framed according to the will of God by the help of the Holy Ghost concerning good things apparteining to his glory and our good." (Downame: 1656, 2). He defines invocation as calling upon the name of God – this whole process of naming, lifting up one's heart to God and praising has been synecdochically replaced in English by the word 'prayer'. Further, lifting up of the hands, or eyes, or the heart, Downame says, is done by a metonymy of the sign. Rhetorical discussion is followed by logical description of general and proper; the general description of prayer is that it is religious speech. It is of two types: man unto man in the name of God – that is preaching; man unto God in the name of Christ that is praying. Both kinds of religious speeches have been called in the Scriptures prophesying. Downame's discussion thus avoids a mechanical partition of the topic but brings us to the same knowledge through rhetorical, logical and in other words, literary treatment of it. (Downame: 1656, 2–3). However, Downame does not neglect any resource as he next proceeds to give us a scholastic treatment of the topic. He says that six substantial topics or six scholastic questions give us a complete idea of the topic of prayer. These are *Quis, Quem, Cujus nomine, Quomodo, Cujus ope, De quibus*; that is 'Who must pray, Whom we must pray unto, In whose name, In what manner, By whose help and For what.' (Downame: 1656, 4–5). From Chapter II the discussion proceeds through the reason, use, objection and answer structure. The reasons of prayer are four-fold: (a) natural law; (b) worship of God is the end of man's creation and redemption; (c) prayer is enjoined by moral law in both the first two commandments; and (d) God's commandment to call him and his promise to hear us makes it obligatory upon us to call him or invoke and pray (Downame: 1656, 8–10). After a detailed discussion of the efficaciousness of prayer, and refutation of the Papist notion of prayer being satisfactory and meritorious when looked upon as penance and ensuring eternal life, Downame comes to speak of the two-fold righteousness echoing but without mentioning Luther; legal righteousness is that by which man can be righteous only by following what the Mosaic law prescribes. Evangelical righteousness is that which is ensured by the revelation of the Gospel and by this believing sinners and penitent sinners are accepted by God as righteous. (Downame: 1656, 34–37). While speaking on the knowledge required in prayer, like Brinsley, Downame also condemns those who pray in an unknown tongue, arguing that the practice of praying in Latin in the Roman church is tantamount to private prayer of the priest because the people cannot follow him. Downame even quotes Ovid to prove his point showing his literary taste: "So Ovid in banishment, *Barbarus hic ego sum quia non intelligorulli*, I am barbarous here because I am not understood by any." (Downame: 1656, 91–96).

Stinted and Unstinted Prayers (*statae & vagae orationes*)

On the question whether set forms of prayer may be used Downame takes a flexible approach: he suggests that a set form is better than an *extempore* prayer. Besides, he adds that stinted prayers may be read at set times and unstinted prayers on occasions.

Now if I be asked the question, Whether is better, a set form of prayer or a prayer conceived; I answer by distinction: For if they speak of such a prayer as is conceived *ex tempore* without former study and meditation, by such an one as expecteth extraordinary inspiration, meaning to pray as the spirit shall move him; I answer that set form is to be preferred before such an extemporall prayer. (Downame: 1656, 138–139.)

Downame's reasons for distrust of *extempore* prayer are that such sudden prayers are of the mind than of the heart and may not be dignified enough for the Lord; besides, it also carries with it the danger of encouraging the enthusiasts, Quakers and radicals who believe in direct communication with the Spirit but most Protestants consider it a heresy. This follows a discussion of public and private prayers and their circumstances. The flexible approach to prayer comes out clearly in this conclusion on praying:

Not that we are always to use the voice and gesture of the body; for sometimes it is sufficient to lift up the soul unto the Lord: Which kind of short prayers among the ancient Fathers were called *ejaculations*. And thus if we shall use *statae & vagae orationes*, stinted and unstinted prayers, omitting no just occasions, we shall perform the commandment 1 Thess.5.17. but otherwise we shall break the same, and in so doing we shall incurre the wrath of God. (Downame: 1656, 161.)

After this general doctrine, Downame begins in Chapter 29 the discussion of the special doctrine, distinguishing between prayer and thanksgiving. In the discussion of things required in prayer he provides particular place to faith as a requirement. To strengthen faith that our prayer will be granted we need meditation which must proceed in a structured manner by answering the scholastic questions regarding God's will:

Though our prayer must be fervent and confident, yet with submission to the will of God; *Quid, Quale, Quantum, Quomodo, Quando, Vbi*, what, of what kind, how much, after what manner, when and where is he pleased to give, knowing that he is able ὑπερεκπερισσοῦ [uperekperissou], exceeding abundantly. We are not to limit God or to circumscribe him by circumstances. (Downame: 1656, 176.)

'Stinted Prayer': | 329

With the same volume another work is bound: *A Godly and Fruitful Exposition of the Lord's Prayer (1640);*[15] that this book is in the commentary tradition and follows oratorical rhetoric is made clear at the outset in the Preface;

> In expounding the Lord's Prayer we will observe this order: First, we will expound the words, and shew the true meaning of them, & then we will inferre the uses of Doctrine, Confutation, Instruction in the duties of prayer and of our lives; and lastly, of Reproof, whereby shall be detected the hypocrisie of worldly men, who using these words do not pray in truth. [...]
> The preface conteineth a description of God to whom we pray taken 1. from his relation to us, that he is *Our Father;* 2. from the place wherein his majesty doth especially appear, that he *is in heaven:* the former signifying especially his love; the other, his power. Of which two if in our preparation we do duly meditate, our desire will be kindled and our faith confirmed, considering that he to whom we pray is both able and willing to grant our requests. (Downame: 1640, 230–231.)

The six petitions in the Lord's Prayer are expounded one after another, first literally, then with respect to their uses in prayer and in our lives. There is a brief section on the temptations of evil: temptations accrue mainly from three sources – the Devil, the world and the flesh. Thus Downame's treatise on prayer and its two parts on doctrine and practice or expounding of the Lord's Prayer comprehensively and elaborately deal with the subject. Whereas its anti-Arminian, anti-Papal orientation is obvious, it does not, however, enter into the controversy about the Eucharist.

It is clear that Downame falls within the tradition of what Judith Maltby calls "Prayerbook Protestantism." Even though my argument that the godly Puritans grew more and more intolerant of the Prayer Book holds true, yet it is also true that Protestants particularly in England felt an urge to strike a compromise as the Prayer Book was deeply ensconced in the daily lives of the laity setting forth rituals regarding birth, death, marriage and the sacraments. As Isaac Stephens claims:

> After all, there were many aspects of the *Book of Common Prayer* that were clear breaks with the Catholic past, particularly a liturgy in English that repudiated the mass, the cult of the saints, and any notion of a sacerdotal priesthood. Judith Maltby has also emphasized the extent to which the Prayer Book was a decidedly Protestant document, arguing that it was perhaps the most pervasive agent of change in the period after 1559. Backed by Parliamentary law and the protection of Elizabeth I's long reign, the Prayer Book fundamentally shaped the religious sensibilities of the English laity. [...]

---

15 Downame, *A Godly and Fruitful Exposition of the LORD'S PRAYER; Shewing the meaning of the words, and the duties required in severall Petitions, both in respect of prayer it self, and also in respect of our lives. Printed by Roger Daniel, Printer to the University of Cambridge,* Cambridge, 1640. Though it is included in the 1656 volume I am indicating it separately in the Bibliography and citing in the body of the text as "Downame: 1640" to avoid confusion.

330 | Niranjan Goswami

On the basis of such evidence, Maltby has argued for the existence of a coherent religious identity that spanned the period from the Elizabethan settlement to the Civil War, an identity for which she has coined the term, "Prayer Book Protestantism". (Stephens: 2011, 26. See also Maltby: 1998.)

Congregationalism and Prayer: Shepard's Reply to John Ball

Thomas Shepard (1605–1649), one of the most influential puritan ministers was the spiritual heir to John Cotton as he was led to the Congregational church by hearing one of John Preston's sermons, who was similarly converted earlier by Cotton. In his autobiography Shepard writes that he was leading a dissolute life:

The Lord therefore sent Doctor Preston to be master of the Colledge; & mr Ston & others commending his preaching to be most spirituall & excellent, I began to listen vnto what he sayd, & the first sermon he preached was Rom: 12: be renewed in the spirit of your mind; in opening which point viz: the change of hart in a Christian, the Lord so bored my eares as that I vnderstood what he spake & the secrets of my soule were Iayd vpon before me the hypocrisy of all my good things I thought I had in me; as if on had told him of all that euer I did of all the turnings & deceeipts of my hart insomuch as that I thought he was the most searching preacher in the woorld. & I began to loue him much, & to blesse god I did see my frame & my hypocrisy & selfe & secret sins; although I found a hard hart & could not be affected with them. (Shepard: 1927–1930, 362.)

This change of heart was considered by the Puritans as a mark of sanctification. Besides, the "boring of the ear" alludes to the Puritan belief of God entering the heart of a Christian through hearing of sermons. Thus transformed, Shepard took a leading part in New England and converted many Indians. Shepard's *A Treatise of Liturgies, Power of the Keys, and of Matter of the Visible Church. In Answer to the Reverend Servant of Christ, Mr. John Ball* (1652/3) was, as is apparent, part of a discussion with other Puritans regarding the nature of the Congregational Church of Massachusetts. Shepard is considered one of the founders of the First Church in Cambridge and he was also instrumental in founding Harvard College in Cambridge or then New Town.

Shepard, in collaboration with John Allin[16] in the Preface answers to the objection that New England churches only receive visible saints as members by saying that "haters of all godliness and reformation" and visible saints cannot stay together as Christ and Belial cannot stay together (Shepard: 1652/3, 10). Next, to the

---

16 Mather mentions the collaborator to be John Allin in his *Brief Discourse* to be discussed below, whereas the name is printed as Thomas Allin in this 1652–1653 volume. Either Mather made a mistake or the printer is wrong.

'Stinted Prayer': | **331**

objection to the church government of New England churches where each congregation is independent and other churches can give only brotherly counsel, Shepard says that it is difficult to see why such church government be a general hindrance to Reformation (Shepard: 1652/3, 11). Answering Ball's apprehension about the separatist tendency of New England churches like Robinson, Shepard denies such a possibility (Shepard: 1652/3, 12). He also dismisses the notion that a congregational church rejects a Pastor for no fault (Shepard: 1652/3, 13). In narrating the state of the great number of ungodly people in England Shepard approvingly quotes from Brinsley's *True Watch Part 3*. In the "Advertisement to the Reader" Shepard names Melanchthon, suggesting that his use of discretion in not naming many members of his opposition was as pragmatic as that of the German reformer. At the outset Shepard gives the context of the present work. John Ball's treatise on the *Nine Questions* (1636) written a little before his death was answered by Shepard in 1638 and 1639 after which the Reply came to his hand through common friends in 1644. This controversy against Ball was mainly on the issue of English liturgy as stinted or imposed and corruptions in the *Common Prayer Book*.

Shepard's work straightaway enters the issue of John Ball's defence of set forms of prayer which he opposes by saying no Reformed church excepting the English Church uses set liturgy. To the objection that people separate from the English liturgy because it is stinted and not because it is the practice of the English Church, Shepard replies that it is the English Church, which only insists on such prayer. To the objection that the church uses set catechism, confession and profession of faith Shepard replies that the doctrine or faith of the church does not change daily but the affections change daily requiring unconstrained forms of prayer. To the objection that the *Common Prayer Book* has some corruption but also good things in it Shepard's reply is:

> Heare what the Authors of the second admonition to the Parliament say, in Queen Elizabeths days, the Booke of Common Prayer, which of all others must not bee touched, because they have gotten the State to beare it out, yet hee hath but a bad conscience, that in this time will hold his peace, and not speake it for fear of trouble. (Shepard: 1652/3, 38.)

In reply to the second position where stinted prayer is used, not joining in prayer or sacraments is tantamount to moderate separation, Shepard replies that it is the corruption of the stinted prayer that both sides need to abolish rather than fear of moderate separation. Ball's fear that such moderate separation may lead to rigid separation is answered thus:

> [B]ut as it is truly observed in England, it was the justification and pressing of ceremonies and other corruptions that drave so many to separation, not the endeavour of further Reformation; so you may fear too much conformity of Ministers to humane impositions, and justification of the Liturgie, &c. have and will more dangerously alienate godly minds from your Churches and Ministery, and so drive to separation. (Shepard: 1652/3, 41.)

The origin of Shepard's objection to the *Book of Common Prayers* lies in Cartwright's answer to Whitgift on the unlawfulness of set liturgy where he argued that these are taken out of Popish Mass Book and one might rather follow the Turks' ritual of worship than such prayers. Cartwright also objected to the absurd manner of chopping and interrupting the prayers. (Shepard: 1652/3, 45–46). Thus, Shepard expresses wonder:

How any man can joyne with this whole Liturgie according to Christ's command, who in the second commandement forbids all humane devices in his worship, whereof this Liturgie is so full; it is hard for us to conceive, and strange to see it affirmed: and that libertie from Christ to bee absent cannot be shewed. (Shepard: 1652/3, 58.)

Shepard gradually comes to oppose the objection that some parts of the Common Prayer were good and parts of the Church's legacy and asserts:

First, wee judge the whole booke an Idolothyte, and whence you gather, that wee confesse the contrary of any part of it, as it stands apart in relation to that whole, wee know not .... when we say it was taken out of the Masse-booke, in a large sense, (as it is commonly taken) for to speake narrowly it was collected out of three Popish bookes, the first part of publique Prayers, *exbreviario*; the second part, *viz.* the order of administring Sacraments, Matrimony, visiting the sick and burials, *è Rituali*; 3. the order of consecration in the Supper, the Epistles and Gospels, and Collects, *è Missali*, as the forme of consecration of Bishops and Priests was taken *è Pontificali*, as the author of *Altare Damasc.* shews, pag. 612. (Shepard: 1652/3, 63.)

By undertaking a thorough examination of the *Common Prayer Book* Shepard demonstrates how most of the book had a pagan origin:

We finde all the principal parts of the Masse to be borrowed from the Idolatrous Pagans, and to have their originals from *Numa Pompilius* that Conjurer, who lived 700 years before Christ, to adorn and deck (as the Bishops thought) the Religion of Christ Jesus to the which with much ado at last the *Romans* were converted. To which principall parts, *viz.* Vestments, Holy Water, the Confiteor, Organs, Incense, Offertory &c. other deckings were added also, as diverse Letanies and the Kurie Elyson to be sung nine times, invented by *Gregory* a Monk at first, well studied in the laws of *Numa* and *Tullus Hostilius: Damasus* (as *Platina* and *Sabellius* shew) inriched it with *Gloria Patri* &c. i.e. Glory be to the Father, Son, and Holy Ghost. *Sergius*, with an *Agnus Dei*, to be sung three times. *Alexander* and other Bishops added the Canon of the Masse, others, the Epistles and Gospels: the Graduall and Collects were added by *Gelasius*, *anno* 493. The *Gloria in Excelsis* by *Symmachus* 508. At last came the Host in about 1062. (Shepard: 1652/3, 66.)

Thus, Shepard's learned discussion of the sources proves that most of the *Common Prayer Book* was corrupted in the sense that these parts originated from pagan sources. This attitude, which we have seen was initially not there, gradually hardened into an uncompromising Puritanical approach to the prayer book as a

'Stinted Prayer': | **333**

corrupt text; a papal device to be shunned by a true Christian. The rest of Shepard's treatise deals with issues of baptism and other doctrines of Congregational Churches and is not directly relevant for the present purpose.

Increase Mather goes the way of Thomas Cartwright[17]

Increase Mather (1639–1723), the father of influential Cotton Mather, upholder of Puritan orthodoxy in Massachusetts during its decline, President of Harvard College and leader of the Congregational Church took it upon himself in his *A Brief Discourse*[18] to prove the unlawfulness of Common Prayer worship. Increase, even though not much original, was thoroughly versed in the earlier works on the subject. Many of his arguments and examples are taken from Shepard's *A Defence of Nine Positions* with the "Preface" by John Allin and Shepard himself (1645). At the very outset Increase states the reason why the *Book of Common Prayer* is unacceptable:

Its true, that as the Mass Book is taken in a more strict sense, a great part of the English Liturgie is not to be found therein. But as the Missal is put for the whole Roman Liturgie … it cannot be denied but that the Common prayer Book is from thence derived. There are things … in the Roman Liturgie which are not Translated into English, but very little is in the English, which is not to be found in the other. This is particularly cleared up by the Learned Author of the Book called *Altare Damascenium* which goeth under the name of *Didoclavius*, but Mr. David Calderwood was the true Author. Also there are many treatises in English, which may bee consulted concerning this matter; Particularly, a Book called *A Parallel between the Mass Book and the Liturgie*, And the *Anatomy of the Service Book* which goeth under the name of Dwarphinhamis and Mr. John Allin of Dedham in N.E. His *Defence of the Nine Positions* p. 62. 66. And *A Discourse of Liturgies* by H.D. (Mather: 1689, 2–3.)[19]

Not only is Increase familiar with all current literature on the controversy, but he also points out some aberrations of the Prayer Book. He states that in the catechism

---

17 Thomas Cartwright (1535–1603) first gave a call for Presbyterianism and was deprived of his fellowship by John Whitgift (1530–1604), the Master of Trinity for his criticism of the English Church. He also sympathised with John Field and Thomas Wilcox, notorious authors of *An Admonition to the Parliament* (1572).

18 The EEBO – TCP version I use is made from a Bodleian Library copy and it does not have the name of the author, place and date of publication. The Title page simply states 'By a Reverend and Learned Divine.' The ascription to Mather in the opposite page is probably by a librarian.

19 The Preface jointly written by John Allin and Thomas Shepard to this work has been erroneously ascribed to Thomas Allin and Thomas Shepard in this 1652/3 edition that I have seen on EEBO – TCP. Apparently, the Preface is a reprint from Defence of the answer made unto the Nine Questions (1645) [1648]. I have not seen the 1645 treatise.

334 | Niranjan Goswami

the words in the Fourth Commandment were changed from "the Lord blessed the Sabbath Day" into "the Lord blessed the Seventh Day" – and he finds this a gross violation. He goes on to point out many of the practices prescribed by the Prayer Book during marriage, burial, wearing the surplice, etc. as superstitious and Jewish rather than Christian (Mather: 1689, 17–18.):

> For men to appoint a Religious Ceremony, is a direct violation of the Second Commandment, which forbids all humane Inventions in Divine worship, as any part thereof. And the Arguments which are brought against the use of Oyle, Cream, Salt, Spittle in Baptism (practised by the Papists) hold as well against the Cross. (Mather: 1689, 20.)

Increase mentions one "supreme superstition" i.e. the practice of kneeling at the sacrament. Men pretend that they kneel out of reverence to Christ, but Christ himself was Personally present, when his Disciples did partake of the Lords Supper, yet they did not kneel, but used the Table gesture then customary amongst the Jews.' Increase refers to the testimony of John Cotton:

> Mr. Cotton in his Book against sett forms of Prayer, does truly and Judiciously observe, that Paul in practising a few Ceremonies out of the Book of the Law, did thereby declare his Subjection to the whole order of worship prescribed by the Authority of that Law. Acts 21.24.6. in doing of which undoubtedly hee had sinned, if God had not warranted the continuance of that worship for a Season. (Mather: 1689, 27.)

After giving a long list of Puritan priests who suffered because they would not commit sin by complying with the Liturgy, Increase mentions some of them who refusing to abide by the *Common Prayer Book* were forced to exile themselves to America:

> *The 9 Positions* (though written by *Mr. Davenport*) had the Approbation of the rest of the *Elders* in *New England*, and therein Reasons are given why it is unlawfull to be present at the Common Prayer worship or any part thereof.
> Mr. *John Cotton of Boston* (a man deservedly Famous in both Englands) has done the like. And Mr. *John Allin of Dedham in New England* (Mr. *Shepard of Cambridge* Joyning with Him) in his *defence of the 9 Positions* has Expressly declared the unlawfulnes of being present at the Common prayer Worship. (Mather: 1689, 31.)

Having established the tradition of Puritan opposition to Common Prayer worship Increase Mather comes to assert the opposition to stinted prayer:

> I might here also have added, that *a stinted Liturgy is Opposite to the Spirit of Prayer*. The Scripture teacheth that Christians should pray with all Prayer and Supplication in the Spirit. Ephes. 6.18. which they cannot do if they tye themselves up to a set Form never to bee varied from. I let pass that Argument, *from the Mischief of a Prescript Liturgy*; It is the Instrument of a foolish Shepherd. An Idol and a Dumb Ministry is thereby continued in the Church. (Mather: 1689, 33.)

'Stinted Prayer': | **335**

We see that from John Brinsley to Increase Mather the attitude to set prayers has undergone a shift by degrees towards intolerance. Whereas for Brinsley and Downame it was an academic question rather than an abomination, for Preston, the issue was still open. With Shepard one finds a full reversal to the position of Cartwright and Increase sounds the dead-serious Puritan who abhors any form of idolatry. By referring to older theologians, Shepard and Increase keep harping on the pagan sources of the rituals and prayers of the English Church. Cartwright, himself was a Presbyterian[20] and did not approve of the Independents and Congregationalists; but it is these latter groups who mostly made use of his theological radicalism to set themselves apart from the English Church.

In spite of Increase Mather's extreme reaction to set prayers, we should not end with the impression that this was the universal position in the seventeenth century. In reality the situation was more nuanced and flexible, particularly, in England. Cynthia Garrett pointed out that the Calvinistic belief in the unchangeability of God made human emotions and communication with God problematic and almost redundant. Calvin suggested that the Christian's emotions would alter from distress to relief and again to distress. Because of such radical uncertainty in the theological matrix of emotions no single form of prayer could be sufficient. The duality of soteriological understanding of emotions compelled the Calvinistic Protestant to retain both forms of prayer. As Cynthia Garrett writes:

Despite their valorization of interior prayer and their suspicion of outward show, the English prayer guides are reluctant to resign the use of set prayers from Scripture or popular contemporary collections and the careful composition of one's own devotions in favor of a strictly spontaneous, internal invocation to God. While they unequivocally state that prayer is not outward form alone and often insist that it can exist without form, they do not reject the use of language and gesture in prayer and indeed offer advice for the most appropriate kinds to use. Puritan and Anglican may disagree on the use of liturgical prayer in public worship, but both generally accept the view that private prayer can be either extempore or premeditated, conceived or set (in the terms they often use) and that these very different kinds of prayer are valuable and even necessary. (Garrett: 1993, 349.)

Balancing both sides of the argument, Maltby also agreed with most historians like Haigh (Haigh: 1975, 1993) that the godly found no merits in the Book of Common

---

20 "Presbyterianism is a part of the Reformed tradition within Protestantism, which traces its origins to Great Britain, particularly Scotland. Presbyterian churches derive their name from the Presbyterian form of church government, which is governed by representative assemblies of elders. A great number of Reformed churches are organized this way, but the word *Presbyterian*, when capitalized, is often applied uniquely to churches that trace their roots to the Church of Scotland, as well as several English dissenter groups that formed during the English Civil War. Presbyterian theology typically emphasizes the sovereignty of God, the authority of the Scriptures, and the necessity of grace through faith in Christ." https://en.wikipedia.org/wiki/Presbyterianism (Last accessed 19.08.20.)

336 | Niranjan Goswami

Prayer. Both scholars have effectively accepted that the views of men like Field, Wilcox, and Bernard on the Prayer Book typified all Puritans. (Stephens: 2011, 27.)

Whereas Stephens begins and ends with such English Puritans as Richard Baxter,[21] John Field and Thomas Wilcox, I choose to end with New England Puritans like Thomas Shepard and Increase Mather. The result is not much different as in both countries in the seventeenth century an extreme Protestantism with its aversion to the Prayer Book existed side by side with an aptitude among Protestants for moderately using the Prayer Book.

Bibliography

BRINSLEY, JOHN (1607), Second Part of the True Watch containing the perfect rule and summe of Prayer (1607), Brinsley_John-The_second_part_of_the_true_watch-STC-3776-1196_07-p1to74.pdf] (EEBO – TCP). (Last accessed 09.01.11.)

COLLINSON, PATRICK (1967), The Elizabethan Puritan Movement, London: Jonathan Cape.

DOWNAME, GEORGE (1640), A Godly and Learned Treatise of Prayer, which both containeth in it the Doctrine of Prayer, and also sheweth the Practice of it in the exposition of the Lord's Prayer, London. Downame_George-A_godly_and_learned_treatise_of-STC-7117-1304_17-p1to224.pdf (EEBO – TCP). (Last accessed 28.01.11.)

DOWNAME, GEORGE (1656), The Doctrine of Practical Praying: together with a learned exposition on the LORD'S PRAYER by the Right Reverend Father in God, George Downam, Late Lord Bishop in Derry in Ireland. Printed by W.H. for Nicholas Bourne at the South entrance of the Royal Exchange Downame_George-A_godly_and_learned_treatise_of-STC-7117-1304_17-p1to224.pdf, (EEBO – TCP). (Last accessed 28.01.11.)

DOWNAME, GEORGE (1640), A Godly and Fruitful Exposition of the Lord's Prayer; Shewing the meaning of the words, and the duties required in several Petitions, both in respect of prayer itself, and also in respect of our lives. Printed by Roger Daniel, Printer to the University of Cambridge. This is reprinted as the second part of the above 1656 volume.

GARRETT, CYNTHIA (1993), The Rhetoric of Supplication: Prayer Theory in Seventeenth-Century England, Renaissance Quarterly, 46 (2), 328–357.

HAIGH, CHRISTOPHER (1975), Reformation and Resistance in Tudor Lancashire, New York: Cambridge University Press.

HAIGH, CHRISTOPHER (1993), English Reformations: Religion, Politics, and Society under the Tudors, Oxford: Clarendon Press.

KETLEY, REV. JOSEPH (1844), The Two Liturgies A.D. 1549 and A.D. 1552 with Other Documents Set Forth by Authority in the Reign of King Edward VI viz. The Order

---

21 Baxter is the author of *The Saints Everlasting Rest: Or a Treatise of the Blessed State of the Saints in Their Enjoyment of God in Glory* (1650).

of Communion, 1548, the Primer, 1553, The Catechism and Articles, 1553, Catechismus Brevis, 1553, Cambridge: The University Press. – https://archive.org/details/twoliturgiesad1500chur/page/n7/mode/2up (Last accessed 19.08.20.)

Macculloch, Diarmaid (2003), Reformation: Europe's House Divided 1490–1700, London: Allen Lane, Penguin Books.

Maltby, Judith (1998), Prayer Book and People in Elizabethan and Early Stuart England, Cambridge: Cambridge University Press.

Mather, Increase (1689), A Brief Discourse concerning the Unlawfulness of Common Prayer Worship and of Laying the Hand on, and Kissing the Booke in Swearing, [London] – https://quod.lib.umich.edu/e/eebo2/A50188.0001.001/1:1?rgn=div1;view=fulltext.

Miller, Perry (1939, 1954), The New England Mind: The Seventeenth Century, New York: Macmillan.

Miller, Perry (1953), The New England Mind: From Colony to Province, Cambridge, Mass.: Harvard University Press.

Ong, Walter J. S. J. (1958), Ramus, Method and the Decay of Dialogue, Cambridge, Mass.: Harvard University Press.

Perkins, William (1607), The Arte of Prophesying or A Treatise Concerning the Sacred and Onely True Manner and Method of Preaching, London. Perkins_William-The_arte_of_prophecying_or_A_treatise-STC-197354-1823_09-p1to83.pdf, (EEBO – TCP). (Last accessed 01.12.10.)

Preston, John (1630), The Saints Daily Exercise A Treatise Unfolding the whole duty of Prayer Delivered in Five Sermons upon 1 Thess.5.17. The fourth edition corrected, Preston_John-The_saints_daily_exercise-STC-20254-1330_10-p1to82.pdf, (EEBO – TCP). (Last accessed 09.01.11.)

Shepard, Thomas (1927–1930), Autobiography printed in Colonial Society of Massachusetts, Vol. 27, Transactions, The Autobiography of Thomas Shepard, https://www.colonialsociety.org/node/460. (Last accessed 04.07.18.)

Shepard, Thomas (1652–1653), A Treatise of Liturgies, Power of the Keys, and of Matter of the Visible Church. In Answer to the Reverend Servant of Christ, Mr. John Ball (London: Printed 1653 but cancelled by a line and written over it in a seventeenth-century hand, November, 1652').

Stephens, Isaac (2011), Confessional Identity in Early Stuart England: The "Prayer Book Puritanism" of Elizabeth Isham, Journal of British Studies, 50 (1), 24–47.

Kathrin Chlench-Priber
Institut für Germanistik, Universität Bern

Gebetsliteratur im Spätmittelalter:
Ein Resümee aus literaturwissenschaftlicher Sicht

Anlass für die internationale Konferenz „Gebetsliteratur im Spätmittelalter" war die Handschrift Klausenburg (Cluj-Napoca, Kolozsvár) Universitätsbibliothek, Ms. 683, ein bebildertes deutschsprachiges Gebetbuch vom Ende des 15. und beginnenden 16. Jahrhundert. Es bildete den Ausgangspunkt, um über die Geschichte der Gebetskultur im siebenbürgischen und ostungarischen Raum des ausgehenden Spätmittelalters und der nachreformatorischen Zeit nachzudenken. Die im Tagungsband dargebotenen Beiträge bieten vielfältige Einzelstudien, die sich nicht nur auf dieses spezielle Gebetbuch oder Gebetsliteratur in einem engeren Sinne beziehen, sondern Frömmigkeitsmedien und Praxen des Betens in den Blick nehmen. Aus ihnen lässt sich ein regelrechtes Gepräge der spezifischen vor- und nachreformatorischen Gebetskultur dieses Raumes in seinen kulturellen Verflechtungen mit dem weiteren europäischen Kontext erschließen. In der Rückschau der Einzelbeiträge lassen sich ausgehend von der deutschsprachigen Gebetbuchhandschrift Ms. 683 einige Überlegungen festhalten, die charakteristische Verflechtungen hinsichtlich der Gebetskultur nochmals verdeutlichen.

Anders als der heutige Aufbewahrungsort vermuten lassen könnte, stammt das Gebetbuch ursprünglich nicht aus Siebenbürgen, sondern aus dem süddeutschen Raum – genauer aus Augsburg –, wie der Beitrag von Regina Cermann zeigen konnte. Erst im 19. Jahrhundert, nach 1841, gelangte es mutmaßlich durch den Antiquar Sámuel Literáti Nemes über Wien und Pest nach Siebenbürgen (vgl. den Beitrag von Katalin Luffy). Dieser Befund ist insofern paradigmatisch (vgl. die Beiträge von Adrian Papahagi und Constantin Ittu), als sich in Siebenbürgen nahezu keine und im Gebiet Ungarns im Spätmittelalter nur sehr wenige lateinische oder volkssprachige Gebetbücher nachweisen lassen. Zudem unterscheiden sich auch die in jener Zeit gelebten Konzepte von Gebetsfrömmigkeit samt ihrer Medien grundlegend von der Form, die in dem Gebetbuchexemplar des süddeutschen Raumes repräsentiert ist (vgl. die Beiträge von Adinel Dincă, Paula Cotoi und Maria Crăciun). In Siebenbürgen und auch Ungarn wurde Religion – und damit auch das Gebet – in weiten Teilen der Bevölkerung überwiegend öffentlich, d. h., in einem durch Kleriker kontrollierten und begleiteten Rahmen des Gottesdienstes praktiziert. Schriftlich überlieferte Predigttexte der ungarischen Franziskanerbrüder Pelbart von Temeswar und Oswald von Laska thematisieren namentlich das Beten der „sogenannten Standardgebete" *Pater noster*, *Credo* und *Ave-Maria*, die als Reihen-, Zähl- und Wiederholungsgebete etwa beim Rosenkranz persolviert werden konnten, sowie die Andacht vor Gegenständen und Bildern (vgl. die Beiträge von Carmen Florea und Paula Cotoi). Diese Gebetspraktiken, die mit Gebärden oder meditativen Techniken kombiniert werden konnten und durchaus auch im süddeutschen Raum verbreitet sind,[1] erfordern nur ein Minimum an Textkenntnis und sind nicht an die Fähigkeit gebunden, selbst lesen zu können. Auch wenn der Alphabetisierungsgrad der Bevölkerung im 16. Jahrhundert sicherlich höher veranschlagt werden muss als im Spätmittelalter, ist die Frömmigkeit in Siebenbürgen gleichermaßen nach der Reformation nicht durch die persönliche Lektüre der Gläubigen – auch nicht die der Bibel – geprägt. Vielmehr dominieren in der religiösen Praxis weiterhin klerikal begleitete Formen. Bibelwissen wird vornehmlich in Predigtgottesdiensten oder im Rahmen von katechetischen Unterweisungen mündlich vermittelt und – wie Maria Crăciun in ihrem Beitrag plausibel machen konnte – mit visuellen, teils mnemotechnischen Praxen kombiniert, so dass textliche Zugänge zur Religion zwar im Vergleich zur vorreformatorischen Zeit deutlich gestärkt werden, aber visuelle keinesfalls ersetzen und erst recht nicht die private Andacht durch Lektüre in den Mittelpunkt rücken.

Die Situation im süddeutschen Sprachraum, aus dem die Klausenburger Handschrift stammt, gestaltet sich – wie mehrere Hundert überlieferte volkssprachige und daneben auch lateinische Gebetbuchexemplare belegen – im ausgehenden 15. und beginnenden 16. Jahrhundert großenteils anders. Während vor dem 14. Jahrhundert im gesamtdeutschen Sprachraum gar kein Gebetbuch mit überwiegend deutschen Gebetstexten und im 14. Jahrhundert nur eine überschaubare Anzahl von etwa 40 Gebetbüchern überliefert ist, die zumeist aus dem Besitz von adeligen, in Klosterkonventen lebenden oder der städtischen Oberschicht angehörenden Frauen stammen, nimmt die Gebetbuchproduktion im 15. Jahrhundert massiv zu (Chlench-Priber: 2020, 16–26). In ihr dokumentiert sich eine Frömmigkeitspraxis des Gebets, die insofern als privat charakterisiert werden kann, als die Gebete zwar Bezug zur Liturgie nehmen können, aber jenseits ihrer textlichen Gestaltung vollkommen unabhängig von einer klerikalen Regulierung gebetet werden konnten und der persönlichen, vertieften Andacht dienten. Diese Art des persönlichen Betens setzt selbstverständlich die Lesefähigkeit ihrer Benutzerinnen und Benutzer voraus, die im süddeutschen Raum zumindest für die städtische Bevölkerung relativ hoch zu veranschlagen ist. Darüber hinaus zeigt die Wahl der Volkssprache, dass die Gebetstexte auch inhaltlich verstanden werden sollten, um eine vertiefte

---

1 Vgl. Lentes:1996. Insbesondere finden sich weitere mit den Reihengebeten verbundenen Gebetspraktiken wie beispielsweise in der ‚Geistlichen Badestube'; in diesem Text stehen die kanonischen Gebete für Bestandteile einer Badestube, in der der Gläubige sich reinigen kann und seiner Andacht nachgehen kann. Vgl. Schnyder: 1977–2008, Sp. 503f.

Andacht auch außerhalb der öffentlichen Gottesdienste zu fördern. Dieser Aspekt der direkten, persönlichen Auseinandersetzung mit Gott bzw. seinem göttlichen Wort wird nicht erst in der Reformation und in postreformatorischen Zeiten ausgiebig debattiert (zur Diskussion in Neuengland vgl. den Beitrag von Nirajan Goswami; zur Situation im postreformatorischen Siebenbürgen vgl. den Beitrag von Maria Crăciun), sondern im Prager Raum bereits unter Kaiser Karl IV. (1316–1378) ausdrücklich gefördert. Er selbst beauftragt Übersetzungen lateinischer und religiöser Texte ins Deutsche und Tschechische. Sein Hofkanzler Johannes von Neumarkt (um 1310–1380), der auch eines der in Ms. 683 überlieferten Gebete verfasste, aber auch weitere seiner hochrangigen Kanzleischreiber, wie Johann Militsch von Kremsier (um 1320–1374), schaffen volkssprachige Gebete, die Eingang in eine sich rasch entwickelnde Gebetbuchkultur im Prager – und später auch gesamten süddeutschen – Raum finden und dem weiteren Kontext der charismatischen Spiritualität in Böhmen der vorreformatorischen Zeit zuzurechnen sind (vgl. Nechutová: 1997). Dieser Raum darf vor, in und nach der Reformation insbesondere für die Textproduktion von volkssprachigen geistlichen Gemeindeliedern als bedeutsam gelten (vgl. den Beitrag von Ulrich A. Wien). Aus ihm wurden aus dem Umfeld der böhmisch-mährischen Brüder-Unität und dem Täufermilieu stammende Lieder für das 1543 in Kronstadt gedruckte Achtlieder-Gesangbuch Andreas Moldners entlehnt. Anhand dieses ersten und frühesten Kronstädter Gesangbuchs lässt sich sehr gut nachvollziehen, wie reflektiert Quellen selektiv ausgewählt und in die Reformationsbewegung lokal integriert wurden. Denn die Inhalte der volkssprachigen Lieder lassen deutliche Rückschlüsse auf eine Positionierung in reformatorischen Glaubensfragen zu, die durch das Medium Lied Gemeindemitgliedern vermittelt wurden.

Volkssprachige Gebetexte jenseits von *Paternoster*, *Credo* und *Ave Maria* verfügen zwar inhaltlich ebenfalls über eine größere thematische Breite, jedoch steht die Vermittlung von Inhalten zumeist nicht in deren Zentrum. Vielmehr können sie als sprachlich vorgeformte Hilfsmedien für unterschiedliche Gebetanlässe gelten, durch die sich ein Betender artikulieren und in eine persönliche vertiefte Andacht eintreten kann und soll (vgl. den Beitrag von Volker Leppin zum *Hortulus animae*). Eine innerlich vollzogene andächtige Haltung wird in Gebetsbeischriften immer wieder als notwendige Voraussetzung für angemessenes, aufrichtiges Beten eingefordert. Dabei kommt auch der textlich-stilistischen Gestaltung bzw. Literarizität der Gebete eine bedeutsame Rolle zu, da sie den Grad der Affektivität der Betenden vorprägt. Wie auch andere zeitgenössische Texte unterliegen Gebete und ihre Überlieferung den Regeln des Literaturbetriebes. Sie werden nicht etwa „spontan" gebetet und dann aufgeschrieben, sondern zeigen in der Regel eine Abhängigkeit von schriftlichen (lateinischen) Quellen und wurden für eine schriftliche Weitergabe konzipiert. Konnte ein Gebet mit einem namhaften Autor verbunden werden, beispielsweise einem Kirchenvater, Papst oder Bischof, so wurde dies oftmals in einer dem Gebetstext vor- oder nachgestellten Beischrift vermerkt. Damit wurde nicht nur der Text selbst weitergegeben, sondern gewissermaßen auch seine Legitimation verbürgt. Dasselbe gilt für Ablassversprechen, die mit bestimmten Gebeten verbunden und deren Wirksamkeit in Beischriften durch Autoritäten verbürgt wurden. Ferner gehören Anweisungen, wie, wann und wo ein Gebet zu sprechen sei, auch in diesen Rahmen, der einen adäquaten Gebrauch – d. h. einen andächtigen Vollzug – sicherstellen sollte. Insofern wird der persönlichen, inneren Haltung beim Beten die höchste Bedeutung beigemessen und dem bloßen äußerlichen Beten als Form einer veräußerlichten Frömmigkeit eine klare Absage erteilt. In dieser Hinsicht wären die volkssprachigen Gebete durchaus an Konzepte der von Luther betonten Innerlichkeit anschlussfähig, auch wenn dieser sich selbst gegen zeitgenössische Gebetbücher wandte (vgl. den Beitrag von Volker Leppin).

Blickt man auf die Zusammenstellung bzw. Überlieferungsgemeinschaft der Gebete, dann darf das aus Augsburg stammende Gebetbuch Ms. 683 – wie auch der *Hortulus animae* oder seine deutschsprachige Übersetzung, das *Seelenwürzgärtlein* – durchaus als ein typisches handschriftliches Gebetbuch des süddeutschen Raumes gelten. Wie Regina Cermann in ihrer detaillierten Untersuchung herausgearbeitet hat, sind die unterschiedlichen Gebetstexte nicht etwa unikal in Ms. 683 tradiert, sondern sie weisen eine breite Parallelüberlieferung auf. Mit Gebetstexten von Johann von Indersdorf (1382–1470) und insbesondere Johannes von Neumarkt sind prominente Gebetsautoren vertreten, deren Texte im süddeutschen Sprachraum vielfach – seltener im mitteldeutschen – überliefert sind und über einen hohen Verbreitungsgrad verfügen. Am Beispiel der beiden genannten Gebetsautoren lässt sich das typische Muster der Überlieferung von Gebeten erläutern. Sowohl Johann von Indersdorf als auch Johannes von Neumarkt, beide Vertreter eines hochgradig affektiven Gebetsstils, konzipierten ihre Gebete als Ensemble, das sie nach spezifischen Kriterien, etwa zur Kommunionvorbereitung oder als Sammlung von Marien- oder Seelengebeten, zusammenstellten (Weiske: 1993, 135–143; Haage: 1968, 50–52, 533–534; Chlench-Priber: 2020, 315–320). Sehr schnell wurden einzelne Gebete aus diesen Ensembles herausgelöst und in Gebetbuchhandschriften mit anderen Gebeten neu kombiniert. So darf es geradezu als paradigmatisch gelten, dass sich für das Klausenburger Gebetbuch kein Manuskript mit exakt derselben Textsammlung findet, da Gebetbuchhandschriften insgesamt in der Regel keine unveränderten Abschriften sind, sondern variieren. Vielfach liegen handschriftlichen Gebetbüchern eigene Ordnungskriterien zugrunde, die entweder den Wünschen und Bedürfnissen ihrer Benutzerinnen und Benutzern angepasst oder aber auch Schreibprozessen geschuldet sein können, etwa wenn freie Seiten des Buchs von Schreibern mit kürzeren Gebetstexten aufgefüllt werden oder deren Besitzer selbst Gebetstexte ohne stringentes Konzept sammeln und ein- bzw. nachtragen (Wiederkehr: 2013, 116–120). So können in Gebetbüchern einerseits die Strukturen von Vorlagenhandschriften aufschei-

Gebetsliteratur im Spätmittelalter: | 343

nen, andererseits ist aber immer auch mit einem mehr oder weniger ausgeprägten Grad an Textvarianz zu rechnen. Ms. 683 scheinen unterschiedliche, nicht miteinander harmonisierte Ordnungsprinzipien zugrunde zu liegen. Ein Prinzip ist mutmaßlich die Ordnung nach dem Kirchenjahr, die die Abfolge der Gebete zu Christi Geburt bis zu den Pfingstgebeten zu erklären vermag. Darin eingeschoben finden sich aber Mess-, Kommunion- und Ablassgebete, die diese Ordnung unterbrechen. Auf die Gebete zum Schutzengel, zum Eigenapostel und zu Maria folgen jedoch nicht weitere Fürsprechergebete zu Heiligen, wie es erwartbar wäre, sondern Kommuniongebete; erst danach schließen sich Heiligengebete an. Diese hier nur exemplarisch skizzierten „Ordnungsbrüche" sind wahrscheinlich vorlagenbedingt zu erklären. Demnach scheint für den Gebetbuchproduzenten die stringente Ordnung der Gebete nicht entscheidend gewesen zu sein, sondern eher ein vielfältiges Angebot von inhaltlich unterschiedlichen Texten, die er gemäß eines Vorlagenexemplars übernommen hat. Zwar reicht das Klausenburger Gebetbuch in der Breite und Anzahl der in ihm dargebotenen Stücke keinesfalls an etwa zeitgleich gedruckte volkssprachige Gebetbücher, wie „Das Seelenwürzgärtlein", heran (vgl. nochmals den Beitrag von Volker Leppin), beinhaltet aber ebenfalls ein umfassendes Angebot für alle erdenklichen Gebetszwecke und ließe sich damit quasi als volkssprachliches „Universalgebetbuch" bezeichnen.

Demnach muss die Klausenburger Handschrift trotz ihrer relativ späten Entstehungszeit als typische Vertreterin eines spätmittelalterlichen Gebetbuchs gelten. Obwohl es Ende des 15. und zu Beginn des 16. Jahrhunderts bereits gedruckte deutschsprachige Gebetbücher wie den überaus auflagenstarken *Hortulus animae* gibt, sind volkssprachige, handschriftliche Gebetbücher zunächst noch weiter verbreitet als Gebetbuchdrucke und werden stetig bis weit ins 16. Jahrhundert und auch darüber hinaus produziert. Besonders ist Ms. 683 jedoch in der Hinsicht, als sie nicht auf die spezifischen Bedürfnisse eines konkreten Benutzers oder einer Benutzerin zugeschnitten zu sein scheint, sondern mutmaßlich trotz ihrer Ausstattung mit zahlreichen Miniaturen als Standardware für den freien Markt produziert wurde (vgl. den Beitrag Regina Cermanns). Wäre dies noch wenige Jahrzehnte vorher undenkbar gewesen, hat sich das Angebot an volkssprachigen Gebetbuchexemplaren sowohl hinsichtlich ihrer Quantität als auch ihrer Qualität an der Wende vom 15. zum 16. Jahrhundert maßgeblich verändert. Zwar finden sich bereits in einigen der frühesten deutschsprachigen Gebetbücher des 14. Jahrhunderts des süddeutschen Sprachraumes Abbildungen, jedoch steht deren Qualität auch noch im 15. Jahrhundert deutlich hinter der zeitgleicher französischer oder flämischer Gebet- oder Stundenbücher, wie sie Kata Szűcs und Constantin Ittu in ihren Beiträgen besprechen, zurück. Ab den 1470 Jahren des 15. Jahrhunderts lassen sich dann jedoch vereinzelt auch solch qualitativ hochwertig ausgestatteten deutschsprachigen Exemplare im süddeutschen Raum nachweisen. Gefertigt wurden diese Stundenbücher in Paris, speziell für den süddeutschen Markt, da ihre Kalender für

Nürnberg eingerichtet wurden (Cermann: 2010). Insofern repräsentiert das Klausenburger Gebetbuch also keinesfalls den höchsten verfügbaren Ausstattungsgrad eines Gebetbuchs, gleichwohl einen gehobenen, für den es in der prosperierenden Handelsstadt Augsburg auf dem freien Markt durchaus Abnehmer gegeben haben mag.

Wie die Beiträge im vorliegenden Band gezeigt haben, wäre es zu kurz gegriffen, wollte man das Fehlen vergleichbarer Gebetbücher im ostungarischen und siebenürgischen Raum im 16. Jahrhundert allein dadurch erklären, dass sie als Medien der vorreformatorischen Frömmigkeit nach der Reformation keinen Absatz finden. Zu unterschiedlich sind die sozial und historisch gewachsenen Traditionen der lokalen Gebetsfrömmigkeit, die dennoch Schnittstellen aufweisen und die Möglichkeit für Adaptionsprozesse sogar in unvermuteten Bereichen bieten. So haben die Beiträge von András Bándi und Edit Szegedi zur gewandelten Bedeutung des Heiligengedenkens in der nachreformatorischen Liturgie Siebenbürgens die Kompromissfähigkeit zur Integration von religiösen vorreformatorischen Elementen bzw. Elementen der anderen Konfession eindrucksvoll vor Augen geführt.

Als jedoch das ehemals Augsburger Gebetbuch im 19. Jahrhundert nach Siebenbürgen gelangte, dürften Aspekte der Integrierbarkeit in herrschende religiöse Praxen nicht mehr bestimmend gewesen sein. In erster Linie sind es der kunsthistorische Wert der Handschrift, ihre Ausstattung als auch ihre mutmaßlichen Vorbesitzer, die der Käufer der Handschrift, der Buchhändler Sámuel Literáti Nemes, wohl im Umfeld des Königs Ludwig II. von Böhmen und Ungarn vermutete (vgl. den Beitrag von Katalin Luffy). Insofern kommt dem Klausenburger Gebetbuch nicht nur eine Bedeutung als Dingmedium der spätmittelalterlichen Gebetsfrömmigkeit zu, sondern es wurde auch als wertvoller Kodex von musealem Wert rezipiert.

Bibliographie

Cermann, Regina (2010), Über den Export deutschsprachiger Stundenbücher von Paris nach Nürnberg, Codices Manuscripti 75, 9–24.

Chlench-Priber, Kathrin (2020), Die Gebete Johanns von Neumarkt und die deutschsprachige Gebetbuchkultur des Spätmittelalters, (Münchener Texte und Untersuchungen 150), Wiesbaden: Reichert.

Haage, Bernhard (1968), Der Traktat „Von dreierlei Wesen der Menschen". Inauguraldissertation zur Erlangung der Doktorwürde der Philosophischen Fakultät der Ruprecht-Karl-Universität Heidelberg, Heidelberg.

Lentes, Thomas (1996), Gebetbuch und Gebärde. Religiöses Ausdrucksverhalten, in Gebetbüchern aus dem Dominikanerinnen-Kloster St. Nikolaus in undis zu Straßburg (1350–1550). Inaugural-Dissertation zur Erlangung der theologischen Doktorwürde der Katholisch-Theologischen Fakultät der Westfälischen Wilhelms-Universität, Münster in Westfalen.

NECHUTOVÁ, JANA (1997), Die charismatische Spiritualität in Böhmen in der vorreformatorischen Zeit, Österreichische Osthefte 39, 411–419.

SCHNYDER, ANDRÉ (2004): Art. „Die geistliche Badestube",11, Berlin/New York: De Gruyter, 503f.

WEISKE, BRIGITTE (1993), Bilder und Gebete vom Leben und Leiden Christi, in: Walter Haug, Burghart Wachinger (ed.), Die Passion Christi in der Literatur und Kunst des Spätmittelalter, Tübingen: De Gruyter, 113–168.

WIEDERKEHR, RUTH (2013), Das Hermetschwiler Gebetbuch. Studien zu deutschsprachiger Gebetbuchliteratur der Nord- und Zentralschweiz. Mit einer Edition, Berlin/Boston: De Gruyter.

Christopher Ocker
Institute for Religion and Critical Inquiry, Australian Catholic University

Prayer Literature and the History of Prayer:
Material Conditions and Subjectivities

It is often said that there existed a fundamental tension in late medieval Christianity: a tension between internal spirituality and external form, charismatic authority and institutionalized power, or individual liberty and normative discipline (Holl: 1923; Leppin: 2017, 171–188; Melville: 2020, 139–155; Hamm: 2004, 1–49, 153–178, 254–272). The early Protestants tried to resolve this medieval tension, many scholars might add, but whether and to what extent they did so remains a matter of stubborn, subtle debate. Was there a moment when Luther self-consciously moved himself and his followers from "medieval Catholicism" toward internalized ethics and spiritual freedom, as the Leipzig historian of law Rudolf Sohm argued over a century ago; and was this "Reformation breakthrough," as some have called it, born out of time or compromised by confessionalization and Protestant orthodoxy (Sohm: 1912; / Dillenberger Welch: 1988; Stjerna: 2022)?[1] Was this the seed of a liberating modernity, the catalyst of the twentieth century's technocratic, autocratic atrocities and nightmares, or simply the raw material of "the Protestant self," a mode of life flowing from a free and assured conscience? (Hering: 2008, 381)[2] To what extent did medieval spirituality anticipate or begin the trend toward interiority?

These questions have allowed scholars to evaluate the impact of Protestant innovations on European culture and clarify linkages as well as differentiations across confessions, but they are not quite right. The tension between external form and internal experience has a history, to be sure, but this tension is natural and can never be resolved. I mean this not in terms of a Hegelian dialectic, but as a biological outcome (Kyongsuk Min: 2004). An internal-external paradox seems to be inevitable and endemic to human consciousness, grounded as it is in the difference between the abstract, imaginatively patterned content of human self-awareness, thought, memory, and emotion, on the one hand, and the environment

---

1 Dillenberg/Welch: 1988, adapting an argument familiar from Ernst Troeltsch's distinction between new and old Protestantism. See Troeltsch: 2001.
2 Paraphrasing *der Protestantische Mensch* of Kurt Leese, student of Ernst Cassirer and Ernst Troetsch, critic of confessional orthodoxy and sacramental religion, "Liberalist und Judenfreund," as the Nazi commission dismissing him from his Hamburg teaching position put it in 1940. See Leese: 1938/1948.

348 | Christopher Ocker

acting upon the senses and the systems of the human body that physically enact our thinking and feeling. At an unknown point of human evolution, a desire to transcend the materiality of objects that represent invisible or absent conditions and beings emerged out of the mental broth of self-awareness and memories physically linked to the living organism's stimuli, senses, nerves, and brain (Deacon/Cashman: 2010; Skowronski/Sedikides: 2019).[3] At a certain point, the desire to transcend became associated with special objects, redolent images, and narratives recursively rebounding on desire, accreting external content and structure, simultaneously expressing transcendence and reiterating the aspiration to reach beyond oneself and the material world again and again.[4] To think historically about the expressions and experiences that are encompassed by the name 'religion' is to interpret behaviours, concepts, and feelings within their temporal and physical entanglements. Religiosity, one could say, expresses and performs this internalexternal paradox. The issue for the historian, therefore, is not a kind of either-or dilemma: to distinguish internal from external religion. It is not a kind of therapeutic calculus of proportions: to determine the proper balance of external action to internal motivation, to identify when it was imbalanced, and to show how balance was restored. A human being will always adjudicate the external-internal relationship. The question is, what is the content of both the subjective experiences expressed and the physical things and conditions of those expressions as they existed and changed, and continue to exist and change, in particular places and times?

The study of the history of prayer puts a spotlight on the content and context of these external-internal adjudications. Prayer goes beyond niggling petitions and apotropaic requests aimed at the world of spirit(s). It expresses longings that link a person's concrete desires to ineffable feelings, encouraging the one who prays to pursue those desires with particular words and gestures, often in a special place, applying a learned method and posture, yet pursuing desire in some absolute form. Prayer enacts a longing for a timeless, tranquil state of being (union with God) and a longing for human perfections like the seven virtues of medieval theologians and moral writers, qualities of an embodied human soul training itself toward divine nature, marking the difference of people from angels, who have spiritual or intel-

---

3 Skowronski/Sedikides: 2019, 4–21for recent research on the role of evolutionary selection and social responses to environment in the development of linguistic representation of knowledge, including self-knowledge, together with traits shared with animals, such as self-recognition, awareness of time, awareness of agency. The dates used by this last article for the appearance of humans in the evolutionary record may be too recent. Consider Gowlett: 2016 (http://dx.doi.org/10.1098/rstb.2015.0164, accessed 13 January 2021).

4 Consider Matthew Engelke's observations on materiality and divine "presence" in Christianity and in Hinduism, and in Christianity in contemporary Ghana, Engelke: 2011, 213–214, 223–227, 221–223. For the relation of consciousness to materiality in the study of religion, consider Elm/Ocker: 2020, 14–19 and the literature noted there.

Prayer Literature and the History of Prayer: | **349**

lectual rather than material being (angels do not need to cultivate moral virtue).[5] And yet, the mystical refinement cultivated through prayer is bound to concrete things, even in modes of religion that emphasize free experience and spontaneous expression.[6] Because it happens in a body, it is conditioned by organic processes and daily and seasonal planetary movements, and by clocks, sounds, rooms and buildings, ornaments and trinkets, pictures, inscriptions, books, and the stories and concepts they communicate in deliberate, methodical arrangements – all things that belong to the history of prayer.[7] The historian captures the periodic convergence of motions, places, objects, images, symbols, texts, and the overlapping messages they communicate among those who pray. In a word, prayer yields a remarkably intricate freeze-frame image of human sensibility and environment.

This book describes a chapter in the history of prayer. Its wide horizon includes vivid, detailed snapshots from prayer books, a popular manual of spirituality (the *Hortulus animae*), the cult of the saints in prayer books and Lutheranism, the practice of indulgences, the late medieval reform of monastic observance, Lutheran churches and spirituality in the long history of a *medieval* German diaspora, liturgy, hymnody, and more. A Berkeley medievalist, reflecting on the aspirations of his own writing, once commented on the value of strong juxtapositions like these. "If ever I have enough nerve," he wrote, "I shall write history completely without transition … Its pattern does not require, in many places, more than the juxtaposition of contrasting figures" (Brentano: 1988, 378). The daring juxtaposition of themes in this volume may be most informative when its particular stories stand each on its own without links and transitions. What impresses me in this diverse collection is its implicit evidence for the inevitability of the bond of internal states to external forms, as well as the explicit and implicit content of the 'screen capture' of cultural elements gathered here. The array put on display is at once culturally western European, linguistically Latinate and German, and regionally eastern-Hungarian and Transylvanian. This volume's juxtaposition of Catholic and Lutheran, medieval and early modern objects, practices, and themes underscores the contingent quality of the past and the hybridity of the convergence that occurs in the history of prayer.[8]

---

5 For example, according to Thomas Aquinas, *Summa Theologiae,* 1a2ae q. 5 a. 6. Rose: 2013. Consider also Drumond: 2016, 2930, Lang: 1983. With regard to individuality, cognition, and the mind-body problem, Adams: 1992, 14–17.

6 Luhrmann: 2004. Luhrmann: 2012, 72–100 and passim.

7 Illustrated on a Flemish example by Champion: 2017.

8 I mean contingency in the sense of Otto-Gerhard Oexle, as the historically conditioned character of human thought and action, and hybridity in the broad sense of Peter Burke, as a product of the interactions, positive and negative, that always accompany co-existence. Oexle: 1996, 18–72. Burke: 2016, 11–41. I think of hybridity as a quality of historical complexity that embraces conflict. Consider Ocker: 2018, 7–8, and the literature noted there, and Ocker: 2020, 179–209.

350 | Christopher Ocker

The sources of late medieval prayer discussed here are more like libraries than posters. Their layered, composite structures leave them susceptible to multiple uses in distant places. Perhaps this suggests their capacity to enact competing identities big and small over a great expanse of time. Cluj-Napoca Ms. 683 is a kind of miscellany prayer book (Luffy) most likely produced in Augsburg (Cermann). Cluj-Napoca MS. 684 is an illuminated Book of Hours illustrated in the Dutch style (Papahagi). The south-German tastes in saints and figuration on view in Ms. 683, like the Flemish style of MS. 684, is indicative of the breadth of a late-medieval biogeography of Christian prayer, which through artefacts like these joined vastly separated places. Elizabeth of Hungary was a prayer-warrior and heroine of self-denial. She appears in neither manuscript, yet her presence in Books of Hours from western Europe, as well as the Flemish origin and Dutch success of an innovative motif, her three crowns, which identify her standing among martyrs, virgins, and priests (Szűcs), point us to a certain western valorisation, perhaps even a kind of western 'presence' of the troubled Hungarian kingdom. The bonds of spiritual affinity reached far. The mercantile networks of an imperial free city like Augsburg and the shared tastes of aristocratic and other religious consumers implicitly indicated the continent as life world, materializing a linkage of western minds with a European east, where the expanding Ottoman Empire, the Kingdom of Poland, the Grand Duchy of Lithuania, and the Principality of Moldavia confronted one another. In the essays gathered here, physical artefacts of that world quietly bear eloquent testimony, not merely to the eastward movement of western books and liturgies, but also to the entanglements of distant cities and regions. A modern habitation of Ms. 683 in Romania suggests additional links with museum politics and the complexities of nineteenth-century Romanian, Hungarian, and Austro-Hungarian state-building (Luffy). Could the Central European 'flavour' of some of this codex's texts (Cermann) also have contributed to its lingering precocity during the conflict of national identities in the nineteenth century, when it found its way from a Viennese bookseller to Count Imre Mikó's Magyar academy of history and science, the Erdélyi Múzeum-Egyesület (in German, Siebenbürgerischer Museumsverein)?[9] A book containing prayers of the eloquent mid-fourteenth-century imperial chancellor of Emperor Charles IV, Johann von Neumarkt, written when the court at Prague was, for a brief generation, a dominant cultural force in Europe, retains something of a modified 'aura' five hundred years later in the museum-academy (Benjamin: 1980, 477–478. Dorrian: 2014, 187–201). Miscellany codices of Transylvania and Hungary, the model sermons of Nicholas von Dinkelsbühl, one of the principal theologians of the young university of Vienna and a Habsburg-court influencer at the time of the Hussite Crusade, stand with east-central European classics by Frater Siboto, Nicholas von Graetz, Johannes de Kwidzyn, and the Ob-

---

9 Bátor: 1990, 580–581.

Prayer Literature and the History of Prayer: | 351

servant Franciscans Pelbartus de Theswar and Osvald de Lasko (Cotoi). To whom do cultural artefacts such as these ultimately belong? Are they European, Hungarian, Austro-Hungarian, Romanian, diasporic German, Catholic, Christian? They can be, in fact, any and all of these by turns.

The mendicant orders, among the most widely and reliably networked organizations of late medieval Europe, make a cameo appearance in this book, which revolves around Transylvania. They make their appearance through the understudied agency of Observant Franciscan laywomen in greater Hungary (Florea). We have long known that friars, as elsewhere, occupied a special role in towns across Europe and that the movement of Observance contributed to their advantage in the religious marketplace.[10] Their presence in the urban east was not merely a reflection of a medieval-German-urban diaspora but a token of on-going religious connectedness, and a reminder that such presence cannot be gendered as exclusively male.

The accent falls on the continuities that withstood the processes of religious differentiation. The continuities keep pointing us back to physical things. Prayer books in Transylvania were rare, which raises the importance of church buildings and their decoration over against the written word, not merely in late medieval and Catholic churches (Dincă), but also, before the eighteenth century, in Reformation-Lutheran churches, where if literacy was growing, it continued to be limited and partial, while "sensuality remained a significant feature of worship," in the east as in the west (Crăciun). And so, the scriptural orientation of Lutheran faith, we learn, was integrated to a spatial sensorium, in the form of biblical and orthodox *Kernstellen* (gospel passages, eucharistic texts, the Decalogue, and the Creed) both memorized in catechisms and inscribed on (often polemical) paintings and church furniture (Crăciun) in once Catholic churches. They were not the only things that triggered awareness of a Catholic past while teaching the legitimacy of evangelical reforms. Saints days and collects that retained texts from the divine office or the mass could also trigger an abiding feeling that the Lutheran congregant was in a church both familiar and novel, not in a meeting room (Bándi, Szegedi). Aurality continued to govern prayer among semi-literate communities after the Reformation (Crăciun). Hymnody was an essential instrument of early Lutheran pedagogy and identity (Boyd Brown: 2005). But in Transylvania, the very earliest Protestant hymnal, Andreas Moldner's *Gesangbuch* (1543), was eclectic in both its sources and the after-history of its hymns (Wien). It seems to have extended a kind of Erasmian pedagogy, which could hold further clues to how the remarkable coexistence of Eastern-Catholic-Lutheran-Reformed orthodoxies and anti-Trinitarian unorthodoxies grew in the seedbed of Transylvania during its Ottoman vassalage.

---

10 E.g. the Augustinian friars in Körmönd in 1517. Erdélyi: 2012. For German examples, consider Ocker: 2003, 69–94, and the literature noted there.

352 | Christopher Ocker

The gap separating Lutheran from Catholic prayer can narrow at the sharpest point of on-the-ground, clashing pieties: the indulgenced prayer. The *Hortulus animae* was a text calibrated to users of different capacities, and it liberally offers indulgences for prayers, in quantities of number, frequency, and duration. Rather than simply exemplify blathering, unchristian prayer, as Luther alleged, the overwhelming mass of indulgences provoked the individual to turn toward God and Christ's passion internally, and an immeasurable quantity of prayers "finally leaves the aspect of quantification behind" (Leppin). An indulgence is quite literally a material object, an ecclesiastically sanctioned writ, whether promised in a book, drawn up as a charter, painted on a narrative panel, or etched onto the wall of a church. A church, a church order, a hymnal, a book are things, and they are party to the apperceptions that occur in prayer. In these essays, theological ideas yield ground to practices, environment, and liturgical performers and performances, which in turn remind us to link doctrines not merely to positions but to the subjectivity cultivated by prayer. External things lead to internal states through the activity of prayer.

The distinctively western prayer literature and liturgies examined in this volume will help the historian reintegrate the fifteenth century into the better-known sixteenth-century history of the Kingdom of Hungary and Transylvania, and reintegrate both into the cultural and religious history of Europe. They also offer an invitation to reconsider 'confessional' Europe, and its forms of prayer, through a Transylvanian lens. This seems especially important to the historian outside Europe. It seems inevitable that the historian in North America or Australia would be drawn to the religious liberties of the east, where "anyone may remain in one's own faith, given and confirmed by God, lest one person be molested by another with prejudice," as the principality's estates said in assembly on the Feast of the Circumcision in 1552, confirming rights acknowledged by the voivode of Transylvania and the Hungarian king.[11] These liberties were as turbulent as confessional competition in western Europe was, to which they were intellectually linked by books, synodal decisions, laws, letters, and political structures. The intention of this 1552 pronunciation and others like it was to ameliorate conflict between Lutherans and Catholics and unite them in opposition to Calvinists; and it failed, overcome by a forced Lutheran-Reformed-Socinian-Jesuit pluralism in the next decades.[12] It was

---

11 The king at the time was, of course, Ferdinand, also king of Bohemia, king of the Romans, and archduke of Austria and veteran of three years of religious controversy in Germany. *Monumenta comitalia*, vol. 1: 383 (art. 3). Keul: 2009, 242–243.

12 As determined by the in the diets of Turda (Torda) and Alba Iulia (Gyulafehérvár/Karlsburg) in 1558, by which time Calvinist-leaning, Cluj (Kolozsvár/Klausenburg) was already separating from a Lutheran center at Sibiu (Nagyszeben/Hermannstadt). Keul: 2009, 88, 244. A decade later, the Hungarian Kolozsvár pastor Ferenc Dávid (later to oppose prayer to Jesus as a form of idolatry, splitting the Unitarian faction in the late 1570s) was leading the anti-

Prayer Literature and the History of Prayer: | **353**

not a condition of laissez-faire toleration. Pluralism provoked theological debate in the east no less intense than debate in Geneva, Wittenberg, Jena, or Leuven. If anything, its energy was greater than that produced in the triathlon of Catholic-Lutheran-Reformed orthodoxies in western Europe, thanks to the threat of openly sanctioned anti-Trinitarian opinion and the presence of Eastern Orthodox Romanians. The bi-confessional *Simultaneum* in Germany may have been more common than earlier generations of church historians have appreciated, but it was still relatively rare. Compromise in Transylvania simply happened on an exponentially greater scale. This made Transylvania "a laboratory of religious heterogeneity," in Ulrich Wien's compelling phrase (Wien: 2019). This amounted to much more than a stubborn refusal to reorient itself "to the Asiatic world of the Ottomans" during Türkish vassalage (Bátor: 1990, 286). It amounted to more than German nostalgia for the west mechanically reproduced in a tardy reception of Renaissance architecture, art, and literary tastes upon its Carpathian borderland plateau. It was not a laboratory that created new life from dead matter, like the workshop of Mary Shelley's fabled Ingolstadt professor. It was a clinical laboratory, where specimens were tested, and diagnoses were made. Its samples were both local and exotic. They came from all of Christendom.

We might think of the evidence gathered here in this book as representing a first stage in the prayer experiment conducted in Transylvania. The first stage suggests the importance of western texts and sources in Europe's fifteenth-and sixteenth-century east. A second stage might reach beyond the classically European, Catholic and Lutheran sources foregrounded here and include even more heterogeneous contexts, and prayers.

In recent years, the biblicizing Christian primitivism of Faustus Socinus, Giorgio Biandrata, Ferenc Dávid, and other Renaissance, proto-Enlightenment free thinkers, has been complemented by a growing awareness of their affinity to Islam.[13] Knowledge of Islam among these anti-Trinitarians was often second-hand and "profoundly coincidental": its long fibrils intertwined with Jewish and Muslim scholarship and polemic over centuries, now complemented by new sources of information, like the letter-writing Mustafa Beg, alias Adam Neuser, a Heidelberg preacher turned anti-Trinitarian refugee in Transylvania before his Ottoman capture and conversion (Mulsow: 2014, 577–578. Wien: 2019, 32. Graf: 2017, 154). A second-hand source communicated assimilated knowledge. It left the perception of Socinian-Muslim likeness no less real. The most daring contributors to reforming Transylvania as a heterodox haven "behind the Ottoman curtain" were exiles like Socinus, Biandrata, and Dávid (Wien: 2019). To the haven, heterodox

---

Trinitarian faction (in defense of the Apostle's Creed!) recognized by János II Zsigmond in 1569. Keul: 2009, 106–116.

13 Mulsow: 2014. Mulsow: 2010, 559 for the quotation.

refugees, and Muslims and Jews, kept on coming, until the end of Ottoman vassalage in the late seventeenth century. A glance to the southwest reminded the Transylvanian that tribute was much better than direct rule. Eastern Hungary's Ottoman subjection, with its mosques made from former churches, seemed considerably harsher (Keul: 2009, 241). The contrast with the Holy Roman Empire and the famous aphorism used to describe the Peace of Augsburg's principle of toleration is not merely striking but informative. That famous aphorism is used to summarize its terms as a statement about ruling authority and social coherence, but it never fit its context all that well. How singular could the confession indicated by *cuius regio, eius religio* be, when a prince's family had more than one confession through marriage, when a prince's estates formed or protected non-conforming enclaves, when a different orthodoxy seemed politically expedient, when no orthodoxy seemed expedient at all? Confessional politics in the Holy Roman Empire belonged to the near constant flux of aristocratic friendships, families sometimes more supportive of Habsburg peace and Lutheran-Catholic detente, sometimes less supportive, and sometimes embracing a "Reformed" confession while leaning hard toward France, challenging the Habsburg hegemony. Religious and political compromises among the Empire's estates tell us more about its political culture than the confessional orthodoxy embraced by a state ever could (Ocker: 2018, 100–299). In Transylvania, the impracticality of state-wide religious uniformity was always on display. In this place of quantum social weirdness, when viewed from the vantage of confessional social ideals, a newly Calvinist prince might have a Reformed bishop, like István Geleji Katona, who strategically tolerated the vestiges of Catholicism in Lutheran churches, the feast-days of biblical saints, which he despised, because the "exponent of episcopal absolutism" was also "bishop of all confessions" (Szegedi). Lutheran churches might be relatively bare, but *adiaphora*, such as modified saints' observances and paintings, could become not-so-indifferent markers of an anti-Calvinist or anti-Socinian orthodoxy, alongside the emphatically essential Lutheran doctrine of real presence in the eucharist (Szegedi in this volume and Wetter, 2016). The religious experiment that was Transylvania confirms the diagnosis that Europe reproduced religious differences when it tried to reduce and eliminate them (Ocker: 2018, 230–299). Europe resembled Transylvania.

"Materiality" is "an immersive environment with no outside position," says the anthropologist (Reinhardt: 2016, 78). It is not the external cause or reflection of an inward state, but inseparable from the subjective content associated with a thing, for example a prayer book, a church building, or perhaps even the city and the territory in which the prayer book 'lives'. This volume's accent on often subtle medieval-Reformation continuities has external geographical coordinates that run between eastern and western Europe before and after the conflict between Luther and the papacy. Artefacts and texts of prayer invite us to think of this as a subjective topography, a wide space of shared attitudes, aspirations, and feelings. They invite us to see books, texts, paintings, buildings, and furniture as tools of spiritual, emotional management shared across the continent. Expanding this to heterodox and Eastern Orthodox Christians, Jews, and Muslims in Transylvania in the late sixteenth and seventeenth centuries will link these coordinates to another geography, that of the northern part of the Ottoman world. The second stage of the experiment could help us understand Europe's entanglements beyond Christendom, on its human template, at the intimate point of prayer.

Bibliography

BÁTOR, GÁBOR et al. (1990), Kurze Geschichte Siebenbürgens, trans. Albrecht Friedrich, Budapest: Akadémiai Kiadó.

BENJAMIN, WALTER (1980), Das Kunstwerk im Zeitalter seiner technischen Reproduzierbarkeit, in: Gesammelte Schriften 1–2, Frankfurt: Suhrkamp, 471–508.

BOYD BROWN, CHRISTOPHER (2005), Singing the Gospel: Lutheran Hymns and the Success of the Reformation, Cambridge: Harvard University Press.

BRENTANO; ROBERT (1988), Two Churches; England and Italy in the Thirteenth Century, Berkeley: University of California Press.

BURKE, PETER (2016), Hybrid Renaissance, Budapest: Central European University Press.

CHAMPION, MATTHEW (2017), The Fullness of Time: Temporalities of the Fifteenth-Century Low Countries, Chicago: University of Chicago Press.

DEACON, TERRENCE W./CASHMAN, TYRONE (2010), The Role of Symbolic Capacity in the Origins of Religion, Journal for the Study of Religion, Nature, and Culture 3, 490–517.

DILLENBERGER, JOHN/WELCH, CLAUDE (1988), Protestant Christianity: Interpreted through Its Development, New York: Macmillan.

DORRIAN, MARK (2014), Museum Atmospheres: Notes on Aura, Distance and Affect, The Journal of Architecture 19, 187–201.

DRUMOND, IAN CHRISTOPHER (2016), John Duns Scotus and the Role of Moral Virtues Ph.D. dissertation, University of Toronto.

ELM, SUSANNE/OCKER, CHRISTOPHER (2020), Christianity and the Material: Medieval to Modern, in: Material Christianity: Western Religion and the Agency of Things, Amsterdam: Springer, 1–25.

ENGELKE, MATTHEW (2011), Material Religion, The Cambridge Companion to Religious Studies, ed. Robert A. Orsi, Cambridge: Cambridge University Press, 209–229.

EOE (1878–1898), Erdélyi Országgyűlési Emlékek = Monumenta Comitialia Regni Transilvaniae, 21 vols. ed. Szilágyi Sándor, Budapest: MTA.

ERDÉLYI, GABRIELLA (2003), The Consumption of the Sacred: Popular Piety in a Late Medieval Hungarian Town, Journal of Ecclesiastical History 63, 31–60.

356 | Christopher Ocker

GOWLETT, J.A.J. (2016), The Discovery of Fire by Humans: A Long and Convoluted Process, Philosophical Transactions of the Royal Society B371, (http://dx.doi.org/10.1098/rstb.2015.0164, accessed 13 January 2021).

GRAF, TOBIAS P. (2017), The Sultan's Renegades: Christian-European Converts to Islam and the Making of the Ottoman Elite, 1575–1610, Oxford: Oxford University Press.

HAMM, BERND (2004), The Reformation of Faith in the Context of Late Medieval Theology and Piety, ed. Robert J. Bast, Leiden: Brill.

HERING, RAINER (2008), Vom Umgang mit theologischen Außenseitern im 20. Jahrhundert, Kirchliche Zeitgeschichte (20. Jahrhundert), ed. Rainer Hering, Inge Mager (Hamburgische Kirchengeschichte in Aufsätzen, 5), Hamburg: Hamburg University Press, 375–398.

HOLL, KARL (1923), Luther, Gesammelte Aufsätze zur Kirchengeschichte, Tübingen: J. C. B. Mohr.

KEUL, ISTVÁN (2009), Early Modern Religious Communities in East-Central Europe: Ethnic Diversity, Denominational Plurality, and Corporative Politics in the Principality of Transylvania (1526–1691), Leiden: Brill.

LANG, HELEN S. (1983), Bodies and Angels: The Occupants of Place for Aristotle and Duns Scotus Viator, 14, 245–266.

LEESE, KURT (1938/1948), Die Religion der Protestantischen Menschen, Berlin/Munich.

LEPPIN, VOLKER (2017), Transformationen. Studien zu den Wandlungsprozessen in Theologie und Frömmigkeit zwischen Spätmittelalter und Reformation, Tübingen: Mohr Siebeck.

LUHRMANN, TANYA (2004), Metakinesis: How God Becomes Intimate in Contemporary U.S. Christianity, American Anthropologist 106, 518–528.

LUHRMANN, TANYA (2012), When God Talks Back: Understanding the American Evangelical Relationship with God, New York: Alfred A. Knopf.

McCORD ADAMS, MARILYN (1992), The Resurrection of the Body according to Three Medieval Aristotelians: Thomas Aquinas, John Duns Scotus, William Ockham, Philosophical Topics 20, 1–33.

MELVILLE, GERT (2020), The Charismatic Leader and the *Vita religiosa*: Some Observations about an Apparent Contradiction between Individual and Institutions in: A. Fitzpatrick/J. Sabapathy (ed.), Individuals and Institutions in Medieval Scholasticism, London: University of London Press, 139–155.

MIN, ANSELM KYONGSUK (2004), Hegel's Dialectic of the Spirit: Contemporary Reflections on Hegel's Vision of Development and Totality, Language and Spirit, ed. D.Z. Phillips, Mario von der Ruhr, London: Palgrave Macmillan, 8–38.

MULSOW, MARTIN (2014), Socinianism, Islam, and the Origins of Radical Enlightenment, Religious Obedience and Political Resistance in the Early Modern World: Jewish, Christian and Islamic Philosophers Addressing the Bible, Turnhout: Brepols.

MULSOW, MARTIN (2010), Socinianism, Islam and the Radical Uses of Arabic Scholarship, *Al-Qantara* 31, 549–586.

OCKER, CHRISTOPHER (2003), Religious Reform and Social Cohesion in Late Medieval Germany, in: Thomas A. Brady, Jr./Katherine Brady/Susan Karant-Nunn/James D. Tracy, The Work of Heiko A. Oberman, Leiden: Brill, 69–94.

OCKER, CHRISTOPHER (2018), Luther, Conflict, and Christendom, Cambridge: Cambridge University Press.

OCKER, CHRISTOPHER (2020), Disruption and Engagement: Christendom's Experience of Islam at the End of the Middle Ages, in: Mirko Breitenstein / Jörg Sonntag (ed.), Disorder. Expressions of an Amorphous Phenomenon in Human History, Münster: Aschendorff, 179–209.

OEXLE, OTTO-GERHARD (1996), Geschichtswissenschaft im Zeichen des Historismus. Studien zu Problemgeschichten der Moderne, Göttingen: Vandenhoeck & Ruprecht.

REINHARDT, BRUNO (2016), Don't Make It a Doctrine: Material Religion, Transcendence, Critique, Anthropological Theory 16, 75–97.

ROSE, MARIKA (2013), The Body and Ethics in Thomas Aquinas' *Summa Theologiae*, New Blackfriars 94, 540–551.

SKOWRONSKI, JOHN J./SEDIKIDES, CONSTANTINE (2019), On the Evolution of the Human Self: A Data-Driven Review and Reconsideration, Self and Identity 18, 4–21.

SOHM, RUDOLF (1912), Wesen und Ursprung des Katholizismus, Leipzig: B.G. Teubner.

STJERNA, KIRSI (2021), Lutheran Theology: A Grammar of Faith, London: T. and T. Clark.

TROELTSCH, ERNST (2001), Schriften zur Bedeutung des Protestantismus für die moderne Welt (1906–1913), ed. Trutz Rendtorff, Berlin: De Gruyter.

WETTER, EVELIN (2016), Staging the Eucharist, *Adiaphora,* and Shaping Lutheran Identities in the Transylvanian Parish Church, Parish Churches in the Early Modern World, ed. Andrew Spicer, Farnham: Ashgate, 119–145.

WIEN, ULRICH A. (2019), Flucht hinter den 'Osmanischen Vorhang'. Glaubensflüchtlinge in Siebenbürgen, Journal of Early Modern Christianity 6, 19–41.

Gesamtbibliographie

ABAFFY, CSILLA N. (ed.) (1996), Festetics-kódex, 1494 előtt. A nyelvemlék hasonmása és betűhű átirata bevezetéssel és jegyzetekkel, Budapest: Argumentum, Magyar Nyelvtudományi Társaság.

ACHTEN, GERARD (1980), Das christliche Gebetbuch im Mittelalter. Andachts- und Stundenbücher in Handschrift und Frühdruck, Wiesbaden: Reichert.

ÁDÁM, EDINA (2009), Pelbart of Temesvar and the Use of Images in Preaching, Annual of Medieval Studies at CEU 15, 131–143.

ADAMSKA, ANNA (2004), The Study of Medieval Literacy: Old Sources, New Ideas, in: Anna Adamska/Marco Mostert (ed.), The Development of Literate Mentalities in East Central Europe (Proceedings of the Fourth Utrecht Symposium on Medieval Literacy, 28–30 June 2001), Turnhout: Brepols, 13–47.

ADAMSKA, ANNA (2016), Intersections: Medieval East Central Europe from the Perspective of Literacy and Communication, in: Katalin Szende/Gerhard Jaritz (ed.), Medieval East Central Europe in a Comparative Perspective: From Frontier Zones to Lands in Focus, Abingdon, UK: Routledge, 225–238.

AGENDA (1547) für die Seelsorger und Kirchendiener in Sybembürgen, Kronstadt: [Honter].

AGENDA (undatiert), Das ist: Kirchen-Ordnung, wie sich die Seelen-Sorger in ihren Diensten halten sollen, für die Diener und Prediger der kirchen zu Schaesburg gestellet, Zentralarchiv der Evangelischen Kirche A. B. in Rumänien (ZAEKR), 400/109–200.

AGENDA MINISTRORUM ECCLESIAE CORONENSIS (1695), Archiv der Honterusgemeinde Kronstadt (AHK), Signatur: I-F-50.

AGENDA SACRA (1653), das ist Kirchen Ordnung in Hermanstadt, Auffs new vbersehen, gebessert und auffgelegt, Hermannstadt, Marcus Pistorius, 1653. ZAEKR, 612-II-286.

AGENDA SACRA (1653) Das ist: Kirchen Ordnung in Hermannstadt Auffs new ubersehen, gebessert und augelegt, gedruckt bei Marcus Pistorius, [Hermannstadt].

AGENDA SACRA (1748), das ist: Kirchen-Ordnung zum heiligen Gebrauch der Herrmannstädtischen, sowie auch der übrigen evangelischen Kirchen in Siebenbürgen von neuem übersehen, vermehrt und aufgelegt, Herrmannstadt, Stadt-Druckerey Samuel Sardi, ZAEKR, 612-III-2.

AGENDA SACRA (1748). Das ist: Kirchen Ordnung zum heiligen Gebrauch der Hermannstädtischen, wie auch der übrigen Ewangelischen Kirchen in Siebenbürgen, von neuem übersehen, vermehret, und aufgelegt im Jahr 1748, Hermann-Stadt: Samuel Sardi.

[AGENDE], DENNDORF, ZAEKR, 601-C-11.

[AGENDE], RODE, ZAEKR, 400/278-29.

[AGENDE], SELIGSTADT, ZAEKR, 400/118–293.

AINSWORTH, MARYAN W./MARTENS, MAXIMILIAAN P.J. (1995a), Jan van Eyck et atelier. Vierge à l'Enfant avec sainte Barbe, sainte Elisabeth et Jan Vos, in: Maryan W. Ainsworth/Maximiliaan P. J. Martens, Petrus Christus, Ghent/New York/Ludion: Metropolitan Museum of Art, 72–78.

360 | Gesamtbibliographie

Ainsworth, Maryan W./Martens, Maximiliaan P.J. (1995b), Portrait d'un donateur, Portrait d'une donatrice, in: Maryan W. Ainsworth/Maximiliaan P. J. Martens, Petrus Christus, Ghent/New York/Ludion: Metropolitan Museum of Art, 131–135.

Ainsworth, Maryan Wynn/Christiansen, Keith (ed.) (1998), From Van Eyck to Bruegel: Early Netherlandish Painting in the Metropolitan Museum of Art, New York: Metropolitan Museum of Art.

Alexander, Jonathan J.G., Medieval Illuminators and Their Methods of Work, New Haven/London: Yale University Press, 1992.

Amtsschriften (1593–1698) des Mühlbacher Bezirkskonsistoriums, ZAEKR, DA-209-14.

Andrássy, Manó, Graf (1861), Kiadatlan magyar érmek és pecsétgyűrűk saját gyűjteményemből, Archeológiai Értesítő 2, 49–64.

Angenendt, Arnold (2004), Grundformen der Frömmigkeit im Mittelalter, 2nd ed., München: R. Oldenbourg.

Approbatae Constitutiones (1815): Regni Transylvaniae & Partium Hungariae Eidem Annexarum. Ex Articulis ab Anno Millesimo Quingentissimo Quadragesimo, ad praesentem huncusque Millesimum Sexcentessimum Quinquagesimum tertium conclusis, compilatae. (…) in Generali Dominorum Regnicolarum, ex Edicto Celsissimi Principis, D.D. Georgii Rákóczi II. Dei Gratia Principis Transylvaniae, (…) in Civitatem Albam Juliam ad diem decimum quintum mensis Januarii Anni praesentis 1653. Congregatorum, in: Fronius Mátyás/Érfalvi Halmágyi Mihály (ed.), Erdély Országának Három Könyvekre osztatott Törvényes Könyve Melly Approbata, Compilata Constitutiokbol és Novellaris Articulusokbol áll. Mostan újjabban, minden Haza-Fiaknak hasznokra ki-botsáttatott, Kolosváratt: Királlyi Lyceum Betüivel.

Arnold, Jochen (2011), Was geschieht im Gottesdienst? Zur theologischen Bedeutung des Gottesdienstes und seiner Formen, Göttingen: Vandenhoeck & Ruprecht.

Articul (2002), so in der Visitation beschlossen, Acta Capituli Barcensis in: Gross, Juilus/Nussbächer, Gernot/Marin, Elisabeta (ed.) Quellen zur Geschichte der Stadt Kronstadt, VIII/2, Annales ecclesiastici, Kronstadt: Aldus.

Arz, Gustav (1955), Series Pastorum. Die Pfarrer der evangelischen Gemeinden A. B. in der R. V. R. von der Reformation bis zur Gegenwart, in: Siebenbürgische Familienforschung, mehrere Jahrgänge, Hermannstadt: [Typoskript] Druck.

Assmann, Aleida/Assmann, Jan (1994), Das Gestern im Heute. Medien und soziales Gedächtnis, in: Klaus Merten/Siegfried J. Schmidt/Siegfried Weischenberg (ed.), Die Wirklichkeit der Medien. Eine Einführung in die Kommunikationswissenschaft, Opladen: Westdeutscher Verlag, 114–140.

Assmann, Jan (1999), Das kulturelle Gedächtnis. Schrift, Erinnerung und politische Identität in frühen Hochkulturen, München: C.H. Beck.

Aston, Margaret (1977), Lollardy and Literacy, History LXII/206, 347–371.

As-Vijvers, Anne Margreet W. (2017), Creation by Variation: The Uses of Models in Ghent-Bruges Marginal decoration, https://hnanews.org/wp-content/uploads/2017/08/Abstracts-of-Antwerp-Conference-Papers.pdf.

As-Vijvers, Anne Margaret W./Korteweg, Anne S. (2018), Splendour of the Burgundian Netherlands: Southern Netherlandish Illuminated Manuscripts in Dutch Collections, Zwolle: Wbooks/Utrecht: Museum Catharijneconvent.

Gesamtbibliographie | 361

BAIER, KARL (2009), Meditation and Contemplation in High to Late Medieval Europe, in: Eli Franco (ed.), Yogic Perception, Meditation and Altered States of Consciousness, Wien: Österreichischen Akademie der Wissenschaften, 325–349.

BÁNDI, ANDRÁS (2016), Lectura saşilor în secolul al XVIII-lea, PhD thesis, Universitatea Babeş-Bolyai, Cluj-Napoca.

BÁNDI, ANDRÁS/MONOK, ISTVÁN/VERÓK, ATTILA (ed.) (2021), Lesestoffe der Siebenbürger Sachsen (1575–1800). Kronstadt und Burzenland/Adattár XVI–XVIII. századi szellemi mozgalmaink történetéhez = Materialien zur Geschichte der Geistesströmungen des 16–18. Jahrhunderts in Ungarn, 16/6. – Erdélyi könyvesházak = Bibliotheken in Siebenbürgen, VI, Budapest, MTA Könyvtár és Információs Központ = Bibliothek und Informationszentrum der Ungarischen Akademie der Wissenschaften.

BÁRCZI, ILDIKÓ (2009), Morálteológiai tanítások Laskai Osvát és Temesvári Pelbárt Szent Erzsébet-napi beszédmintáiban, in: Dávid Falvay (ed.), Árpád-házi Szent Erzsébet kultusza a 13–16. században. Saint Elizabeth of Hungary's Cult in the 13th-15th Century. Az Eötvös Loránd Tudományegyetem Bölcsészettudományi Karán 2007. május 24-én tartott konferencia előadásai, Budapest: Magyarok Nagyasszonya Ferences Rendtartomány, 83–104.

BARTLETT, ANNE CLARK/BESTUL, THOMAS H. (ed.) (1999), Cultures of Piety: Medieval English Devotional Literature in Translation, Ithaca: Cornell University Press.

BARTSCH, ADAM (1808), Le peintre graveur, 21 Bde, Wien: Verl.-Dr. Würzburg, 1802–1821: Bd. 7 (1808), S. 141, Nr. 120; Bd. 7 (1808), S. 127–130, Nr. 60–75.

BASCHET, JÉRÔME (2008), L'Iconographie médiévale, Paris: Gallimard.

BAST, ROBERT J. (ed.) (2004), The Reformation of Faith in the Context of Late Medieval Theology and Piety. Essays by Berndt Hamm, London/Boston: Brill.

BÁTOR, GÁBOR et al. (1990), Kurze Geschichte Siebenbürgens, trans. Albrecht Friedrich, Budapest: Akadémiai Kiadó.

BATTHYÁNY, IGNÁC (ed.) (1827), Leges Ecclesiasticae Regni Hungariae et Provinciarum Adiacentium, Albae-Carolinae.

BÄUML, FRANZ H. (1980), Varieties and Consequences of Medieval Literacy and Illiteracy, Speculum, 55, 237–265.

BEIER, CHRISTINE (2004), Missalien massenhaft. Die Bämler-Werkstatt und die Augsburger Buchmalerei im 15. Jahrhundert, in: Codices Manuscripti 48/49, Textbd., 55–78, Taf.-bd., 67–78, Abb. 1–42.

BELTING, HANS (1994), Likeness and Presence. A History of the Image before the Era of Art, Chicago/London: University of Chicago Press.

BELTING, HANS (2002), Macht und Ohnmacht der Bilder, Historische Zeitschrift 33, 11–32.

BELTING, HANS (2011), An Anthropology of Images: Picture, Medium, Body, Princeton/Oxford: Princeton University Press.

BENJAMIN, WALTER (1980), Das Kunstwerk im Zeitalter seiner technischen Reproduzierbarkeit, in: Gesammelte Schriften 1–2, Frankfurt: Suhrkamp, 471–508.

BENRATH, KARL (1886), Zur Geschichte der Marienverehrung, Theologische Studien und Kritiken 59, 7–94, 197–267.

BERHIDAI, LAJOS PIUSZ (2013), Bonaventura-hagyomány Laskai Osvát prédikációiban, in: Judit Bogár (ed.), Misztika a 16–18. századi Magyarországon, Piliscsaba: Pázmány Péter Katolikus Egyetem. Bölcsészet- és Társadalomtudományi Kar, 31–41.

362 | Gesamtbibliographie

BESTUL, THOMAS H. (1996), Texts of the Passion: Latin Devotional Literature and Medieval Society, Philadelphia: University of Pennsylvania Press.

BILLER, PETER (1994), Heresy and Literacy. Earlier History of the Theme, in: Peter Biller/ Anne Hudson (ed.), Heresy and Literacy, 1000–1530, Cambridge: Cambridge University Press, 1–19.

BINDER, LUDWIG (1990), Die Geistliche Universität, in: Wolfgang Kessler (ed.), Gruppenautonomie in Siebenbürgen. 500 Jahre siebenbürgisch-sächsische Nationsuniversität, Köln/Wien: Böhlau, 45–63.

BINDER, LUDWIG (1996), Johannes Honterus. Schriften, Briefe, Zeugnisse, durchgesehen und ergänzt von Gernot Nussbächer, Bukarest, Kriterion.

BINSKI, PAUL (1999), The English Parish Church and Its Art in the Later Middle Ages: A Review of the Problem, Studies in Iconography 20, 1–25.

BINZ, GUSTAV (1907), Die deutschen Handschriften der Öffentlichen Bibliothek der Universität Basel, Bd. 1: Die Handschriften der Abteilung A, Basel: Universitätsbibliothek.

BIRÓ, LAJOS (1937), Neves jezsuita-plebánosok és írók a székely anyavárosban, Székely Közélet 20.41 (9 Oct.), 3.

BISCHOF, JANIKA (2013), Testaments, Donations and the Values of Books as Gifts. A Study of Records from Medieval England before 1450, Frankfurt am Main: Peter Lang.

BOD, PETRUS (1890), Historia Hungarorum ecclesiastica, inde ab exordio Novi testamenti ad nostra tempora ex monumentis partim editis, partim vero ineditis, fide dignis, collecta studio et labore Petri Bod de Felső-Csernáton, Lugduni-Batavorum, Brill.

BORECKY, ANNA (2018), Book Culture in Medieval Hungary, in: Xavier Barral i Altet/Pál Lővei/Vinni Lucherini/Imre Takács (ed.), The Art of Medieval Hungary, Roma: Viella, 283–306.

BOSSY, JOHN (1991), Christian Life in the Later Middle Ages. Prayer, Transactions of the Royal Historical Society 1, 137–148.

BOTTIGHEIMER, RUTH B. (1993), Bible Reading, "Bibles", and the Bibles for Children in Early Modern Germany, Past & Present 139, 66–89.

BOYD BROWN, CHRISTOPHER (2005), Singing the Gospel: Lutheran Hymns and the Success of the Reformation, Cambridge: Harvard University Press.

BRACALONI, LEONE (1932), Origine, evoluzione ed affermazione della Corona francescana mariana. Studi francescani 21, 257–295.

BRANDSCH, GOTTLIEB (1941–1944), Die Agende Stephan Ludwig Roths, in: Archiv des Vereins für Siebenbürgische Landeskunde, Fünfzigster Band, Erstes Heft. Hermannstadt und Bistritz: Michaelis, 149–238.

BRANTLEY, JESSICA (2007), Reading in the Wilderness: Private Devotion and Public Performance in Late Medieval England, Chicago: University of Chicago Press.

BRENTANO, ROBERT (1988), Two Churches; England and Italy in the Thirteenth Century, Berkeley: University of California Press.

BRINSLEY, JOHN (1607), Second Part of the True Watch containing the perfect rule and summe of Prayer (1607), Brinsley_John-The_second_part_of_the_true_watch-STC-37 76-1196_07-p1to74.pdf (EEBO – TCP). (Last accessed 09.01.11.)

BROADHEAD, P.J. (2005), Public Worship, Liturgy and the Introduction of the Lutheran Reformation in the Territorial Lands of Nuremberg, The English Historical Review 120/486, 277–302.

Gesamtbibliographie | 363

BROWN, JACOB M. (2013), From Incense to Idolatry: The Reformation of Olfaction in Late Medieval German Ritual, The Sixteenth Century Journal 44/2, 323–344.

BRÜCKNER, WOLFGANG (2007), Lutherische Bekenntnisgemälde des 16. bis 18. Jahrhunderts. Die Illustrierte Confessio Augustana, Regensburg: Schnell und Steiner.

BUNYITAY, VINCZE/RAPAICS, RAJMUND/KARÁCSONYI, JÁNOS (ed.) (1902–1904), Monumenta Ecclesiastica tempora innovatae in Hungaria religionis illustrantia, vol. I–II, Budapest: Szent István-Társulat.

BURKE, PETER (2001), Eyewitnessing. The Uses of Images as Historical Evidence, Ithaca, NY: Cornell University Press.

BURKE, PETER (2016), Hybrid Renaissance, Budapest: Central European University Press.

CAMERON, EVAN (1991), The European Reformation, Oxford: Clarendon Press.

CAMILLE, MICHAEL (1996), The Gregorian Definition Revisited: Writing and the Medieval Image, in: Jérôme Baschet/Jean Claude Schmitt (ed.), L'Image. Fonctions et usages des images dans l'Occident médiéval, Paris: Léopard d'Or, 89–107.

CANNON, JOANNA (2010), Kissing the Virgin's Foot: Adoration Before the Madonna and Child. Enacted, Depicted, Imagined, Studies in Iconography, 31, 1–50.

CAREY, HILARY M. (2010), Astrology in the Middle Ages, History Compass, 8/8, 888–902.

CERMANN, REGINA (in Vorbereitung), Das Stundenbuch deutsch.

CERMANN, REGINA (2010), Über den Export deutschsprachiger Stundenbücher von Paris nach Nürnberg, in Codices Manuscripti 75, 9–24.

CERMANN, REGINA (2018), Unter Druck? Buchmalerei im Wettstreit mit Reproduktionsmedien, in: Hamburger, Jeffrey F./Theisen, Maria (ed.), Unter Druck. Mitteleuropäische Buchmalerei im 15. Jahrhundert. Tagungsband zum internationalen Kolloquium in Wien, Österreichische Akademie der Wissenschaften, 13.1–17.1.2016, Buchmalerei des 15. Jahrhunderts in Mitteleuropa 15, Petersberg: Michael Imhof Verlag. (Abbildungsteil zu dem gleichnamigen Beitrag online unter der URN ⟨urn:nbn:de:bsz:16-artdok-49267⟩ bzw. URL ⟨http://archiv.ub.uni-heidelberg.de/artdok/volltexte/2017/4926⟩ bzw. DOI ⟨10.11588/artdok.00004926⟩, Heidelberg 2017).

CERMANN, REGINA (1998), Der Verfasser der Gebete: Thomas von Kempen, in: Das Glockendon-Gebetbuch, Biblioteca Estense Universitaria, alpha. U.6.7, Kommentar zum Faksimile, Luzern: Faksimile-Verlag, 7–30.

CHAMPION, MATTHEW (2017), The Fullness of Time: Temporalities of the Fifteenth-Century Low Countries, Chicago: University of Chicago Press.

CHARTIER, ROGER (1987), The Culture of Print. Power and the Uses of Print in Early Modern Europe, Oxford: Polity Press.

CHAZELLE, CELIA (1990), Pictures, Books and the Illiterate: Pope Gregory I's Letters to Serenus of Marseilles, Word and Image 6, 138–153.

CHLENCH-PRIBER, KATHRIN (2020), Die Gebete Johanns von Neumarkt und die deutschsprachige Gebetbuchkultur des Spätmittelalters, (Münchener Texte und Untersuchungen 150), Wiesbaden: Reichert.

CHRISTIANSEN, CARL C. (1979), Art and the Reformation in Germany, Athens, Ohio: Ohio University Press.

CLANCHY, MICHAEL T. (1979), From Memory to Written Record. England 1066–1307, Cambridge: Harvard University Press.

CLARK, GREGORY T. (2013), Variant Litany Readings and the Localization of Late Medieval Manuscript Books of Hours – The d'Orge Hours, in: Sandra Hindman/James H.

364 | Gesamtbibliographie

Marrow (ed.), Books of Hours Reconsidered, London/Turnhout: Harvey Miller, 213–233.

CLICHTOVE, JOSSE VAN (1911), Article "Châtelet – Constantine", Encyclopædia Britannica, vol. 6, 507.

CLICHTOVEUS, JODOCUS (1575), Homiliae seu sermones Iudoci Clichtovei. Colonae: apud Heredes Iohannis Quentely et Geruuinum Calenium.

COLE, RICHARD G. (1984), Reformation Printers: Unsung Heroes, The Sixteenth Century Journal 15/3, 3127–3139.

COLLINSON, PATRICK (1967), The Elizabethan Puritan Movement, London: Jonathan Cape.

CONFESSIO (1986): oder Bekanntnuß des Glaubens etlicher Fürsten und Städte uberantwort Kaiserlicher Majestat zu Augsburg Anno 1530. Confessio fidei exhibita invictissimo Imperatori Carolo V. Caesari Augusto in comitiis Augustae Anno MDXXX in: Bekenntnisschriften der evangelisch-lutherischen Kirche, Göttingen: Vandenhoeck&Ruprecht.

CORBELLINI, SABRINA (2013), Cultures of Religious Reading in the Late Middle Ages: Instructing the Soul, Feeding the Spirit and Awakening the Passion, Turnhout: Brepols.

CORBELLINI, SABRINA (2012), Instructing the Soul, Feeding the Spirit and Awakening the Passion: Holy Writ and Lay Readers in Late Medieval Europe, in: Bruce Gordon/Matthew MacLean (ed.), Shaping the Bible in the Reformation: Books, Scholars and Readers in the Sixteenth Century, Leiden/Boston: Brill, 15–39.

CORBELLINI, SABRINA/HOOGVLIET, MARGRIET (2015), Holy Writ and Lay Readers in Late Medieval Europe: Translation and Participation, in: André Lardinois/Sophie Levie/Hans Hoeken/Christoph Lüthy (ed.), Texts, Transmissions, Receptions. Modern Approaches to Narratives, Leiden/Boston: Brill, 259–280.

COTOI, PAULA (2021), The Book as Object of Lay Devotion in Late Medieval Transylvania (15th – 16th centuries), Studia Universitatis Babeş-Bolyai. Historia 66 (Sp. Issue), 27–42.

COTOI, PAULA (2019), Predica medievală între oralitate și scris. Abordări metodologice și perspective transilvănene, Anuarul Institutului de Istorie "George Barițiu". Series Historica 58/Supl., 159–174.

COTOI, PAULA (2019), So Near and Yet so Far Away. The Reception of the Homiletic Works of Pelbartus de Themeswar and Osualdus de Lasko in Transylvania, Philobiblon: Transylvanian Journal of Multidisciplinary Research in Humanities 24/2, 311–335.

COVACIU, CĂTĂLINA (2018), Bunuri fără preț. Relicvele în context privat în Transilvania medievală, Buletinul Cercurilor Științifice Studențești 24, 139–162.

CRĂCIUN, MARIA (2010), Attitudes to Religious Art and the Confessional Identity of the Saxon Community. Passion Cycles in the Context of Lenten Observance and Easter Celebrations in Late Medieval and Early Modern Transylvania, Yearbook of the New Europe College, GE-NEC 2 Program, 13–70.

CRĂCIUN, MARIA (2013), Communities of Devotion: The Saxons in Early Modern Transylvania, Studia Universitatis Babeş-Bolyai. Historia 58 (Sp. Issue), 156–195.

CRĂCIUN, MARIA (2008), The Construction of Sacred Space and the Confessional Identity of the Transylvanian Lutheran Community, in: Evelin Wetter (ed.), Formierungen des Konfessionellen Raumes in Ostmitteleuropa, Stuttgart: Franz Steiner, 97–124.

Gesamtbibliographie | 365

CRĂCIUN, MARIA (2010), The Cult of St Barbara and the Saxon Community of Late Medieval Transylvania, in: Ana Marincović/Trpimir Vedriš (ed.), Identity and Alterity in Hagiography and the Cult of Saints, Zagreb: Hagiotheca, 137–163.

CRĂCIUN, MARIA (2002), Eucharistic Devotion in the Iconography of Transylvanian Polyptych Altarpieces, in: José Pedro Paiva (ed.), Religious Ceremonials and Images: Power and Social Meaning (1400–1750), Lisbon: Palimage Press, 191–230.

CRĂCIUN, MARIA (2010), Eucharistic Iconography and the Confessional Identity of the Saxon Community in Early Modern Transylvania, in: Jaroslav Miller/László Kontler (ed.), Friars, Nobles and Burghers-Sermons, Images and Prints. Studies of Culture and Society in Early Modern Europe. In memoriam István György Tóth, Budapest: Central European University, 49–71.

CRĂCIUN, MARIA (2008), Frații minori și societatea seculară: impactul spiritualității mendicante în Transilvania medievală târzie, in: Ovidiu Cristea/Gheorghe Lazăr (ed.), Vocația Istoriei. Prinos Profesorului Șerban Papacostea, Brăila: Istros, 191–220.

CRĂCIUN, MARIA (2017), "Historiae Vero Sacrae et Similes Retineantur": Funcția imaginilor produse pentru bisericile luterane ale Transilvaniei în epoca modernă timpurie, Studii și Articole de Istorie LXXXIV, 18–38.

CRĂCIUN, MARIA (2016), Imaginea și Reforma Luterană în Transilvania Modernității Timpurii, Cluj-Napoca: Editura Mega.

CRĂCIUN, MARIA (2012), Marian Imagery and its Function in the Lutheran Churches of Early Modern Transylvania, in: Andrew Spicer (ed.), Lutheran Churches in Early Modern Europe, Farnham: Ashgate, 133–164.

CRĂCIUN, MARIA (2011), Mendicant Piety and the Saxon Community of Transylvania, c. 1450–1550 in: Maria Crăciun/Elaine Fulton (ed.), Communities of Devotion. Religious Orders and Society in East Central Europe, 1450–1800, Farnham: Ashgate, 55–99.

CRĂCIUN, MARIA (2021), The Minister's Reading List: Religious Books in the Libraries of Transylvanian Lutheran Clergy, in: Howard Louthan/Drew Thomas/Elizabeth Dillenburg (ed.), Print Culture at the Crossroads: The Book and Central Europe, Leiden/Boston: Brill, 42–71.

CRĂCIUN, MARIA (2015), "Non in Mensis Ligneis sed in altaribus administratem esse Coena Domini": L'altare nelle chiese luterane della Transilvania nella prima età moderna, in: Ioan-Aurel Pop/Ovidiu Ghitta/Ioan Bolovan/Ana Victoria Sima (ed.), Dal cuore dell'Europa. Omaggio al Professor Cesare Alzati per il compimento dei 70 anni, Cluj-Napoca: Presa Universitară Clujeană, 209–228.

CRĂCIUN, MARIA (2012), "Ora pro nobis sancta Dei genitrix": Prayers and Gestures in Late Medieval Transylvania, in: Gerhard Jaritz (ed.), Ritual, Images and Daily Life. The Medieval Perspective, Wien/Zurich: Lit Verlag, 107–138.

CRĂCIUN, MARIA (2005), Polipticul și devoțiunea euharistică în Transilvania evului mediu târziu, Caiete de Antropologie Istorică 4/1, 45–110.

CRĂCIUN, MARIA (2018), The Polyptych of Dobârca and the Issue of the Text-Retable in Early Modern Transylvania, Brukenthal Acta Musei XIII/2, 179–207.

CRĂCIUN, MARIA (2014), Ritual și Recuzită: practica liturgică luterană din Transilvania modernității timpurii (secolele XVI-XVII), Ars Transsilvaniae XXIV, 133–176.

CRĂCIUN, MARIA (2015), Transylvanian Lutheran Liturgical Practices in Comparative European Perspective, in: Irene Dingel/Ute Lotz-Heumann (ed.), Entfaltung und zeitgenössische Wirkung der Reformation im europäischen Kontext / Dissemination and

366 | Gesamtbibliographie

Contemporary Impact of the Reformation in a European Context, Gütersloh: Gütersloher Verlagshaus, 345–375.

CRĂCIUN, MARIA (2021), The Voice of Pulpits. Word and Image in the Construction of Confessional Identity of Lutheran Communities in Early Modern Transylvania, in: Ulrich A. Wien (ed.), Common Man, Society and Religion in the Sixteenth Century/ Gemeindermann, Gesellschaft und Religion in 16. Jahrhundert. Piety, morality and discipline in the Carpathian Basin/Frömigkeit, Moral und Sozialdisziplinierung im Karpatenbogen, Götingen: Vandenhoeck & Ruprecht, 385–413.

CRĂCIUN, MARIA/GHITTA, OVIDIU/MURDOCK, GRAEME (2002), Religious Reform, printed books and confessional identity, in: Maria Crăciun/Ovidiu Ghitta/Graeme Murdock (ed.), Confessional Identity in East-Central Europe, Aldershot: Ashgate, 1–30.

CRESSY, DAVID (1986), Books as Totems in Seventeenth-Century England and New England, The Journal of Library History, 92–106.

CROCKETT, WILLIAM R. (1989), Eucharist: Symbol of Transformation, New York: Pueblo Publishing Company.

CUNNINGHAM, DAVID S. (1995), On Translating the Divine Name, Theological Studies, 56/3, 415–440.

CSEPREGI, ZOLTÁN (2004), Die Auffassung der Reformation bei Honterus und seinen Zeitgenossen, in: Ulrich A. Wien/Krista Zach (ed.), Humanismus in Ungarn und Siebenbürgen: Politik, Religion und Kunst im 16. Jahrhundert, Siebenbürgisches Archiv 37, Köln/Weimar/Wien: Boehlau, 1–18.

D'AVRAY, DAVID (1995), Method in the Study of Medieval Sermons, in: Nicole Bériou/ David D'Avray (ed.), Modern Questions about Medieval Sermons. Essays on Marriage, Death, History and Sanctity, Spoleto: Centro Italiano di Studi Sull'Alto Medioevo, 8–14.

DAHL, GINA (2011), Books in Early Modern Norway, Leiden/Boston: Brill.

DAVIS, THOMAS J. (1999), "The Truth of the Divine Words": Luther's Sermons on the Eucharist, 1521–28 and the Structure of Eucharistic Meaning, Sixteenth Century Journal 30/2, 323–342.

DE CEVINS, MARIE-MADELEINE (2008), Les franciscains observants hongrois de l'expansion à la débâcle (vers 1450–vers 1540), Roma: Istituto Storico dei Cappuccini.

DE CEVINS, MARIE MADELEINE (2011), The Influence of Franciscan Friars on Popular Piety in the Kingdom of Hungary at the End of the Fifteenth Century, in: Maria Crăciun/Elaine Fulton (ed.), Communities of Devotion. Religious Orders and Society in East Central Europe, 1450–1800, Farnham: Ashgate, 71–90.

DE CEVINS, MARIE-MADELEINE (2017), Le rayonnement des Franciscains de l'Óbservance en Hongrie à l'aune des entrées dans la confraternité de l'Ordre (v. 1450–v.1530), in: György Galamb (ed.), Chronica. Franciscan Observance between Italy and Central Europe. Proceedings of International Conference 4–6 December 2014, Franciscan Monastery of Szeged-Alsóváros (Hungary)/L'Osservanza Francescana fra Italia ed Europa Centrale. Atti del Convegno internazionale 4–6 dicembre 2014, Convento Francescano di Szeged-Alsóváros (Ungheria), Szeged: University of Szeged, 105–125.

DE CEVINS, MARIE MADELEINE (2001), La religion des laïcs, vue par les prédicateurs franciscains hongrois de la fin du Moyen Âge, Specimina Nova 1, 147–168.

Gesamtbibliographie | **367**

DE CEVINS, MARIE MADELEINE (2003), Le stéréotype du bon laïc dans les sermons franciscains hongrois de la fin du Moyen Âge, in: M. Grandière/M. Molin (ed.), Le stéréotype, outil de régulations sociales, Rennes: Presses Universitaires de Rennes, 15–49.

DE CEVINS, MARIE-MADELEINE (2011), Les travaux sur les ordres mendiants en Transylvanie médiévale au regard des tendances actuelles de la recherche européenne, Studia Universitatis "Babeş-Bolyai". Historia, vol. 56/1, 1–25.

DE HAMEL, CHRISTOPHER (1997), A History of Illuminated Books, 2nd edn., London: Phaidon.

DE MAERE, JAN (2007), Flämische Kunst in Siebenbürgen. Das Brukenthal-Museum in Hermanstadt/Sibiu, Antwerpen.

DEACON, TERRENCE W./CASHMAN, TYRONE (2010), The Role of Symbolic Capacity in the Origins of Religion, Journal for the Study of Religion, Nature, and Culture 3, 490–517.

DEANE, JENNIFER (2013), Pious domesticities, in: Judith M. Bennett/Ruth Mazo Karras (ed.), The Oxford Handbook of Women and Gender in Medieval Europe, Oxford: Oxford University Press, 262–278.

DELAISSÉ, L. M. J. (1974), The Importance of Books of Hours for the History of the Medieval Book, in: Ursula E. McCracken/Lilian M. C. Randall/Richard H. Randall, Jr. (ed.), Gatherings in Honor of Dorothy E. Miner, Baltimore: The Walters Art Gallery, 203–225.

DELAISSÉ, L. M. J. (1959), Le siècle d'or de la miniature flamande: Le mécénat de Philippe le Bon, Bruxelles: Palais des Beaux-Arts.

DENZINGER, HEINRICH/HÜNERMANN, PETER (ed.) (2017), Kompendium der Glaubensbekenntnisse und kirchlichen Lehrentscheidungen = Enchiridion symbolorum definitionum et declarationum de rebus fidei et morum, Freiburg/Basel/Wien: Herder.

DERBES, ANNE (1996), Picturing the Passion in Late Medieval Italy. Narrative Painting, Franciscan Ideologies, and the Levant, New York: Cambridge University Press.

DEROLEZ, ALBERT (2003), Masters and Measures. A Codicological Approach to Books of Hours, Quaerendo 33, 83–95.

DEROLEZ, ALBERT (2003), The Palaeography of Gothic Manuscript Books from the Twelfth to the Sixteenth Century, Cambridge: Cambridge University Press.

DERRIDA, JACQUES (1988), The Ear of the Other, trans. by Peggy Kamuf, Lincoln: University of Nebraska.

DIAS, ISABEL (2016), Le sermon "De sanctis martyribus quinque fratribus" de Pelbart de Themeswar, in: Eleonora Lombardo (ed.), Models of virtues. The roles of virtues in sermons and hagiography, Padova: Centro Antoniani, 189–210.

DIEDERICHS-GOTTSCHALK, DIETRICH (2005), Die protestantischen Schriftaltäre des 16. und 17. Jahrhunderts in Nordwestdeutschland. Eine Kirchen und kunstgeschichtliche Untersuchung zu einer Sonderform liturgische Ausstattung in der Epoche der Konfessionalisierung, Regensburg: Schnell und Steiner.

DILLENBERGER, JOHN/WELCH, CLAUDE (1988), Protestant Christianity: Interpreted through Its Development, New York: Macmillan.

DINCĂ, ADINEL C. (2018), "Biblioteca oraşului Sibiu" în evul mediu. Câteva consideraţii pe marginea unei confuzii istoriografice, in: Lupescu Makó Mária (ed.), Cluj – Kolozsvár – Klausenburg 700: várostörténeti tanulmányok = studii de istorie urbană, Cluj-Napoca: Erdélyi Múzeum-Egyesület, 431–436.

368 | Gesamtbibliographie

DINCĂ, ADINEL C. (2019), Codex Altemberger, in: Ginel Lazăr (ed.), Codex Altemberger. Primul cod de legi al sașilor din Sibiu, București: MNIR, 24–50.

DINCĂ, ADINEL C. (2021), Dorfkirche und Schriftlichkeit in Siebenbürgen um 1500, in: Ulrich A. Wien (ed.), Common Man, Society and Religion in the 16th century. Piety, morality and discipline in the Carpathian Basin / Gemeiner Mann, Gesellschaft und Religion im 16. Jahrhundert. Frömmigkeit, Moral und Sozialdisziplinierung im Karpatenbogen, Göttingen: Vandenhoeck & Ruprecht, 39–54.

DINCĂ, ADINEL C. (2011), Formen und Funktionen der Schriftlichkeit in spätmittelalterlichen Hermannstadt. Zum Schriftgebrauch in einer vormodernen Rechtsgemeinschaft, Berichte und Forschungen. Jahrbuch des Bundesinstituts für Kultur und Geschichte der Deutschen im östlichen Europa, 18, 290–296.

DINCĂ, ADINEL C. (2019), Illuminating the Page in Transylvania around 1500. The First Contact, Étude bibliologiques / Library research studies 1, 5–38.

DINCĂ, ADINEL C. (2017), The Medieval Book in Early Modern Transylvania. Preliminary Assessments, Studia Universitatis Babeș-Bolyai, Historia 1, 23–34.

DINCĂ, ADINEL C. (2015), Medieval Literacy in Transylvania. Selective Evidence from the Parish Church, Transylvanian Review 24/1, 109–121.

DINCĂ, ADINEL C. (2015), Notaries Public in Late Medieval Transylvania: Prerequisites for the Reception of a Legal Institution, Anuarul Institutului de Istorie "George Barițiu". Series Historica, Supplement 1, 33–47.

DINCĂ, ADINEL C. (2022), Die Prädikatur in der siebenbürgisch-sächsischen Pfarrkirche vor der Reformation. Quellenauswertung und locale Zesammenhänge in: Ulrich A. Wien (ed.), Anfänge der Reformation in Siebenbürgen, Berlin: De Gruyter, forthcoming.

DINCĂ, ADINEL C. (2015), Reading Nicholas of Dinkelsbühl in Medieval Transylvania: Surviving Texts and Historical Contexts, in: Monica Brînzei (ed.), Nicholas of Dinkelsbühl and the Sentences at Vienna in the Early XVth century, Turnhout: Brepols, 453–471.

DINCĂ, ADINEL C. (2015), Scrieri autografe în Transilvania medievală: de la cele mai timpurii mărturii, până în secolul al XVI-lea, in: Susana Andea / Avram Andea / Adinel Dincă (ed.), Autographa et signaturae Transilvaniae (sec. XIV–XVII), Cluj-Napoca / Gatineau: Argonaut / Symphologic Publishing, 11–85.

DINCĂ, ADINEL C. (2020), Scrisori private din Transilvania medievală în context local și european, Anuarul Institutului de Istorie "George Barițiu" din Cluj-Napoca, Series Historica, vol. LIX, 361–384.

DINCĂ, ADINEL C. (2019), La Transilvania nel commercio europeo di libri intorno al 1500. Stampe veneziane nella Sibiu (Cibinium – Nagyszeben – Hermannstadt) medievale, in: I Convegno della medievistica italiana. Bertinoro (Forlì-Cesena), 14–16 giugno 2018, Roma: Open Archive di Reti Medievali, 580–599.

DINCĂ, ADINEL C. (2019), The University and the Parish. The Medieval Books from Heltau / Cisnădie, Philobiblon: Transylvanian Journal of Multidisciplinary Research in Humanities, 24/2, 337–352.

DOGAER, GEORGES (1987), Flemish Miniature Painting in the 15th and 16th Centuries, Amsterdam: B.M. Israël.

DONDI, CRISTINA (2016), Printed Books of Hours from Fifteenth-century Italy. The Texts, the Books, and the Survival of a Long-lasting Genre, Florence: Olschki.

Gesamtbibliographie | 369

DORRIAN, MARK (2014), Museum Atmospheres: Notes on Aura, Distance and Affect, The Journal of Architecture 19, 187–201.

DOWNAME, GEORGE (1640), A Godly and Fruitful Exposition of the Lord's Prayer; Shewing the meaning of the words, and the duties required in several Petitions, both in respect of prayer itself, and also in respect of our lives. Printed by Roger Daniel, Printer to the University of Cambridge. This is reprinted as the second part of the above 1656 volume.

DOWNAME, GEORGE (1656), The Doctrine of Practical Praying: together with a learned exposition on the Lord's Prayer, London: Nicolaus Bourne. – https://quod.lib.umich.edu/cgi/t/text/text-idx?c=eebo;idno=A36465.0001.001.

DRUMOND, IAN CHRISTOPHER (2016), John Duns Scotus and the Role of Moral Virtues Ph.D. dissertation, University of Toronto.

DUBA, WILLIAM B. (2019), Fragmentarium. Das Mittelalter. Perspektiven mediävistischer Forschung 24/1, 221–223.

DUFY, EAMON (2006), Elite and Popular Religion: The Book of Hours and Lay Piety in the Later Middle Ages, Studies in Church History 42, 140–161.

DUFY, EAMON (2006), Marking the Hours: English People and Their Prayers 1240–1570, New Haven/London: Yale University Press.

DUFFY, EAMON (1992), The Stripping of the Altars. Traditional Religion in England 1400–1580, New Haven/London: Yale University Press.

DÜRR, RENATE (2006), Politische Strukturen in der Frühen Neuzeit: Kirchenräume in Hildesheimer Stadt- und Landgemeinden 1550-1750, Gütersloh: Gütersloher Verlagshaus.

ECO, UMBERTO (2003), Vegetal and Mineral Memory: the Future of Books, Al-Ahram, November 20–26, 665 (http://www.umbertoeco.com/en/bibliotheca-alexandrina-2003.html

EDWARDS, MARK U. Jr. (1994), Printing, Propaganda, and Martin Luther, Berkeley/Los Angeles: University of California Press.

EHLICH, KONRAD (1993), Text und sprachliches Quellen. Die Entstehung von Texten aus dem Bedürfnis nach Überlieferung, in: Aleida Assmann/Jan Assmann/Christof Hardmeier (ed.), Schrift und Gedächtnis. Beiträge zur Archäologie der literarischen Kommunikation, München: Fink, 24–43.

EHRSTINE, GLENN (2012), Passion Spectatorship between Private and Public Devotion, in Elina Gertsman/Jill Stevenson (ed.), Thresholds of Medieval Visual Culture: Liminal Spaces, Woodbridge: Boydell and Brewer, 302–320.

ELM, KASPAR (2001), Riforme e osservanze nel XIV e XV secolo. Una sinossi in: Giorgio Chittolini/Kaspar Elm (ed.), Ordini religiosi e società politica in Italia e Germania nei secoli XIV e XV, Bologna: Il Mulino, 489–504.

ELM, SUSANNE/OCKER, CHRISTOPHER (2020), Christianity and the Material: Medieval to Modern, in: Material Christianity: Western Religion and the Agency of Things, Amsterdam: Springer, 1–25.

ENENKEL, KARL A.E./MELION, WALTER (2010), Meditatio – Refashioning the Self: Theory and Practice in Late Medieval and Early Modern Intellectual Culture, Leiden: Brill.

ENGELKE, MATTHEW (2011), Material Religion, The Cambridge Companion to Religious Studies, ed. Robert A. Orsi, Cambridge: Cambridge University Press, 209–229.

Gesamtbibliographie

ENTZ, GÉZA/KOVÁCS, ANDRÁS (1995), A kolozsvári Farkas utcai templom címerei, Budapest: Balassi Könyvkiadó/Kolozsvár: Polis Könyvkiadó.

ERDEI, KLÁRA (1990), Auf dem Wege zu sich selbst: Die Meditation im 16. Jahrhundert: Eine funktionsanalytische Gattungsbeschreibung, Wiesbaden: Otto Harrassowitz.

ERDÉLYI, GABRIELLA (2012), The Consumption of the Sacred: Popular Piety in a Late Medieval Hungarian Town, Journal of Ecclesiastical History 63, 31–60.

ERLER, MARY C. (1999), Devotional Literature, in: Lotte Hellinga/J. B. Trapp (ed.), The Cambridge History of the Book in Britain, Vol. III: 1400–1557, Cambridge: Cambridge University Press, 495–525.

FALVAY, DÁVID (ed.) (2009), Árpád-házi Szent Erzsébet kultusza a 13–16. században: az Eötvös Loránd Tudományegyetem Bölcsészettudományi Karán 2007. május 24-én tartott konferencia előadásai, Budapest: Magyarok Nagyasszonya Ferences Rendtartomány.

FARA, ANDREA (2008), L'ordine e la Confraternita del Santo Spirito dalle origini allo sviluppo di una vocazione di frontiera ai confini orientali della Christianitas latina: la Transilvania tra Medioevo e prima Età moderna (XIV–XVI secolo), in: Cesare Alzati/Gabriella Rossetti (ed.), Profili istituzionali della santità medioevale. Culti importati, culti esportati e culti autoctoni nella Toscana Occidentale e nella circolazione mediterranea ed europea, Pisa: Edizioni ETS, 369–442.

FARKAS, GÁBOR (2015), Új kérdések II. Lajos rejtélyes halálával és temetésével kapcsolatosan, Magyar Könyvszemle, 381–396.

FARQUHAR, JAMES DOUGLAS (1977), The Manuscript as a Book, in: Sandra Hindman/James Douglas Farquhar, Pen to Press. Illustrated Manuscripts and Printed Books in the First Century of Printing, College Park: University of Maryland Press, 67–75.

FASSLER, MARGO (2004), Psalms and Prayers in Daily Devotion: A Fifteenth-Century Devotional Anthology from the Diocese of Rheims, Beinecke 757, in: Karin Maag/John D. Witvliet (ed.), Worship in Medieval and Early Modern Europe, Change and Continuity in Religious Practice, Notre Dame, Indiana: University of Notre Dame Press, 15–40.

FATA, MÁRTA (2000), Ungarn, das Reich der Stephanskrone, im Zeitalter der Reformation und Konfessionalisierung. Multiethnizität, Land und Konfession 1500–1700, Katholisches Leben und Kirche im Zeitalter der Glaubensspaltung 60, Münster: Aschendorf.

FIELD, RICHARD S. (1965), Fifteenth Century Woodcuts and Metalcuts: from the National Gallery of Art, Washington, D.C., Washington DC: National Gallery of Art.

FINUCANE, RONALD C. (2011), Contested Canonizations: the Last Medieval Saints, 1482–1523, Washington D.C.: Catholic University Press.

FIREA, CIPRIAN (2010), Art and its Context. Late Medieval Transylvanian Altarpieces in their Original Setting, New Europe College. GE-NEC Program, 2004–2007, 317–360.

FIREA, CIPRIAN (2010), Arta Polipticelor medievale din Transilvania (1450–1550), PhD thesis, Universitatea Babeş-Bolyai, Cluj-Napoca.

FIREA, CIPRIAN (2013), "Donatio pro memoria": lay and female donors and their remembrance in late medieval Transylvania. Research on visual and documentary evidence, Studia Universitatis Babeş-Bolyai. Historia 58 {Sp. Issue}, 107–135.

FIREA, CIPRIAN (2012), The Great Altarpiece of the Passion from Sibiu and its Painters, Brukenthal. Acta Musei VII/2, 229–246.

FIREA, CIPRIAN (2012), Liturgie médiévale et architecture gothique dans l'église paroissiale de Sibiu (1350–1550), in: Arhitectura religioasă medievală din Transilvania/

Gesamtbibliographie | **371**

Középkori egyházi építészet Erdélyben/Medieval Ecclesiastical Architecture of Transylvania, V, Satu-Mare: Ed. Muzeului Sătmărean, 275–318.

FIREA, CIPRIAN (2018), The Pietà of Sibiu: Patronage of the Urban Elite in Transylvania around 1400, in: Susan Marti/Richard Němec/Marius Winzeler (ed.), Pražská Pieta v Bernu: předmět obchodu – modla – muzejní exponát / Die Prager Pietà in Bern: Handelsgut – Götzenbild – Museumsexponat, Praze: Národní Galerie, 191–202.

FIREA, CIPRIAN/DINCĂ, ADINEL C. (2015–2016), Breslele artistice din Transilvania medievală și regulamentele lor. Un statut nou descoperit de la Bistrița, Ars Transsilvaniae, 28, 173–184.

FLÓRA, ÁGNES (2014), The Matter of Honour. The Leading Urban Elite in Sixteenth Century Cluj and Sibiu, PhD thesis, Central European University, Budapest.

FLOREA, CARMEN (2013), Beyond the late medieval economy of salvation: the material running of the Transylvanian mendicant convents, Hereditas Monasteriorum 3, 97–110.

FLOREA, CARMEN (2013), Civic Control of Sainthood in Late Medieval Transylvania, Studia Universitatis Babeș-Bolyai. Historia 58, 136–156.

FLOREA, CARMEN (2009), The Construction of Memory and the Display of Social Bonds in the Life of Corpus Christi Fraternity from Sibiu (Hermannstadt, Nagyszeben), in: Lucie Doležalova (ed.), The Making of Memory in the Middle Ages, Leiden/Boston: Brill, 283–309.

FLOREA, CARMEN (2008), Identitate urbană și patronaj marian în evul mediu târziu [Urban Identity and Marian Patronage in the Late Middle Ages], Studia Universitatis Cibiniensis, Series Historica V, 59–81.

FLOREA, CARMEN (2011), The Third Path: Charity and Devotion in Late Medieval Transylvanian Towns, in: Maria Crăciun, Elaine Fulton (ed.), Communities of Devotion. Religious Orders and Society in East Central Europe, 1450–1800, Farnham: Ashgate, 91–120.

FODOR, ISTVÁN (2015), Marosvásárhelyi krónikás füzetek I – II, in: Sebestyén Mihály (ed.), Erdélyi Ritkaságok 9, Neumarkt am Mieresch: Mentor.

FRANKE, ERHARD (2004), Kirchliches und schulisches Musizieren der Siebenbürger Sachsen im 16. Jahrhundert, in: Ulrich A. Wien/Krista Zach (ed.), Humanismus in Ungarn und Siebenbürgen: Politik, Religion und Kunst im 16. Jahrhundert, Köln/Weimar/Wien: Boehlau, 65–134.

FREEDBERG, DAVID (1971), Johannes Molanus on provocative paintings. De historia sanctarum imaginum et picturarum, book II, chapter 42, Journal of the Warburg and Courtauld Institutes, 34, 229–245.

GALAMB, GYÖRGY (1997), San Giacomo della Marca e gli eretici di Ungheria, in: Silvano Bracci (ed.), San Giacomo della Marca nell' Europa del'400. Atti del Convegno internazionale di studi. Monteprandone, 7–10 settembre 1994, Padova: Centro Studi Antoniani, 211–220.

GARRETT, CYNTHIA (1993), The Rhetoric of Supplication: Prayer Theory in Seventeenth-Century England, Renaissance Quarterly, 46 (2), 328–357.

GAVRILUȚĂ, NICU (2003), Fractalii și timpul social, Cluj-Napoca: Dacia.

GAVRILUȚĂ, NICU (2015), Mit, magie și manipulare politică, Iași: Institutul European.

GEARY, PATRICK (1994), Living with the Dead in the Middle Ages, Ithaca/London: Cornell University Press.

372 | Gesamtbibliographie

GECSER, OTTÓ (2007), Aspects of the Cult of St. Elizabeth of Hungary with a Special Emphasis on Preaching, 1231 – ca. 1500, PhD thesis, Budapest: Central European University.

GECSER, OTTÓ (2005), Il miracolo delle rose, in: Annuario 2002–2004: Conferenze e convegni, Roma, 240–247.

GECSER, OTTÓ (2014), Predicazione, formazione scolastica e modelli culturali nell'Osservanza francescana ungherese alla fine del medioevo, in: Francesca Bartolacci/Roberto Lambertini (ed.), Osservanza francescana e cultura tra Quattrocento e primo Cinquecento: Italia e Ungheria a confronto. Atti del Convegno Macerata-Sarnano, 6–7 dicembre 2013, Roma: Viella, 33–52.

GESTA (2009), Making Thoughts, Making Pictures, Making Memories: A Special Issue in Honor of Mary J. Carruthers, 48/2.

GINZBURG, CARLO (1979), Clues: Roots of a Scientific Paradigm, Theory and Society 7/3, 273–288.

GÖHLER, JOHANNES (1990), Ringstedt. Geschichte eines Kirchsspiel an der Oberen Geeste von der Christianisierung, bis zum Jahre 1900, Ringstedt.

GÖHLER, JOHANNES (1997), Aus der Geschichte des Kirchspiels, Debstedt.

GORDON, BRUCE/MARSHALL, PETER (2000), The Place of the Dead: Death and Remembrance in Late Medieval and Early Modern Europe, Cambridge: Cambridge University Press.

GOULD, KAREN (1989), Roger Wieck, Time Sanctified: the Book of Hours in Medieval Art and Life (Book Review), The Papers of the Bibliographical Society of America 83/1, 233–237.

GOW, ANDREW (2005), Challenging the Protestant Paradigm: Bible Reading in Lay Urban Contexts of the Later Middle Ages, in: T.J. Heffernan/T.E. Burman (ed.), Scripture and Pluralism. Reading the Bible in the Religiously Plural Worlds of the Middle Ages and Renaissance, Leiden/Boston: Brill, 161–91.

GOWLETT, J.A.J. (2016), The Discovery of Fire by Humans: A Long and Convoluted Process, Philosophical Transactions of the Royal Society B371, (http://dx.doi.org/10.1098/rstb.2015.0164, accessed 13 January 2021).

GRAF, TOBIAS P. (2017), The Sultan's Renegades: Christian-European Converts to Islam and the Making of the Ottoman Elite, 1575–1610, Oxford: Oxford University Press.

GROSS, JULIUS (1886), Seltene Druckwerke in der Bibliothek des evang. Gymnasiums A. B. in Kronstadt, Korrespondenzblatt des Vereins für siebenbürgische Landeskunde IX/1, 1–5.

GROSS, JULIUS (1887), Zur ältesten Geschichte der Kronstädter Gymnasialbibliothek, Archiv des Vereins für siebenbürgische Landeskunde 21, 591–708.

GROSS, JULIUS (1927), Honterus Schriften, Gross Julius (ed.), Schriften des Johannes Honterus, Valentin Wagner und Markus Fronius, Kronstadt, Gutenberg.

GROSS, JULIUS, (ed.) (1896), Quellen zur Geschichte der Stadt Kronstadt 3: Rechnungen aus (1475), 1511–1550 (1571), Kronstadt: Zeidner.

GROSS, LIDIA (2003), Confreria Capitlului de Sibiu, Anuarul Institutului de Istorie "George Barițiu", Series Historica XLII, 161–170.

GUDOR, BOTOND KUND (2012), Az eltűnt Gyulafehérvári Református Egyházmegye és egyházi közösségei. Inquisitoria Dioceseos Alba-Carolinensis Reformatae relatoria, Kolozsvár – Barót: Kriterion.

GÜNDISCH, GUSTAV (1977), Die Bibliothek des Superintendenten der evangelischen Kirche Siebenbürgens, Matthias Schiffbäumer (1547–1611), Revue des Études Sud-Est Européennes XV/3, 463–478.

GÜNDISCH, GUSTAV (1987), Die Bibliothek des Damasus Dürr (1585), in: Gustav Gündisch, Aus Geschichte und Kultur der Siebenbürger Sachsen. Ausgewählte Aufsätze und Berichte, Köln/Wien: Böhlau, 340–350.

GÜNDISCH, GUSTAV (1987), Die Oberschicht Hermannstadts im Mittelalter, in: Gustav Gündisch, Aus Geschichte und Kultur der Siebenbürger Sachsen. Ausgewählte Aufsätze und Berichte, Köln/Wien: Böhlau, 182–200.

GÜNDISCH, GUSTAV (1987), Eine siebenbürgische Bischofsbibliothek des 16. Jahrhunderts. Die Bücherei des Lukas Unglerus, in: Gündisch, Aus Geschichte und Kultur der Siebenbürger Sachsen, Köln/Wien: Böhlau, 351–362.

GÜNDISCH, GUSTAV/NÄGLER, DOINA (1992), Die Bücherei des Hermannstädter ev. Stadtpfarrens Petrus Rihelius (1648) und seiner Söhne, Zeitschrift für Siebenbürgische Landeskunde 15/1, 41–62.

GÜNDISCH, GUSTAV/NÄGLER, DOINA (1994), Die Bibliothek des Hermannstädter ev. Stadtpfarrens Andreas Oltard (1660) und seiner Familie, Zeitschrift für Siebenbürgische Landeskunde 17/2, 121–143.

HAAGE, BERNHARD (1968), Der Traktat "Von dreierlei Wesen der Menschen", Inauguraldissertation zur Erlangung der Doktorwürde der Philosophischen Fakultät der Ruprecht-Karl-Universität Heidelberg, Heidelberg.

HABERKERN, ERNST (2003), Die "Wiener Schule" der Pastoraltheologie im 14. und 15. Jahrhundert: Entstehung, Konstituenten, literarische Wirkung, I – II, Göppingen: Kümmerle.

HAEMIG, MARY JANE (2004), Jehoshaphat and His Prayer among Sixteenth Century Lutherans, Church History 73/3, 522–535.

HAEMIG, MARY JANE (2016), Little Prayer Book. 1522, in: Mary Jane Haemig (ed.), The Annotated Luther volume 4 Pastoral Writings, Minneapolis, Minnesota: Fortress Press, 159–165.

HAIGH, CHRISTOPHER (1993), English Reformations: Religion, Politics, and Society under the Tudors, Oxford: Clarendon Press.

HAIGH, CHRISTOPHER (1975), Reformation and Resistance in Tudor Lancashire, New York: Cambridge University Press.

HAIGH, CHRISTOPHER (2001), Success and Failure in the English Reformation, Past & Present 173, 28–49.

HAIMERL, FRANZ X. (1952), Mittelalterliche Frömmigkeit im Spiegel der Gebetbuchliteratur Süddeutschlands, (Münchener theologische Studien I,4.), München: Zink.

HAMBURGER, JEFFREY (2013), Another Perspective. The Book of Hours in Germany, in: Sandra Hindman/James Marrow (ed.), Books of Hours Reconsidered, Studies in Medieval and Early Renaissance Art History, Turnhout: Harvey Miller, 97–152.

HAMBURGER, JEFFREY (1998), The Visual and the Visionary: Art and Female Spirituality in Late Medieval Germany, New York/London: Zone Books.

HAMBURGER, JEFFREY (1989), The Visual and the Visionary: The Image in Late Medieval Monastic Devotion, Viator 20, 161–182.

HAMM, BERNDT (2016), Ablass und Reformation – Erstaunliche Kohärenzen, Tübingen: Mohr Siebeck.

374 | Gesamtbibliographie

HAMM, BERNDT (2004), Lazarus Spengler (1479–1534). Der Nürnberger Ratsschreiber im Spannungsfeld von Humanismus und Reformation, Politik und Glaube, Spätmittelalter und Reformation. NR 25, Tübingen: Mohr Siebeck.

HAMM, BERNDT (2004), The Reformation of Faith in the Context of Late Medieval Theology and Piety, ed. Robert J. Bast, Leiden: Brill.

HAMM, BERNDT (2011), Religiosität im späten Mittelalter. Spannungspole, Neuaufbrüche, Normierungen, Reinhold Friedrich / Wolfgang Simon (ed.), Tübingen: Mohr Siebeck.

HAMM, BERNDT / LENTES, THOMAS (ed.) (2001), Spätmittelalterliche Frömmigkeit zwischen Ideal und Praxis, Tübingen: Mohr Siebeck.

HANER, GEORG (1694), Historia ecclesiarum Transylvanicarum. Francofurti et Lipsiae, Fölginer.

HARBISON, CRAIG (1985), Visions and Meditations in Early Flemish Paintings, Simiolus 15, 87–118.

HARTHAN, JOHN (1977), Books of Hours and Their Owners, London: Book Club Associates.

HAUG, WALTER / WACHINGER, BURGHART (ed.) (1993), Die Passion Christi in Literatur und Kunst des Spätmittelalters, Tübingen: M. Niemeyer.

HEINZER, FELIX (1989), Aus Handschriften und Inkunabeln der Historischen Lehrerbibliothek des Ludwig-Wilhelm-Gymnasiums, Vortragsreihe der Historischen Lehrerbibliothek des Ludwig-Wilhelm-Gymnasiums in Rastatt 1, Rastatt: Stadtverwaltung Rastatt, 46–49.

HEITZMANN CHRISTIAN / KRUSSE, BRITTA-JULIANNE / LESSER, BERTRAM (ed.) (2015), Bilder lesen: deutsche Buchmalerei des 15. Jahrhunderts in der Herzog August Bibliothek Wolfenbüttel: Katalog zur Ausstellung in der Herzog August Bibliothek vom 22. November 2015 bis 28. Februar 2016, Buchmalerei des 15. Jahrhunderts in Mitteleuropa 13, Luzern: Quaternio.

HENNECKE, A. B. D., (ed.) ([1792]), Breviarium Ecclesiæ Cathedralis Halberstadiensis Juxta Ritum Antiquum Una Cum Missis Festorum Principalium Singularumque Dominicarum, Halberstadii: Delianus.

HENRIET, PATRICK (2006), Prière, expérience et fonction au Moyen Âge: Remarques introductives, in: Jean-François Cottier (ed.), La prière en latin, de l'Antiquité au XVIe siècle. Formes, évolutions, significations, Turnhout: Brepols, 197–207.

HERBERT, HEINRICH (1883), Die Reformation in Hermannstadt und dem Hermannstädter Capitel: Festschrift zur 400-jährigen Gedächtnißfeier der Geburt Dr. Martin Luthers, Hermannstadt: von Closius.

HERING, RAINER (2008), Vom Umgang mit theologischen Außenseitern im 20. Jahrhundert, Kirchliche Zeitgeschichte (20. Jahrhundert), ed. Rainer Hering / Inge Mager, (Hamburgische Kirchengeschichte in Aufsätzen, 5), Hamburg: Hamburg University Press, 375–398.

HINDMAN, SANDRA (2013), Books of Hours: State of the Research. In Memory of L. M. J. Delaissé, in: Sandra Hindman / James H. Marrow (ed.), Books of Hours Reconsidered, London: Harvey Miller, 5–16.

HOLL, KARL (1923), Luther, Gesammelte Aufsätze zur Kirchengeschichte, Tübingen: J. C. B. Mohr.

HOLLSTEIN, F[RIEDRICH] W[ILHELM] H[EINRICH] (1954), German Engravings, Etchings and Woodcuts ca. 1450–1700, Bd. 1 ff. Amsterdam: Sound & Vision Publishers.

Gesamtbibliographie | 375

HONÉE, EUGÈNE (1994), Image and imagination in the medieval culture of prayer: a historical perspective, in: Henk van Os (ed.), The Art of Devotion in the Late Middle Ages in Europe 1300–1500, London: Merrell Holberton, 157–174.

HONEMANN, VOLKER (1978), Art. "Beda", VerLex 1, Berlin/New York: De Gruyter, 660–663.

HONTERUS, JOHANNES (1896), Reformatio Ecclesiae Coronensis ac Totius Barcensis Provinciae, Coronae MDXLIII, in: Oskar Netoliczka (ed.), Johannes Honterus's ausgewählte Schriften. Im Auftrage des Ausschusses zur Errichtung des Honterusdenkmals in Kronstadt, Hermannstadt, 11–28.

HOOGVLIET, MARGRIET (2013), Encouraging Lay People to Read the Bible in the French Vernaculars: New Groups of Readers and Textual Communities, Church History and Religious Culture 93/2, 239–274.

HOOGVLIET, MARGRIET (2013), The Medieval Vernacular Bible in French as a Flexible Text: Selective and Discontinuous Reading Practices, in: Eyal Poleg/Laura Light (ed.), Form and Function in the Late Medieval Bible, Leiden/Boston: Brill, 283–306.

HORTULUS ANIME | zu tewtsch Selen wuertz-| gertlein genant/mit viel schoe | nen gebeten vnd figuren, Nürnberg: Peypus, 1519.

HORVÁTH, JÁNOS (1931), A magyar irodalmi műveltség kezdetei, Budapest: Magyar Szemle Társaság.

HOUSTON, RAB (1983), Literacy and Society in the West 1500–1850, Social History 8/3, 269–293.

HUPFER, GEORG (2003), Zur Geschichte des antiquarischen Buchhandels in Wien, Diplomarbeit zur Erlangung des Magistergrades der Philosophie aus der Studienrichtung Deutsche Philologie eingereicht des Geistes- und Kulturwissenschaftlichen Fakultät der Universität Wien. – https://www.wienbibliothek.at/sites/default/files/files/buchforschung/hupfer-georg-antiquariat-wien.pdf (30.01.2020).

HUTTON, RONALD (1987), The Local Impact of the Tudor Reformation, in: Cristopher Haigh (ed.), The English Reformation Revised, Cambridge: Cambridge University Press, 114–138.

ITTU, CONSTANTIN (2017), Instantia Crucis, Sibiu: Editura Andreiana, Editura Universităţii Lucian Blaga.

ITTU, CONSTANTIN (2012), Omilii nerostite, Sibiu: Editura Andreiana.

JAKÓ, ZSIGMOND (1977), Tiparul cu litere latine din Sibiu în secolul al XVI-lea, in: Zsigmond Jakó, Philobiblon Transilvan, Bucureşti: Kriterion, 93–116.

JAKOBI-MIRWALD, CHRISTINE (2004), Das mittelalterliche Buch. Funktion und Ausstattung, Stuttgart: Reclam.

JENEI, DANA (2004), Art and Mentality in late Middle Age Transylvania, Getty-NEC Yearbook, 2000–2001, 2001–2002, Bucureşti: NEC, 13–71.

JENEI, DANA (2014), The Passion, Death and Resurrection of Jesus Christ painted inside St. Matthias Church in Râşnov (1500), Studii şi Cercetări de Istoria Artei. Artă Plastică, 4(48), 9–27.

JENEI, DANA (2014), Thèmes iconographiques et images dévotionnelles dans la peinture murale médiévale tardive de Transylvanie (deuxième partie du XVe siècle – premier quart du XVIe siècle), Revue Roumaine d'Histoire de l'Art: Série Beaux-Arts 51/1, 11–35.

376 | Gesamtbibliographie

Jürgens, Henning P. (2015), Das Evangelium singen. Gesangbücher und bezahlter im europäischen Kontext, in: I. Dingel/U. Lotz-Heumann (ed.), Entfaltung und zeitgenössische Wirkung der Reformation im europäischen Kontext = Dissemination and Contemporary Impact of the Reformation in a European Context. Schriften des Vereins für Reformationsgeschichte 216, Gütersloh: Gütersloher Verlagshaus, 103–123.

Karácsonyi, János (1924), Szent Ferenc rendjének története Magyarországon 1711-ig, Budapest: Magyar Tud. Akadémia.

Karant-Nunn, Susan (1997), The Reformation of Ritual. An interpretation of early modern Germany, London: Routledge.

Karteizettel (undatiert), Staatsarchiv Klausenburg: Bestand des Siebenbürgischen Museum-Vereins, Nr. 298, Ordner 94: Alphabetische Karteizettel der Spender des Siebenbürgischen Museum-Vereins.

Katona Geleji, István (1638), Praeconium Evangelicum in quo Evangelia omnia Anniversaria, vulgo Dominicalia vocitata, concionibus CCXII ... explicantur ac enarrantur; ... quod quidem in Aedificationem imprimis Aulae Transsylvanicae, ac Ecclesiae Albae-Juliensis ... enuntiatum, nunc vero ... recognitum, auctum, ac in gratiam neophitorum verbi Dei Praeconum publici juris et usus factum per Stepanum Katona Gelejinum ... (Praeconii evangelici tomus primus, seu pars hymealis ac vernalis continens omnium evangelium Dominicalium a Dominica I. Adventus ad festum usque Pentecostes novae ... concionibus C. et XIX. comprehensam analysin ac exegesin, cum indice triplici... studio et opera Stephani Katona Geleji ..., Albae-Juliae: [typis principis].

Kelberg, Karsten (1983), Die Darstellung der Gregorsmesse in Deutschland, Münster: Univ. Diss.

Kelecsényi, Ákos (ed.) (1988), A hamisítások és Literáti Nemes Sámuel, in: Múltunk neves könyvgyűjtői, Budapest: Gondolat, 108–114.

Kelecsényi, Ákos (1971), Literáti Nemes Sámuel útinaplója, in: Az Országos Széchenyi Könyvtár évkönyve, 1968–1669, Budapest: OSZK, 317–330.

Kelecsényi, Ákos, (1975), Egy magyar régiségkereskedő a 19. században. Literáti Nemes Sámuel (1794–1842), in: Az Országos Széchenyi Könyvtár évkönyve – 1972, 307–327. Budapest: OSZK.

Kelecsényi, Ákos (1988), Literáti Nemes Sámuel 1794–1842, in: Múltunk neves könyvgyűjtői, Budapest: Gondolat, 102–107.

Keller, Hagen/Grubmüller, Klaus (ed.) (1992), Pragmatische Schriftlichkeit im Mittelalter. Erscheinungsform und Entwicklungsstufen, München: Fink.

Kemperdick, Stephan (2007), Kreis und Kosmos. Ein restauriertes Tafelbild des 15. Jahrhunderts, mit einem Beitrag von Amelie Jensen zu Maltechnik und Restaurierung, Kunstmuseum Basel, 18.8.–11.11.2007, Petersberg: Michael Imhof Verlag.

Kennedy, Kirsten (2015), 'Seeing is Believing': The Miniatures of the Cantigas de Santa Maria and Medieval Devotional Practices', Portuguese Studies 31/2, 169–182.

Kenyeres, Ágnes (ed.) (1967), Magyar életrajzi lexikon, Budapest: Akadémiai.

Kertész, Balázs (2017), The 1499 Constitutions of the Hungarian Observant Franciscan vicariate, in: György Galamb (ed.), Chronica. Franciscan Observance between Italy and Central Europe. Proceedings of International Conference 4–6 December 2014, Franciscan Monastery of Szeged-Alsóváros (Hungary)/L'Osservanza francescana fra Italia

Gesamtbibliographie | **377**

ed Europa Centrale. Atti del Convegno internazionale 4–6 dicembre 2014, Convento Francescano di Szeged-Alsóváros (Ungheria), Szeged: University of Szeged, 173–187.

KETLEY, REV. JOSEPH (1844), The Two Liturgies A.D. 1549 and A.D. 1552 with Other Documents Set Forth by Authority in the Reign of King Edward VI viz. The Order of Communion, 1548, the Primer, 1553, The Catechism and Articles, 1553, Catechismus Brevis, 1553, Cambridge: The University Press.

KEUL, ISTVÁN (2009), Early Modern Religious Communities in East-Central Europe: Ethnic Diversity, Denominational Plurality, and Corporative Politics in the Principality of Transylvania (1526–1691), Leiden: Brill.

KIECKHEFER, RICHARD (1989), Major Currents in Late Medieval Devotion, in: Jill Raitt et alii (ed.), Christian Spirituality: High Middle Ages and Reformation, New York, London: Routledge & Kegan Paul, 75–108.

KINGDON, R.M. (1966), Patronage, Piety and Printing in Sixteenth Century Europe, in: D. H. Pinkney/T. Rupp (ed.), A Festschrift for Frederick B. Artz, Durham, N.C.

KINGDON, ROBERT (2004), Worship in Geneva before and after the Reformation, in: Karin Maag/John D. Witvliet (ed.), Worship in Medieval and Early Modern Europe. Change and Continuity in Religious Practice, Notre Dame, Indiana: University of Notre Dame Press, 41–62.

KIRCHENORDNUNG (1554), Wie es mit Christlicher Lere, reichung der Sacrament, Ordination der Diener des Euangelij, ordenlichen Ceremonien, in den Kirchen, Visitation, Consistorio vnd Schulen, Jm Hertzogthumb zu Meckelnburg etc. gehalten wird, Wittenberg, Hans Lufft.

KIRCHENORDNUNG (1559), Wie es mit Christlicher Lere, reichung der Sacrament, Ordination der Diener des Euangelij, ordenlichen Ceremonien, in den Kirchen, Visitation, Consistorio vnd Schulen, zu Witteberg, vnd in etlichen Chur vnd Fuerstenthum, Herrschafften vnd Stedte der Augsburgischen Confession verwand, gehalten wird, Wittenberg, Hans Lufft. Bibliothek der Kreisdienststelle Hermannstadt des Rumänischen Nationalarchivs (rum. Arhivele Naţionale ale României, Serviciul Judeţean Sibiu, biblioteca, Signatur: II--4899.

KLANICZAY, GÁBOR (2004), Proving sanctity in the canonization processes. (Saint Elizabeth and Saint Margaret of Hungary), in: Klaniczay, Gábor, Procès de canonisation au Moyen Âge. Aspects juridiques et religieux – Medieval Canonization Processes. Legal and Religious Aspects, Roma: École Française de Rome, 117–148.

KLANICZAY, GÁBOR (2000), Az uralkodók szentsége a középkorban. Magyar dinasztikus szentkultuszok és európai modellek, Budapest: Balassi.

KLAPPER, JOSEPH (1935), Schriften Johanns von Neumarkt. Vierter Teil: Gebete des Hofkanzlers und des Prager Kulturkreises. Vom Mittelalter zur Reformation, Forschungen zur Geschichte der deutschen Bildung, Bd. VI,4, Berlin: Weidmann.

KLEIN, KARL KURT (1935), Der Humanist und Reformator Johannes Honter. Untersuchungen zur siebenbürgischen Geistes- und Reformationsgeschichte, Hermannstadt: Krafft und Drotleff.

KNAPE, JOACHIM/WILHELMI, THOMAS (2015), Sebastian Brant Bibliographie. Werke und Überlieferungen, Gratia 53, Wiesbaden: Harrassowitz.

KNODT, GERHARD (1998), Leitbilder des Glaubens. Die Geschichte des Heiligengedenkens in der evangelischen Kirche, Stuttgart: Calwer.

378 | Gesamtbibliographie

Kodres, Krista (2006), Lutheran Internationalism of Estonian Art Production in the 16th – 18th centuries: the Pulpit, in: Jan Harasimowicz/P. Oszczanowski/Marcin Wisłocki (ed.), On Opposite Sides of the Baltic Sea. Relations between Scandinavia and Central European Countries, Wroclaw: Via Nova, 381–393.

Koerner, Joseph Leo (2004), The Reformation of the Image, London: Reaktion Books.

König, Eberhard (1997), Augsburger Buchkunst an der Schwelle zur Frühdruckzeit, in: H. Gier/J. Janota (ed.), Augsburger Buchdruck und Verlagswesen: von den Anfängen bis zur Gegenwart, Wiesbaden: Harrassowitz, 173–200.

Konrád, Eszter (2017), The Representations of the Saints of the Mendicant Orders in Late Medieval Hungary, Doctoral Dissertation, Medieval Studies Department, Central European University, Budapest.

Kónya, Anna (2017), Eucharistic references in the representations of saints: A case study of Late Gothic wall paintings in Transylvania, Acta Historiae Artium Academiae Scientiarum Hungaricae AHistA 58/1, 85–113.

Kootz, Julius (1890), Kirchenvisitationen im siebenbürgisch-deutschen Unterwald. Ein Beitrag zur Kirchen- und Kulturgeschichte des 17. Jahrhunderts, in: J. Wolff (ed.), Programm des vierklassigen Evangelischen Gymnasiums und der damit verbundenen Elementarschule in Mühlbach (Siebenbürgen) für das Schuljahr 1889/90, Hermannstadt: Krafft, 5–32.

Köpeczi, Béla et al. (ed.) (1994), History of Transylvania, Budapest: Akadémiai Kiadó.

Korányi, András (2005), Egy XVI. századi ferences beginaszabályzat in: Őze Sándor/ Medgyesy-Schmikli Norbert (ed.), A ferences lelkiség hatása az újkori Közép-Európa történetére és kultúrájára, Budapest – Piliscsaba: PPLE – METEM, 130–143.

Korondi, Ágnes (2016), Misztika a késő középkori magyar nyelvű kolostori kódexirodalomban, Kolozsvár: Egyetemi Műhely Kiadó, Bolyai Társaság.

Kren, Thomas/Mckendrick, Scot (2003), Illuminating the Renaissance: The Triumph of Flemish Manuscript Painting in Europe, Los Angeles: Paul Getty.

Kühne, Hartmut/Bünz, Enno/Müller, Thomas T. (ed.) (2013), Alltag und Frömmigkeit am Vorabend der Reformation in Mitteldeutschland. Katalog zur Ausstellung "Umsonst ist der Tod", Petersberg: Michael Imhof Verlag.

Kühnel, Harry (ed.) (1992), Bildwörterbuch der Kleidung und Rüstung: vom Alten Orient bis zum ausgehenden Mittelalter, Stuttgart: Alfred Kröner.

Kührer-Wielach, Florian (2015), Siebenbürgen als administrative Einheit und diskursives Konzept, in: Oliver Jens Schmitt/Michael Metzeltin (ed.), Das Südosteuropa der Regionen. Wien: Verlag der Österreichischen Akademie der Wissenschaften, 349–409.

Lähnemann, Henrike (2016), The Materiality of Medieval Manuscripts, Oxford German Studies, 45/2, 121–141.

Landmann, Florenz (1927), Zum Predigtwesen der Straßburger Franziskanerprovinz in der letzten Zeit des Mittelalter, Franziskanische Studien 14, 297–332.

Láng, Benedek (2014), Invented Middle Age in Nineteenth-century Hungary. The Forgeries of Sámuel Literáti Nemes, in: M. János Bak/Patrick J. Geary/Gábor Klaniczay (ed.), Manufacturing a Past for the Present. Forgery and Authenticity, in Medievalist Texts and Objects in Nineteenth-Century Europe, Leiden/Boston: Brill, 129–155.

Lang, Helen S. (1983), Bodies and Angels: The Occupants of Place for Aristotle and Duns Scotus, 14, 245–266.

Gesamtbibliographie | 379

LAUGERUD, HENNING/RYAN, SALVADOR/SKINNEBACH, LAURA KATRINE (ed.) (2016), The Materiality of Devotion in Late-Medieval Northern Europe: Images, Objects and Practices, Dublin: Four Courts.

LE LOUP, WILLI (1981), Vlaamse kunst op perkament. Handschriften en miniaturen te Brugge van de 12de tot de 16de eeuw, Brugge: Gruuthusemuseum.

LEESE, KURT (1938/1948), Die Religion der Protestantischen Menschen, Berlin/Munich.

LENTES, THOMAS (1996), Gebetbuch und Gebärde. Religiöses Ausdrucksverhalten, in Gebetbüchern aus dem Dominikanerinnen-Kloster St. Nikolaus in undis zu Straßburg (1350–1550). Inaugural-Dissertation zur Erlangung der theologischen Doktorwürde der Katholisch-Theologischen Fakultät der Westfälischen Wilhelms-Universität, Münster in Westfalen.

LENTES, THOMAS (2007), Verum Corpus und Vera imago. Kalkulierte Bildbeziehungen in der Gregorsmesse, in: A. Garmans/Th. Lentes (ed.), Das Bild der Erscheinung. Die Gregorsmesse im Mittelalter, Berlin: Reimer, 13–35.

LEPPIN, VOLKER (2017), Die fremde Reformation. Die mystischen Wurzeln Martin Luthers, München: C.H. Beck.

LEPPIN, VOLKER (2017), Transformationen. Studien zu den Wandlungsprozessen in Theologie und Frömmigkeit zwischen Spätmittelalter und Reformation, Tübingen: Mohr Siebeck, 2. Aufl.

LEPPIN, VOLKER (2015), Die Wittenberger Reformation und der Prozess der Transformation kultureller zu institutionellen Polaritäten, in: ders., Transformationen. Studien zu den Wandlungsprozessen in Theologie und Frömmigkeit zwischen Spätmittelalter und Reformation, Spätmittelalter, Humanismus, Reformation 86, Tübingen: Mohr Siebeck.

LEROQUAIS, VICTOR (1927), Les Livres d'heures manuscrits de la Bibliothèque Nationale, 3 vols., Paris: s.n.

LIPSIUS, JUSTUS (1605), Diva virgo Hallensis: Beneficia eius & miracvla fide atque ordine descripta. Antverpiae: ex Officina Plantiniana, apud Ioannem Moretum.

LIST, GERHARD (2018), Die Handschriften der Stadtbibliothek Mainz, Bd. IV: Hs I 351 – Hs I 490. Überarbeitung, Nachträge und Register von Annelen Ottermann unter Mitarbeit von Christoph Winterer, Wiesbaden: Harrassowitz.

LISTE (1860–1890), Staatsarchiv Klausenburg: Bestand des Siebenbürgischen Museum-Vereins, Nr. 298, Ordner 241: Liste der Spenden (Bücher, Manuskripte, Museumsstücke).

LOBRICHON, GUY (1994), La religion des laïcs en Occident : XIe–XVe siècles, Paris: Hachette.

LUHRMANN, TANYA (2004), Metakinesis: How God Becomes Intimate in Contemporary U.S. Christianity, American Anthropologist 106, 518–528.

LUHRMANN, TANYA (2012), When God Talks Back: Understanding the American Evangelical Relationship with God, New York: Alfred A. Knopf.

LUPESCU MAKÓ, MÁRIA (2017), The Book Culture of the Dominican Order in Transylvania, Philobiblon: Transylvanian Journal of Multidisciplinary Research in Humanities, 22/1, 187–204.

LUPESCU MAKÓ, MÁRIA (2004), Death and Remembrance in Late Medieval Sighişoara (Segesvár, Schässburg), Caiete de Antropologie Istorică 1–2, 93–106.

LUPESCU MAKÓ, MÁRIA (2001), "Item lego…". Gifts for the Soul in Late Medieval Transylvania, Annual of Medieval Studies at CEU 7, 161–185.

380 | Gesamtbibliographie

LUPESCU MAKÓ, MÁRIA (2013), The Transylvanian Nobles: Between Heavenly and Earthly Interests in the Middle Ages, Studia Universitatis Babeş-Bolyai. Historia 58 (Sp. Issue), 78–106.

LUPESCU, RADU (2003), A tövisi ferences kolostor középkori történetének és építéstörténetének néhány kérdése, Református Szemle 6:96, 830–844.

LUTHER, MARTIN (1905), Acht Sermone D. M. Luthers von ihm gepredigt zu Wittenberg in der Fasten, 1522, WA 10/III, 1–64.

LUTHER, MARTIN (1907), Betbüchlein, 1522, WA 10/2, 331–501.

LUTHER, MARTIN (1897), Deutsche Messe und Ordnung Gottesdiensts, 1526, WA 19, 70–113.

LUTHER, MARTIN (1891), Formula missae et communionis, 1523, WA 12, 205–220.

LUTHER, MARTIN (1912), Eine einfältige Weise zu beten für einen guten Freund, 1535, WA 38, 351–375.

LUTHER, MARTIN (1884), Ein Sermon von dem hochwürdigen Sakrament des heiligen wahren Leichnams Christi und von den Bruderschaften, 1519, WA 2, 738–741, 742–758.

MACCULLOCH, DIARMAID (2003), Reformation: Europe's House Divided 1490–1700, London: Allen Lane, Penguin Books.

MACHAT, CHRISTOPH (1985), Auswirkungen der Reformation auf die Ausstattung siebenbürgischen Kirchen, in: Renate Weber/Georg Weber (ed.), Luther und Siebenbürgen. Ausstrahlungen von Reformation und Humanismus nach Südost Europa, Köln/Wien: Böhlau, 309–326.

MAGER, INGE (1986), Lied und Reformation. Beobachtungen zur reformatorischen Singbewegung in norddeutschen Städten, in: Alfred Dürr/Walter Killy (ed.), Das protestantische Kirchenlied im 16. und 17. Jahrhundert: text-, musik- u. theologiegeschichtliche Probleme, Wiesbaden: Harrassowitz, 25–38.

MÂLE, ÉMILE (1948), L'art religieux du XIIIe siècle en France. Étude sur l'iconographie du Moyen Âge et sur ses sources d'inspiration, Paris: Armand Colin.

MALTBY, JUDITH (1998), Prayer Book and People in Elizabethan and Early Stuart England, Cambridge: Cambridge University Press.

MARKUS, ROBERT AUSTIN (1990), The End of Ancient Christianity, Cambridge: Cambridge University Press.

MARROW, JAMES (1979), Passion Iconography in Northern European Art of the Late Middle Ages and Early Renaissance: A Study of the Transformation of Sacred Metaphor into Descriptive Narrative, Brussels: Van Ghemmert.

MARTIN, JESSICA/RYRIE, ALEC (ed.) (2012), Private and Domestic Devotion in Early Modern Britain, Farnham and Burlington, VT: Ashgate.

MARX, DÁNIEL/KRÉN, EMIL (2015), Master of Mary of Burgundy, Biography, Web Gallery of Art, searchable fine arts image database, last accessed on 2015.07.10.

MATHER, INCREASE (1689), A Brief Discourse concerning the Unlawfulness of Common Prayer Worship and of Laying the Hand on, and Kissing the Booke in Swearing, [London] – https://quod.lib.umich.edu/e/eebo2/A50188.0001.001/1:1?rgn=div1;view=fulltext

MATTER, STEFAN (2017), Transkulturelle Gärten. Zu den frühen Ausgaben des *Hortulus animae*, des Seelengärtleins und des Wurtzgartens, in: Ingrid Kasten/Laura Au-

Gesamtbibliographie | 381

teri (ed.), Transkulturalität und Translation. Deutsche Literatur des Mittelalters im europäischen Kontext, Berlin/Boston: De Gruyter, 293–299.

MAZURKIEWICZ, ROMAN (2014), The Newly Identified Latin Prototype of the Marian Homilies of Jan of Szamotuły, Studia Slavica Academiae Scientiarum Hungaricae 59/1, 93–112.

MCCORD ADAMS, MARILYN (1992), The Resurrection of the Body according to Three Medieval Aristotelians: Thomas Aquinas, John Duns Scotus, William Ockham, Philosophical Topics, 20, 1–33.

MEISTER ECKHART (1994), Die deutschen und lateinischen Werke. Die lateinischen Werke Bd. 3: Expositio Sancti Evangelii secundum Iohannem, Karl Christ u. a. (ed.), Stuttgart: Kohlhammer.

MELVILLE, GERT (2020), The Charismatic Leader and the *Vita religiosa*: Some Observations about an Apparent Contradiction between Individual and Institutions in: A. Fitzpatrick/J. Sabapathy (ed.), Individuals and Institutions in Medieval Scholasticism, London: University of London Press, 139–155.

MERKL, ULRICH (1999), Buchmalerei in Bayern in der ersten Hälfte des 16. Jahrhunderts. Spätblüte und Endzeit einer Gattung, Regensburg: Schnell und Steiner.

MERKL, ULRICH/OBHOF, UTE/NEIDL, MICHAELA (2002), Das deutsche Gebetbuch der Markgräfin von Brandenburg. Hs. Durlach 2, Badische Landesbibliothek Karlsruhe. Kommentar [zum Faksimile], Luzern: Faksimile-Verlag.

MESSLING, GUIDO (2004), Leonhard Beck als Buchmaler. Eine Untersuchung zu zwei Hauptwerken der religiösen Buchmalerei Augsburgs vom Ende des 15. Jahrhunderts, in Münchner Jahrbuch der bildenden Kunst 55, 73–114. [2006 erschienen].

MICHALSKI, SERGIUSZ (1996), Inscriptions in Protestant Paintings and in Protestant Churches, in: Arja Leena Paavola (ed.), Ars Ecclesiastica. The Church as a Context for Visual Arts, Helsinki: University Press, 34–47.

MIHÁLY, FERENC (2014), Contribuţii la cercetarea polipticelor medievale transilvănene. Observaţii privind tehnicile de execuţie şi intervenţiile de restaurare, Ars Transsilvaniae XXIV, 75–94.

MIHÁLY, TIBOR (2012), A lelki és szellemi élet szolgálatában. Adatok az Oroszhegyi család történetéhez, Areopolisz 12, 45–59.

MILLER, MATTHIAS/ZIMMERMANN, KARIN (2007), Die Codices Palatini germanici in der Universitätsbibliothek Heidelberg (Cod. Pal. germ. 304–495), Kataloge der Universitätsbibliothek Heidelberg VIII, Wiesbaden: Reichert-.

MILLER, PERRY (1953), The New England Mind: From Colony to Province, Cambridge, Mass.: Harvard University Press.

MILLER, PERRY (1939, 1954), The New England Mind: The Seventeenth Century, New York: Macmillan.

MIN, ANSELM KYONGSUK (2004), Hegel's Dialectic of the Spirit: Contemporary Reflections on Hegel's Vision of Development and Totality, Language and Spirit, ed. D.Z. Phillips, Mario von der Ruhr, London: Palgrave Macmillan, 8–38.

MISSALE ECCLESIAE STRIGONIENSIS (1507), Venetiis: Luc'Antonius de Giunta.

MISSALE secundum chorum almae ecclesiae Strigonienis, (1486), Venetiis: Erhardus Radtolt.

MITCHELL, W. J.T. (1994), Picture Theory. Essays on Verbal and Visual Representation, Chicago: University of Chicago Press.

382 | Gesamtbibliographie

Molanus, Johannes (1594), De Historia sanctorum: Imaginum et picturarum. Lovanii: apud Ioannem Bogardum, Typographum iuratum.

Monok, István/Ötvös, Péter/Verók, Attila (ed.) (2004), Lesestoffe der Siebenbürger Sachsen (1575–1750, I–II), Adattár XVI–XVIII. századi szellemi mozgalmaink történetéhez = Materialien zur Geschichte der Geistesströmungen des 16.–18. Jahrhunderts in Ungarn; 16/4.1-4.2 – Erdélyi könyvesházak = Bibliotheken in Siebenbürgen, IV/1-2, Budapest, Országos Széchényi Könyvtár.

Moore, R. I. (1994), Literacy and the Making of Heresy, in: Peter Biller/Anne Hudson (ed.), Heresy and Literacy, 1000–1530, Cambridge: Cambridge University Press, 19–37.

More, Alison (2014), Institutionalizing Penitential Life in Late Medieval and Early Modern Europe: Third Orders, Rules, and Canonical Legitimacy, Church History 83:2, 297–323.

Morgan, Nigel/Panayotova, Stella et al. (2009), Illuminated Manuscripts in Cambridge: A Catalogue of Western Book Illumination in the Fitzwilliam Museum and the Cambridge Colleges, Part One, Volume Two: The Meuse Region, Southern Netherlands, London: Harvey Miller/The Modern Humanities Research Association.

Morrison, Elisabeth (2006), Iconographic Originality in the Oeuvre of the Master of the David Scenes, in: Elisabeth Morrison/Thomas Kren (ed.), Flemish Manuscript Painting in Context/Recent Research, Los Angeles: Paul Getty.

Müller, Friedrich (1877), Die Incunabeln der Hermannstädter "Capellenbibliothek", Archiv des Vereins für siebenbürgische Landeskunde, N. F., 14, 293–358, 489–543.

Mulsow, Martin (2014), Socinianism, Islam, and the Origins of Radical Enlightenment, Religious Obedience and Political Resistance in the Early Modern World: Jewish, Christian and Islamic Philosophers Addressing the Bible, Turnhout: Brepols.

Mulsow, Martin (2010), Socinianism, Islam and the Radical Uses of Arabic Scholarship, Al-Qantara 31, 549–586.

N. N. (1808), Nekrolog auf Georg Preidt, in: Siebenbürgische Provinzialblätter, III. Band, Hermannstadt: Hochmeister, 52–62.

Nechutová, Jana (1997), Die charismatische Spiritualität in Böhmen in der vorreformatorischen Zeit, Österreichische Osthefte 39, 411–419.

Nelson, Janet L. (1990), Literacy in Carolingian Government, in: R. McKitteridge (ed.), The Uses of Literacy in Early Medieval Europe, Cambridge: Cambridge University Press, 269–270.

Nemes, Balázs J. (2012), Mittelalterliche deutsche Handschriften in rumänischen Bibliotheken: eine vorläufige Bestandsübersicht, in Astrid Breith (ed.), Manuscripta germanica. Deutschsprachige Handschriften des Mittelalters in Bibliotheken und Archiven Osteuropas, Zeitschrift für deutsches Altertum und deutsche Literatur, Beiheft/15, Stuttgart: S. Hirzel, 61–72.

Nemes, Balázs (2002), Die mittelalterlichen Handschriften des Miklós Jankovics im Spiegel zeitgenössischer Kataloge I., Magyar Könyvszemle, 387–410.

Nemes, Balázs (2003), Die mittelalterlichen Handschriften des Miklós Jankovics im Spiegel zeitgenössischer Kataloge II., Magyar Könyvszemle, 67–88.

Noble, Bonnie (2009), Lucas Cranach the Elder. Art and Devotion in the German Reformation, Lanham: University Press of America.

Gesamtbibliographie | 383

NUSSBÄCHER, GERNOT (1977), Johannes Honterus, Bucureşti: Kriterion.

NUSSBÄCHER, GERNOT/MARIN, ELISABETA (ed.) (1999), Quellen zur Geschichte des Stadt Kronstadt, vol. IX, (1420–1580), Kronstadt: Aldus.

NUSSBÄCHER, GERNOT/PHILIPPI, ASTRID (ed.) (1983), Odae Cvm Harmoniis 1548, Honterus, faksimile Nachdruck, Übertragen, Bukarest, Kriterion.

OCHSENBEIN, PETER (1983), Art. 'Hortulus animae', VerLex Tl. 4, Berlin/New York: De Gruyter, 147–154.

OCHSENBEIN, PETER (2004), Das Gebet "Christus am Kreuz" – ein frühes Prosagebet aus Böhmen?, in: V. Bok/H. J. Behr (ed.), Deutsche Literatur des Mittelalters in und über Böhmen II. Tagung in České Budějovice/Budweis 2002, Schriften zur Mediävistik 2, Hamburg: Kovač 2004, 185–198.

OCKER, CHRISTOPHER (2020), Disruption and Engagement: Christendom's Experience of Islam at the End of the Middle Ages, in: Mirko Breitenstein/Jörg Sonntag (ed.), Disorder. Expressions of an Amorphous Phenomenon in Human History, Münster: Aschendorff, 179–209.

OCKER, CHRISTOPHER (2018), Luther, Conflict, and Christendom, Cambridge: Cambridge University Press.

OCKER, CHRISTOPHER (2003), Religious Reform and Social Cohesion in Late Medieval Germany, in: Thomas A. Brady, Jr./Katherine Brady/Susan Karant-Nunn/James D. Tracy, The Work of Heiko A. Oberman, Leiden: Brill, 69–94.

ODENTHAL, ANDREAS (2011), Liturgie vom Frühen Mittelalter zum Zeitalter der Konfessionalisierung. Studien zur Geschichte des Gottesdienstes, Tübingen: Mohr Siebeck.

ODENTHAL, ANDREAS (2005), Die Ordinatio Cultus Divini et Caeremoniarium des Halberstädter Domes von 1591. Untersuchungen zur Liturgie eines gemischtkonfessionellen Domkapitels nach Einführung der Reformation, Münster: Aschendorff.

OESER, WOLFGANG (1971), Das 'a' als Grundlage für Schriftvarianten in der gotischen Buchschrift, Scriptorium 25, 25–45, 250–52.

OEXLE, OTTO-GERHARD (1996), Geschichtswissenschaft im Zeichen des Historismus. Studien zu Problemgeschichten der Moderne, Göttingen: Vandenhoeck & Ruprecht.

OGÁYAR, JUANA HIDALGO (1983), Libro de Horas de William Hastings, Goya: Revista de arte, 177, 127–131.

OLDENBOURG, M[ARIA] CONSUELO, Hortulus animae [1494]–1523. Bibliographie und Illustration. Hamburg: Hauswedell.

OLTARD, ANDREAS (1650), Concio solennis et extraordinaria complectens Initia et progressum reformationis prima ecclesiarum Saxonicarum in Sede Cibiniensi, in Transilvania, constitutarum. Elaborata et habita Cibinii Anno 1650. Ipsa Dominica Jubilate, quaeerat dies 8. MaiJ, dam ibidem Visitationem Ecclesiarum Saxonicarum, ordiretur et auspicaretur bono cum Deo, Reverendus et Clarissimus Vir Dominus Christianus Barthius Pastor Birthalbensis, Episcopus et Superintendens earundem. Ab Andrea Oltardo, Pastore Cibiniensi, nec non eiusdem Capituli Decano, Cibinii Transylvaniae, imprimebat Marcus Pistorius, Anno 1650, 41, 56–62.

ONG, WALTER J. S. J. (1958), Ramus, Method and the Decay of Dialogue, Cambridge, Mass.: Harvard University Press.

ORDEANU, MARIA (2007), Gloria in Excelsis Deo. Liber horarum Brukenthal, Sibiu/Alba Iulia: Altip.

384 | Gesamtbibliographie

Ötvös, Ágoston (1859), Geleji István élete és levelei I. Rákóczi Györgyhöz, Új Magyar Muzeum IX, I, 199–329.

Pächt, Otto (1964), *Vita Sancti Simperti: eine Handschrift für Maximilian I*, Berlin: Dt. Verlag für Kunstwissenschaft.

Pakora, Jakub (1987), Word and picture as keys for solving the ideological programme of Protestant Pulpits in Silesia, 1550–1650, Polish Art Studies 8, 45–56.

Pál, József/Újvári, Edit (ed.) (2001), Szimbólumtár: Jelképek, motívumok, témák az egyetemes és a magyar kultúrából, Budapest: Balassi.

Pallmann, Heinrich (1887), Art. Peypus, Friedrich, ADB 25, 569.

Palmer Wandel, Lee (2006), The Eucharist in the Reformation. Incarnation and Liturgy, Cambridge: Cambridge University Press.

Papahagi, Adrian (2017), A Fragment of the Graduale Varadiense at the Romanian Academy Library in Cluj (Kolozsvár), Magyar Könyvszemle 133, 455–459.

Papahagi, Adrian (2013), Manuscrisele medievale occidentale aflate in colecțiile Bibliotecii Centrale Universitare din Cluj-Napoca, Revista română de istorie a cărții IX/9, 32–46.

Papahagi, Adrian/Dincă, Adinel C./Mârza, Andreea (2018), Manuscrisele medievale occidentale din România: Census, Iași: Polirom.

Paradisus anime: pro orationum | delitijs affluit : velut alter delitia-| rum ortus: operandus et custodiensus, Basel: Jakob Wolff 1498.

Parker, Geoffrey (1992), Success and Failure during the First Century of the Reformation, Past & Present 136, 43–82.

Parks, Malcolm B. (1973), The Literacy of the Laity, in: D. Daiches/A.K. Thorlby (ed.), Literature and Western Civilization. The Medieval World, London: Aldus Books, 555–576.

Parshall, Peter W./Schoch, Rainer (2005), Die Anfänge der europäischen Druckgraphik. Holzschnitte des 15. Jahrhunderts und ihr Gebrauch. (Ausstellungskatalog) National Gallery of Art, Washington, 4. September – 27. November 2005; Germanisches Nationalmuseum, Nürnberg, 15. Dezember 2005.–19. Mä. Nürnberg.

Pásztor, Lajos (1940), A magyarság vallásos élete a Jagellók korában, Budapest: Királyi Magyar Egyetemi Nyomda.

Paul, Hermann/Moser, Hugo/Schröbler, Ingeborg/Grosse, Siegfried (1982), Mittelhochdeutsche Grammatik, Sammlung kurzer Grammatiken germanischer Dialekte. A: Hauptreihe Nr. 2. Tübingen: Niemeyer.

Paulus, Nikolaus (1923), Geschichte des Ablasses im Mittelalter. Bd. 3: Geschichte des Ablasses am Ausgange des Mittelalters, Paderborn: F. Schönigh.

Perkins, William (1607), The Arte of Prophesying or A Treatise Concerning the Sacred and Onely True Manner and Method of Preaching, London.

Pettegree, Andrew (2005), Reformation and the Culture of Persuasion, Cambridge: Cambridge University Press.

Pettegree, Andrew/Hall, Matthew (2004), The Reformation and the Book: a Reconsideration, The Historical Journal 47/4, 785–808.

Petzet, Erich (1920), Die deutschen Pergament-Handschriften Nr. 1–200 der Staatsbibliothek in München, Catalogus codicum manu scriptorum Bibliothecae Monacensis V,1, München: Palm.

Gesamtbibliographie | 385

Pieper, Lori (2000), A New Life of St. Elizabeth of Hungary, Archivum Franciscanum Historicum 93, 29–78.

Pitagora (2013), Imnurile Sacre, București.

Plajer, Dietmar (1980), Zur Geschichte des Kronstädter Gesangbuches, in: Christoph Klein (ed.), Bewahrung und Erneuerung. Festschrift für Bischof D. Albert Klein, Beihefte zu den Kirchlichen Blättern 2, [Hermannstadt], 223–236.

Poos, Raymond Lawrence (2001), Social History and the Book of Hours, in: Roger S. Wieck, Time Sanctified: The Book of Hours in Medieval Art and Life, New York: Braziller, 33–38.

Possas, Stephanie (2018), Art of the Northern Renaissance: Courts, Commerce and Devotion, London: Laurence King Publishing.

Preston, John (1630), The Saints Daily Exercise A Treatise Unfolding the whole duty of Prayer Delivered in Five Sermons upon 1 Thess.5.17, London: Nicolas Bourne.

Radosav, Doru/Hentea, Ioan (1995), La Bibliothèque Centrale Universitaire "Lucian Blaga" de Cluj-Napoca. Bref historique, Transylvanian Review 4.2, 14–28.

Randall, Lilian M.C. (1992). Medieval and Renaissance Manuscripts in the Walters Art Gallery. Vol. II, France, 1420–1540, Baltimore: Johns Hopkins University Press/Walters Art Gallery.

Razovsky, Helaine (1998), Remaking the Bible: English Reformation Spiritual Conduct Books, Renaissance and Reformation/Renaissance et Réforme 22/4, 5–25.

Rechberg, Brigitta (1983), Königstochter, Fürstin, Heilige Bemerkungen zum Drei-Kronen-Attribut dér hl. Elisabeth, in: Elisabeth in der Kunst – Abbild, Vorbild, Wunschbild. Ausstellung im Marburger Universitätsmuseum für bildende Kunst, Marburg: Elwert, 109–134.

Reeves, Andrew (2010), Teaching the Creed and the Articles of Faith in England (1215–1281), in: Ronald Stansbury (ed.), A Companion to Pastoral Care in the Late Middle Ages (1200–1500), Leiden/Boston: Brill, 41–72.

Rehberg, Andreas (2012), Religiosi stranieri a Roma nel Medioevo: problemi e prospettive di ricerca, Rivista di storia della chiesa in Italia 66/1, 3–63.

Reinburg, Virginia (2012), French Books of Hours: Making an Archive of Prayer, c. 1400–1600, Cambridge: Cambridge University Press.

Reinburg, Virginia (1993), Hearing Lay People's Prayer, in: Barbara Diefendorf/Carla Hesse (ed.), Culture and Identity in Early Modern Europe 1500–1800. Essays in Honor of Natalie Zemon Davis, Ann Arbor: Michigan University Press, 19–39.

Reinerth, Karl (1931), Eine Agende der Kirchengemeinde Streitfort, Vierteljahrschrift. Korrespondenzblatt des Vereins für siebenbürgische Landeskunde 20/1, 130–134.

Reinerth, Karl (1972), Das älteste siebenbürgisch-deutsche evangelische Gesangbuch, Jahrbuch für Liturgik und Hymnologie 17, 221–235.

Reinerth, Karl (1973), H. Andreas Moldenhauer aus Kronstadt und sein Gesangbüchlein aus dem Jahr 1543, Korrespondenzblatt des Arbeitskreises für Siebenbürgische Landeskunde 3, 1–10.

Reinerth, Karl (1979), Die Gründung der Evangelischen Kirchen in Siebenbürgen, Studia Transylvanica 5, Köln/Wien: Böhlau, 13–18.

Reinerth, Karl (1976), Nochmals: Das älteste siebenbürgisch deutsche Gesangbuch, Jahrbuch für Liturgik und Hymnologie 20, 172–176.

386 | Gesamtbibliographie

REINERTH, KARL (1929), Die reformationsgeschichtliche Stellung des Johannes Honterus in den Vorreden zu Augustins Sentenzen und Ketzerkatalog, Korrespondenzblatt des Vereins für siebenbürgische Landeskunde 52/7–8, 97–114.

REINHARDT, BRUNO (2016), Don't Make It a Doctrine: Material Religion, Transcendence, Critique, Anthropological Theory 16, 75–97.

REISS, ATHENE (2008), Beyond "Books for the Illiterate": Understanding English Medieval Wallpaintings, The British Art Journal 9/1, 4–14.

REMPEL, JOHN D. (2011), Anabaptist Religious Literature and Hymnology, in: John D. Roth/James A. Stayer (ed.), A Companion to Anabaptism and Spiritualism, 1521–1700, Leiden/Boston: Brill, 389–424.

RESKE, CHRISTOPH (2007), Die Buchdrucker des 16. und 17. Jahrhunderts im deutschen Sprachgebiet. Auf der Grundlage des gleichnamigen Werkes von Josef Benzing, Beiträge zum Buch- und Bibliothekswesen 51, Wiesbaden: Harrassowitz.

REXROTH, KARL HEINRICH (1981), Das Kronenattribut der heiligen Elisabeth in der Kunst des Spätmittelalters und der Renaissance, Hessische Heimat 31/4–5, 116–121.

RINGBOM, SIXTEN (1969), Devotional Images and Imaginative Devotions: Notes on the Place of Art in Late Medieval Piety, Gazette des Beaux Arts 673, 159–170.

RITTGERS, RONALD K. (2012), The Reformation of Suffering: Pastoral Theology and Lay Piety in Late Medieval and Early Modern Germany, New York/Oxford: Oxford University Press.

ROBINSON, PAUL W. (2008), Sermons on the Lord's Prayer and the Rogation Days in the Later Middle Ages, in: Roy Hammerling (ed.), A History of Prayer. The First to the Fifteenth Century, Leiden: Brill, 441–462.

ROEST, BERT (2011), Appropriating the Rule of Clare, Canterbury Studies in Franciscan History 3, 63–92.

ROEST, BERT (2018), Observances "féminines" dans la famille franciscaine: phénomènes bouleversants, pluralistes et multipolaires, Mélanges de l'École française de Rome. Moyen Âge 130:2.

ROEST, BERT (2007), The Discipline of The Heart: Pedagogies of Prayer in Medieval Franciscan Works of Religious Instruction, in: Timothy J. Johnson (ed.), Franciscans at Prayer, Leiden: Brill, 413–448.

ROEST, BERT (2005), Franciscans between Observance and Reformation: the Low Countries (ca. 1400–1600), Franciscan Studies 63, 409–442.

ROEST, BERT (2009), Observant Reform in Religious Orders, in: Miri Rubin/Walter Simons (ed.), The Cambridge History of Christianity, Cambridge: Cambridge University Press, 446–457.

ROMAN, TOMA COSMIN (2007), Sibiul între siguranță și incertitudine în zorii epocii moderne 1528–1549, Alba Iulia: Editura Altip.

ROMHÁNYI, BEATRIX F. (2016), Das Konstanzer Konzil und die Ankunft der Franziskaner-observanz im mittelalterlichen Ungarn in: Attila Bárányi/Balázs Antal Bacsa (ed.), Das Konzil von Konstanz und Ungarn, Debrecen, 237–251.

ROMHÁNYI, BEATRIX F. (2017), Social Network and Resources of the Observant Franciscans in Hungary at the End of the Middle Ages, in: György Galamb (ed.), Chronica. Franciscan Observance between Italy and Central Europe. Proceedings of International Conference 4–6 December 2014, Franciscan Monastery of Szeged-Alsóváros (Hungary)/L'Osservanza francescana fra Italia ed Europa Centrale. Atti del Convegno internazionale 4–6 dicembre 2014, Convento Francescano di Szeged-Alsóváros (Ungheria), Szeged: University of Szeged, 125–137.

ROSE, MARIKA (2013), The Body and Ethics in Thomas Aquinas' *Summa Theologiae*, New Blackfriars 94, 540–551.

ROTH, ERICH (1954), Die Geschichte des Gottesdienstes der Siebenbürger Sachsen, Göttingen: Vandenhoeck & Ruprecht.

ROTH, HARALD (1996), Kleine Geschichte Siebenbürgens, Köln / Weimar / Wien: Böhlau.

ROTH, VICTOR (1916), Siebenbürgische Altäre, Strassburg.

ROTHER, CHRISTIAN (2002), Siebenbürgen und der Buchdruck im 16. Jahrhundert. Mit einer Bibliographie Siebenbürgen und der Buchdruck, Wiesbaden: Harrassowitz.

ROTHKEGEL, MARTIN (2001), Ein 'schwärmerischer' Vorfahr des siebenbürgischen Gesangbuches: Täuferische und böhmisch-brüderische Lieder in einem Kronstädter Druck von 1543, Freikirchenforschung 11, 195–207.

RUBIN, MIRI (1991), Corpus Christi: The Eucharist in Late Medieval Culture, Cambridge: Cambridge University Press.

RUBIN, MIRI (2012), Popular Attitudes to the Eucharist, in: Ian Levy / Gary Macy / Kristen Van Ausdall (ed.), A Companion to the Eucharist in the Middles Ages, Leiden: Brill, 447–468.

RUBLACK, ULINKA (2010), Grapho-relics: Lutheranism and the Materialization of the Word, Past & Present, Supplement 5, 144–165.

RUGE, REINHARD (1985), Der wiederentdeckte Schriftaltar, Festschrift Ludgerikirche, 14–24.

SAENGER, PAUL (1987), Books of Hours and the Reading Habits of the Later Middle Ages, in: Roger Chartier (ed.), The Culture of Print. Power and the Uses of Print in Early Modern Europe, Oxford: Polity Press, 141–173.

SAENGER, PAUL (1982), Silent Reading. Its Impact on Late Medieval Script and Society, Viator. Medieval and Renaissance Studies 13, 367–414.

SALLAY, DÓRA (2012), V. Manuscript Illumination, in: Vladimir Baranov / Kateřina Horníčková/Elena Lemeneva / Gerhard Jaritz (ed.), Medieval Manuscript Manual [online], Budapest: Central European University, Department of Medieval Studies.

SALONTAI, MIHAELA SANDA (2017), Repere dispărute din topografia ecleziastică a Brașovului medieval: capela Corpus Christi și claustrul Franciscanilor observanți, Historia Urbana XXV, 119–133.

SAND, ALEXA (2014), Vision, Devotion, and Self-Representation in Late Medieval Art, New York: Cambridge University Press.

SCARISBRICK, J.J. (1984), The Reformation and the English People, Oxford: Blackwell.

SCARPATETTI, BEAT MATTHIAS VON / LENZ, PHILIPP (2008), Die Handschriften der Stiftsbibliothek St. Gallen. Bd. 2, Abt. III / 2, Codices 450–546: Liturgica, Libri precum, deutsche Gebetbücher, Spiritualia, Musikhandschriften, 9.–16. Jahrhundert, Wiesbaden: Harrassowitz.

SCHEDEL (TOLDI), FERENC (1841), Literáti Nemes Sámuel, 's a' közel legrégibb Magyar naptár, Athenaeum, 17. August, 333–335.

SCHEURL, CHRISTOPH (1867) Christoph Scheurl's Briefbuch, ein Beitrag zur Geschichte der Reformation und ihrer Zeit (1867), Franz von Soden / J.F.K. Knaake (ed.). Zweiter Band: 1517–1540, Potsdam: Gropius. Neue Edition: Aalen: O Zeller, 1962.

SCHILLING, JOHANNES (2016), "Die Musik ist eine herrliche Gabe Gottes": Luther und die Reformation der Musik, in: von Dietrich Korsch / Jan Lohrengel (ed.), Das Evangelium in der Geschichte der Frömmigkeit: Kirchengeschichtliche Aufsätze, Leipzig: Evangelische Verlagsanstalt, 187–201.

SCHLACHTA, ASTRID VON (2020), Täufer: Von der Reformation ins 21. Jahrhundert, Tübingen: A. Francke.

SCHLECHTER, ARMIN / STAMM, GERHARD (2000), Die kleinen Provenienzen: die Handschriften der Badischen Landesbibliothek in Karlsruhe XIII, Wiesbaden: Harrassowitz.

SCHMIDT, PETER (2003), Gedruckte Bilder in handgeschriebenen Büchern. Studien zum Gebrauch von Druckgraphik im 15. Jahrhundert, Pictura et poësis 16, Köln / Weimar / Wien: Böhlau.

SCHMIDT, PETER (1998), Rhin supérieur ou Bavière? Localisation et mobilité des gravures au milieu du XVᵉ siècle, Revue de l'art 120, 66–88.

SCHMIDT, VICTOR M. (2001), Painting and Individual Devotion in Late Medieval Italy: the Case of St Catherine of Alexandria, in: Andre Landes / Shelley Zurow (ed.), Visions of Holiness: Art and Devotion in Italy, Athens: University of Georgia, 21–36.

SCHMITT, JEAN-CLAUDE (1981), Du bon usage du *Credo*, in: Faire croire. Modalités de la diffusion et de la réception des messages religieux du XIIe au XVe siècle. Actes de table ronde de Rome (22–23 juin 1979), Rome: École Française de Rome, 337–361.

SCHMOLL, FRIEDRICH (1914), Zur Ikonographie der heiligen Elisabeth im 13. bis 16. Jahrhundert. Dissertation, Giessen: Hof- und Universitätsdruckerei Otto Kindt.

SCHNEIDER, KARIN (1995), Berufs- und Amateurschreiber. Zum Laien-Schreibbetrieb im spätmittelalterlichen Augsburg, in Literarisches Leben in Augsburg während des 15. Jahrhunderts, Johannes Janota / Werner Williams-Krapp (ed.), Studia Augustana 7, Tübingen: Niemeyer, 8–26.

SCHNEIDER, KARIN (1988), Deutsche mittelalterliche Handschriften der Universitätsbibliothek Augsburg: die Signaturengruppen Cod. I. 3. und Cod. III. 1, Die Handschriften der Universitätsbibliothek Augsburg, Bd. 2,1. Wiesbaden: Harrassowitz.

SCHNEIDER, KARIN (1999), Paläographie und Handschriftenkunde für Germanisten: eine Einführung, Sammlung kurzer Grammatiken germanischer Dialekte. B: Ergänzungsreihe Nr. 8. Tübingen: Niemeyer.

SCHNYDER, ANDRÉ (2004): Art. "Die geistliche Badestube",11, Berlin / New York: De Gruyter, 503 f.

SCHOCH, RAINER / MENDE, MATTHIAS / SCHERBAUM, ANNA (2002), Albrecht Dürer. Das druckgraphische Werk. Bd. 2, Holzschnitte und Holzschnittfolgen. München / Berlin / London / New York: Prestel.

SCHREINER, KLAUS (ed.) (2002), Frömmigkeit im Mittelalter: Politisch-soziale Kontexte, visuelle Praxis, körperliche Ausdrucksformen, München: Fink.

SCHREINER, KLAUS (ed.) (1992), Laienfrömmigkeit im späten Mittelalter. Formen, Funktionen, politisch-soziale Zusammenhänge, München: R. Oldenbourg.

SCHULLERUS, ADOLF (1923), Geschichte des Gottesdienstes in der siebenbürgisch-sächsischen Kirche, Archiv des Vereins für siebenbürgische Landeskunde, Neue Folge 41/2–3, Hermannstadt: Michaelis und Dück, 299–522.

SCHULZ, FRIEDER (2003), Das Gebet. A. Das Kollektengebet, in: Hans-Christoph Schmidt-Lauber / Michael Meyer-Blanck / Karl-Heinrich Bieritz (ed.), Handbuch der

Liturgik. Liturgiewissenschaft in Theologie und Praxis der Kirche, Göttingen: Vandenhoeck & Ruprecht, 742–762.

SCHUSTER, PETER KLAUS (1983), Abstraktion, Agitation und Einfühlung. Formen protestantischer Kunst im 16. Jahrhundert in: Werner Hofmann (ed.), Kopie der Lutherzeit. Katalog der Ausstellung in der Hamburger Kunsthalle, München, 115–125.

SCILLIA, DIANE G. (2002), Gerard David's "St. Elizabeth of Hungary" in the "Hours of Isabella the Catholic", Cleveland Studies in the History of Art 7, 50–67.

SCOTT-STOKES, CHARITY (2006), Women's Books of Hours in Medieval England, Cambridge: Boydell & Brewer.

SCRIBNER, ROBERT (1989), For the Sake of Simple Folk. Popular Propaganda for the German Reformation, Cambridge: Cambridge University Press.

SCRIBNER, BOB (1994), Heterodoxy, literacy and print in the early German Reformation, in: Peter Biller / Anne Hudson (ed.), Heresy and Literacy 1000–1530, Cambridge: Cambridge University Press, 225–278.

SCRIBNER, R. W. (1987), Oral Culture and the Diffusion of Reformation Ideas, in: R. W. Scribner, Popular Culture and Popular Movements in Reformation Germany, London: Hambledon Press, 49–70.

SCRIBNER, BOB (1989), Popular Piety and Modes of Visual Perception in Late Medieval and Reformation Germany, The Journal of Religious History 15/4, 448–469.

SERAPHIN, FRIEDRICH WILHELM (1891), Kronstädter Schulen vor der Reformation, Archiv des Vereins für siebenbürgische Landeskunde, Neue Folge XXIII, 791–792.

SERIES PASTORUM VERDENSIS (1865), Pfarrarchiv Werd, ZAEKR, 400-246-99.

SHEPARD, THOMAS (1652–1653), A Treatise of Liturgies, Power of the Keys, and of Matter of the Visible Church. In Answer to the Reverend Servant of Christ, Mr. John Ball, London: E. Cotes for Andrew Crooke.

SHEPARD, THOMAS (1932), The Autobiography of Thomas Shepard, the celebrated Minister of Cambridge, Transactions, Vol. 27, Boston: Prince and Parker. https://www.colonialsociety.org/node/460. (Last accessed 04.07.18.)

SIMON, ZSOLT (2007), Primele tipărituri din Transilvania (Sibiu, 1525), Anuarul Institutului de Istorie "George Barițiu" din Cluj-Napoca, Series Historica 46, 89–106.

SIMROCK, KARL (1988), Die deutschen Sprichwörter, Stuttgart: Reclam.

ŞINDILARIU, THOMAS (2017), Der Beginn der Reformation in Kronstadt: Ansätze zu einer Neubewertung, in: Bernhard Heigl / Thomas Şindilariu (ed.), Quellen zur Geschichte der Stadt Kronstadt, Band VIII, Beiheft 2: Johannes Honterus, Reformatio ecclesiae Coronensis ac totius Barcensis provinciae. Corona 1543, Kronstadt: Aldus, 1–32.

SIPOS, GÁBOR (ed.) (2009), Az Erdélyi Múzeum-Egyesület gyűjteményei, Klausenburg, SMV.

SITZUNGSPROTOKOLL (1870), Staatsarchiv Klausenburg: Bestand des Siebenbürgischen Museum-Vereins, Nr. 298, Ordner 17: Sitzungsprotokoll, 1870.

SKOWRONSKI, JOHN J./SEDIKIDES, CONSTANTINE (2019), On the Evolution of the Human Self: A Data-Driven Review and Reconsideration, Self and Identity 18, 4–21.

SMEYERS, MAURITS (1998), L'art de la miniature flamande du VIIIᵉ au XVIᵉ siècle, Tournai: La Renaissance du Livre, 1998.

SMEYERS, MAURITS (1981), De arte illuminandi, in: Vlamse kunst op pergament. Handschriften en miniaturen te Brugge van de 12de tot de 16de eeuw, Brugge: Gruuthusenmuseum, 19–43.

390 | Gesamtbibliographie

SMEYERS, MAURITS (1999), Flemish Miniatures from the 8th to the Mid-16th Century: The Medieval World on Parchment, Turnhout: Brepols.

SNOEK, GODEFRIDUS J. C. (1995), Medieval Piety from Relics to the Eucharist: A Process of Mutual Interaction, Leiden: Brill.

SOHM, RUDOLF (1912), Wesen und Ursprung des Katholizismus, Leipzig: B.G. Teubner.

SÖLLER, BERTRAM (1989), Art. "Paradisus animae", VerLex Tl. 7, Berlin/New York: De Gruyter, 293-298.

SOÓS, ZOLTÁN (2003), The Franciscan Friary of Târgu Mureş (Marosvásárhely) and the Franciscan Presence in Medieval Transylvania, Annual of Medieval Studies at CEU vol. 9, 249-274.

SPICER, ANDREW (ed.) (2012), Lutheran Churches in Early Modern Europe, Farnham: Ashgate.

SPIELMANN, MIHÁLY/BALÁZS, LAJOS/AMBRUS, HEDVIG/MESAROŞ, OVIDIA (2001), Catalogus Librorum Sedecimo Saeculo Impressorum Bibliothecae Teleki-Bolyai Novum Forum Siculorum, Târgu-Mureş: Lyra.

STAYER, JAMES M. (2011), Swiss-South-German Anabaptism, 1526-1540, in: John D. Roth/James A. Stayer (ed.), A Companion to Anabaptism and Spiritualism, 1521-1700, Leiden/Boston: Brill, 83-117, 99-109.

STEGMÜLLER, OTTO (1958), Aus Handschriften der Rastatter Gymnasialbibliothek, in Humanitas. 1808-1958. 150 Jahre Ludwig-Wilhelm-Gymnasium Rastatt, Rastatt: Pabel, 74-82.

STEIGER, JOHANN ANSELM (2010), Christophorus – ein ebenbild aller christen. Ein nichtbiblisches Bild und dessen Relevanz für die Schrift-und Bildhermeneutik. Aufgezeigt an Texten Martin Luthers und Sigmund von Birkens, in: Torbjörn Johansson/Robert Kolb/Johann Anselm Steiger (ed.), Hermeneutica Sacra. Studien zur Auslegung der Heiligen Schrift im 16. und 17. Jahrhundert. Studies of the Interpretation of Holy Scripture in the Sixteenth and Seventeenth Centuries, Berlin/New York: De Gruyter, 5-32.

STEIGER, JOHANN ANSELM (2002), Fünf Zentralthemen der Theologie Luthers und seiner Erben. Communicatio – imago – figura – Maria – exempla, Leiden/Boston/Köln: Brill.

STEIN, WENDY (2017), The Book of Hours: A Medieval Bestseller, Heilbrunn Timeline of Art History, New York: Metropolitan Museum of Art.

STEPHENS, ISAAC (2011), Confessional Identity in Early Stuart England: The "Prayer Book Puritanism" of Elizabeth Isham, Journal of British Studies 50 (1), 24-47.

STJERNA, KIRSI (2021), Lutheran Theology: A Grammar of Faith, London: T. and T. Clark.

STONE, LAWRENCE (1964), The Educational Revolution in England, 1560-1640, Past & Present 28, 41-80.

STONE, LAWRENCE (1969), Literacy and Education in England 1640-1900, Past & Present 42, 69-139.

STRANDENAAES, THOR (2002), Translation as Interpretation, in: Mogens Müller/Henrik Tronier (ed.), The New Testament as Reception, New York: Sheffield Academic Press, 181-200.

STRAUSS, GERALD (1984), Lutheranism and Literacy: A Reassessment, in: Kaspar von Greyerz (ed.), Religion and Society in Early Modern Europe 1500-1800, London: George Allen and Unwin, 109-123.

STRAUSS, GERALD (1975), Success and Failure in the Reformation, Past & Present 67, 30-63.

Gesamtbibliographie | 391

STRAUSS, GERALD/GAWTHROP, RICHARD (1984), Protestantism and Literacy in Early Modern Germany, Past & Present 104, 31–55.

SYNODI GENERALI (1765–1801), Mühlbacher Bezirkskonsistorium, ZAEKR, DA-209-64.

SZABÓ, KÁROLY (1866–1870), [Biblioteca Centrală Universitară, Cluj] – Registru inventar-achiziții cărți, începând cu 27 aprilie 1866-31 decembrie 1872, Signatur: Col. Doc. 105, Lucian Blaga Zentrale Universitätsbibliothek, Klausenburg.

SZEGEDI, EDIT (2009), Comemorarea sfinților în Transilvanian protestantă (sec. XVI–XVII), Banatica 19, 95–115.

SZEGEDI, EDIT (2009), Hungarian and Saxon Culture in the Sixteenth Century, in: Ioan Aurel Pop/Thomas Nägler/András Magyari (ed.), The History of Transylvania, vol. II (from 1541 to 1711), Cluj-Napoca: Center for Transylvanian Studies, 273–280.

SZEGEDI, EDIT (2006), Konfessionsbildung und Konfessionalisierung im städtischen Kontext. Eine Fallstudie am Beispiel von Kronstadt in Siebenbürgen (ca. 1550–1680), in: Jörg Deventer (ed.), Berichte und Beiträge des Geisteswissenschaftlichen Zentrums Geschichte und Kultur Ostmitteleuropas an der Universität Leipzig. Heft 2, Konfessionelle Formierungsprozessen im Frühneuzeitlichen Ostmitteleuropa. Vorträge und Studien, Leipzig: GWZO, 126–253.

SZEGEDI, EDIT (2008), Was bedeutete Adiaphoron/Adiaphora im siebenbürgischen Protestantismus des 16. und 17. Jahrhunderts, in: Evelin Wetter (ed.), Formierungen des konfessionellen Raumes in Ostmitteleuropa. Forschungen zur Geschichte und Kultur des östlichen Mitteleuropa (FGKOME) 33, Stuttgart:Franz Steiner, 57–74.

SZEGEDI, EDIT (2012), Wohin gehört die Kronstädter Reformation? Versuch einer theologischen Zuordnung von Johannes Honterus und der Reformation in Kronstadt, Banatica 22, 77–85, 78.

SZENDE, KATALIN (2009), Integration through Language: The Multilingual Character of Late Medieval Hungarian Towns, in: Derek Keene/Balázs Nagy/Katalin Szende (ed.), Segregation – Integration – Assimilation. Religious and Ethnic Groups in the Medieval Towns of Central and Eastern Europe, Farnham: Ashgate, 205–234.

SZENDE, KATALIN (2018), Towns and Urban Networks in the Carpathian Basin between the Eleventh and the Early Sixteenth Centuries, in: Xavier Barral i Altet/Pál Lővei/Vinni Lucherini/Imre Takács (ed.), The Art of Medieval Hungary, Roma: Viella, 65–82.

SZINNYEI, JÓZSEF (1891–1914), Magyar írók élete és munkái, Budapest: Hornyánszky Viktor.

SZŐCS, TAMÁS (2009), Kirchenlied zwischen Pest und Stadtbrand. Das Kronstädter Kantional I.F.78 aus dem 17. Jahrhundert, Studia Transylvanica 38. Köln/Weimar/Wien: Böhlau.

SZÖGI, LÁSZLÓ (2011), Magyarországi diákok németországi egyetemeken és akadémiákon 1526–1700, Magyarországi diákok egyetemjárása az újkorban 17, 7–29.

TEUTSCH, FRIEDRICH (1881), Die Hermannstädter Buchdrucker und Buchhändler, Korrespondenzblatt des Vereins für Siebenbürgische Landeskunde IV/1, 1–4.

TEUTSCH, FRIEDRICH (1921), Geschichte der evangelischen Kirche in Siebenbürgen, I, Hermannstadt: Michaelis, 1150–1699.

TEUTSCH, GEORG DANIEL (1853), Das Testament des Denndorfer Pfarrers Antonius Schwartz vom 8. Dezember 1570, Archivs des Vereins für siebenbürgische Landeskunde, Neue Folge 1, Kronstadt: Michaelis, 363–374.

392 | Gesamtbibliographie

TEUTSCH, GEORG DANIEL (1862, 1883), Urkundenbuch der Evangelischen Landeskirche A.B. in Siebenbürgen, I–II, Hermannstadt: Michaelis.

THAYER, ANNE T. (2010), Support for Preaching in Guido of Monte Rochen's Manipulum Curatorum, in: Ronald J. Stansbury (ed.), A Companion to Pastoral Care in the Late Middle Ages (1200–1500), Leiden/Boston: Brill, 123–144.

THAYER, ANNE T. (2012), The Medieval Sermon: Text, Performance and Insight, in: Joel Thomas Rosenthal (ed.), Understanding medieval primary sources: using historical sources to discover medieval Europe, London: Routledge, 43–58.

THOSS, DAGMAR (1987), Flämische Buchmalerei: Handschriftenschätze aus dem Burgunderreich. Ausstellung der Handschriften- und Inkunabelsammlung der österreichischen Nationalbibliothek, Prunksaal, 21. Mai – 26. Oktober 1987, Graz: ADEVA.

TOMASZEWSKI, JACEK (2016), Girdle Books and Leather Overcovers in Poland, Relics and Iconographic Sources, Polish Libraries, 4, 84–180.

TONK, SÁNDOR (1996), Siebenbürgische Studenten an ausländischen Universitäten, in: Walter König (ed.), Beiträge zur siebenbürgischen Schulgeschichte, Köln/Weimar/Wien: Böhlau, 119–121.

TÓTH, ISTVÁN GYÖRGY (2007), The Correspondence of Illiterate Peasants in Early Modern Hungary, in: Francisco Bethencourt/Florike Egmond (ed.), Correspondence and Cultural Exchange in Europe, Cambridge: Cambridge University Press, 313–332.

TRAUSCH, JOSEF (1852), Geschichte des Burzenländer Capituls, Kronstadt: Gött.

TRAUSCH, JOSEPH (1983), Schriftsteller-Lexikon oder biografisch-literärische Denk-Blätter der Siebenbürger Deutschen, Kronstadt, 1870, unveränderter Nachdruck: Schriftsteller-Lexikon der Siebenbürger Deutschen, Schriften zur Landeskunde Siebenbürgens 7/II, Köln/Wien: Boehlau.

TRIO, PAUL/SMET, MARJAN (ed.) (2006), The Use and Abuse of Sacred Places in Late Medieval Towns, Leuven: Leuven University Press.

TROELTSCH, ERNST (2001), Schriften zur Bedeutung des Protestantismus für die moderne Welt (1906–1913), ed. Trutz Rendtorff, Berlin: De Gruyter.

VALENTE BACCI, ANNA MARIA (1993), The Typology of Medieval German Preaching, in: Jacqueline Hamesse/Xavier Hermand (ed.), De l'homélie au sermon. Histoire de la prédication médiévale: Actes du Colloque international de Louvain-la-Neuve (9–11 juillet 1992), Louvain-la-Neuve: Université catholique de Louvain, 313–329.

VAN BUEREN, TRUUS (2005), Care for the Here and a Hereafter: A Multitude of Possibilities, in: Truus van Bueren (ed.), Care for the Here and a Hereafter: Memoria, Art and Ritual in the Middle Ages, Tournhout: Brepols, 13–28.

VAN HOOREBEECK, CÉLINE (1997), Un corpus de vingt livres d'heures manuscrits du XVe siècle du diocèse de Tournai: catalogue descriptif, hypothèses de localisation et modalités d'utilisation, unpublished BA dissertation, Louvain-la-Neuve: Université catholique de Louvain.

VAN OS, HENK et alii (1994), The Art of Devotion in the Late Middle Ages in Europe. 1300–1500, Princeton, NJ: Princeton University Press.

VANVIJNSBERGHE, DOMINIQUE (2015), Reconstructing Local Styles in the Southern Low Countries. The Importance of Books of Hours, in: Delmira Espada Custódio/Maria Adelaide Miranda (ed.), Livros de Horas. O imaginário da devoçao privada, Lisbon: Biblioteca Nacional de Portugal, 123–43.

VANWIJNSBERGHE, DOMINIQUE (2018), The Tastes of the Upper Classes, in: Splendour of the Burgundian Netherlands: Southern Netherlandish Illuminated Manuscripts in Dutch Collections, Zwolle: Wbooks/Utrecht: Museum Catharijneconvent, 110–119.

VERÓK, ATTILA (2020), Melanchthon-Rezeption bei den Siebenbürger Sachsen im Reformationsjahrhundert, in: Andrea Seidel/István Monok (ed.), Reformation und Bücher: Zentren der Ideen – Zentren der Buchproduktion, Wolfenbütteler Schriften zur Geschichte des Buchwesens 51, Wiesbaden: Harrassowitz, 123–138.

VLAICU, MONICA (ed.) (2003), Documente privind istoria orașului Sibiu II. Comerț și meșteșuguri în Sibiu și în cele Șapte Scaune, 1229–1579, Sibiu: Editura Hora. Societatea de Studii transilvane din Heidelberg.

VLAICU, MONICA/GÜNDISCH, KONRAD (ed.) (2007), Der Nachlaß Samuel von Brukenthals: Einblicke in Haushalt und Lebenswelt eines siebenbürgischen Gouverneurs der Barockzeit, Sibiu: Hora.

VOLF, GYÖRGY (ed.) (1884), Teleki codex, Budapest: MTA.

VULIĆ, KATHRYN R./USELMANN, SUSAN/GRISÉ, C. ANNETTE (ed.) (2016), Devotional Literature and Practice in Medieval England: Readers, Reading, and Reception, Turnhout: Brepols.

WACHINGER, BURKHARD (2004), Art. "Der himmlische Rosenkranz", VerLex[2] 11, Berlin/New York: De Gruyter, 676–680.

WACKERNAGEL, PHILIPP (1870), Das deutsche Kirchenlied von der ältesten Zeit bis zum Anfang des XVII. Jahrhunderts, Bd. 3, Leipzig: Teubner.

WAGNER, ERNST (1998), Die Pfarrer und Lehrer der Evangelischen Kirche A.B. in Siebenbürgen, I: Von der Reformation bis zum Jahre 1700, Köln/Weimar/Wien: Böhlau.

WAGNER, PETER (1996), Introduction: Ekphrasis, Iconotexts and Intermediality – the State(s) of the Art(s), in: Peter Wagner (ed.), Icons-Texts – Iconotexts. Essays on Ekphrasis and Intermediality, Berlin/New York: Walter de Gruyten, 1–42.

WAGNER, VALENTIN (1554), Praecepta vitae Christianae Valent, Corona: [Wagner]. (RMNY 105)

WATSON, ROWAN (2011), Victoria and Albert Museum: Western Illuminated Manuscripts, London: V&A Publishing, vol. 1.

WAUTERS, ALPHONSE (1899), Article "Molanus, Joannes", Biographie Nationale de Belgique, vol. 15, Brussels.

WEBB, DIANA (2005), Domestic Space and Devotion, in: S. Hamilton/A. Spicer (ed.), Defining the Holy: Sacred Space in Medieval and Early Modern Europe, Aldershot: Ashgate, 27–47.

WEHLI, TÜNDE (1986), A flamand hóráskönyv: kísérőtanulmány az Országos Széchényi Könyvtárban őrzött Cod. lat. 205-ös jelzetű Gent-brüggei kódex hasonmás, Budapest: Helikon.

WEHMER, CARL (1955), Ne Italo cedere videamur: augsburger Buchdrucker und Schreiber um 1500, in Clemens Bauer/Bernhard Josef/Hermann Rinn (ed.), Augusta 955–1955: Forschungen und Studien zur Kultur- und Wirtschaftsgeschichte Augsburgs, Augsburg: Rinn, 145–173.

WEISKE, BRIGITTE (1993), Bilder und Gebete vom Leben und Leiden Christi, in: Walter Haug, Burghart Wachinger (ed.), Die Passion Christi in der Literatur und Kunst des Spätmittelalter, Tübingen: De Gruyter, 113–168.

394 | Gesamtbibliographie

WETTER, EVELIN (2016), Staging the Eucharist, *Adiaphora,* and Shaping Lutheran Identities in the Transylvanian Parish Church, in: Andrew Spicer (ed.): Parish Churches in the Early Modern World, Farnham: Ashgate, 119–145.

WETTER, EVELIN/KIENZLER, CORINNA/ZIEGLER, ÁGNES (ed.) (2015), Liturgische Gewänder in der Schwarzen Kirche zu Kronstadt in Siebenbürgen, Riggisberg: Abegg-Stiftung.

WETTER, EVELIN/SCHOLTEN, FRITS (ed.), (2017), Prayer Nuts, Private Devotion and Early Modern Art Collecting, Riggisberg: Abegg-Stiftung.

WIECK, ROGER S. (1997), Painted Prayers. The Book of Hours in Medieval and Renaissance Art, New York: George Braziller.

WIECK, ROGER S. (2008), Prayer for the People. The Book of Hours, in: Roy Hammerling (ed.), A History of Prayer. The First to the Fifteenth Century, Leiden/Boston: Brill, 388–416.

WIECK, ROGER S. (1991), The Savoy Hours and Its Impact on Jean, Duc du Berry, The Yale University Library Gazette 66, 159–180.

WIECK, ROGER S. (1988), Time Sanctified. The Book of Hours in Medieval Art and Life, New York: George Braziller.

WIEDERKEHR, RUTH (2013), Das Hermetschwiler Gebetbuch. Studien zu deutschsprachiger Gebetbuchliteratur der Nord- und Zentralschweiz. Mit einer Edition, Berlin/Boston: De Gruyter.

WIEN, ULRICH A. (2019), Flucht hinter den 'Osmanischen Vorhang'. Glaubensflüchtlinge in Siebenbürgen, Journal of Early Modern Christianity 6, 19–41.

WIEN, ULRICH A. (2015, 2020), Der Humanist Johannes Honterus, in: Robert Offner/Harald Roth/Thomas Șindilariu/Ulrich A. Wien (ed.), Johannes Honterus. Rudimenta Cosmographica: Grundzüge einer Weltbeschreibung, Corona/Kronstadt, 1542, Hermannstadt/Bonn: Schiller, 11–37.

WILHELM, JOHANNES (1983), Augsburger Wandmalerei 1368–1530: Künstler, Handwerker und Zunft, Abhandlungen zur Geschichte der Stadt Augsburg 29, Augsburg: Mühlberger.

WILKINS, DAVID G. (2002), Opening the Doors to Devotion: Trecento Triptychs and Suggestions Concerning Images and Domestic Practice in Florence, Studies in the History of Art 61, 370–393.

WILLIAMSON, BETH (2004), Altarpieces, Liturgy and Devotion, Speculum 79/2, 341–406.

WILLIAMSON, BETH (2013), Sensory Experience in Medieval Devotion: Sound and Vision, Invisibility and Silence, Speculum 88/1, 1–43.

WINSTON-ALLEN, ANNE (1998), Stories of the Rose. The Making of the Rosary in the Middle Ages, University Park, PA: Pennsylvania State University Press.

WINSTON, ANNE (1993), Tracing the Origins of the Rosary: German Vernacular Texts, Speculum 68/3, 619–636.

WISSE, JACOB (2002), Burgundian Netherlands: Court Life and Patronage, Heilbrunn Timeline of Art History, New York: The Metropolitan Museum of Art. Gebet im späten Mittelalter zwischen Ablassverheißung und identifikatorischer Internalisierung.

ZACH, KRISTA (2002), Protestant vernacular catechisms and religious reform in sixteenth-century east-central Europe, in: Maria Crăciun/Ovidiu Ghitta/Graeme Murdock (ed.), Confessional Identity in East Central Europe, Aldershot: Ashgate, 49–63.

ZANDER-SEIDEL, JUTTA (1990), Textiler Hausrat. Kleidung und Haustextilien in Nürnberg von 1500–1560, München: Dt. Kunstverlag.

ZARRI, GABRIELLA (2015), Ecclesiastical Institutions and Religious Life in the Observant Century, in: James D. Mixson/Bert Roest (ed.), A Companion to Observant Reform in the Late Middle Ages and Beyond, Leiden/Boston: Brill, 24–59.

ZÖHL, CAROLINE, (2018), Das Catholicon-Projekt – eine Augsburger Kooperation im frühen Medienwandel, in Hamburger, Jeffrey F./Theisen, Maria (ed.), Unter Druck Mitteleuropäische Buchmalerei im 15. Jahrhundert. Tagungsband zum internationalen Kolloquium in Wien, Österreichische Akademie der Wissenschaften, 13.1.–17.1.2016, Buchmalerei des 15. Jahrhunderts in Mitteleuropa 15, Petersberg: Michael Imhof Verlag, 224–238.

Index

Orte / Places

Abtsdorf *siehe/see* Țapu
Agnethen *siehe/see* Agnita
Agnita 210, 284, 289, 300 f, 303
Alba Iulia 79 f, 159, 251, 352
Albești 155, 194, 196
Alessandria 95
Amiens 79, 108, 110
Atea 197 f
Atya *siehe* Atea
Augsburg 7 f, 27, 33–36, 39–41, 46–48, 57, 59, 61, 63, 73, 268, 339, 342, 344, 350, 354
Australia 352
Austria 193, 352

Baia Mare 203
Baltimore 79, 88
Barcaság *siehe/see* Țara Bârsei
Basel 37 f, 50, 69, 157, 193, 222–224, 268
Baumgarten *siehe/see* Bungard
Belgium 94, 110
Berethalom *siehe/see* Biertan
Beszterce *siehe/see* Bistrița
Biertan 209, 211, 299 f, 303
Birthälm *siehe/see* Biertan
Bistrița 223
Bistritz *siehe/see* Bistrița
Bodeln *siehe/see* Budila
Bodola *siehe/see* Budila
Boldogváros *siehe/see* Seliștat
Bongárd *siehe/see* Bungard
Brașov 16, 154 f, 195, 209, 213, 216, 221, 223 f, 228 f, 231–235, 252, 295, 298, 303, 341
Brassó *siehe/see* Brașov
Bratislava 216
Broos *siehe/see* Orăștie
Bruges 9, 79, 83–88, 100, 106, 109 f, 114
Bruxelles 84, 86, 106, 121
Buda 224
Budapest 25, 80, 151
Budila 251 f, 257 f
Bungard 222
Burzenland *siehe/see* Țara Bârsei
Busd *siehe/see* Buzd
Buzd 227, 295, 303

Cambridge 34, 85, 92, 325 f, 329 f, 334
Cenad 79, 200
Cincșor 300, 303
Cisnădie 159 f, 170
Clermont 116, 136
Cluj 7 f, 21–23, 28, 31, 33 f, 40, 42, 46, 48, 50, 56, 58–60, 62, 67, 70, 80–88, 91, 151, 157, 195 f, 203, 209, 227, 306, 339 f, 342–344, 350, 352
Compostela 157
Constance 193
Coșeiu 194 f
Csanád *siehe/see* Cenad
Csicsóholdvilág *siehe/see* Țapu
Csíksomlyó *siehe/see* Șumuleu Ciuc
Csíkszentlélek *siehe/see* Leliceni

Daia 212 f, 216
Dallas 37, 40, 46, 48, 51, 77
Darlac *siehe/see* Dârlos
Dârlos 277, 280
Denndorf *siehe/see* Daia
Deutschland / Germany 302, 314, 352 f
Dobârca 277 f, 280, 284, 289, 292, 295, 302–306
Doboka *siehe/see* Dobârca
Dobring *siehe/see* Dobârca
Dreikirchen *siehe/see* Teiuș
Dupuș 299, 303
Durles *siehe/see* Dârlos

Egypt / Ägypten 95, 99 f
Eisenmarkt *siehe/see* Hunedoara
England 16, 269, 311, 321–323, 325 f, 329, 331, 335
Erfurt 268

Fehéregyháza *siehe/see* Albești
Felfalu *siehe/see* Suseni
Frankreich / France 38, 79, 83, 108, 110, 116, 160, 272, 309, 323, 354
Frauenbach *siehe/see* Baia Mare
Freiburg 31, 33, 57, 60, 67

Galt *siehe/see* Ungra
Gand 79

398 | Index

Genf/Geneva 353
Ghent 83, 100, 109f, 114
Großlogdeser *siehe/see* Ludoș
Großscheuern *siehe/see* Șura Mare
Großwardein *siehe/see* Oradea
Gyulafehérvár *siehe/see* Alba Iulia

Haag, Den (The Hague) 84
Hagenau 185, 201
Hălchiu 299f, 303
Hațeg 194
Hatzeg *siehe/see* Hațeg
Hátszeg *siehe/see* Hațeg
Heidelberg 37, 41, 47, 49–50, 353
Heldsdorf *siehe/see* Hălchiu
Heltau *siehe/see* Cisnădie
Hermannstadt *siehe/see* Sibiu
Holy Roman Empire 8, 354
Hunedoara 195
Hungary/Ungarn 151

Ingolstadt 353
Iowa City 47, 49, 78
Italien/Italy 95, 105, 110, 193, 272, 309

Jena 216, 353
Jidvei 295, 303

Karlsruhe 34, 37, 43
Kronstadt *siehe/see* Brașov
Kusaly *siehe/see* Coșeiu

Leipzig 248, 250, 268, 347
Leliceni 81
Leuven/Löwen 117, 353
Liège 108, 110
Lille 117
Ludos 215
Lyon 79

Mainz 47, 49, 76
Malibu (LA) 83
Mantua/Mantova 32, 37, 42, 50
Marburg 229
Marosvásárhely *siehe/see* Târgu Mureș
Medgyes *siehe/see* Mediaș
Mediaș 195f, 200, 294, 299f, 303, 306
Mediasch *siehe/see* Mediaș
Mercheașa 212
Meschen *siehe/see* Moșna
Meșendorf 300, 303
Mirkvásár *siehe/see* Mercheașa
Mohács 27, 194, 223

Moșna 211
Muzsna *siehe/see* Moșna
Mühlbach *siehe/see* Sebeș
München 34f, 39, 46, 48, 51, 53, 63–65, 69, 80

Nagybánya *siehe/see* Baia Mare
Nagycsűr *siehe/see* Șura Mare
Nagydisznód *siehe/see* Cisnădie
Nagyludas *siehe/see* Ludoș
Nagyszeben *siehe/see* Sibiu
Nagyvárad *siehe/see* Oradea
Nemes *siehe/see* Nemșa
Nemșa 211, 299f, 303
Netherlands/Niederlande 84, 272
Neumarkt am Mieresch *siehe/see* Târgu Mureș
New England 16, 321f, 324f, 330f, 334, 336
New York 20, 46f, 49, 78, 83
Niederlande/Netherlands 8f, 79, 83, 88, 105f, 108–110, 115f, 118f, 309
Nieppe 116
Nimesch *siehe/see* Nemșa
North America 352
Nürnberg 14, 32, 34, 36, 39, 56, 132f, 225, 228, 268, 344

Oderhellen *siehe/see* Odorheiu Secuiesc
Odorheiu Secuiesc 80f
Ofen *siehe/see* Buda
Oradea 79
Orăștie 211

Paris 36, 46, 79, 86, 106, 110, 116, 343
Pavia 157
Pápa 203
Pest 25f, 339
Piliscsaba 151
Pisa 165, 193
Poland 193, 350
Pozsony *siehe/see* Bratislava
Prag/Prague 341, 350
Pränzdorf *siehe/see* Suseni
Prázsmár *siehe/see* Prejmer
Prejmer 252
Preßburg *siehe/see* Bratislava

Racoș 223
Radeln-Schäßburg *siehe/see* Roadeș-Sighișoara
Rádos *siehe/see* Roadeș-Sighișoara
Rákos *siehe/see* Racoș

Rakosch *siehe/see* Racoș
Rastatt 37, 50
Roadeș-Sighișoara 212 f
Rode *siehe/see* Zagăr
Roma 84, 86 f, 112, 160
Romania 8, 151, 350
Rouen 79

Schässburg *siehe/see* Sighișoara
Schomlenberg *siehe/see* Șumuleu Ciuc
Sebeș 303
Segesvár *siehe/see* Sighișoara
Seligstadt *siehe/see* Selistat
Seliștat 212–216
Sibiu 96, 152, 154–160, 163, 165, 170,
 209 f, 217, 222 f, 264, 277 f, 284, 298,
 302–306, 352
Siebenbürgen *siehe/see* Transilvania
Sighișoara 155, 212 f, 222
Slimnic 157
Sorbonne 116
St. Gallen 37, 41, 46, 50
Stolzenburg *siehe/see* Slimnic
Straßburg 38 f, 73, 132, 144, 268
Straßburg am Mieresch *siehe/see* Aiud
Streitfort *siehe/see* Mercheașa
Șumuleu Ciuc 194–196, 213
Șura Mare 222, 292, 295, 303, 307
Suseni 194, 196
Szászbuzd *siehe/see* Buzd
Szászdálya *siehe/see* Daia
Szászsebes *siehe/see* Sebeș
Szászugra *siehe/see* Ungra
Szászváros *siehe/see* Orăștie
Székelyudvarhely *siehe/see* Odorheiu
 Secuiesc
Szentágota *siehe/see* Agnita

Táblás *siehe/see* Dupuș
Tartlau *siehe/see* Prejmer
Târgu Mureș 25–27, 194–196, 199 f, 213
Teiuș 194 f

Thuringia 113
Tobsdorf *siehe/see* Dupuș
Torda *siehe/see* Turda
Tournai 94, 110, 115 f, 287
Tours 79
Tövis *siehe/see* Teiuș
Transilvania 8 f, 11–13, 16 f, 21 f, 25, 80 f,
 88, 96, 151–161, 169–172, 176 f, 180,
 182–184, 194–196, 204 f, 211, 214,
 221–224, 229, 251 f, 254, 267, 269–273,
 275 f, 280, 297, 302, 304–307, 309,
 311–313, 339–341, 344, 349–355
Troyes 79
Turda 352
Țapu 277, 280 f
Țara Bârsei 216, 224–226

Ungarn/Hungary 12, 80, 120, 155, 163,
 172, 182 f, 193–197, 201–204, 206, 223,
 255, 339, 344, 350–352, 354
Ungra 303
Utrecht 110
Újlak 198

Vajdahunyad *siehe/see* Hunedoara
Vărd 210
Venedig/Venice 96
Vérd *siehe/see* Vărd
Vienna *siehe/see* Wien

Weißenburg *siehe/see* Alba Iulia
Weißkirch *siehe/see* Albești
Werd *siehe/see* Vărd
Wien 8, 25–27, 33, 39, 49, 56, 66, 68 f, 73
 80, 83, 109, 151, 157, 169, 223, 339, 350 f
Wittenberg 15, 133, 209 f, 222–224, 230,
 233, 235, 268 f, 298, 306, 353
Wolfenbüttel 24

Zagăr 213, 216
Zágor *siehe/see* Zagăr
Zürich 268

Personen/Names

Abaffy, Csilla 153
Abraham (biblische Figur) 99
Achten, Gerard 132
Adam (biblische Figur) 98
Adamska, Anna 152

Ainsworth, Maryan W. 106, 116
Albelius, Simon 252
Albert de Sarteano/Alberto of Sarteano
 193
Alexander VI. (Papst/Pope) 138

400 | Index

Allin, John 330, 333 f
Allin, Thomas 330
Altemberger, Thomas 160
Altdorfer, Albrecht 33
Amandus de Maastricht (Heilige)/Saint
 Amandus 88
Ambrosius/Ambrose (Heilige/Saint) 88
Amsdorff, Nicolaus von 133
Andreas/Andrew (Apostel/Apostle) 254 f,
 260
András, II./Andreas II/Andrew II (König
 von Ungarn/King of Hungary) 105
Andrássy, Manó 27
Angenendt, Arnold 156
Anna/Anne (Heilige/Saint) 199
Antonius Eremita 33, 44
Antonius von Padua/Anthony of Padua
 (Heilige/Saint) 88
Apollonia von Alexandria/Saint Apollonia
 33–34, 44, 48, 73
Arnold, Jochen 211
Arz, Gustav 211
Assmann, Aleida 152
Assmann, Jan 152
Aston, Margaret 271
As-Vijvers, Anne-Margareet W. 84, 100 f
Audomarus van St-Omer/Saint Omer 87 f
Augustinus von Hippo/Augustine of Hippo
 (Heilige/Saint) 88, 224
Ádám, Edina 182
Ägidius von St-Gilles, (Heilige)/Aegydius,
 Saint Giles 88

Baier, Karl 153, 156
Ball, John 330 f
Barbara von Nikomedien/Saint Barbara
 34, 36, 44, 48, 71
Barnabas (Apostle/Apostel) 213
Bartholomäus/Bartholomew (Heilige/Saint)
 216, 254 f
Bartlett, Anne Clark 151
Bartsch, Adam 32, 56
Baschet, Jérôme 265
Batthyány, Ignác 197 f, 202 f
Bavo von Gent/Bavo of Ghent (Heilige/
 Saint) 88
Baxter, Richard 336
Bayer, Christian 133
Bämler, Johannes 34–35, 41, 72–73
Bäuml, Franz H. 152
Bándi, András 16, 222, 271, 344, 351
Bárczi, Ildikó 172
Báthori, István, ecsedi 27

Báthory, Zsófia 81
Beck, Georg 35, 64
Beckmann, Otto 133
Beier, Christina 34
Belting, Hans 102, 267, 277, 281, 287, 291
Benedikt von Nursia/Benedict of Nursia
 (Heilige/Saint) 88
Bening, Alexander 111, 113 f
Bening, Simon 109, 111–113
Benjamin, Walter 350
Bernard von Clairvaux (Heilige/Saint) 88,
 156, 237
Bernard, Richard 326
Bernhardin von Siena/Bernardino of Siena
 (Heilige/Saint) 193, 202 f
Bertin (Heilige/Saint) 87 f
Bertschi, Nikolaus 35–36, 39, 69
Besenyő, Mihály/Michael 201
Bestul, Thomas 151, 159
Béldi, János 251
Biandrata, Giorgio 353
Binder, Ludwig 226, 257
Binski, Paul 265
Binz, Gustav 37
Biró, Lajos 81
Bischof, Janika 12, 34
Bombrecher, Laurentius 209
Bonaventura (Heilige/Saint) 199,
 201–203, 205
Boreczky, Anna 12, 155, 161
Borosnyai, Pál 8, 23 f, 26 f
Bossy, John 9
Bottigheimer, Ruth B. 268–270, 275, 299
Bracaloni, Leone 176
Brandsch, Gottlieb 211
Brant, Sebastian 38 f, 132
Brantley, Jessica 152
Bredow-Klaus, Isabel von 31
Brentano, Robert 349
Brigitta von Schweden (Heilige)/Bridget of
 Sweden (Saint) 140, 144
Brinsley, John 324, 335
Broadhead, P.J. 276, 307, 309
Brown, Jacob M. 265
Brukenthal, Samuel von 96, 161
Brückner, Wolfgang 281, 284
Bucur, Mirel 278
Budacherus, Andreas 306
Bueren, Truus van 177
Bünz, Enno 160
Bunyitay, Vince 198, 200, 203, 222 f
Burke, Peter 287, 349

Index | 401

Cameron, Evan 269
Camille, Michael 265
Cannon, Joanna 292
Carey, Hilary M. 97
Carlstadt, Andreas 133
Cartwright, Thomas 332 f, 335
Cashman, Tyrone 348
Cassirer, Ernst 347
Cermann, Regina 7, 27, 34–36, 39, 41, 339,
342–344, 350
Chaderton, Laurence 325
Champion, Matthew 349
Charles I/Karl I (King of England/König von
England) 323
Chartier, Roger 14, 16
Chazelle, Celia 265
Chlench-Priber, Kathrin 340, 342
Christ/Jesus Christus 14 f, 19, 37, 39–43,
46–47, 99, 101, 134, 136, 139–143,
145–148, 152, 159, 171, 173, 176 f, 180,
182 f, 187, 197, 203–205, 209–211, 214,
216, 226, 231, 233, 247, 254, 256, 261, 265,
292, 300, 302, 304, 306, 310, 313, 322–325,
327, 330, 332, 334 f
Christiansen, Keith 106
Christensen, Carl C. 277, 291
Christophorus/Christopher (Heilige/Saint)
33–34, 44, 48, 254, 256
Christus, Petrus 106
Clanchy, Michael T. 152
Claravallensis, Alcherus 171
Clark, Gregory T. 79, 85
Cleves, Catherine of 108, 110 f
Clichtoveus, Jodocus 116 f
Cole, Richard G. 268
Collinson, Patrick 322
Corbellini, Sabrina 156, 163, 266, 271 f,
309 f
Corvinus, Matthias I,/Matei Corvin/
Hunyadi Mátyás 195
Costa, Alvaro da 109, 112
Cotoi, Paula 8, 12 f, 18, 154, 169–172,
339 f, 351
Cotton, John 325, 330, 334
Covaciu, Cătălina 157
Cranmer, Thomas 321 f
Crăciun, Maria 17 f, 151, 157, 169, 177,
180, 183, 204, 273 f, 276–278, 280 f, 296,
298–300, 311, 339–341, 351
Crockett, William R. 180
Cunningham, David S. 98
Csepregi, Zoltán 224 f

Dahl, Gina 15
David (biblische Figur) 96, 98, 100
David, Gerard 106, 111, 114
Davis, Thomas J. 273
Dávid, Ferenc 353
De Cevins, Marie Madeleine 13, 172, 178 f,
194–200, 203 f
De Hamel, Christopher 79
De Maere, Jan 96, 98
Deacon, Terrence W. 348
Deane, Jennifer 152
Delaissé, Léon 79, 81
Delaissé, L. M. J. 81, 83 f, 86, 88
Denziger, Heinrich 142, 146
Derbes, Anne 177
Derolez, Albert 82 f
Derrida, Jacques 98
Des Trompes, Jan 114
Dias, Isabel 172
Diederichs-Gottschalk, Dietrich 277, 284,
302
Diemer, Georg 33, 40
Dietl, Cora 232
Dillenberg, John 347
Dincă, Adinel 8, 12 f, 18, 79 f, 152–157,
159–161, 170 f, 271, 339, 351
Dinkelsbühl, Nikolaus de 159, 170, 350
Dogaer, Georges 79, 83
Doltz, Johann 133
Dominikus von Kastilien/Dominic de
Guzmán (Heilige/Saint) 88
Dondi, Cristina 151
Donne, John 325
Dorothea von Cäsarea/Dorothea of Caesarea
(Heilige/Saint) 174, 254
Dorothea von Mansfeld 39
Dorothea von Preußen/Dorothea of
Denmark 39
Dorrian, Mark 350
Downame, George 324, 326–329, 335
Drumond, Ian Christopher 349
Duffy, Eamon 9–11, 79, 151, 156, 160,
265 f, 269 f, 272, 299
Duprat, Antoine 116
Dürer, Albrecht 32–33, 56
Dürr, Renate 253

Ebran, Elisabeth 37
Eco, Umberto 95
Edward IV (King/König) 110–112, 114
Edward V (King/König) 110, 112
Edwards, Mark U. Jr. 268, 270, 272
Ehlich, Konrad 152

402 | Index

Ehrstine, Glenn 152
Eisenstein, Elizabeth 266
Eligius von Noyon (Heilige)/Saint Eligius 88
Elisabeth (biblische Figur) 256
Elizabeth I (Queen of England/Königin von England) 321f, 324, 329
Elisabeth von Ungarn/Elizabeth of Hungary (Heilige/Saint) 15, 105–109, 113–119, 350
Elm, Susanne 348
Enenkel, Karl 159
Engelke, Matthew 348
Erasmus, Desiderius Roterodamus 224, 228, 231
Erdei, Klára 159
Erdélyi, Gabriella 21, 80, 152, 351
Erler, Mary C. 151
Esau (biblische Figur) 100
Esra/Ezra (Prophet) 100
Eugen IV/Eugene IV (Papst/Pope) 193
Eva/Eve (biblische Figur) 98

Falvay, Dávid 105
Fara, Andrea 160
Fassler, Margo 9
Fata, Márta 223
Ferdinand I. (König/Kaiser) 27, 223
Field, John 333, 336
Fillastre, Guillaume 287
Finucane, Ronald C. 201
Firea, Ciprian 155, 157, 160, 169, 180, 278, 298
Florea, Carmen 13f, 157, 160, 176, 180, 183, 340, 351
Flóra, Ágnes 271
Francis of Sepsiszentgyörgy 199, 201f
Franciscus/Franz von Assisi/Francis of Assisi (Heilige/Saint) 88, 174, 193, 201
Franke, Erhard 221, 227f
Frater Siboto 158, 170, 350
Freedberg, David 117
Friedrich Peypus 133
Fronius, Marcus 298
Fuchs, Johannes 224

Galamb, György 194
Garrett, Cynthia 335
Gavriluță, Nicu 97
Gawthrop, Richard 268f, 311
Gecser, Ottó 105, 172
Geleji Katona, István (Bischof) 251–253, 257f, 354

Georg (Heilige)/Saint George 34, 44, 48
Ghitta, Ovidiu 276
Ginzburg, Carlo 287
Giovanni da Capestran/John of Capistrano (Saint)/Johannes von Capistrano (Heilige) 193
Gordon, Bruce 177
Goswami, Niranjan 16, 341
Gould, Karen 97
Gowlett, J. A. J. 348
Graetz, Nicolaus de 170f, 350
Gregor der Große/Gregor I/Gregory I (Papst/Pope) 88, 101, 141
Gregor III./Gregory I (Papst/Pope) 140
Grisé, Anette C. 151
Gross, Julius 154, 221, 224, 226–228
Gross, Lidia 160
Grosse, Siegfried 35
Grubmüller, Klaus 152
Grünerberg, Georg 268
Grünerberg, Hans 268
Grünerberg, Johann 268
Gudor, Botond 251
Gutknecht, Jobst 39
Gündisch, Gustav 153, 161, 271, 306f, 316

Haage, Bernhard 342
Haberkern, Ernst 157
Haemig, Mary Jane 14–16
Haigh, Christopher 269, 275, 309, 311, 335
Haimerl, Franz X. 37–38, 42–44, 51
Hall, Matthew 270
Haller, Petrus 221
Hamburger, Jeffrey 9, 47, 266
Hamm, Berndt 133, 140f, 151, 197, 204, 347
Harbison, Craig 266
Harnung, Martin 298
Harthan, John 79, 86
Hastings, William 110
Hätzer, Ludwig 227f, 232, 234
Hebler, Matthias 304, 306
Hecht, Johannes 222
Heinzer, Felix 37
Heisterbach, Caesarius von 115
Heitzmann, Christian 36
Helth, Kaspar/Heltai, Gáspár 227
Hennecke, A. B. D. 214, 216
Henriet, Patrick 181f
Henry VIII (King of England/König von England) 321f
Hentea, Ioan 80
Herbert, Heinrich 222f

Index | **403**

Hering, Rainer 347
Hermann, Nicolaus 254
Herod/Herodes (biblische Figur) 100
Herzog Wilhelm III. von Bayern 37, 42–43
Hieronymus (Heilige)/Jerome of Stridon (Saint) 88
Hindman, Sandra 46, 79, 93, 151
Hirscher, Lukas 224
Holbein, Hans 35, 64
Holcot, Robert 171
Honée, Eugène 9, 265
Honemann, Volker 143
Honn, Michael 215 f
Honterus, Johannes 16, 209, 211, 213, 221, 223–226, 233–235, 275, 304, 306
Hoogvliet, Margriet 266, 271 f, 287, 299, 309–311
Hoorebeeck, Céline van 86
Huet, Georg 222
Hunyadi János/Ioan de Hundoara/John of Hunedoara/Johannes Hunyadi 194
Hupfer, Georg 25
Hus, Jan 228
Hutton, Ronald 266
Hünermann, Peter 142, 146

Iohannes Baptista/Johannes der Täufer 33, 48, 134, 139, 254, 256, 259
Isaac/Isaak (biblische Figur) 100
Isabella I. of Castilen/von Kastilien (Queen/Königin) 15, 107, 110, 114
Isabella of/von Portugal (Empress and Queen/Kaiserin und Königin) 116
Ittu, Constantin 8 f, 95, 99, 102, 339, 343

Jacob/Jakob (biblische Figur) 100, 254 f, 259
Jacobus de Marchia/Jakobus von der Mark/James of the Marches (Heilige/Saint) 193 f
Jacobus de Voragine 158
Jagelló Anna (Queen of Hungary/Königin von Ungarn) 24, 27
Jagiellon Isabella 223
Jakobi-Mirwald, Christine 151
Jakó, Zsigmond 271
James (Saint, James the Great, Apostle)/Jakobus der Ältere (Apostel) 174
James IV of Scotland/Jakob IV von Schottland 111
Jankovich, Miklós 25, 27
Jean, Count of Dunois 110

Jekel, Hieremias 225
Jenei, Dana 157, 160
Jerney, János 25
Johann Friedrich I. (Sachsen) 228
Johann von Neumarkt 341, 350
Johanna I of Castile/von Kastilien 109 f, 112
Johannes (Apostel)/John (Apostle) 37, 44, 48, 145
Johannes IV/John IV (Papst/Pope) 38
Johannes von Indersdorf 36, 42–44
Johannes von Neumarkt 36, 41, 43, 342
Josef/Joseph (biblische Figur) 100
Judas Iscariot (Apostel/Apostle) 254 f
Jürgens, Henning 227

Karl I. von Baden, Markgraf 32, 37
Karant-Nunn, Susan 276
Karl IV./Charles IV (römisch-deutscher Kaiser/Holy Roman Emperor) 341, 350
Karácsonyi, János 195 f, 198, 200, 203, 222 f
Katharina von Alexandrien (Heilige/Saint) 32, 34, 36, 44, 48, 56–57, 59, 214
Káldi, György (Georgius Káldi) 80 f
Kelecsényi, Ákos 26
Keller, Hagen 152
Kemény, József 22
Kemény, Sámuel 22
Kemperdick, Stephan 36
Kennedy, Kirsten 266
Kenyeres, Ágnes 26, 81
Kertész, Balázs 193, 197, 202
Keul, István 352–354
Kieckhefer, Richard 151, 171, 184
Kienzler, Corinna 226
Kingdon, Robert M. 266
Kinizsi, Pál 153
Klaniczay, Gábor 105
Klapper, Joseph 36, 43
Klein, Karl Kurt 224
Knape, Joachim 132
Knodt, Gerhard 254
Koberger, Anton 133
Koberger, Johann 133
Kodres, Krista 289
Koerner, Joseph Leo 273–277, 284, 287, 298–300, 305
Konrád, Eszter 201 f
Kootz, Julius 211
Korányi, András 199, 202–204
Korondi, Ágnes 199 f, 202
Korteweg, Anne S. 84
Kovács Bányai, Réka 27

404 | Index

Kónya, Anna 180
König, Heidrun 278
Köpeczi, Béla 271
Kren, Thomas 96, 99, 106, 109, 113, 118
Krén, Emil 113
Kühne, Harmut 160
Kühnel, Harry 33
Kührer-Wielach, Florian 151
Kwidzyn, Iohannes de 170 f, 350

Lajos, I./Ludwig I./Louis the Great/Louis I
of Hungary 194
Landmann, Florenz 171
Laskai, Osvát/Osvaldus de Lasko
172–183, 185, 193, 197, 201 f, 339, 351
Laugerud, Henning 153
Láng, Benedek 26
Lázár, Miklós (Graf) 23
Leese, Kurt 347
Lefèvre d'Etaples, Jacques 116
Lehmann, Zacharias 306
Lentes, Thomas 141 f, 151, 340
Lenz, Philipp 37, 46
Leo I., der Große (Papst/Pope 88
Leo X (Papst/Pope) 157, 193, 198
Leonhard von Limoges/Leonard of Noblac
44, 48, 65-65, 88
Leppin, Volker 14, 131, 137 f, 341–343,
347, 352
Leroquais, Victor 79, 86
Lesser, Bertram 36
Lipsius, Justus 117
List, Gerhard 47
Lotter, Melchior 268
Louis IX/Saint Louis of France 88
Ludwig II. (König von Ungarn / King of
Hungary) 24, 26 f, 344
Ludwig IV von Thüringen/Louis IV
Landgrave of Thuringia 113
Ludwig der Bayer/Louis IV 105
Lufft, Hans 268, 270, 306
Luffy, Katalin 7 f, 278, 339, 344, 350
Luhrmann, Tanya 349
Lukas/Luke (Evangelist) 214
Lunguvitius (Lungwitz), Matthaeus 275
Lupescu Makó, Mária 154, 160, 169, 196
Lupescu, Radu 195
Luther, Martin 14 f, 116, 131-133, 138,
222, 225, 227 f, 231, 233 f, 252, 254, 266,
268-270, 272-274, 276, 284, 287, 298 f,
305-307, 312, 325, 327, 342, 347, 352, 354
Lyly, William 324

MacCulloch, Diarmaid 323
Machat, Christoph 277
Mager, Inge 226
Makarios von Alexandria (Heilige)/Saint
Macarius 199
Maltby, Judith 329 f, 335
Manuel I of Portugal/von Portugal 109
Maria, Mutter Jesu/Mary, Mother of God
19, 34, 36, 40, 42–44, 48, 62, 81, 86, 88, 96,
99, 107, 115, 138 f, 145, 152, 175 f, 193, 199,
213 f, 256, 259–262, 266, 300
Maria Magdalena 34, 37, 44, 48, 59, 66-67,
213
Maria, Erzherzogin von Österreich, Königin
von Ungarn und Böhmen, Statthalterin der
Niederlande 27
Markus, Robert Austin 100 f
Markus/Mark (Evangelist) 213
Marrow, James 151, 157
Marshall, Peter 177
Martens, Maximilan P.J. 116
Martin von Tours/Martin of Tours (Heilige/
Saint) 88
Martin, Jessica 152
Marx, Daniel 113
Mary of Burgundy/Maria von Burgund
113
Mather, Increase 324, 330, 333-336
Matthäus/Matthias (Apostle) 254 f
Maximilian I (Holy Roman Emperor/Kaiser)
35, 64, 109, 111
Mátray, Gábor 26
Mâle, Émile 265
Mârza, Andreea 31, 79 f, 170 f
McKendrick, Scot 96, 99, 106, 109, 113,
118
Meister Eckhart 131
Melanchthon, Philipp 225, 228, 268, 331
Melion, Walter 159
Melville, Gert 347
Memling, Hans 106
Mende, Matthias 32
Merkl, Ulrich 35-36
Mets, Guillebert de 111, 114
Meyer (Agricola), Daniel 171
Michael (Erzengel/Archangel) 254-256,
258
Michalski, Sergiusz 278, 284, 299
Mihály, Tibor 81
Mikó, Imre (Graf) 21 f, 350
Milič, Jan/Milicius, Johannes/Militsch,
Johannes von Kremsier 341
Miller, Mathias 37, 49

Min, Anselm Kyongsuk 347
Mitchell, W. J. T. 287, 294
Molanus, Johannes 117
Moldner, Andreas 16, 221, 225–231, 233–235, 243, 341, 351
Moler, Benedictus 298
Molitor, Heinrich 35
Monok, István 222
Moore, R.I. 270f
More, Alison 198
Morgan, Nigel 85
Morrison, Elisabeth 98–100
Moser, Hugo 35
Moses (biblische Figur) 230
Mulsow, Martin 353
Murdock, Graeme 276
Müller, Friedrich 103, 154
Müller, Thomas T. 160

Nagel von Waltdorff, Gabriel 46
Nägler, Doina 271, 306
Nechutová, Jana 341
Neidl, Michaela 36
Nemes, Balázs 25, 31
Nemes Literáti, Sámuel 8, 24–27, 339, 344
Nemes Literáti, Zsuzsanna 26f
Nerlich, Michael 294
Netoliczka, Oskar 273–276, 304
Neuber, Valentin 228
Nicholas (Heilige)/Saint Nicholas 88
Nikolaus V/Nicholas V (Papst/Pope), 193
Nussbächer, Gernot 233, 271, 274f

Obhof, Ute 36
Ochsenbein, Peter 132f, 140
Ocker, Christopher 348, 351, 354
Odenthal, Andreas 212, 214
Oekolampad, Johannes 39
Ogáyar, Juana Hidalgo 114
Oldenbourg, Maria Consuelo 132f
Ong, Walter J. S. J. 326
Ordeanu, Maria 96
Otmar, Hans 33, 40
Ottilie/Odile (Heilige/Saint) 34, 44, 48
Ötvös, Ágoston 251f
Ötvös, Péter 222

Pakora, Jakub 294
Pallmann, Heinrich 133
Panayotova, Stella 85
Papahagi, Adrian 7–9, 31, 79f, 94, 154, 161, 170f, 339, 350
Parisiensis, Guillelmus 171f

Parker, Geoffrey 267–269, 274, 309, 311
Parks, Malcom B. 271
Parshall, Peter 117
Paul, Hermann 35
Paulus (Apostel/Apostle) 34, 44, 59, 254f, 258, 260, 304
Pál, József 108
Pásztor, Lajos 152
Pächt, Otto 35, 96
Pempflinger, Markus 223
Perkins, William 324
Peters, Anna 117
Petrus (Apostel/Apostle) 139, 254f, 260
Petrus Christus 116–119
Pettegree, Andrew 12, 267, 270, 272f
Petzet, Erich 46
Philip (Evangelist) 98, 255, 259
Philip III (Philippe le Bon/Duke of Burgundy) 79, 106, 116
Philippi, Astrid 233
Pieper, Lori 105
Pius II./Aeneas Sylvius Piccolomini (Papst/Pope) 24, 32, 37–38, 40, 42, 46, 50–51
Pius V. (Papst/Pope) 79
Plajer, Dietmar 221
Possas, Stephanie 157
Preidt, Georg 216
Preston, John 325f, 330, 335, 337
Prokopp, Gyula 27
Pythagoras 95

Radosav, Doru 80
Ramser, Matthias 225
Randall, Lilian M.C. 88
Rapaics, Rajmund 198, 200, 203, 222f
Razovsky, Helaine 266
Rákóczi, Ferenc/Francis I. (Fürst, Siebenbürgen/Prince of Transylvania) 80, 88
Rákóczi, György, I/Georg I. (Fürst, Siebenbürgen/Prince of Transylvania) 251
Rákóczi, György, II/Georg II. (Fürst, Siebenbürgen/Prince of Transylvania) 80
Rebecca/Rebekka (biblische Figur) 100
Rechberg, Brigitta 116
Reeves, Andrew 170
Rehberg, Andreas 160
Rehner, Wolfgang H. 217
Reinburg, Virginia 15, 79
Reinerth, Karl 171, 212, 221f, 224, 227, 229f, 234

406 | Index

Reisner, Adam 24
Reiss, Athene 266
Remigius von Reims (Heilige/Saint) 88
Rempel, John D. 227
Renner Hans 35–36, 61, 68
Renner, Narziß 35–36, 68
Reske, Christoph 133
Rexroth, Karl Heinrich 116
Rély, Jean de 272
Ringbom, Sixten 266
Rittgers, Ronald K. 159
Robinson, Paul W. 173f, 331
Roest, Bert 181, 193f, 199, 202, 204
Romhányi, Beatrix F. 194
Rose, Marika 349
Roth, Erich 210
Roth, Stefan Ludwig 211
Roth, Victor 278, 303
Rother, Christian 156, 271
Rothkegel, Martin 227, 230
Rozsondai, Marianne 25
Rubin, Miri 180
Rublack, Ulinka 266f, 270, 299
Rubliov, Andrei 99
Ruppel, Berthold 38
Ryan, Salvador 153
Ryrie, Alec 152

Saenger, Paul 11, 16, 181
Salontai, Mihaela Sanda 195
Samuel (biblische Figur) 100
Sand, Alexa 160, 266
Sarah/Sara (biblische Figur) 99
Saul (biblische Figur) 100
Scarisbrick, J.J. 266
Scarpatetti, Beat Matthias von 37, 46
Scherbaum, Anna 32
Scheurl, Christoph 133
Schiemer, Leonhard 228
Schilling, Johannes 221
Schlachta, Astrid von 227
Schlechter, Armin 37
Schmidt, Peter 33
Schmidt, Victor 266
Schmoll, Friedrich 115
Schneider, Karin 35, 46
Schnyder, André 340
Schoch, Reiner 32, 117
Scholten, Frits 157
Schröbler, Ingeborg 35
Schullerus, Adolf 209, 222f, 225f, 234
Schulz, Frieder 255
Schwartz, Antonius 213

Scillia, Diane G. 114
Scott-Stokes, Charity 155
Scribner, Robert 265f, 270–272, 291
Sebastian (Heilige/Saint) 33–34, 38–40, 43, 48, 58
Sedikides, Constantine 348
Seller, Martinus 306
Seraphin, Friedrich Wilhelm 271
Shelley, Mary 353
Shepard, Thomas 324, 330–333, 335f
Silvester I., Papst/Saint Sylvester, Pope 88
Simon (Apostel/Apostle) 254f
Simon, Zsolt 109, 111–113, 156
Simonius, Johannes (Juratus notaries Cibiniensis) 257
Simó, Ferenc 80
Sipos, Gábor 22
Sixtus IV (Papst/Pope) 201
Skinnebach, Laura Katrine 153
Skowronski, John J. 348
Smet, Marjan 151
Smeyers, Maurits 79, 83
Socino, Fausto/Faustus Socinus 353
Sohm, Rudolf 347
Sohmargued, Rudolf 347
Soós, Zoltán 195
Sorg, Anton 39–40
Söller, Bertram 132
Spalatin, Georg 133
Spicer, Andrew 276
Spielmann, Mihály 171
Stamm, Gerhard 37
Statilaeus, Johannes 224
Staupitz, Johann 133
Stayer, James A. 227
Stegmüller, Otto 37
Steiger, Johann Anselm 254, 256
Stein, Wendy 107
Steiner, Heinrich 39
Steinmetz, Jörg 229
Stephens, Isaac 326, 329f, 336
Stjerna, Kirsi 347
Stone, Lawrence 266
Strandenaes, Thor 97f
Strauss, Gerald 268–270, 274f, 309–311
Stuntz, Melchior 61, 68
Șindilariu, Thomas 223
Szabó, Károly 8, 23f
Szapolyai, János (I. János)/Johann/John/Ioan Zápolya (König von Ungarn/King of Hungary) 223

Index | **407**

Szapolyai János Zsigmond (II. János)/Johann
 Sigismund Zápolya (König von Ungarn/
 King of Hungary)   353
Szathmári Ilyés, Mihály   26
Szegedi, Edit   16, 224, 253f, 273–276, 307,
 344, 351, 354
Szende, Katalin   153, 272, 307
Széchényi, Ferenc   25
Szilágyi, Erzsébet/Elizabeth   195
Szinnyei, József   26
Szőcs, Tamás   254
Szűcs, Kata   7, 15, 343, 350

Taler, Ulrich   35, 65, 67
Temesvári, Pelbárt/Pelbartus de Themeswar
 172–175, 177–184, 201, 339, 351
Teutsch, Friedrich   212f, 222, 255, 271, 273
Teutsch, Georg Daniel   269f, 273–276, 304f
Thayer, Anne T.   154, 170
Thomas (Apostel/Apostle)   254f
Thomas Aquinas (Heilige/saint)   349
Thonhäuser, Petrus   222
Thoss, Dagmar   83
Toldy (Schedel), Ferenc   25f
Tomaszewski, Jacek   155
Tonk, Sándor   271
Trausch, Joseph   226, 252
Trio, Paul   151
Troeltsch, Ernst   347

Ulrich VII. von Montfort-Tettnang   33
Ulrich von Augsburg   34, 44, 59
Unglerus, Lukas   304, 306
Urban II. (Papst/Pope)   38f, 136
Uselmann, Susan   151
Újvári, Edit   108

Valente Bacci, Anna Maria   170
Valerius Maximus   84
Van Eyck, Jan   106, 116, 118f
Van Os, Henk   20, 157
Vanvijnsberghe, Dominique   83, 86f
Vedastus (Heilige/Saint)   88
Vermeulen, Hendrik   117
Verók, Attila   222, 225

Viallet, Ludovic   193, 197, 203
Volf, György   204
Vos, Jan   116
Vulič, Kathryn R.   151

Wachinger, Burckhard   133, 159, 171
Wackernagel, Philipp   227, 229
Wagner, Ernst   271
Wagner, Leonhard,   35, 64f
Wagner, Peter   287, 294
Wagner, Valentin   221, 232, 234
Wal, Thomas   158
Wauters, Alphonse   117
Wähinger, Johann   38–39
Webb, Diana   156
Wehli, Tünde   107f
Wehmer, Carl   35
Weiske, Brigitte   342
Weiße, Michael   227–229
Welch, Claude   347
Wetter, Evelin   135, 154, 157, 226, 354
Whitgift, John   333
Wieck, Roger S.   9–11, 14, 79, 86, 153
Wied, Hermann von/of   322
Wiederkehr, Ruth   342
Wien, Ulrich Andreas   16, 223, 351, 353
Wilcox, Thomas   333, 336
Wilhelm III. von Bayern   37, 42–43
Wilhelm, Johannes   35
Wilhelmi, Thomas   132
Wilkins, David G.   266
Williamson, Beth   152, 265f
Winston-Allen, Anne   9, 176f
Wisse, Jacob   106

Zainer, Günther   35, 39, 72
Zander-Seidel, Jutta   33
Zach, Krista   276
Zarri, Gabriella   198
Ziegler, Ágnes   226
Zimmermann, Karin   37, 49
Zschampi, Margaret   37
Zultner, Martin   210
Zwingli, Ulrich   234